repair & renovate

your

home

repair &
renovate
your
home

BY

Julian Cassell

Peter Parham

Mark Corke

Mike Lawrence

MURDOCH
BOOKS

contents

introduction

Home improvement is fast becoming a national pastime with more and more people tackling jobs that would previously have been left to the services of professional tradespeople. Taking on a job yourself can be cheaper and more rewarding than hiring a professional – ensuring that the finished effect is how you envisaged and falls within a budget that does not incur additional labour costs.

repair & renovation issues

This revolution has been fuelled by a booming DIY retail sector, which tries to convince us that no job is too difficult and any practically-minded person can set about full scale home renovation. Although it is true to say that there is indeed huge scope for applying oneself to home improvement tasks, it is always important to know your limitations right from the outset. It is best to approach DIY as a learning curve, building up your experience and knowledge before tackling jobs of greater difficulty.

Repair issues can be neatly separated from those of renovation – the former is concerned primarily with making good existing features, and the latter is related to adjusting the appearance of certain areas in your home. Renovation therefore leans more heavily on the creative side of your abilities, whereas repairs generally tend to be dependent on your ability to apply yourself practically to restoring a particular finish or structure.

Most people are able to recognize when a particular area of their home needs adapting or changing, but realizing or envisaging what that change should be exactly can often be more difficult. Therefore, inspiration for change needs to be balanced with the potential options available, which in turn relate firmly to budget, personal choice, your ability to tackle the work and how much professional advice or input may be required for the task. It is best to try and tackle each of these areas in turn.

The smallest of renovation or home improvement tasks will always cost some money and therefore it is impossible to begin work without deciding on a budget. Right from the start, budgetary constraints will be the major governing factor in deciding on the extent of work.

Personal choice is clearly of the utmost importance when you come to repairing and renovating your house. Work out your ideal situation, and then compromise as necessary, taking into consideration the wishes of other people who will be affected and the relative value of your house. Decide whether your plans are to renovate purely to cater for your needs, or whether you are aiming to provide a general level of improvement that will also appeal to others, including potential buyers.

Next comes the question of your ability to tackle home improvement tasks. This book takes into account a wide variety of options and techniques covering all aspects of renovation. However, some techniques are clearly more demanding than others. It is always advisable to seek professional advice when needs dictate, even if it is just to provide a guiding hand rather than full scale employment. The areas of plumbing and electrics are specific examples where professional help will almost certainly be required. There is also a clear safety issue here and safety is one area where there is no room for compromise when renovating.

LEFT *The wall between these two rooms has been knocked through, allowing more light into both rooms and turning the two living rooms into one area.*

The layout of this book has been designed to give project instruction in as comprehensive yet straightforward a manner as possible. The illustration below provides a guideline to the different elements incorporated in the page design. Colour photographs and diagrams combined with explanatory text, laid out in a clear, step-by-step order, provide easy-to-follow instructions. Each project is prefaced by a blue box containing a list of tools so that you will know in advance the range of equipment required for the job. Other boxes of additional text accompany each project, and are aimed at drawing your attention to particular issues. Pink safety boxes alert the reader to issues of safety and detail any precautions that may need to be taken. They also indicate where a particular job must be carried out by a tradesperson. Green tip boxes offer professional hints for the best way to go about a particular task involved in the project. Boxes with an orange border describe alternative options and techniques, relevant to the project in hand but not demonstrated on the page.

difficulty rating

The following symbols are designed to give an indication of difficulty level relating to particular tasks and projects in this book. Clearly what are simple jobs to one person may be difficult to another, and vice versa. These guidelines are primarily based on the ability of an individual in relation to the experience and degree of technical ability required.

Straightforward and requires limited technical skills

Straightforward but requires a reasonable skill level

Technically quite difficult, and could involve a number of skills

High skill level required and involves a number of techniques

A list of tools is provided at the beginning of each job.

Option boxes offer additional instructions and techniques for the project in hand.

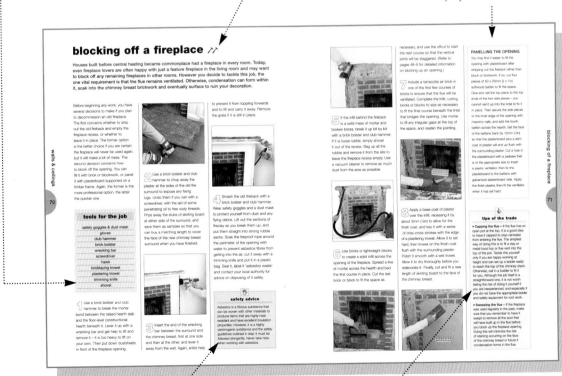

Safety boxes, pink for emphasis, draw attention to safety considerations.

Tip boxes provide helpful hints developed from professional experience or highlight areas where more traditional methods can be used.

planning

Careful planning is crucial for any type of repair or renovation because there are so many issues that need close consideration. In addition to gauging tool and material requirements, it is also important to establish whether planning permission will be necessary, whether you are capable of carrying out all the work yourself, and what the total cost and time frame will be. The extent and nature of a project will be highly dependent on at least some, if not all, of these considerations. This section provides some basic guidelines in all of these areas and helps to provide a framework for decision making and setting about a renovation project.

The careful use of mirrors, as shown here, can create the illusion of space for your bathroom.

how to start

Before commencing any project, it is important to plan your overall approach to the job and a specific order of work. Simple repairs or minor renovations tend not to raise too many problems, but inadequate planning on larger scale projects can produce very real difficulties. Even if the physical work itself is organized, issues such as building regulations and planning permission may need to be addressed.

planning permission

Before any construction project can begin, some consideration must be given to whether the particular work will need planning permission. The majority of projects inside the home do not need planning approval, and so this is not an issue for most works that you are likely to carry out. However, there are some circumstances which you should be aware of before beginning renovations.

restrictions

Most restrictions are applied to houses that are listed buildings and/or are in conservation areas, national parks, or areas of outstanding natural beauty. If your property fits into any of these categories, always call the local authority planning department before commencing any plans.

However, even in these cases, formal permission is rarely required for internal alterations, minor improvements, and general repairs and maintenance. Projects that definitely require planning permission are generally those in which an area of the house has a 'change of use', normally when business purposes are proposed. For example, if you wish to divide off a section of your home for business use, or you want to create a separate bedsit or flat. So generally speaking, in addition to the restrictions mentioned here, as long as the external appearance of the building is not changed, internal work may be carried out relatively free from too many planning obstacles. However, if you are in any doubt about what is permissible, it is best to contact your local authority.

External work can often be subject to strict building restrictions. Always check with an appropriate body before embarking on work that may require authorization.

building regulations

While most internal renovation is unlikely to require actual planning permission, all construction work should adhere to building regulations. So whenever you plan to carry out any construction work, contact the Building Control Officer at your local council, who can provide any necessary guidelines for potential work.

making a scale drawing

It is always sensible to make a scale drawing of a proposed construction job, in order to get a firm idea of material quantities. This does not have to be up to architectural standards, but it should provide enough detail to give you a good idea of the effect a project will have, and how it will change the existing look of your home. Graph paper always makes any technical drawing easier, and allows for more accurate measurement. It can often be helpful to add furniture to the diagram, so that you can gauge the effect of the alteration on the overall layout of the room – this can be especially important when dividing an existing room into two separate areas, as the amount of space is obviously reduced.

timescales

Always consider the timescale required to complete a project, as this can influence the most convenient time to commence the job. For example, while some projects can be completed in a weekend, other jobs will take longer, causing disruption to the household for several days. Most projects in this book are designed to be completed within a weekend, although the actual finishing may take longer, as

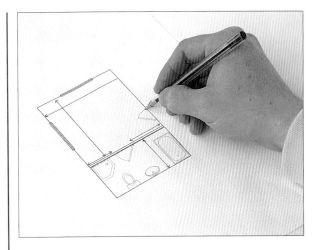

Making a scale drawing can help you to visualize the effect of any work on the surrounding environment. Adding furniture to the diagram will also help.

you return to the job for final decorating. As soon as you begin to combine a number of projects, or work on large areas, completing jobs can become more difficult. This is especially true of projects that run between weekends or evenings, so it is advisable either to break them down into smaller sections which can be completed as part of an overall larger renovation, or take time away from day-to-day work in order to make headway into the particular task. Otherwise, pressure to finish the job and minimize disruption can lead to inadequate work with poor finishing. Never underestimate the time involved in a project, and consider it an important part of the planning procedure to decide on dates and times when the work can be done, and within what timescale it can be finished.

budgeting

The greatest expense in a construction project is usually the price of the labour itself, and therefore by reducing this input costs are reduced. If professional trades are required, this should be given priority in terms of your overall budgeting strategy. Aside from this, material costs can be calculated relatively easily so long as accurate measurements are taken. Remember that bulk buying of particular materials should mean financial discounts, and it is always worth shopping around for the best deals. This is especially the case with common items such as general timber and plasterboard because the market is so competitive, and suppliers can vary their prices from week to week. If your planning is comprehensive, you have a better chance of remaining within your budget. However, it is always worth building in a slight surplus requirement to your figures so that if work does take longer – or require more materials – you are able to complete the project without delay.

Many DIY tasks will cause some inevitable disruption to the household. Bear this in mind when planning a job, and aim to commence work at a time convenient to all of those involved.

dealing with professionals

Prior to any construction work, it is important to establish what work you are capable of fulfilling, and to what extent you will require professional help. Small renovations or repairs are unlikely to require a great deal of assistance, but when tackling any major renovation, it is almost certain that the services of plumbers, electricians or general builders may be required. In these cases, try to identify the kind of assistance you require, and understand how to get the best service out of them.

architects and surveyors

In some circumstances, it may be necessary to draw on the services of architects and surveyors. Although not considered conventional 'tradespeople', they supply services which enable the practical side of major renovations to be planned and carried out in the correct manner. Architects only really need employing on larger projects where major design features have to be considered. However, on large projects, architects or surveyors can be employed in a kind of project management role, overseeing general work to ensure it meets building regulations (see page 10). Bear in mind that these services cost money and fees for monitoring work can add a further 10 per cent to the original price of drawing up plans. There may also be daily rate charges for site attendance.

Professional advice for major projects is always advisable, particularly for projects that may require planning permission. Bear these costs in mind when planning the work.

finding good tradespeople

Finding good, reliable tradespeople can be difficult – there is no point in hiring the best bricklayer in the area if he never turns up for work. The best method is to use personal recommendations, as you can see or hear about the quality of the work from a genuine customer. The other alternative is to contact three or four advertised companies for separate quotes. However, although this may help to ensure a competitive price, it does not guarantee the quality of the work or the reliability of the tradesperson. Even companies that display particular trade association badges may be no more reliable than other advertisers, so check the credentials with the association itself, and then with an independent body. Always ask to have a look at a person's work, preferably through the property owner, and then perhaps with the builder or tradesperson.

estimates, quotations and prices

Before allowing any tradesperson to begin work in your home, it is essential to know how much the actual job is going to cost. Estimates, quotations and prices can be a minefield – and are frequently the source of customers' disgruntlement. The main factor to bear in mind at this stage is that if you receive an estimate or a quotation, this is exactly the case – they are only estimates or quotations and therefore the price you pay can inflate considerably. If at all possible, it is therefore best to get a specific price from the tradesperson, which should not fluctuate unless you decide to change the specifications for the work. In some circumstances, an estimate may be necessary, as you may not have made final decisions on specifications and need to see how the project develops. However, the closer you can get to deciding on a price before the work begins, the better position you will find yourself in when budgeting for the job and keeping track of payments.

Never make the mistake of paying any money 'up front' unless there are exceptional circumstances. (For example, if the tradesperson is supplying expensive materials, it is only fair that you should make an initial downpayment towards the cost of those materials.) However, generally

Keep the lines of communication open. Although the cost of work may rise slightly as the job progresses, this can be negotiated at each stage, helping you monitor the cost overall.

speaking there is no reason to pay until the job is complete and you are happy with the finished product. For long projects, it is fair to stage payments throughout the job, but always leave the largest payment until completion. Finally, treat builders or tradespeople who insist on cash-only payments with some suspicion. Although there are potential savings to be made in this line, it means you have no comeback in terms of defective work or problems at a later date. Such methods of payment could also suggest illegal transactions in the eyes of the relevant tax authorities.

extras

On making any final payment, seeing the word 'extras' or 'extra work carried out' can add a surprising amount to the figure you were expecting to pay. In many cases, these may be items that you authorized during the overall works. However, it is always best to get a price for extra work before it is done, so that shocks do not occur at the final stage of payment. Alternatively, arrange during the initial price agreement that any extra work has to be carried out on your authority and is charged at a specific hourly rate. This makes it much easier to keep a track of expenses and prevent unexpected surprises with the final bill.

avoiding disputes

Disputes can easily be avoided so long as you follow the recognized 'rules of engagement'. Over half the battle is won if you have chosen the right tradesperson. Further gains can be made by ensuring that the price you are quoted is written and detailed in terms of the work to be carried out. This therefore acts as an accurate referral document for all parties. Aside from this, the only problems which generally arise concern the standard of work compared to what was initially agreed. Most of these problems can be sorted out through discussion and compromise, and it is best to avoid legal wrangles unless absolutely necessary. If you are that unhappy with the work carried out, your only option may be to withhold payment and hand the matter over to a solicitor.

In following these simple guidelines, you should be well equipped for employing the services of people from various trades. Simply remember that, in all occupations, there are both good and bad operators and that the building business gets more than its fair share of criticism. However, if you do have a reliable tradesperson at your disposal, pay them on time and recommend them to friends – in looking after their interests, you will almost certainly be looking after your own.

Professional tradespeople will do a good job for a fair price. However, before agreeing on the terms and conditions of the contract, establish the length of time and expense of the project.

tools & equipment

The range of tools and equipment necessary for completing DIY tasks can be vast and expensive. Yet many of the basic tools are in fact multi-purpose, and make up what might be called a 'household tool kit'. Once this strong base of essential tools has been established, you can go on to purchase more specialized tools as and when they are required. Although it is not necessary to spend a fortune on equipment, it is generally a good rule to buy the best tools that you can afford. Top quality tools tend to last longer and give better results, time and again.

household tools

This general household tool kit contains the essential tools for carrying out any number of small jobs and tasks around the home. Although the kit will not cope with every situation you encounter, it provides a good starting point to which you can add more specific tool requirements.

claw hammer

sanding block

wire brush

slot-head screwdrivers

cross-head screwdrivers

insulated sleeves

nail punch

pipe, joist and cable detector

craft knife

combination pliers

bradawl

carpenter's pencil

side cutters

long-nose pliers

cordless drill/driver

half-round rasp

general purpose chisels

oil stone

plier wrench

sealant dispenser

stepladder

wooden mallet

tape measure

clamp

mini hacksaw

mini level

scraper

mitre block

panel saw

power tools

Power tools are designed to make jobs easier and less time consuming. For most enthusiasts, mid-range tools are ideal, as the very expensive equipment is designed for everyday work, and the very cheap equipment for the occasional DIY person. Even so, the cost of power tools has dropped considerably, and it is possible to buy quality products relatively cheaply. For some tasks, it can even be worth buying a cheap tool for one job before discarding it.

power drill

router

jigsaw

electric sander

brick jointer

external corner trowel

internal corner trowel

pointing trowel

gauging trowel

brick trowel

plastic bucket

shovel

sledge-hammer

plastering trowel

hawk

In order to carry out alterations to walls and ceilings, the household tool kit needs to be supplemented with construction tools for heavy duty tasks. Try to concentrate on specific needs when purchasing such tools, as it can be tempting to fall for gimmicky options or cheap alternatives that will be of minimal use in the long term. Instead, stick to good quality, tried and tested tools which should last for several years of DIY projects. If you are unsure of the best product, consult your retailer.

wood plane

dry wall saw

board and door lifter

wrecking bar

power stirrer

mitresaw

combination square

plumb line

chalk line

hacksaw

caulking blade

water level

spirit level

workbench

bolster chisel

cold chisel

club hammer

taping/coating knife

HIRING TOOLS

For isolated tasks that require particularly heavy duty equipment, or tools that are very expensive to buy, hiring is often the best option. This area has become a growing sector of the DIY market, and hire shops are increasingly catering for home repair enthusiasts, as well as traditional trade customers.

tools & equipment

15

hiring specialist equipment

Certain projects described in this book will require the use of specialist tools and equipment, which are often large and expensive. If the equipment is only needed for the occasional job or one specific task it can be uneconomic to purchase it outright. Hiring a piece of equipment for a week, a day or just a few hours is a viable alternative and the market now caters for this growing practice amongst DIYers. Knowing that you have access to an almost unlimited range of specialist equipment will allow you to plan far more ambitious projects.

when to hire

When planning any job, however large or small, thought should be given to which skills and tools will be needed. In many cases the projects shown in this book can be completed successfully with a basic set of household tools. As your skill levels increase with experience and confidence, you will be amazed at just what can be achieved without recourse to a vast armoury of tools, but at times this is just not enough and a particular task will call for the aid of a specific piece of equipment. Just about any tool can be hired these days but it can be difficult for the amateur to know what is available and recognize when a piece of equipment is a candidate for hiring. Throughout this book you will see references to different tools. A basic tool kit, which is sufficient to complete most projects, is anatomized on page 14. Where larger pieces of machinery are shown

RIGHT *A small-scale concrete mixer can be hired for relatively little cost and will greatly contribute towards a professional finish.*

then it is safe to assume that these can be hired. That said, if you will be using such equipment for an extended period of time, or on a frequent basis, you should consider buying, as there may come a time when the total cost of the hire will be greater than the price tag of the tool.

what to hire

Equipment such as carpet cleaners are popular hire items, but there are plenty of others of which the average person may be unaware. Concrete mixers and floor sanders speed up the work magnificently, putting professional results within reach of the amateur. A small compressor and nail gun can be used to fix a large amount of floorboards down very quickly, whilst a powerfloat will give a smooth, glass-like finish to concrete and screeds.

LEFT *Although this damp-proof fluid injection machine is highly specialized, it is possible to hire one to do the job yourself.*

at the hire shop

Once the preserve of the professional builder, hire shops are increasingly catering for the DIY market, and many stores even offer a home-delivery service at little extra charge for tools too big or too bulky to transport yourself. Before you start using an unfamiliar machine for the first time, it is vital that you fully understand how it operates, so make sure you have this explained to you before leaving the shop. Do not be afraid to ask for a demonstration if you are at all unsure. Staff in hire shops are usually very knowledgeable so do not be afraid to ask for advice. Often they will be able to suggest different methods for completing a task and direct you to tools that you might not know. Explain to them clearly what your project is, what tools you have already and ask them what tools they would suggest you need to hire to complete the job most efficiently. Many stores will have a catalogue, although do not expect this to explain how each piece of equipment works. It is more likely to give details of cost, minimum periods of hire and so forth.

In addition to the machine itself you may need to buy some consumables. In the case of a floor sander this will mean the sanding sheets. Often the shop will give you a selection of these and only charge you for those you

ABOVE RIGHT *You may need to hire a good quality grinder to sharpen tools in your existing tool kit.*

RIGHT *A heavy steel roller is a vital tool for ensuring full adhesion of vinyl flooring, but for just this one job it is best to hire.*

BELOW *An electric floor sander will make light work of an otherwise daunting task. Large, edging and corner versions are available.*

actually use when you return the machine. The store should stock and offer you all the necessary safety gear, such as goggles, kneepads and ear defenders, although it is likely you will be obliged to purchase these.

Finding the nearest tool hire store ought to be as simple as looking in the yellow pages or your local telephone book. Most reputable firms belong to the HSA (Hire Shops Association). If you have difficulty finding an outlet, phone the HSA and they will be able to tell you the location of your nearest member store.

safety considerations

When undertaking any projects around the home safety should be the number one consideration. There is an element of risk to almost any job and it is vital to minimize such risks by taking all necessary precautions. For example, safety equipment should be considered a vital element of your general tool kit and you will also need to maintain a top quality first aid kit. Above all, never carry out any task that common sense indicates will be dangerous.

ladder safety

Ladders and steps are invaluable for gaining access to higher levels. Although simple tools they are often abused and can lead to nasty accidents if used incorrectly. By obeying the following rules you will minimize the risk of injury.

- The distance from the base of the wall or skirting board to the foot of the ladder must be a quarter of the height the ladder rests at.
- The base of the ladder must rest on a level, non-slip surface.
- Both foot pads must touch the ground – you may shim with plywood pads but keep the ladder level.
- Ensure that the top of the ladder has total contact with the wall surface.

- Before mounting a ladder, check all rungs are secure and have not been damaged in any way.
- If using a ladder outdoors watch out for overhead powerlines and telephone cables.
- Never overstretch – if you cannot reach comfortably, move the ladder.
- When working at any height have a helper hold the bottom of the ladder to prevent it moving.

safety advice

The over-enthusiasm of children and curious nature of animals can lead to accidents. Try to keep these 'elements' clear of the working area!

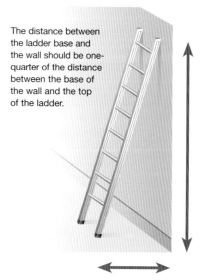

The distance between the ladder base and the wall should be one-quarter of the distance between the base of the wall and the top of the ladder.

Careful ladder positioning is vital for the safety of its user.

safety equipment

A range of safety equipment is available for various DIY tasks. Some items are intended for particular jobs, but many, such as goggles, work boots and protective gloves, should be worn in most situations. It is also essential to have a well stocked first aid kit to deal with grazes and abrasions.

protective gloves

work boots

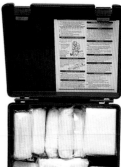
lead test kit

plastic gloves

hard hat

ear defenders

goggles

dust mask

respirator mask

knee pads

first aid kit

lifting

Get help when lifting boards and joists. Do not lift more than you can safely carry and when lifting bend your knees, not just your waist. Wear gloves to protect your hands from rough concrete and timber splinters.

dust

Dust can be deadly so always wear a dust mask, which in Europe should be 'CE' marked. Some of the cheaper masks offer little or no protection against certain dusts. Cut tiles and sheet timber outside if possible, particularly when using power tools.

drilling

Never drill into an area of a wall, floor or ceiling where there are likely to be electric cables or gas and water pipes behind. Use a joist, pipe and cable detector to locate the exact position of such services before starting work.

fire risk

Some of the procedures described in this book utilize heat-producing tools, most notably for the removal of paint. Always have a bucket of water or fire extinguisher close at hand when working with such tools, as a small fire can quickly turn into a big fire if it is not quickly put out.

electric 'cut off'

If using electrically operated power tools, it is a good idea to invest in a special 'cut off' device. In the event of the cable being accidentally cut, the device will shut down the electricity supply to the tool. This is commonly called a residual current circuit device or RCD for short.

toxic materials

Some older properties may contain asbestos products or insulation. If you come across suspected asbestos get it removed by a specialist contractor.

Lead was added to paint until fairly recently and can be released into the atmosphere if an old finish is burnt off. Remove lead-based paints with paint stripper before recoating, rather than with a blow-lamp or hot air gun. Modern paints and varnishes are far less toxic but it is still important to follow the instructions on the can, particularly concerning brush cleaning and disposal of excess paint. Remove paint from skin with a proprietary hand cleaner not white spirit, which strips essential oils from the skin and can lead to dermatitis in extreme cases.

Avoid breathing the heavy vapour from adhesives and work in a well ventilated space whenever possible. If you start to feel light headed, stop work immediately and go outside into the fresh air.

TOOL SAFETY

● Before using any unfamiliar tools read and fully understand the manufacturer's instructions. Tools from hire shops should come with an instruction booklet but if you are in any doubt ask for a demonstration before you leave with the tool.

● Chisels, planes and cutting equipment must always be kept as sharp as possible. More accidents are caused by blunt tools slipping on the surface than by sharp tools. An oilstone is ideal to keep tools such as chisels razor sharp.

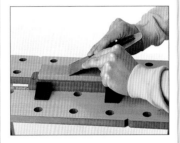

● Power tools require additional precautions. Unplug any tool before changing bits or blades and never operate with safety guards removed. Regularly inspect cables and wires to ensure they are in good condition. If frayed or damaged they should be replaced to prevent the risk of potentially lethal electric shocks. Although just about every power tool is double insulated for safety, never let a cable trail in water or use a power tool outside in the rain. Power tools in general may also require periodic servicing and accessories, such as bits and blades, should be renewed when necessary, as old ones can strain the workings of the tool.

● Hammers can often slip off nail heads when you are knocking them in. To prevent this, sand the striking face of the hammer to clean it and provide a fine key. This technique may be applied to all types of hammer and is useful for any hammering job.

safety considerations

19

walls & ceilings

Many factors affect the anatomy or make-up of the walls and ceilings in your home. Some relate to age, with practices that were once common building practice or regulation now being out-of-date or superseded by improved design and modern materials. Architectural preference can also make a significant difference, which means that even buildings of the same age can have entirely different wall or ceiling structures. So before embarking on a renovation project, it is important to try and recognize the different types of house structure, so that you can make informed decisions on the extent and type of work that will be required. This section considers the most common varieties of walls and ceilings and how they are constructed.

house construction

Ceilings and walls are, quite obviously, major components in house structure. So before embarking on any alterations, it's important to examine the make-up of your house in its entirety. This will help you to recognize some of the main design features and form a greater understanding of the structure of your home and its particular characteristics.

Most modern houses are referred to either as brick-built or timber-framed. However, there are wide variations on this theme, and older buildings can comprise a number of different structures and features. Understanding the principles of house construction can help with recognizing some of your home's characteristics.

It's important to remember that, regardless of house design, the role of walls can be isolated to one key feature – whether they are loadbearing or non-loadbearing. Non-loadbearing walls act as a partition and do not bear any of the house weight, whereas loadbearing walls play an integral part in supplying general support and bearing the weight of floors. This theme is common to all house structures and is the starting point for deciding on any alterations.

tips of the trade

It can sometimes be difficult to identify a wall that is loadbearing. However, these points may help:

● Consider all external walls as loadbearing.

● Check to see where floorboards run parallel with a wall. This implies that the joists run in the opposite direction (ie at right angles), and are thus supported by the wall.

● Look in the loft to see if roof timbers sit on top of the wall. If so, support for the roof is being supplied by that wall.

● Cut a small inspection hatch in the ceiling at the top of the wall. This allows you to inspect the wall construction, to see where joists are running and to see how much support the wall is creating.

understanding timber & block

The majority of houses combine wood, blocks or bricks in their construction and any of these components can have a loadbearing role to play. In other words, a wall that is timber-framed is as capable of being loadbearing as a wall that is made from block or bricks. Similarly, a wall made of brick or blocks does not, necessarily, have to be loadbearing.

The common misconception that a timber-frame wall has less of a loadbearing capability than one made from solid block or brick must therefore be totally dispelled. Instead of judging walls by the material they are made from, it is more useful to think of walls in terms of the role they play within the total house structure (see the illustration on page 23).

brick-built houses

Modern brick-built houses are based on a cavity wall construction, with an outer layer of brick or block and a secondary, inner layer of brick or block. The cavity between the two walls is usually around 50mm (2in) wide. These houses should not be confused with older brick-built properties where the characteristics are more likely to be those specified under 'solid wall construction' (right).

To ensure structural strength, the cavity between the outer and inner brick walls is spanned by special ties. If the internal wall is loadbearing, it will

be made from block or brick. If it is non-loadbearing, the internal wall may again be built with blocks, or less heavyweight stud partitioning (timber frames) may be used.

timber-framed houses

As the name suggests, the main structural elements of these houses are built using timber frames, though they are also built on a cavity structure comprised of two walls. The internal, wooden wall framework is erected first and the outer wall is then built from brick, block or wood cladding. As with brick-built houses, the exterior walls are generally loadbearing. However, because the internal walls are made from wood, it can sometimes be difficult to determine whether these walls are loadbearing or not.

solid wall construction

This type of construction features in older houses, where there is no cavity and therefore not a two-layer system. Walls in these houses tend to be thicker, often with the stone or brick make-up extending from the outer to the inner face of the wall. Internal walls are either made of similar materials to the external walls or they may be constructed from timber partitioning, demonstrating lath and plaster characteristics (see page 29). Loadbearing walls in these houses nearly always comprise the same stone or brick structure as the external walls.

supports

Entrances in loadbearing walls, such as windows and doors, reduce the strength of the wall. For this reason, additional support will be needed over the window or door, in order to take the structural weight of the wall above.

(Non-loadbearing walls, because of their less structural role, do not always need this additional support.) These extra supports are referred to as lintels, and may be of wood, stone, concrete or metal. The type of material is dependent on the age of the house and the size of the opening. Modern

techniques tend to favour rolled-steel joists (RSJs) for large openings, whereas reinforced concrete lintels or galvanized pressed-steel lintels are generally used for doors and windows. Exterior cavity walls may combine lintel types with concrete on the outer wall and wood on the interior.

house structure

To understand the role and function of ceilings and walls, it can be useful to put them in the context of an entire structure. This cross section of a house shows the integration of walls and ceilings, and highlights those areas of the house that bear weight or help to support the weight of the building.

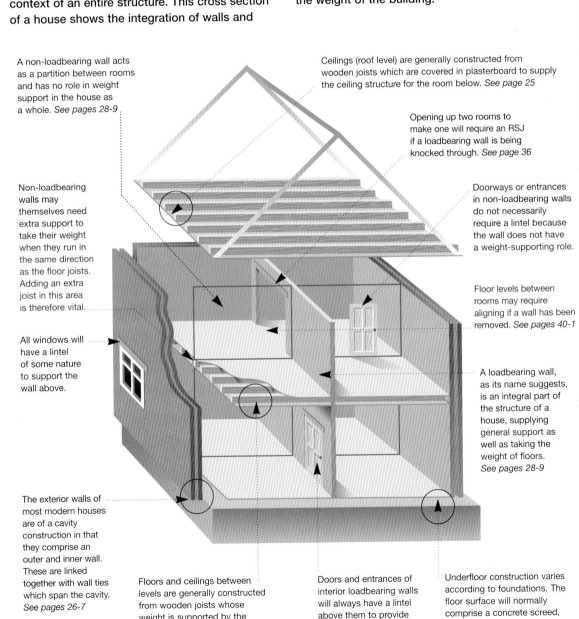

A non-loadbearing wall acts as a partition between rooms and has no role in weight support in the house as a whole. *See pages 28-9*

Non-loadbearing walls may themselves need extra support to take their weight when they run in the same direction as the floor joists. Adding an extra joist in this area is therefore vital.

All windows will have a lintel of some nature to support the wall above.

The exterior walls of most modern houses are of a cavity construction in that they comprise an outer and inner wall. These are linked together with wall ties which span the cavity. *See pages 26-7*

Ceilings (roof level) are generally constructed from wooden joists which are covered in plasterboard to supply the ceiling structure for the room below. *See page 25*

Opening up two rooms to make one will require an RSJ if a loadbearing wall is being knocked through. *See page 36*

Doorways or entrances in non-loadbearing walls do not necessarily require a lintel because the wall does not have a weight-supporting role.

Floor levels between rooms may require aligning if a wall has been removed. *See pages 40-1*

A loadbearing wall, as its name suggests, is an integral part of the structure of a house, supplying general support as well as taking the weight of floors. *See pages 28-9*

Floors and ceilings between levels are generally constructed from wooden joists whose weight is supported by the exterior walls and internal loadbearing walls. *See pages 24-5*

Doors and entrances of interior loadbearing walls will always have a lintel above them to provide support for the wall above.

Underfloor construction varies according to foundations. The floor surface will normally comprise a concrete screed, wooden floorboards or building boards.

ceiling & floor construction

The structure of a house dictates that the ceiling of one room will generally combine to make up the floor of the room above. Since alterations to one room can thereby affect the structure of another, it is vital to consider both ceiling and floor anatomy when planning changes. All the structures shown here have wooden joists which make up the framework of the ceiling. Quite a few modern homes, however, incorporate solid concrete ceilings — so there will be some variation on the themes outlined below. As with most designs, trends vary with time and the basic ceiling structure will be very dependent on the age of the building.

lath and plaster ceilings

An old design, lath and plaster ceilings are now avoided in modern techniques of construction. However, they are still commonly found in older houses and may well feature in a house that is intended for renovation.

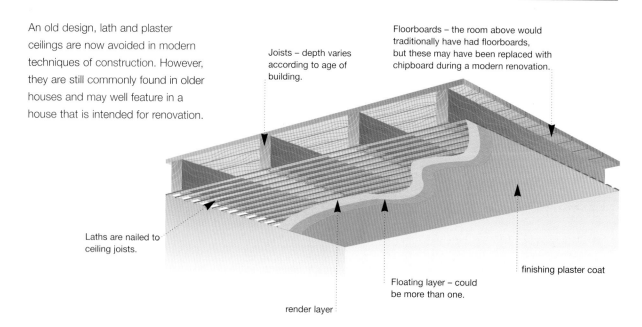

Joists – depth varies according to age of building.

Floorboards – the room above would traditionally have had floorboards, but these may have been replaced with chipboard during a modern renovation.

Laths are nailed to ceiling joists.

render layer

Floating layer – could be more than one.

finishing plaster coat

plasterboard and plaster ceilings

The invention of plasterboard made lath construction an out-of-date and time consuming method for building ceilings. Therefore, most modern ceilings have a plasterboard base, which is either plastered as shown here, or dry lined as shown on page 25.

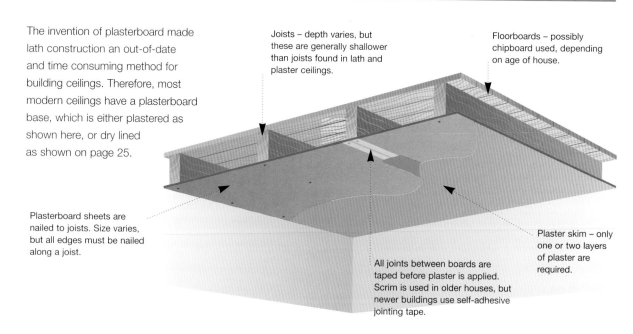

Joists – depth varies, but these are generally shallower than joists found in lath and plaster ceilings.

Floorboards – possibly chipboard used, depending on age of house.

Plasterboard sheets are nailed to joists. Size varies, but all edges must be nailed along a joist.

All joints between boards are taped before plaster is applied. Scrim is used in older houses, but newer buildings use self-adhesive jointing tape.

Plaster skim – only one or two layers of plaster are required.

dry lined ceilings

Similar to plastered plasterboard ceilings, dry lined ceilings are finished using a slightly different technique. Dry lining tape over the tapered edges seals the join and produces a smooth surface ready for decoration. This is probably the easiest ceiling structure for a home improvement enthusiast to tackle.

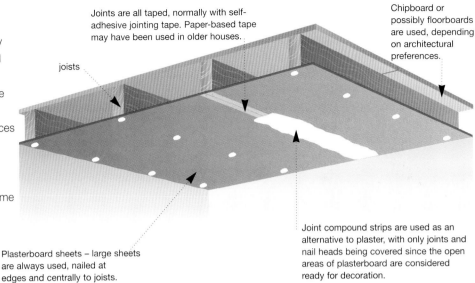

Joints are all taped, normally with self-adhesive jointing tape. Paper-based tape may have been used in older houses.

joists

Chipboard or possibly floorboards are used, depending on architectural preferences.

Plasterboard sheets – large sheets are always used, nailed at edges and centrally to joists.

Joint compound strips are used as an alternative to plaster, with only joints and nail heads being covered since the open areas of plasterboard are considered ready for decoration.

wooden ceilings

Not all ceilings have a plasterboard or plaster-based finish, and wood is a common alternative to this type of finish. In fact, wood is often used as a cladding mechanism for finishing the ceiling, with tongue and groove boards being a popular surface choice.

Floorboards – wooden board choice for ceiling will often mean a wooden board bias above.

joists

Tongue and groove boards are interlocked to create a neat finish. The boards are nailed to joists either 'invisibly' through tongues or through the board face.

Board lengths join lengthways with straight cuts measured to meet at joists.

top floor ceilings

The ceiling between the top floor of a house and the loft space is often slightly different in make-up to the other ceilings in the house. The overall structure will depend on the age of the building and may therefore look like any of those already shown. The main difference will be the presence of an insulating layer between ceiling and loft, and a basic chipboard floor may be fitted on the upper layer.

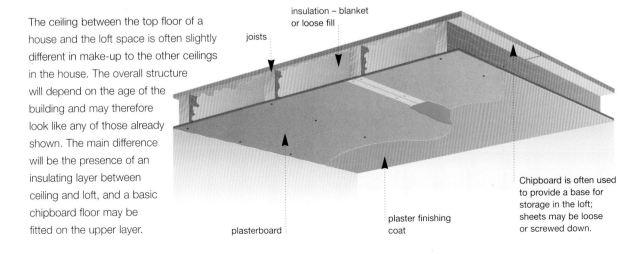

insulation – blanket or loose fill

joists

plasterboard

plaster finishing coat

Chipboard is often used to provide a base for storage in the loft; sheets may be loose or screwed down.

external walls

Wall purpose and structure can be categorized as to whether the wall is internal or external. Much like ceilings, the age of the property can affect the type of structure considerably, as can architectural or design considerations. This is particularly the case for external walls, which are visible as a finished product, whereas interior walls are constructed to provide a flat surface which will then be further decorated. That said, external walls can generally be identified by two simple categories — whether they are of a solid or cavity structure.

walls & ceilings

26

solid walls

Solid external walls, or those with no cavity, tend to be found in older buildings. Depth and make-up is varied, but most show similar characteristics to the examples outlined below.

cavity walls

Nearly all modern houses have external walls which are constructed with a cavity. This means that the external wall effectively consists of two layers, with a void or cavity between the layers for insulation.

There are many possible combinations for how these two layers are constructed but the examples on the following page demonstrate the most common variations that occur.

brick/block solid wall

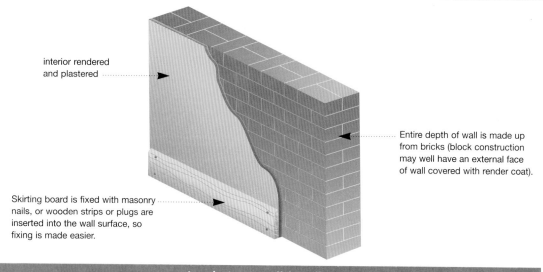

interior rendered and plastered

Entire depth of wall is made up from bricks (block construction may well have an external face of wall covered with render coat).

Skirting board is fixed with masonry nails, or wooden strips or plugs are inserted into the wall surface, so fixing is made easier.

natural stone solid wall

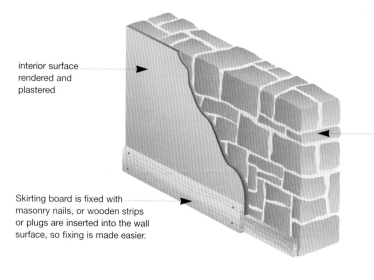

interior surface rendered and plastered

Entire depth of wall is made up from stone (interior make-up of wall is usually made from less attractive pieces of stone – the best is therefore kept for the outer facing layer).

Skirting board is fixed with masonry nails, or wooden strips or plugs are inserted into the wall surface, so fixing is made easier.

brick/block cavity with render & plaster

This type of cavity wall employs solid wall construction materials to provide a brick outer layer for the finished exterior of the house, and a block inner layer which requires further rendering and plastering before decoration can be applied.

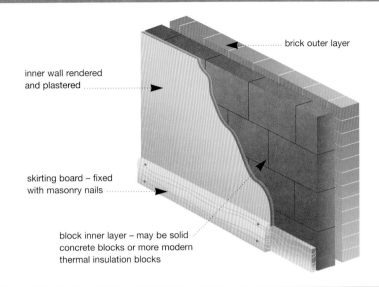

brick outer layer

inner wall rendered and plastered

skirting board – fixed with masonry nails

block inner layer – may be solid concrete blocks or more modern thermal insulation blocks

brick/timber cavity

This is a popular form of construction in modern houses, where the exterior wall layer is made from a solid facing material such as brick, and the interior layer takes the form of a wooden framework.

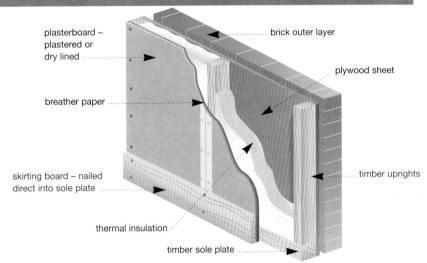

plasterboard – plastered or dry lined

breather paper

skirting board – nailed direct into sole plate

thermal insulation

timber sole plate

brick outer layer

plywood sheet

timber uprights

brick/block cavity – dry lined

This example shows that block walls can be combined with dry lining techniques for finishing purposes. Outer and inner wall construction is similar to that shown for the first example of cavity walls, but the internal finishing is clearly different.

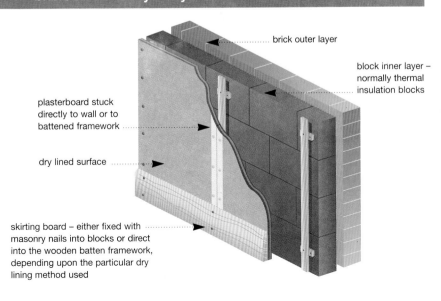

plasterboard stuck directly to wall or to battened framework

dry lined surface

skirting board – either fixed with masonry nails into blocks or direct into the wooden batten framework, depending upon the particular dry lining method used

brick outer layer

block inner layer – normally thermal insulation blocks

internal walls

Internal walls are usually constructed as a single layer and therefore do not have the same depth as external walls. Many characteristics are similar, but there tends to be a wide variety of structure in terms of the internal make-up of the wall itself. Much is dependent on whether the wall is loadbearing or non-loadbearing, and therefore what structural requirements it has in relation to the rest of the building.

solid construction

As the name suggests, these walls are made from solid materials, blocks or bricks. The main structural differences depend on how the outer faces of the wall are finished.

hollow construction

Hollow wall construction is very common in modern houses, with most homes containing some form of 'hollow' wall. However, this does not necessarily mean that the wall is non-loadbearing, and it is important to check such issues out before commencing work. The examples on the page opposite illustrate the most common types of internal hollow wall.

block

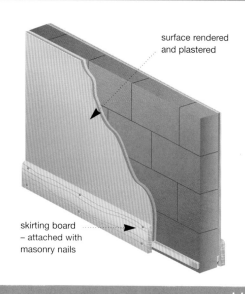

surface rendered and plastered

skirting board – attached with masonry nails

brick

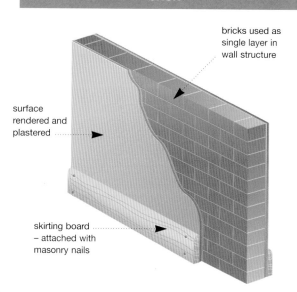

bricks used as single layer in wall structure

surface rendered and plastered

skirting board – attached with masonry nails

block/dry lined

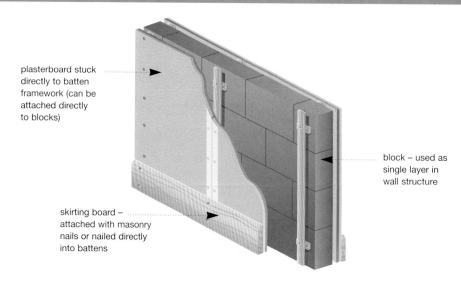

plasterboard stuck directly to batten framework (can be attached directly to blocks)

block – used as single layer in wall structure

skirting board – attached with masonry nails or nailed directly into battens

plasterboard/stud partition

Probably the most commonly occurring of all modern internal hollow walls. Easy to build and adaptable to most circumstances.

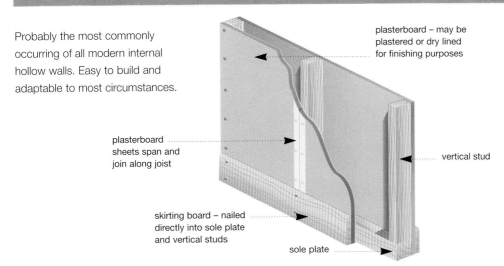

plasterboard – may be plastered or dry lined for finishing purposes

plasterboard sheets span and join along joist

vertical stud

skirting board – nailed directly into sole plate and vertical studs

sole plate

dry partition wall

A lightweight and simply built wall. Its make-up still provides a rigid finished product.

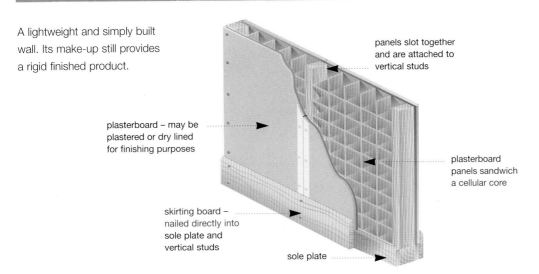

panels slot together and are attached to vertical studs

plasterboard – may be plastered or dry lined for finishing purposes

plasterboard panels sandwich a cellular core

skirting board – nailed directly into sole plate and vertical studs

sole plate

lath and plaster partition

As with ceiling structures, lath and plaster dates back to older houses before the advent of plasterboard.

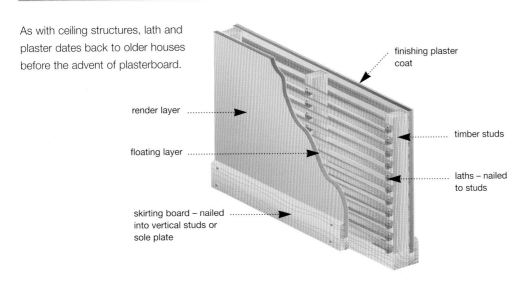

finishing plaster coat

render layer

floating layer

timber studs

laths – nailed to studs

skirting board – nailed into vertical studs or sole plate

altering the structure of a wall

The type and extent of work required to alter a wall structure will largely depend on the existing structure. Before deciding on the exact changes you would like to make, it is important to identify the kind of wall you currently have, so that you can gauge the best procedures for transformation. As always, the key issue is whether the wall is loadbearing or non-loadbearing – only once this has been established can planning commence for alteration. This chapter covers a range of projects, some with more structural implications than others, but many deal with the more aesthetic aspects of altering the structure of walls within your home.

Open plan dining and living areas create a very relaxed and comfortable feel for your home and surroundings.

recognizing problems – 1

Cracks and faults in wall and ceiling surfaces can often look more problematic than they actually are. However, while the main concern may appear to be aesthetic, cracks should also be seen as signs of potential structural problems – such as movement – so it is important to try to determine their cause. Many cracks form for particular reasons and can easily be identified and categorized. The diagram below shows common areas where cracking occurs.

testing cracks and movement

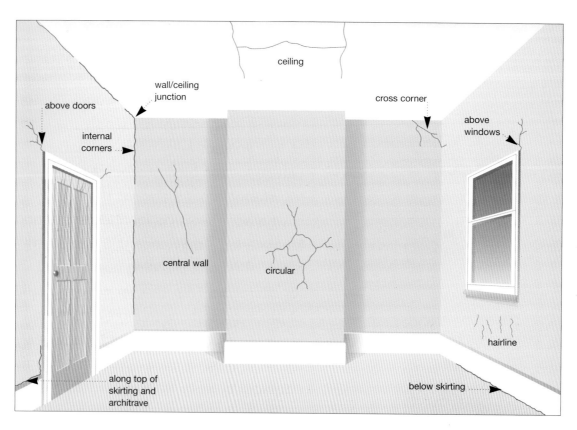

ceiling

wall/ceiling junction

cross corner

above doors

above windows

internal corners

central wall

circular

hairline

along top of skirting and architrave

below skirting

Determining where there is movement and how cracks – if any – develop can obviously be difficult. Movements tend to be slight and cracks take time to develop, making it virtually impossible to monitor them accurately. For this reason, proprietary crack monitoring systems which enable accurate measuring of any movement can now be bought. Although manufacturers' guidelines do vary, the general principles of use remain the same for most commercial brands. If in doubt, contact the product manufacturer or a structural surveyor for further assistance.

1 Screw the detector in place, with the detection scale roughly positioned over the crack. Do not overtighten the screws at this stage.

2 Shift the scale on the detector so that it sits precisely in line with the crack. Tighten the screws when you are happy with the position.

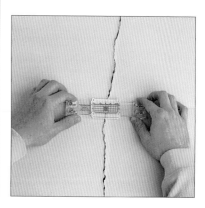

3 Remove the plastic lugs from the edge of the detector to free the two-plate mechanism. If movement does occur, the scale on one plate will move in relation to the other, thereby making it possible accurately to observe the extent and timespan of any movement. Detectors, of slightly varying designs, can also be used across corners or at ceiling and floor level.

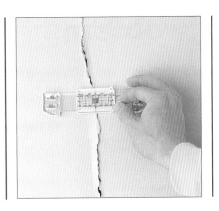

safety advice

Always seek professional advice about cracks that may be caused by structural problems. Detecting subsidence or structural faults is a skilled profession, not work for amateurs. Failure to gauge the gravity of the situation could present long-term dangers to both the structure of the house and the health of its inhabitants.

type	causes of cracks & remedies
internal corners	These cracks are often a result of settlement in new homes and therefore can be filled and decorated. Persistent cracking should be monitored.
ceiling	Ceiling cracks which are very directional, in that they have a relatively straight course or turn at right angles, tend to result from slight board movement in the ceiling structure. These can be filled and decorated or, if they persist, lining can normally prevent them from reappearing.
cross corner	Cracks which extend across a corner from one wall to another can represent a subsidence problem, especially if lines of brick or blockwork can be picked out. In such cases, seek professional advice.
above windows	Cracks are often visible extending from the corners of windows up towards ceiling level. So long as they are relatively small, they generally represent slight settlement or movement. However, large cracks that show a vertical shift should be investigated further.
hairline	These cracks are common, multi-directional, and suggest slight movement of a plaster surface. Numbers tend to increase with the age of the building. Most are superficial and do not represent any cause for alarm. However, if new plaster surfaces display a number of persistent cracks, this could suggest that the plaster was poorly mixed or has not bonded correctly to the wall. In such cases, replastering may be necessary.
below skirting	Gaps below skirting tend to suggest that the skirting was poorly fitted. However, cracks that continue to develop could reflect floor problems or some subsidence. Those which continue to grow should be investigated by a professional.
circular	Cracks that form irregular, circular shapes tend to reflect areas of plaster blowing away from the wall background. This is common in old lath and plaster walls, where age has taken its toll and the plaster surface has become unstable in localized areas. The affected area can be removed and patch-plastered.
central wall cracks	These may occur for any number of reasons and should simply be monitored to check that they do not grow wider. Seek professional advice in extreme cases.
along top of skirting and architrave	Cracks occur in these places either because of age and slight building movement or because the materials are new and take a little time to settle to the atmospheric conditions of the particular room environment. Unless the cracks persist or grow after filling and redecoration, there is generally no cause for alarm.
above doors	See explanation for cracks around windows.
wall/ceiling junction	These cracks commonly occur during settlement in new houses, and as a result of age in older ones. Small cracks can be filled and redecorated, whereas larger types should be monitored to check that they do not expand, thus requiring structural repair.

recognizing problems – 2

In addition to movement, damp and insect or fungal infestation can also have structural effects on the home. Many such problems are easily remedied but others can have wider consequences and be extremely damaging to the building structure, especially if they are left untreated. These sorts of problems can take many forms and affect different areas of the home, but the diagram below outlines many of the key areas to look out for.

damp and infestation

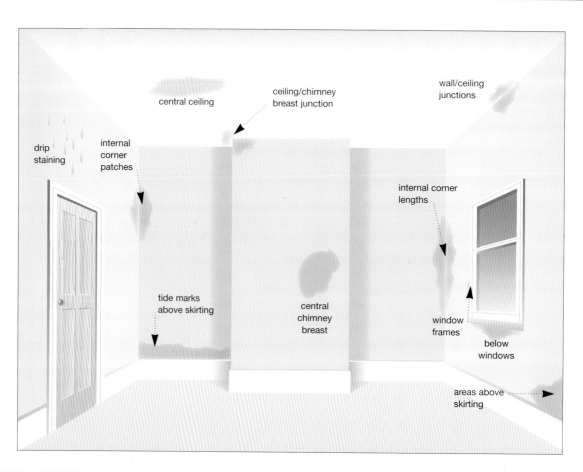

central ceiling

ceiling/chimney
breast junction

wall/ceiling
junctions

drip
staining

internal
corner
patches

internal corner
lengths

tide marks
above skirting

central
chimney
breast

window
frames

below
windows

areas above
skirting

other problems of infestation

Aside from those problems usually associated with damp, there are other potential problems that can be linked to insects and fungal attack.

dry rot

This is an exceptionally damaging form of decay which mainly affects timber but also spreads across masonry.

While identifying and counteracting the source will remedy the problem, dry rot attacks with actual fungicidal spores which spread the disease very quickly, making it difficult to eradicate. Dry rot does initially take hold in areas of damp and poor ventilation. It is identified by thin, white strands which spread along surfaces, rather like a spider's web. The effect breaks down building structure irreparably. Treatment should therefore be hasty, involving the cutting out and destroying of all infected areas. New timber and

materials should be treated to protect it against dry rot infection.

woodworm

These are basically the larvae of particular beetles, and so there are two methods for discovering if you have the problem. Either the appearance of the beetles provides evidence of their presence, or more commonly, the actual flight holes are visible, indicating their existence in the household woodwork. Action against woodworm must be swift as the parasite can quickly break down timber and spread throughout the entire house. Spray infected areas and any unaffected woodwork nearby with the appropriate insecticide, to prevent further spreading. When replacing any timbers, always ensure that the new material has been preserved properly. If in any doubt, seek professional advice.

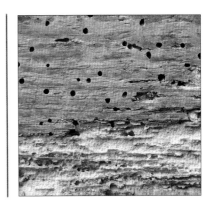

type	causes of damp & remedies
central ceiling	These patches tend to be a result of leaking pipes in the ceiling, or at top floor level they may be a roof leak dripping on to surfaces below. Consult a plumber for fixing pipework, and make any necessary tile repair work at roof level.
ceiling/chimney breast junction	Damp patches which develop in these areas may be a result of a gap in flashing around the chimney. Therefore inspect the area and effect a repair if required.
wall/ceiling junctions	At top floor level, this is often a result of a blocked gutter. Unblock the gutter to eliminate the resulting damp penetration. This sort of damp may also result from a lean-to building, where the flashing at the point where it joins the main building has deteriorated. Check the flashing and repair if necessary.
internal corner lengths	Elongated damp patches along internal corners often indicate a blocked or cracked downpipe on the exterior of the building. Dripping water therefore gradually penetrates, causing a persistent damp wall stain. Unblock or replace the downpipe as required.
window frames	Damp penetration is common around the edges of windows due to a build-up of condensation or because of a break in the seal around the edge of the window frame itself. Check that the window is sealed correctly and reapply silicone sealant if necessary. If the problem is more condensation-based, install better ventilation systems for the room or simply open windows more often.
below windows	Seals beneath windows may be damaged or the drip guard below the sill may be blocked. Check both areas and clear or re-seal as required.
areas above skirting	Large damp patches above skirting are often a result of the build-up of material, such as piles of soil, on the external side of the wall surface. This bridges the damp course and causes damp penetration. Simply remove the obstructive material, and ensure soil levels are kept below damp course level.
central chimney breast	These patches commonly develop in disused chimneys where the chimney and fireplace have been blocked off. The disused chimney void therefore has no ventilation, causing the moist damp air to penetrate through the chimney breast. To cure this problem, install an air vent in the chimney breast in order to improve air flow and circulation.
tide marks above skirting	If these are not a result of the damp course being bridged on the other side of the wall, then it may be straightforward rising damp. This is common in older houses with no damp course or in houses where the damp course is damaged and therefore allowing water penetration. Various damproofing injection systems are the most effective cure. These systems are always best carried out by professionals.
internal corner patches	Small damp patches in walls often result from patches of damaged pointing or render on the exterior of the building. Simple repair of the appropriate material should cure the problem.
drip staining	Visible stains from drips or running moisture on the walls tends to point in the direction of a condensation problem. This commonly occurs in kitchens and bathrooms. Simply install better ventilation systems and open windows more often.

removing a loadbearing wall ⁄⁄⁄⁄

Removing a loadbearing wall is not a project that should be tackled lightly, and professional advice and instruction should be sought before carrying out this procedure. Total wall removal is rare, and it is more common to knock through a loadbearing wall in order to open up the floor layout and convert two rooms into a single area with a more open plan design. The work involved is strongly based around supportive measures.

The most important factor when taking on work of this kind is to ensure that there is adequate support, both while the area of wall is being removed and when the work is complete. This latter point is crucial – an RSJ (rolled steel joist) or beam of some nature will be required to act as the permanent support. Its size and make-up can depend on two major factors, namely the structure of the wall you are wishing to remove and the span of the opening you need to make. Both these factors require serious calculation, and the beam type and construction should be decided in consultation with a structural engineer. Once the necessary safety precautions, procedures and planning have been finalized, the actual work itself is possible for most practically minded, home improvement enthusiasts. Work may therefore be divided into two stages. Firstly the opening has to be made, and secondly the supportive RSJ must be inserted.

making the opening

Preparation and planning is essential for this procedure, and because the nature of the work is relatively demanding in a physical sense, two people are much better than one in this instance. Also keep the working area clear of any obstacles as much as possible, as this will help to reduce the likelihood of accidents.

1 Mark out the size of the opening on the wall surface.

2 Knock holes through the wall above the proposed opening.

3 Insert needles through the holes.

4 Support the needles by props on both sides of the wall.

5 Use a stone cutter or club hammer and bolster chisel to cut around the edge of the opening.

6 Remove the blocks or bricks by first loosening them with a club hammer and bolster chisel and then levering them out with a wrecking bar or lifting them by hand.

7 Continue to remove blocks until the entire area is clear.

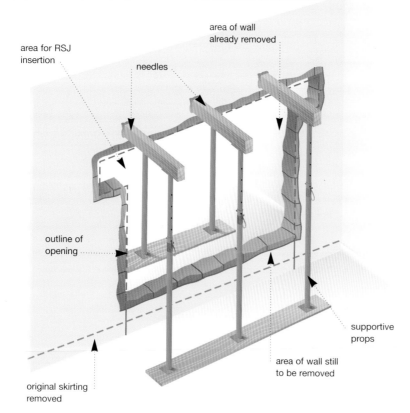

area for RSJ insertion

needles

area of wall already removed

outline of opening

supportive props

area of wall still to be removed

original skirting removed

Two people or more will definitely be required for this stage of the project as even the smallest lintels are surprisingly heavy. It is also a time-consuming process when setting the RSJ in position. Make sure that you check the level of the RSJ because problems will be difficult to rectify later.

1 At the top corners of the opening, take out bricks or blocks to accommodate the RSJ ends.

2 Check and re-check measurements to ensure that the lintel will fit into the required space.

3 Apply a bed of mortar to the area before lifting the RSJ into place.

4 Check that the RSJ is level. Use cut bricks or blocks, wedged beneath the end of the RSJ, to rectify if necessary.

5 Apply more mortar around the RSJ ends to ensure it will be held securely in place.

6 Make good with plasterboard and/or render and plaster around the RSJ.

7 Make good with plasterboard and/or render and plaster around the cut blocks or bricks which make up the sides of the opening.

8 Remove needles and patch in holes.

patched-in holes where needles had been

RSJ

cut away edge of wall

RSJ supported by cut bricks and mortar (sometimes structural engineers may specify the need for padstones for RSJ support)

factors to consider

In addition to the practical considerations of how to support your wall, there are also a number of other issues that should be carefully addressed.

needle requirement

The number of needles that you will require for the support will depend on the width of the opening that you plan to create. The actual needle dimensions should not be less than 15cm x 10cm (6in x 4in), but you should consult a structural engineer in order to establish the exact needle requirements of your wall.

propping

Steel props can be hired at a relatively low cost, and their adjustable nature makes them ideal for these supporting purposes. Make sure that the bases of the props are positioned on scaffold planks so that the weight distribution is evened out. Most prop bases have nail holes so that they can be nailed into the scaffold planks to eliminate any risk of them moving.

RSJ support

In many cases the new RSJ may be accommodated in the existing wall structure with no extra support below it. However, in some cases it may be necessary to install extra concrete support or padstones. Consult a structural engineer for correct requirements in your circumstances.

safety equipment

This sort of work requires close attention to safety and all the necessary precautions must be taken. Wear protective gloves, goggles and a hard hat when taking down the wall. A dust mask may also be needed, especially when clearing away the rubble and dust caused by wall removal. As with any DIY task, the area must be kept as clear as possible from obstructions, and rubble should be removed regularly. (See page 18 for more practical health and safety advice.)

removing a non-loadbearing wall

Before embarking on this project it is vital to ensure that the wall is definitely non-loadbearing. Once this is established, removal requires little more than a simple methodical approach. However, it is important to bear in mind that there will undoubtedly be a certain amount of making good to do once the wall has gone, so try to minimize the amount of damage caused to the ceiling and other wall surfaces.

The techniques required for removing a non-loadbearing wall will largely depend on whether the wall is of a stud construction or built from solid bricks or blocks. Once this has been established, ensure that electrical sockets, switches and pipework have been removed and re-routed as necessary by an electrician or plumber.

👍 tips of the trade

Never underestimate the amount of mess and dust that can be generated by projects such as wall removal. Plan the task to fit in conveniently with your busy household (such as at a weekend, when disruption will not be a problem) and take the time to remove all furniture and floorcoverings from the room(s) in which you will be working.

removing a stud wall

The lightweight construction of stud walls means that their removal tends to be a fairly straightforward job, so long as you follow an organized, basic order of work.

tools for the job

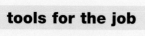

wrecking bar

joist detector

panel saw

1 Begin by removing any features on the wall surface such as picture rails, coving and skirting boards. A wrecking bar is the ideal tool to prise

skirting away from the wall. Try not to damage the skirting as it can be saved and possibly re-used on another wall.

2 Locate a central stud in the wall, either by using a joist detector or by tapping along the wall surface with the head of the wrecking bar – areas between studs will sound hollow, whereas stud positions will make the noise of a dull thud. Dig into the wall

by the stud with the end of the bar and lever the plasterboard away from the stud framework.

3 When all the plasterboard has been removed, begin to take out the wooden studs by sawing through

each one in a suitable place. Cut slightly above the joint/nogging cross section – if you cut too tight to the joint, the saw may catch the nails or screws in the studs.

4 To remove the floor plate, it is often easier to saw it into separate sections. This helps to reduce the strength of its bonding 'power' with the floor surface.

✋ safety advice

When carrying out any sort of demolition job, wear gloves, goggles and a hard hat to protect yourself from any flying debris or sharp edges.

5) Use the wrecking bar to lever the sections of the plate away from the floor surface. A similar technique may be used for the ceiling plate and wall plates as required.

part removal of a solid block wall

Non-loadbearing block or brick walls may be totally or partially removed to create a larger room space. Partial removal can provide a more aesthetically pleasing finish because, instead of producing a completely open new room, it creates two areas with character and interest.

tools for the job

pencil or chalk line
....
wrecking bar
....
club hammer
....
bolster chisel
....
angle bead
....
hacksaw
....
plastering trowel
....
spirit level
....

Removal of blocks can be harder work than that of a simple stud wall, and you will need additional tools such as a club hammer and bolster to break down the joints. It is always best to start at the top and work down, removing single blocks if possible. When partially removing a wall, draw guidelines directly on to the wall surface using a chalk line or pencil and level. A stone cutter can be used to make an accurate cut down these guidelines, but in most cases it is easy enough to follow the line using the club hammer and bolster chisel.

1) Once the main area of wall has been removed, straighten up the block edges as much as possible, and remove any loose mortar.

2) Use a hacksaw (see page 113) to cut some angle bead to the required height of the wall edge and position it along the edge using bonding plaster to hold it in place. It may be necessary to use a spirit level in order to gain a truly vertical position for the bead. Position another angle bead on the adjacent edge. Hold the angle beads in position while the bonding plaster dries.

3) Mix and apply PVA solution (5 parts water to 1 part PVA) to the edges of the trimmed blocks. Work the solution into every crevice and allow to dry to a tacky consistency.

4) Then apply more bonding plaster along the entire wall edge. A perfect finish is not required at this stage, so just ensure a good coverage of the whole edge. Score the bonding plaster (see page 111) before allowing it to dry.

5) Mix and apply finishing plaster over the top of the bonding coat, creating a smooth, flat finish. Use the rigid frame of the angle beads on which to rest the edges of the plastering trowel so that the finish is flush. Apply plaster along the adjacent edges of the angle bead, feathering it with the original wall.

aligning floors

Once a wall has been removed – whether totally or partially – it can be common for the floors between what were once two rooms to vary slightly in level. This happens most often in older houses, where either there has been some slight subsidence, or an extension has been built with slightly different floor levels to that of the original house. The reasons for variation in levels is not that important, but making good the situation is vital in order to obtain a suitable floor join.

Even when floor levels are similar, it is likely that you may need to fill the gap left by the old wall. This is often the case when a block wall has been removed – either the blocks break off at ground level, producing a rough surface, or the blocks drop below the floor level, leaving a gap to fill between the two rooms. The techniques required for such tasks will be mainly dependent on whether the floors are concrete- or wood-based.

concrete floors

tools for the job

dusting brush
bolster chisel
club hammer
paint brush
gauging trowel
wooden batten
plastering trowel

After removing a stud wall, little reparation is normally required because the wall would have been built on top of an existing concrete screed. However, when removing a block wall, it can be common to find that the concrete screed was laid after the block wall was erected. This means the block removal either leaves a large hole along the line of what was the wall base, or the blocks are broken away leaving a rough, unfinished joint across the floor. In either situation, some repair work will be required.

1 Dust out as much debris and loose material as possible from the old block wall base. Ensure that none of the broken block edges protrude above the surrounding floor surface. Trim such protrusions using a bolster chisel and club hammer.

2 Mix up a PVA solution (5 parts water to 1 part PVA) and apply it generously along the entire broken block joint, allowing the solution to overlap the edges of the concrete screed on both sides of the joint.

3 Mix up some mortar (5 parts building sand to 1 part cement) and press it firmly into the joint. Use the edge of a gauging trowel to

'chop' the mortar in, thus ensuring it gets into every area along the length of the joint. Allow the mortar to protrude slightly above the surrounding concrete.

4 Cut a length of batten, slightly longer than the width of the joint, and position it across the joint. Slowly push it along the length of the joint, agitating the batten slightly from side to side so that it gradually removes the excess mortar, to create a flush join between the existing screed

and the new mortar. This process may need to be repeated two or three times to produce a finish that is totally smooth and flat.

5 Once dry, mix up some self-levelling compound and apply it along the joint, allowing a large overlap on to the surrounding screed. Gently spread the compound using a plastering trowel. Allow it to settle and dry, providing a perfectly smooth and level joint.

making a slope

Where floor levels vary slightly, a slope or step may need to be constructed. Slopes can be created by simply feathering the edges of the self-levelling compound to produce an even drop between the two levels. Alternatively, the floors can be evened by applying a greater depth of compound to the entire surface of the lower concrete screed level.

wooden floors

tools for the job

cordless drill/driver

claw hammer

wrecking bar

One of the key considerations when working on a wooden floor is whether the surface will be exposed – thus making aesthetic considerations important. If it is to be covered, a firm, level joint is the only major concern, but exposed floors need more care.

reparation of a covered floor

1 Attach lengths of 5cm x 2.5cm (2in x 1in) batten to the wooden joists on either side of the old wall joint. Ensure that the top edge of each length of batten sits directly flush with the top of the joist and therefore precisely below the wooden boarding.

2 Filling the gap will depend on its dimensions. Ideally, nail a new floorboard in position along the joint, allowing the nails to go through the board and into the battens that have been attached to the joists. Different gap dimensions may require you to cut a board such as chipboard to the appropriate size before nailing it in position along the gap.

reparation of an exposed floor

Most exposed floors are made up of traditional floorboards, so filling gaps may also entail adjusting the original board position.

1 Attach lengths of 5cm x 2.5cm (2in x1in) batten to the wooden joist on the floorboard side of the old wall joint. Use a wrecking bar to lift every other board carefully along the joint junction and to lift the chipboard flooring. (Alternatively you may find the boards need to be unscrewed and for this a wrecking bar is inappropriate.)

2 Use a claw hammer to remove any old nails that are protruding from the floor joists.

3 Cut boards to length and use them to infill across the floor surface, creating a neat finish.

building a stud wall – 1

Stud walls are built in two main stages, and the following four pages explain each step. Before any work can begin, however, you must first establish the direction of the ceiling and floor joists – this will determine whether the head and sole plates are to run parallel or at right angles to them. Use a proprietary joist detector for this task. These simple tools contain sensor pads which trigger a light every time they pass over a joist.

walls & ceilings

42

When the wall runs parallel to the joists, it is best to position the sole plate directly above a joist and the head plate below a joist. On first floors, a further joist below floor level should be used to provide extra strength (see page 23).

When the wall is to run at right angles to the joists there is greater flexibility because fixings will be made on subsequent joists across the span of the room. So be prepared to find a compromise between your desired position for the wall and the most practical location for fixing.

making the frame

tools for the job

joist detector

hammer

chalk line

spirit level

pencil

panel saw

cordless drill

tape measure

board lifter (optional)

plumb line (optional)

Studs may either be 10cm x 5cm (4in x 2in) or 7.5cm x 5cm (3in x 2in) in dimension, and are generally made from sawn softwood. Traditionalists choose sturdy, thicker studs whereas most modern buildings will contain the smaller ones. The distance between the studs is vital – if you are covering the frame with plasterboard that is 9.5mm (⅜in) thick, the studs must be

a maximum of 40cm (1ft 4in) apart. However, if you are using 12.5mm (½in) plasterboard, the studs should be no more than 60cm (2ft) apart.

1 Use a joist detector to trace the position of joists and any cables or pipes above the ceiling surface.

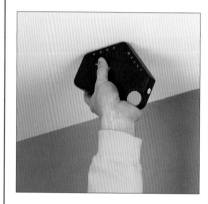

2 Having decided on the wall position, knock a nail into the ceiling close to the wall junction, at what will be the centre of the head plate position. Do the same at the opposite ceiling/wall junction.

3 Attach a chalk line between the two nails and snap a guideline on to the ceiling surface. This line will

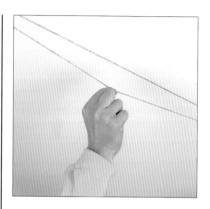

help to provide the exact position for the head plate.

4 Use a spirit level and pencil to continue this guideline down both walls at each end of the ceiling guideline. Continue the lines down to floor level.

5 Hold a stud section at skirting board level, and direct the wall pencil guideline so that it bisects the centre of the stud. Make a pencil guideline on either side of the stud, thus marking the skirting board. Remove the stud and cut out this section of skirting board in order to accommodate the sole plate. Repeat this process on the opposite wall. The guidelines should now indicate the

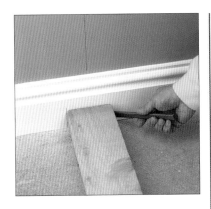

position of the head plate (ceiling), sole plate (floor) and wall plates.

6 Cut a timber stud to the exact length between the opposing walls. Position it, allowing the cut skirting board sections to accommodate each end of the timber length. Mark on this piece of timber (the sole plate), the exact position of any doors that may be required. Remember to allow for the door lining and the door frame.

7 Screw the sole plate into the floor at 40cm (1ft 4in) intervals. For concrete floors, drill and plug the holes before screw insertion.

8 Cut a timber stud to the exact length between the opposing walls at ceiling level, and make a pencil mark bisecting the centre of the stud at each end. Align this mark with the wall guideline, before fixing the stud or head plate in position.

9 Cut two studs to the exact length between the head and ceiling plate on each wall and fix them into position.

10 Mark off along the sole plate at 40cm (1ft 4in) intervals to indicate the positions for

the vertical studs. If a door position has been marked, work away from each side of the door frame guidelines until you reach each wall.

11 Cut small blocks of timber and nail them in position at the side of each stud guideline. This is not essential, but it will help to make fixing the vertical studs in place much easier. The frame is now complete and ready to be filled in (see page 44 for the next stage).

USING A PLUMB LINE

It is also possible to create guidelines using a plumb line or bob. Once you have established the ceiling guideline (steps 1–2), attach the plumb line to each of the nails in turn and mark along, and at the bottom of, the line to gain a vertical guide. The plumb line may also be used from a central ceiling position to mark sole plate guidelines along the floor. Ensure that the plumb line is stationary before marking off.

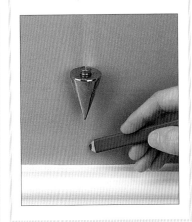

building a stud wall – 2 ↗↗↗

Once the outer framework of the stud wall has been installed, attention can be turned to filling in the framework and plasterboarding. Make a final check on levels of the frame and its positioning, because any slight adjustments are best made at this stage rather than later. See page 42 for a list of tool requirements.

filling the frame

1 Measure each vertical stud and cut the required lengths. Fix them at the base, holding them against the block supports to prevent them from moving. Use 10cm (4in) nails and knock or 'skew' them in at an angle on both sides of the stud, so that the fixings penetrate into the sole plate.

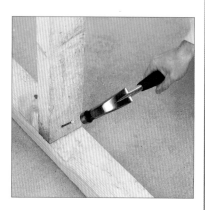

2 With the stud fixed at its base, hold a level against the length in order to find the precise vertical fixing

position in the head plate. Skew nails into each side of the stud and into the head plate.

3 Keep checking the level and adjusting the stud until it is precisely vertical, before securing it finally in place.

4 To make the door frame, cut a length of timber to the exact size between the two vertical studs on either side of the door opening. Remember to check the correct height measurement for the door (including the door lining), and nail the length in place, ensuring that it is level.

5 To add strength, fix a further length vertically between the door head and the head plate. Nails may be inserted into the base of the vertical stud, whereas at ceiling level the nails need to be skewed through the vertical length, into the head plate.

6 Extra strength will also need to be added to the full-length studs, so cut short lengths of timber to fit horizontally between them. These noggings should be positioned half way between the sole and head plates.

7 Once you have completed the framework, work on providing access for any services or electrical cables that may need to run through the wall. Drill holes through studs and noggings as required.

walls & ceilings

44

8 Thread cables through the holes drilled in the studs. (Check with a qualified electrician the exact cable requirements for the services you require.)

fixing the plasterboard

As discussed on page 42, ensure that you are using the correct depth of plasterboard according to the position of the studs. Bear in mind that if you are planning to use dry lining, the plasterboard should also have tapered edges (see page 96).

Invariably, sheets of plasterboard need to be cut to fit so careful measuring is required. As most ceilings or wall surfaces undulate slightly and are not completely square, the edge of plasterboard sheets will often need to be 'scribed' in order to produce a precise fit. This is most important at ceiling level and corners because the joint needs to be as tight as possible, whereas at floor level there is some leeway because skirting board will cover the joint.

tips of the trade

Although it is often easier and more practical to have two people fixing plasterboard, it can be achieved while working on your own with the aid of a board lifter. This allows you to lever plasterboard sheets into position on the wall surface, while leaving your hands free for fixing purposes.

1 Holding the plasterboard sheet as close to the ceiling as possible (so that it touches), slide a small wooden block and pencil along the sheet, keeping the block resting against the ceiling surface. The pencil guideline produced will thereby mimic the profile of the ceiling, providing a guideline to cut the plasterboard for the perfect fit.

2 Use plasterboard nails to fix the sheets in place. Fixings should be made between 12mm and 25mm (½in to 1in) from the board edges and at 15cm (6in) intervals or centres along all edges and studs. Fix plasterboard around a door opening so that the join is above the centre of the door. Although this is technically more difficult to measure and cut, after dry lining or plastering, a central board join such as this will be less likely to crack than joints that run vertical from the door opening corners.

3 When one side of the wall is completely covered, drill the necessary holes in the plasterboard

for any electrical cables. Then, before plasterboarding the other side of the stud wall, install insulation blankets between all the studs. Finally, plasterboard the wall, ready for plastering (see page 96) and dealing with the door opening.

tips of the trade

- **Extra noggings** – Fix extra noggings between studs where heavy items are to be fixed on the wall surface. For example, ensure that an extra nogging is positioned to accommodate fixings for such fittings as sinks or basins.

- **Flush joints** – When positioning all the studs and noggings, take extra care to ensure that the surfaces of all the particular joints are flush. Uneven joints may cause bows in the plasterboard, making fixing difficult and causing weak spots.

- **Secure nailing** – When knocking in plasterboard nails, ensure that their heads are slightly below surface level for a secure fixing, but not so far that the head of the nail causes the plasterboard to crumble and reduces the strength of the fixing.

- **Screwing alternative** – Dry wall screws instead of nails can be used to fix plasterboard. This can often be easier when working on your own and reduces the risk of damaging plasterboard with hammer blows.

- **Marking off** – It can be difficult to locate the exact position of studs when plasterboarding, as the plasterboard itself is covering them. So when the stud framework has been completed, mark off where the centre of each stud is located on the floor with a pencil. Then use a level to draw a pencil guideline on each board from floor to ceiling as you work.

making a serving hatch ⁄⁄⁄

Serving hatches provide ideal access for serving food from a kitchen into a dining area. Although they are still used for this purpose in many cases, they can also make attractive decorative features and may be constructed in a range of different styles. Building a hatch in a solid block wall or loadbearing wall will require greater endeavour (see opposite page). However, carrying out such a project in a non-loadbearing wall is a very straightforward exercise.

serving hatch in a non-loadbearing stud wall

tools for the job

joist/cable detector
pencil
spirit level
tape measure
dry wall saw
panel saw
hammer
cordless drill/driver
mitre block or mitresaw

1 Work out your preferred position for the hatch, then use a joist detector to find stud positions in the wall and also to check for services such as wires and pipes. Be prepared to make some small adjustments according to the position of the wall studs and these services. (It is almost certain that you will need to cut through some studs, but try to adjust your measurements so that the sides of the hatch correspond with the edges of the studs.)

2 Use a pencil and spirit level to draw a guideline on the wall to show the exact size of the hatch. It is essential to get dimensions and measurements as vertical and level as possible at this stage – this will help to make constructing the hatch quite simple when the necessary hole has been knocked through.

3 Use a dry wall saw to cut around the pencil outline. (This type of saw is used instead of a panel saw because its sharp point pierces the plasterboard easily.) If you come across a stud obstruction, use the very end of the saw to score the plasterboard until you penetrate through to the stud surface. Once

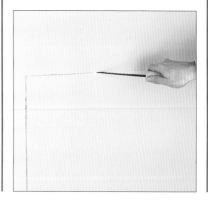

the plasterboard panel has been cut around, it may be removed and discarded. Repeat the procedure for the other side of the wall. If the wall was insulated, remove the insulatory blanket as required.

4 Remove noggings by first sawing centrally through them with the panel saw. Then lever out the noggings with a wrecking bar or hammer. If you try to saw too closely to the vertical stud, it is likely that you will come into contact with nail or screw fixings and damage the saw blade. Instead, remove such fixings with a hacksaw.

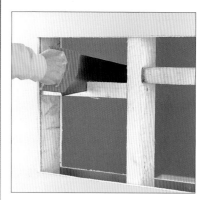

5 Leaving the central stud in place, cut and fit noggings to either side of it at the top and bottom of the hatch. It is best to use screws for this purpose, because trying to skew in nails with a hammer can push the noggings below the edge of the hatch, making them difficult to pull out of the wall and back into the required position. Provide pilot holes for the screws first, as this will help to avoid applying too much pressure on the noggings when fixing them in place.

6 Cut out the central stud, keeping the saw blade flush with the top and bottom of the hatch.

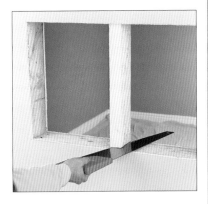

7 Line the hatch with 12.5cm x 2.5cm (5in x 1in) planed softwood. Nail measured lengths in position, beginning with the base followed by the top of the hatch and finishing with the two sides. Lost-head wire nails are best for fixing purposes, so their heads can be filled before decorating the hatch.

8 Use the mitresaw to cut architrave and fit it around the hatch on both sides to finish off the

project. Wire nails can again be used for fixing purposes. In addition to nailing the architrave through the front, use one smaller nail at each corner of the hatch, going through one section of architrave and into the adjacent section. This will help to pull the corner joints together and reduce the risk of any movement, which can potentially cause cracking.

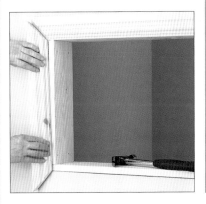

LOADBEARING WALLS

The illustrations shown here provide instruction for inserting a serving hatch in a non-loadbearing stud wall. However, if the hatch is to be inserted into a loadbearing wall, or a block or brick wall, the technique will need to be modified. In fact, the procedure is very similar to that for removing a loadbearing wall (see page 36). Clearly, the scale of the project will be reduced because you are dealing with a much smaller opening for a serving hatch. However, a lintel of some nature will be required – the size of which depends on the dimensions of the hatch. When removing blockwork, remember to wear the necessary protective equipment such as goggles, gloves and a hard hat.

A serving hatch provides a useful and attractive access point between two rooms. It can also draw light into dark areas of the home and makes a handy display area.

soundproofing walls ⚒⚒⚒

The best time to soundproof a wall is during its construction, but unless you are physically building a new wall yourself, this option does not often arise. Manufacturers have now come to recognize this rather basic problem and have, accordingly, developed a number of systems to make soundproofing existing walls a feasible and effective procedure, including better insulation slabs, which are now tested to a much higher standard.

By far the greatest need for wall soundproofing tends to arise with walls that you share with a neighbour.

soundproofing a party wall

tools for the job

wrecking bar
tape measure
pencil
panel saw
cordless drill/driver
spirit level
protective gloves
dust mask
hacksaw
sealant gun

Traditionally, soundproofing a party wall would usually mean building a new stud wall in front of the existing party wall, and using insulation blankets to fill the gap. The dimensions involved would almost certainly mean losing a sizeable area of your own room, as well as requiring some fairly major construction. However, the method below only encroaches 5cm–7.5cm (2in–3in) into the room space, and is therefore rarely noticeable in terms of the overall room dimensions. Proprietary plasterboard panels are used for this technique – these consist of two different thicknesses of plasterboard joined together, with another soundproofing layer sandwiched in between. Although this is the

ideal material, you can use normal plasterboard sheets so long as the bottom layer is of a greater thickness than the top layer. (This adheres to a basic soundproofing theory – when layering similar materials, never use the same depth of material twice.)

1 Use a wrecking bar to remove the skirting board from the base of the wall. Try not to damage the board as this can be re-used later, when the soundproofing is complete.

2 Starting at floor level, use a pencil to make a series of measurements along the corner of the wall, at 60cm (2ft) intervals. It is unlikely that the height of the wall will

fit exactly into divisibles of 60cm (2ft), so simply make the last mark directly at ceiling level.

3 Cut a soundbreaker bar to the exact length of the wall you wish to soundproof, and fix it in position at floor level. Make sure that the open side of the soundbreaker is facing up, and that the fixings are made just above the floor level. Screw the fixings through the foam pads on the soundbreaker bar.

4 Position a second bar at the next measurement along, this time ensuring that the open side of the soundbreaker is facing down to floor level. Use a spirit level to ensure

that the bar is positioned precisely level. Continue to fix soundbreakers at the marked-off intervals right up to ceiling level. All bars from the second one up should have the open side facing downwards.

5 Fit 120cm x 60cm x 10cm (4ft x 2ft x 4in) soundproofing slabs, beginning at floor level. Lip the bottom edge of the slab into the open side of the floor level soundbreaker, and fit the top edge of the slab into the open side of the soundbreaker above. So long as your measurements have been correct, a precise fit should be achieved. Wear protective gloves for this process as the soundproofing slab fibres can be irritating to the skin, and the bar edges can be sharp.

6 When the bottom section of the wall is complete, progress to the next level, inserting slabs in a similar fashion. Bear in mind that at this and subsequent levels, it is not possible to lip the bottom edge of the slab into the soundbreaker. However, the top edge will be lipped into the bar,

allowing the bottom edge of the slab to rest flush on the top edge of the bar below. Continue to fit slabs until the entire wall is covered.

7 Once trimmed and cut to fit, attach the double plasterboard panels to the wall. Using plasterboard screws, fix through the lower level of plasterboard and into the soundbreaker bar. Screws should be long enough to fix the board firmly to the bar, but not so long that they reach the original party wall. Otherwise, an automatic channel for sound transference will be created.

8 Lip the staggered edge of the next panel over the first, butting it up tightly to create a flush join. It may be easier to put marks along the previous sheet, identifying the exact position of the last fixing. These will indicate the position of the soundbreaker bars and therefore allow you to position the next fixing exactly. Continue to fit panels as required, fixing along the soundbreaker bars at 15cm–20cm (6in-8in) intervals.

9 Finally, apply a bead of mastic around all the new joints made between the plasterboard panels and the existing floor, walls and ceiling. The wall may then be plastered or dry lined, its skirting reapplied, and decorated as required.

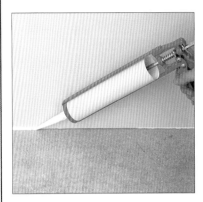

CARPET SOUNDPROOFING

Bear in mind that soundproofing efficiency will benefit from laying good quality underlay and carpet in the room. This situation may be further improved by using a specially designed acoustic flooring underlay system. Even though underlay and carpet are more generally concerned with the floor of a room, they will indirectly assist the soundproofing of a wall. This is especially the case if the floor is suspended, which enables noise to travel more easily from one room to another level. So deal with floor soundproofing issues at the same time as dealing with walls.

tips of the trade

Different tools will be required for marking and cutting different materials. For example, soundbreakers should be marked with a felt tip pen before cutting with a hacksaw. However, soundproofing slabs should be marked with chalk and cut with a panel saw – a dust mask is also vital for this process. Plasterboard panels can be marked with a pencil and cut with a panel saw.

building a block wall /////

Although stud walls (see pages 42–5) are easier to construct than solid block walls, there are some instances when a block structure may be more appropriate or even preferred. For example, in a house where all existing walls are of a block or brick construction, a stud wall may be rather out of character. Block walls also provide better soundproofing qualities and are better suited to supporting heavy objects or multiple fixings.

tools for the job

spirit level
pencil
tape measure
cordless drill/driver
spanner or plier wrench
hammer
gauging trowel
bricklaying trowel
club hammer
bolster chisel
goggles
protective gloves

1 Use a spirit level and pencil to draw a vertical line on the wall from the floor to the ceiling. This will be the line on to which the wall profile is attached, helping to 'tie in' the blocks to the existing wall structure. Profiles vary slightly in design but most will require holes to be drilled, ready for fixing. (Use the masonry bit specified by the manufacturers of the profile.) Hold the profile steadily in position on the wall surface and carefully drill through it into the wall surface beneath.

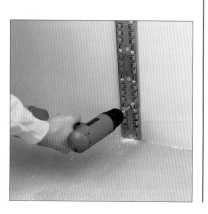

2 Plug the holes and insert the supplied fixings. Coach screws are often provided for this purpose, and are used in combination with a large washer to add extra strength and rigidity to the fixing. Position them by hand and tighten with a spanner or a plier wrench. Continue to add coach screws up the entire length of the profile. Once the profile is fixed in place, repeat steps 1 and 2 to fix the second profile to the opposing wall.

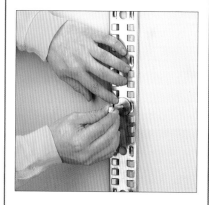

3 Attach a string line to the wall to one side of the profile. It should be in such a position that when the first block is positioned, the line will

safety advice

Block walls are quite heavy, so it is important to check that the weight is supported by the floor below. At ground level this is less of a problem, especially on a solid concrete base, but building on a suspended wooden floor is a different matter and you should seek professional advice. Also, when building on first floors or above, similar approval should be sought because joists may need additional strengthening.

correspond to the face of the block and slightly below its top edge. A block may be positioned 'dry' to gain the appropriate fixing point. The other end of the line should be attached to the corresponding position next to the other wall profile. This line will help with positioning the first layer.

4 Apply a strip of mortar to the floor, extending away from the profile, and of a width and length slightly wider than a standard block. Try to keep this mortar base a consistent but uncompacted level.

5 Take the first block and mould a cap of mortar on to one end using a gauging trowel. This process

is known as 'buttering' and is an integral part of the block- or brick-laying technique.

6 Lift and position the buttered end of the block tight up against the wall profile, while settling the base of the block into the mortar bed. The block weight will force mortar out from underneath it while finding a good, solid resting position.

7 Tap the block with the butt end of the bricklaying trowel to help it settle and check that the front face of the block just rests against the string line, and that it is level.

8 Use a spirit level to make any final adjustments, ensuring that the block is both level and vertical across the appropriate dimensions as required. After final positioning, continue along the floor adding blocks, checking levels and adjusting as necessary until the entire first course of blocks is complete. Trim excess mortar with a trowel as you progress and use it as the base for the next block, together with any extra fresh mortar that is required.

9 Apply a layer of mortar along the top of the first course of blocks to a similar depth as used at ground level. Also, use the ties provided by the profile kit to link into the profile itself and bed into the mortar layer.

10 The most essential rule of block wall construction is to ensure that mortar joints on adjacent levels never coincide. Therefore, before starting the second layer, cut a half block using a club hammer and bolster chisel. Always wear goggles when carrying out this

procedure to protect your eyes from flying debris. Use a sturdy surface to prevent the block from toppling.

11 Add the half block before continuing along with full blocks for the remainder of the course. Keep checking levels at regular intervals and move up the string line to correspond with the next block level. Never lay more than five courses of blocks in one session, and allow them to dry before progressing with further courses.

openings

It is likely that an opening of some sort will be required in the wall. Simply mark out the dimensions on the floor and build up to these guidelines, while leaving the area of the opening free. Once you have reached the required height for the entrance, a lintel will need to be installed over the top of the opening before you can continue adding blocks across the opening and building up to ceiling level.

installing wall ventilation ⚒

Effective ventilation is an essential part of any household construction, both for general efficiency and health and safety. Before double glazing and improvements to insulation, installing ventilation systems was rarely necessary because draughts were a 'natural' feature of most houses. However, increased efficiency of insulation in most modern houses means that artificial devices must be installed as substitutes for what was once an automatic system.

AREAS FOR VENTILATION

Key areas for ventilation include:

● **Bathrooms and kitchens** – Bathrooms are an environment in which air tends to be moist. Adequate ventilation is therefore vital to prevent mould or damp infestation, and condensation which can ruin decoration. Similarly, kitchens can be exposed to steam and condensation, as well as cooker fumes, and need good ventilation. Both rooms tend to require mechanical ventilation, such as an extractor fan that actually takes air out of the room and to the exterior of the house.

● **Suspended floors** – Suspended or sprung floors require ventilating beneath them using air bricks in the exterior wall. Failure to install air bricks or allowing them to become blocked can cause problems such as dry rot.

● **Chimney breasts** – When a fireplace has been blocked off, it will be necessary to install a vent in the chimney breast to allow air circulation in the chimney void. The same ends can be achieved by installing air bricks on the external wall into the chimney void. However, the interior method tends to be easier to carry out and is equally effective.

● **Boilers and solid fuel fires** – These systems must be vented correctly to ensure that fumes are not allowed to build up inside the house. Always seek professional advice from a qualified engineer and get appliances checked regularly.

installing a through-wall vent

tools for the job

joist detector

tape measure

pencil

core drill and bit

protective gloves

goggles

dust mask

hacksaw

sealant gun

1 Mark off on the wall the centre point for the ventilation shaft. Check for any cables with the joist detector and ensure that the height and position of the hole adheres to any relevant building regulations.

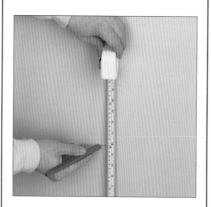

2 Attach the core drill bit to the main drill body, ensuring that it is correctly fitted in place. Read the guidelines provided by the manufacturer for this process as techniques vary with heavy duty tools.

3 Position the pilot drill point on the marked wall point and commence drilling. The pilot drill will make the initial hole in the wall to secure the core drill in place and allow the larger round core drill bit to begin cutting the hole in the wall surface. Be sure to hold firmly on to the drill as it is both heavy and can 'kick' as it bites into the wall surface. Goggles must be worn to protect your eyes from flying debris, and a mask is also important as the drill can generate a lot of dust as it it eats through the wall.

When the drill reaches the other side of the wall, there is a danger that it will blow out the exterior render or bricks, thus causing a larger hole than required, which will need repair. To prevent this from happening, the core drill can be used from both sides of

safety advice

It is important to get professional advice before installing or changing ventilation systems. This is vital when dealing with the requirements for fuels such as gas, oil or solid fuels as failure to vent correctly can endanger life.

plastic so that it cannot be closed off and inhibit ventilation. Plastic vents may be painted to match and therefore blend with the wall colour, making them a less noticeable feature.

8 On the exterior, fit a cowled cover over the hole. This enables a good throughflow of air while limiting strong gusts of wind. It also prevents rain from penetrating through the vent into the room.

the wall, so that the breakthrough point is inside the wall itself rather than directly on the outside. However, this will obviously require careful and accurate measuring and marking on both sides of the wall.

4 Remove the cut core by hand. It should come out in one or two large pieces depending on the wall make-up. If you are drilling through a cavity wall, ensure that no large pieces of the core fall into the cavity.

bought as part of a kit and the manufacturer's guidelines for positioning should be included.

6 Seal around the edge of the ducting with silicone, ensuring a good unbroken seal. Carry out this process on both the interior and exterior of the wall. (If areas around the edge of the hole broke away or became damaged while drilling, repair them with mortar followed by all-purpose filler, before applying sealant.)

9 Again, seal around the cowled cover with more silicone sealant to ensure a completely rainproof seal.

5 Line the hole with some ducting, cutting it to the right size with a hacksaw. The ducting is normally

7 Internally, fix a louvre vent to cover the hole. This must be a static ventilator made of metal or

tips of the trade

Installing a static ventilator in an exterior wall is straightforward, so long as you have the correct equipment and tools. It will be necessary to hire a core drill and bit from your local hire shop – such equipment is expensive to buy, and not worth purchasing for such 'one off' jobs.

tips of the trade

Where electrically operated extractor fans need to be fitted, it will be necessary to seek the help of a qualified electrician in order to ensure that the fan is wired up safely and correctly. An electrician will also provide advice on the positioning and type of extractor fan required to provide sufficient air flow and circulation for the room in question.

inserting a doorway – 1 ⁄⁄⁄⁄

Inserting a doorway in a loadbearing wall is not a task that should be taken on lightly because of the structural nature of the work. It is important to follow the correct procedures and techniques when tackling a project such as this. It is always advisable to seek some professional guidance before beginning work, as the procedure will vary slightly depending on the make-up of the wall and its exact position in the house structure as a whole.

The work involved depends strongly on supportive measures. This means supplying the necessary temporary support while the part of the wall for the doorway is removed, and supplying the necessary permanent support for above the doorway in the future. For the permanent support you will need to use a lintel of some nature to act as the permanent support. Its size and make-up will depend on two factors, namely the structure of the wall to be removed and the span of the proposed opening. Both of these require serious calculation, and the question of lintel type and construction should be decided in consultation with a structural engineer. Once all the necessary safety precautions and procedures are in place, and permission has been gained from a Building Control Officer, the actual work itself is eminently achievable. This can be divided into two stages: firstly, the opening has to be made and secondly, the lintel inserted.

making the opening

A methodical approach is required for this procedure and it is important to follow guidelines in the correct order. The work will produce a lot of dust and rubbish, so use dust sheets and arrange for the rubble and broken masonry to be disposed of.

1 Mark out the size of the opening on the wall surface.

2 Knock holes through the wall above the proposed opening.

3 Insert needles through the holes.

4 Support the needles by props on both sides of the wall.

5 Use a stone cutter or club hammer and bolster chisel to cut around the edge of the opening.

6 Remove the blocks or bricks by first loosening with a club hammer and bolster chisel and then levering them out with a wrecking bar or lift by hand.

7 Continue to remove blocks until the entire area is clear.

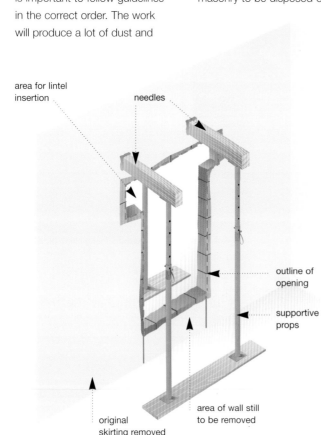

area for lintel insertion

needles

outline of opening

supportive props

original skirting removed

area of wall still to be removed

It is essential for two people to be involved when inserting the lintel as they are surprisingly heavy. It is also much easier to carry out this procedure whilst working from some sort of access platform, rather than using stepladders.

1 At the top corners of the opening take out bricks or blocks to accommodate the lintel ends.

2 Check and re-check measurements to ensure that the lintel will fit into the required space.

3 Apply a bed of mortar to this area before lifting the lintel into place.

4 Check that the lintel is level. Use cut bricks or blocks, wedged beneath the end of the lintel to rectify this if necessary.

5 Apply more mortar around the lintel ends to ensure it will be held securely in place.

6 Make good with plasterboard and/or render and plaster around the lintel.

7 Make good with plasterboard and/or render and plaster around the cut blocks or bricks that make up the sides of the opening.

8 Remove the needles and patch in the holes.

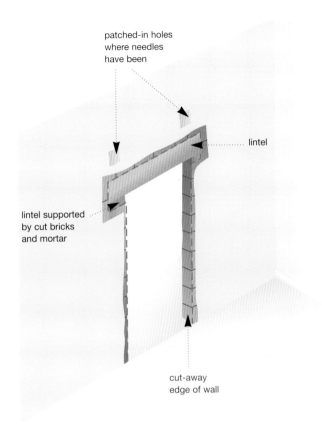

patched-in holes where needles have been

lintel

lintel supported by cut bricks and mortar

cut-away edge of wall

In addition to the practical considerations of how to support your wall, there are also a number of other issues that should be carefully addressed.

needle requirement

The number of needles required for support will depend on the width of the opening. Needle dimensions should not be less than 15cm x10cm (6in x 4in), but consult a structural engineer on exact requirements.

propping

Steel props can be hired at low cost and their adjustable nature makes them ideal for supporting purposes. Make sure that the bases of the props are positioned on scaffold planks so that weight distribution is evened out. Most prop bases have nail holes so that they can be nailed into the scaffold planks to eliminate any risk of them moving.

lintel support

In many cases the new lintel may be accommodated in the existing wall structure with no extra support below it required. However, in some cases it may be necessary to install extra concrete support. Consult a structural engineer for the correct requirements in your particular circumstances.

safety equipment

This sort of work requires close attention to safety and all the necessary precautions must be taken. Wear protective gloves, goggles and a hard hat when taking down the wall. A dust mask may also be needed, especially when clearing away the rubble and dust caused by wall removal.

inserting a doorway – 2

Inserting a doorway in a non-loadbearing wall is much easier than the technique used for a loadbearing wall. However, before work begins, you must be certain that the wall is non-loadbearing and it is always best to take professional advice to check this. For solid, block, non-loadbearing walls, a lintel is generally required and therefore the procedure is similar to that shown on pages 54–5. The example shown here deals with cutting an entrance into a non-loadbearing stud wall.

safety advice

As always, check that there are no services running through the stud wall, which will otherwise require re-routing before work can begin.

tools for the job

joist detector

bradawl

pencil

spirit level

panel saw

tape measure

wrecking bar

cordless drill/driver

1 Use a joist detector in order to locate the position of the vertical studs in the wall. It is essential that you locate a stud close to or directly where the hinged side of the door will eventually come to hang. Once the position of this stud has been located, all your other measurements should be taken from this point and will guide the process.

2 On the main stud, locate the exact edge of the timber by inserting a bradawl through the plasterboard at the detection points that you located by using the joist detector.

3 Join up the line of holes with a pencil and spirit level. A well-constructed stud wall should show this line to be exactly vertical. If this is not the case, the stud may require slight repositioning once exposed.

4 Measure out the rest of the entrance dimensions on the wall surface. For a standard internal door and doorway, remember to allow for the dimensions of the door plus the

thickness of the door lining, leaving an additional 6mm (¼in) to allow for a gap between door and frame. Remove the section of plasterboard by accurately sawing along the guidelines with a panel saw.

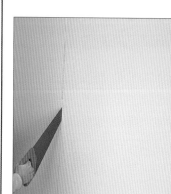

5 The other side of the wall will require cutting out as well. From 'inside' the wall, use a bradawl to pierce the plasterboard at the corners and positions corresponding to the initial opening. It is then possible to join these markings with a pencil on the other side of the wall, and again cut out the area with a panel saw. Remember to keep the edge of the saw tight against the stud.

6 Remove any vertical studs or noggings from the entrance with a panel saw, trimming back precisely to the plasterboard edge.

7 Cut away the sole plate with the panel saw, back to the edge of the plasterboard. If the sole plate is fixed in the entrance, it may be necessary to use a wrecking bar to prise it free. It is also recommended to add some fixings into the sole plate at the bottom corners of the 'entrance'. In this way, the cut sole plate will be secured firmly back in position.

8 Although the stud creating the hinging side of the entrance is precisely aligned with the edge of the

plasterboard, it is unlikely that your measurements will have allowed the stud on the opposite door to align as accurately as possible. Therefore, it may be necessary to insert a vertical stud along this edge. Cut the timber to size and skew some screws in at the bottom of its length, which will make fixing easier and help you to secure the stud in place.

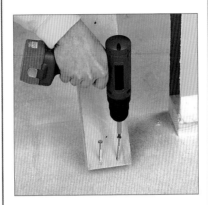

9 Skewing the screws in at an angle before the stud is positioned makes it easier to tighten the screws once it is in position. Depending on the wall structure it will then be necessary to fix the stud at the top of the entrance. Usually, there will be an existing wall nogging to help you. Alternatively, you may need to insert another nogging for secure fixing purposes.

10 Fill in the top part of the frame by cutting lengths of timber to the required size. Again skew screws into these lengths before tightening and driving them into position once the length is in

place. Ensure that the screwheads enter into the wood so that they are below surface level.

11 Where vertical studs extend down to the top of the entrance, it is necessary to add further fixings to ensure rigidity. Fit a further length on the other side of the vertical length to finish off the entrance frame.

STUD WALL ISSUES

● **Dimensions** – Stud walls are generally constructed of timbers that are either 10cm x 5cm (4in x 2in) or 7.5cm x 5cm (3in x 2in) in dimension. Therefore before purchasing or re-using any wood to make the entrance, ensure that you know which stud dimensions will be required.

● **Use** – Entrances may be left open, doors inserted or other features such as arches added. When measuring for the entrance, calculating specific size requirements is vital, especially for doors, as sizes vary so much.

inserting a door lining ⤳⤳⤳

A door lining houses the hinges and closing mechanism, and provides the general perimeter for a door when 'positioned' in a wall surface. Linings tend to be supplied in a very simple kit form, and are then fitted to the precise aperture requirements. Although this is a very straightforward procedure, accuracy is essential as any deviation from totally vertical and square positioning will cause major problems when it comes to hanging a door.

walls & ceilings

58

tools for the job

wooden mallet

hammer

tape measure

pencil

panel saw

spirit level

cordless drill/driver

door linings

The sections that make up a lining are often referred to by different terms. For our purposes, the top part of the lining is called the 'head' and the side sections the 'stiles'.

1 Assemble the three parts of the lining on the floor. Put the stile ends into the pre-made slots in the head. They should fit relatively snugly but may need one or two blows with a mallet to ensure the joint is tight.

2 Secure the stiles in place by nailing through the top of the head into the stiles. Alternatively,

screw fixings may be used for this purpose. Ensure that each stile is secured with at least two fixings.

3 Measure the exact distance between the stiles at the head end of the lining. Transfer this measurement to the floor level of the lining and nail a length of batten between the stiles, securing them in position at this required width. Ensure that the batten does not extend past the outer edge of the lining, as this will hinder fitting the lining when it is positioned in the wall aperture.

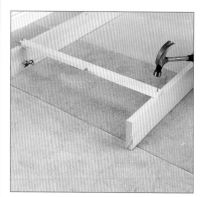

4 To ensure that the lining is totally 'square', it is necessary to make further measurements and fixings at

the top of the lining. Measuring away from the top corner of the lining, mark off one point at 30cm (12in) along the head, and another at 40cm (16in) along the stile. Adjust the distance between the 40cm (16in) mark and the 30cm (12in) mark on the head and ensure that it is exactly 50cm (20in). With these three measurements exact, this means that the lining itself is totally square.

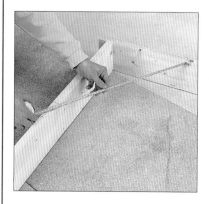

5 Cut a length of batten to fit across the angle of the head and stile. Nail it in place, checking to ensure that the diagonal measurement of 50cm (20in) is maintained. The lining is now firmly braced at both the top and bottom.

6 Use a panel saw to cut off the excess head. Make sure that you cut right back to the corners of the lining, as leaving any excess will hinder its positioning in the wall.

7 Lift up the lining and position it in the wall opening. Concentrate on the 'hinged' side of the door. Use a spirit level to check that the lining is exactly vertical and the front edge is level with the wall surface on both sides.

8 Fix the 'hinging' side of the lining in place with screws, through the stile and into the timber below.

9 Depending on the precision of your measurements, it is likely that there will be a small gap between the stile and wall on the opposite side of the lining. Before trying to rectify this situation, make the fixing easier by starting off screws for fixing at intervals along the stile. Allow them to penetrate into the stile, but not through to the other side.

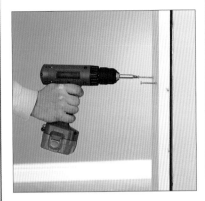

10 Cut some wooden wedges from offcuts and position them in the gap between the stile and wall. Position wedges at the screw fixing points. The best technique is to apply two wedges in each case, inserted from the opposite sides of the wall. In this way when the wedges meet, they can be gradually pushed in together to form a rigid support between the stile and wall.

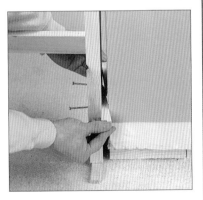

11 When all the wedges have been inserted, you can then secure the frame in place by continuing to insert the screw fixings, so that they go through the wedges and into the vertical stud of the wall.

Again, while you are inserting the screws continue to check the lining position with a spirit level.

12 Use a panel saw to cut off wedge excess as required (trim back flush). Add some final fixings to the head, screwing through into the horizontal stud above. Use wedges to pack out any spaces.

SOLID BLOCK WALLS

The technique for inserting door linings into solid block or brick walls is exactly the same as that shown here except that there will be a different fixings requirement. In order to deal with masonry, concrete anchor screws or frame fixings should be used for securing the lining in place.

• **The right lining** – Linings are sold in kit form and are thus, to a certain extent, standardized to correspond to modern wall and door dimensions. In older properties it may be necessary to make your own customized lining.

making an arch profile

As well as fitting doors into wall openings, arch profiles can be used as an alternative to traditional doors or square openings, providing more of a feature between rooms. In the past it would have been a highly skilled procedure to produce a framework for an arch and finish it with subsequent coats of plaster. Today, however, manufacturing innovation has made the process much easier. Arch formers can be bought, positioned and plastered over to create perfect profiles.

making an arch profile in a stud wall

tools for the job

cordless drill/driver
screwdriver
hacksaw
hammer
tape measure
filling knife
plastering trowel

Although arch profiles may be built onto existing wall openings, beginning from scratch and building them into a new stud wall is by far the easiest procedure. A new wall, if erected correctly, is more likely to be true and square compared to older walls, thereby making the process of fitting the arch much more straightforward.

1 Most formers will have pre-drilled holes to accommodate fixings. Hold the former in position whilst drilling four pilot holes into the timber studs. Ensure that the front lip of the

arch former corresponds to the manufacturer's guidelines in terms of encroaching up to the level of the plasterboard on either side of the wall.

2 Secure the former in place with wood screws. Use a screwdriver rather than a cordless drill/driver to tighten the screws, as overtightening could crack the plaster former. Greater control of movement can be achieved by using a simple hand tool in situations like this.

3 From the base of the arch former to the floor, it will be necessary to cut and fit plasterboard so as to cover the wooden stud and bring its surface up to the same

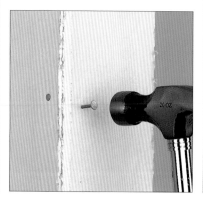

depth as the base of the arch former. Fix this strip in place with plasterboard nails in the usual manner taking care not to damage the plaster.

4 Cut angle bead to the correct length (former base to floor) and attach it on both edges of the opening. Fix it in position using plasterboard nails, ensuring that the apex of each angle bead aligns precisely with the respective bottom corners of the former.

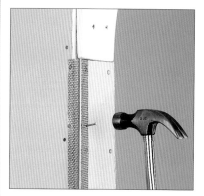

5 Repeat steps 1–4 to fit the second former and entrance lining. It is rare that the dimensions of the formers will join exactly and therefore it is almost certain that there will be a gap between the top edges

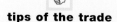

tips of the trade

Dry lined arches – This is an alternative technique to make an arch profile. Instead of using angle bead along the vertical arch edges, use corner tape and jointing compound. The internal area of the former can also be filled with plaster bonding coat before being finished with jointing compound.

of the formers. Use the same technique as for the studs on each side of the entrance to fill the gap between the formers – in other words, fill the gap with plasterboard and use angle bead to form the edges.

6 Once the formers, plasterboard lining and angle beads have all been positioned and aligned, fill the arch former holes with all-purpose filler or bonding coat plaster.

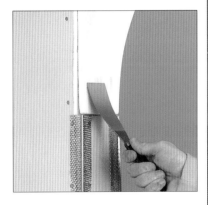

7 Tape the plasterboard joints with self-adhesive jointing tape, and also the joints between the plasterboard and the arch formers.

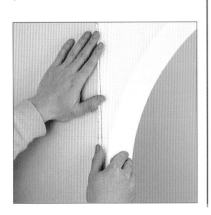

8 Apply plaster to the walls, making sure that you extend the plaster over and onto the arched formers. The actual arched face of the formers may not require plastering depending on the type of former you have used. Once the plaster has been 'polished' and dries, the arch is ready for decoration. With some formers, it may be necessary to apply two coats of plaster.

Arches add shape to rooms and soften edges, producing a relaxed and comfortable atmosphere. They also help to link decoration between two living areas.

closing up a doorway – 1

When a doorway needs to be blocked up, the first consideration is whether the wall itself is of a solid block or brick construction, or is composed of a stud framework. If the former is the case, it is always best to close up the opening using blocks or bricks, as the dimensions of the materials you use will be more suitable than stud work, and employing similar materials to those used in the construction of the rest of the wall will generally make the project far easier to carry out.

tools for the job

wrecking bar
cordless drill/driver
screwdriver
hammer
trowel
spirit level
plastering trowel

1 The first task is to remove the door and frame from the entrance. The door may simply be unscrewed from its hinges, but the frame, or the door lining, will almost certainly require levering free from the surrounding blockwork. A wrecking bar is the ideal tool for this purpose and should be able to prise the lining away and remove any fixings.

2 The blocks which are inserted will require some form of tying in to the existing wall for strength and stability. There are a number of different frame tie designs, and the types used here require screwing into the blocks in the entrance. Drill a series of holes for the plugs at the

mortar levels, so that the ties will be inserted at the same level for tying into the new mortar between the blocks used in the entrance.

3 Insert the plastic wall plug into the drilled hole and screw in the wall tie tight up to the collar. You may need to use some sort of lever mechanism to make the last few turns of the tie. Holding a screwdriver across and between the V-shape of the tie design, and using it to rotate and lever the tie into position, should produce a firm fixing.

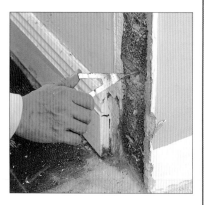

4 Mix up and apply a bed of mortar along the floor between the two sides of the entrance. The

mortar should be laid at about the width of a block and be generous enough to provide a good bedding for block placement.

5 Butter the end of the first block with mortar, giving it a good 'cone'-shaped coverage. Be fairly generous with the mortar, without applying too much of an excess so that it keeps falling off and away from the top of the block. Use a gauging trowel for this purpose, smoothing around the edge of the block to form good adhesion between the mortar and the block. This is also a good test to see if your mortar mix is of the correct consistency. It should hold a firm but pliable shape on top of the block.

filling the aperture

1 Remove door, door lining and architrave.

2 Build up blocks in aperture, using frame ties to tie them in with the surrounding blockwork or by removing blocks at alternate levels on either side of the aperture so that new blocks are tied in with the existing wall structure.

3 Fill area between the top level of blocks and the lintel with bricks.

4 Render blocks or apply plaster scratch coat.

5 Apply final plaster skim to render.

6 Fill in with missing section of skirting or replace entire section of skirting along length of wall.

7 Sand new plastered area and decorate as required.

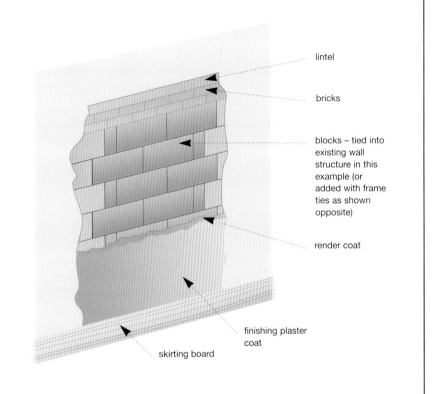

- lintel
- bricks
- blocks – tied into existing wall structure in this example (or added with frame ties as shown opposite)
- render coat
- finishing plaster coat
- skirting board

63

6 Position the block on the bed of mortar under the first frame tie, forcing the buttered end of the block tight up against the entrance surface. Use a spirit level to ensure the block is correctly positioned. Continue to build up levels until the entrance is filled. Remember to insert frame ties at each level to ensure that the new blockwork forms a strong bond with the existing wall. Also make sure that the vertical joints between successive levels of blockwork are staggered.

FURTHER POINTS TO NOTE

• Frame tie alternatives
Instead of using frame ties, it is just as effective to remove the first block on every other course, and in this way create a staggered effect allowing the new blocks to be tied into the old wall.

• Cutting blocks
Concrete blocks may either be cut with a stone cutter, which you will probably have to hire, or using a club hammer and bolster chisel. For either method, be sure to wear goggles for safety.

• Wooden floors
When closing up an opening on a wooden floor, you will need to insert a wooden sole plate across the bottom of the entrance, which will help to provide a more rigid base, and build up your blockwork on top of this. Otherwise, the flexibility of a wooden floor may fracture the joints in the blockwork as you progress.

• Neat joints
Although the blockwork will be covered with both render and plaster, it is still important to make the joints between the blocks as neat as possible. Smooth, finished joints will be much easier to render over than if you leave any rough mortar edges between blocks. Therefore, after each block has been positioned, be sure to use a trowel to remove excess mortar from the face of the joints before it dries out.

• Improving the finish
However proficient your blockwork and plastering skills are, making a blocked-up entrance in a wall completely 'disappear' after redecoration is a difficult task. Make sure that after plastering you undertake some fine filling and sanding along the join between the new and old walls. You might also want to consider lining the wall before painting, as this will again make any joins less noticeable.

closing up a doorway – 2

When closing up a doorway in a stud wall, it is a case of filling in the wood and plasterboard framework to provide as flat a finish as possible. One of the most important considerations is to ensure that the studs and plasterboard you use are of similar dimensions to the actual wall. Different stud walls have varying depths depending on the house and its particular age. It is essential therefore to check the dimensions carefully before purchasing the materials.

tools for the job

screwdriver

wrecking bar

panel saw

cordless drill/driver

hammer

craft knife

straight edge or spirit level

scraper

plastering float

tips of the trade

Remember that when you fill in or close up an old entrance, it is likely that services will need re-routing. For example, light switches – which are normally found close to an entrance – will look out of place once the opening has been closed up. You should therefore make the appropriate arrangements before starting the closing up project, to have switches moved and any other services that are affected adjusted.

1 Unscrew the door from its hinges and remove it from the opening. Use a wrecking bar to lever the

architrave away from the wall surface. Take care not to allow the wrecking bar to dig into and damage the existing wall surface.

2 Once again use the wrecking bar to lever the door lining away from the studs. The ease with which this comes away will depend upon whether the lining wad is fixed in position with nails or screws. If nails have been used, lining removal tends to be much easier.

3 Fill in the missing section of sole plate by cutting a piece of timber to length and fitting it at the base of the entrance. Pilot hole and screw it securely in position.

4 Cut a vertical length of timber to the height of the frame and secure it in position, again with screws. Add another length on the other side of the frame, and then a central stud running from the middle of the new section of sole plate up to the centre of the stud which was above the door frame.

5 Add extra rigidity to the three new vertical studs by fitting noggings between each one. Skew screws through the noggins and into the vertical studs in order to provide extra strength of fixing. Nails may also be used for this purpose as long as they hold the noggings very securely in position.

6 Rather than using a large plasterboard sheet, which would require accurate cutting to fit into the framework aperture, use smaller laths fitted horizontally. These are easier to handle and trim to size. Hold a lath in position at the top of the aperture and accurately mark off the cutting requirement using a pencil.

7 Lay the lath flat on the floor and use a craft knife to score a line in the plasterboard between the pencil guidelines. A spirit level provides an excellent straight edge to guide the blade of the craft knife. Once scored, turn the lath over and snap it upwards to break it along the scored line.

8 Place the cut lath back in the aperture and carefully nail it into position. Continue to measure and fit more laths until the aperture is filled. Carry out the same procedure on the other side of the wall – you may wish to fill the void with insulation blanket before this second part of the plasterboarding process. If you do choose to insulate the wall, remember to wear protective gloves as the insulation fibres may otherwise cause skin irritation.

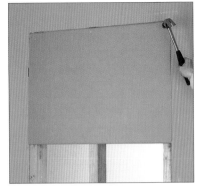

9 Apply self-adhesive jointing tape along all the joins, both between the plasterboard laths and the existing wall, and along the join between each lath. Smooth the tape to ensure there are no lumps or wrinkles in its surface.

10 You now have the choice of dry lining or plastering the plasterboard. Dry lining should only be considered an option if the new plasterboard level is flush with that of the existing wall. Otherwise, the old entrance will appear slightly recessed into the wall surface once decorated. Plastering the whole area is thus normally a more suitable option. Before applying a skim, fill along all the taped joints with some bonding plaster to provide a good base for the plaster. Once this has dried, apply a skim of finishing plaster to the whole area, feathering a join with the existing wall surface. Repeat this procedure on the other side of the wall. Once all the plaster has dried, the missing skirting board can be filled in and the walls decorated.

PREPARING TO DECORATE

To achieve a good finish and make the 'closing' as unnoticeable as possible, there are a few final procedures that will improve the 'invisible' effect.

● **Fine sanding** – Although a standard procedure for preparation, sanding is even more vital when trying to blend in an old doorway. The application of some fine filler, followed by further sanding, will improve the smooth nature of the final finish.

● **Closed doorway painting** – When painting over a stud wall in an old doorway, even if you are using an identical colour to that of the rest of the wall, the old doorway will still show up. It is best to prime the newly plastered area, apply a first coat of finishing paint and then apply the top coat over the entire stud wall. This may sound extravagant, but it does tend to make such old doorways less noticeable in the overall finish.

● **Lining** – The best option is to line the entire wall after the old doorway has been closed up. The thickness of the lining paper (1000–1200 microns is ideal) helps to smooth the wall surface further and reduces the likelihood of the closed-up area remaining apparent. Once lined, all the walls may be painted.

building a glass block wall ⁄⁄⁄

Translucent glass blocks are attractive and provide an unusual alternative to more traditional wall structures, producing a highly decorative finish that adds character to any room surroundings. They cannot be used for structural support, but they do fulfil the majority of roles required by most walls and make ideal shower walls or room dividers. Extremely versatile, they can even be used to construct curves – thus adding further interest.

tools for the job

spirit level
pencil
nail and line
hammer
cordless drill
gauging trowel
sponge

1 Use a spirit level and pencil to draw a precise vertical line on the wall surface, extending from ground level to the finished wall height. As with block walls (see pages 50–1), attach a string line at a height just below the top of where the first course of glass blocks will be, and where it will touch the face of the blocks. You may wish to hold a glass block in position to obtain the correct height and position measurements. Secure the line in the corresponding position on the opposite wall.

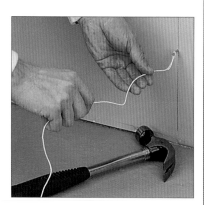

2 To add strength to the finished wall, it will be necessary to build a rigid steel framework inside the glass block structure. These steel rods

need to be positioned every four to five courses (depending on the manufacturer's guidelines). In order to get the bottom course position for these rods, hold a block 'dry' in position at the base of the wall – on top of spacers – to ensure that it is at the correct height. Hold a steel rod on top of the block and mark the position at which it touches the wall surface.

3 Remove the block, spacers and rod, and drill into the wall surface at the marked-off point. Measure the area required for the block and spacer, and mark off further points at which the rods will be inserted. Drill these holes at this stage rather than leaving till later.

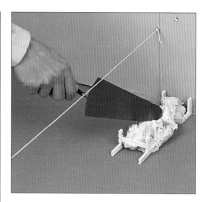

4 Mix up some mortar. (Use white cement as this produces a more pleasing finish with translucent bricks than the other, traditional types of mortar.) Use the spacers to position a block accurately. Then remove the brick and apply mortar to the area between the spacers.

5 Take a glass block and 'butter' one side with some mortar, ensuring a good even coverage, while trying to keep the mortar off the glass faces of the block.

6 Position the block back on the spacers so that the buttered end is against the wall, with the adjacent edge bedding down into the mortar

on the floor level. Ensure that the block is level and vertical using the spacers – the block should rest against the edge of each spacer.

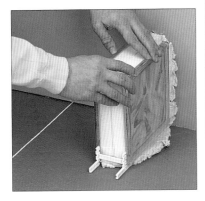

7 Position spacers and add blocks until the entire first course is complete. Use a spirit level to ensure that the block positions are precise. The top edge of each block should also rest against the string line. Insert a steel rod into the pre-drilled hole at the top of the first course of blocks.

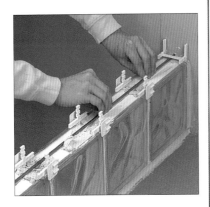

8 Once the wall is complete, remove the face plates of the spacers by twisting them.

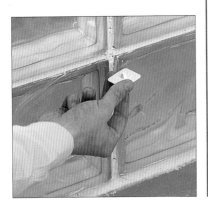

9 Once the blocks have dried out, they can be grouted using a similar mortar mix as used for the building process. Work mortar into any gaps in the joints and smooth to a finish with a clean, damp sponge. The blocks will need wiping over several times to remove all mortar residue and leave a clean, bright glass block surface. If the wall is to be used in a

shower cubicle, use waterproof tiling grout, and seal the edge of the wall with silcone sealant.

wooden floors

When building on wooden floors, fix a wooden sole plate to the floor to act as the base for the block wall. Ensure that the wood is the same width as the glass blocks.

spacers

The spacers provided with glass block walls are designed so that they can be adapted to make both 'T' and 'L' shapes, and therefore deal with all requirements in a block wall construction. Simply snap off the parts of the spacer which you do not require.

Glass block walls make a very distinctive feature, helping to lighten rooms and creating an attractive, decorative finish.

opening up a disused fireplace ⤢

If your house has a fireplace that was blocked off the last time fireplaces went out of fashion, reinstating it is a relatively straightforward job. The amount of work involved depends on how the fireplace opening was blocked off, and on whether the old fireback was removed or left in position. Opening up a fireplace is very messy, so remember to roll back the carpet and put down a dustsheet before you begin work.

removing the infill

Tap the face of the chimney breast to discover if the infill is solid or hollow. Prize off the skirting board across the face of the chimney breast, saving it for later reinstatement at either side of your new fireplace. There should be an air brick or ventilator in the face of the chimney breast to ventilate the flue. Start work by removing this – chop out a masonry brick from a solid infill, and unscrew a metal or plastic ventilator from a board infill. Then shine in a torch to see if the old fireback is still in place. If it is, you will only have some making good to do once the recess is reopened. If it is not, you will have to buy and fit a replacement, or get a builder to do the job for you.

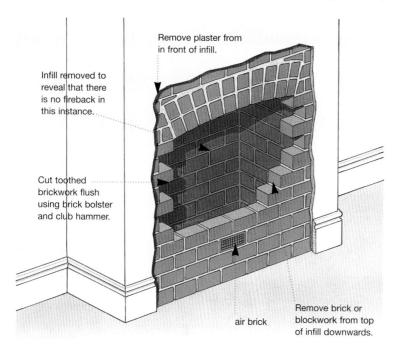

Remove plaster from in front of infill.

Infill removed to reveal that there is no fireback in this instance.

Cut toothed brickwork flush using brick bolster and club hammer.

air brick

Remove brick or blockwork from top of infill downwards.

1 With masonry infill, chop off the plaster at skirting board level, working from the centre of the chimney breast outwards. This will reveal the edges of the infill.

2 Chop off plaster up the sides of the infill until you reach the top, where the infill will have been butted up against the lintel spanning the original fireplace opening.

3 If there was no air brick to break out earlier, chop out an infill brick or block at one top corner of the infill. Chisel out its mortar joints after drilling a series of almost-overlapping holes into them with a drill and masonry drill bit, and lever it out.

4 Work across and down the infill, chipping out one brick or block at a time. If the fireback is still present, take care not to knock pieces of masonry inwards against it or you might crack it. Clear away the debris as you proceed.

5 If infill bricks have been toothed (bonded) into the masonry at each side of the opening, cut them flush with the original brickwork with a sharp downward blow using a brick bolster and club hammer.

REMOVING BOARD INFILL

With board infill, make a test drilling to see if plasterboard or a manufactured timber board has been used. If it is plasterboard and there was no air vent to remove, make a hole in the centre of the panel with a hammer and simply pull the pieces of plasterboard away. If plywood or another type of board was used, insert a padsaw or power jigsaw blade into the drilled hole and cut outwards towards the edges of the infill. Prize the cut sections of board away. Then look to see how the supporting framework of battens has been attached to the edges of the recess, and undo any screws you can locate. If there are no screws, assume that masonry nails have been used and lever the battens away carefully with a wrecking bar.

If the original fireback remains, you may have to patch it up in places. If it is missing, you will obviously have to buy a replacement one and install it. Start by measuring the width of the opening and order a new fireback to fit the space. Standard fireback widths are 400 and 450mm (16 and 18in), but larger sizes are available if you want a more impressive fireplace. You will also need some lightweight mortar (made with vermiculite and lime), some corrugated cardboard, fireproof rope, brick rubble (use the infill you removed earlier) and fire cement.

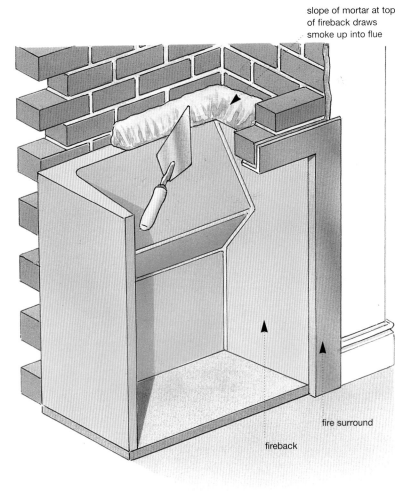

slope of mortar at top of fireback draws smoke up into flue

fire surround

fireback

altering the structure of a wall

PATCHING UP AN OLD FIREBACK

If an existing fireback is sound but cracked, you can repair it with fire cement. Let the fireback cool for a couple of days if it has had a real fire in it. Brush off soot with a wire brush and rake out the cracks with an old screwdriver, undercutting the edges. Wet the cracks to help the cement to stick, then fill them flush with fire cement. Smooth the filler with a wet paintbrush and allow it to harden for several days before relighting the fire.

69

safety advice

Wear safety gloves, goggles and a face mask when removing infill to prevent dust inhalation and injuries from flying debris. This is particularly important when working with masonry infill. It is also a good idea to enlist advice from a professional builder if you intend to have a real or fuel-effect fire installed, to ensure that the flue is sound and safe to use.

1 Separate the two halves of the fireback by tapping along the recessed cutting line with a club hammer and brick bolster.

2 Mix some mortar using four parts vermiculite (a lightweight granular insulation material) and lime, and place a bed of it where the base of the fireback will sit. Set the fireback in place, then pull it forward and trap lengths of fireproof rope between it and the edge of the fireplace opening.

3 Cut two strips of corrugated cardboard to match the height of the fireback and place them behind it, held against it with dabs of mortar. This will burn away when the fire is lit to leave an essential expansion gap behind the fireback. Then fill the space behind the fireback with mortar, bulked out with broken brick – you can use the remains of the masonry infill for this.

4 Bed some mortar on top of the lower half of the fireback and stand the top half in place on it. Neaten the joint and carry on filling behind the fireback.

5 Once the infill is level with the top of the fireback, add more mortar to form a slope up to the rear face of the flue. This forms a narrow throat that draws the smoke from the fire up into the flue.

6 Use fire cement to seal the edges of the new fireback to the fire surround, and to cover the fireproof rope.

blocking off a fireplace ⚒

Houses built before central heating became commonplace had a fireplace in every room. Today, even fireplace lovers are often happy with just a feature fireplace in the living room and may want to block off any remaining fireplaces in other rooms. However you decide to tackle this job, the one vital requirement is that the flue remains ventilated. Otherwise, condensation can form within it, soak into the chimney breast brickwork and eventually surface to ruin your decoration.

Before beginning any work, you have several decisions to make if you plan to decommission an old fireplace. The first concerns whether to strip out the old fireback and empty the fireplace recess, or whether to leave it in place. The former option is the better choice if you are certain the fireplace will never be used again, but it will make a lot of mess. The second decision concerns how to block off the opening. You can fill it with brick or blockwork, or panel it with plasterboard supported on a timber frame. Again, the former is the more professional option, the latter the quicker one.

tools for the job

safety goggles & dust mask
gloves
club hammer
brick bolster
wrecking bar
screwdriver
hawk
bricklaying trowel
plastering trowel
trimming knife
shovel

1 Use a brick bolster and club hammer to break the mortar bond between the raised hearth slab and the floor-level constructional hearth beneath it. Lever it up with a wrecking bar and get help to lift and remove it – it is too heavy to lift on your own. Then put down dustsheets in front of the fireplace opening.

2 Use a brick bolster and club hammer to chop away the plaster at the sides of the old fire surround to expose any fixing lugs. Undo them if you can with a screwdriver, with the aid of some penetrating oil to free rusty threads. Prize away the stubs of skirting board at either side of the surround, and save them as samples so that you can buy a matching length to cover the face of the new chimney breast surround when you have finished.

3 Insert the end of the wrecking bar between the surround and the chimney breast, first at one side and then at the other, and lever it away from the wall. Again, enlist help

to prevent it from toppling forwards and to lift and carry it away. Remove the grate if it is still in place.

4 Smash the old fireback with a brick bolster and club hammer. Wear safety goggles and a dust mask to protect yourself from dust and any flying debris. Lift out the sections of fireclay as you break them up, and put them straight into strong rubble sacks. Soak the fireproof rope around the perimeter of the opening with water to prevent asbestos fibres from getting into the air, cut it away with a trimming knife and put it in a plastic bag. Seal it, label it 'asbestos waste' and contact your local authority for advice on disposing of it safely.

🖐 safety advice

Asbestos is a fibrous substance that can be woven with other materials to produce items that are highly heat resistant and have excellent insulation properties. However, it is a highly carcinogenic substance and the safety guidelines outlined in step 4 must be followed stringently. Never take risks when working with asbestos.

5 If the infill behind the fireback is a solid mass of mortar and broken bricks, break it up bit by bit with a brick bolster and club hammer. If it is loose rubble, simply shovel it out of the recess. Bag up all the rubble and remove it from the site to leave the fireplace recess empty. Use a vacuum cleaner to remove as much dust from the area as possible.

6 Use bricks or lightweight blocks to create a solid infill across the opening of the fireplace. Spread a line of mortar across the hearth and bed the first course in place. Cut the last brick or block to fit the space as

necessary, and use the offcut to start the next course so that the vertical joints will be staggered. (Refer to pages 62–5 for detailed information on blocking up an opening.)

7 Include a terracotta air brick in one of the first few courses of bricks to ensure that the flue will be ventilated. Complete the infill, cutting bricks or blocks to size as necessary to fit the final course beneath the lintel that bridges the opening. Use mortar to fill any irregular gaps at the top of the space, and neaten the pointing.

8 Apply a base coat of plaster over the infill, recessing it by about 3mm (⅛in) to allow for the finish coat, and key it with a series of criss-cross strokes with the edge of a plastering trowel. Allow it to set hard, then trowel on the finish coat flush with the surrounding plaster. Polish it smooth with a wet trowel. Allow it to dry thoroughly before you redecorate it. Finally, cut and fit a new length of skirting board to the face of the chimney breast.

PANELLING THE OPENING

You may find it easier to fill the opening with plasterboard after stripping out the fireback rather than block or brickwork. If so, cut four pieces of 50 x 25mm (2 x 1in) softwood batten to fit the space. Glue and nail the top piece to the top ends of the two side pieces – you cannot nail it up into the lintel to fix it in place. Then secure the side pieces to the inner edge of the opening with masonry nails, and add the fourth batten across the hearth. Set the face of the battens back by 12mm (½in) so that the plasterboard plus a skim coat of plaster will end up flush with the surrounding plaster. Cut a hole in the plasterboard with a padsaw that is of the appropriate size to insert a plastic ventilator, then fix the plasterboard to the battens with galvanized plasterboard nails. Apply the finish plaster, then fit the ventilator when it has set hard.

tips of the trade

• **Capping the flue** – If the flue has an open pot at the top, it is a good idea to have it capped to stop rainwater from entering the flue. The simplest way of doing this is to fit a clay or metal hood top or flue vent into the top of the pot. Tackle this yourself only if you are happy working at height and can set up a ladder easily to reach the top of the chimney stack. Otherwise, call in a builder to fit it for you. Although the job itself is a straightforward one, it is not worth taking the risk of doing it yourself if you are inexperienced, and especially if you do not have the appropriate ladder and safety equipment for roof work.

• **Sweeping the flue** – If the fireplace was used regularly in the past, make sure that you remember to have it swept to remove all the soot that will have built up in the flue before you block up the fireplace opening. Doing this will minimize the risk of staining occurring on the face of the chimney breast in future if condensation forms in the flue.

installing a fireplace ⚒

Fireplaces have always had a dual function – in addition to providing heat, they also provide a focal point and therefore contribute decoratively to the room as a whole. The advent of central heating meant that many fireplaces were blocked up, but they are now enjoying a revival for their aesthetic value. Solid fuel and gas fires require professional installation, but building a fireplace for aesthetic or ornamental purposes is relatively straightforward.

fitting a surround

Some of the most attractive modern fireplaces are based on a marble hearth and back panel design. Marble is a heavy stone and often requires two people for lifting and positioning. It is also fragile, so provide plenty of support while it is being positioned, and while you are waiting for any mortar to dry. The surround is either made of painted MDF or, as in this case, stained softwood.

tools for the job

pencil & tape measure
gauging trowel
sponge
spirit level
pointing trowel
screwdriver
sealant gun
sponge

1 Having chosen your location for the fireplace, mark its central position on the wall surface.

2 Taking measurements from the marked point on the wall surface, draw in the dimensions of the hearth on the floor. Use a gauging trowel to apply a number of blobs of mortar within the confines of this hearth guideline. Make sure the blobs are of a consistent size, so that when the hearth is positioned, it will sit and bed down as evenly as possible.

3 Lift the hearth into place and check that it is positioned central to the wall mark with a tape measure. Allow the hearth to bed down into the mortar. Check for any mortar squeezing out from under the hearth edges and remove with a clean, damp sponge before it dries.

4 Use a spirit level to check the hearth positioning across all dimensions, side to side, front to back and diagonally, as it will not be possible to make adjustments later.

5 Add blobs of mortar to the back panel and position it centrally on the hearth. Allow the panel to secure to the wall surface, but do not press it finally into position. Check it is sitting vertically by using a spirit level.

6 Carefully lift the fire surround into position, pushing the back panel on to the wall until the surround is flush against the wall surface. This will also help to force the back panel into its correct position.

7. Remove the fire surround and seal around the edges of the back panel using some more mortar (a pointing trowel is ideal for this process). However, take care not to get any mortar on to the marble face – if this happens, remove it immediately with a clean, damp sponge before it dries.

8. Re-position the fire surround on the back panel. Secure it in place using glass plate fixings, which will help it to sit flush on the wall surface. Attach the fixings under the mantel shelf so that they will not be too conspicuous.

9. Finally, attach the internal brass surround to the back panel with some silicone sealant. The surround can be pressed into position by hand. Be sure to remove any excess silicone that squeezes out with a dry cloth, before it sets.

MORTAR CHOICE

Mortar made from white cement is ideal for marble fireplaces because of its aesthetic qualities. Fireplaces may also be positioned using bonding coat plaster, but when using light-coloured marble, bear in mind that the marble can become stained. Also, some marble types have transparent characteristics which will mean that the fixing material may be visible in places. For this reason, a light-coloured mortar is best as it should be less noticeable than many of the darker types of adhesive. White cement is generally available from good DIY outlets.

Once blended into the rest of the decoration, a fireplace can make a stunning impact on the look and feel of a room. Painting the internal 'fireplace' matt black creates the impression of an authentic old fire instead of a newly positioned reproduction.

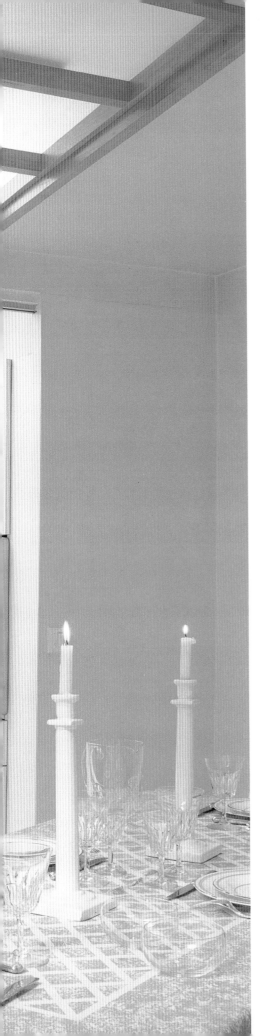

altering the structure of a ceiling

When redesigning a room layout or planning a new colour scheme, it can be common to neglect ceilings or assume that their finish will be led by other design elements in the room. However, this does not have to be the case, and entering any renovation project should include close consideration of ceiling improvements and potential alterations. Therefore, appropriate heights, soundproofing, access and insulatory properties are all considered in this chapter.

75

Different patterns and designs make suspended ceilings an unusual alternative to traditional ceiling finishes.

lowering a ceiling – 1

The most common reason for lowering a ceiling is quite simply the desire to reduce the height of a room for decorative or soundproofing purposes. High ceilings are most common in older properties, but this is not always the case and ceiling levels can be adjusted in any room – regardless of age – provided the practicalities of head clearance and final appearance are considered. A two-part process, the first step is to construct a framework for the plasterboarding.

walls & ceilings

76

making the frame

Before focusing on the ceiling itself, consider the existing wall construction. The new ceiling will be supported primarily by fixings to the walls in the room, and so the strength of these fixings is vital. For solid block walls, concrete anchors or frame fixings can be used with confidence as the strength of the fixing will be consistent on all wall areas. If you are fixing to stud walls, however, it will first be necessary to pinpoint the studs. Wall plates can then be fixed directly into the studs, rather than the surrounding, weaker plasterboard. Furthermore, for ceilings with a greater span than 2.4m (8ft), it will be necessary to attach timber hangers between the new framework and the existing ceiling, in order to provide extra support.

ensuring accuracy

Taking extra time to ensure accurate measurements, and that the joists are correctly aligned, will be highly beneficial when it comes to applying plasterboard to the framework. Even small discrepancies between joist levels will be accentuated once the plaster sheeting has been applied. It is also vital that the joists are not fixed in the hangers in a twisted position. Otherwise, when plasterboard is applied it will not fit flush against the bottom of the joist, resulting in weak fixings along the entire joist length.

joists set at 60cm (2ft) centres

wall plates acting as fixing point for joists

wall hangers fixing joists in place

joists spanning shortest dimension of room

tools for the job

tape measure

pencil

spirit level

panel saw

cordless drill/driver

hammer

1 Having decided how far you wish to bring the ceiling level down, use a pencil and spirit level to mark out a guideline around the entire perimeter of the room. Never simply measure the distance at different points and join them together,

as slight undulations in most ceiling surfaces mean that these measurements do not provide a true level. It is better to mark off height at one point and use the level from that point on.

tips of the trade

Modern ceilings are normally 2.4m (8ft) high and manufacturers make most building boards to these dimensions. This is a good guideline when deciding on the height to set your ceiling. The timbers used for the frame here are 10 x 5cm (4 x 2in) but thinner joists can be used. However, thin joists will need to be fixed at closer intervals and timber hangers used to attach the joists to the existing ceiling. Plasterboard thickness can affect the position of joists. For 12.5mm (½ in) plasterboard, fix the joists at 60cm (2ft) intervals, for 9.5mm (⅜ in) plasterboard, the joists should be adjusted to intervals of 40cm (1ft 4in).

2 Fix lengths of 10 x 5cm (4 x 2in) sawn timber to each wall width with the bottom edge of each timber running precisely along the pencil guideline. Make fixings at 40 cm (1ft 4in) intervals along the timber. In this example, the wall plates are being attached with concrete anchors because the walls are solid block construction. If you are attaching to stud walls, use a joist detector to find the studs and therefore the ideal positions for fixing.

3 The joists for the frame should always span the room across its shortest dimension. Along the appropriate opposing wall plates, therefore, mark off at 60cm intervals to denote the position for the metal hangers, which will be used to support the joists.

4 At each marked-off point on the two wall plates, nail a hanger in place – fix only to the underside of the wall plate for the moment.

5 Cut joists to the exact size between the opposing wall plates, positioning the cut joist inside the hangers. First, nail the hanger into the sides of the joist to clamp it in place. Then nail the hanger into the wall plate face for a secure, final fixing. Continue to attach joists to hangers across the rest of the ceiling framework.

6 To add extra rigidity to the framework, you can position some noggings between joists at staggered 1m (3ft 3in) intervals. The ceiling can now be considered ready for plasterboarding.

split level ceilings

Some people choose split level ceilings as an alternative to a complete ceiling level change. This is ideal for rooms in which high windows prevent the possibility of lowering the entire ceiling, or for people who want variation in the room height. The same basic system can be used to construct the frame, with some slight modifications to the main structure.

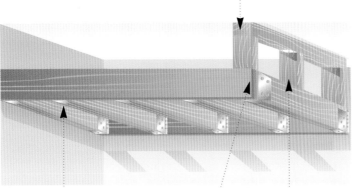

Attach timber to ceiling, making a head plate.

Position joists and wall hangers as for total ceiling lowering.

Draw vertical guideline on wall at 'step' position and attach wall plate up to existing ceiling.

Attach noggings between edge of lowered ceiling and head plate.

lowering a ceiling – 2 ↗↗

Once the frame of your lowered ceiling is in place, plasterboard needs to be fixed in position, before dry lining or plastering can begin. Large sheets of plasterboard can be difficult to handle (see below) but laths are an ideal option in many instances. This is also the point at which additional features such as soundproofing or lighting fixtures should be considered. All of these tasks are quite straightforward, provided you plan ahead.

walls & ceilings

PLASTERBOARDING

If you are using regular-sized plasterboard, you will need to employ the assistance of a helper to lift and manoeuvre the boards. Nail the sheets at 150mm (6in) intervals along all the joists, while the joins between each board should be made half-way across the width of the joists. This will ensure that the edges of the two sheets join along a single joist.

plasterboarding with laths

Laths are much smaller and easier to handle than large plasterboard, which makes them better for manoeuvring and enables you to work alone. They are also ideal to use when joists are set at 60cm (2ft) centres because they tend to be supplied in 120cm x 60cm (4ft x 2ft) sheets, which means they do not require cutting, except for around the perimeter of the ceiling.

tools for the job

hammer
screwdriver (optional)
panel saw
protective gloves

1 Starting in one corner of the room, attach a single lath across three ceiling joists. Plasterboard nails are ideal for this process, or alternatively, plasterboard screws can be used.

2 Continue to add laths to the joists, staggering the joints so as to create a brick bond pattern. This means that as you reach the perimeter of the ceiling, you will need to measure and cut laths to fill the various gaps.

soundproofing

Lowering a ceiling also provides the perfect opportunity to add some soundproofing to the room. By inserting soundproofing slabs into the ceiling space before plasterboarding, you can make a substantial difference to the amount of noise audible from the room above. (An alternative soundproofing technique is outlined on pages 82–3 where lowering the ceiling level is not an option.)

1 Weave 120cm x 60cm x 10cm (4ft x 2ft x 4in) soundproofing slabs between the top of the joists and the existing ceiling. If you have not been able to bring the ceiling down this far, use soundproofing slabs of the same size but with a 5cm (2in) depth instead of 10cm (4in). Rest the slabs in position, so that they are loosely joined but wedged securely above each joist.

2 Nail plasterboard sheets to the ceiling in the usual manner (see box). Bear in mind that it is important to use large sheets in this case, rather

than laths, as the fewer the joins, the greater the soundproofing effect. Then apply a second layer of plasterboard (see step 5 page 82).

dealing with ceiling roses

(see step 5 page 82).

safety advice

Before beginning any work on or around the ceiling rose, turn off the electrical supply at the consumer unit, and do not turn it back on until all the electrical work has been completed.

Ceilings tend not to have too many obstacles, and therefore lowering one can be a fairly trouble-free task. The main exception is a ceiling rose, which needs to be adjusted or lengthened in order to be of use for the new ceiling level. This work should be carried out after the new joists have been positioned, but before plasterboarding has begun.

tools for the job

screwdrivers (various)

cordless drill

hammer

pencil

tape measure

1 Unscrew the ceiling rose by hand, allowing the cover to slide down the wire to the fitting itself.

2 Unscrew the retaining screws that are keeping the rose plate secured to the old ceiling. Put the screws safely to one side as they will be needed again later.

3 Release the electrical wires from the rose by unscrewing the relevant terminals, allowing the wires to drop free. The pendant should now be separate from the electrical cable, and can be put to one side.

4 Use insulation tape to tape up each wire in the electrical supply cable. Ensure that each wire is completely separated from the others.

tips of the trade

It may be worth changing light fittings for flush-mounted spotlights, which will generally be less intrusive. However, always consult a qualified electrican before commencing work.

5 Plasterboard the ceiling until you come to a point where the old electrical cable is about to be totally obscured. Drill through the plasterboard directly below the cable, using a bit which is wide enough to accommodate the cable.

6 Pull the cable through the hole before continuing to apply plasterboard across the rest of the ceiling. If the cable is too tight in its original position and does not have the required excess to pull down to the new ceiling level, it will be necessary to add some extra cable to the existing one, joined with a junction box. Once the ceiling has been plasterboarded or dry lined, the pendant can be reconnected.

building a suspended ceiling ⫻

Suspended ceilings are traditionally linked with shopfitting, offices and commercial buildings. However, such ceiling structures are becoming increasingly popular in private dwellings. They are an ideal option for lowering ceilings, and require less structural work than alterations using joists and plasterboard. The tiles provided for suspended ceilings also tend to have both thermal and sound insulating properties and therefore make a useful alternative to traditional ceilings.

The construction of a suspended ceiling is a straightforward exercise so long as sufficient planning time has been allowed. It is worth drawing a scale diagram of the room in order to work out tile positioning and thus the ideal location for the main bearers in the framework (see diagram below).

tools for the job

tape measure
spirit level
cordless drill/driver
hacksaw
side cutters
pliers
panel saw

1. Draw a level pencil line around the perimeter walls at the prospective suspended ceiling height. Fix angle sections along this line at 40cm (1ft 4in) intervals. Fixings in solid block walls should be quite easy but you will need to follow the stud pattern (see page 76) on stud walls.

2. Fix angle brackets into the existing ceiling at measured intervals above the position where the main bearers will be.

3. Cut a section of hanger wire to a manageable length – 2–3m (6 –10ft) is suitable – and secure one end to a heavy object such as a workbench. Push the other end of the wire into a cordless drill and tighten the chuck until it is held securely in position. Slowly start the drill, causing the wire gradually to tauten until it is completely rigid. This will ensure that the wire has no slack and will make a rigid support when joined between the bearers and the ceiling.

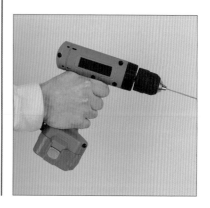

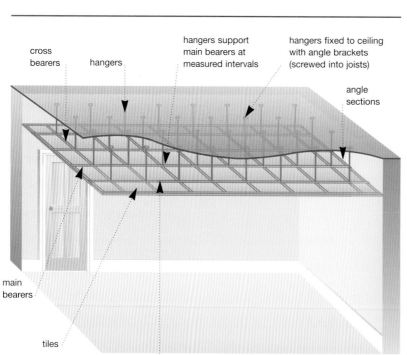

cross bearers

hangers

hangers support main bearers at measured intervals

hangers fixed to ceiling with angle brackets (screwed into joists)

angle sections

main bearers

tiles

bearer framework laid out so that cut tiles are an equal distance from wall around entire perimeter of room

4 Use side cutters to cut the wire down to the required lengths. Allow an excess of 10cm (4in) at each end of the length for attaching to the bearers and angle brackets.

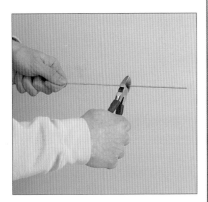

5 At each angle bracket, thread a section of wire through the bracket hole and tighten it in position by wrapping the end of the wire on to the main vertical section with pliers.

6 Position the main bearers on the angle sections. Thread the end of the hanger wires through the appropriate holes and wind the ends back on to the vertical length.

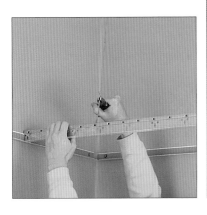

7 Fit the smaller cross bearers in position, at the appropriate intervals between the main bearers. The intervals should correspond to the tile dimensions.

8 Simply drop the tiles in place, feeding them above the suspended ceiling level first and then lowering them into position between the bearers. There is no particular insertion order, but it is always best to position the full tiles first before working around the edges. (The edge tiles may be cut using a panel saw before they are fitted in place.) Some manufacturers provide clips that fit on top of the bearers to hold the tiles down in position.

👍

tips of the trade

Main bearers need to be cut so that they can fit precisely between the angle sections on opposing walls. Mark off the length requirement on the bearer, and cut using a hacksaw.

Different patterns and designs make suspended ceilings an unusual alternative to traditional ceiling finishes.

soundproofing a ceiling ⚒

If you are unable to combine soundproofing with lowering a ceiling (see page 78) it may be necessary to use other techniques for minimizing sound travel. One method is to lift the floor above and soundproof from above the ceiling in question. Alternatively, it is possible to work from below, taking the existing ceiling down and starting from scratch.

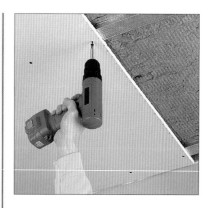

working from below

Soundproofing from below requires the removal of the old ceiling's plasterboard cladding. Once you have broken through the first piece of plasterboard, the task becomes a straightforward case of removing sections and sheets with a hammer or wrecking bar.

tools for the job

claw hammer
wrecking bar
cordless drill
protective gloves

1 Carefully remove the old ceiling with a wrecking bar. Then check between the joists for the presence of cables or pipes. Remove any remaining nails with a claw hammer – all joists must be free from obstructions before work begins so that new fixings can be inserted unhindered.

2 Starting on one side of the ceiling, fix soundbreaker bars across the joists at 40cm (1ft 4in) intervals. Fix the bars in place using drywall screws, ensuring that the screws are inserted through the felt pads and into the joist.

3 Weave 120cm x 60cm x 10cm (4ft x 2ft x 4in) soundproofing slabs above the soundbreaker bars and between the joists. Try to ensure that the slabs meet and join, above the bars. Continue to position slabs until the whole area is covered. Wear protective gloves for this process as the fibres in the slabs can cause skin irritation.

4 Fix 12mm (½in) plasterboard sheets to the ceiling using drywall screws. Fix the screws through the plasterboard and into the soundbreaker bars at 15cm (6in) intervals. Allow the screws to bite sufficiently to hold the plasterboard securely in place, but without the screwhead breaking into the surface and creating a weak fixing.

5 Fix 9mm (⅜in) plasterboard sheets over the first layer of plasterboard, staggering joints so that none of the second layer joints correspond with the first. Longer drywall screws will be required to penetrate both layers of plasterboard and fix into the soundbreaker bars. The ceiling may now be dry lined or plastered in the usual way.

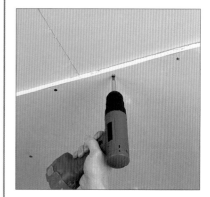

👍
tips of the trade

Coving is a useful way to introduce an additional soundproofing seal around the edge of the ceiling (see pages 100–1).

working from above

If possible, working from above a ceiling is an easier option for adding soundproofing. Although this involves lifting a floor in order to gain access to the ceiling space, it tends to be less messy than taking a whole ceiling down. Soundproofing slabs are therefore slotted between joists from above, before the floor is relaid. However, where joist depth or the ceiling space is particularly large, sand pugging may be combined with sound insulation slabs to create a more effective soundproofing system.

tools for the job

bolster chisel
panel saw
hammer
cordless drill/driver
dust mask
protective gloves

1 Strip the floor back to the floorboards and remove the boards using a bolster chisel. Take care not to damage any of the boards as they will be repositioned once soundproofing is complete.

2 Cut sections of 5cm x 2.5cm (2in x1in) batten with a panel saw. Fix the lengths in place along the bottom of the joists, just above the plasterboard ceiling.

3 Cut and fit 12mm (½in) plyboard strips between the joists, fixing them in place by nailing through the ply and into the battens.

4 Line the face of the plyboard with a plastic membrane sheet. Tuck the membrane into the corners and allow it to encroach up to the top of the floor joists. Only nail in position at the top of the joists.

5 Carefully pour kiln-dried sand on to the plyboard between each joist, spreading out the sand into a layer about 5cm (2in) deep. A small piece of batten cut to the width of the

space between the joists makes an ideal tool for spreading the sand across the area and producing a consistent level.

6 Fit 120cm x 60cm x 10cm (4ft x 2ft x 4in) soundproofing slabs in between the joists and on top of the sand. The slabs may need to be cut to fit – use a panel saw and wear a dust mask when cutting. Protective gloves should also be worn whilst fitting the slabs. Then replace the floorboards – a thick underlay and good quality carpet will also add to the soundproofing effect.

83

safety advice

Remember that sand adds a great deal of weight to the ceiling, so check with a structural engineer that your ceiling will be able to cope with the load. Furthermore, this technique should not be used in ceilings containing water pipes. Any small leaks soaking into the sand over time will increase the weight further and could result in ceiling collapse.

insulating a ceiling ↗

Trying to make your home as energy efficient as possible provides benefits on a financial level and contributes towards protecting the environment. One of the simplest ways to increase energy efficiency is to ensure that you have adequate loft insulation. This is easy to lay but requires some thought about how to deal with obstacles.

blanket insulation

Blanket insulation is the most commonly used form of loft insulation material as it is the simplest to handle and can be laid very quickly. Roll length measurements provided by the manufacturer make it easy to estimate the amount required. When measuring up, be sure to choose rolls that are the same width (or slightly wider) than the joist gap in your loft. This will help to avoid extra cutting.

tools for the job

protective gloves
dust mask

1 Roll out the insulation blanket between the joists. Do not compress it because much of its effectiveness is provided by maintaining its depth. Carefully tear the blanket by hand whenever a division is required.

2 Greater efficiency can be achieved by laying a second layer over, and at right angles to, the first. This technique obscures all the joists, so if you choose this option you may need to build access bridges in your loft.

loose fill insulation

Loose fill insulation offers an alternative to blankets. Although it can be used in most situations as a direct alternative, it is mainly used in lofts where there are a number of awkward spaces to fill, making it a more practical option than blanket insulation. It is made of similar material to the blankets, but has been shredded into smaller pieces.

🖐
safety advice

Always wear gloves and a dust mask when handling loft insulation as the fibres in its construction can be irritating to both skin and the respiratory system.

tips of the trade

When installing loft insulation, do not cover any ventilation access. Most roof spaces are ventilated through grills or openings in the loft, or at the junction between the roof and exterior walls. Covering these areas can lead to damp and condensation problems, so keep filling safely away.

1 Pour the loose fill directly from the bag into the gaps between the joists.

2 Use a piece of batten, cut to the same length as the width of the gap between the joists, to even the loose fill out in the joist gap.

tips of the trade

Just as ventilation inlets must be kept clear of lagging, flush electrical fittings must also be given clearance, so that they do not overheat. Cut around flush fittings, leaving plenty of clearance between the insulation material and the fitting.

3 Insulation must always be on top of obstacles rather than below, so make some cardboard bridges for pipes, before covering over them with the loose fill.

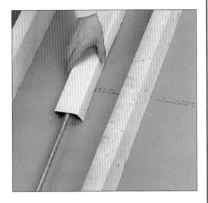

loft hatches

Loft hatches have to be movable, so it is clearly not possible simply to lay insulation over the top of the hatch. However, insulation is still necessary if it is to be effective throughout.

tools for the job

panel saw
hammer
protective gloves
dust mask

1 Cut four pieces of 12.5cm x 2.5cm (5in x 1in) planed softwood to the dimensions of each side of the loft hatch. Nail them in position to create a shallow box.

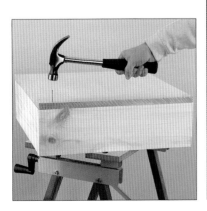

2 Insert a section of blanket insulation inside the box. Loose fill insulation may be used.

3 Cut a piece of plyboard to size, attach it to the top and position the box as the hatch.

DEALING WITH PIPES

Pipes situated between and below joist level are best dealt with as shown left. However, pipes situated above the joists need another method of insulation.

Fit pipe lagging over and around any exposed pipes, butt joining sections as required.

Where a junction is required, mitre the lagging so that a precise joint is achieved. Lagging can be cut using a craft knife or scissors.

insulating water tanks

The growing popularity of combination boilers means that modern houses are less likely to have loft-situated water tanks. However, the majority of older houses still have water tanks which feed the various systems in the house. It is therefore important to ensure that the tank is insulated correctly.

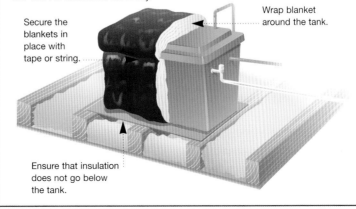

Secure the blankets in place with tape or string.

Wrap blanket around the tank.

Ensure that insulation does not go below the tank.

building a loft hatch ⁄⁄⁄

Lofts are increasingly recognized as areas of under-utilized space. Many people now look to the idea of converting such areas into extra rooms, or into special storage areas in order to free-up other rooms. Most lofts have some sort of access built into the design of the house, but renovation may make it necessary to install a proper loft hatch.

cutting in a hatch

tools for the job

joist detector
....
tape measure
....
pencil
....
spirit level
....
plasterboard saw
....
panel saw
....
cordless drill/driver
....
hammer
....

Before beginning the process of installing a new hatch, it is important to make all the necessary calculations and judgements in terms of the suitability of its position. If ladder access is required, ensure that your chosen site has suitable provision for storing and/or supporting such equipment. Similarly, check to see what is directly above the proposed hatch, as all precautions must be taken to ensure that services will not be interfered with or disrupted.

Dimensions clearly require the hatch to be large enough to allow comfortable access for both yourself and any household items that need to be passed through the opening. The structure of the ceiling is vital because some joists will have to be cut in order to make room for the access area. It is therefore advisable to take some professional advice before embarking on the project, in order to ensure that the ceiling structure will sustain a loft hatch construction. In older homes,

where joist depth tends to be more substantial, this is rarely a problem. In newer homes, however, joists tend to be thinner and so it is necessary to check the strength of the structure.

1 Use a joist detector to pinpoint the joist position on the ceiling. Mark out the proposed position of the hatch, ensuring that two of the opposing sides are directly below the edges of two joists. In this way, it will only be necessary to cut through one central joist to create the opening.

2 Use a dry wall saw to cut around the pencil guideline. On the two sides of the square that run in

the same direction as the joists above, try to rest the saw against the joists, thereby following directly along their edge. This should help to achieve an exact cut to the precise joist width.

3 Having removed the plasterboard 'hatch', use a panel saw to cut out the central joist. This will now provide access through the hole and into the roof space. Trim back the cut joist (from above) a further 5cm (2in) at either side of the hatch, so that when noggings are inserted to create the opposing sides of the hatch, they will be positioned back from the ceiling opening, and also supply a more rigid structure.

4 Use the panel saw to cut noggings to size, and then screw them in place to form the hatch frame. In addition to fixing the noggings centrally into the cut joists, it will also be necessary to fix in the corners. Skew screws through the noggings and into the joists at all four corners of the hatch frame using a cordless screwdriver.

5 Cut 12.5cm x 2.5cm (5in x 1in) planed softwood to the internal dimensions of the hatch. Fix it in place by nailing or screwing directly through the lengths and into the joists and noggings. Ensure the bottom edge sits flush with the ceiling to produce a smooth lining upon which to attach the remaining hatch features.

6 Cut a 2.5cm x 0.5cm (1in x ⅜in) batten to the internal dimensions of the lining. Make a pencil guideline around the lining, half-way up its height. Then nail the batten in place, so that the bottom edge sits precisely on the pencil guideline. This batten will act as the ledge upon which the finished loft hatch will rest.

7 Measure and cut architrave to fit around the lining. Allow the architrave front edge to bisect the edge of the lining, in order to create a neat and balanced finish.

8 Tighten the mitred joints of the architrave by nailing further fixings at each corner, thus pulling the mitre into a secure, finished position.

9 Finally, cut a sheet of MDF (medium density fibreboard) to the dimensions of the hatch and drop it into place above the ledge created by the batten. This can be primed and decorated as required.

loft ladders

Access through a loft hatch can be made by means of a portable ladder or by a permanent, custom-designed ladder. Many manufacturers provide easy-to-install ladder systems, but make sure that your ladder is accessible and that the loft has enough clear storage capacity, without obstructing joists. If possible, choose your ladder design before building a hatch because many manufacturers stipulate particular dimensions and positioning in order to achieve the best access results.

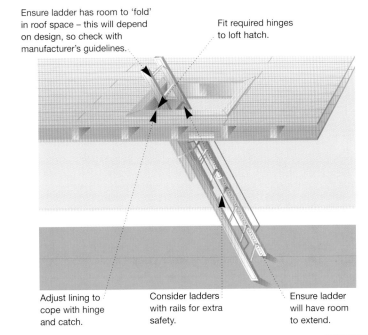

Ensure ladder has room to 'fold' in roof space – this will depend on design, so check with manufacturer's guidelines.

Fit required hinges to loft hatch.

Adjust lining to cope with hinge and catch.

Consider ladders with rails for extra safety.

Ensure ladder will have room to extend.

constructing a slatted ceiling ⁄⁄⁄

Slatted ceilings offer a purely decorative option to traditional ceiling structure. They can be useful when trying to 'lower' a particularly high ceiling, and require less structural consideration than lowering the ceiling in its entirety (see pages 76–9). However, slatted ceilings do require a large quantity of wood and the jointing mechanism and measurements used in their construction need to be accurate, in order to achieve the best possible effect.

tools for the job

pencil
spirit level
panel saw
combination square
mitresaw
chisel
wooden mallet
cordless drill/driver

1 Draw a level guideline around the perimeter of the room using a pencil and spirit level. This line will be the bottom edge of the slatted ceiling, and therefore its positioning should be considered carefully. Height suitability is really determined by the existing ceiling height in your home. Older, more traditional houses vary in ceiling height but modern houses tend to be about 2.4m (8ft).

3 Pencil in a central bisecting line through an offcut of 7.5cm x 2.5cm (3in x 1in) prepared softwood. Hold the offcut next to each guideline on the full length in turn, marking a second guideline across the length to denote the width of the slats. Then, using the pencilled bisecting line on the offcut, mark where this line meets the pencilled guidelines on the full length on either side of the offcut.

5 Use a chisel to cut out each sawn section of the length. Ensure that the chisel blade dimensions fit exactly between the sawn cuts so as to produce a precise, accurate finish. One light tap with a mallet on the chisel is usually enough to remove this small section of wood. Repeat steps 2–5 for the length of wood required for the opposing wall. It may pay to sand the cut-out area lightly to remove any rough edges.

2 Cut a piece of 7.5cm x 2.5cm (3in x 1in) prepared softwood to the length of the longest wall dimension. Use a combination square to make guidelines at 15cm (6in) intervals along the length.

4 Use a mitresaw, set at the 90 degree angle, to cut down to the marks on each slat guideline on the length. Be exact with this cut, not allowing it to encroach further than the marked-off points.

6 Screw the notched lengths into position on the wall, allowing the bottom, uncut edge of the lengths to run along the pencil guideline. Screw in fixings below every other notch using concrete anchor

screws or plugs and screws as required. On the two opposing walls – as yet untouched – fix full lengths of 7.5cm x 2.5cm (3in x 1in) prepared softwood between the notched lengths, flush against the wall.

7 Measure exactly between the opposing notches on the two opposing lengths (from wall to wall). Cut lengths of 7.5cm x 2.5cm (3in x1in) prepared softwood accordingly. At the ends of these lengths, measure in exactly the width of the length – 2.5cm (1in) in this case – and bisect the width of the length to produce an L-shaped pencil guideline. Cut this portion away, at each end.

8 Position the length between the appropriate notches, allowing the length to drop down into position.

9 A couple of knocks with a mallet may be required finally to position the length – pins should not be necessary. Repeat this process across the entire ceiling.

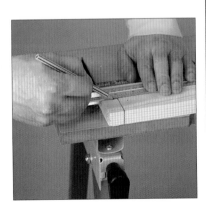

tips of the trade

Dropping the ceiling level will mean that ceiling-fitted lighting will also need adjusting. This may require the lengthening of pendants or fluorescent fittings. Alternatively, a switch to wall-mounted fittings could be an option. Consult an electrician before embarking on this work.

tips of the trade

For ceilings where the slat length is more than 3m you may need to add extra support. Fix a length of 50mm x 50mm planed softwood across the top of the slats, and attach it to the ceiling with 'hangers'.

Painting the original ceiling above the slats can enhance the desired effect. The slats themselves can also be used as a system from which to hang further decoration.

plastering & lining

Before walls and ceilings can be decorated
with paint, wallpaper or other finishes, they
have to be given a smooth, flat surface.
On brickwork and blockwork walls, plaster
does the job. This is a powder based on
gypsum that is made into a plastic mix
with water and applied to wall and ceiling
surfaces, where it dries to a hard coating.
On timber-framed walls, a rigid sheet
material called plasterboard is used to clad
both sides of the wall structure. Plasterboard
is also used to form ceilings beneath timber
floor joists, and to line the inside of exterior
walls as an alternative to plastering. There
are several other plaster-based products
that are used around the house for their
decorative effect, including coving, ceiling
centres and panel mouldings. This chapter
tells you how to use them.

91

*Ornate coving complements the elegant
grandeur of this room, but plain coving
would suit a more modern decor.*

plastering masonry ⚹⚹⚹

The type of plaster most widely used for masonry is a mix based on a mineral called gypsum. This is usually applied as a two-coat system, with a thick undercoat applied first and thinner finish coat on top. Different types of plaster are used for undercoats and finish coats, and there are different undercoats for different backgrounds such as brick, aggregate blocks and thermal blocks. Ask your supplier for advice to ensure that you select the correct plaster for the job.

The job of the plaster undercoat is to smooth out any irregularities in the wall surface and even out differences in the rate at which the masonry and pointing absorbs water, thereby allowing the thin finish coat to dry out evenly and without cracking.

A professional plasterer will plaster a wall in one continuous operation, gauging the thickness they are applying as they work. However, the amateur plasterer will find it easier initially to divide the wall surface up into a series of bays using slim timber battens called grounds. These act as depth guides to help you apply an even thickness of plaster to each bay. They are removed once the plaster has set, and the narrow channels are then filled with more plaster, ready for the finish coat to be applied.

tools for the job

tape measure
tenon saw
claw hammer
spirit level
bucket
power drill & mixer attachment
spot board
workbench
garden spray gun
hawk
plasterer's trowel
stepladder
wooden rule
(1.5m/5ft length of 75 x 25mm/
3 x 2in planed softwood)
wooden plasterer's float
angle trowel

1 Nail 25 x 10mm (1 x ⅜in) planed timber battens to the wall you are plastering at roughly 1m (3ft) intervals, using 25mm (1in) long masonry nails. Check that they are vertical using a spirit level, and insert cardboard or hardboard packing behind them if the wall surface is uneven. Fit a batten right in the angle of internal corners, and pin on a length of expanded metal angle bead at external corners – this acts as a depth guide during plastering, and remains in place when the wall has been plastered to reinforce the corner.

2 Mix your first batch of plaster. As a guide to quantities, 50kg (110lb) of undercoat plaster will cover around 8sq m (86sq ft) of wall surface in a layer about 10mm (⅜in) thick. Half-fill your bucket with clean water, then sprinkle handfuls of dry plaster into it, stirring as you do so by hand or with a power drill and mixer attachment. Add more plaster until the mix takes on the consistency of porridge. Tip it out onto your spot board, which should be set on a portable workbench, close to the wall you are plastering.

3 Wet the surface of the masonry in the first bay using a garden spray gun. Wetting the masonry will cut down substantially the absorption rate of the wall, thus preventing moisture from being sucked out of the undercoat too quickly, which will result in poor adhesion and cause the plaster to crack.

4 Hold your hawk under the edge of the spot board and scoop a trowelful of plaster onto it. Then transfer the plaster off the hawk and onto your trowel, tilting the hawk so that it is nearly vertical as you slide the almost horizontal trowel upwards across its surface. This procedure may take a little practice.

5 Resting the right-hand edge of the loaded trowel against the right-hand batten at floor level, tilt the blade until it is at an angle of about 30° to the wall. Push the trowel upwards to press the plaster against the masonry, gradually tilting the blade towards the vertical so that the plaster is squeezed out between its lower edge and the wall. The blade will be vertical when the plaster runs out. Load and apply a second band of plaster to the left of the first. Work your way up the bay to the next batten, applying parallel bands of plaster and blending them together. Over-fill the centre of the bay so that the plaster is proud of the battens. Use steps to reach the top of the bay.

6 When the bay is complete, hold a wooden rule across the guide battens at floor level and slide it upwards, at the same time moving it from side-to-side with a sawing motion. This will remove any high spots from the plaster. Fill obvious low spots with more plaster and then drag the rule across the bay again.

7 Drive five or six wire nails through a wooden float in a line 25mm (1in) in from one end of the blade, so that they protrude about 3mm (1/8in). Use this to key the surface of the fresh plaster. Wet the base of the float and hold it flat against the plaster. Then move it around in a circular motion so that the nails score shallow marks.

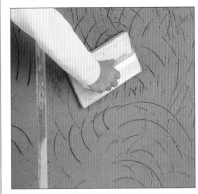

8 Repeat steps 3 to 7 to apply undercoat to the remaining bays. Prize out the battens and fill the channels with plaster. Use an angle trowel to plaster internal angles. Plaster external corners using a batten and the angle bead as depth guides.

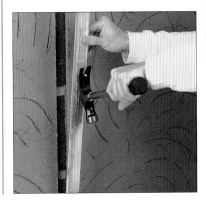

9 Undercoat plaster takes about two hours to set hard, so you should be able to start applying the finish coat to the first bay by the time you have completed the undercoat for the final bay. Mix up a quantity of finishing plaster to the consistency of melting ice cream. Load your hawk and trowel as before, applying a coat with a maximum thickness of 3mm (1/8in). Start at the bottom of the wall and work upwards, again with broad sweeping arm movements. Cover about 2sq m (22sq ft), then apply another, even thinner, coat over the top of the first. Trowel off any ridges and splashes, and repeat the process until the entire wall is covered. Finally, wet the trowel and polish the finish plaster with the blade held flat against the surface.

MOVING BATTENS

As you become more proficient at plastering and gain in confidence, try using the moving batten technique. Put up two battens about 1.2m (4ft) apart and plaster the area between them. Then remove both battens and reposition one on the wall 1.2m (4ft) away from one edge of the plaster, which will act as a depth guide at one side of the next bay. Plaster this next section, then reposition the batten to the same distance again. Continue working around the room, bay by bay. When you return to your start point, the edge of the plaster in the first bay will act as your final depth guide.

working with plasterboard ⚒

Plasterboard is a rigid sheet material used for cladding the surfaces of timber-framed partition walls and for surfacing ceilings. It has a lightweight plaster core, sandwiched between two sheets of strong paper that also cover the longer edges of the board. Grey-faced plasterboard is intended for plastering over, while ivory-faced board can be painted or wallpapered directly. Ivory-faced boards with a tapered edge allow the joints to be taped and filled flush, ready for decorating.

types of plasterboard

Standard plasterboard, also known as wallboard, has one grey and one ivory face and is the most widely used type. It comes in standard 2.4 x 1.2m (8 x 4ft) sheets and a range of smaller sizes useful for repair jobs. You can also get longer sheets for rooms with high ceilings. Wallboard is available with square or tapered edges, in 9.5 and 12.5mm ($^3/_8$ and $^1/_2$in) thicknesses.

Baseboard is used for lining ceilings, and will be given a skim coating of finish plaster. It is available only as a square-edged board and has grey paper on both faces. The most common size is 1.2 x 0.9m (4 x 3ft). It comes in just the 9.5mm ($^3/_8$in) thickness.

Both types are available with a vapour barrier. Vapour-shield boards are used mainly for upstairs ceilings (to prevent condensation in the loft) and for dry lining exterior walls (see pages 98–9). Thermal board has a layer of rigid insulation bonded to one face and also incorporates a vapour barrier. It is used for walls where extra insulation is needed.

storing plasterboard

Plasterboard is fragile until it is fixed to a supporting framework. Always carry sheets on edge – they may snap if you carry them flat. Store them on edge, closely packed against each other and leaning against a wall at a slight angle. If you are using ivory-faced boards, stack them with these faces together. Take care not to damage the paper-covered edges as you handle them.

fixing plasterboard

To line a partition wall or ceiling, plasterboard sheets are nailed to supporting timbers – vertical studs and horizontal top and bottom plates in a timber-framed wall, and joists in a ceiling. These are usually positioned at 400mm (16in) centres so that the edges of 1.2m (4ft) wide boards can be butt-jointed over the centre of every third timber and nailed to the intermediate ones. They are fixed with galvanized plasterboard nails, which have a jagged shank to grip the timber and a flat head that should be driven so that it dimples the face of the board. These are then filled with plaster to conceal them. Nails should be placed every 150mm (6in), 9mm ($^3/_8$in) in from paper-covered edges and 12mm ($^1/_2$in) from cut ends.

cutting plasterboard

You can cut plasterboard with a fine-toothed saw, resting it on trestles to leave the cutting line clear. However, it is easier to cut through the paper and into the plaster core along the cutting line and then to snap the board over the edge of a length of wood. Cut through the paper on the other face to separate the two pieces. Use a padsaw, jigsaw or knife to make cut outs for light switches, socket outlets and so on.

MAKING A FOOT LIFTER

A foot lifter is a double wedge used to lift plasterboard sheets tight against the ceiling. Make one from a short length of 75 x 50mm (3 x 2in) wood, tapered into a wedge shape from the centre towards each end so that it rocks like a seesaw. Rest the sheet on one end of the wedge, then press down on the other end with your foot to lift the board into position. The small gap at the bottom of the board is concealed with skirting boards later.

cladding a partition wall

With the wall framework in place, fix the first board beside the doorway if the wall has one, as in this example, or in a corner if not.

tools for the job

tape measure
pencil
long straight edge
fine-toothed saw
trimming knife
foot lifter (see box above)
hammer

1 Measure the floor-to-ceiling height and subtract 20mm ($^3/_4$in), then cut the board to length. Offer it up to the frame with one edge aligned with the door stud, lift it tight against the ceiling using a foot lifter and mark the position of the door head on this

edge. Cut a 25mm (1in) wide strip off this side of the board between the mark and the top edge. This cut edge will be centred on the upper section of the stud above the door opening.

2 Set the board back in place and nail it to the framework. Repeat the process for the board at the other side of the door opening.

3 Fix more whole boards in place, working from the doorway towards the corners. Butt tapered-edge boards together, but leave a 3mm (⅛in) gap between square-edged boards (to be plastered later).

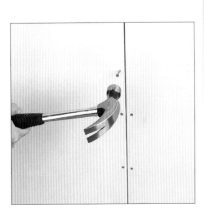

4 Cut the last boards down in width to fit the space at the room corners, and nail them in place. See pages 96–7 for how to fill joints and plaster plasterboard.

See pages 96–7 for how to fill joints and plaster plasterboard.

cladding a ceiling

When cladding a ceiling, the boards should be fixed with their long edges at right angles to the joists, and with board ends meeting at the centre of a joist. To support the long edges, fix 50mm (2in) thick supports – called noggings – between the joists along the side walls, and across the room at centres to match the board width. You will also need steps or a platform of scaffold boards to work from, plus a spare pair of hands to help support the boards while each is fixed.

1 Offer up the first board in one corner of the room. Nail it to the joists and to the noggings, working from the centre of the board outwards. This stops the board from sagging as you fix it.

2 Complete the first row of boards, trimming the last one to fit if necessary. Butt-join tapered-edge boards, but leave a 3mm (⅛in) gap between square-edged ones.

3 Start the next row with a board trimmed to reach the centre of a joist. This avoids having all the joints between boards aligned along just one joist. Continue in this way.

4 Finish the ceiling with a row of boards cut down in width to fit between the last row of boards and the wall. See pages 96–7 for how to fill joints and plaster plasterboard.

plastering plasterboard ⚋⚋⚋

Plasterboard can be given a thin overall coat of board finish plaster if it is fixed with the grey side facing outwards. If tapered-edge boards are fixed ivory side out, however, only the joints need filling before the boards are painted or papered. In both cases it is vital to tape all the joints first, using proprietary paper joint tape or self-adhesive joint mesh, to avoid the risk of the joints opening up in the future due to movement of the ceiling structure.

safety advice

The step-by-step sequences on these two pages demonstrate how to apply a plaster or taped finish to a plasterboard wall. Exactly the same techniques are used to finish a plasterboard ceiling, with the only difference being that you are working above your head. This has certain safety implications, however, since it is essential that you have a safe working platform so that you can reach the ceiling surface comfortably and without stretching. Scaffold boards or staging set on adjustable trestles, or a low mobile work trolley on lockable castors, are all ideal. Check out what your local plant hire company has available.

tools for the job

stepladders & boards
for working platform
bucket & mixer
spot board
plasterer's trowel
hawk
scissors for joint tape
or joint mesh
angle trowel (optional)
garden spray gun
filling knives
close-textured sponge

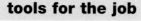

plastered finish

Set up a working platform, ensuring that it is steady, and mix some finish plaster in a bucket to the consistency of melting ice cream.

1 Apply a thin band of finish plaster with a trowel along each joint line, then cut joint tape to the required length and bed it into the plaster band using the end of the trowel to press it into place. If you are using self-adhesive joint mesh, dispense with the plaster band and stick the tape directly onto the board surface. Repeat for all the joints.

2 Spread a thin layer of plaster along each joint, wide enough to cover the tape or mesh. It should also be just thick enough to hide the tape or mesh completely. Smooth the plaster out on either side of the joints with the trowel held flat against the surface of the plasterboard.

3 Repeat steps 1 and 2 to bed tape or mesh into the wall/ceiling angle all around the room. Bed tape or mesh into the external and internal corners of the room in the same way. Do not be tempted to omit any of these angles – if you do not tape these joints, you are sure to get cracks opening up there as time goes by.

4 Apply finish plaster to the bays between the joints, working from the bottom upwards if you are plastering walls and from one edge outwards if you are plastering a ceiling. Use the same technique as for applying finish plaster over undercoat (see pages 92–3).

5 Return to your starting point and apply a second, thinner coat of plaster over the entire surface. Work with the trowel held almost flat to the surface to control the plaster thickness and ensure a flat finish.

6 Neaten the angles between wall and ceiling and in internal corners by running the edge of the trowel along each surface in turn. Alternatively, use an angle trowel.

7 Wet the blade of the trowel and the plaster surface using a garden spray gun, and polish the surface of the plaster until smooth.

taped finish

Use joint filler instead of finish plaster to fill the joints between tapered-edge boards. You can use either paper or self-adhesive mesh tape – the former is bedded in a band of joint filler, the latter is stuck straight to the plasterboard surfaces.

1 If you are using paper tape to fill the plasterboard joints, apply a narrow band of filler down the joint line and bed the tape into it with a filling knife, making sure that you exclude any air bubbles. Then apply another band of filler over the top with a wider knife to fill the tapered edges of the joint flush with the board surfaces at each side.

2 If you are using mesh tape to fill the plasterboard joints, stick the tape in place and fill the joint using the same technique as for paper tape. If you have to make a joint in the tape, butt the ends rather than overlapping them.

3 Finish all the joints with a thinner, wider band of filler, applied with a plasterer's trowel or a coating knife that will bridge the tapered edges of the boards. Then smooth out the edges of the filler with a slightly damp sponge.

PLASTERBOARD FINISHES

• **Sealing plasterboard** – To even out differences in porosity between the board and the filled joints, you should seal the wall before it is decorated, to prevent paint or wallpaper paste from drying too quickly as water is sucked into the board surface. To seal the plasterboard, use a thin coating of joint filler, applied and rubbed into the surface with a sponge. Alternatively, apply proprietary plasterboard primer with a brush or roller, or use emulsion paint diluted with 10 per cent water. Use two coats of paint to ensure uniform surface porosity.

• **Tiling plasterboard** – Plasterboard has very little strength if it gets wet, which can happen if a plasterboard wall is covered with ceramic tiles and the grouting is not waterproof. If you intend to tile an existing plasterboard wall, treat its surface with a coat of solvent-based paint first to seal the surface against water penetration. If you are cladding a new wall and plan to tile it, use special waterproof tile backing board instead of plasterboard to provide a surface that can withstand water penetration.

dry lining walls ⟋⟋⟋

This technique involves lining external masonry walls with plasterboard as an alternative to traditional plastering. It is used mainly in older properties to improve the insulation performance of solid walls. The boards are nailed to a framework of sawn timber battens fixed to the wall surface at centres to suit the board widths. Standard vapour-shield wallboard is commonly used for this purpose, with glass fibre insulation batts sandwiched between the boards and the masonry.

Dry lining can be installed over existing plaster if this is sound, but crumbly or damp plaster should be removed and, if damp, the problem must be treated and the wall allowed to dry out before dry lining is installed. The space between the dry lining and the masonry can be used to conceal cable runs to switches and sockets.

The timber used for wall battens should be pre-treated with wood preservative. It should be 50 x 50mm (2 x 2in) if glass fibre insulation is to be placed behind the plasterboard, and 50 x 32mm (2 x 1¼in) if thermal board is being used. Fix the battens with masonry nails long enough to penetrate the masonry by at least 25mm (1in), or with nail wall plugs.

If you are using insulation batts, wedge them in place between the wall battens all around the room before you start cutting and fixing plasterboard. Insulation is not used at the sides and heads of door and window openings.

Alternatively, thermal board with a layer of polystyrene or polyurethane insulation and a vapour barrier bonded to the rear face can be used to combine wall lining and insulation.

tools for the job

tape measure & pencil
straight edge
hand saw or power saw
spirit level
plumb line
cordless drill/driver
foot lifter (see box page 94)

1 Cut the vertical battens to a length about 150mm (6in) less than the room height and fix them in place, leaving a 75mm (3in) gap above and below each batten. Space the battens at 400mm (16in) centres for 9.5mm (⅜in) thick plasterboard in sheets 1.2m (4ft) wide, and at 600mm (2ft) centres for 12.5mm (½in) thick plasterboard in sheets of the same width. Start fixing the battens at door and window openings and work out towards the room corners.

2 When fixing battens at the corners of the room, fix a batten on each wall about 50mm (2in) away from the internal angle.

3 Cut and fit the horizontal battens at floor and ceiling level, fixing them in the gaps that you left above and below the vertical battens.

4 Add short horizontal battens above doorways and above and below window openings. Lastly, fit short vertical battens above these openings, offset by 25mm (1in) so that they will support the edges of boards that are fixed flush with the edges of the opening below as well as the infill panel above the opening.

5 Start fixing boards beside a door or window opening if there is one, and in a corner otherwise.

Cut the board to the required length, then use a foot lifter to hold it tightly up against the ceiling. Once it is in the correct position, drive in the fixings. Repeat the process at the other side and above the opening.

6 Cut strips of plasterboard to the required size to line the sides and head of the reveal opening around any windows or doorways. Place dabs of plaster on the reveals.

7 Fix the boards to the sides of the reveal so that their paper-covered edges lap the cut edges of the wall lining.

8 Prop the piece lining the head of the reveal in place with wooden battens until the plaster sets.

9 Work towards each corner of the room, fixing as many whole boards as possible. Cut the last board 20mm (³⁄₄n) narrower than the distance between the last whole board and the next wall. Fix it in place with its cut edge facing the corner.

10 Start the next wall with a whole sheet, butting the board against the face of the board already in place (but repeat from step 5 if there is an opening in the wall).

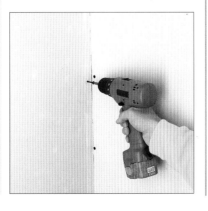

11 At external corners, fix one board with its cut edge flush with the face of the batten on the other wall. Then fix a board with a paper-covered edge to this wall so that the edge laps the cut edge of the first board. If using thermal board, you will have to cut away some of the insulation from the back of the board to allow board-to-board contact.

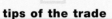

tips of the trade

If there are any switches or socket outlets on the wall that you are dry lining, make cutouts in the plasterboard to fit around them. If these are flush-mounted, remove the faceplates after turning the power off at the mains and draw the cable forward through the cutout. Fit a plastic cavity wall box in the cutout, feed in the cable and reconnect the faceplate to the new box.

FIXING BOARDS WITH ADHESIVE

If the existing wall surfaces are flat and true, you can fix ordinary plasterboard directly onto the wall surface using panel adhesive applied with a cartridge gun. Thermal board can be fixed with special adhesive applied to the wall in bands behind the centre and edges of the boards. This method reduces slightly the amount of floor area lost by dry lining a room, and saves the cost and time of fitting battens.

fitting coving ↗

Coving is a decorative moulding that is fixed into the angle between wall and ceiling, framing the ceiling in the manner of a picture frame. It is generally a plain quadrant in cross-section, and may be made from plaster with a paper cover, or from a foamed plastic resin. More elaborate mouldings are generally referred to as cornices and have three-dimensional surface designs. They are traditionally formed in fibrous plaster but foamed plastic types are also available.

Coving and cornice is usually sold in lengths of 2 or 3m (2 or 3yds), which are butt-jointed along each wall of the room. It is mitred at internal and external corners, although some moulded plastic cornice has pre-formed corner pieces. Plasterboard and plastic coving are fixed in place with adhesive, but the weight of fibrous plaster mouldings makes fixing with screws and wall plugs essential. Old wallcoverings must be removed from the area beneath the coving so that the adhesive can bond to solid plaster or plasterboard. There is no need to fill cracks in the wall-ceiling angle – the coving will hide these.

fixing plasterboard coving

Measure the perimeter of the room and calculate how many lengths of coving will be required. Allow for the loss of about 150mm (6in) of coving for every mitre joint. Buy enough adhesive to fix the quantity of coving. Plasterboard coving is fixed with either powder or ready-mixed tub adhesive, while plastic coving usually has its own special adhesive.

tools for the job

tape measure
pencil
long straight edge
spirit level
trimming knife
wallpaper scraper
filling knives
mitre box (see box below)
fine-toothed saw
stepladders
hammer

1 Hold a length of coving in place in the wall/ceiling angle and mark pencil lines on the ceiling and wall along its top and bottom edges. Use a straight edge (plus a spirit level for the wall lines) to extend these lines around the room. If there is wallpaper on either surface, cut along the pencil lines with a trimming knife and dry-strip as much wallpaper between the lines and the wall/ceiling angle using a scraper. Soak any patches that remain to soften the paste, but take care not to wet the wallpaper outside the guidelines.

MAKING A MITRE BOX

If you cannot find a mitre box that will cope with standard 100 and 125mm (4 and 5in) plasterboard coving, make one from scrap wood using a combination square to mark the 45° cutting lines. Cut the saw guides right down to the base of the box so that you can saw the mitres cleanly.

2 Use the edge of a filling knife to score the plaster surface with a series of criss-cross cuts in between the guidelines on the wall and ceiling. This will help the coving adhesive to bond well to the plaster and thereby achieve a secure enough fixing to hold the coving in place.

3 Start work on the longest wall in the room. Refer to the guidelines for cutting mitres on the opposite page to ensure that you cut the first mitre in the right direction – mistakes are wasteful and expensive. Place the coving in the mitre box with the ceiling edge in the base of the box, and cut with a fine-toothed saw. Smooth the edges with sandpaper.

4 Use a wide filling knife to butter a generous amount of adhesive along the rear faces of the coving. Draw the knife towards the outer edge of the coving so that excess adhesive will mainly be squeezed into the triangular space between the coving and the wall-ceiling angle.

5 Align the bottom edge of the coving with the pencil line on the wall, slide the tip of the mitre into the corner and push the coving firmly upwards and backwards to compress the adhesive and ensure a good bond to the wall. This is a job for two people if you are working with 3m (3yd) lengths of coving. Scrape off excess adhesive along the wall and ceiling edges of the coving and check that it is lined up with the pencil lines. The adhesive should grab strongly enough to support the weight of the coving, but if you want to reinforce it while it sets, drive two or three masonry nails through its lower section and into the wall. Only drive them part-way in so that you can remove them and fill the holes later.

6 Measure the distance from the square end of the first length to the next corner. If it is more than one length away but less than two, cut a mitre on the next length to fit the corner and stick it in place as in step 5. If it is less than one length away, cut the mitre as before, then hold the length in position and mark where it meets the first length. Cut the coving squarely at this point and fit it in place, filling the joint between the two lengths with coving adhesive.

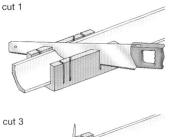

7 If you need a short infill piece to bridge the gap left between two full lengths, measure the gap and cut a piece of coving to fit it. Fix in place, filling the joints with coving adhesive.

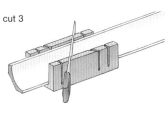

8 Move to the next wall and cut the correct mitre to fit into the corner, then repeat steps 3 to 7 to fix coving around the rest of the room. Finally, fill all joints with adhesive and remove any masonry nails you used to support long lengths of the coving.

CUTTING MITRES

Take care that you cut mitres in the correct direction. The cutting diagrams below show the order of mitre cuts needed to cove a chimney breast (right), when working from left to right.

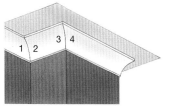

cut 1

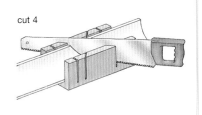

cut 2

cut 3

cut 4

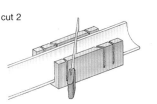

adding plaster features ↗

There are several other types of plaster feature that you can add to a room to complement the effect of coving (pages 100–1). These include decorative ceiling centres, wall plaques, corbels to support door heads, panel mouldings to frame areas of wall or ceiling, and even decorative plaster niches to display a favourite ornament. There is a wide range of styles available, from traditional to modern, formed in fibrous plaster or foamed plastic resin.

Ceiling centres and roses are widely available. They are produced in a wide range of different styles to suit every budget and taste, from traditional ornate examples to simpler, more modern varieties. Their function is twofold – they provide visual adornment to a ceiling and also conceal the electrical connections to a pendant light or chandelier. The smallest, lightest types can be stuck to the ceiling in the same way as coving, but large centres – especially those made from fibrous plaster – need to be screwed to the ceiling joists.

Wall plaques, being smaller and lighter than ceiling centres, are generally stuck in place, as are panel mouldings. Corbels fitted to support a door head or flat arch between rooms need screws driven into wall plugs, while plaster niches are generally fixed using mirror plates or similar fixings. Check the manufacturer's instructions when you choose the plaster feature you plan to install.

tools for the job

tape measure
....
string
....
drawing pins
....
pencil
....
wide filling knife
....
wallpaper scraper
....
bradawl
....
power drill & twist drill bits
....
screwdriver
....
fine-toothed saw
....
stepladder
....

fixing a ceiling centre

1 If your room has no central pendant light, the first step is to find the centre of the ceiling – a ceiling centre will look odd if it is not carefully positioned. To do this, find the mid-points of opposite walls and pin string lines between them. Where they cross is the ceiling centre. With the string lines still in place, hold the ceiling centre over them so that you can position it precisely central. Draw a light pencil line on the ceiling around its perimeter, then take it and the string lines down. (See the sequence on the opposite page for what to do if there is a central pendant light.)

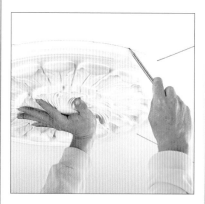

2 If the ceiling is painted, use the edge of a filling knife to score the surface inside the line in a criss-cross pattern and provide a key for the adhesive. If there is wallpaper present, cut along the pencil line and scrape off as much of the wallpaper as you can. Soak the remains with a wet sponge and scrape them off too. Then key the plaster as before.

3 If the ceiling centre you are fitting is lightweight to medium-weight, simply fix it in place with adhesive. Apply a generous band of adhesive all around the edge of the ceiling centre with a filling knife, and add a blob in the middle too. Offer the ceiling centre up to the marked outline and press it firmly upwards against the ceiling surface. Hold it for a few seconds to give the adhesive a chance to grab, then scrape off excess adhesive around the perimeter and use it as a filler in any gaps between the centre and the ceiling.

4 If you are installing a heavy plaster ceiling centre, follow steps 1 and 2 to position it, then

locate the joist positions at either side of the ceiling's central point. Use a bradawl within the pencil outline to probe for solid timber, and mark the joist positions at the perimeter of the outline. Hold the ceiling centre in place and mark where to drill holes for screws that will pass into the centre of the joists – use at least two, but preferably four, screws.

5 Take down the ceiling centre and carefully drill countersunk holes through it at the marked points. Spread a generous layer of adhesive on the back of the ceiling centre as described in step 3, then get a helper to hold the ceiling centre back in place while you drill pilot holes into the joists and drive in the fixing screws. Press the ceiling centre tightly against the ceiling as you do this, but take care not to overtighten the screws or you may crack the plaster.

6 Fill any gaps around the edge of the ceiling centre with adhesive, then wipe away the excess with a damp sponge for a smooth finish.

7 Finally, fill the fixing screw holes with a little adhesive and sand it smooth when it has set hard.

coping with a pendant light

1 Turn off the power at the mains and disconnect the pendant flex from its terminals, making a sketch of which cable cores are connected to which terminal on the baseplate first. Poke the wires up through the hole in the ceiling. Gain access to the ceiling void and connect the cables to the terminals of a four-terminal junction box, referring to your sketch to see which cables go to which terminal. This will restore the mains supply and switch control to the light when the power is restored later. Screw the

safety advice

Always consult a qualified electrician if in any doubt about carrying out wiring and electrical work yourself.

base of the junction box to the side of a nearby joist. Drill a hole in the middle of the ceiling centre for the pendant flex, and fit the ceiling centre as described on the opposite page.

2 Pass the end of a new piece of cable down through the ceiling. Connect the cores to the live, neutral and earth terminals of the junction box. Fit the cover on the box.

3 Return to the room below and connect the cable to the new baseplate. Screw this to the ceiling centre, connect the flex and fit the cover. Restore the power supply.

fitting skirting boards ⁊⁊⁊

Skirting board is the most effective material for finishing the junction between walls and floors. It helps to protect the bottom of the wall from scuffs and knocks, but it also provides a decorative feature. This means that, like coving, there is a wide range of designs available and profiles can be chosen to match similar designs for architrave around doors, dado rails and even picture rails. Once the correct design has been chosen, it's important to spend time fitting it properly.

MITRE CUTTING

If the length of skirting is to butt up against a straight edge such as architrave, a simple, straight saw cut at the correct measurement along the length is all that is required. However, when lengths need to join at a corner it is necessary to make a more complicated cut.

• **Mitred cuts** – Either a mitre block and panel saw or a specially designed mitresaw can be used for cutting 45 degree angles in skirting board lengths. The mitresaw locks in place to allow a perfect cut to be made at the correct angle through the skirting board length. The direction of the cut will also be dependent on whether a mitre for an internal or external corner is required.

👍 tips of the trade

Most manufacturers now produce skirting board with different profiles on each side. This saves wood but can make measuring and cutting confusing. For this reason, keep checking your board as you measure, cut and fix, to ensure that the correct profile is always being used.

profile cutting

This method is most suitable for simple, undetailed profiles on internal corners. In a simple square corner, allow the first length of skirting board to butt straight up against the wall surface. The second length must now be cut to fit against and around the profile that the first length creates in the corner junction.

tools for the job

tape measure
pencil
panel saw
jigsaw
plane (optional)
hammer
cordless drill/driver
mitresaw

1 Measure the length of skirting required. Then take a cut-off section of skirting board, position it over the length, and draw around its outline with a pencil.

2 Cut the skirting board along the pencil guideline. A jigsaw is ideal for this purpose as it makes it easy to follow the curve of the guideline, producing an accurate cut.

uneven floors

In some instances, an undulating floor can make fixing skirting board a more difficult task. This is because the bottom edge of the board is 'machined' to a straight edge and any dips or bumps in the floor will either show as gaps or push the skirting board up. This means that the board will be out of position when it comes to meeting the next length in a corner. In such circumstances, it is necessary to scribe the bottom edge of the skirting board so that it will sit flush against the undulating floor surface.

1 Cut the board to the correct length requirement and temporarily position it at the base of the wall. Take an offcut of wood whose depth is the same as the largest gap between the bottom edge of the skirting board and the floor.

Holding a pencil on top of the offcut, start in one corner and drag the block and pencil across the floor, next to the skirting, allowing the pencil to draw a guideline on the skirting board surface. This guideline reveals the line to cut along, so that when the board is fitted, it will follow the profile of the floor without leaving any gaps.

2 Remove the skirting board and fix it to a workbench. If a substantial amount of wood needs to be removed, cut along the guideline using a jigsaw. If it is only a small amount, shave off the unwanted material with a plane.

fixing skirting boards

Once cut to fit, the skirting board needs to be fixed securely in position. The type of fixing will depend on the wall structure. For stud walls, it is best to fix through the wall, into the sole plate and vertical studs. With masonry, the fixings can be anywhere, so long as they are secure.

nail fixings

Oval wire nails are ideal for nailing into studwork as their heads are easily concealed for decorative purposes, and they tend not to split wood. If hammering into block or brickwork, masonry nails should be used. The number and frequency of nails required will be dependent on the strength of each fixing – nails every 60cm (24in) will usually suffice.

screw fixings

Screws are often better for fixing skirting board to masonry walls. This is because there can be a tendency for nails to 'bounce' the skirting away from the wall as subsequent nails are inserted. In other words, you may gain a good fixing with one nail, but the vibration caused by inserting the next nail can weaken the fixing of the first, thus pulling it away from the wall. So use screws, first drilling pilot holes and either fixing in place with concrete anchor screws or plugs with tightly positioned screws.

difficult joins

In addition to normal, internal corners, there are other areas of the wall where skirting board requires a different approach to fixing, to ensure that the skirting is secure.

external corners

Mitre joins at external corners using a mitresaw. Once nailed in position on the wall, pull the mitre join together with panel pins inserted through the face of one piece of skirting board and into the mitre join with the second length.

open wall joins

Rather than butt joining lengths on open walls, it is always best to make a mitred join. This is because butt joining tends to crack quickly after decoration, leaving an unsightly join. Instead, mitre the join and apply some wood glue, before fixing the join with two panel pins through the mitre.

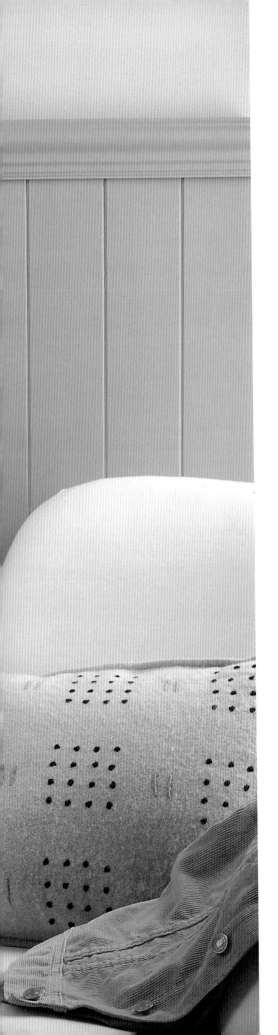

repair & restoration of walls & ceilings

Not all constructional tasks involve the complete rebuilding of entire ceilings and walls. Indeed, most jobs are concerned with repairs and alterations to localized areas, such as restoring surfaces and areas of damage. This type of work is often quick to carry out but nevertheless important in maintaining or restoring the appearance of walls and ceilings. This chapter covers many of the more common repair projects which occur around the home, and provides instruction on the best means of dealing with damaged areas. Many of the methods used have been briefly mentioned in earlier chapters, but slight variations are often required when it comes to finding the best techniques for repairs.

Whether painted or stained, tongue and groove provides an attractive and hardwearing finish, to an entire room.

making minor repairs to plaster ↗

Plastered wall surfaces can be damaged by accidental impacts that leave dents and scrapes, and may develop other defects with age. Ceilings are less prone to damage, but can suffer from popped nail heads and from cracks developing along board edges, at the wall/ceiling junction or in line with the laths in an old lath-and-plaster ceiling. All can be repaired quickly and easily, and are well within the capabilities of even those who are less experienced in DIY.

tools for the job

nail punch
hammer
pliers
filling knife
trimming knife
old paintbrush
caulking blade
coating blade
belt sander

ceilings

The two main causes of ceiling defects are vibration caused by traffic on the floor above, and movement in the timber structure that supports the ceiling surface. Trouble can also arise if the joints in a plasterboard ceiling were not properly sealed when the ceiling was first put up.

popped nail heads

If you have plasterboard ceilings, you may find occasional tell-tale discs of plaster on the floor – evidence that one of the nails used to fix the boards to the joists has popped and dislodged the plaster skim covering it. This happens if the nail was not driven fully in when the ceiling was put up, so that the boards have moved slightly and loosened it.

1 Use a nail punch and hammer to drive the nail in until its head just dimples the surface of the plasterboard. If it has popped far

enough for you to grip the head with pliers, pull it out and drive it in again just next to the original hole. Make sure its head is indented in the plaster skim.

2 Apply a little ready-mixed filler over the nail head with a filling knife, leaving it slightly proud of the ceiling surface. When it has set hard, sand it down flush and apply paint over the patch.

cracked ceilings

Cracks in plasterboard ceilings generally follow the edges of the plasterboard sheets, and are caused by movement in the ceiling structure

as temperature and humidity changes. In lath-and-plaster ceilings, the cracks may be irregular or run parallel to the laths to which the plaster is bonded. See pages 118–19 for larger-scale repairs.

1 Draw the blade of a trimming knife along the crack, undercutting each edge slightly so that the filler will be locked in place when it sets. Then use an old paintbrush to brush any dust from the crack. On lath-and-plaster ceilings, brush some water along the crack to stop the dry plaster from sucking moisture out of the filler and making it crack as it sets.

2 Load up a filling knife with filler and press it well into the crack, drawing the blade across it as you work. After filling a short section of crack in this way, draw the knife blade along the crack to smooth the filler level with the surrounding surface. Carry on in this way until you have filled the whole crack. Allow the filler to set hard, then sand the repair smooth and redecorate to conceal it.

tips of the trade

If cracks open up repeatedly along plasterboard joint lines, apply self-adhesive mesh joint tape along them and cover the tape with a wide band of filler applied with a caulking blade (see joint cracks below). Alternatively, apply a flexible textured coating to bridge and disguise the cracks, or put up lining paper.

walls

The main problem with walls is damage caused by collisions with the plaster surface. The cause could be anything – carelessly moved furniture, boisterous children playing or general wear and tear. Solid walls can also suffer from hairline cracking in the plaster, while hollow walls can develop cracks along the joints between the plasterboard sheets. All are relatively easy to rectify.

dents & cracks

All you need to repair small-scale surface damage to solid and hollow walls is some filler and a filling knife, or a caulking blade for hairline cracks.

1 Remove any loose material from the damaged area using an old paintbrush. Then fill it slightly proud of the surrounding surface with filler, and allow it to set hard. Sand the repair flush with the surface using fine-grade glasspaper, then redecorate.

2 Where an area of wall is suffering from extensive hairline cracking, tap the surface with your knuckles to check that the plaster is still sound. If it sounds hollow, its bond to the masonry beneath has probably failed (see pages 110–11 for how to repair it). If it is sound, use a caulking blade to apply the filler over the affected area, working it in different directions to ensure that all the cracks are filled. Allow it to set, then sand smooth as before.

joint cracks

Long, straight cracks often appear in plasterboard walls along the lines of the joints between adjacent plasterboard sheets – a sure sign that they were not taped before the plaster skim coat was applied. The best solution to this problem is to tape these cracks and skim a coating of filler over them.

1 Use a belt sander to sand off 1–2mm ($\frac{1}{16}$in) of plaster along the joint line, as wide as the sanding belt.

This ensures that the tape and filler lie flush with the wall surface when the repair is complete.

2 Stick a length of self-adhesive mesh joint tape down the cracked joint. Press the tape firmly into position, butt-joining lengths if necessary to cover the crack.

3 Use a coating or caulking blade to apply filler over the tape, running the blade down the wall at an angle so that the filler is finished flush with the surrounding wall surface. Allow it to set hard, then sand and redecorate for an invisible repair.

patching plaster ↗

If you discover areas of plaster on solid walls that sound hollow when tapped, or areas of plaster that have fallen away from the wall completely, the solution is to patch the affected area with new plaster. This is a relatively easy job to tackle, even if you have never used plaster before, because you have a solid base onto which to apply it, and the surrounding sound plaster to act as a guide to enable you to achieve a smooth, level finish.

tools for the job

club hammer
cold chisel
work gloves
safety goggles
old paintbrush
bucket & mixer
hawk
gauging trowel
plastering trowel
length of batten
to use as straight edge

1 Use a club hammer and cold chisel to chop away all of the unsound plaster back to a sound edge. It is important to wear gloves to protect your hands and safety goggles to protect your eyes from any flying chips of plaster. Make sure that you remove any plaster that remains stuck to the masonry within the area you are stripping.

2 Use an old paintbrush to remove the remaining dust from the hole, especially along the bottom edge where the majority of falling dust will collect. If this is not done, the new plaster will not bond properly to the masonry surface at the base of the hole and will eventually fail again.

3 Dilute some PVA (polyvinyl acetate) building adhesive with water, 1 part PVA to 5 parts water, and brush a coat of this solution liberally onto the masonry, making sure that you reach right to the edges of the hole. This seals the surface, preventing it from sucking moisture out of the new plaster too quickly, which would cause the plaster to crack as it set. Allow it to dry before proceeding with the plastering.

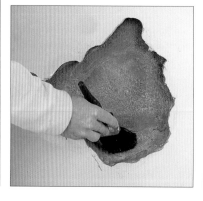

4 Mix some bonding plaster in a bucket until it is the consistency of thick porridge. Follow the manufacturer's guidelines regarding quantities, but remember that it is worth mixing a little more than you think you will need to ensure that you have a sufficient amount. Make sure that you stir the plaster thoroughly so that it is free from lumps – adding the plaster to the water rather than the other way around helps to avoid lumps in the mix. Scoop some of the plaster onto a hawk and use a gauging trowel to press the plaster into the hole. Start work at the edges of the hole, gradually filling the entire area to within 2–3mm (⅛in) of the surrounding surface.

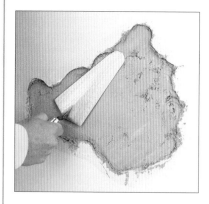

5 When you have filled the hole evenly, lightly score the plaster surface with the tip of the gauging trowel in a criss-cross pattern. This process is called keying and is used to give the finish coat of plaster a better chance of bonding well to the underlying surface. Leave the undercoat plaster to set for a couple of hours before applying the finish coat.

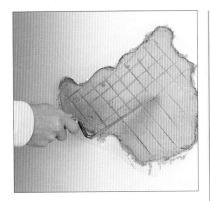

6 Mix a small quantity of finish plaster, this time to the consistency of melting ice cream. Once again, make sure you stir the plaster thoroughly to remove any lumps. Load some onto the hawk, scoop it off with the plastering trowel and apply it over the patch with a smooth, upward movement of the trowel. Tilt the blade towards the vertical as you finish the application to squeeze the plaster out between trowel and wall. Apply a second or third coat if necessary, with the end of the float resting on the surrounding plaster to help you finish the patch level with it.

7 Cut a piece of batten long enough to span the hole and use it as a ruler to scrape off any excess plaster that is sitting proud of the surrounding wall surface. This will also reveal if there are any hollow areas in your patch. If there are, apply an additional skim of finish plaster to fill them, then scrape the batten ruler across the patch once more to remove any excess.

8 Leave the repair to dry for a few minutes. Wash your plastering trowel clean, then use an old paintbrush to wet it with clean water, ready to give the repair its final polish.

9 Hold the trowel flat to the wall surface and use it to flatten and polish the patch to a smooth, hard finish. Flick more water onto the wall with the brush as necessary to keep the trowel wet, and do not be afraid to press hard with the trowel as you work. Leave the plaster to set hard, then sand off any flecks of plaster from the patch or the surrounding wall surface, ready for redecorating.

tips of the trade

- **Ready-mixed plaster** – Unless you have a fairly large number of patches to repair, it is not usually worth buying separate supplies of bonding and finish plaster, since the smallest size generally available is 10kg (22lb). This quantity of bonding plaster is enough to cover about 1.5sq m (16sq ft); the same quantity of finish plaster will cover approximately 5sq m (54sq ft). It is therefore more economical to buy a tub of ready-mixed, lightweight, one-coat plaster and use this to fill the patch in one go. This type of plaster contains latex and other additives that are designed to prevent the plaster from slumping out of the hole when applied relatively thickly. Over-fill the patch slightly, leave the repair to set hard, then sand back with fine sandpaper until the repair is flush with the surrounding wall surface.

- **Storing plaster** – If you are using dry bagged plaster rather than a ready-mixed variety, store any leftover plaster in a tightly sealed plastic bag to prevent it from becoming damp and setting hard in the bag. Date the bag, and throw it away after six months if you have not used it by then – plaster does not keep well once opened.

CHECKING FOR DAMP

One possible cause of failed plaster is dampness in the masonry. This may be the result of penetrating damp due to defects in the house structure – typical problems are water penetration around door or window frames, or roof defects allowing water to penetrate ceilings or down chimney breasts. Damp patches low down on downstairs walls may be caused by rising damp, due to defects in the damp-proof course. Whatever the cause, it is essential to put the defects right before patching the plaster, as continuing dampness will only cause the repair to fail again (see pages 132–3). If you are unsure as to whether a wall is damp, hire a damp meter from a local plant hire shop and use this to check all suspect areas.

repairing corners ↗

The most vulnerable parts of any plasterwork are external corners, especially in doorways where the angles are most likely to be knocked and damaged. Older homes are especially vulnerable, because the original plaster is often both thicker and softer than modern plasterwork and is also not likely to have been reinforced. Internal corners are less likely to suffer damage, which is generally limited to cracking in the angle due to differential movement in the house structure.

patching small-scale damage

If the damage is superficial, restoring the corner is a simple two-stage job. If the wall is papered rather than painted, first strip the wallpaper off in the region of the repair.

tools for the job

old screwdriver or small cold chisel
old paintbrush
tenon saw
power drill & masonry drill bits
hammer
filling knife

1 Chip away any loose plaster from the damaged area with an old screwdriver or a small cold chisel until the area has a clean, sound edge. Then brush away any dust from the area with an old paintbrush.

2 Cut a piece of batten twice as long as the damaged section and at least 50mm (2in) wide so that

the nails fixing it to the wall do not break away more plaster from the corner. Drill pilot holes near each end of the batten and push in a masonry nail. Hold the batten against one face of the corner with its edge flush with the other face and tap in the nails far enough to hold the batten in place. Leave the heads projecting so that you can remove them easily later.

3 Mix some filler and use a filling knife to pack it into the hole between the damaged edge and the batten on one face of the wall. Run the blade along the wall and batten surface so that the filler is flush with them. Press the knife in firmly to ensure that the filler bonds well.

4 Allow the filler to become touch-dry, then carefully remove the batten and reposition it on the other face of the corner, covering the section you have just filled and with its edge flush with the surface of the adjacent wall. Fill the rest of the hole as before, again running the knife on the wall and batten surfaces to leave a smooth, level finish to the repair.

5 When the filler has set, carefully prize off the batten and remove the nails from it. Fill the nail holes with more filler, then lightly sand the repair with fine-grade glasspaper, aiming to round off the repaired section slightly to match the profile of the rest of the corner angle.

repairing the entire corner

If the corner is extensively damaged, it is best to strip and repair the corner from floor to ceiling, incorporating a strip of metal angle bead beneath the repair plaster to make future damage less likely. Unless you have powder plaster available, buy a tub of ready-mixed repair plaster for this job.

tools for the job

tape measure

portable workbench

hacksaw

bolster chisel

club hammer

hawk

gauging trowel

plastering trowel

corner trowel (optional)

1 Measure the height of the corner. Clamp the angle bead in a portable workbench and cut it to length using a hacksaw. Saw through the bead first, then cut the expanded metal mesh wings that flank either side of the bead one at a time.

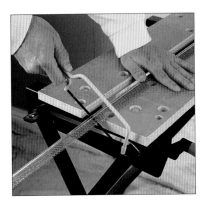

2 Use a bolster chisel and club hammer to chip off a band of plaster about 40mm (1½in) wide on each side of the corner. Draw pencil guidelines on each wall and cut along each line first, then remove the plaster from the corner.

3 Apply dabs of plaster at 300mm (12in) intervals on either side of the corner using a gauging trowel.

4 Press the angle bead into place until the plaster oozes through the mesh wings. The wings should almost touch the masonry to ensure that the bead is at the correct level.

5 Use the tip of the gauging trowel to flatten the extruded plaster over the mesh and to remove excess. Check that the bead is vertical and make any necessary adjustments. Allow the plaster to set for an hour before proceeding any further.

6 Next, fill the gap between the bead and the existing plaster. Work from the bottom up on one side of the corner, holding the plastering trowel at a 45° angle as you push it upwards and force plaster into the space between the bead and the existing plaster. Repeat the process on the other side of the corner.

7 Wet the float of the trowel with water and polish the repaired plaster to a smooth, flat finish. When the plaster has set hard, complete the job by using a damp cloth to wipe any plaster off the exposed quarter of the angle bead.

repairing hollow walls ↗

Most houses have some hollow walls with timber frames. In older houses, these were covered with slim timber laths that were then plastered over – a finish known as lath-and-plaster. In houses built since the 1930s, sheets of plasterboard have been used instead of lath-and-plaster. Both are prone to damage from impacts, which causes the plaster to break away from lath-and-plaster walls and generally makes a hole in plasterboard.

repairing lath-and-plaster

As long as the laths are not damaged, replastering is a straightforward job because the laths support the plaster. If any are broken, you need to provide support to prevent the plaster from falling into the void behind the laths.

tools for the job

trimming knife
old paintbrush
pencil
scissors or tin snips
cordless drill/driver
bucket & mixer
hawk
gauging trowel
plastering trowel

1 Use a trimming knife to cut away loose plaster from the edge of the damaged area, until it is surrounded by plaster that is still bonded to the laths behind. Poke any lumps of plaster trapped between the laths into the void behind.

2 Use an old paintbrush to remove dust and remaining debris from the hole and the laths. Take care that you dust the area thoroughly because loose material left in the hole will prevent the new plaster from bonding to the laths properly, and may lead to premature failure of the repair.

3 Hold a piece of fine metal mesh over the hole and draw a pencil line on it just inside the perimeter of the hole. Cut it to size with scissors or tinsnips, hold it in place and drill several slim pilot holes through the mesh and into the laths. Secure the mesh to the laths with short, slim countersunk screws.

4 Wet the edges of the hole with water to prevent the repair plaster from drying out and cracking. Mix some bonding plaster, and press it into the hole with a gauging trowel, working from the edges inwards. Fill the hole to within 2–3mm (⅛in) of the surrounding plaster. Score the surface of the wet plaster with the tip of the trowel in a criss-cross pattern to provide a good key for the finish coat.

5 Allow the bonding coat to set hard, then mix some finish plaster and use a plastering trowel to skim-coat the patch and leave it flush with the surrounding wall. Allow it to harden, then wet the trowel and polish the surface to a smooth finish.

tips of the trade

When repairing lath-and-plaster walls, buy a tub of ready-mixed one-coat plaster if you do not have powder plaster available. Apply a single thick coat to the hole with a plastering trowel, pressing it firmly against the laths so that some plaster squeezes between them to form a key. Finish the repair flush with the surface and leave it to set hard before redecorating.

repairing plasterboard

If you have a hole in a plasterboard wall, there will be nothing behind it to support the repair plaster. The solution is to insert a piece of plasterboard or other board in the hole and bond it into place, then to fill the hole in the usual way.

tools for the job

pencil & ruler
trimming knife or padsaw
hand saw
cordless drill/driver
filling knife

1 Draw a square or rectangle around the hole and cut along the lines with a trimming knife. Use a padsaw to cut 12.5mm (½in) thick plasterboard, which is too thick to cut easily with a knife. Remove the cut section of plasterboard.

2 Cut a patch of plasterboard or other sheet material such as hardboard to the appropriate size – about twice the height of the hole in one dimension, and a fraction less than its width in the other. Drill a hole in the centre of the board and thread a loop of string through the hole. Tie the cut ends of the string around a nail and pull the string until the nail lies flat up against the face of the patch of board.

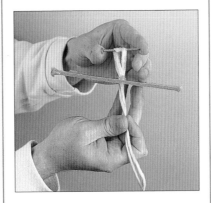

3 Apply some instant-grip adhesive to the other side of the patch along the two shorter edges. This will bond it to the inner face of the wall board when it is inserted in the hole.

4 Carefully feed the patch into the hole while holding the string in your other hand so that you do not lose it in the void. Manoeuvre it so that the two short edges press against the inner face of the wall board above and below the hole. Pull hard on the string to bond the patch in place. With instant-grip adhesive it should stay safely in place after a minute or so. Allow it to set for the time recommended on the tube.

5 When the adhesive has set, cut off the string. Mix some filler and fill the hole in two stages – first to about half its depth and then, when this layer is touch-dry, to just proud of the surrounding surface. Allow it to set hard, then sand it flush.

tips of the trade

If the hole in a plasterboard wall is larger than about 100mm (4in) across, it is better to use the technique for patching damaged ceilings (see page 118). Make horizontal cuts in the plasterboard above and below the hole, back to the adjacent studs at either side, then cut down the centre line of the studs to leave a rectangular hole. Cut noggings to fit between the studs behind the top and bottom edges of the hole and fix them to the studs with screws driven in at a 45° angle. Cut some plasterboard to fit the hole, nail it to the studs and noggings, then apply a skim coat of plaster over the repair.

making solid wall repairs ↗↗↗

In many ways, solid wall repairs are easier to carry out than equivalent damage in hollow walls. This is because you do not need to worry about providing support while the plaster dries. However, it can still be challenging to produce a finish that blends with the surrounding wall area. Whether the damaged wall is brick, stone or block based, the same technique may be used for repair.

tools for the job

club hammer

cold chisel

protective gloves

safety goggles

dusting brush

old paint brush

gauging trowel

plastering trowel

1 Remove any loose debris from the hole. Use a club hammer and cold chisel to knock off any rough areas of old render or plaster. Always wear safety equipment such as goggles and gloves during this process, to protect yourself from bits of debris that tend to fly away from the wall surface.

2 Use a dusting brush to clean out the hole as thoroughly as possible. Pay particular attention to the area around the edges, where dirt and dust tend to collect. Before any work can commence, all loose material must be cleared away so that the hole is totally dust free.

3 Mix up some PVA solution (5 parts water to 1 part PVA) and use an old paint brush to apply the solution liberally in the hole. Again, pay particular attention to the edges of the hole, allowing the solution to extend slightly on to the surrounding wall.

4 Mix up some bonding coat plaster, and press it firmly into the hole using a gauging trowel. Ensure that the bonding coat is moulded into all areas of the hole, and that it is brought up to a level which is slightly below that of the surrounding wall surface. You may find it easier to combine use of the gauging trowel with a plastering trowel to ensure an even surface finish.

5 Score the surface of the bonding coat, before it dries, using the edge of the gauging trowel. At the same time ensure that none of the bonding coat is pushed above wall level, as this will affect the finish when you apply the top plaster coat.

👍 tips of the trade

If you do not have bonding coat and multi-finish plaster, it is possible simply to build up the patch with layers of one-coat plaster. This will not produce the same totally smooth, flush finish as that of multi-finish plaster, but its slightly rougher surface may be more appropriate on wall surfaces in older, less smooth properties.

6 Mix up and apply a coat of multi-finish plaster, using a plastering trowel to press it firmly into position. For holes of this size, rest the edges of the plastering trowel on the wall to the sides of the hole, thereby enabling you to produce a neat finish.

7 This finish can be further levelled-off by cutting a length of batten to slightly longer than the hole diameter, and gradually drawing the batten across the plaster surface, again making it as flush with the surrounding wall as possible.

9 Smooth or 'polish' the plaster patch with the wettened trowel until a totally even and flush finish is achieved. Once the plaster dries, a light sand will be necessary to smooth the surface before redecoration can be carried out as required.

HOLE TYPES

• **Deep holes** – Where depth is greater than that shown above, it may well be necessary to apply a render coat to the hole before plaster can be applied. As always, it is better to apply thin layers rather than try to speed up the process with thicker ones. Over-application simply causes the render or plaster to bulge and makes it impossible to achieve a smooth finish when applying subsequent coats.

• **Shallow holes** – Where the top layer of plaster has blown away from the layers underneath, it may only be necessary to apply a single finishing coat. In such cases, however, it is common to find that if one area of top layer plaster has come away, this may be the case for most of the rest of the wall surface. Tapping the surface with the butt end of a trowel and listening for hollow reverberations will give some indication as to the stability of the surface. If the plaster is indeed 'loose', it is better to remove and re-plaster at this stage rather than redecorate and face a similar patching problem in the near future.

8 Allow the plaster to dry off slightly. Then use an old paintbrush to wet the surface of a plastering trowel with some clean water.

tips of the trade

Rendering or plastering is always a messy job, so it is important to keep surfaces and tools clean at all times. When applying plaster or render to a hole, keep a clean sponge handy so that you can wipe away any excess material that gets on to the surrounding wall surface. It is always better to clean such messes off the wall while they are still wet – if the render or plaster is allowed to dry, their removal will be much more difficult and may require a combination of sanding and scraping to attain a flat surface.

FINISHING OFF

• **Drying naturally** – The temptation when patching a small area is to try to 'force' the drying process by applying heat directly to the patch. This can have the effect of cracking the render and plaster, which will then require further repairs in order to achieve the desired finish. It is much better to allow the patch to dry naturally at room temperature so that any cracking can be avoided.

• **Priming** – Once dry, ensure that the newly plastered area is primed before further coats of paint are applied. A dilute acrylic coat (10 parts paint to 1 part water) is perfectly adequate for priming purposes in this instance.

• **Lining option** – On walls that may have a number of patch repair requirements, it may be necessary to consider lining the wall after repairs are complete, in order to smooth the surface further. On particularly undulating walls, woodchip or textured paper is a further possibility in terms of providing a more even wall finish.

patching ceilings

Ceilings can be damaged by water leaks, or sometimes on an old lath and plaster ceiling the plaster can simply come away from the laths if the plaster key fails with age, but the most common cause of damage to a ceiling is when someone's foot slips off a rafter onto an unboarded area of the loft and ends up poking through – the stuff of many a TV comedy sketch! After the comedy of the moment, however, there is no need for panic as a simple patch repair will return the ceiling to a finish as good as new. Whatever has caused the damage, the best solution is to cut away the affected area and to fit a plasterboard patch.

tools for the job

pipe, cable & joist detector
pencil
straight edge
safety goggles
padsaw
trimming knife
claw hammer
tape measure
panel saw
power drill & twist drill bits
screwdriver
self-adhesive mesh
joint tape
filling knife
plastering trowel
hawk

1 Locate the joists on either side of the hole, either by using an electronic joist detector or, if the loft is unboarded, by making holes down through the ceiling alongside the joists so that their positions are visible in the room below. Draw a pencil line along the centre line of each joist, extending beyond the damaged area.

safety advice

You must also check whether there are any services, such as water pipes or electricity cables, in the immediate vicinity of the hole before drawing guidelines for cutting. If the ceiling is below the loft these checks can be made manually, otherwise a cable, pipe and joist detector can be used.

2 Draw two further lines at right angles to the first, joining up the joist lines to form a rectangle outline of the area you plan to cut out. Use either a long ruler, a timber straight edge or a spirit level.

3 Cut out from the hole towards one of the pencil guidelines using a padsaw, then cut along the line in each direction until you reach the joists. Repeat the process at the other side of the hole. Use a trimming knife to cut the plasterboard along the guidelines indicating the joist centres. Look out for concealed fixing nails as you do this.

4 Pull down the cut-out section of board and use the claw of a hammer to prise out the old fixing nails from the undersides of the joists. Lever them out with the hammer head against the joist, not the plasterboard.

5 Cut two lengths of sawn softwood so that they form a tight fit between the joists on either side of the hole. These will act as noggings to support the edges of the plasterboard patch. They should be at least 50 x 50mm (2 x 2in) in cross section, but 100 x 50mm (4 x 2in) is ideal. Hammer them in until they are half concealed by the edge of the hole.

6. To secure each nogging in place you will first need to drill a clearance hole through one end at 45° to the joist, then drive in a long screw to secure the end of the nogging to the joist it butts up against. Repeat the process to fix the other end of the nogging to the opposite joist. Don't worry if the noggings move slightly as you screw them in place – there will still be enough exposed wood to which the plasterboard patch may be nailed.

7. Measure and cut a piece of plasterboard to fit the hole. Test its fit and, if necessary, trim the sides down to size with the aid of a trimming knife. Lift the piece of plasterboard into place and nail it to both the joists and noggings with 30mm (1¼in) galvanized plasterboard nails. Position the nails a distance of at least 10mm (⅜in) from the edges of the plasterboard, and drive them into the wood until their heads just dimple the paper. Nail the existing plasterboard to the noggings along the edges of the hole too.

8. Stick lengths of self-adhesive mesh joint tape over the joints to stop cracks opening up in the future. Then use a filling knife to apply a band of filler over the tape both to conceal it and to fill the gaps around the patch.

9. Plaster over the patch with a skim coat of finish plaster if you have it, or use a one-coat ready-mixed plaster. Feather out the edges of the plaster onto the surrounding ceiling surface to make the patch less noticeable. Wet the trowel and use it flat to the ceiling to polish the repair, leaving a smooth finish. Leave to dry and then decorate to match.

WATER DAMAGE

If a part of the plasterboard ceiling has been soaked by penetrating damp or a plumbing leak, the surface finish will still be badly stained by the water even if the actual plasterboard has remained intact. It is not enough simply to reapply water-based paint as the stains will keep bleeding through. The solution is to seal the stains in with a proprietary stain-block aerosol, or to cover them with a coat of any solvent-based primer or paint. Once the stains are sealed you can then paint over the area with water-based paint to match the rest of the ceiling.

LATH-AND-PLASTER

If the ceiling is of a lath and plaster construction, the technique for making the repair is slightly different:

1. Pull down as much loose material as you can to begin with, then mark out the area to be removed as for plasterboard ceilings.

2. Make the saw cuts parallel to the laths first, inserting the padsaw between adjacent laths and cutting through the plaster. Dislodge as much plaster as possible between these cuts and the hole to expose the laths that need to be removed.

3. Simply pull broken laths downwards so that they snap where they are nailed to the joists – they are usually very dry and brittle. Saw through the centre of any undamaged laths and snap them off in the same way.

4. Clean up the broken ends of the laths beneath the joists with your trimming knife, then cut and fit the plasterboard patch as normal.

If a patch of plaster breaks away because the key to the laths has failed, the rest of the ceiling may be close to failure too. If this is the case, the best solution is to pull down the entire ceiling and replace it with a plasterboard ceiling.

restoring plaster mouldings ↗↗

Many older properties have highly detailed plaster cornices and other ceiling and panel mouldings as original features. These would have been moulded in fibrous plaster and then screwed into place – most are too heavy to be supported solely by plaster adhesive. Unfortunately, years of repainting will often gradually obscure the fine detail. Many may also have been damaged by the building of partition walls to subdivide large rooms. However, restoration is usually possible.

cleaning mouldings

If you have mouldings that are clogged with layers of old paint, be prepared for some slow and fiddly restoration work. The first thing you have to do is to find out what sort of paint you have to contend with. In an unrestored property it will probably be distemper, but in renovated ones you could find anything from eggshell to modern emulsion paint.

tools for the job

work platform
garden spray gun
improvised picks & scrapers
old toothbrushes
soft-bristled brush

1 The first thing to try on old mouldings is water applied as a mist with a garden spray gun. This will soften distemper, but will have no effect on other types of paint. Soak a test area and leave it to penetrate for 10–15 minutes.

2 If the water works, use an improvised pick, scraper or toothbrush, as appropriate, to remove the old distemper bit by bit. This will be time-consuming and fiddly work, so tackle just a short section at a time and make sure you are working at a comfortable height – ideally off a work platform rather than a stepladder.

3 After removing as much paint as possible, scrub the surface of the moulding gently with a soft-bristled brush to remove flecks and specks left behind by the picks and scrapers. Repaint it with a thinned coat of emulsion to act as a sealer, followed by a full-strength coat.

safety advice

Always wear PVC work gloves and safety goggles to apply any form of chemical paint stripper.

4 If water fails to make any impression on the old paint, you will need to experiment with chemical strippers. Look for products that come in paste form rather than as runny liquids. The former will stay put on the surface of the moulding as they soften the paint, while the latter will splash everywhere and make a thoroughly unpleasant mess. Brush the stripper on liberally, then work it into the recesses of the moulding with a stippling action of the brush.

5 Some strippers are designed to be used in conjunction with special fibrous tissue strips that you bed into the layer of stripper. These not only help to prevent the stripper from drying out too quickly, they also allow you to peel strip and stripper away in one go after the stripper has done its work, making the restoration job much less labour-intensive.

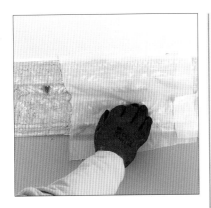

restoring damaged cornices

If the damage to the cornice is minor, you may be able to make it good with filler or plaster of Paris, moulding the repair material to match the originals. However, if this is not possible, the best option is to replace the damaged section with a new piece of cornice that matches the original as closely as possible.

There are several manufacturers who produce modern replicas of traditional cornices in fibrous plaster, so unless your particular cornice is very unusual you may be able to find a suitable replacement from one of these suppliers. Another possible source of matching cornices is architectural salvage companies, who rescue and sell period details from old houses. Both solutions are likely to prove expensive, however.

1 If you are able to obtain a length of suitable replacement cornice to match the damaged cornice in your home, remove the damaged section by carefully cutting it away piece by piece with a brick bolster and club hammer. Remember to wear protective gloves and safety goggles to protect you from dust and flying debris. Depending on how the cornice was put up, you may find wall and ceiling plaster coming away as you work. Look out for fixing screws buried in the coving. Break the plaster away around them, then cut them off flush with the wall or ceiling surface with a hacksaw.

2 When you have removed the damaged section of cornice, clean up the newly exposed wall and ceiling surfaces so that the new cornice can fit closely against them. Cut the new cornice to length and offer it up to check its fit – this is a job for two pairs of hands. If the old cornice was put up after plastering, you will then have to replaster the areas that came away in step 1.

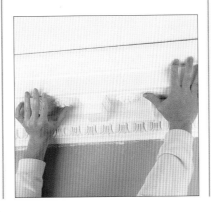

3 Make sure that any replastering has fully hardened before installing the length of replacement cornice. When it is ready, drill fixing holes through the cornice at the spacings recommended by the manufacturer. Hold the coving back in place and mark the corresponding hole positions on the wall. Drill the holes and insert wall plugs, then apply the adhesive recommended by the manufacturer to the rear faces of the cornice and offer it up to the wall and ceiling surfaces, pressing it firmly into place. Secure it with long screws countersunk beneath the surface of the cornice.

4 Insert filler into the screw holes and the joints between the old and new sections of cornice, then make good the wall and ceiling plaster alongside the repaired section. Finally, paint the cornice with a coat of diluted emulsion paint to seal the surface, followed by a full-strength coat. Brush the paint out well so that you avoid the clogging that overpainting can cause.

improving ceilings

Making sure that a ceiling has a good surface for decorating may require more work than simply minor repairs. Severely sagging old ceilings can require demolition and reconstruction but some surfaces have other potential options. For example, applying a new plaster skim over a rough ceiling surface is one way of restoring it to a flatter finish. Alternatively, the projects considered below may be more appropriate to your needs.

old textured ceilings

Textured ceilings suit some people more than others. For this reason, you may find it desirable to restore a textured or patterned ceiling back to a flat surface. One technique for removing textured coatings is to use a wallpaper stripper. However, when using such appliances, pay close attention to the manufacturer's operating instructions and adhere to all the required safety procedures – goggles and gloves are essential protective equipment.

Alternatively, if the coating is particularly well stuck to the ceiling surface, it can be easier and less time consuming to simply plaster over the top of it. To do this, refer to the plastering techniques described on pages 92–103, but you may also need to adopt the refining technique described below.

tools for the job

scraper

large paint brush or pasting brush

plastering trowel

mixing equipment

1 Use a scraper to knock off all the high points from the textured coating. The degree to which you have to do this will depend on the depth of finish but, generally, removing as much texture as possible will make the plastering process much easier later on.

2 Brush a coat of PVA solution (5 parts water to 1 part PVA) on to the textured surface to seal it and stabilize it in readiness for the plaster.

3 Mix up plaster (see page 92) and apply it to the ceiling with a

plastering trowel. A fairly deep plaster coat is required in order to 'take up' the roughness or texture on the ceiling, and therefore two coats of plaster may be needed.

THE TEXTURED OPTION

On badly cracked or rough ceilings, there is an option to use proprietary textured paint to help 'take up' the roughness or undulations of the ceiling surface. The texture produced is not the finish of standard textured coatings, but it is enough to fill minor cracks and provide a more even-looking finish, without going to the expense or time of re-plastering. It is worth bearing in mind that plastering a ceiling is by no means a job for the beginner and so textured paint is a serious and economic option for people with less experience.

using textured paper on ceilings

Just as lining paper can be used to smooth a ceiling surface, textured paper can be used to add pattern and interest to the ceiling surface.

The structure of this type of paper is three dimensional, so some care is required when hanging it. It may be necessary to line the ceiling first to achieve the best possible results.

tools for the job

chalk line

pasting brush

paperhanging brush

scissors

pencil

craft knife or scissors

1 Use a chalk line to gain a precise guideline across the ceiling surface. Secure the paper in the wall/ceiling junction, making sure that the edge of the length runs precisely along the chalk line.

2 Brush out the paper in the usual manner, applying enough pressure to secure it in position and to remove bubbles from beneath, but not so much pressure that the

pattern texture becomes crushed. Continue along the length to the other end.

3 Draw a pencil guideline along the wall/ceiling junction, peel the length back and cut along the guideline with a craft knife or scissors. Once trimmed, brush the end of the paper back in place and repeat the process at the other end of the length.

4 When joining lengths, take care not to crush the relief with the brush. Wipe off excess paste from the wall and paper surfaces as you work.

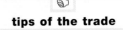

tips of the trade

Remember that textured paper needs a stronger mix of paste than normal paper because of its weight.

Textured paper offers a uniform, patterned finish which gives a greater focus to the ceiling and helps to distract the eye from undulations in the surface.

repairing wooden features ⟋⟋⟋

Wooden wall features often need repair and require quite different techniques of restoration compared to those for walls or plaster surfaces. Wood, whether in the form of panelling, skirting board or any other feature, tends to suffer from wear-and-tear such as general knocks, scrapes and splits. Minor knocks can be treated with the relevant filler, but more serious damage may require replacement sections of wood in order to restore the surface to an attractive finish.

skirting boards

The function of skirting board is to add a finish at the wall/floor junction, and to protect the base of the wall from any damage. Unsurprisingly, the skirting itself can become damaged over time and in need of repair. For short sections of damaged board, the most economical technique is to replace the entire length. However, on long stretches of skirting board this can be seen as wasteful, and inserting a replacement section is better.

tools for the job

wrecking bar & protective gloves
panel saw
mitre block
hammer
tape measure
damp cloth
nail punch

1 Ease the skirting board away from the wall using a wrecking bar to prise a gap between skirting and wall.

(Wear protective gloves for this process.) Position two pieces of cut-off batten behind the skirting and wedge the skirting board free from the wall surface.

2 Position a mitre block in front, and to one side, of the damaged section of skirting board. Cut down through the skirting board with a panel saw. Move the mitre block to the other side and then cut on the opposite mitre angle through the skirting board. Remove the damaged section.

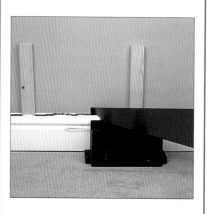

3 Nail the skirting board back in position on either side of the gap you have created. Take accurate

measurements for the new piece of skirting you require and cut a length to fit, remembering to mitre each end correctly, so as to fit snugly in the gap.

4 Before fixing in place, test to see that your new section fits. Apply some wood glue along the cut edge of the new piece and position it, removing any excess adhesive with a damp cloth.

5 Fix the section permanently in place by nailing panel pins through the mitred join at either end of the new section. Three pins along each side should be sufficient. Punch in the pin head before redecorating the skirting.

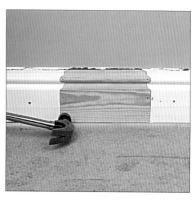

repairing tongue and groove

Damaged tongue and groove panelling presents a different set of problems because removing the panels – which have a concealed fixing mechanism – can be tricky. Some ingenuity is therefore required so that boards can be replaced, while avoiding any further damage to surrounding panels.

tools for the job

cordless drill

dry wall saw or padsaw

wrecking bar

claw hammer or pliers

panel saw

wooden mallet

chisel

1 Drill a hole to the side of the damaged board and along the joint it makes with the adjacent board. Choose a drill bit large enough to accommodate either a padsaw or a dry wall saw.

2 Use a dry wall saw or padsaw to cut through the join. Work up and down along the joint, until total separation between the two lengths has been achieved. Accuracy is not vital as the aim is simply to gain access to the damaged board in order to make your repair.

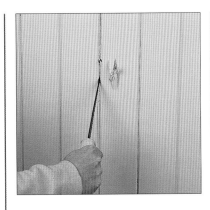

3 Use a wrecking bar to lever out the damaged board. You may also need to work a little on the other side of the board, because there will be other fixings holding the panel in place. However, with one edge loose, a combination of levering and easing should result in the board coming free. It is also worthwhile removing the board adjacent to the broken one, as the damage caused during cutting is likely to be noticeable.

4 After both boards have been removed, use a claw hammer or pliers to take out any pins or nails that may still be present in the exposed

battens beneath the tongue and groove cladding. Failure to remove them will hinder progress later.

5 Cut two new lengths of tongue and groove to size. Use a mallet and chisel to trim the tongue off one of the lengths – this is because damage caused in removing the old lengths may have affected the actual interlocking mechanism of the tongue and groove system. By removing the tongue on one length, it should then be possible to insert the strip into the existing panelling.

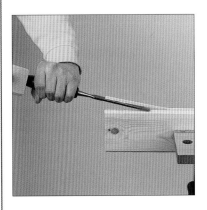

6 Interlock the two new sections into the panelling, and secure them in place with panel pins. The new panelling may then be primed and repainted.

tips of the trade

Tongue and groove is supplied in a range of thicknesses, so always check your requirements before purchasing replacement strips.

repointing brickwork ✗✗

The mortar joints between bricks – the pointing – is the weakest link in any exterior wall. If it fails for any reason, water can penetrate the bricks and winter frosts can lead to their faces splitting off – a condition known as spalling. The problem may have been caused by poor workmanship, by use of the wrong mortar mix or simply by rain erosion. Make a point of inspecting your brickwork each spring, and tackle any areas showing signs of deterioration before serious problems arise.

tools for the job

safety goggles
work gloves
cold chisel
club hammer
stiff brush
bucket & mixer
garden spray gun
hawk
pointing trowel
profiling tools

1 If you find an area of pointing that is loose and crumbly, the first job is to chip it out back to sound mortar – to a minimum depth of about 20mm (¾in) – using a sharp cold chisel and a club hammer. Wear work gloves and safety goggles to guard against flying debris. Work along the horizontal joints first, then along the vertical ones.

2 Use a stiff-bristled brush – but not a wire one, which will mark the bricks – to clean dust and debris from all the joints you have worked on. Then mix a small batch of mortar

and allow it to dry to see how well it matches the existing mortar. Use a ratio of 1 part cement to 5 parts soft sand, and experiment with different coloured sands to get as close a match as possible.

3 When you have a suitable mortar formula, mix about half a bucketful at a time – repointing is slow work, and unused mortar that has begun to dry out cannot be resuscitated by adding more water. Then spray water from a garden spray gun onto the area where you plan to start work. This helps to cut the suction of the brickwork and prevents the mortar from drying out too quickly.

tips of the trade

• **Tackling large areas** – If you have a large area of wall to repoint, you can speed up the chopping out process by hiring a power tool called a mortar raker. This has a tungsten carbide cutter that grinds out the old mortar to a pre-set depth in a fraction of the time the job takes by hand. Wear safety goggles, a dust mask and ear defenders when using this equipment.

• **Access equipment** – Repointing brickwork is a slow job, and working off steps or a ladder can make your feet and back ache. Work off trestles and staging instead for areas up to about 3m (10ft) above ground level, and use a slot-together platform tower for work higher up. Not only do these access options enable you to stand or kneel in comfort, they also provide a surface for placing tools and materials conveniently to hand. Both types of equipment can be hired.

4 Put some mortar onto a hawk, and take a sausage shape of mortar off it with a pointing trowel. Press the mortar firmly into one of the horizontal joints, and draw the tip of the trowel over it to bed it in and bond it to the underlying mortar. Repoint all the horizontal joints first.

5 Use the same technique to fill the vertical joints, one at a time. Press the mortar in well, leaving it almost flush with the surface of the bricks. Trim off excess mortar as you work, but leave any that gets on the face of the bricks to dry. You can then remove it with a dry brush and avoid staining the wall face.

6 When you have completed about 1sq m (10sq ft) of wall, it is time to finish the pointing to match the existing brickwork's joints. In a weathered joint, the pointing has a slope outwards from top to bottom, with the top recessed by about 5mm (¼in) and the bottom flush with the face of the brick below. Form this type of joint by drawing the tip of the trowel along the newly filled joint, with the flat of the trowel resting on the top edge of the brick below the joint.

7 To match a V-shaped recess, draw the tip of the pointing trowel along the centre of the new mortar joint, removing some mortar to leave a neatly shaped recess.

8 A joint with a concave profile is one of the most common joint finishes and is easy to match. Simply draw a rounded object such as an offcut of garden hose along the joint, leaving it with a semicircular cross-section. A recessed joint is set back from the face of the bricks by up to 10mm (⅜in). It is formed by drawing a wood offcut or similar implement along the joint to rake out the mortar to a uniform depth. This type of joint should not be used on brickwork in exposed locations.

👍 tips of the trade

If you are having trouble matching the colour of your existing pointing, try adding a mortar pigment to your mix. These powders are available in black, brown, green, yellow and red, and come in 1.25kg (3lb) packs that will tint 50kg (110lb) of cement. Make a few trial batches first using different amounts of pigment, allowing them to dry out before you compare the final colour. Measure the ingredients accurately – too much or too little pigment will change the colour of the finished mortar noticeably.

Identify the type of joint in the existing brickwork and try to match it as closely as possible. The recessed joints in this brickwork are formed using an offcut of wood.

replacing damaged bricks ⟋⟋⟋

If failed pointing has allowed rainwater to penetrate behind the face of your brickwork, and subsequent frost has split off the faces of some of the bricks – known as spalling – the only way you can restore the appearance of the wall is to chop out the damaged bricks and replace them. The job itself is a relatively straightforward one. The biggest problem lies in finding replacement bricks that are a good match for your existing ones.

walls & ceilings

128

tools for the job

safety goggles
work gloves
cold chisel
club hammer
hammer drill & masonry drill bits
brick bolster
bucket & mixer
spot board
hawk
bricklaying trowel
pointing trowel
profiling tools

1 Chop out the pointing all around the damaged brick using a sharp cold chisel and a club hammer. Make sure that you wear work gloves to protect your hands, and safety goggles to keep flying debris out of your eyes.

2 To make it easier to remove the damaged brick from the wall, drill a series of closely spaced holes down the middle of the brick to a depth of about 100mm (4in) using a hammer drill and a large

masonry drill bit. Take care that the drill bit does not slip onto any of the surrounding bricks and cause further damage.

3 Try to split the brick in half by chopping along the line of the drill holes with a brick bolster and club hammer. When you have done so, hold the bolster on this central split at an angle towards the ends of the brick and chop out sections one by one, taking care not to damage the surrounding bricks. Take care on cavity walls not to drive pieces of brick into the cavity, where they could drop and act as a damp bridge between the inner and outer parts of the wall.

👍
tips of the trade

It can be difficult to remove whole bricks from solid walls, especially walls in which the bricks are laid end-on (known in the trade as headers). The best way of repairing a damaged header is to drill it as described in step 2, and then to chop it out to a depth of about 100mm (4in) – roughly half the length of the brick. Chop the replacement brick in half and test its fit in the recess, cutting it down further in length if necessary to allow for a mortar bed behind it. Butter mortar into the base of the recess and onto the top, sides and back of the replacement brick, and slide the brick into place. Check that it is centred in the recess, adjust if necessary, and then tap the brick gently home until it is flush with its neighbours. Point all around it, matching the existing pointing as closely as possible, to complete the repair.

4 When you have removed the damaged brick, chop away as much of the remaining pointing as possible from the top, bottom and sides of the recess. Once again, if you are repairing a cavity wall, take care not to let any debris drop down into the cavity.

5 Mix a small amount of mortar and let it dry to see how well it matches the colour of the existing pointing. See the tips of the trade box on page 127 for more information on matching the colour of mortar. When you have a satisfactory formula, mix another small batch and place it on a spot board – a piece of old plywood or similar board close to where you are working. Place a bed of mortar on the base of the recess using a bricklaying trowel, and butter more mortar onto the top and ends of the new brick.

MATCHING BRICKS

Unless your house is relatively new, the brickwork will have weathered and changed colour over the years to the point where a new brick – even if it is a close match to the originals – will look highly noticeable next to its aged neighbours. Look out for advertisements in local papers offering second-hand bricks, which may be a closer match to yours. Architectural salvage firms may also be able to help. If all else fails, tour your area looking for demolition work in progress – you may well find the bricks you want lying in a skip somewhere.

Once you have found an appropriate second-hand brick, you will need to clean it if any mortar is stuck to its surface. To do this, use a brick bolster and club hammer to chip off the old mortar. Make sure you wear appropriate safety goggles and work gloves to protect yourself from flying debris when you performing this task.

6 Carefully slide the new brick into place in the recess, centring it and then tapping it backwards with the handle of the club hammer until it fits flush with its neighbours. Check that it is horizontal and that the joints around it are an even thickness, repositioning it slightly if necessary to achieve this. Use a pointing trowel to add mortar as necessary to the joints around the new brick, then finish the pointing to match the rest of the wall.

Try to match the type of pointing on the existing brickwork. Refer to steps 6–8 on pages 126–7 for more details on how to create different pointing profiles.

patching rendering ↗↗

Many houses have a rendered finish applied to their exterior walls, either to make poor quality masonry more weatherproof or simply as a decorative feature. It is a layer of mortar applied to the surface of bricks or blocks using a two-coat system to give a final layer up to 25mm (1in) thick. The surface may be trowelled smooth or textured. It may have pebbles or other fine aggregate pressed into the surface to create the finish known as pebble-dash.

Weathering and slight movements in the masonry can eventually cause rendering to crack. This allows water to penetrate and seep down behind the rendering, and if it freezes it can cause patches to lose their grip on the masonry. These sound hollow when tapped, and may break away altogether as time goes by.

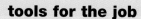

tools for the job

safety goggles

work gloves

claw hammer

chalk

brick bolster

club hammer

stiff brush

old paintbrush

bucket & mixer

hawk

pointing trowel

timber straight edge

plastering trowel

texturing tools

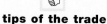

tips of the trade

If your rendering is in generally poor condition, with a number of blown or missing areas, it will take forever to patch up and the apparently sound areas are probably on the verge of failing too. Your best bet is to hack off all the old rendering, and to call in a builder to apply a fresh coat. This job is beyond all but the most dedicated DIY enthusiast because of the large quantities of materials involved and the need for scaffolding to provide safe access for the work to be carried out.

1 Identify areas of rendering that have 'blown' – lost their bond to the masonry behind – by tapping the surface with the handle of a hammer. Mark around any areas that sound hollow with chalk. Use a ladder to reach rendering at first floor level.

2 Wearing safety goggles and gloves, use a brick bolster and club hammer to chop away the rendering until you reach a sound edge. Undercut the edges of the hole slightly to help key the new mortar patch to the old rendering, then brush all loose material out of the hole, paying particular attention to the bottom edge where most of the debris will collect.

3 Mix some sealant solution by diluting 1 part PVA (polyvinyl acetate) building adhesive with 5 parts water. Use an old paintbrush to apply this sealant onto the masonry and the cut edges of the rendering. This will help the patch of new render to bond well to the masonry, and will also help to stop it from drying too quickly and cracking as it does so.

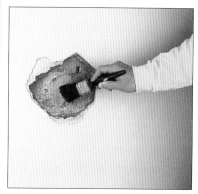

4 Mix some mortar in the ratio 1 part cement to 4 parts sharp (concreting) sand, and add some liquid plasticizer to the mix to improve its workability. For small repairs, buy a bag of dry ready-mixed mortar for rendering and just add water. Load

some mortar onto a hawk and start trowelling it into the hole. Fill the edges first, then the centre, aiming to leave the first coat about 6mm (¼in) below the surface of the surrounding rendering. Score the surface with the corner of the trowel in a criss-cross pattern to provide a key for the second coat of render.

5 Apply the second coat so that it finishes a little proud of the surrounding rendering, then use a timber straight edge to rule off the excess mortar. Hold its edge against the wall just below the patch and move it slowly upwards, while at the same time moving it from left to right in a see-saw action. This removes excess mortar without any risk of disturbing the underlying patch.

PAINTING RENDERING

If you have bare rendering, it will be much more weather resistant – and look better – with a coat of masonry paint applied to it. Kill any green algal growth on north-facing walls with a proprietary fungicide, then apply a coat of stabilizing solution to the rendering to seal its surface and reduce its porosity. You can then apply the paint, using a brush, a long-pile roller or a spray gun. The last is the quickest method, but you need to employ special spraying equipment – the fillers used in masonry paints will clog an airless spray gun. You will also have to spend time masking doors, windows, eaves, woodwork and downpipes, but the effort will be worth it, especially if you have pebble-dash or heavily textured rendering, which is time-consuming to paint by brush or roller because of the need to work the paint into all the crevices. If you do not have time to paint the whole house in one go, try to do it wall by wall rather than stop in the middle of a wall, since the join may show up in the finished surface.

6 Fill any hollows revealed by the ruling off with a little more mortar, then float the surface of the repair smooth with a plastering trowel, wetting it first to stop the mortar from sticking to it as you work. Make the mortar as smooth as possible. If the existing surface has a texture, imitate it on the patch using whatever tools

are appropriate – perhaps a stiff brush, a sponge, a textured paint roller or a pointing trowel. If the house is pebble-dashed, load some matching pebbles onto a hawk and push them off it and into the rendering with a plastering trowel. Use the flat of the trowel to bed them well into place.

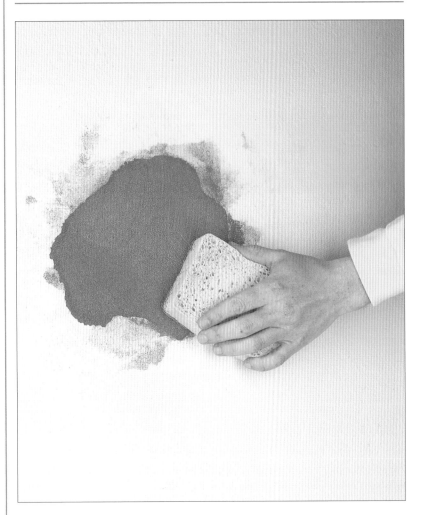

Finish the patched area of render to match the existing surface. This could mean using a sponge to texture the surface, as in this example, or perhaps applying pebble-dash.

dealing with rising damp ⤢

Houses built since the late 19th century have a waterproof layer called the damp-proof course (DPC) built into their walls just above ground level to stop ground water from being absorbed into the masonry. In older houses, the DPC is either a double layer of slate or a couple of courses of dense water-resistant engineering bricks. In modern houses it is a strip of strong plastic. A similar damp-proof membrane is incorporated in the structure of solid concrete ground floors.

tackling DPC bridges

Rising damp shows up as damp patches on interior walls, usually rising to a height of about 1m (3ft) above floor level. However, finding this type of dampness does not necessarily mean that the DPC has failed. It could have been bridged in some way, allowing ground water to bypass it and rise into the wall structure. The illustration below shows some common causes of DPC bridges. The step-by-step sequence at the bottom of the page outlines how to tackle them.

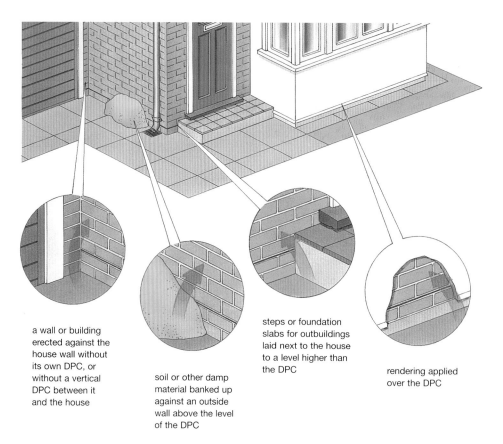

a wall or building erected against the house wall without its own DPC, or without a vertical DPC between it and the house

soil or other damp material banked up against an outside wall above the level of the DPC

steps or foundation slabs for outbuildings laid next to the house to a level higher than the DPC

rendering applied over the DPC

1 Begin by clearing soil or other material that has been piled against the walls above DPC level, and make sure that air bricks have not been blocked. These are essential for providing ventilation to suspended timber floors, which can develop rot if they become damp.

2 Where walls or slabs have been built against the house and they bridge the DPC, chisel out the mortar or concrete between the two and insert a vertical DPC. Then seal the joint with non-setting mastic.

3 Treat brickwork above a path or patio that is less than 150mm (6in) below DPC level with two coats of clear silicone water-repellent sealer to stop it from absorbing water. Alternatively, lift one row of slabs next to the house and replace them with a layer of gravel.

4 Cut away rendering to just above the level of the DPC with a brick bolster and club hammer. The DPC is usually visible in the mortar joint in which it is bedded. Fix a steel and expanded metal mesh external render stop bead to the wall, level with the DPC, and render down to it to leave a neat horizontal edge.

dealing with a failed DPC

If your damp problem persists despite tackling any possible damp bridges, then it is likely that the DPC has actually failed. You can call in a damp treatment firm to install a new DPC for you, who will inject waterproof chemicals into the masonry at DPC level. However, since the work is very labour intensive and you can hire the same injection equipment the specialists use, it makes sense to do the job yourself. The tool hire companies that supply the equipment also stock the chemicals you need – you buy them on a sale-or-return basis when you hire the equipment.

Before you begin you need to find out whether you have solid or cavity walls by examining their structure – if brickwork is exposed and it consists entirely of bricks laid end to end, it is a cavity wall. If the bricks are not visible, measure the wall thickness – it will be around 240mm (9½in) if it is solid, and about 290mm (11½in) if it is a cavity wall.

tools for the job

DPC injection machine (hired)
....
hammer drill
....
long masonry drill bits
....
depth stop
....
pointing trowel

1 Hire the DPC injection machine and collect enough DPC fluid for the job. You may need up to 3 litres per square metre (5¼ pints per 10sq ft) of wall if the brickwork is very porous. Hire a professional-quality drill, too – you may well overload a DIY model. Buy masonry drill bits in a diameter to match the size of the injection nozzles and long enough to drill to a depth of 200mm (8in). Make sure the hire company shows you how to operate the machine.

2 Carry out the first stage of the injection process by drilling holes 75mm (3in) deep at about 150mm (6in) intervals along the wall at DPC level. The injecting may be done from the inside or outside. Insert the shorter nozzles supplied, secure them in place and start injecting the fluid. When complete, move the linked nozzles along to the next set of holes and repeat.

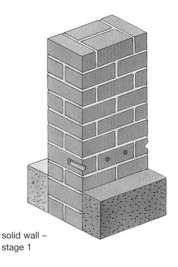

solid wall –
stage 1

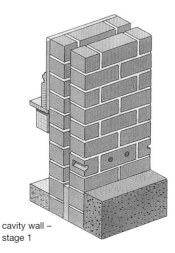

cavity wall –
stage 1

3 When you have injected all the holes, drill through the same holes to a depth of 150mm (6in) in solid walls and 200mm (8in) in cavity ones. Repeat the injection process using the longer nozzles supplied with the machine. When injection is complete, fill the holes with mortar.

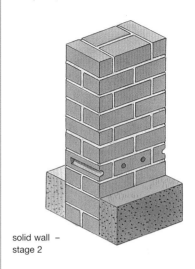

solid wall –
stage 2

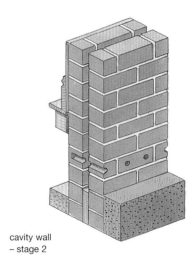

cavity wall
– stage 2

👍 tips of the trade

• **Internal walls** – If solid internal walls also show signs of rising damp, lift floorboards alongside them and inject fluid using holes about 50mm (2in) deep in a one-brick thick wall.

• **Damaged plaster** – If plaster has been damaged by rising damp, hack it off and replace it with a waterproofed cement rendering. Cover this with a coat of finish plaster when the wall has dried out.

133

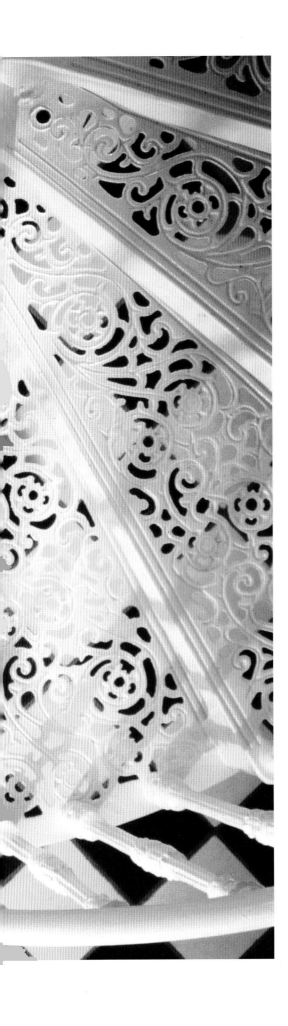

floors & stairs

Floors and stairs are used every day with little thought given to how they are constructed. To some degree their design will be determined by the building codes and regulations in force at the time the house was built and the materials that were available. Within these parameters, however, there is substantial scope for variation in construction to satisfy different purposes and functions, while the preferences of the architect and the relationship of the building to its surroundings will also have an impact.

estimating quantities

Once you have decided that you are going to alter or renovate your floors, whether you are rebuilding them entirely or just replacing the floor coverings, your first task will be to work out the overall size of the floor area. This will allow you to make accurate estimates of the quantities of materials required and thus you will be able to estimate the cost of the project.

planning quantities

In the rush to get started on a new project it is all too easy to miss out on sensible planning. Carefully estimating the amount of materials that will be needed is a vital element of the planning stage, so that you can then place an accurate order – standing in the builder's merchant or DIY store is not the time to be working this out. With expensive items, such as quarry tiles and carpet, it is especially important not to over-order or you will be left with costly surplus. Some projects are easier than others when it comes to working out the amount of materials you will need. In the case of a floor in a perfectly square or rectangular room, for instance, simply multiply the width by the length to get the total area. Working in three dimensions is only slightly more complicated – just remember to multiply width by length by depth. The best way to plan for quantities is to take accurate measurements and transfer these to a scale plan, from which you can calculate the amounts.

tips of the trade

Always add about 10% to the final figure when calculating quantities – this will account for cutting and waste and will leave you with a little spare material for future repairs.

SPECIAL CONSIDERATIONS
• **Patterned flooring** – Plan for greater wastage allowance if laying patterned flooring, so that you can match up the design as it is laid.

• **Fitted furniture** – If laying the floor covering in a room with fitted furniture, for example in a kitchen or bathroom, you can cover the entire floor prior to installation, or cut around the furniture leaving a short margin that will run underneath. If the latter, then either incorporate the fitted elements into your plan, if you have an accurate idea of their dimensions, or measure up after installation.

MAKING CALCULATIONS

Depth of joists

The capacity for a joist to support weight is more dependent on depth than thickness, which tends to remain constant at about 50mm (2in). Follow the formula shown below to work out the depth of joist you will need. The number of joists that you require will depend on the size of the room and the centre-to-centre spacing.

Formula for calculating depth of joists:

$$\text{Depth in units of 25mm (1in)} = \frac{\text{Span of joists in units of 300mm (1ft)} + 2}{2}$$

Example for room span of 3m (10ft):

$$\text{3m (10ft) divided by 300mm (1ft)} = \frac{10 \text{ units}}{2} = 5 + 2 = 7 \text{ units}$$

7 units x 25mm (1in) = 175mm (7in)

Floor covering

To calculate the amount of floor covering that you need, multiply the width by the length then add 10% for cutting and waste.

Example for a room measuring 3m x 7m (10ft x 23ft):   3 x 5m = 15sq m + 1.5 = 16.5sq m
(10ft x 23ft = 230sq ft + 23 = 253sq ft)

making a scale drawing

In order to make an accurate calculation of the amount of flooring material needed, it is a good idea to formulate a detailed two-dimensional diagram of the room with measurements for each of the different areas indicated. Even professional builders will make a scale drawing of the room showing the location of principal features. If the room includes permanently fitted furniture, or will do so, these should be included on the diagram, especially if it is not your intention to lay floor covering underneath. Using graph paper to draw the plan will help ensure accuracy. If you take the plan, with all the measurements marked on, along when going to buy materials, this will enable you to place an accurate order so that you do not end up with too little or excess surplus.

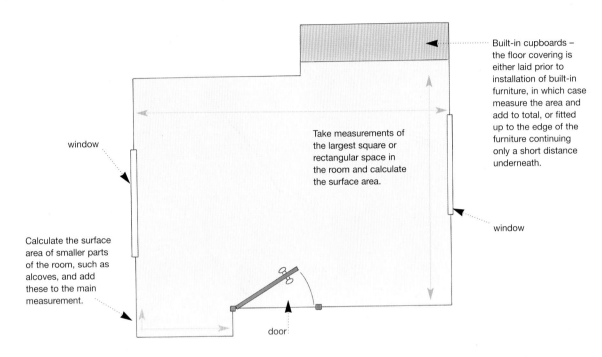

window

Take measurements of the largest square or rectangular space in the room and calculate the surface area.

Calculate the surface area of smaller parts of the room, such as alcoves, and add these to the main measurement.

Built-in cupboards – the floor covering is either laid prior to installation of built-in furniture, in which case measure the area and add to total, or fitted up to the edge of the furniture continuing only a short distance underneath.

window

door

estimating quantities

137

calculating floor covering for stairs

To work out the amount of floor covering needed for a staircase, add together the total run (the sum of the depth of each step) to the total rise (the sum of the height of each step). The total run and total rise can be calculated either by measuring the total width and height of the staircase or by taking measurements for one step and multiplying this by the total number of steps. This will give the 'length' of material required but you will need to multiply this by the width of the steps to give the total surface area. If laying a trim, whereby strips of the staircase are left exposed either side of the covering, adjust the width measurement accordingly. Add 5% to the total for cutting and waste.

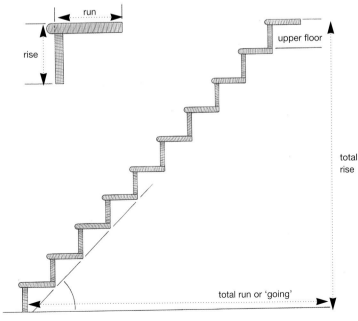

run

rise

upper floor

total rise

total run or 'going'

ground floor level

timber floor construction

In the vast majority of homes the floors will be constructed from timber. Until quite recently a timber floor meant just that – a floor constructed out of solid wood floorboards nailed on top of solid wood joists. However, technological advances have altered many of the traditional methods of construction so that chipboard and plyboard are commonly used instead of timber. The age of the property will have a bearing on the method of construction, with newer houses tending to make use of sheet flooring, which provides a smooth base over which to lay a floor covering.

traditional timber floor

The diagram below illustrates the traditional method of constructing a timber floor. Floorboards may be either square-edged or joined to each other with the aid of a tongue and groove joint, which helps to cut down on draughts. New houses tend not to have floorboards as it is a much slower and more expensive process to lay floorboards than laying sheet flooring. Where renovations have taken place quite often you will find that floorboards have been ripped out and chipboard sheets laid instead, although recently there has been a vogue for plain, exposed floorboards in interior design. Where an upper storey floor has been constructed using this traditional method, it is likely that the ceiling below will follow the old-style lath and plaster construction.

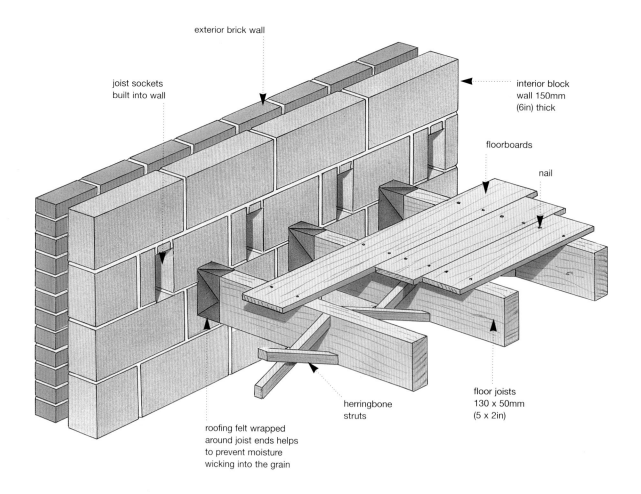

exterior brick wall

joist sockets built into wall

interior block wall 150mm (6in) thick

floorboards

nail

herringbone struts

floor joists 130 x 50mm (5 x 2in)

roofing felt wrapped around joist ends helps to prevent moisture wicking into the grain

floor supported by joist hangers

Suspended floors in modern houses are commonly supported by joist hangers. These prevent the timber joists from coming into direct contact with the brickwork or blockwork, so that moisture cannot wick into the ends of the joists. The joists will often be thinner than those used in traditional construction, and sheet chipboard in place of floorboards acts as a stressed component tying everything together. Where the floor forms a ceiling for the room below this will be of plasterboard skimmed with a plaster finish.

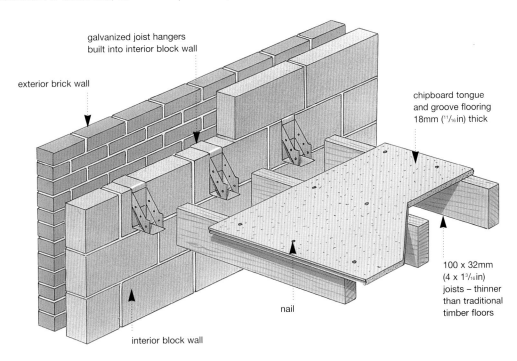

galvanized joist hangers built into interior block wall

exterior brick wall

chipboard tongue and groove flooring 18mm ($^{11}/_{16}$in) thick

100 x 32mm (4 x 1$^{3}/_{16}$in) joists – thinner than traditional timber floors

nail

interior block wall

139

modern 'I' beam construction floor

This type of floor is found in houses that utilize timber framing for structural walls and is common in the USA. It may look inferior but in actual fact 'I' beam construction is extremely strong and stiff. The beams can be made on site but are most often manufactured under controlled conditions and bought in. As with floors supported by joist hangers, sheet materials will usually be employed as flooring and ceiling for beam floors.

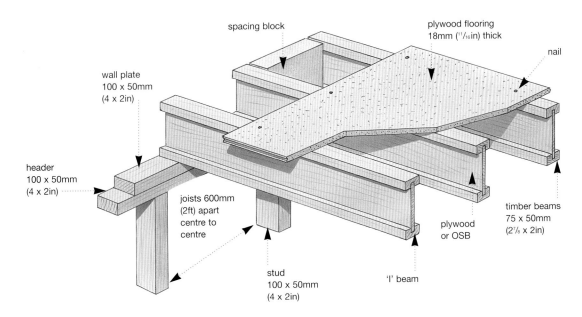

spacing block

plywood flooring 18mm ($^{11}/_{16}$in) thick

nail

wall plate 100 x 50mm (4 x 2in)

header 100 x 50mm (4 x 2in)

joists 600mm (2ft) apart centre to centre

stud 100 x 50mm (4 x 2in)

'I' beam

plywood or OSB

timber beams 75 x 50mm (2$^{7}/_{8}$ x 2in)

timber stairs

In private homes the majority of staircases are manufactured from timber. If the stairs are in particularly bad shape then replacing them entirely is often a more economical option than attempting to repair or refurbish them. With most older stairs you will find the structure is sound but there are just a few creaks. These can be effectively repaired and given a new finish by being sanded and then painted or stained, and when this is combined with a new set of spindles and newel post or panelling under the stairs, a total revamp can be achieved for relatively little cost.

closed tread

Closed tread stairs are the simplest to make and are undoubtedly the most common – most modern houses include a staircase with a single straight flight of stairs of closed tread construction. More traditional closed tread stairs tend to be made from solid timber, but with the invention of relatively inexpensive manufactured building boards, on many modern staircases treads and risers will often be made from MDF or plywood.

Building regulations state that a staircase with over sixteen treads must incorporate a landing. Few domestic staircases are greater then twelve treads but they may still include a landing if the stairs turn a corner.

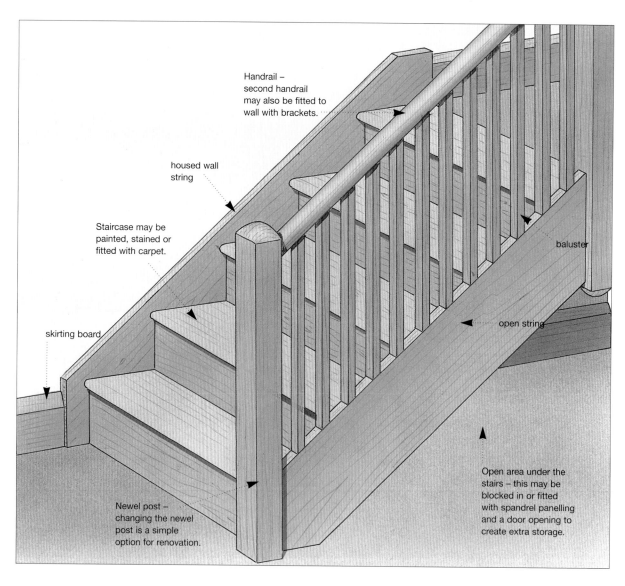

Handrail – second handrail may also be fitted to wall with brackets.

housed wall string

Staircase may be painted, stained or fitted with carpet.

skirting board

Newel post – changing the newel post is a simple option for renovation.

baluster

open string

Open area under the stairs – this may be blocked in or fitted with spandrel panelling and a door opening to create extra storage.

Open tread stairs are similar to closed tread stairs except that more of a feature is made of the staircase. Although once very popular, nowadays domestic staircases are seldom built with an open tread construction, partly because of changing trends and fashions and partly because of the increased cost of production. Lacking the support of risers, the treads must be more stoutly constructed to be able to cope with the loads placed upon them without deflecting. For obvious reasons open tread stairs are not usually covered with carpet, but the treads tend to be made of hardwood which can be stained, varnished, polished or painted. The absence of risers means that these stairs cannot be boxed in with any great success. Indeed, the very idea of the open tread is to allow the eye to see other parts of the room and the structure of the building.

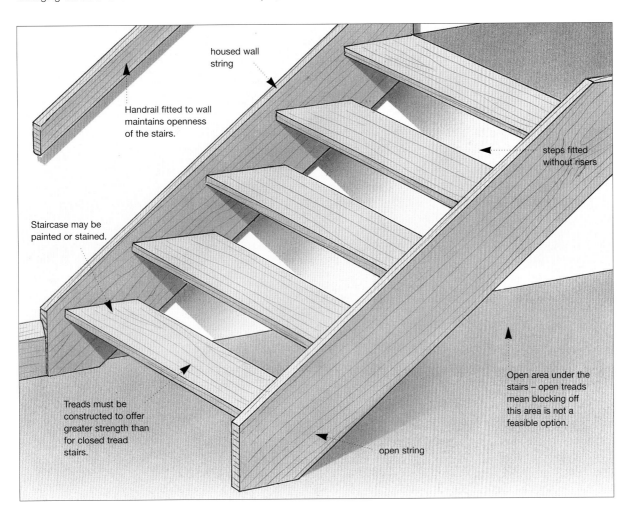

housed wall string

Handrail fitted to wall maintains openness of the stairs.

steps fitted without risers

Staircase may be painted or stained.

Treads must be constructed to offer greater strength than for closed tread stairs.

Open area under the stairs – open treads mean blocking off this area is not a feasible option.

open string

CHOOSING TIMBER

Stairs can be so much more than just a means to travel from one level to another. There is a huge range of timbers suitable for stair construction if you are considering installing a new staircase or completely replacing an existing one. You may buy a pre-constructed stairway, or you may choose to have one custom-made.

The cost depends on the type of timber you choose. If you select a hardwood timber such as oak, be prepared to pay a premium price. Conversely, softwood timber such as pine will be far more affordable. You can always use cheaper wood or manufactured boards if the stairs are to be painted, but a pine stair will look good stained or varnished.

RENOVATING A STAIRCASE

Another option is to dress up the stairway you already have. Many DIY stores offer stair part kits to transform the look of a staircase. Without touching the treads and risers it is possible to remove the existing newel, balusters and handrail, replacing these with something else better suited to your taste and the surrounding decor.

concrete & cast iron stairs

Concrete stairs are usually seen in commercial properties but they can be found in residential properties too. Popular in the 1930s they have recently seen something of a renaissance. Stairs constructed from cast iron are more often located outside a property, as an exterior fire escape or as a means of accessing an upper-storey flat. If cast iron stairs are installed internally it is most often in the form of a spiral staircase.

concrete stairs

If you are aiming for a minimalist, functional interior style then concrete stairs will contribute greatly to such a look. However, it is possible to soften their harsh appearance with wooden cladding or carpet, clever use of timber handrails and other details. Concrete stairs can be mass-produced off site and then installed by a builder, but for a one-off job it is more economic to construct the stairs in situ. The usual method of construction is to construct timber formwork to act as a mould for the wet concrete, which is then removed once the concrete has set.

Concrete stairs are durable but not without their problems. Spalling occurs when moisture gets into minute cracks in the surface and then freezes in cold weather, causing the surface of the concrete to break away. Spalling can be difficult to stop, for once the surface has broken off more water can find its way in. Another problem is the corrosion of reinforcing bars or mesh embedded into the concrete, which can cause serious structural failure. This problem is rare, but when it does occur the entire staircase will have to be replaced.

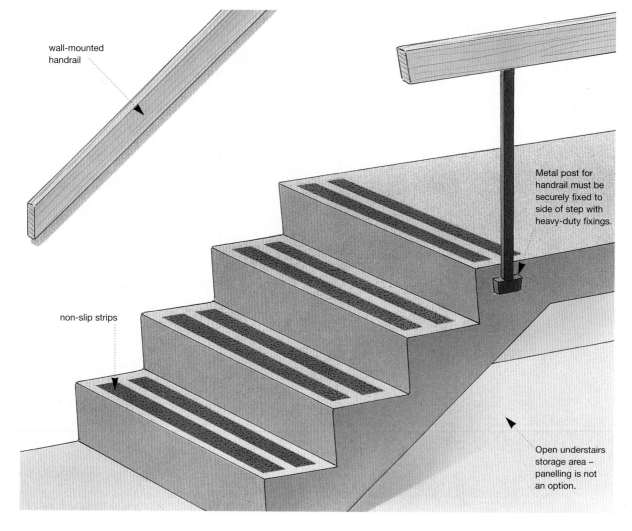

wall-mounted handrail

Metal post for handrail must be securely fixed to side of step with heavy-duty fixings.

non-slip strips

Open understairs storage area – panelling is not an option.

A newly built cast iron staircase can be expensive to buy, but if you are very lucky you may be able to buy a second-hand example. Old Victorian industrial buildings often contain cast iron spiral stairs, so it is worth enquiring with reclamation yards to see if they have anything that might be suitable. Cast iron stairs are constructed the same, whatever their shape and size, from sections bolted together. Virtually maintenance free, the only thing you may have to do is tighten or replace some of the nuts and bolts, particularly at handrail junctions.

ornate patterned fretwork on risers and treads

'turned' handrails and balusters

balusters bolted onto treads – all sections of staircase bolted together

spiral stairs

Installing a spiral staircase will make an unusual and impressive addition to a house, opening up new possibilities in the use of interior space. Spiral stairs rise in their own space and so take up much less floor area then any other type of stairway, hence one of the prime reasons for installing such a staircase is the need to cope with a lack of space.

The idea of installing spiral stairs rarely occurs to homeowners, and when it does it is usually dismissed out of hand. Certainly, as the main staircase linking the ground and first floors spiral stairs are not really a practical option, especially in a household that includes children, the elderly or disabled people. Yet for a secondary staircase when space options are limited, spiral stairs will make an original and ornate feature. In a small house which does not have space for a straight flight staircase, a spiral staircase can be used to gain access to the loft or attic space. Not having to use a loft ladder each time makes this space much more user-friendly, and the fact that a previously uninhabitable room has been made usable means the cost of the staircase is easily recouped. One of the main disadvantages is that, with the steepness of the rise and the continuous turn, moving larger items of furniture to the upper floor is a real problem. Spiral stairs may be constructed from either wood, metal or concrete. They can also be built against a wall, in which case the outside edge will be supported by the wall structure, or they may be built free-standing with all structural support deriving from the central post.

BELOW *Strips of carpet attached to each tread make it easier on the feet and less noisy to ascend and descend these spiral stairs.*

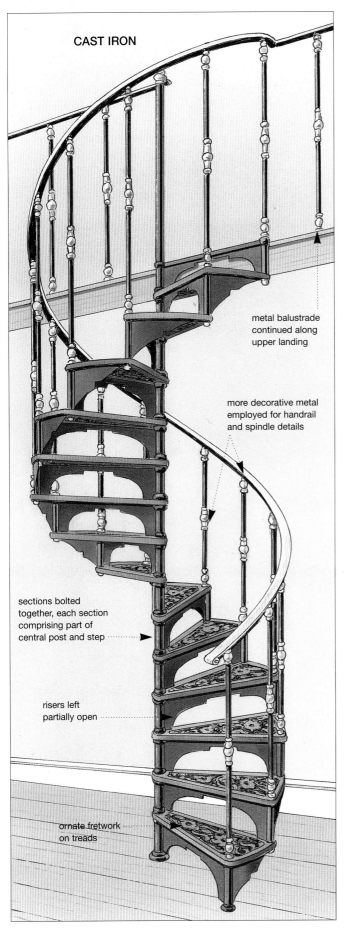

CAST IRON

metal balustrade continued along upper landing

more decorative metal employed for handrail and spindle details

sections bolted together, each section comprising part of central post and step

risers left partially open

ornate fretwork on treads

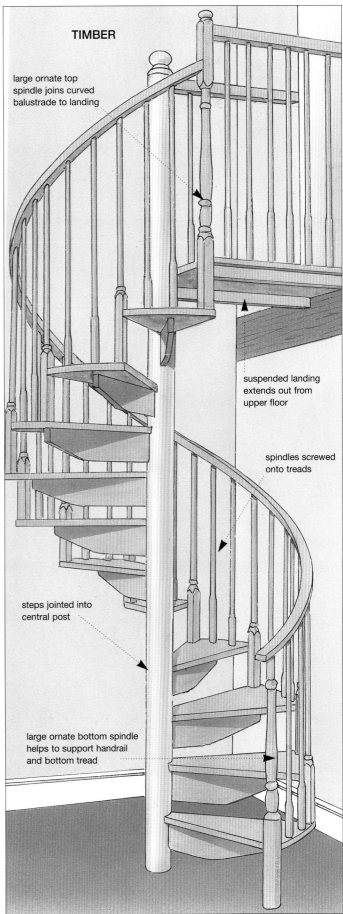

TIMBER

large ornate top spindle joins curved balustrade to landing

suspended landing extends out from upper floor

spindles screwed onto treads

steps jointed into central post

large ornate bottom spindle helps to support handrail and bottom tread

landings

The term landing traditionally describes the area created by extended treads at a point where there is a turn in the staircase, but is also used to describe the part of an upstairs hallway immediately adjacent to the staircase. Where landings form an integral part of the staircase their construction will be similar to the rest of the stairs, although there are occasions when they will have been built as part of the structure of the house, particularly where they form short hallways between separate flights of stairs.

Landings perform several different functions. Where space is limited they may be installed to allow the stairs to change direction. They may also be installed into the staircase purely as a design feature, forming a visual break to the run of the stairs. The landing of your staircase is a good place to establish the decor of your home.

The upstairs landing is the first place you arrive at when you reach the top of the stairs and it leads on to the other rooms. As such it can be used to good effect either to set the tone for the decoration in adjacent rooms or to offer a contrast. Generally people match landing and downstairs hallway decoration, but not always. Victorian

houses often have large windows that give good natural light to landings and stairways, something that can tend to be lacking in newer properties. If your landing is dark, try brightening the colour scheme and installing additional light fixtures. A more radical approach would be to make an opening in a bulkhead wall to allow more light in.

LANDING TYPES

There are different types of landing for each kind of 'turn' in staircases with more than one flight. A quarter space landing is the most common, which is where the second flight continues up at right angles. A quarter space landing is a small square landing, equal in width to the stairs. Half space landings allow a 180° turn in the flights and their length is equal to two flights. A variation of these two is the half-turn open-well staircase with two quarter space landings. This allows for a 180° turn but over three flights, often with a shorter flight between two landings. The least common is a flying landing where the stairs continue straight. In between landings and steps are winders, which are really extended, wedge-like steps that describe a short turn at the top of a staircase.

LEFT *The staircase carpet has here been extended along the landing hallway and into the adjacent room to provide continuity of decoration.*

safety advice

Like those on the main staircase, for safety reasons balusters on landings are subject to building regulations. They must be no less than 900mm (2ft 11½in) high. The gap between each baluster should also be small enough so that a 100mm (4in) ball cannot pass through them at any point. Older properties are not subject to these rules but if handrails and balusters are being replaced then you will need to comply.

RIGHT *A chair and desk have been installed in what would otherwise be redundant landing space to create a bright study area.*

BELOW *Rather than having two quarter landings, this staircase combines a landing with winders to make the 180° turn between flights.*

making changes to floors

Making changes to existing flooring, or replacing the floor altogether, is often the first step towards more general renovation of a room. For example, if you are converting an upper-storey room into a bathroom you will need to consider strengthening joists to cope with the weight of a bath filled to capacity. You may be forced to make changes due to adverse circumstances, such as damp penetration in a suspended floor, the best remedy for which is often to replace it altogether with a solid concrete floor. Prevention is the best cure, however, and another project described in this chapter is how to add ventilation to the underfloor area in order to avoid damage from damp.

By installing a plywood floor over the concrete subfloor, this garage has been transformed into a comfortable workroom.

laying floors in bathrooms

If you feel confident about laying floors in any other room in the house then the bathroom should present no particular problem. However, there are a few special considerations, most of which relate to all the water involved in the day-to-day activities that take place – bathrooms can be extremely wet and measures need to be taken to minimize the amount of moisture damage to the floor. The damp air, leaking pipes from baths and basins and the weight of the tub all conspire to cause damage to both the subfloor and floor covering.

dealing with moisture

To ensure the longevity of flooring in a bathroom, an adequate ventilation system is essential to eradicate the presence of condensation. Care over plumbing work and regular inspections will make sure that all pipework connections are tight and leak free. Laying bath mats will go some way to minimize the damage due to splashes from baths and basins, but more important is to ensure the floor covering is waterproof or resistant to moisture and that all areas where moisture can penetrate are adequately sealed. Before laying any new floor covering carefully inspect the existing subfloor for water damage and rot. Remove the bath panel and check below the bathtub. Leaking pipes should be obvious and need to be rectified immediately. A musty smell is a sure sign of problems and must not be ignored: sections of the floor that are soft or rotten will need to be replaced. If you are buying sheets of manufactured board, remember to tell your supplier that these are being laid in a bathroom, as there are special water resistant grades which are better suited to the damp environment.

ABOVE RIGHT *Naturally water resistant, hard tiles are a good option for bathrooms, but make sure you seal the grout joints.*

the bathroom suite

If the flooring is being replaced or re-laid as part of an overall bathroom refurbishment the suite is probably also being replaced at the same time. If not, then before the floor can be replaced you will need to remove the bathroom suite and any other cabinets and fixtures attached to the floor. Elsewhere in this book you will find instructions on renewing the subfloor and provided you follow these closely you should encounter few problems. When flooring is to be replaced as part of a much larger refurbishment program it can be a good idea to lay the floor covering before the installation of toilet, bath, bidet and basin pedestal. Though not always practical, where it is you avoid having to lay the floor covering in what is often a tight space that will require lots of fiddly cutting.

LEFT *A neater job will often result if floor coverings can be laid before the installation of the bathroom suite.*

By using whole sheets the lack of cutting means you are able to put down the floor much faster and will end up with a neater finish. Moreover, because the suite sits on top of the flooring there will be less chance of water finding its way onto the subfloor. The only drawback is that you need to be careful not to damage the floor during the installation of the suite and when the plumbing and decoration is carried out, but even then the floor may be protected with just a few sheets of hardboard.

weight considerations

If you are installing a larger bath you will need to take into account the stresses this may impose on the floor. Replacing a standard bath with a jacuzzi will add about an extra 225kg (500lb) when the bath is full. It is quite likely that you will need to add some local strengthening to the joist, and the floorboards may be too thin to support the weight of the feet. If you are at all concerned then you should consult a structural engineer, who will be able to assess the risks and recommend a course of action. You will have to pay for this of course but it is better than having the bath end up in the downstairs living room!

ABOVE RIGHT *A bathroom looks far neater when pipework is concealed behind wall panels and under floorboards.*

MIDDLE RIGHT *A bath holds a considerable amount of water, which puts an enormous load on the floor and may mean you need to add extra strengthening around large bathtubs.*

BELOW *If you are leaving exposed timber floorboards in a bathroom you will need to apply a water-resistant finish.*

types of flooring

Almost any type of flooring can be used in a bathroom – even hardwood floors can be treated with a water-resistant finish. Check with your supplier whether the flooring you intend to buy is suitable for bathrooms. Carpet is best avoided as water can soak through and rot both the carpet and the subfloor underneath, although there are varieties of carpet specifically designed for bathrooms which are water, mildew and stain resistant with a backing that does not allow water to seep into the pad. Tile and sheet vinyl floors are probably the best choices as they are easy to clean and effectively resist staining and moisture penetration. Whatever flooring you choose, always use waterproof adhesives and grout, and seal holes with silicone where pipes come through the floor. Moisture resistant flooring and MDF have a green tinge to them, so can be easily identified against standard products which are usually biscuit colour.

laying floors for garages & workrooms ⚒

Most garage floors are made from concrete, which is fine for the car but can be hard on feet and legs. Moreover, a concrete floor tends to be cold and damp and if you are storing tools or machinery this is liable to cause them to rust. A plywood floor will make for a drier, more comfortable room.

Garages are often used for hobby rooms and children's play areas, but without some modification they can be cold and uninviting. By adding a floating floor the garage can be transformed into a comfortable activity area. Plywood floors are easier on the knees and allow for a floor covering. They are simple to lay and since they are not fixed to the subfloor, they can be removed at a later date.

tools for the job

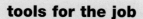

club hammer & bolster chisel

mixing equipment

broom

tape measure & pencil

trimming knife

handsaw

cordless drill/driver

1 Use a club hammer and bolster chisel to knock off any high points on the concrete that could puncture the plastic membrane. Fill any large indentations with a concrete or mortar mix. Sweep the floor to remove any dust and debris.

2 Lay down the damp-proof membrane (DPM), allowing it to lip up the wall by at least 150mm (6in). Trim off any excess with a trimming knife. If you need to attach two sheets together, tape along the join with duct tape, then fold the second sheet over on itself three or four times so that you end up with a seam 100mm (4in) wide, before taping again.

3 Starting at one wall, place 100 x 50mm (4 x 2in) timbers side down on top of the DPM at 600mm (2ft) intervals. Use a handsaw to cut them to length. Then cut some noggins to provide support at the end joints and between timbers, attached at 1.2m (3ft 11in) intervals.

4 Cut some polystyrene insulation panels to fit between the timbers and lay them in position. 50mm (2in) thick panels will sit level with the top of the timbers and provide additional support for the flooring. You can omit the insulation if you wish, but it does make a big difference to the warmth of the room and provides some measure of sound insulation.

5 Take 18mm (¹¹⁄₁₆in) shuttering plywood and, with its best side uppermost, drill pilot holes at 200mm (8in) intervals, 50mm (2in) in from the edge and across the centre of the board. Screw down the boards using 32mm (1⁵⁄₁₆in) no 8 screws. Unless the room is perfectly square, you may find that you have to trim the edges of some of the boards.

✋ safety advice

When cutting the heavy plywood sheets, make sure they are well supported on a sawhorse, workmate or trestles. You will be able to cut more accurately and the sheets are much less likely to slip and cause an injury.

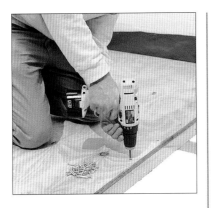

6. Moulding or skirting boards provide a neat trim and help to hold down the edges of the floor. Screw through the skirting boards and damp-proof membrane into the wall. Fold but do not cut the plastic at the corners of the room, tucking it neatly behind the skirting as you fix it back.

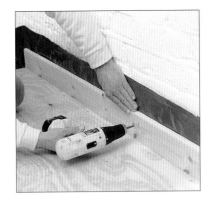

7. Run a sharp trimming knife around the top of the skirting to trim off any excess plastic flush. If you do not like the look of the DPM sandwiched between the skirting board and the wall, this can be disguised by running a bead of mastic along the top of the skirting.

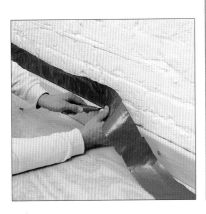

8. At door openings, fit threshold cover strips to hide the edges of the plywood. If the new floor is higher than the floor level in an the adjoining room, then you will need to make a ramped reducer strip and cut the bottom of the door to suit. With garage up-and-over doors, screw or nail a thin strip of timber to cover the joint between timber and ply. Ensure the plastic is sandwiched in-between, then trim the plastic level with the finished floor.

FLOOR COVERINGS

If the room is to be used for a children's play area you could cover the plywood with stick down tiles or vinyl sheeting. For a deluxe finish a piece of carpet will offer a measure of thermal and noise insulation.

tips of the trade

Cutting polystyrene can be messy as the white lumps stick to everything. Rather than use a saw, which generates large amounts of static, use a sharp, serrated bread knife which is almost as fast.

Sturdy and damp-proof, a plywood floor is ideal for transforming a garage into a workshop, and a further covering of vinyl will add extra warmth and comfort.

replacing a suspended floor with concrete ⁄⁄⁄⁄

There may be several reasons for replacing a suspended floor with concrete. One of the most likely scenarios is when the original floor has suffered from rot or infestation and will have to be replaced. In older houses unprotected by a damp-proof course a concrete floor might be installed as part of the overall damp-proofing measures in the property.

1 Before stripping out the old flooring, make a pencil mark 1m (3ft) up the wall. Draw a line around the room at this height with a spirit level – this is your datum mark.

2 Strip out the old floorboards and joists. Joists are easier to handle cut into sections, especially on older floors where they will need to be pulled out of wall sockets. Ensure all traces of the old joists have been removed, this is especially important if dry rot has been present.

3 Shovel in a layer of hardcore so that its top level is 1.3m (4ft 3in) below the level of the datum mark on the wall. Use a punner to tamp it down and break up any large lumps.

4 The next stage is to lay on the sand blinding. Shovel builder's sand on top of the hardcore to a depth of 100mm (4in), all the time checking the height against the datum marks on the wall. You may find it helpful to cut a batten to 1.2m (3ft 11in) rather than keep measuring with the tape measure. Smooth it down with the back of your shovel as you go and use a long board to make certain that the sand is flat.

5 Lay a sheet of plastic damp-proof membrane on top of the sand, taking care not to puncture the sheet. Ensure that it lips up the wall by about 300mm (1ft). Use some strips of duct tape to hold the membrane against the wall.

6 Reinforcing bars strengthen the concrete and prevent it from cracking. Place the bars raised up on concrete garden slabs. Make a criss-cross pattern, at 400mm (1ft 4in) centres, tying any joints with binding wire. Keep the bars at least 100mm (4in) clear of any wall. Once finished, the grid should be fairly rigid and should not sag if you walk on it.

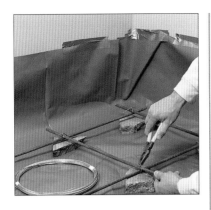

7 Provided another person helps, for a small room it is perfectly feasible to mix the concrete yourself with a small mixer. Use a mix of 1 part ordinary Portland cement, 1 part building sand and 3 parts aggregate. There is no need to be too precise, just measure each of the components out by the shovel-full. Do not make the concrete overly wet – add just enough water to mix the components into a grey creamy consistency.

8 Rather than simply spreading the concrete in a random fashion, start in one corner of the room and work back towards the doorway. Use the shovel to work the concrete down between the reinforcing bars, forcing out any trapped air.

9 Check the top level of the concrete against the datum with a batten cut to 1m (3ft), to ensure the finished floor will not be lower than adjacent rooms.

10 Tamp the concrete surface with a board or piece of 18mm ($^{11}/_{16}$in) thick ply. Starting at one end of the room, work the top of the concrete with the tamp edge. Do not apply great force but simply stipple the surface slightly. If the room is over 2.5m (8ft) wide you will need a helper. If you work towards the doorway tamping as you go, the holes left by your boots will refill.

11 After a couple of hours water will have come to the surface before it starts to sink back into the concrete. At this point you can trowel the surface to a smooth finish with metal plasterer's trowels. Spread your weight on two ply boards about 800mm (2ft 7in) square. Gently lift the leading edge of the trowel to stop it digging in as you drag it across. Work back towards the doorway, moving the boards as you go.

12 You can walk on the concrete the next day, but leave at least three days before trimming off the plastic and fitting skirting. Wait at least three weeks if laying carpet as moisture remaining in the concrete will rot the backing.

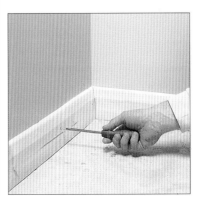

installing joist hangers

On most modern houses the ends of the joists are supported on metal brackets called joist hangers. Even if you are replacing the entire floor in an older house where joist hangers were not originally fitted, you can still fit them using the method described below. There are several different types of hangers and each type comes in different sizes, so make sure you fit the correct joist hangers for your application.

The most common reason for installing joist hangers is when a new floor is being built, either for a new room or because the original joists need replacing. Joist hangers are typically fixed to either masonry or timberwork. In new houses the joist hangers are built into the wall, or if the house is timber-framed special hangers are nailed to the studwork. In older house where joists are fitted into pockets in the wall, by installing joist hangers the ends are kept away from potentially damp brickwork and masonry. Joist hangers also allow you to space the joists so that the joints of sheet flooring fall directly onto the centreline of a joist.

tools for the job

tape measure & pencil

spirit level

cordless drill/driver

panel saw

hammer

trimming knife

1 Allow for the width of the plasterboard by measuring up 12mm (⁹⁄₁₆ in) from where the underside of the ceiling will be, then mark a level line at this point all around the room using a spirit level. Mark out the centre spacing for the joists along this line no more than 400mm (1ft 4in) apart centre to centre. You may need additional joists close to the wall in order to support the edge of the boards.

tips of the trade

• **Positioning joists** – Joists typically run across the shortest span of the room, but loadbearing walls must always support the ends. If you are replacing a floor the new joists should run the same way as the original joists. Consult an architect or structural engineer for advice if you are unsure.

• **Spacing joists** – The spacing of floor joists is always quoted as centre to centre. This is the spacing between the imaginary centreline of each joist. To gain the actual distance between joists, deduct the total thickness of one complete joist.

2 To ensure the finished floor ends up level, nail or screw a temporary batten to the wall so that the top edge is level with your datum mark. Hold the joist hangers on top of the batten at the centreline reference marks and screw or nail them to the wall. If using screws you may find it easier to mark the screw position before drilling the hole and inserting a wall plug. Use a hammer or percussion drill fitted with a bit specifically designed for masonry when drilling into brick or blockwork.

If the hole has been drilled correctly you should be able simply to push in the wall plug for a snug fit.

3 Get a helper to hold the end of the tape measure while you check the length of the joists. Measure by holding the tape across the room and checking the distance between the back plates of the joist hangers. As it is unlikely that the room will be completely square, hence lengths will vary slightly, do not just measure the first joist and assume all the others will be the same length. Deduct 4mm (³⁄₁₆ in) from the overall measurement and mark this on the joist before cutting to length with a panel saw.

safety advice

The chemical used in pressure-treated timber for joists can be poisonous if ingested. Wear gloves if possible and always wash your hands after work and before eating and drinking.

4 If you have cut it correctly the joist should drop in without the need for hitting it with a hammer. If the joist wobbles from side to side slightly in the hanger, you can make it a better fit by wrapping roofing felt around the end and securing it in place with nails. Parcelling the end in felt also has the added advantage of preventing moisture from wicking into the end grain of the joist.

5 Nail the joists into position through a couple of the holes on either side of the hangers. Galvanized nails have a better grip due to their rough finish and are more resistant to rust than conventional brightwire nails. Nails should be no more than half the thickness of the joist or there is a risk of splitting the timber. Do not drive them right home at this stage. Place the spirit level across all the joists and check for level, repeating this at several places in the room. If any joists are high, pull the nails and either trim a little from the underside of the joist where it sits in the hanger or reposition the hanger. When you are certain of the fit, drive home the temporary nails and hammer nails through the remaining

holes in the sides of the joist hangers. To avoid splitting the wood try blunting the ends of the nails with light hammer blows.

6 For any span more than 3m (10ft), nail herringbone struts between each of the joists to add extra strength and to prevent twisting (see pages 208–9). The joists are now ready to receive the flooring and ceiling, but before doing this run in any cables and plumbing work.

LATERAL RESTRAINT STRAPS

For extra stability in the completed floor you may want to add lateral restraint straps. These come in the form of galvanized steel straps, fitted and screwed to the wall, and are available from any good builder's merchant. Such restraint straps are intended to be fitted at a perpendicular angle to the joists.

Provided they are fitted with care and accuracy, joist hangers will form a sturdy suspended floor with the added benefit of providing a damp-proof barrier.

cutting an access hatch ⁄⁄⁄⁄

There can be lots of reasons for wanting to gain access to the area underneath a floor, but the most common is for the repair or installation of services such as plumbing or wiring. Before the introduction of chipboard and ply floors, accessing was usually a simple matter of lifting and replacing a few boards. Sheet materials, which cover larger expanses, make access a more complicated affair, since removing sections is not really an option and small access hatches need to be cut into the floor instead.

Using the speed and versatility of an electric router, cutting an access hatch in a chipboard, ply or laminate floor need not be complicated. The techniques demonstrated here allow access to be gained with a minimal amount of disruption to the overall floor. Cutting permanent hatches also means that the area under the floor can be easily accessed whenever the need arises in the future.

chipboard & ply floors

tools for the job

tape measure & pencil
screwdriver
electric router & 'rout-a-bout' jig

1 A 'rout-a-bout' is a type of jig specially made for use with an electric router. It is fast and easy to use for those with some previous experience with routers. First mark the position of the access hatch on the floor. Attach the electric router to the special base plate, then loosely screw the plate to the floor, directly over the area you wish to cut. Rotate the router around the screw until the disc is cut all the way round.

2 Remove the disc and drop in a special plastic ring, which will come supplied with the 'rout-a-bout'.

3 Finally, drop the cut disc so that it rests on the plastic ring. No glue or fixing of any kind is required and the area surrounding the hatch is almost as strong as the floor prior to the hole being cut. Access to the underfloor area is available at any time by simply lifting out the disc.

laminate floors

When a laminate or solid timber floor has been laid over a ply or chipboard subfloor, it is vital to be as neat as possible. The cut out section can be any size, but making it as small as is practicable will mean it is ultimately less obtrusive.

tools for the job

safety equipment
tape measure & pencil
carpenter's square
fine-toothed panel saw
double-sided tape
router
wood chisel
handsaw

1 Mark out a square on the floor 300mm (1ft) along each side. Check each corner is a perfect right angle with a carpenter's square. Two of the sides must also be parallel with the line of the laminate strips.

2 Prepare some battens 60mm (2½in) wide and no less than 10mm (½in) thick. Stick the battens to the floor with double-sided tape, ensuring that the inside edges exactly align with the pencil marks.

3 Insert a 10mm (½in) thick straight cutter into the router and attach the template guide bush to the base plate. Keeping the base plate down on the battens with the bush against the inside of the battens, cut through the laminate floor and the subfloor.

safety advice

Using a router is noisy and dusty so wear always a dust mask, goggles and ear defenders.

tips of the trade

Make sure that the router cutters are sharp to avoid splintering the top surface of the laminate.

4 Remove the section of floor and put to one side. Carefully peel off the battens and double-sided tape. Change the router cutter to a bearing-guided cutter and run a rebate around the inside of the opening, cutting down to the same depth as the thickness of the laminate.

5 Use a sharp wood chisel to square up the rounded internal corners of the laminate left by the circular router cutter.

6 Form a section of flooring from some laminate offcuts that is at least 2.5cm (1in) larger all round than

the hole in the floor. Glue the tongues together with wood glue, then glue this in turn onto the section of chipboard or ply subfloor that you saved. Put a heavy weight on top and allow the glue to dry.

7 Make a paper or card template so that it just drops into the rebated opening in the floor, then clearly mark the positions of the joint lines onto the top edges. Transfer the template to the replacement floor section, noting the position of the joints but keeping it as near the centre as possible. Mark around the outside before finally cutting with a fine-toothed panel saw. Sand up the edges to remove any rough spots.

8 Provided that the cutting and marking have been accurate, the panel should simply drop into position and require no further fixing. If you are confident that you will never need access later, it could be glued in place. If the panel is quite large you may want to use small brass screws at each corner to retain it.

soundproofing a floor

Noise pollution can be a cause of friction between neighbours, especially in apartment blocks and properties that have been divided into separate flats, though the problem can be just as bad within a family home. Adding some soundproofing to a floor helps to cut down noise transmitted from above and will go some way to solving your noise pollution problem. Using the technique shown here almost any floor can be soundproofed.

Noise is either transmitted through the air or through the materials used in the construction of a house. With the method of soundproofing shown here, sand and insulation blanket combine to form an effective barrier against the transmission of noise throughout the house. A floor can be soundproofed from below, but this means destroying the ceiling, and working above your head is tiring on the arms and neck. Moreover, by soundproofing from above, sand can be used as an insulating material, which is both a cheap and effective sound-deadening medium.

safety advice

The soundproofing method shown here will increase the weight of the floor. Before starting any work you must check that this will not adversely affect the structural integrity of the property. If you are in any doubt then contact a structural engineer.

tools for the job

pipe, cable & joist detector

crayon

circular saw

trimming knife

gloves

prybar

bolster chisel

hammer

handsaw

cordless drill/driver

dust mask

1 Unless they are immediately obvious, use a pipe and wiring detector to check the position of plumbing and electrical circuits. Then mark their positions on the floor surface with a crayon, so that when cutting into the floor you will be able avoid damaging these services.

2 If the floor is constructed of chipboard or tongue and groove boards, run a circular saw set to the thickness of the flooring down the joints between boards. Do not cut round more than one or two boards at this stage, for once you start lifting the first couple of boards you may find that the rest can be removed without cutting off the tongues.

3 Use a prybar and bolster to gently lift the flooring, trying not to damage too many boards. Remove any nails that remain poking out of the joists with the claw end of a hammer.

tips of the trade

With all the floorboards removed it can be difficult to move around the room. Have a couple of loose boards to hand that you can position across the joists to walk on as you work in the room.

4 Screw 50 x 25mm (2 x 1in) battens to either side of the ceiling joists. Make sure the bottom edge is just clear of the ceiling below.

5 Cut 12mm (⁹/₁₆in) plywood strips to sit on top of the battens. Fix the strips in place with nails.

6 Cut plastic membrane material to line the troughs, pressing it into the corners and allowing it to lip up the sides of the joists. Nail or staple it into position using a minimum of fastenings near the top edge. Trim off excess plastic membrane so that it is level with the top of the joists.

7 Pour in kiln dried sand to about 50mm (2in) deep. Cut a piece of ply so it rests on top of the joists with the bottom edge 50mm (2in) higher

than the bottom of the trough. Use this to to achieve consistent results when levelling out the sand.

8 Place slabs of rock wool on top of the sand. They should not be any higher than the top of the joists or refixing the boards will be difficult. If cutting the slabs, use a fine handsaw and make sure you wear a dust mask.

9 With the two layers of insulating material in place, you can refit the flooring on top of the joists. Any split or damaged boards will need to be replaced. When refixing boards make sure that all joints are tight and there are no gaps. Covering the floor with some thick, good quality underlay and carpet will further enhance the soundproofing properties.

If appropriate to the type of floor covering, a thick underlay stapled to the subfloor will further enhance the sound insulation properties of the floor.

adding ventilation to floors

Ventilation is essential in any floor space. Stagnant air can lead to rot, unpleasant smells and damp, which can destroy floor finishes and carpets, and in some cases the floor itself, if left untreated. Some floors suffer from a lack of ventilation more than others, such as those in bathrooms and kitchens. Before starting on major work it is worth checking that poor ventilation is not simply a case of existing air bricks being blocked by soil and dirt.

fitting a floor grille

Though not as effective as an exterior air brick, a grille fitted into floorboards will allow air to circulate in the floor space, which might otherwise be a potential breeding ground for rot and infestation. If the grille is installed under a window or a radiator then the convection currents will help to draw air into the room.

tools for the job

joist detector

tape measure & pencil

cordless drill/driver

jigsaw or padsaw

bradawl or small drill

screwdriver

1 Determine the positions of the joists. These are often indicated by the position of the floor fixings or you can use a joist detector. Measure in and draw a parallel line 150mm (6in) out from the skirting board. Place the top edge of the grille on this line and draw a pencil line round it, keeping

the ends equally spaced between the run of joists where these run at right angles to the wall.

safety advice

When determining the position of the grille, use a detector to locate pipes and cables to avoid cutting through these services by accident.

2 Set the grille to one side and draw another line 12mm ($^9/_{16}$in) inside the grille outline. Drill a hole at each corner with a 12mm ($^9/_{16}$in) drill bit, ensuring that the edges of the bit stay inside the second guideline.

3 Cut out the waste area within the second guideline, using either a jigsaw or padsaw. Work from each drilled hole. At the last hole the waste section is liable to fall through into the ceiling area. To prevent this, particularly if the grille is so small that you will not be able to get your hand into the hole to remove the cut out section, partially screw in a large wood screw to give you something to hold as the block is cut away.

tips of the trade

When a grille is to be fitted into a polished floor you will want to get the best finish possible. Special jigsaw blades are available that cut on the down stroke and prevent splintering to the floor surface.

4 Remove any rough edges from the hole with abrasive paper before screwing on the grille. Align the edges of the grille with the pencil guideline. Use a bradawl or small drill to make a pilot hole for the screws and fix the grille in position. For a neater appearance, align all the screw slots so that they face the same way.

5 Where carpet is to be refitted, cut out the hole in the carpeting prior to fitting the grille in place. Then screw down the grille so that the carpet is sandwiched between grille and floorboards. If the carpet is quite thick pile, you may find that you need to use slightly longer screws than those that were originally supplied with the grille.

fitting an air brick

Exterior air bricks are the traditional means of ventilating the space under suspended floors at ground level. Alterations to the house or garden may mean that the original bricks are no longer performing their function. As a general rule there should be an air brick every 2.5m (8ft) along an external wall. If there are less air bricks in the walls of your house, or if you have signs of mould or damp due to lack of air movement, you should consider fitting additional bricks. Air bricks come in a variety of sizes but the easiest to fit are the smaller ones, used here, which have the same overall dimensions as a common house brick.

tools for the job

cordless drill/driver

club hammer & bolster chisel

protective gloves & goggles

pointing trowel

jointing trowel

1 To install an additional air brick, or replace one that is missing, first select a suitable standard brick to remove, 2–2.5m (6½–8ft) from the nearest existing air brick. It should also be at least one course below the damp-proof course and below the level of the floor inside. Drill lots of holes to break up the brick, using an electric drill with a large masonry bit.

2 Remove the remainder of the brick with a club hammer and bolster chisel, taking great care not to damage the adjacent brickwork. Most of the mortar holding the brick in place will probably come away with the brick. Remove any remaining mortar so that you have a clean hole ready to receive the air brick.

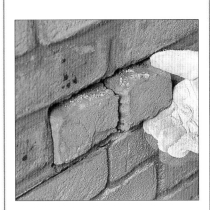

safety advice

When chopping out old bricks with a hammer and chisel, make sure you wear gloves to protect your hands and, more importantly, goggles to protect your eyes from flying chips.

3 Mix up some mortar using 3 parts sand to 1 part cement. Cut a couple of strips of timber 50mm (2in) long with a square section the same thickness as the existing mortar courses in the brick wall. Place the strips in the bottom of the hole and hold them in place with a little mortar. Damp down the new brick and spread mortar onto the top and ends.

4 Slide in the brick, ensuring it stays flush with the existing brickwork. Check with a straightedge that the brick is not too far in or sitting proud. Work in additional mortar to the joint with a pointing trowel, if necessary. After about an hour when the mortar has just started to harden, finish with a jointing trowel.

tips of the trade

When pointing brickwork, leave the mortar to 'go off' a little before finishing. In this way you will not drag mortar out of the join and the finish will be smoother.

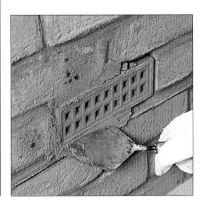

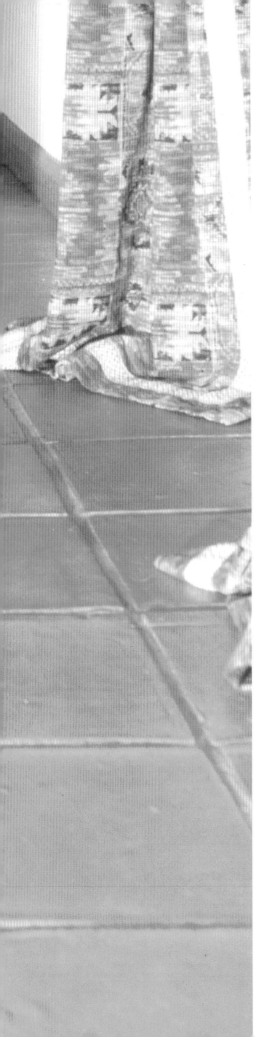

floor finishes

There are probably more choices of floor covering available today then there have ever been. Improvements and innovations within manufacturing mean that materials previously deemed unsuitable are now commonly used for flooring. Many homeowners still make carpet their first choice and it is easy to see why – luxurious underfoot, a carpet will lend any room a warm and cosy feel. Other types of floor covering are also finding their way into homes. Laminate flooring, which has always been popular in Scandinavia, is now common in other European countries. Many people still tend to avoid sheet flooring, but this too has had something of a renaissance in recent years, and a huge range is now available that has little in common with the linoleum of old.

Floor finishes need not start and end with carpets – hard tiles, for example, can make a stylish and original flooring option.

comparing floor coverings

When planning alterations to a room it is essential to know which types of floor covering are appropriate for the particular subfloor, what are the specific qualities of each type and how much it is all likely to cost. The following table examines each of the main types of floor covering available, listing the cost, positive and negative aspects, suitability and how difficult it is to lay, so that you can easily compare types and make your choice.

PROS & CONS	COST	DURABILITY	LAYING	SUITABLE SUBFLOORS
CARPET ▽				
Pros Warm and soft to the touch. Luxurious look. Vast range of colours and patterns to suit any colour scheme. Helps to keep down draughts. Available in wide rolls. **Cons** Not waterproof but special carpets are available for bathrooms. Can mark and stain easily.	Wide range of costs from cheap to very expensive.	Moderately durable. Carpets with a high wool content last longest and can be shampooed.	May be undertaken by a skilled amateur but more expensive carpets are best left to a professional. Cheaper foam-backed carpet is glued to double-sided tape at the edges. Woven backed carpet is attached to gripper rods at the edges of the room.	Concrete screed, plywood, chipboard and solid timber floors are all suitable, but carpet is generally laid on top of underlay.
WOODBLOCK ▽				
Pros Very hardwearing. Easy to maintain. Can be stained or bleached to give different look. **Cons** Limited range of options as not all timbers are suitable for floors.	Expensive but some modern equivalents are slightly cheaper.	Very durable – ideal for high traffic areas. When worn, scuffed and dirty can be refinished to bring back to a condition that is good as new.	Laying proper woodblock flooring is a professional job requiring hot pitch. An experienced amateur using a latex adhesive can lay small areas.	Concrete screed. Not suitable for upper floors or for laying on wooden floorboards.
VINYL TILES ▽				
Pros Hardwearing. Easy to maintain and keep clean. Waterproof when correctly laid. Ideal for kitchens and bathrooms. **Cons** Not suitable for living areas as they can look rather clinical. Cold and hard.	Costs are moderate considering the life span and compared to other coverings.	Very durable – ideal for high traffic areas. Mopping or wiping with a cloth is all that is required in the way of maintenance.	Easy to lay, provided the subfloor is in good condition and the setting out is correct. Self-adhesive tiles are the cleanest and easiest to lay for the amateur. Others are set into adhesive.	Concrete screed. Ply or chipboard. Solid floorboards should be covered with ply or hardboard before laying.

PROS & CONS	COST	DURABILITY	LAYING	SUITABLE SUBFLOORS
SHEET VINYL ▼				
Pros Hardwearing. Easy to maintain. Waterproof when correctly laid – ideal for kitchens and bathrooms. Available in wide rolls. **Cons** Not as resilient as tiles. Not suitable for living areas as it can look uninviting.	Moderate considering the life span and compared to other coverings.	Very durable – ideal for high traffic areas. Mopping or wiping with a cloth is all that is required in the way of maintenance.	Not as easy to lay as tiles as it can be unwieldy. Often best to make a template first. Some can be loose laid but others are glued to the subfloors with special adhesive.	Concrete screed. Ply or chipboard. Solid timber floorboards should be covered with ply or hardboard before laying.
LAMINATE ▼				
Pros Hardwearing. Easy to maintain. Look of solid wood without the expense. Does not need to be laid by a professional. **Cons** Difficult to affect an invisible repair. Can be noisy and slippery. Limited range of finishes.	Moderate considering the life span and in comparison with other coverings. The cheaper laminates are better suited to low-usage rooms.	Durable. Ideal for high traffic areas. Mopping or wiping with a cloth is all that is required in the way or maintenance.	Straightforward to lay. Some of the new versions clip together and do not require glue, making them even easier. All should be laid on a thin underlay which varies according to the type of subfloor.	Concrete screed. Ply or chipboard. Solid timber floorboards should be covered with ply or hardboard before laying.
PLYWOOD ▼				
Pros Hardwearing. Best suited for workrooms and garages. **Cons** Dusty if not coated. Fixings cannot be concealed.	Cheap to moderate depending on the thickness and grade of ply chosen.	Very durable. Ideal for high traffic areas. Waterproof when a suitable paint or varnish is applied.	Simple with no complicated joints but take care fitting around pipes. Nailed or screwed to the subfloor or joists.	Laid directly onto joists or flooring. DPM underneath if laid on floor liable to become damp.
QUARRY TILES ▼				
Pros Hardwearing. Easy to maintain. Waterproof when correctly laid and sealed. Ideal for kitchens and entrances. **Cons** Noisy, hard and cold. Slippery when wet. Crockery dropped onto it will smash.	Highly expensive.	Very durable. Ideal for high traffic areas. Unsealed tiles need periodic sealing with a proprietary product in order to retain their appearance and prevent the surface staining.	Not a suitable job for novice. Tiles are laid in wet mortar rather than an adhesive.	Concrete screed. Ply or chipboard. Solid timber floorboards should be covered with ply or hardboard before laying.

laying chipboard & ply floors

Chipboard or plywood may be used as a cheaper substitute for floorboards when laying the subfloor of a room. Many new houses are already being built with floors made from such sheet materials. Plywood is dimensionally stable so makes an ideal base for other floor coverings such as laminated floors and tiles. Whilst it is possible to lay chipboard and ply over existing flooring, bear in mind that this could make access to underneath the floor difficult in the future.

tools for the job

tape measure & pencil

cordless drill/driver

hammer

prybar

panel saw or circular saw

carpenter's square

nail punch

chipboard floors

Flooring grade chipboard is generally 18mm ($^{11}/_{16}$in) thick and comes in sheets 2.4m x 600mm (7ft 10$^1/_2$in x 2ft). Tongue and groove joints provide extra support to the edges. Larger sheets makes it much quicker to lay than standard timber floorboards.

1 Chipboard floors are most likely to be fitted directly to joists. Lay one or two boards down without fixing them to walk around on.

2 Lay the first board at right angles to the run of the joists, starting in one corner. Ensure that the board is placed with the tongue facing away from the wall, and note that all boards should be laid printed side down.

3 Screw or nail the board in place. Screws should be 25mm (1in) longer than the flooring thickness, so a floor 18mm ($^{11}/_{16}$in) thick will require 32mm (1$^3/_8$in) screws. Drive these in at 200mm (8in) centres. Make fixings no closer than 50mm (2in) to any edge.

4 Run a bead of PVA adhesive into the end groove of the next board and push this up to the first board. Endure the joint is tight with no gaps showing on the face where the two boards meet. If hand pressure alone is not enough, tap the end of the board with a hammer. Insert a scrap of wood between the hammer and board to avoid damaging the tongue.

5 Carry on till one row is finished then start on the next. If the last board of the first row was cut to length then start from this end on the second row in order to stagger joints. Do not worry if joints do not occur on joists as the tongues provide support.

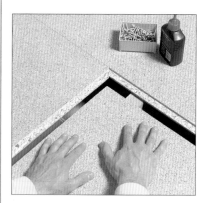

6 Cut the last boards to width 1cm ($^1/_2$in) less than the overall measurement. Run glue into the groove of each board and place them onto the joists tight against the wall. Force the board onto the tongue of the next board with a prybar.

plywood floors

Very popular in the USA, plywood is often used as a quick method of covering a floor. It provides a very stable and strong subfloor over which tiles, carpet and almost any other floor covering may be laid. Stronger than chipboard, it is better suited to damp environments and can withstand greater weights being placed upon it. If better quality ply is used it can even be varnished and left without any additional floor covering.

1 Ensure the plywood is laid to best advantage. If sheets are being laid over an existing floor then where

the joints fall will not matter. Where ply is being laid directly onto joists the joints must fall onto a joist. Lay down a few sheets dry, orienting them in different directions to check.

2 Newer houses have joists placed at close spacing. In older houses floors tend to be constructed using joists with a larger section but spaced farther apart. Fit noggings to reinforce ply edges where necessary, providing additional support. Use 75 x 50mm (3 x 2in) timbers on edge cut to fit between the width of the joists. Skew nail on each side, through the top of the nogging and into the side of the joist. Keep the top of the noggings level with the joists.

3 Boards can be fixed down by hammering wire nails into the joists and punching the heads below the surface. Alternatively, by drilling pilot holes and screwing them down, gaining access below the floor will be that much easier. Place screws at 200mm (8in) centres with no screw closer than 15mm (⅝in) to any edge.

4 Fit the remaining boards, maintaining a 2mm (⅛in) gap along all joints to prevent the boards from squeaking and to allow for any slight movement. Cut a couple of pieces of scrap timber 2mm (⅛in) thick and place these between the boards to keep the gap consistent as you fit. It also saves having to keep checking the measurement repeatedly.

5 Replace the skirting if this was removed, or install it now if fitting new skirting. Press it down to the floor as you fix it to the wall but do not insert fixings into the floor. If the skirting was left in situ, install a small quadrant or Scotia moulding to hide the joint between ply and skirting.

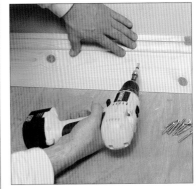

tips of the trade

Running a small bead of mastic around the room will seal the joint between any skirting board or moulding and the floor. This helps to prevent dirt and dust from finding its way into the room and soiling carpets or other floor covering.

laying a laminate floor ⁄⁄⁄

Until recently the materials available for laying a wooden floor were limited to parquet and other solid timbers, which required a healthy bank balance to buy and specialist knowledge to fit. The recent innovation of timber laminate flooring, which comprises lengths of decorative timber bonded to a cheaper backing, has addressed both these points, providing an easy-to-fit and relatively cheap wooden flooring that looks good, is hardwearing and with minimal care will outlast many other floor coverings.

The general principals of laying a laminate floor are the same irrespective of the manufacturer, but there are subtle differences between makes so do not mix types. Some of the most recent types have tongue and groove joints that require no glue and simply snap together. If you use this type then follow the instructions shown below omitting the stages that refer to adhesives. Strips should be laid up and down the room, and it often looks best if they run in the direction of the longest dimension. If the room is square, run the strips away from the strongest light source.

tools for the job

tape measure & pencil
club hammer & bolster chisel
claw hammer or screwdriver
straightedge
bucket
metal plasterer's trowel
mallet
panel saw

1 If laying on a concrete screed, carefully remove any protruding nibs that might prevent the floor from laying level. On wooden subfloors, nail or screw down any sections that are loose and ensure that all raised nail heads are punched below the surface. Lay a straightedge across the floor at several points checking for humps and hollows – if any are greater than 6mm (⁵⁄₁₆in) the floor will need levelling. Mix up latex levelling

compound in accordance with the manufacturer's instructions and, using a metal plasterer's trowel, spread it across the entire floor. It sets fast so do not mix too much at once or try to spread it on too thickly.

2 Once the compound has dried, roll out the recommended underlay, which will provide an even, soundproof cushion. Underlay material is usually either polystyrene or thin cork. Lay it across the room at 90° to the eventual direction of the laminate strips, holding it in position with sticky tape. Do not overlap any joints, butt them instead and attach them with a little more tape.

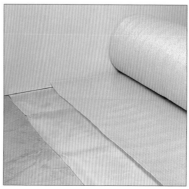

3 Lay the first row of boards with the grooved side towards the wall. Place the wedges behind this first strip, if supplied, otherwise use some scraps of timber to give a 12mm (⁹⁄₁₆in) expansion gap at the wall.

4 Run a bead of white wood PVA glue into the end groove, then push it by hand onto the tongue of the board already laid. If there is still a gap, place a scrap of flooring against the edge of the board and tap home. Use a plastic, rubber or wooden mallet and be careful not to damage the edge of the boards. Continue until you have laid a complete row of strips down one edge of the room.

tips of the trade

Kneeling on the section of floor you have just completed will hold it in place and make tapping in the new sections just that little bit easier. If you bought the fitting kit then the manufacturer will have supplied a hammering block to protect plank edges as you knock them together. Otherwise use an offcut of flooring.

5 The edges of the boards are glued in the same way but ensure that joins with adjacent boards are staggered brickwork fashion for strength and appearance. No joint should be any closer than 150mm (6in) to any other joint. Wipe off any glue that squeezes out of the joints straight away with a damp cloth.

6 Use a sharp panel saw to cut any boards to length. When cutting to size remember to maintain the 12mm (⁹⁄₁₆in) expansion gap. Provided the offcut board is more than 150mm (6in), it may be used to start the next row.

7 You may need to cut the last row to width. Check the distance from the wall to the face edge of the last full board and transfer these marks to the closing board, measuring from the grooved edge. Deduct 12mm (⁹⁄₁₆in) for the expansion gap and cut to size. Run glue into the joint, drop the board into the gap and use the wrecking bar to force the tongue into the groove.

8 Leave the room for a minimum of 12 hours, during which time you should try to avoid walking on the laminate flooring to give the glue a chance to set. The final step is to cover the expansion joint with strips of moulding. Do not nail the moulding into the floor, rather fix it into the wall or skirting to allow for expansion and contraction of the new flooring.

Laminate flooring is easy-to-clean, hardwearing and soft underfoot, which makes it an ideal floor covering for use in a nursery or children's playroom.

laying vinyl tiles

Vinyl tiles have undergone something of a revival in recent years and are now available in a variety of styles and sizes. Some tiles come with a self-adhesive backing, otherwise they are laid by bedding them into a special adhesive. The quality and longevity of the finished floor will depend on the thoroughness of your preparatory work, so make sure any necessary repairs to the subfloor are carried out before you start to lay your tiles.

tools for the job

tape measure & pencil

hammer or cordless drill/driver

jigsaw or padsaw

chalk lines

carpenter's square

serrated adhesive trowel

hot air gun or hair-drier

trimming knife

vinyl roller

wallpaper roller

1 Vinyl tiles are ideal for laying on concrete and hardboard, but cannot be laid on floorboards. If you have floorboards, cover them over with hardboard or ply before laying vinyl. Cut around any pipes or other obstructions. Nail or screw the boards every 150mm (6in) in every direction. Ensure fixings finish below the surface.

2 Jumble up the tiles from several boxes so that slight variations in colour will not be noticeable. Lay a few out for a trial run – you can often vary the look of the floor by alternating how the surface pattern or texture flows.

3 Lay out dry two rows of tiles between opposing walls to form a cross. Leave an even gap between the tile and wall at each end. Mark round the tile at the centre of the cross – this is your key tile.

4 Remove the tiles and, using the key tile marks as a guide, snap a chalk line along the length of the floor. Make sure the line is at right angles to any main doorway or window. You might need to adjust the line a little, but provided the temporary layout was correct then any adjustments will be minimal. With the aid of a large carpenter's square, snap another chalk line at right angles to the first, using the pencil marks as a reference.

5 Spread out a quantity of tile adhesive with a serrated adhesive trowel. Cover an area large enough to lay down the first eight or nine tiles, including the key tile. Work from the intersection of the chalk lines, keeping all the adhesive restricted to one quadrant of the room for the moment. Do not apply the adhesive too thickly – spreading rates are generally given on the tub.

safety advice

Many tile adhesives are petroleum based and give off heavy vapours. Work in a well-ventilated room and extinguish all naked lights.

6 Bed in the key tile, exactly lining up the corners with the right angle of the chalk lines. Then lay tiles adjacent to the key tile, keeping each tile tight to the next. Twist the tiles as you push them into the adhesive – this helps them to bond properly and ensures an even coating of adhesive.

7 Continue laying tiles, one quadrant at a time, wiping away adhesive that squeezes out through the joints. End with full tiles, leaving a gap at the edge of the room.

8 Lay down the last complete tile then align another tile on top so that it touches the wall. Cut through the bottom tile using the top tile as a straightedge. Discard the offcut, then swap the tiles around before gluing.

tips of the trade

Vinyl tiles remain stiff when cold. Warming them with a hair-drier or hot air gun makes the tiles more flexible, easier to cut and improves bonding.

9 To fit the tiles around pipes, start by making a card template, then copy this onto a tile with a chinagraph

pencil and cut out. Cut just one slit down to a pipe hole and spring the tile open as you bed it into the adhesive. Tiles cut in this way should fit perfectly, with little trace of the cut.

10 Immediately you have finished tiling go over the floor with a heavy steel roller to ensure full adhesion. Proceed slowly, moving left to right and up and down the length of the room. Wipe up adhesive that oozes from the joins. Any tiles that the big roller cannot reach, press down with a wallpaper roller.

These tiles have been laid at 90° to each other according to the direction of the 'grain'. For less obvious joins, lay the tiles so that the pattern runs in the same direction.

laying vinyl sheet flooring

Vinyl sheet flooring is ideal for kitchens and bathrooms, since it is easy to keep clean and resistant to moisture. Many modern varieties of sheet flooring have a cushioned back, which makes them easy on the feet and legs if working in the kitchen for any length of time. Making a template is by far the easiest method for laying sheet vinyl as it avoids costly mistakes. As with tiles, getting the subfloor in good condition is of paramount importance.

tips of the trade

- **Vinyl care** – Never fold sheet vinyl as this puts permanent puckers into it. Avoid walking on it and make sure that nothing sharp is trapped underneath.

- **Heating** – Laying the vinyl sheet out flat, pattern side-up, for an hour or two in a warm room, makes it easier to cut.

- **Paper template** – Building paper is ideal as it is reinforced, but you can use almost any thick paper.

tools for the job

tape measure & marker pen

trimming knife

serrated adhesive trowel

vinyl roller

wallpaper roller

1 Cut and join together sheets of building paper to form a template of the floor space 150mm (6in) bigger than the overall size of the room. Join sheets with masking tape, allowing a good overlap and applying tape to both sides of the joint to prevent it from moving.

2 Cut some windows near the edge of the paper about 50mm (2in) square. Attach the template to the floor through these windows with masking tape. The spacing is not crucial, but make sure that you have enough windows to hold the paper template in position so that it does not slip around.

3 Press the paper into the edges of the room. Trim off the excess with a trimming knife where it lips up the skirting board or around built-in pieces of furniture. You may find that you have to cut 'darts'– vertical relieving cuts – up from internal and external corners to get the template to lay on the floor properly.

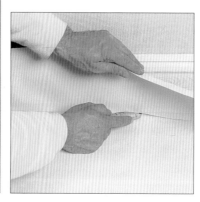

4 When you are happy with the fit, slowly peel the template from the floor, being careful not to tear the paper. Lay the template on top of the sheet flooring and orient it to best effect, noting the position of any lines or pattern, then tape it in place.

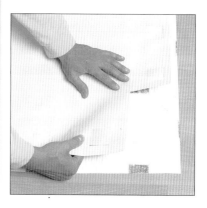

5 Draw around the template onto the vinyl with a marker pen. Discard the template and cut the flooring with a knife. Lay a scrap of hardboard or ply under where you are making cuts to avoid damaging the floor below. Even if you are doing this on the garage floor the board is still a good idea to save dulling the knife edge. When you have cut the vinyl to size, roll it up and carry it to the room.

6 Roll out the flooring, then gently fold back the vinyl from the longest wall to uncover a 1m (3ft) wide strip of subfloor. Spread adhesive onto the exposed area of subfloor with a serrated adhesive trowel.

7 Lay the flooring into the adhesive, smoothing it down with the heel of your hand to force out any air bubbles. If you need to make small adjustments to the fit now is the time to do it, before the adhesive sets. Roll the rest of the flooring back on itself and spread on the remaining adhesive. Smooth the flooring into the adhesive from the centre to the edges to force out any trapped air.

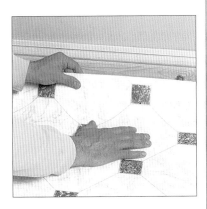

👍

tips of the trade

If you have to join two sections of flooring together, overlap one on top of the other and cut through both pieces at the same time to ensure a perfect butt seam. Peel back the top sheet, remove the offcut from the bottom sheet, then fix to the subfloor with adhesive in the usual way.

8 Once the vinyl is laid, ensure full adhesion by pressing down on the flooring with a vinyl roller. Move slowly over the floor, making passes in different directions. Employ a wallpaper roller against the edges of the room and in any hard to reach areas, using firm hand pressure.

9 Wipe away the inevitable splashes of adhesive from skirting boards, fitted furniture and the surface of the flooring, using the solvent recommended by the manufacturer and a clean rag.

SEALING THE VINYL

In bathrooms and kitchens, seal the vinyl with a bead of clear silicone mastic around the edge.

Vinyl is especially good for laying in bathrooms as it produces a watertight floor surface. Soft underfoot and easy to clean it is also a good option for a children's playroom.

laying hard tiles ///

Hard tiles are ideal for wet areas because of their durability and looks. However, you need to plan work thoroughly and use the correct techniques in order to maximize both these qualities. If the tiles are unglazed, it is important to seal them with a proprietary sealing solution. Otherwise, their surface can become ingrained with adhesive and grout, which can be difficult to clean off. The majority of floor tiles are supplied with a glazed surface, which makes application more simple.

where to start

Most rooms are not totally 'square', so starting by laying full tiles along a skirting/wall junction is not usually an option since slight imperfections in wall alignment will become magnified as the tile design progresses across the floor. You should therefore start by finding the centre of the room. Attach a chalk line between centre points on opposing walls, pull it taut and snap the line onto the floor surface to provide a guideline. Repeat between the other two walls. The point at which the lines bisect is the centre of the room. All tiling designs should be planned from this point. Lay them dry first in order to determine the best starting point, which is ideally on a wall with few obstacles. You can then draw another guideline to show the starting line for the first full row of tiles. This line should be adjusted so that any cut tiles needed around the edge of the room are balanced.

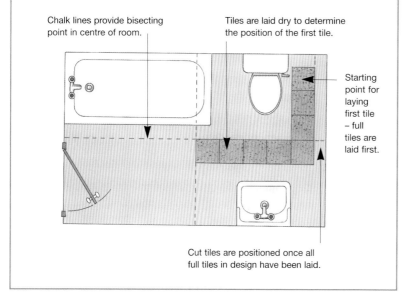

Chalk lines provide bisecting point in centre of room.

Tiles are laid dry to determine the position of the first tile.

Starting point for laying first tile – full tiles are laid first.

Cut tiles are positioned once all full tiles in design have been laid.

2 Position the first tile, allowing it to bed into the adhesive before pressing it firmly in place.

3 Continue to add tiles, keeping consistent gaps between each tile using pieces of card as spacers.

laying the tiles

tools for the job

adjustable spanners

basin wrench

tile cutter & tile saw

1 In this example, standard tiles are being laid onto a plywood subfloor (see pages 150–1 for more on laying bathroom floors). Secure wooden battens along the starting guideline and at right angles to this line to provide a good edge to butt the tiles against. Apply adhesive with a notched spreader in the area where the first tiles are to be laid.

4 Every now and again use a spirit level to check that all surfaces are flush. Make sure that no tile edges protrude above surface level or sink below it.

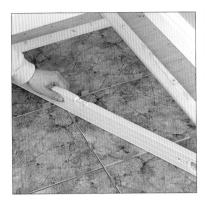

5 When all the whole tiles have been laid, fill in around the edge of the room with cut tiles. It is best to let the main body of tiles dry overnight before completing the edge, since you will have to stand on the tiles when measuring.

6 Draw guidelines on tiles that need to be cut. Use a tile cutter to score and snap along the lines.

7 A tile saw is the ideal tool for cutting curves. First make a paper template of curved shapes such as the toilet pedestal and use it as a guide for cutting.

8 Once all the tiles have been laid and the adhesive is dry, mix some grout and fill the joints between the tiles. Press the grout firmly in place and wipe away any excess.

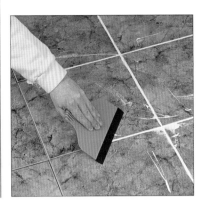

Hard tiles can also be applied to the walls and boxed-in areas of a bathroom for an integrated, watertight and easy-to-clean finish. See pages 420–1 for tiling walls.

laying mosaic tiles ⚞

Some manufacturers now produce mosaic tiles suitable for floor use. They are supplied in sheets, which allows a large number to be laid at any one time – single tile application would be a very labour-intensive and time-consuming project, even for the smallest of rooms. When laying mosaic tiles, your first concern must be to make sure that they are laid as evenly and flat as possible so that they are comfortable underfoot.

👍

tips of the trade

If the edges of mosaic tiles lift above floor level, their small size means that they will be uncomfortable underfoot, so it is vital that the surface onto which they are laid is level. Concrete or plywood subfloors are ideal as other types rarely provide enough rigidity. Make sure there are no protruding nails or bumps in the floor's surface.

tools for the job

tape measure & pencil
hammer
notched spreader
mini roller
grout spreader
scissors
tile nibblers
sponge

1 Choosing a suitable starting point when tiling with mosaics is vital and varies slightly from the approach taken when laying larger floor tiles. However, as with larger tiles, it is important to start laying the mosaics from one wall in the room, using a batten to act as an initial supporting barrier to butt the tiles up against. Position the batten close to the wall, ideally about two or three tile widths away from the skirting board. (When the batten is removed it will be easy to fill the remaining gap with the small tiles.)

Tile sheets are not applied directly next to the skirting because, if the room is not totally square, even a

small angle of difference will become exaggerated in the finished tile design. The second batten shown here (fixed at 90° to the first) provides a good guideline for producing a square design that will appear balanced and in alignment with the walls of the room, even if they are not totally square. Spread adhesive onto the subfloor in the area where the first mosaic sheets are to be positioned.

2 Remove the backing from the first sheet of mosaic tiles. This backing may be made of plastic or paper and its only function is to make the sheets easier to handle before being laid in place.

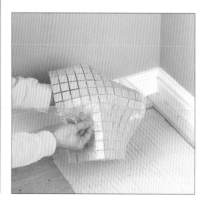

3 Position the sheet of mosaic tiles, adhesive side down, so that the edges of the tiles on two sides of the sheet rest against the right angle formed by the battens. A mosaic sheet is not rigid like a standard floor tile, so pay particular attention that each tile edge is in the correct place and that none is skewed out of position. Fix any that are misaligned before the adhesive has a chance to dry.

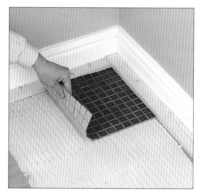

4 Run a mini roller over the surface of the sheet. Apply even pressure across its expanse to bed the mosaic tiles into the adhesive and ensure that each tile is as flat as possible.

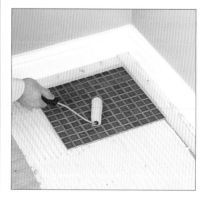

5 Lay the next sheet of tiles in the same way, inserting pieces of cardboard as spacers between each sheet to maintain a consistent gap between them.

6 As mentioned before, the flexible nature of a mosaic sheet can allow single tiles to move slightly out of position. Rather than checking and repositioning individual tiles one at a time, use a grout spreader to maintain consistent and straight gaps between rows of tiles. Where tiles appear out of position, simply press the blade of the spreader into the gaps between them to straighten any tile edges that are not aligned.

7 Once the central floor area is complete, apply tiles around the edge of the room. It is best to leave the full mosaic sheets to dry overnight before tackling the edges in case you dislodge them from position. Remove the battens, then cut tile sheets to the desired size to fit in the gap between the full sheets and skirting board edge.

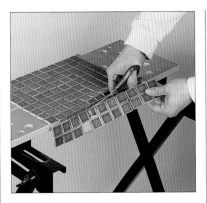

8 Apply adhesive along the gap in the usual way and carefully position the strips of tiles. Again, use a mini roller to make sure that they are bedded in sufficiently and level with the surrounding tiles. Check that they are aligned correctly with the tiles that have already been laid.

9 You may need to use single tiles cut to size to follow the curved profile of obstacles such as a basin pedestal or the base of a toilet pan. Single tiles are too small to be cut with a tile cutter, so use tile nibblers to trim the unwanted portion of the tile before putting it in position.

10 Grout the floor with a grout spreader, by pushing the grout firmly into all the joints and making sure that they are all evenly filled. Try to keep the level of the grout flush with the mosaic tiles rather than raised above them. This will provide a smoother feel underfoot. Wipe away excess grout from the tiled surfaces using a damp sponge, then allow to dry overnight.

COLOURED GROUT

Try finishing mosaic tiles with coloured grout for a different finish. The colour itself is normally supplied as a powder and mixed with white grout to achieve the required intensity. Matching the wall colour can create a good effect.

ALL-OVER MOSAIC

For an all-over effect, use the same type of tiles on the walls as those used on the floor.

MOSAIC BORDER

Mosaic tiles may be used selectively on floors rather than as an overall design. For example, using large tiles in the centre of the floor with mosaic tiles around the edge can be extremely effective.

CHANGING PATTERNS

Although mosaics are supplied in sheet form, patterns can be created by using a selection of different coloured sheets or cutting single tiles from sheets and replacing them with another colour.

fitting carpet

The choice of carpet colours and patterns is virtually limitless so it is easy to coordinate a carpet into the chosen decorative scheme of a room. Carpets made from artificial fibres are now suitable for high traffic areas and rooms once considered inappropriate, such as bathrooms and kitchens. Often considered a professional job, carpet laying can in fact be undertaken by a skilled amateur.

First you will need to estimate the quantity of carpet, gripper and underlay you need (see pages 136–7). Carpet and underlay are usually sold by the square metre, although it is still made in widths of 12 and 15ft (3.7 and 4.6m). Gripper has different length pins for different depths of carpet pile, so seek your supplier's advice. Carpet comes in different weights – the heavier the weight, the greater the wear.

tools for the job

tape measure & pencil

secateurs or handsaw

hammer

sealant gun

trimming knife

staple tacker

protective gloves

knee kicker

edge trimmer

bolster chisel

screwdriver

1 Fit gripper all the way around the room. Cut strips to length as necessary with secateurs or a small handsaw. On chipboard and wooden floors, nail it down ensuring that the slanted gripper pins point towards the wall. Leave a gap two-thirds the thickness of the carpet between the back of the gripper and the wall.

safety advice

The pins on gripper are extremely sharp – always wear gloves and safety glasses when handling and cutting it.

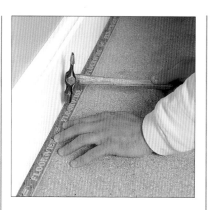

tips of the trade

To ensure you fit gripper the correct distance from the wall, make a spacer two-thirds the thickness of the carpet and use this when nailing it down.

2 On hard floors such as concrete use a special adhesive designed for sticking down gripper. Work fast as the adhesive generally only stays workable for ten minutes.

3 Special gripper strips, often called naplocks, are fitted at doorways for a neat appearance. Nail the strip to the floor so that it will be covered completely by the bottom of the door when it is closed.

4 Cover the floor inside the gripper with underfelt, cutting to fit with a craft knife. Leave no gaps but do not overlap, as this will cause an unsightly bulge. Fix the underfelt to the subfloor using a staple tacker.

5 Lay the carpet with the nap sloping away from the main source of light. Trim off excess with the trimming knife leaving 150mm (6in) turned up the wall at each edge.

tips of the trade

The 'nap' of a carpet refers to the way the pile slopes. Make sure that the nap all faces the same way when two pieces are joined together.

6 Press the carpet onto the gripper along the straightest wall with the ball of your hand. Wear gloves to avoid friction burns.

7 Position a knee kicker about 150mm (6in) from the opposite wall and kick the carpet forward with your knee so that it is stretched and held by the gripper. Stretch out the whole width of the carpet.

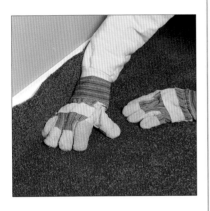

8 Cut the carpet to size with a carpet edge trimmer. Use the trimming knife to get into the corners of the room. Stretch and fit the carpet to the other wall in the same manner.

9 Force down the edge of the carpet between the gripper and the wall/skirting board with a bolster

chisel. Hand pressure is usually fine, but if the gripper is tight to the wall you may have to tap the chisel.

10 To fit carpet around pipes and other obstructions, cut a slit in the carpet the distance from the wall to the obstruction with a trimming knife, then make small cuts across the edges of the slit. Use a screwdriver to tuck the carpet down around the pipe for a neat finish. Unless the pipe is larger than about 20mm (³⁄₄in) it is unlikely that you will have to cut out a circle of carpet.

Carpet can add colour and warmth to a room. Deep pile carpets are the most luxurious, but more hardwearing varieties are available where durability is important.

altering a staircase

There can be a variety of reasons for wishing to alter a staircase, and a staircase can be altered in a variety of ways. For example, you might want to fit a balustrade for reasons of safety and appearance, or to convert the area underneath a stairway into a cupboard, or you may have decided that a cosmetic change is all that is needed and would like to paint or stain the stairs a different colour. Before any such projects can be undertaken, you must first check that the basic structure of the staircase is sound and make any necessary repairs. Once you have satisfied that requirement you may proceed with any number of projects for altering the staircase.

Spandrel panelling may be fitted underneath these stairs to create extra storage or closet space for minimal investment.

installing a handrail ⚒

Handrails are an essential aid for climbing and descending a stairway in safety and with ease. During the 1970s there was a trend towards doing away with handrails altogether. Whilst this is fine for the young and agile, it can be dangerous and difficult for children and the elderly. Handrails are traditionally built on top of the balusters, but if you want to do away with tradition you can fix a handrail directly to an adjoining wall with the use of brackets. Alternatively, you may want to add another handrail to complement an exisiting balustrade, as shown here.

The instructions on these pages refer to a solid wall. If you are attaching the handrail to a hollow stud wall with plasterboard cladding, then you must modify the position of the brackets so that they can be screwed into the upright studs. Alternatively, use one of the many fixing mechanisms designed especially for hollow walls. Handrails come in a variety of styles and can be purchased from most DIY stores or builder's merchants.

safety advice

A handrail is more than a decorative feature and should be chosen as much for its strength and security of fixing as for its style and appearance. It should be strong enough and sturdy enough to take the weight of someone falling against it, and should provide a secure hand hold that is easily grasped. For thinner handrails, stairs higher than average or weak walls, consider installing additional support brackets.

tools for the job

tape measure & pencil

cordless drill/driver or hammer

string or chalk line

spirit level

bradawl

handsaw

1 Measure up vertically 850mm (2ft 10in) from the top and bottom tread and make a pencil mark at both points on the wall. Insert a nail or screw temporarily

into the wall at these marks – do not drive them all the way in, but make certain that they are secure.

2 Stretch a string or chalk line tightly between these two fixings. Check the height at some of the intermediate treads. You may have to adjust one of the fixings up or down if the measurements are not all the same.

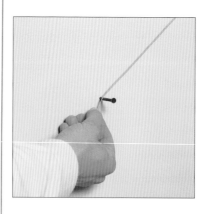

3 Plumb lines up from the front of the second riser at the bottom of the staircase and the penultimate riser at the top of the staircase. Draw a line at both points where the level bisects the string line.

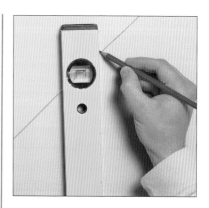

4 Fix brackets at the points just marked. Align the top plate of the bracket flush with the underside of the string line, keeping the wall fixing plate centrally over the vertical reference line.

5 Mark the wall through the holes on the fixing plate with a bradawl. Remove the bracket and drill the fixing holes, making sure you fit the correct size of bit for the screws. Screw the bracket to the wall, double-checking that the top plate is still in line with the string. With the top and bottom brackets fitted, divide the gap between them into three and fit two more brackets, giving four in all.

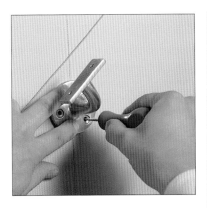

ROPE HANDRAIL

Although not as sturdy as wooden or metal varieties, a rope handrail is a handy option for curved stairways. To fit, screw the brackets to the wall as described. If you are fitting it to a curved stairway, measure the vertical height from each tread to find the correct bracket location. Thread the rope through the brackets and tie a decorative knot at the top and bottom to prevent it being pulled out. Leave 5cm (2in) of slack between each bracket to avoid straining the screws.

6 Remove the string line and temporary fixings and place the handrail on top of the brackets. Get a helper to hold it in position or wind masking around each bracket to keep it in place temporarily. With the handrail secure, use a spirit level to mark plumb cuts in line with the first and last riser.

safety advice

After the handrail is installed, carefully remove any sharp edges on the surface of the wood with abrasive paper, which could otherwise cause injury or give splinters. Once you have sanded any obvious nicks, put on a thick pair of gloves and run your hand up and down the rail several times to make sure nothing catches on the glove material. If it does, sand over the surface once again.

7 Remove the handrail and cut through the pencil marks with a fine handsaw. Smooth down the cut ends using abrasive paper. Place the handrail back into position and drill pilot holes up into the underside of the handrail, before finally screwing it in place on the bracket.

tips of the trade

While the handrail is in position to mark the plumb cuts, you can also mark on the screw positions. This makes it possible to insert the screws without having to use a drill upside down, while the holes will provide reference marks to ensure the handrail is repositioned correctly.

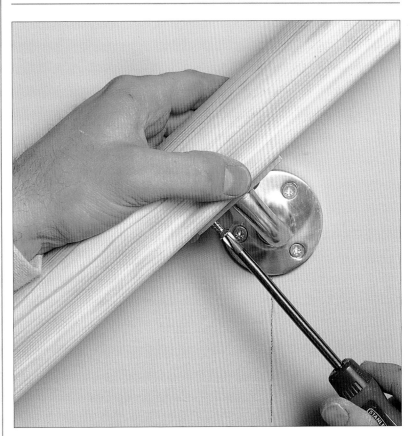

Once the handrail is fixed securely to each of the brackets, it provides a vital support that will make the stairs safer and more comfortable for all who use them.

fitting handrail bolts ⁄⁄⁄⁄

Handrail bolts represent the more traditional method for joining together two sections of handrail. Although, to a certain extent, their use has been superseded by other methods, when properly executed handrail bolts remain an unsurpassed joining mechanism. Requiring no glue, they are ideal for joining a straight section of handrail to a curve at the junction of a landing or at the junction between different flights of a staircase.

Joining sections of handrail together using the bolt method requires a high degree of skill, and accuracy is essential for best results both in the marking out and cutting. Therefore this project should only be attempted if you are confident of your abilities, and this is certainly not a job for a beginner. You are unlikely to be able to find handrail bolts in your local general DIY store. These will most probably need to be bought from a specialist hardware retailer.

tools for the job

panel saw

mitre box

tape measure & pencil

square

cordless drill/driver

6mm (⁹⁄₁₆in) chisel

nail punch

1 Take the two sections of handrail and, using a panel saw, cut the ends to be joined so that they are precisely square. Make the cuts in a mitre box using the right angle cut

guide, then check how the ends butt together. Rest the sections on a flat surface and bring together the two ends. There should be no gaps, and if there are you will need to recut the joints until perfect.

2 Establish a centreline on the flat underside of one handrail section. Draw a neat pencil mark down this line to approximately 100mm (4in) from the cut end.

tips of the trade

A trick for finding the centreline of anything is to measure across at an angle until the measurement is easily divisible by two, then make a pencil mark at this point. This will give the exact centre irrespective of the actual half measurement.

3 Transfer this mark from the underside onto the cut face using a square, continuing the pencil mark until you reach the top surface. Accurately measure up half the height of the handrail and mark on this point square to the guideline.

4 Repeat steps 2 and 3 for the other section of handrail, then briefly put the sections to one side. Now take the handrail bolt and screw both nuts onto either end, screwing them so that a couple of threads are projecting past the nuts at either end. Carefully measure the distance between the inside edge of both nuts, divide this by two and mark the dimension onto the underside of the handrail along the centreline.

5 Drill into the end face of each handrail section at the centre point marked in step 3. Use a drill bit 2mm (¹⁄₁₆in) larger than the diameter of the bolt and 10mm (½in) deeper than half the overall length of the bolt.

6 Use a 6mm (⁵/₁₆in) chisel to cut a pocket in the underside of one of the handrail sections, into which the square nut will be dropped. Chisel out the timber at the point marked in step 4. Note that the pocket should be on the side of the line furthest from the end of the handrail. Once the pocket is complete, drop the square nut into it, allowing the bolt to poke through the hole and enter the thread.

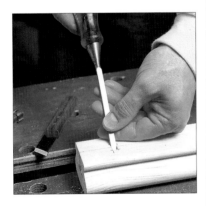

7 In the same way, cut the pocket for the round serrated nut on the other handrail section. The pocket should be slightly larger to allow the nut to turn on the bolt.

8 Use a small nail punch to tighten the serrated nut so that the two halves of the handrail are pulled up tight. Do not overtighten or you may split the timber. Proving that you have been accurate, the two sections should form a perfect fit.

9 Use a sanding block and abrasive paper to sand across the completed joint in order to blend any slight irregularities. Finally, fit the handrail into position on the stairs. Should the joint open up in the future, gently retighten the serrated nut.

A 'reef' is the section of handrail that goes around a corner and connects one straight section to another. A handrail bolt is ideal for joining these sections together.

changing a newel post ⚡⚡

Replacing a newel post can alter the overall appearance of just about any staircase. This project is much less drastic and expensive than replacing all the balusters and handrails. Swapping, for example, a contemporary square post with a classic turned newel can soften what might otherwise be seen as a boxy design.

Changing newel posts is a popular project and is often accompanied by changing baluster spindles (see pages 190–1). Larger DIY stores now offer a wide selection of newel posts that are specifically manufactured to replace existing posts.

tools for the job

tape measure & pencil
....
panel saw
....
wood chisel & mallet
....
cordless drill/driver & bore bit
....
square

1 Measure the vertical height of the existing handrail adjacent to the existing newel. It is important to do this before you start work on removal of the old newel as you will need this measurement at a later stage.

2 Cut the top off the old newel squarely, about 10mm (½in) above the level where the handrail enters the post. You should be able visually to estimate where to cut. If not, draw a line as a guide around the newel and cut along the line.

3 Do the same below the handrail, but leave 25mm (1in) on the inside of the newel post to cut later.

4 Use a wood chisel and mallet to split away the timber carefully on either side of the newel post in order to expose the tenon.

5 Do a little at a time and be careful not to damage the tenon as you get closer to it, since you will need to slot it into the new newel post.

6 Square a line around the remaining newel post 25mm (1in) above where the string enters and cut at this point. Be accurate as the new post will sit on top of this cut stump.

7 Use a sharp chisel or plane to flatten the stump of the existing newel post. Check the surface is flat with a square so that the new newel post will fit properly on top of the old base. If the stump is perfectly flat this will make the job of drilling for the dowel a lot easier. Draw diagonal lines across the top of the stump and bore a hole 25mm (1in) in diameter about 75mm (3in) deep at this centre point. Ensure the drill bit goes in upright.

8 Mark and chisel out from the new newel post the mortise for the handrail tenon. Transfer measurements from the existing tenon to the newel.

9 Measure the height you took in step 1 and transfer this to the new post less the distance left on the stump. Before cutting off the waste from the bottom of the new newel, double check your markings by holding the new post up against the stump. Measure across the diagonals and drill.

tips of the trade

If you are at all unsure about your marking out, tape the new post alongside the old one while it is still in position and transfer the positions of the handrail, string and 25mm (1in) high cut line prior to removal.

10 Fit a 25mm (1in) dowel 140mm (5½in) long to hold the base of the newel. Carry out a dry run to make sure that all the parts fit together. Take it apart and glue the newel in position with wood glue or

epoxy resin. Once the job is completed, sand the new newel post and apply your chosen finish. If you are replacing the newel post, then the finish should match as closely as possible the balusters and handrails. For additional information about finishing see pages 212–13.

safety advice

The strength and durability of epoxy resin is unsurpassed, however, some people may experience allergic reactions to certain products. To avoid this problem wear latex gloves or apply barrier cream when handling these materials.

tips of the trade

If you plan to paint or stain your newel post it is wise to sand it before it is installed, as the shape of the post makes it difficult to sand once it is connected to the handrail.

It is important to ensure a close match between the finish on the replacement newel post and the existing finish on the rest of the balustrade.

installing balusters ✂✂

It is often the case that balusters are changed at the same time as the newel posts to alter entirely the look of the stairs. The style of spindles you ultimately go for will depend on personal preference and your budget. You should consider which type of spindles will contribute best to the overall style that you are trying to achieve. Buying the most expensive hardwood balusters could be a waste of money if you are going to end up painting them, when cheaper softwood spindles would have given the same result for less money.

You will need to fit two spacer blocks and two baluster spindles for each stair tread, plus the string capping and a new handrail if this is being replaced at the same time (see also pages 184–7). All the parts should be available from good DIY stores.

tools for the job

tape measure & pencil

handsaw

nail punch

hammer

spirit level

sliding bevel

sanding block

1 Place the capping that houses the bottom of the balusters on top of the string, and slide it down until it touches the newel. Holding a scrap of timber against the newel, mark then cut the necessary bevel.

2 Repeat the process at the top of the stairs, then nail through the capping into the top of the string, setting the nails below the surface of the capping with a nail punch.

3 Mark a plumb line with a spirit level on both the handrail and string capping. The position of this line does not matter as it is simply a guideline to help you mark the length of the balusters. Draw equivalent lines across the top of the capping and underside of the handrail.

4 Use two lengths of thin batten to act as a pinch rod for measuring the height of the balusters. Hold the two sections together and then slide them apart until they touch the plumb line marks made on the capping and handrail. Tape together the two pieces to preserve the measurement.

5 Hold the pinch rod against one of the balusters and transfer the height measurement. Set a sliding bevel to the angle between the newel post and string capping, and transfer this bevel to the baluster. Note that the top and bottom bevels slope in the same direction.

tips of the trade

Store the balusters indoors for a few days so that they can acclimatize to the temperature and humidity of the house prior to fitting. This will ensure they do not shrink afterwards, which will cause them to rattle.

6 Cut the bevels onto each end of the baluster and then place it between the handrail and capping to check for fit. Hold a spirit level against the baluster when in position to make sure that it is plumb. If you are happy with the fit, use this first baluster as a pattern for cutting all the others.

themselves. Only the spacer blocks are fixed in place as these are sufficient to hold the balusters.

9 When all the balusters have been fitted, give them a light rub over with a sanding block and abrasive paper, then apply your chosen finish.

tips of the trade

If you have chosen barley twist-style balusters, make sure that the twists all start in the same position at the bottom. This makes for a neater and more professional appearance.

safety advice

Make sure that the spindles are not spaced too far apart, as this could allow a child to fall through.

7 Starting at the bottom of the staircase, nail the first two spacer blocks, one to the underside of the handrail and the other to the string capping. Use a nail punch to set the nail heads below the surface.

8 Add the first baluster, then follow this with the next spacer block, and so on until you reach the top of the stairs. No fixings are made through the balusters

Combined with a decorative handrail and newel post, balusters provide an ornate finish to a staircase. They also represent a safety option, especially if you have children.

blocking in the underside of a staircase ⚒

In smaller homes it may not be appropriate to fit spandrel panelling underneath a staircase if this would cause a portion of the main living space to be blocked off. You may instead want to consider leaving the side of the stairway open and disguising the architecture and construction details on the underside with the addition of a flat panel. If your needs change or you feel more confident in your DIY abilities, there is always the option to add spandrel panelling at a later date.

Plasterboard is commonly used to form the panel, although it is heavy and difficult to handle, and many other materials will do just as well. For the project demonstrated on these pages the panels have been cut from thin plywood instead. Lightweight and easy-to-handle, working with plywood means it is perfectly feasible for a DIYer of average skill to undertake this project single-handed and easily complete it over a weekend. Timber battens form the framework for fixing the panels, and since these are small and thin it is important to use good quality timber with minimal defects.

tools for the job

tape measure & pencil
....
handsaw
....
screwdriver
....
hammer
....
nail punch
....
wallpaper brush & roller

1 Cut small sections of 25 x 25mm (1 x 1in) battens to act as set-backs, against which cross pieces will be fixed at 200mm (8in) centres to form the framework for the panels. You will need to cut two for each cross piece – make a template to save having to measure each individual piece when cutting. When you have cut enough pieces, measure and mark midway between each step the distance these pieces will need to be set back from the edge of the

string to accommodate the cross pieces. Since the cross pieces are cut from the same batten, this will be 25mm (1in). Glue and screw each set-back in the marked positions.

2 Measure and cut sufficient cross pieces to provide supports at 200mm (8in) centres. Fix these into position by skew nailing or screwing through each end at an angle into the set-back sections of batten.

3 Cut 6mm (⁵⁄₁₆in) ply to fit across the width of the stairs, from string edge to string edge, so that any joints meet on the cross pieces.

4 Mark the centrelines of the cross pieces a little way onto the sides of the strings. Spread wood glue onto the face of each cross piece and fix the panels into position on the strings with 20mm (³⁄₄in) panel pins. Join up the pencil marks across the face of the panels with a straightedge. These will act as guidelines for fixing panel pins into the cross supports.

tips of the trade

On older stairs where access might be needed later, omit the glue and fix the panels with small screws.

5 Set the pin heads just below the surface of the plywood with a nail punch. Disguise the holes left by the nails by smoothing in enough wood filler so that it sits slightly proud. Leave to dry then sand smooth.

6 Nail on some trim to cover the exposed joints between ply and string. This also helps to cover the slots left by the router for the treads and risers when the stairs were built.

👍
tips of the trade

If you plan to wallpaper the plywood panelling, it is a good idea to apply a coat of emulsion paint to the side of the panel that will face the back tread of the stairs prior to fixing. This may seem like an unnecessary job as it will never be seen; however, it will prevent the wood from warping and this in turn ensures the panel remains flat and the wallpaper does not peel.

👍
tips of the trade

When fixing delicate trim use veneer pins instead of panel pins, as they are thinner and less obtrusive and require less filler to disguise the nail heads.

7 Finally, decorate the surface of the finished panelling to match or blend with the existing decoration in the room for a unified look. If applying wallpaper as shown, buy a good quality wallpaper to ensure an adequate bond with the plywood.

UNDERSTAIRS LIGHTING

If the underside of the stairs could do with some additional illumination, one idea is to fit recessed lights. You will need to run the necessary wiring before you fit the panels. Use a jigsaw to cut the hole into the ply panel as instructed by the manufacturer. Installing electrical lighting is a complicated procedure and you must not take chances with electricity – employ a qualified electrician for wiring up the lights and final connection.

Finished with the appropriate decoration, blocking in both conceals the underside of a staircase and incorporates the stairs more into the overall decor of the room or hall.

fitting spandrel panelling – 1

Spandrel panelling is really just another name for the panels that can be fitted to fill in the area below the stairs and create cupboard space. Once common in older houses, it often does not feature in modern properties because of cost considerations. Although this is probably one of the more complex projects featured in the book, you will find the attractive finish and extra storage space created ultimately makes the effort worthwhile.

Before starting on this project it is advisable to clear as far as possible the room of furniture and other items, in order to give yourself enough space to work comfortably. Also remove any floor covering in the vicinity and check and repair the subfloor, if necessary before starting on the panelling. Use planed timber for all the studwork to give a neater appearance on the inside of the cupboard, and it should be high quality, since wood that is warped or twisted makes the job of getting the panel to lay flat impossible.

tools for the job

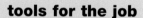

tape measure & pencil

plumb bob & line

fine handsaw

cordless drill/driver

pipe, cable & joist detector

spirit level

sliding bevel

claw hammer

small hammer

1 Hold a plumb bob and line against the open string of the staircase and, with the bottom of the bob resting just clear of the floor, mark reference points with a pencil at two or three places along the floor between the newel post and the wall. Join up the marks with a straightedge to form a reference line for the sole plate of the panelling. At the same time, plumb a line up the wall between this sole plate guideline and the outside bottom edge of the string where it bisects the wall.

2 If skirting board is fitted around the back wall of the stairway, as here, it must be removed. Use a fine handsaw to cut the skirting board at the pencil mark you have just made and discard the section from under the stairs. Sometimes you can cut the skirting board in situ by easing it away from the wall. To avoid uneven cuts it is neater and easier to remove the section completely. You may then cut it to length and replace.

3 Decide upon the position of the cupboard door and mark this on the sole plate reference line on the floor. As a guide, an opening about 750mm (2ft 5½in) wide and 250mm (10in) from the wall is about right.

4 Cut sections of timber to form the sole plate, using 50 x 50mm (2 x 2in) timber. Screw these sections to the floor with a cordless drill/driver, leaving a gap for the door at the point marked in step 3. Before screwing into the floor check with a pipe, cable and joist detector that there are no plumbing or electrical services directly underneath. The timbers will need to be set back slightly from the sole plate reference line made in step 1 to allow for the thickness of the cladding. Use a scrap of 9mm (⁷⁄₁₆in) ply or MDF as a guide to ensure a consistent gap.

5 Screw a timber upright to the wall below the open string. Again, keep this back 9mm (⁷⁄₁₆in) from

the reference line. You will need to fix the upright to the wall at three points 450mm (1ft 6in) apart, and fix it at the bottom to the sole plate, screwing at an angle down into the timber.

6 Screw another piece of 50 x 50mm (2 x 2in) timber onto the back of the open string, making sure that the bottom edge is level with the bottom of the string. Onto this last piece of 50 x 50mm (2 x 2in) timber screw on another piece of timber, set back the same 9mm (⁷⁄₁₆in) from the edge of the open string as for the sole plate. This will be the string plate to which the uprights of the framework will be nailed at the top. Check with a spirit level that it is fitted straight.

7 Cut further studs from 50 x 50mm (2 x 2in) timber and nail them at 200mm (8in) centres to the string plate at the top and sole plate at the bottom. Make sure the outside edges of the uprights are aligned with the edge of the string and sole plates. Fit an upright on either side of the door opening, checking with a spirit

level that these are fitted plumb. To draw the correct angle at the top, use a sliding bevel set to the same angle as that between the wall plate and underside of the string.

8 To form the head of the cupboard door frame, measure down 200mm (8in) from the open string on the longest of the studs that comprise either side of the door opening, marking this point with a pencil. Cut and fit a timber to form the head across at this point, checking with the spirit level that it is perfectly level. Fix the head section in place, screwing it to the stud and into the string plate at an angle. As you look at the door opening you should have a rectangle with one corner cut off.

9 Clad the outside of the frame with either 9mm (⁷⁄₁₆in) ply or MDF. Screw it to the framework with 25mm (1in) screws. Use a countersink bit to sink screw heads below the surface. Make sure that vertical joints meet on a stud. Fit a nogging behind any unsupported horizontal joints.

10 Nail 60 x 20mm (2¹⁄₂ x ³⁄₄in) timber around the inside of the opening to form a door frame, keeping it flush with the cladding.

11 Fit skirting, architraves around the door frame, and a cover strip over the joint between string and cladding.

tips of the trade

If there is room, you may find it easier to construct the whole panel flat on the floor, before lifting it up and screwing it into place on the framework.

fitting spandrel panelling – 2 ✏✏✏

With the basic panel below the stairs completed you could just decorate it to match the room. However, adding a door, fielded panelling and other details will create a more finished appearance and you can choose the look which best suits the overall style of your home.

tools for the job

tape measure & pencil
fine handsaw or jigsaw
sharp plane
hammer
G-cramps
nail punch
screwdriver

making the door

1 Check the opening is square and plumb. If the frame is not perfectly upright withdraw the nails and adjust. Take accurate measurements from the door opening and transfer these to thin ply or MDF, 3mm (⅛in) thick is ideal but otherwise use 6mm (⁵⁄₁₆in). Cut around the door outline using a fine handsaw or jigsaw with a fine-toothed blade. Use a sharp plane to create a 3mm (⅛in) gap all round.

2 Check against the door opening that the first panel is a correct fit. Then make an exact copy using the panel as a template. Ensure both panels are identical as discrepancies may impart a twist in the final door.

tips of the trade

When trying for fit, to prevent the door falling through the frame hammer two nails part way in either side of the door, leaving about 10mm (½in) to support the leaning door.

3 Using one of the door panels as a guide, cut 25 x 40mm (1 x 1½in) timber to form an internal framework for a door 50mm (2in) thick. Run the strips for the two long edges first and cut the cross pieces to meet these. If your woodworking skills are good, cut mitres at the top corners. Spread PVA wood glue around the edges of one of the panels and pin the timber sections in place, holding them in position with G-cramps.

4 Spread PVA wood glue around the edge of the timber then pin the second panel into position, again holding the timber in place with G-cramps as you drive the pins in. Set the pin heads below the surface with a nail punch.

5 Fit a hinge on the high side of the door, 150mm (6in) down from the top and 200mm (8in) up from the bottom. Surface-mounted hinges, as shown here, are the easiest to fit. You can use traditional hinges that are let into the edge of the door and frame, but these are harder to fit and require a greater degree of skill.

6 Attach a magnetic latch at the inside top edge of the door to retain it in the closed position. Then fix your chosen door handle no more than 1m (3ft) from the floor and 100mm (4in) in from the opening edge.

adding trim

Adding trim will take some of the boxiness out of what might otherwise be a rather bland, flat panel. Correctly executed and tastefully applied details can enhance your work. Try to pick up from existing details and decor in the room or hallway where the spandrel panelling is located. Matching skirting boards or base moulding along the bottom of the panel will tie everything together. Similarly, you may choose to match up nearby architraves and use this to frame your doors.

1 One option to break up the expanse of flat panels is to add some faux fielded panels. First cut some 6mm (⁵⁄₁₆in) thick MDF 100mm (4in) smaller all round than the overall size of the door and panels. Plane a small bevel all around the edge before gluing and pinning it into position.

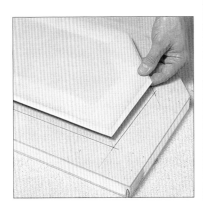

2 To give the appearance of fielded panels, cut some pieces of small bolection moulding to size, then glue and pin them so that they just cover the edge of the panel fitted in step 1. Be careful cutting the mitres at the corners, as they will show up badly if poorly executed. Finally, check the finished door fits into the opening, planing the edges if required, then decorate the door as desired and screw it into position.

UNDERSTAIRS STORAGE

Many DIY stores stock metal shelving systems that are both lightweight and sturdy. These systems are ideal for areas like the underside of stairs since they can be easily adapted as storage needs change. Stores also offer a great variety of wooden shelving, but these are often quite expensive and with very little effort you can create your own at less than half the cost. If you intend to install coat racks or shelving, do this prior to hanging the door so you do not block access.

Decorated to match the surrounding area, spandrel panelling will neaten the look of a staircase and can provide additional storage space if fitted with a door opening.

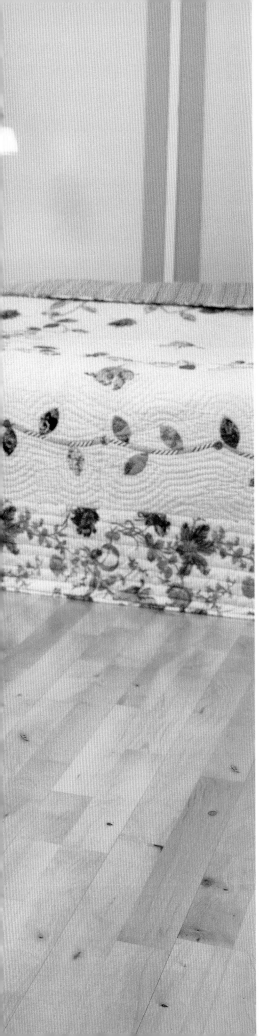

repairing floors & stairs

Every home, whatever its age, will need some degree of regular maintenance – the amount will usually depend on how well and how often repairs were carried out in the past. It is well worth taking your time to ensure the job is done effectively, as there is nothing more irritating than having to carry out the same repair for a second time just a few months later. Carrying out repairs will in itself breathe new life into older floors and stairs, but if you also wish to alter the look then this chapter offers several easy renovation ideas.

Old floorboards can be made to look good as new by replacing any damaged boards and stripping and varnishing the wood surface.

recognizing problems with floors & stairs

A house is probably the biggest investment that you will ever make so it pays to look after it. Major repairs are always more costly than catching a problem before it goes too far – as the saying goes, an ounce of prevention is worth a pound of cure. Cracks, damp and squeaking stairs are all things that should be investigated immediately. If caught early enough then repairs are often straightforward, but when ignored they can lead to structural failure.

problems with floors

cracks

Most cracks in the plaster of a room, especially in newer homes, will be due to the natural settlement of materials or, in older houses, due to plaster that has been poorly mixed and applied. Such cracks often appear at the corners of the room or around door frames and should be no larger than hairline. Some cracks, however, especially ceiling cracks, are caused by slight movement in the floorboards rather than general settlement or poor plastering. These are usually no cause for alarm and may simply be patched, as a certain amount of seasonal movement is normal in solid timber floors. If the house is new, floor movement can probably be attributed to natural shrinkage once the property starts to dry out and the moisture content of the timber is reduced. In older properties, however, ceiling cracks accompanied by springy flooring in the room above may signal rotten joists or boards that have come loose of joists due to rusted nails. Persistent cracks under skirting may also indicate floor problems or even subsidence, and cracks in subfloors made from manufactured boards are generally indicative of more serious problems. If you cannot easily find the root cause of a crack or it continues to widen, this may indicate serious structural problems and you should seek professional advice.

damp

Wet and damp skirting boards are a sure sign of rising moisture in the fabric of the wall, which could be caused by a bridged or missing damp-proof course. Such damp is far more noticeable on walls facing the prevailing wind, especially after heavy rain when moisture is driven through the wall. If the wall is noticeably damp on these occasions it may be the joists are absorbing water. If this is allied to blocked air bricks and poor ventilation in the floor space, rot could soon follow. On upper floors a damp spot in the centre of the ceiling is a good indicator of a leaking pipe. Although most damage is likely to be to the ceiling itself, moisture may also be seeping into the joist timbers. Houses built after 1920 are less prone to damp since their cavity wall structure is designed to channel any water that penetrates the outer wall down its inner face to ground level.

problems with floorboards

Gaps between floorboards are most often caused by timber shrinkage. Insert wider boards or lift all the boards, close up the gaps and re-lay the floor. Alternatively, insert small stealers coated with glue to seal gaps. If a board is badly split then remove and replace, but if the split is minor simply apply extra fixings to prevent

further movement. If a floorboard has sprung up, then the fixing has failed or is missing and the problem can be sorted with new fixings.

EMPLOYING A SURVEYOR

Surveyors do not exist merely to assess properties when they are about to be bought or sold, but may also be contacted to examine suspected problems in your current home and offer advice on how to treat them. The services of suitably qualified surveyors are often quite expensive, but they will be able to take a professional look at the structure of your house, carry out specialist tests and provide you with a written report on the condition of your property – much as a doctor might give you a health check. If you do choose to employ surveyors, make sure that they are members of the Royal Institute of Chartered Surveyors, who will be able to supply you with a list of members in your area.

safety advice

Floors and stairs are major structural elements in a house and are often the site of domestic accidents and injuries. If you notice sudden changes or are at all concerned seek professional advice from a surveyor or structural engineer.

stairs

Internal stresses in the timber can cause a tread to split. If the split is bad then remove and replace the tread, otherwise patch from below or inject epoxy resin into the gap. Squeaking stairs are most often caused by loose or missing glue blocks and wedges below stairs. Investigate the cause from below and renew or replace any missing components. Alternatively, fixing a strengthening timber between the internal joint of tread and riser will often cure the problem. Broken nosing is usually just caused by general wear and tear with no structural ramifications. Simply cut off the damaged area and let in a new section of timber to match the original. Damage to staircase risers is relatively rare as these do not get wear in the same way that treads do. If a riser has split or become loose then there may be something seriously wrong with the overall structure of the stairs. If further investigation indicates no other damage, the split riser can be fixed in the same way as a split tread.

strings

If gaps start to form between the string and the wall, the fixings holding the stairs back to the wall may have failed. To replace these fixings, drill through the string and use a suitable screw and wall plug to pull the string tight to the wall. A gap in the joint between string and tread usually indicates a failed wedge. Replace the wedge from under the stairs, making sure it is coated with glue.

balustrade

Open joints between a handrail and the newel post are often caused by glue failure in the joint or a dowel through the joint may have failed. Drill out the old dowel, squirt in some wood glue and replace with a new dowel. Newel posts on older stairs are held in place by a wedged mortise and tenon joint that goes through to the joists below the floor. It is common for the wedge in this joint to fall out. To cure the problem, remove a section of floorboard adjacent to the newel and replace the missing wedge. Loose, broken and missing spindles are usually caused by broken joints at the top and bottom. Clean off the old glue and recoat the joint with new adhesive, taping the spindle into position until the glue sets.

identifying the problem

You should inspect the state of floors and stairs in your home on a regular basis, perhaps every six months or so. Such inspections are best made when the floor coverings have been removed and the subfloor and stair structure is exposed. It can also be helpful if another person slowly walks up and down the stairs and across the floor while you listen for creaks.

handrail/newel post joint coming apart

tread/riser joint coming apart

loose spindle

gap between string and wall

missing spindle

gap due to broken or missing wedge

broken spindle

split riser

broken nosing

large gap between boards

floorboard sprung up

split board

dealing with infestation & rot

A house is under constant threat from infestation and rot, and even in the best maintained homes such pests can sometimes turn up. Being able to identify which pest has caused the damage, how they have been able to flourish and what effective treatment can be used to eradicate them is essential. Some infestations are more a nuisance than a danger to structures, but others have the ability to destroy your home if left unchecked.

wood-boring insects

Over half of all homes suffer some sort of infestation from wood-boring beetles. It is not the beetles themselves that do the damage but their larvae, which bury into the wood creating elaborate labyrinthine tunnels. The best way to treat the problem is to treat the timbers with a woodworm solution. If you are at all unsure then professional help should be sought.

wet & dry rot

Dry rot thrives in warm and stagnant areas caused, for example, by dripping pipes under a bath or blocked air bricks that prevent the air circulating under a floor. Once dry rot has taken hold it can attack perfectly good timber and can even penetrate walls. At the centre of dry rot is a large fruiting body, white in appearance, from which long, spindly white/grey strands radiate. In the right conditions dry rot can spread at an alarming rate, quickly destroying hitherto healthy timber. If you find dry rot when working on the floor, all the infected timber must be removed and burnt to prevent the spread of the disease.

Wet rot is far less serious and does not have the capacity to spread as quickly as dry rot. Wet rot only occurs in wood with a high moisture content – the rot will cease to spread once moisture levels are lowered.

TYPE	SYMPTOMS	CAUSES	TREATMENT	TELLTALE SIGNS
Furniture beetle A brown beetle no more than 3mm (⅛in) in length. ▼	Destruction of the timber caused by the grubs boring through the interior of a section of timber.	Beetles lay small lemon-shaped eggs in cracks and crevices, which then hatch. Woodworm can be introduced into the home by bringing in old furniture that is already infested. Most active in the early summer, it may enter your home at this time looking for a suitable nesting site.	Spraying or brushing the surface of the infected timbers to kill the grubs and eggs. If the outbreak is serious then hire a specialist contractor.	Flight holes of about 1.5mm (¹⁄₁₆in) in diameter and traces of what looks like very fine sawdust on the timber surface.
Death-watch beetle Brown beetle often with white spots about 5mm (¼in) in length. The grubs are white and about the same length when fully grown. ▼	Destruction of the timber caused by the grubs boring through the interior of a section of timber. Much more destructive than the more common furniture beetle.	Beetles lay eggs in cracks and crevices, which then hatch. Deathwatch beetle favours timber that is already well matured and oak is a favourite habitat – it rarely attacks softwood.	Spraying or brushing the surface of the infected timbers to kill the grubs and eggs. If the outbreak is serious then hire a specialist contractor. You must also notify the local authority.	The grubs cause great destruction with innumerable tunnels about 3mm (⅛in) in diameter, converting the timber to dust in the process.

TYPE	SYMPTOMS	CAUSES	TREATMENT	TELLTALE SIGNS
Powder-post beetle Brown to black beetle about 5mm (¼in) in length. The grubs are white and about the same length fully grown. ▼	Destruction of the timber caused by the grubs boring through the interior of a section of timber. Unlikely to attack mature timber found in buildings, more likely to infect timber while stacked at the timber yard pending transportation.	Bad conditioning of timber or using timber that has a high proportion of sapwood (the wood immediately below the bark).	Treatment is as for other forms of woodworm, using a suitable brush or spray treatment.	Holes of about 2mm (¹⁄₁₆in) in diameter in the surface of the timber. Grubs do not burrow to the same depth as death-watch or furniture beetle, so the whole surface of the timber may fall away when touched, exposing the holes.
Dry rot Consists of minute silky threads covering the surface of the timber in early stages. If conditions are right this will change to what looks like cotton wool balls. In very advanced stages this will further develop into dark red sponge-like bodies. ▼	Musty smell that does not go away. Often working out of sight below flooring and carpets in damp areas, the strands will spread to infect perfectly sound wood. Ultimately leads to total breakdown of joists and floorboards.	Damp stagnant air with poor ventilation. Blocking up air bricks and under-floor vents. Leaking pipes and waste systems below flooring also promote ideal conditions for dry rot to thrive.	Curing the condition that caused the outbreak. Removal of the infected timber at least 1m (3ft) beyond in all directions from the last visible signs of the rot or strands. Scorching of brickwork to kill spores in order to prevent reinfection. Specialist treatment is advised.	Often very few, the greatest indication being a musty smell. Visible surface of timber may change colour, followed by the appearance of small mushrooms.
Wet rot Discoloration of the timber surface, with floorboards often turning black in the advanced stages. When the surface of the timber is broken away the interior will be brown and fibrous. ▼	Soft, crumbly wood with no strength and wet to the touch. Bubbling paint on the surface of the timber.	Leaking pipework and rainwater are the main causes. In the case of floor joists it could be where they are in contact with damp brickwork. Also moisture rising up a wall and being soaked into the ends of the flooring due to a bridged damp-proof course.	Fix the source of the problem before replacing any affected timbers. Brush or spray on a timber preservative to both new and remaining wood. Provide adequate ventilation.	Black spots on paintwork and wallpaper near the affected area, which even when cleaned away return after a few days. Damp in the carpet or floor covering. Where floor tiles have been fitted the damp may cause these to lift.

solving problems with older floors ↗

Older floors will inevitably need repairs as ordinary wear and tear over the years takes its toll. Maintenance is usually straightforward and, since older floors are likely to have been laid before the advent of cheap large sheets of manufactured board, problems will tend to be confined to the solid timber floorboards. Most areas that require attention will be easy to spot once any floor covering is removed, and can be dealt with using a few basic tools.

👍 tips of the trade

• **When to inspect** – The ideal time to inspect and correct problems is when the carpet or other floor covering is being replaced. At this time the boards will be completely exposed and can be given a thorough overall investigation.

• **Removing skirting board** – If you are refurbishing the floor, consider removing the skirting boards before you begin work. This makes it far easier to re-lay the floor as you do not have the problem of tucking new floorboards underneath skirting.

✋ safety advice

Wear knee pads when working on a wooden floor to protect your knees from splinters and projecting nails.

fixing loose boards

One of the main reasons for creaking floors is that floorboards have become loose over time.

tools for the job

hammer

nail punch

Nail down any loose boards using losthead nails, which are specially designed for flooring. Set any heads below the surface with a nail punch.

closing up gaps

Over time floorboards will shrink so that gaps begin to appear between them. Gaps will make carpets more dirty and cause a room to feel colder as draughts blow up the gaps into the living area. There are two methods for sealing up these gaps – either the gaps are filled or the entire floor is taken out and laid again.

tools for the job

tape measure & pencil

handsaw

hammer

floorboard jack

filling the gaps

Regular gaps between floorboards can be filled with a strip of wood. Cut a strip the width of the gap and as thick as the adjacent board, coat it with glue on both edges then tap it into the space with a hammer.

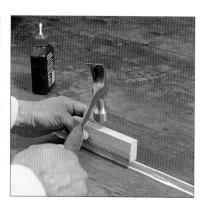

re-laying the floor

Another option is to lift and re-lay all the floorboards in the room. Fit the first board tight to the wall and, using a floorboard jack, butt each one up against its neighbour as it is fitted. Fit new boards into any remaining gaps.

👍 tips of the trade

Tattered edges will often prevent nails from properly securing the boards. By ripping a strip off either side, though this narrows the boards, you will gain fresh edges to ensure a secure fixing.

laying hardboard

Laying sheets of manufactured board, in this case hardboard, over existing floorboards is a worthwhile project. It instantly seals any small gaps, preventing dirt and draughts from coming up from below, and provides a smooth floor over which to lay carpet or other flooring. However, laying hardboard should not been seen as a cure-all. Although it will successfully cover minor flaws and undulations in the existing floorboards, it is essential that any missing floorboards are replaced and any broken or damaged boards are repaired before the hardboard is laid on top.

tips of the trade

- **Preparing the hardboard**
Before being fitted hardboards need to be sprinkled with water to remove internal stresses. This prevents the hardboard from bubbling or puckering up later, which could otherwise damage the floor covering laid on top.

- **Rough side up** – Laying hardboard with the rough side uppermost will provide more grip for the carpet underlay and prevents it slipping. If the floor covering is to be stuck down the rough surface also helps to provide a key for the glue.

tools for the job

tape measure & pencil
staple gun
safety glasses
hammer
coping saw
handsaw

1 Start in one corner of the room and lay a sheet of hardboard smooth side down. The traditional method for laying hardboard is with panel pins to fit it to the floor at 100mm (4in) centres in every direction. To reduce the chance of ripples forming nail from the centre of the sheet towards the edges.

2 Work out from the first sheet, butting the edges of adjacent sheets against it. However, to avoid a ridge forming you must leave a small gap of approximately 3mm ($^3/_{16}$in) between each sheet. If the room is particularly small or you are working alone, you may find that whole sheets of hardboard are difficult to handle and need to cut them down to a more manageable size. If you are using smaller sheets note that you will still need to leave a 3mm ($^3/_{16}$in) gap all around the edge.

3 To fit the hardboard around such obstacles as radiator pipes, first cut out a 100 x 100mm (4 x 4in) piece in the adjacent sheet so that it clears the pipe. Then make a paper template that fits neatly into this cut out and around the pipe. Trace the shape onto an offcut of hardboard before cutting it out and pinning it into place.

LAYING WITH STAPLES

An alternative and quicker method of laying hardboard is with a heavy-duty staple gun. If you are using a staple gun make sure you protect your eyes with protective goggles or safety glasses, as a misfired staple can fly up at your face at high speed and do serious damage.

TURNING OVER THE FLOOR

One way of rejuvenating an old floor without going to the expense of buying all new floorboards is to lift the existing boards and turn them over. Often the underside has no sign of the wear and tear you might find on the original side. If the floorboards are very damaged this may not work, but often it is worth investigating as a cost saving measure.

FURTHER PROBLEMS

While you are inspecting and repairing the floorboards it is a good idea to investigate the supporting structure of the floor at the same time. Make sure that all joists, strutting and associated woodwork are sound – repair and replace if necessary.

replacing a section of floorboard ⚒

Just about every house will include an area of wooden flooring, whether in the form of timber floorboards or manufactured boards such as chipboard. Wooden floors generally require little in the way of maintenance, but there are times when individual boards need attention. For example, you may need to replace a timber floorboard that has split or been irreparably damaged on its surface, or if access is required to pipes underneath the floor then boards may need to be cut out and new ones fitted. Replacing a section of flooring is a relatively straightforward task.

floors & stairs

206

timber floorboards

The procedure for replacing timber floorboards described below applies to boards fitted with a tongue and groove mechanism. These are slightly more difficult to remove and some of the stages mentioned can be omitted if the floor is constructed from straight-edged boards, which makes the job slightly less taxing. In some rooms, especially those that are fairly small, the boards tuck under the skirting along the edges of the room with no intermediate joints. In this case, simply levering up the board in the centre of the room and slipping a scrap of timber underneath will allow you to cut it in half. If you are at all unsure about a section of floorboard then it is wise to replace the whole length.

tools for the job

pipe, joist & cable detector
circular saw
bolster chisel (wide)
square
fine-toothed handsaw
tape measure & pencil
panel saw
cordless drill/driver or hammer

1 Here the board to be replaced is split down the middle. It is unlikely to be split along its entire length, so first inspect the damage to assess whether you can just replace a small section of the board.

2 Identify joist positions, either with the use of a pipe, joist and cable detector or by following the line of nails. Mark with a pencil if any run below the board to be replaced. Locate the joist just beyond the end of the split and mark this too. For safety reasons it is also vital to find out whether any pipes or electric cables run under the boards before cutting.

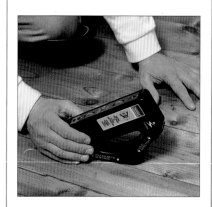

3 Set a circular saw so that it will cut to a depth of approximately 15mm (⅝in). Run the blade along both sides of the split board to cut through the tongues. If the floor has been constructed using square-edged boards then this step can be omitted.

safety advice

Circular saws are safe if used correctly, but not everyone is comfortable with them. If you are unsure, a floorboard saw (a special handsaw with a curved blade) may be used instead.

4 Insert a wide bolster chisel into the cut side and gently lever up the board. Start near the joint and work your way along the board. Hold up the board with a scrap of timber and draw a line across with a square, ensuring any joint will be over the centreline of the joist. Cut this line with a fine-toothed handsaw.

5 Measure and cut a new section of floorboard to fit neatly into the space left by the broken section. If you are using tongue and groove board you will need to cut off the tongue with a panel saw before fitting.

6 Once the new board has been cut to a precise fit, either nail or screw it in position. You may prefer to use screws if access to the underfloor area is likely to be required at some future date.

chipboard floors

It is highly unlikely that a section of chipboard floor will split in the same way that a timber floorboard might, but you may still encounter situations where a section will need to be replaced. For example, you might have to replace one or more boards after cutting through to gain access to the underfloor services, or you might need to cut out and replace boards that have become unsound due to moisture damage.

1 Set a circular saw to an 18mm (³⁄₄in) depth of cut and saw all around the edge of the board to remove the tongue. Be careful not to cut into adjacent boards.

2 Gently lever up the board using wide bolster chisels. Do not lever in just one position but work all around the perimeter. The nails should come up with the board, otherwise pull them out with a claw hammer.

3 Install noggings between joists to support any board edges that do not join on a joist.

4 Saw off the tongues of the replacement board with a panel saw, so that it will fit into the gap.

5 Finally, fit the new board into the hole and fix it in position. Nails can be used as fixings but it is better to screw the board in place.

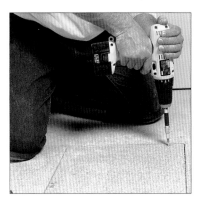

tips of the trade

A screwed board will allow easier access to underfloor services in the future, and screwing avoids the heavy vibrations of hammering, which can cause cracks in the ceiling below.

fitting herringbone struts //

Herringbone struts provide extra stiffness to upper floors in houses. Made from either wood or metal, they serve several purposes. They stop a floor from twisting out of shape, damp down vibration and keep the joists uniformly spaced apart from one another. It is important to fit them properly otherwise they will cause the floor to squeak.

Unless you are constructing an entirely new suspended floor it is unlikely that you will have to completely strut out the floor with herringbone. More often than not you will find that there are just one or two struts loose or missing when the floorboards are lifted. For new floors, fitting herringbone struts is a relatively straightforward job which has been made simpler in recent years with the introduction of ready-made metal struts. Herringbone struts should be fitted to joists prior to the installation of floors or ceilings

safety advice

When fitting herringbone struts there will not be any existing flooring in place. To make the job more safe and easy, lay scaffold boards or temporary flooring across the joists to create a working platform.

wooden struts

tools for the job

tape measure & pencil

chalk lines

pinch rod

sliding bevel

mitresaw

cordless drill/driver

hammer

1 Measure the length of the joists at each end of the room and divide this into three. Snap a chalk line at both points across the bottom of all the joists.

2 Make a pinch rod from two thin strips of wood about 15 x 3mm ($^5/_8$ x $^3/_{16}$in) thick and about 400mm (1ft 4in) long. Use the pinch rod to measure the distance between the top of one joist and bottom of the next joist. Wrap masking tape around the pinch rod to hold it at this setting.

3 Hold the pinch rod diagonally across a piece of 50 x 25mm (2 x 1in) timber and transfer the measurement by marking with a pencil at either end. Set a sliding bevel to a shallow angle and use this to mark the same bevel across the face of the timber at both ends of what will be the strut. Ensure the measurements are correct at this stage as this will act as a template for future struts.

4 After checking for fit, cut the struts using a mitresaw to achieve the bevel – you will need four struts for each joist. Since all bevels are the same, the cut edge of one forms the end cut on the next strut.

tips of the trade

If you have many struts to cut and install it might be cost- and time-effective to hire an electric chop saw. This tool will help you to do the job in half the time.

5 Position the struts where the chalk lines cross each joist and skew nail them between the joists, first drilling pilot holes with the aid of a cordless drill. Leave a small gap between each strut to prevent any squeaking as the floor moves.

tips of the trade

The biggest mistake you can make when installing herringbone struts is to have them touch at the crossing points. This can cause annoying squeaks to develop once the floor is completed. To avoid this problem use a scrap of ply as a guide to maintain an even gap between struts when fixing them into position.

metal struts

Metal struts have now largely taken the place of wooden struts in most new construction. Requiring no cutting, they are faster to fit and can be bought to suit the spacing of floor joists which are typically at 400mm (1ft 4in) 450mm (1ft 6in) or 600mm (2ft) centres.

tools for the job

hammer

chalk line

1 Set out two chalk lines as described above. Starting at one end of the room, nail through the hole in the top of each strut, using glavanized nails to fix them securely to each joist. Work your way along the length of the room.

2 Working from the room below bend the struts until they touch the opposite joist. Nail these in position, again with galvanized nails, taking care to maintain a small gap where the struts criss-cross to avoid any possible squeaking.

tips of the trade

Use a set of long-nosed pliers to hold the nails as you get them started into the joist. This will help to protect fingers from accidental hammer blows.

Herringbone struts provide additional support to joists. They can be constructed from either wood or metal, but metal struts are the easiest to fit.

renovating a woodblock floor

Solid woodblock flooring is seldom fitted in houses today as the cost is often prohibitive, but it is relatively common in larger older houses. Resilient and hardwearing when properly laid, it will last for several lifetimes. Major repair is usually not required, but if it is then this really is a specialist repair best left to the experts. Having said that, it is not beyond the competent DIY enthusiast to replace a few wood blocks or refinish a badly worn floor.

sanding

To sand a woodblock floor effectively you will need to hire specialist machines from tool hire shops. Start with a coarse paper on the sander and finish with a finer grade to remove scratches, after vacuuming the floor surface. A special edging sander is needed to reach those parts that cannot be sanded with the large machine. Sanding can be dirty work and you will almost certainly create a lot of dust. Before you start, remove all furniture and ensure that the floor is clear. Tape up any doors to the rest of the house and open a window to ensure good ventilation. Wear a good quality dust mask and ear defenders when using the sanding machines.

tips of the trade

Any protruding nails or staples will tear the sanding sheets, which are expensive to replace and hire shops often charge extra for the number of sheets used. Examine the entire floor and pull out or punch in anything that could snag on the sanding drum.

sanding procedure

Always turn on the machine tilted back so the drum is off the floor surface. Start at one wall and sand across the room with overlapping passes. If you allow the sander to remain in one spot too long it will cut grooves into the floor.

1 Use floor sander at 45° angle to direction of floorboards, making sweeps across the whole floor.

2 Repeat 45° angle sweep with floor sander in opposite direction.

3 Sand across entire floor surface following direction of floorboards and grain.

4 Use an edging sander to finish the perimeter of the room next to the skirting or wall surface.

5 Use a special corner sander to get tight into corners.

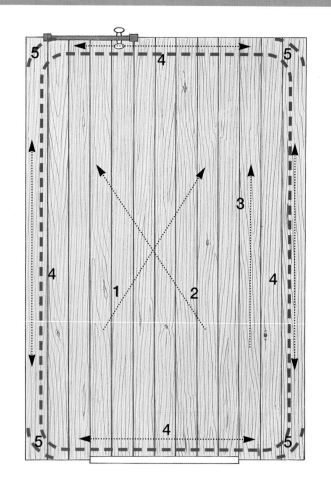

refitting blocks

Blocks are usually laid onto a sand or cement screed with black pitch, but to replace just a few blocks use a ready-mixed latex compound. If blocks are missing your local joinery manufacturer can make replacements, or you might find them in a reclamation yard.

tools for the job

old chisel

paint scraper

old paintbrush

electric sander

1 Remove the loose blocks and scrape off the old pitch from the back of the blocks with an old wood or bolster chisel. Do not use heat as this may set the pitch alight.

2 Spread a layer of latex adhesive into the gap in the floor with a paint scraper, keeping it to a thickness of approximately 4mm (³/₁₆in).

3 Spread a thin layer of latex on the back of the blocks with an old paintbrush, then immediately lay the blocks onto the wet latex in the floor, following the original pattern of the surrounding blocks. In some cases there will be a tendency for the wood blocks to float on top of the adhesive layer.

4 Take a sheet of polythene and sandwich it between the floor and an offcut of ply, which should be slightly larger than the area of the floor being repaired. Then place several bricks on top of the ply to weigh down the blocks until the adhesive has set.

5 When the adhesive has set, fill any small cracks with a two-part wood filler. Finally, sand the blocks to the same level as the rest of the floor, before finishing to match.

With careful finishing to ensure the refitted blocks match the colour of those surrounding them, the woodblock floor will look as good as new.

painting & varnishing floors ↗↗

When the budget for home improvement is tight there can be a tendency to leave the floor until you are better able to afford your ideal floor covering. A good way to give a room a finished feel without spending a fortune is by painting or varnishing the floor. As long as the floor is in a reasonable condition, you will be surprised how striking this can look for little cost. If you have a large expanse then including one or two rugs into the finished scheme can soften the effect.

tools for the job

hammer & nail punch

filling knife

electric floor sander

vacuum cleaner

broom

tack rag

paint roller

paintbrushes

tips of the trade

Almost all fillers change colour when varnish is applied, so it is best to choose a shade slightly lighter than the surrounding timber. Test a discreet section before tackling the whole floor.

5 Close all windows and doors, then go over the surface with a tack rag to pick up any remaining dirt that might otherwise spoil the finish.

varnishing

1 Go over the floor and punch raised nails below the surface. If the floor is screwed down ensure the screws are well below the surface. You may have to withdraw all or some of the screws and recountersink the holes if the heads are any less than 2mm (⅛in) below the surface.

3 Once the filler has dried, sand the floor with electrical sanders, cleaning off the excess filler as you go. Follow the method for sanding a wooden floor described on page 210.

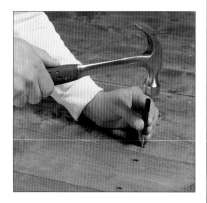

2 Use a filling knife and a flexible filler to cover all nail and screw heads. If the floor is to be painted the filler colour will not matter. If you are varnishing, select a tone that blends in with the surrounding flooring.

4 Vacuum the floor with an industrial cleaner. Use a soft clean broom to dislodge any stubborn dirt and then vacuum once more.

6 Thin down the first coat of varnish by adding about 30% by volume of the recommended thinners. Apply the varnish using a roller with an extension arm. Work back from the main source of light so that you can see those areas that you have missed.

safety advice

Paint and thinners can be dangerous if ingested so never leave opened cans unattended near children.

7 Let the first coat harden, then apply the next coat without thinning the varnish. Again, use a paint roller, but do keep a paintbrush handy so that you can cut in around the edge of the room and apply varnish to those areas you are unable to reach with the roller. Before you apply the third and final coat, sand any rough spots using fine abrasive paper and wipe up any dust with a clean tack rag. Water-based varnishes in particular will raise the grain to quite an extent, so this light sanding will pay dividends in the final finish.

painting

There are special hardwearing paints designed for floors in garages and workshops. Although only available in a limited range of colours, they do provide excellent coverage and can be used in kitchens, bathrooms and play areas. Emulsion paints are quick drying and will last several years provided they are over-coated with a suitable varnish.

stencilling

A coloured base can be livened up by painting or stencilling a border around the room. Either buy ready-made stencils or cut your own from special stencil paper. Tape the stencil to the floor with masking tape, then stipple a little paint with a stencil brush. Remove the stencil immediately.

applying kiln-dried sand

A simple yet highly effective technique for making the floor surface more safe in bathrooms and kitchens is to sprinkle a little kiln-dried sand onto wet paint to create a non-slip finish. When the paint has dried, sweep up the excess sand and seal the surface with a coat of varnish.

Dramatic decorative effects are possible when painting a floor. Colourful painted floorboards such as these will make any room feel warmer and brighter.

solving problems with older stairs

Stairs need very little in the way of maintenance and a new staircase should function for years without any major problems. Fortunately, when problems do occur they tend to be relatively minor and simple to resolve, and basic maintenance is usually easy to accomplish. A squeaking stair or wobbly handrail is often more of an irritation than a danger, but small problems such as these should be fixed promptly for if left untreated more extensive repairs will be required.

Almost all problems related to stairs can be fixed with a basic set of tools – the hardest part is often finding the problem. Squeaking stairs are caused by two pieces of timber rubbing against each other, so if a tread makes a noise when you step on it then it is almost certainly due to the tread being split or a loose wedge on the underside. When there are several problems with a staircase, try to work systematically, rectifying each one before moving onto the next.

tips of the trade

Get a helper to walk up and down the stairs while you carefully watch and listen for trouble spots.

tools for the job

tape measure & pencil

panel saw

cordless drill/driver

wooden or plastic mixing stick

hammer

jigsaw

block plane

rubber mallet

syringe

split treads

1 Split treads are common in older stairs and if the stairs are fitted with carpet a sure sign will be a squeaking tread. They can be easily fixed in two different ways. First remove any floor covering to expose the split.

2 If underside of the tread is accessible a patch can be fitted over the split. Cut a piece of plywood 150mm (6in) wide and as long as will comfortably fit between the strings. Coat the piece with wood glue and screw it in position. Make sure the screws are not too long or they will cut through the face of the tread.

3 Epoxy glue is a good alternative when the only access is from above. Scrape out any dust and dirt from the crack then force epoxy into the joint with a wooden or plastic mixing stick. Allow it to harden overnight then sand flush.

safety advice

Many people are sensitive to the components in epoxy resins. Wear disposable gloves or barrier cream to protect your hands.

tips of the trade

Mix epoxy resin with some sawdust for a stiffer mix to make trowelling into wider joints easier. The glue has quite a runny consistency and this will also prevent it from dripping out.

missing glue blocks

Another major cause of squeaking stairs is missing glue blocks. These triangular blocks reinforce the corner joint between the riser and tread and are fitted to the underside of the staircase. Replace any missing glue blocks by cutting a piece of timber to the correct size. Coat the replacement glue block with wood glue, then knock it into the appropriate channel in the string with a hammer, holding it in position with panel pins until the glue has set.

split or worn nosing

1 To repair a split or worn nosing, use a straightedge to draw a straight line 12mm (9/16in) back from the original line of the front edge. Then cut a 45° splay 10cm (4in) in from each end of the tread down to this line, with a panel saw. Having made these initial cuts, remove the rest of the waste timber using a jigsaw.

2 Cut replacement timber, slightly oversize. Glue this in position, holding it with masking tape until the glue dries. When the glue has set, use a block plane and abrasive paper to replicate the original nosing shape.

loose wedge

A gap between tread and string means a loose wedge. Remove the original wedge or cut a new one. Brush wood glue into the groove and tap home.

wobbly newel

1 To tighten a wobbly newel, measure up 50mm (2in) from the base of the newel. Find the centre line and mark where they meet. Drill a 9mm (7/16in) hole 12mm (9/16in) deep at a 45° angle down to the tread.

2 Continue drilling with a 3mm (1/8in) bit from the centre of this hole down as far as the tread. Then insert a 75mm (2 14/16in) number 8 wood screw into the hole and firmly tighten it up. Shape up and glue a small timber pellet to fit the 12mm (9/16in) hole and cover the screw head.

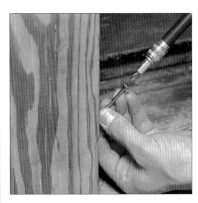

loose baluster

To refix a loose baluster, first detach it from the underside of the handrail by tapping it with a soft mallet and pulling it from the mortise in the tread. Clean off all the old glue and brush on new adhesive before renailing it to the underside of the handrail.

tips of the trade

If the problem requires a repair that involves removing some part of the stair but this cannot be done without extreme difficulty, a good repair can be achieved by squirting epoxy glue into a loose joint with a small syringe.

mending a broken stair tread ⚞

Stairs suffer inevitable wear and tear but they usually remain structurally sound for a very long time. However, if a broken tread is suspected it should be repaired immediately to avoid a potentially serious accident. Replacing a stair tread is an easy enough job for the average DIY enthusiast, but if the fault looks more serious you may need to consult a professional builder.

There are several methods of repairing broken stair treads, but even the simplest will require access to the underside of the stairs. Stairs fitted with spandrel panelling are easy to repair because the underside is readily accessible. For newer stairs that have been blocked in you may have to remove board to gain access and refit it afterwards (see pages 192–3).

safety advice

When working on stairs, tie a ribbon or a bright piece of tape across the top and bottom of the staircase to prevent it being used. A nasty accident could occur if someone were to put their foot through where a tread is missing.

tools for the job

tape measure & pencil

panel saw

cordless drill/driver

hacksaw blade

wood chisel

claw hammer

rubber mallet

padsaw

hammer

quick fix

If the stair tread is split along its length a quick repair is to glue and screw a plywood patch to the underside. Cut this from 9mm (7/16in) ply, making it as large as possible to keep it just clear of glue blocks and wedges.

replacing the tread

Two methods are used to join treads to risers. Some stairs employ a simple butt joint reinforced into the riser to hold the tread secure. The other, more common, approach is for the riser to be tongued or housed into the tread. To check which type you have, try to insert a hacksaw blade between the tread and riser joint. If you cannot work it through then you have the latter type of joint, which must be cut before the tread can be removed.

1 Prise off the moulding fitted under the nosing with a wood chisel. Keep the nosing for refitting later. Pull out any nails left behind.

2 From the underside of the stairs use a chisel and mallet to remove any glue blocks fitted into the corner of the joint between tread and string. Do not try to save these as new ones will have to be fitted later.

3 Drill three or four small holes of about 3mm (1/8in) diameter into the riser and through to the tread joint below the damaged tread – these will enable you to insert the blade of a padsaw. Start making the cut with the padsaw, then when it is long enough use a panel saw to finish off the cut, keeping the blade flat to the underside of the tread. Employ the same procedure to saw through the joint between the tread and the next riser, which you will need to do from

under the stairs. Again, make sure that you keep the saw blade flat on the surface of the stair tread.

4 Chisel out the wedges that hold the tread in place. If your staircase is of the closed string variety, free the tread by giving it a sharp tap with a hammer and block of wood right above and adjacent to the string. With the tread free, drive out to the rear again by tapping the nosing with a block of wood and hammer.

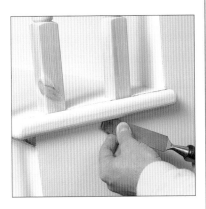

5 If you have an open string staircase the approach is slightly different. Prise off the return moulding on the end of the tread, then remove the balusters by tapping them side ways from the shallow mortises before knocking out the tread from the rear.

6 Cut a replacement tread from timber, using the old tread as a template for the new one. Ensure that the timber has the same dimensions as the existing tread and that the nosing is identical to the original, otherwise it will not fit correctly.

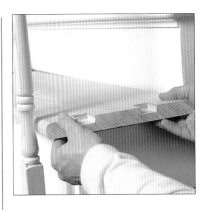

7 Refit the tread following the same procedure for removing it, only in reverse. Cut new wedges and glue blocks, coat these with adhesive, then fit by tapping the wedges firmly home. Finally, replace the balusters and return moulding and Scotia moulding if it was removed earlier.

tips of the trade

If your staircase is old or there is any evidence of infestation or rot, both new and old timber must be treated with a suitable preservative before sealing in the underside of the stairs.

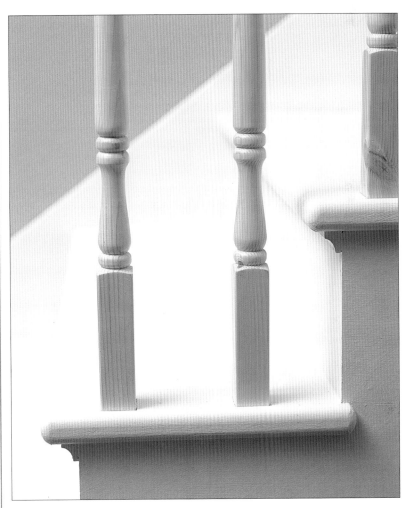

Having made the repair it is a simple matter of returning the new tread to the same finish as the others and the staircase will be good as new.

dealing with squeaking stairs ↗

Irrespective of the quality of their construction, there will inevitably come a time when the treads of a staircase will start to squeak. The main causes of squeaking stairs are simply general wear and tear, coupled with the natural shrinkage and movement of timber, which means that sooner or later almost every staircase made from timber will develop squeaks. In many cases, this is annoying rather than anything to worry over and by spending a little time you should be able to eradicate just about every squeak.

In most cases the best results are obtained if as many of the repairs as possible are made from underneath the stairs. While this is the ideal scenario it is not always a practical option; however many effective smaller repairs can still be carried out from the front. Several different repairs can often be employed to deal with the exact same problem, and most of the options available are demonstrated on these pages.

tools for the job

hammer
cordless drill/driver
saw
screwdriver
wood chisel

👍

tips of the trade

It will help to identify where repairs are needed if someone else walks slowly up and down the stairs whilst you watch and listen to each step in turn. If you have a cupboard under the stairs you may also be able to find open joints by standing inside with the light off to spot any chinks of light filtering in from outside.

loose tread – nailing

One of the simplest of all repairs, which is ideal if you are unable to gain access to under the stairs, is to nail down through the tread into the riser

below. Be careful that the nails do not come through the front of the riser spoiling the appearance. The nails will have better grip if they are inserted in dovetail fashion as shown.

loose tread – screwing

A better method for fixing down a loose tread, again without needing to access under the stairs, is with a row of screws rather than nails. You will first need to drill holes level with the riser just through the surface of the tread and then insert the screws. Use 38mm (1⁷⁄₁₆in) no. 8 screws and make sure that any heads are

countersunk below the surface of the tread. For the ultimate finish use a screw sink and matching plug cutter. The special drill bit drills the correct size of pilot hole for the screw and cuts a straight counter-bore which sits below the surface. Pellets are then cut from matching timber, glued over the screw head and trimmed off flush.

replacing wedges

A gap between the upper surface of the tread and the string indicates a loose or missing wedge. If loose, remove the wedge from under the stairs, clean off the old adhesive, brush on glue and reposition. If missing or damaged cut a new one from hardwood then glue and reposition.

strengthening joints

To strengthen the joint between an open string and tread, cut a block of wood 35mm (1³⁄₈in) square and the width of the tread. Access under the stairs and, at the back of the step in question, screw the wood block into the corner at the joint between tread and string. First coat the block with glue and drill holes for 50mm (2in) no. 8 screws. If you can, get a helper to stand on the tread from above to close up the gap between block and step as you drive the screws home.

Gluing on a section of a quadrant can sometimes reinforce a loose riser joint at the back of the tread. If the stairs are exposed you may want to give each tread the same treatment to match.

You may be able to prise open a joint with a wood chisel and inject adhesive. Clamp the joint until the glue has set. This is effective combined with other repairs, such as replacing glue blocks.

where to insert wedges

Driving in small slip wedges coated with glue is an effective method for tightening joints between tread and riser. Make the wedges about 30mm (1¼in) long tapering from about 3mm (³⁄₁₆in) down to nothing. After the glue has dried use a sharp chisel to trim off the end of any protruding wedges.

BUTT JOINT

small wedge inserted horizontally

small wedge inserted vertically

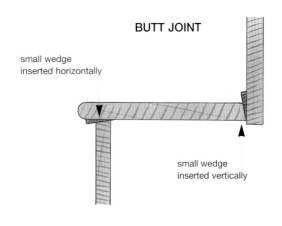

MORTISE & TENON JOINT

small wedge inserted vertically at front

small wedge inserted horizontally

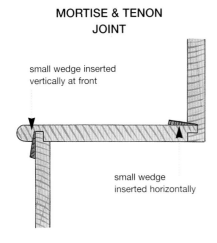

HOUSING JOINT

small wedge inserted vertically at back

small wedge inserted horizontally

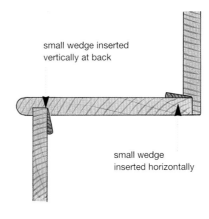

windows & doors

As with any structure in your home, the design and make-up of doors and windows will vary according to a number of factors. The age of your house, decisions taken by previous owners, your own particular preferences regarding appearance, and the specific function of the door or window will all affect the types of doors and windows you have in your home. Before making changes or restoring doors and windows, it is therefore necessary to have some understanding of the different structures which are available and how this relates to your own personal requirements. It is also important to determine how door and window structure relates to the walls they are fitted into, so that when change is implemented, you will have a good understanding of the work that is required to carry out particular tasks.

door types & construction

There is a huge variation in door design, but they all have functions and features in common. Much of the structural variation derives from the materials used. This in turn is related to cost and so, to a certain degree, structure and quality are the variable factors in the design of doors. The examples given here provide a cross-section of door types and help towards understanding the differences in door design.

solid panel doors

Wooden panel doors are very common and manufactured in a wide range of qualities. Softwood varieties are much less expensive than hardwood doors, the latter commonly being used for front doors.

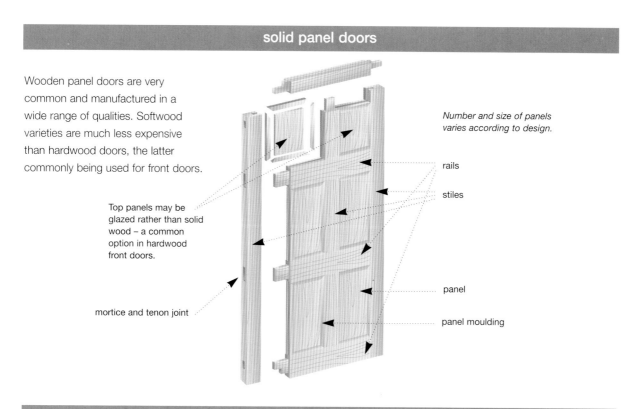

Number and size of panels varies according to design.

Top panels may be glazed rather than solid wood – a common option in hardwood front doors.

mortice and tenon joint

rails

stiles

panel

panel moulding

ledge & brace doors

This more traditional and 'rustic' door design offers a completely different look. The construction is based on a number of different timber sections attached vertically and braced by horizontal and diagonal rails.

Sometimes ledged and braced doors are framed with rails and stiles to make a more substantial structure.

Hinges will be surface mounted on ledges. Those used are not butt hinges but T-hinges (for example, see antique iron hinge page 234).

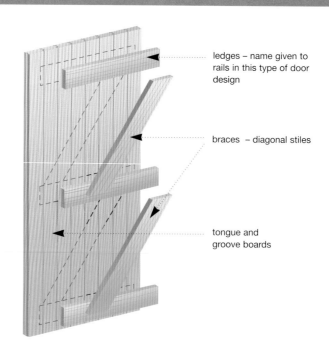

ledges – name given to rails in this type of door design

braces – diagonal stiles

tongue and groove boards

flush door (solid)

Solid flush doors have plain flat surfaces without any sort of panel features. The materials used in their construction do vary, but the framework of the door is usually made from softwood timbers and the actual door surface from ply.

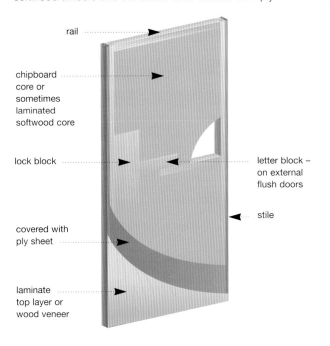

rail

chipboard core or sometimes laminated softwood core

lock block

covered with ply sheet

laminate top layer or wood veneer

letter block – on external flush doors

stile

flush door (hollow)

These cheaper versions of solid flush doors tend only to be used internally and offer an economical option for fitting new doors throughout your home. Though less substantial, they can still be used very effectively.

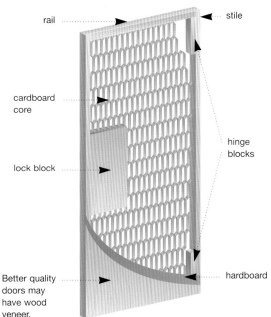

rail

stile

cardboard core

lock block

hinge blocks

Better quality doors may have wood veneer.

hardboard

PVC doors

These doors tend to be used in homes where double glazing and good insulation are a priority. They are moulded and supplied with a fitted frame, ready for installation into a wall aperture. Generally used only as external doors.

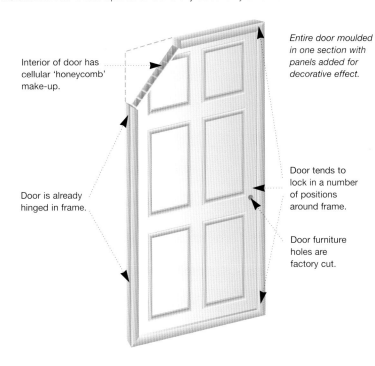

Interior of door has cellular 'honeycomb' make-up.

Door is already hinged in frame.

Entire door moulded in one section with panels added for decorative effect.

Door tends to lock in a number of positions around frame.

Door furniture holes are factory cut.

tips of the trade

Softwood – Most warping problems occur with softwood doors. Therefore, there is a tendency for most exterior wooden doors to be hardwood. Although softwood doors can be used for external use, in these cases be sure to buy good quality decorating materials to ensure that the wood is treated with the best possible exterior decorating system.

safety advice

Fire considerations – Before purchasing a new door it is worth considering what regulations the door conforms to. This is especially important when you are considering its performance in the event of a fire. Some doors are specifically supplied as 'fire doors' because retardant materials are built into their design. It is therefore important to check these issues and consider their relevance to your needs before making a final choice.

how doors are fitted

All doors are fitted into some form of frame or lining, and differences tend to lie in the hinging mechanism and how it works in relation to the frame. Fitting mechanisms also tend to be slightly different for internal and external doors. This factor relates to the differing door structures in each case. The illustrations provided identify many of the factors that differ between doors and show how this affects their relationship to the frame or lining.

internal doors

In this example, a solid wood panel door has been used for illustrative purposes. However, most of the features and mechanisms referred to can be related to other kinds of internal doors. For example, although many flush doors have hollow areas in their structure, the actual door perimeter is solid so that hinges and opening mechanisms may be fitted.

architrave mitred to join at corners

Hinges – most internal doors will have only two hinges. These commonly have three staggered screw holes in each leaf of the hinge.

leading edge of door

hinging edge of door

latch – fitted in leading edge of door

Strike plate accommodates catch when the door is closed.

Lever handle operates latch mechanism.

Door stop provides an edge for the door to close onto.

Door lining – the size chosen should relate to the wall thickness. The vertical sections of the lining are referred to as stiles. The horizontal section is often known as the head.

Architrave (decorative moulding) covers the gap between the edge of the door lining and the wall surface.

External doors tend to have slightly more features than internal doors, as security becomes more of an issue and the door incorporates structures aimed at counteracting the weathering process.

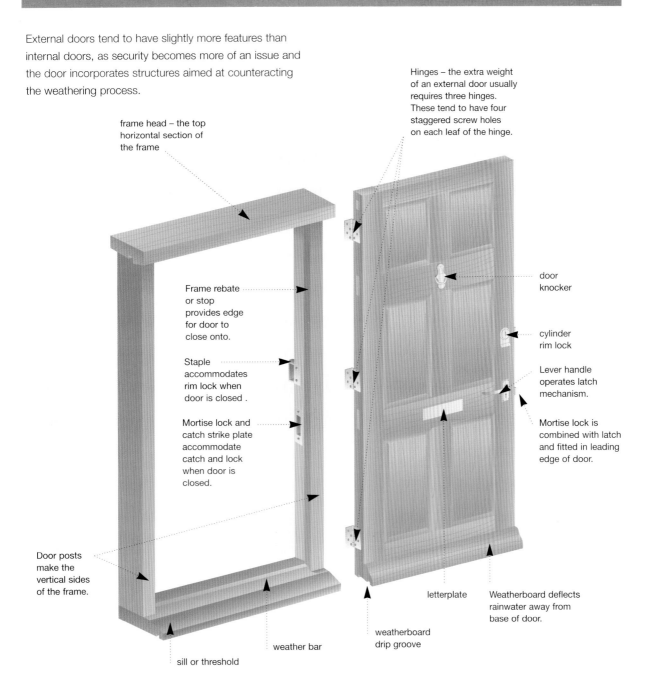

frame head – the top horizontal section of the frame

Hinges – the extra weight of an external door usually requires three hinges. These tend to have four staggered screw holes on each leaf of the hinge.

Frame rebate or stop provides edge for door to close onto.

Staple accommodates rim lock when door is closed .

Mortise lock and catch strike plate accommodate catch and lock when door is closed.

Door posts make the vertical sides of the frame.

door knocker

cylinder rim lock

Lever handle operates latch mechanism.

Mortise lock is combined with latch and fitted in leading edge of door.

letterplate

Weatherboard deflects rainwater away from base of door.

weatherboard drip groove

weather bar

sill or threshold

patio doors

Other common varieties of external door include patio doors. These are sometimes hinged or in many cases are positioned in runners and are therefore opened and closed by a sliding mechanism. In both cases the frame of the door itself is fitted into the wall in a similar manner to any exterior door. In other words, the frame is fixed in the wall aperture and then the doors added. Before purchasing, check that any patio doors you choose have good security features.

garage doors

Garage doors, although completely different in terms of size and style to other forms of external door, do still follow similar fitting principles, with the frame still being fitted before the door is hung. It is at the later stages where variations can occur, because although many garage doors are hinged in a similar position to normal exterior doors, others have automatic opening mechanisms which require completely different fitting techniques.

window types & construction

Much of the variation between window types relates to style and period. There is also a need to consider window function in terms of insulatory properties, and to what extent opening lights and casements are required in the window structure. The examples provided here help to demonstrate many of the variations available and to show the major differences in the construction of each type of window.

casements

The term 'casements' generally refers to windows with hinged opening sections combined with fixed sections. The design within this category can therefore vary considerably.

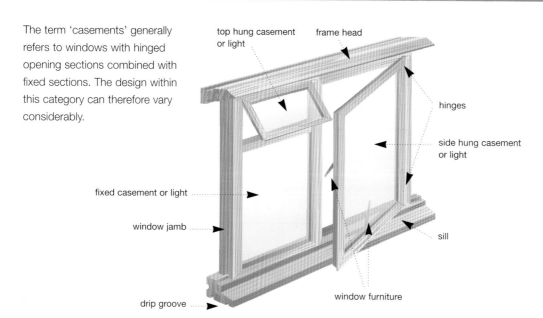

top hung casement or light
frame head
hinges
side hung casement or light
fixed casement or light
window jamb
sill
window furniture
drip groove

sashes

These are traditional-looking windows, which involve the movement of casements or lights in the window frame by means of a cord and pulley mechanism. Modern variations may use chains or have spiral balances.

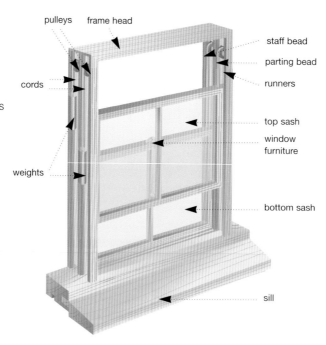

pulleys
frame head
staff bead
parting bead
cords
runners
top sash
window furniture
weights
bottom sash
sill

roof windows

These vary considerably in design from normal windows and are based on the principle that they fit into a pitched roof situation. Tiles are removed and the window is positioned or cut into the roof timbers, with the addition of some extra support.

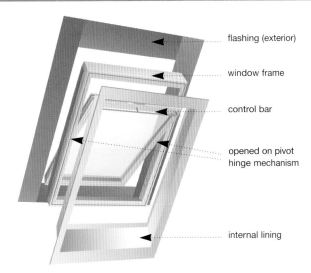

flashing (exterior)

window frame

control bar

opened on pivot hinge mechanism

internal lining

bay windows

Bay windows are large windows which extend out from the front of a house, often positioned on either side of the front door or entrance. Structure tends to take the form of a casement window which has been stuck together in a number of sections.

separate components fixed together to complete shape of window

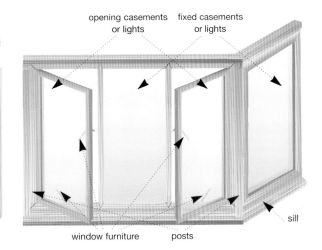

opening casements or lights

fixed casements or lights

window furniture

posts

sill

PVC windows

These windows provide by far the best insulation and can take the form of either casement or sash, depending on the manufacturer's design. As a result of its thermal efficiency and low maintenance requirement, this structure has become increasingly popular for homeowners.

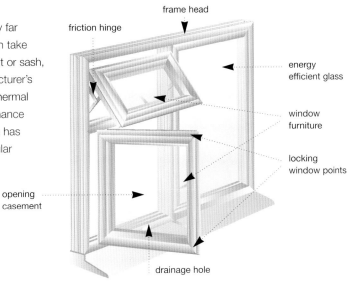

frame head

friction hinge

energy efficient glass

window furniture

locking window points

opening casement

drainage hole

how windows are fitted

Broadly speaking, the main determining factor in the positioning of windows is whether the wall in which they are to be fitted is of a solid or cavity structure. The former situation tends to apply to older houses where solid walls are more prevalent, whereas a cavity wall situation is more likely to be found in modern houses. The general issues for both are outlined here, showing the most important features relevant to the fitting of windows in these two common wall structures.

solid walls

Most new houses are built with a cavity wall structure, but if you need to replace windows in older properties it is necessary to understand how they are fitted so that replacement may be carried out using the correct technique. The main difference here relates to the fact that in older properties, where there is no cavity, it is unlikely that a DPC ('damp-proof course') was used around the window. Therefore replacement merely requires positioning the window in the same place as the previous one was situated. Once the window is in place, the junction between frame and masonry is sealed with mortar and sealant.

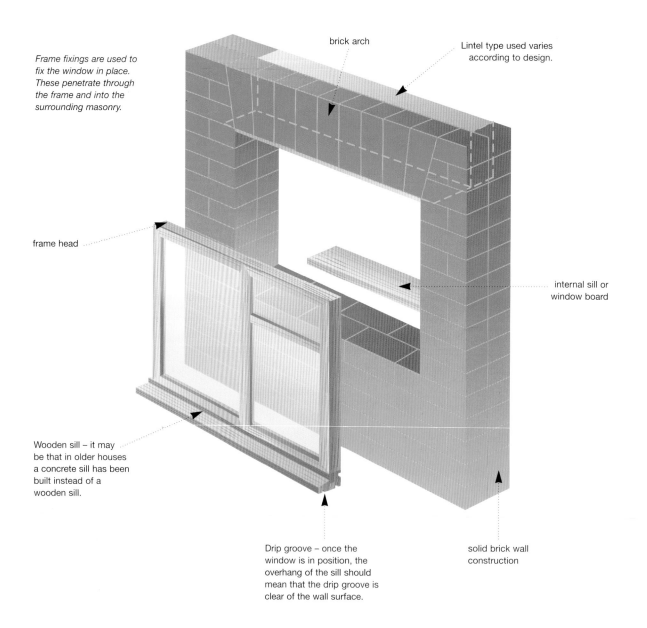

Frame fixings are used to fix the window in place. These penetrate through the frame and into the surrounding masonry.

brick arch

Lintel type used varies according to design.

frame head

internal sill or window board

Wooden sill – it may be that in older houses a concrete sill has been built instead of a wooden sill.

Drip groove – once the window is in position, the overhang of the sill should mean that the drip groove is clear of the wall surface.

solid brick wall construction

With cavity walls, positioning is slightly different and different factors need taking into account when looking at how the window is fixed in position. There will inevitably be slight variations depending on window type but this illustration helps demonstrate the main principles involved. Whether the window is wooden, PVC or metal, similar principles of fixing are used.

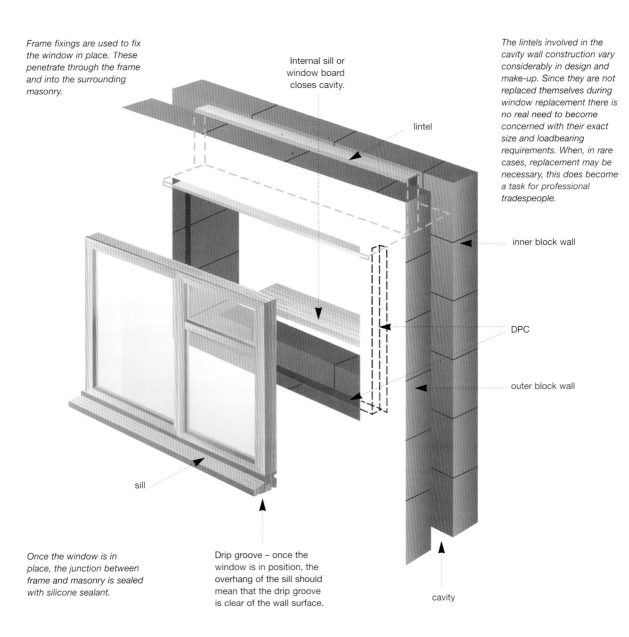

Frame fixings are used to fix the window in place. These penetrate through the frame and into the surrounding masonry.

Internal sill or window board closes cavity.

lintel

The lintels involved in the cavity wall construction vary considerably in design and make-up. Since they are not replaced themselves during window replacement there is no real need to become concerned with their exact size and loadbearing requirements. When, in rare cases, replacement may be necessary, this does become a task for professional tradespeople.

inner block wall

DPC

outer block wall

sill

Once the window is in place, the junction between frame and masonry is sealed with silicone sealant.

Drip groove – once the window is in position, the overhang of the sill should mean that the drip groove is clear of the wall surface.

cavity

bay windows

Although bay windows display many similar characteristics in the way they are fitted, it is important to realise that in some situations the bay window itself does have a weight-supporting and therefore loadbearing part to play in house structure. Simply taking out an old bay window and replacing it with a new one should only be undertaken once the relevant checks have been made. Therefore if you are thinking of replacing a bay window, it is always best to seek some professional advice, thus making sure that you take any measures needed to support the wall structure.

formers

In modern houses it is not uncommon to find an extra part to the framing structure of a window. This extra piece is called a former and is inserted, or more accurately, built into the wall structure to create the correct size of opening for the window to be fitted into.

glass & glazing options

Glass options need a certain amount of consideration as clearly all windows contain some sort of glass, along with many part glazed or totally glazed doors. Modern invention and innovation has allowed for a range of different types of glass to become available, with differing properties of both their finish and function. Decisions therefore need to be made on what type of glass is suitable for your needs in relation to the door or window in question.

clear glass

By far the most common type of glass used in houses is clear, to allow the maximum amount of light into the house and to ensure the view outside is made as clear and open as possible. However, clear glass can in itself be divided into a number of categories which are difficult to pick up instantly with the naked eye.

thickness

Glass thickness is often difficult to spot when it is in position and only when you see the edges of glass panes does it become apparent that there can be considerable variation. In general, thinner clear glass is used for windows and thicker versions are used in doors. This tends to relate to safety considerations, as thinner glass is naturally easier to break and therefore a child mistakenly running into a glass door is less likely to break the glass and cause injury. As well as being thicker, glass used in doors and low-level areas in the home should also be safety glass or toughened, so that if it is broken it shatters into relatively small granular sections which tend not to cause injury compared to the sharper shards common in normal glass breakages.

laminated glass

Laminated glass is in fact two or more panes of glass which have a clear plastic layer fused in between them. This plastic layer binds the panes together as one solid structure. It is available in many different thicknesses and varieties such as clear, patterned and tinted. Laminated glass is difficult to cut and it is therefore advisable to get glass cut to size by your supplier. Although laminated glass is an expensive option, it is an excellent choice in security terms as well as for safety purposes – in glazed doors, for example. It can absorb greater impact than most alternatives and is therefore relatively strong. If it does break under severe impact, the plastic layer holds the glass pieces in position so that it remains in one piece and splinters of glass are not spread all around.

double glazed units

Double glazed units are two panes of glass separated by a void filled with inert gas and then totally sealed off from the surrounding atmosphere. Glass thickness tends to increase according to pane size and so the larger the panes, the thicker the glass. Double glazed units may be fitted into PVC and aluminium framed windows as well as new wooden ones. However, if you wish to change single panes for double glazed units in an existing window, you will need to check that the rebates in the frame are wide enough to accommodate the new unit. If they are too narrow, it will be necessary to fit units with a stepped edge to allow for the difference. Double glazed units significantly improve insulation and can reduce condensation as well as noise pollution.

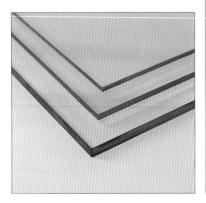

patterned clear glass

Patterned clear glass is often used in a modesty or privacy function. For example, bathroom windows or doors may contain such glass to provide the required privacy whilst still allowing maximum light into the room. With a wide range of designs available, there is considerable room for choice and thus for finding a suitable option for your own personal requirements.

patterned coloured glass

Coloured patterned glass offers a further design option and is often used in conjunction with clear patterned glass when maximum light requirement is not a priority.

lead lights

Lead lights provide a traditional looking window and are often supplied using different coloured glass in varying designs. They can be fitted into appropriately designed casements or are common features in part-glazed front doors. Many companies will provide a 'self design' service allowing you to decide which you require.

etched glass

Etched glass can be considered a more exclusive version of patterned glass and is more commonly used in part-glazed front doors. As well as adding privacy, light is still let in and the availability and attractiveness of designs makes this option a real addition to the overall look of windows or doors.

wired glass

Wired glass has a mesh inside the glass pane to increase its strength, even though the glass itself may still shatter when broken. It is not particularly attractive and tends only to be used in fire doors because of its retardant properties. The wire binds the glass together during a fire and therefore maintains a retardant barrier.

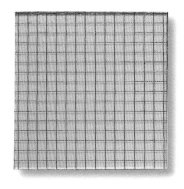

fitting doors

Fitting a door requires a methodical technique that can be adapted to take into account variations in door design and function. The actual principle and method remains similar with all doors but it can be necessary to make variations during installation depending on such factors as whether the door is internal or external and what type of hinges are being used. This chapter looks at many of these variations in door design and use, and demonstrates the most common procedures for fitting not only the door but all the accessories required for its correct functioning. This includes such items as the handles needed for opening and closing, and the relevant security fittings that have become an essential requirement in modern everyday life. Doors are crucial components in how your home functions and therefore close attention to detail will ultimately be rewarding.

Picked up in a salvage yard, this door was trimmed to size and given a makeover with etched-glass panelling.

door furniture & security fittings

Doors clearly need the appropriate fixtures and fittings in order that they can function properly. Although this is a mainly practical concern, there is considerable choice in terms of style and design when it comes to purchasing door furniture. Add to this the relevant security features that may be needed and the options expand further. It is, therefore, necessary to look at some examples of what is available so that you can make the right choices for your particular needs.

handles

Door handles can broadly be placed into two categories – those that have a basic knob design and those that operate in a lever fashion. Nearly all operate the closing and opening mechanism of a door, the latch, by means of a spindle joining the two handles on a door through the latch mechanism. On doors that do not have a latch mechanism, such as cupboard doors which may use a simple spring-loaded ball catch, a spindle is not required and the handles merely act as a secure gripping point to open the door. Shown on the right are some examples of common door handles and the latch sets they may operate in conjunction with. Owing to the fact that there are many different designs available it is possible to combine their style with the relevant security features which may also be used on the door.

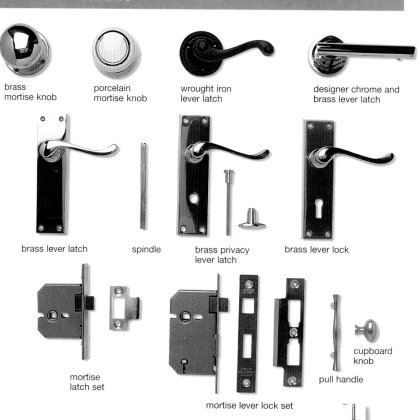

brass mortise knob

porcelain mortise knob

wrought iron lever latch

designer chrome and brass lever latch

brass lever latch

spindle

brass privacy lever latch

brass lever lock

mortise latch set

mortise lever lock set

pull handle

cupboard knob

hinges

Straightforward butt hinges are used as the hinging mechanism on most entrance and cupboard doors in the home. Even though most of the hinge is concealed when the door is shut, there are still some designs that display decorative appeal. Exposed hinges, such as the antique iron one shown, are used most commonly in conjunction with traditional door designs such as a stable door or ledge and brace. Piano hinges are also an option for cupboard doors.

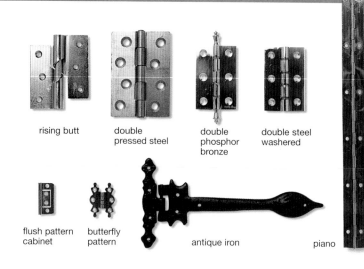

rising butt

double pressed steel

double phosphor bronze

double steel washered

flush pattern cabinet

butterfly pattern

antique iron

piano

Door security features are mainly concerned with external doors, although some items are used in conjunction with rooms of privacy such as bathrooms. Most devices either interact directly with the handle latch mechanism, or are separate to this and used as extra security devices on other areas of the door. Since security is such an important issue in modern society, system designs vary considerably. On the right are examples of the security mechanisms available, catering for many different requirements.

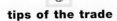

door viewer

door viewer with cover

cylinder pull

door limiter

security chain

knob side flush bolt

door bolt

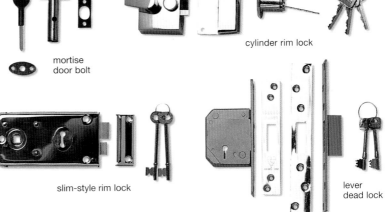

mortise door bolt

cylinder rim lock

slim-style rim lock

lever dead lock

fitting doors

235

accessories

Aside from the essential opening, closing and security aspects of door furniture, there are other items that can be applied to a wide range of door surfaces, either to complement those already mentioned or to fulfil another specific function. Fire doors, for example, will definitely require door closers. Most of these items have a highly decorative aspect to their make-up and so need to be chosen with this aesthetic requirement in mind. All these features are generally less complicated to fit compared to other door furniture. It is therefore worthwhile making these additions to improve the look and give some excess function to the door as a whole.

letter plate

concealed door closer

doorknocker

finger plate

brass escutcheon

brass door closer

brass covered escutcheon

porcelain escutcheon

skirting door stop

cutting to size

It is unlikely that a door will fit perfectly into the door lining or frame and so some cutting to size will probably be required, though trimming a door too much may weaken its structure. This is particularly true of 'hollow' doors that are based on a simple wooden frame. Most doors can be cut down using saws and planes, but for proprietary doors that are steel faced, or made of fibreglass or carbon fibre, the manufacturer's guidelines for fitting should be observed.

internal panel door

Fitting a solid panel door provides an ideal demonstration of the best technique for cutting a door to size. If you have fitted a new lining, then trimming the door to size should be straightforward. Fitting a new door to an old lining can be more complicated, but the same basic technique can be followed in both cases. Firstly, the door must be trimmed to less than the size of the aperture. Once this is achieved, precise fitting can be carried out.

tools for the job

hammer
pencil
tape measure
spirit level or straightedge
wood plane or power plane
board or door lifter

1 Insert two nails into the head of the lining. Their distance from the front of the head should be equal

to the depth of the door. In this way, when the door is placed in position in the lining, it will not fall through and will be supported securely enough to carry out the fitting procedure.

2 Fit the door in the lining, and mark off around the edge of the door to provide a 3mm (⅛in) clearance between the two vertical door stiles and the lining stiles. Depending on the 'squareness' of the lining, this may require more wood to be trimmed in some areas than in others.

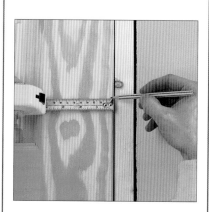

POWER PLANES

A power plane is an excellent tool for trimming down doors quickly and is especially useful when there is more than just a few millimetres to be shaved off.

tips of the trade

Excess trimming – Where the amount of wood to be shaved off a door edge is more than can be done with a plane, it may be necessary to use a jigsaw with a fine cutting blade.

3 Join up the marked-off points along the door edge using a straightedge or spirit level.

4 It may also be necessary to trim the height of the door, depending on whether the lining is square, and/or if the floor is level. Adjust your measurements to account for the required floor clearance.

5 Use a pencil to join markings, so that a precise guideline for trimming purposes is achieved.

6 Plane along the edge of the door to remove wood down as far as the pencil guideline. Clamp the door in a workbench for this procedure as this will hold it steady during the planing process.

7 Plane along the leading edge of the door at a slight angle, so that a little more wood is being taken off the edge, which will eventually be the closing edge of the door. This fractional extra wood removal will make the door clearance slightly larger on the back of the leading edge than on the front. This makes the clearance between door and lining much more even and reduces the risk of the door sticking in the future.

8 Once the door edges have been trimmed to fit and are checked in the entrance for size, trim down the top and/or bottom of the door as required. A plane may also be used for this process. Since this will mean working the plane over the end grain of the vertical stiles, only work the plane in a direction into the door and not towards its edge, which may cause the grain to split and damage the look of it.

9 A board or door lifter is the ideal tool to hold the door in place whilst clearances and preciseness of fit are measured. It also allows you to support the weight of the door, lifting or lowering it into the desired position. It is best to position the door lifter below the central stile and bottom rail.

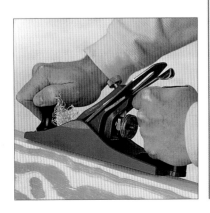

10 Wedge the door in place at the top and bottom, butting it up tightly against what will be the hinged side. Measure the distance between the leading edge and the door lining to check that it is exactly 6mm (¼in), which will allow for a clearance of 3mm (⅛in) on both edges of the door once it is accurately hung in position.

EXTERIOR DOORS

The fitting process for an external door is very similar to that for an interior, except that an external door will always be fitted into a frame rather than into a lining. Apart from this, the same principles of cutting to size are employed. It is also likely that you will need to cut a rebate into the bottom of the door in order to accommodate the weather bar on the door sill. This can be achieved using a router. Some doors will come with 'horns' extending from the ends of the vertical stiles. This elongation of the stiles is simply a measure to protect the end grain before fitting. Accordingly, they should be cut off prior to the fitting process.

Exterior doors are generally much more expensive than interior doors, mainly because they are built to fulfil a more hardwearing requirement than their interior counterparts. Mistakes may therefore be costly, and so it is wise to take extra time in your measuring process, ensuring that you do not waste any materials.

cutting in hinges 🔩🔩🔩

The accuracy of cutting in hinges is the vital factor that ensures the ease and efficiency with which a door opens and closes. External doors should always have three hinges because they tend to be heavier than internal ones. Three hinges also lessen the chances of a new door going out of shape and are therefore a good option if you have purchased relatively cheap doors. However, most internal doors may be hung successfully using two standard butt hinges.

tools for the job

tape measure
combination square
wooden mallet
chisel
cordless drill/driver
door lifter

1 Mark the hinge positions on the door edge, 15cm (6in) from the top of the door and 22.5cm (9in) up from the bottom of the door.

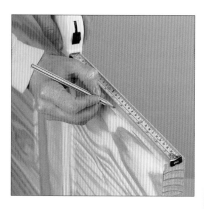

2 At the top marking, position the hinge wrong side up and directly below the 15cm (6in)

measurement. Holding it wrong side up allows the hinge barrel to be held flush against the door edge, which will ensure that the hinge position is marked off in the correct place. Draw a guideline around the edge of the hinge.

3 To measure the depth of the hinges you are using, hold one against a combination square. Adjust the ruler on the square to the depth of the hinge and lock it in position.

4 Hold the combination square perpendicular to the door edge so that the depth measurement for the hinge may be drawn accurately on the face of the door.

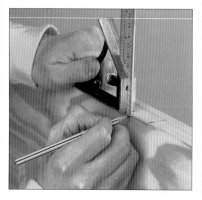

5 Use a wooden mallet and sharp chisel to remove the wood to the marked-off depth by making chisel indentations for the top and bottom edge of the hinge. This prevents the wood splitting when you chisel a guideline along the vertical length of the hinge marking.

6 The wood needs to be removed gradually to ensure accuracy and depth of the cut. Make a number of chisel cuts horizontally along where the hinge position will be, allowing the chisel to penetrate only as far as the depth measurement on the face of the door. Knocking the chisel in too far will cause an uneven surface once the recess wood is removed.

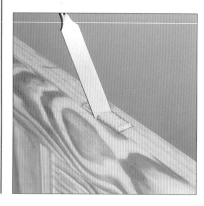

7 Now position the chisel so that its blade can be inserted beneath and at right angles to the horizontal cuts. Carefully lever up and remove the wooden sections, taking care not to allow the chisel to extend over the hinge guidelines.

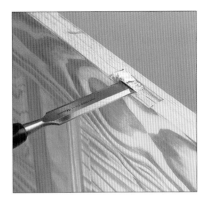

8 Repeat steps 2–7 at the base of the door for the bottom hinge, but hold the hinge above the 22.5cm (9in) measurement. Then put the door in position in the door lining and place an open hinge between the top of the door and the door lining. This gives the measurement for the door clearance at the top and so allows you to mark off the hinge positions accurately on the door lining. Mark off at the top and bottom of the hinge position for both the top and bottom hinge.

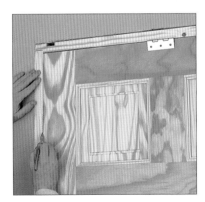

9 Remove the door and – in a similar way to marking off on the door edge – again hold a hinge wrong side up on the door lining and mark around it with a sharp pencil. Measure hinge depth and chisel out as required

in the same manner as used for the door edge. Carry out this process for both the top and bottom hinge.

10 Hold a hinge, right side up and in position, on the door edge. Make pencil marks for the screw positions, allowing the pencil point to move fractionally away from the screw hole centre and towards the back edge of the hinge.

11 Remove the hinge and drill pilot holes for the screws. Be as accurate as possible, ensuring that the drill bit is inserted directly at the marked-off pencil points.

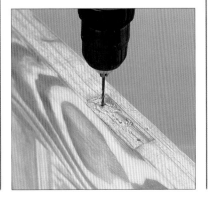

tips of the trade

Rising butts – Instead of fitting standard butt hinges, it may sometimes be necessary to fit rising butts. These lift the level of the door as it is opened. Cutting in rising butt hinges is similar to standard butt hinges but ensure you have right- or left-handed hinges, to suit the way the door opens. Also, bevel the top corner edge of the door (nearest to the hinges) so that it will be able to shut properly.

12 Reposition the hinge and insert screws into the pilot holes. Do not tighten the screws until all three are in place and the hinge is in the correct position. Repeat steps 10–12 for the bottom hinge.

13 Hold the door open but in position in the door lining. Ensure that each hinge fits exactly into the chiselled-out positions. Mark with a pencil and pilot drill, before screwing the hinges in place. The door should open and close into the lining with a perfectly smooth action.

fitting handles – 1 ↗

Handles are fitted in three stages, which relate to the main components required for handles to work. Firstly, it is necessary to fit the latch; secondly, the handles themselves; and, thirdly, the strike plate has to be fitted in the door lining. Although, in the following example, a mortise lever lock has been used, the fitting principals are the same as for a simple mortise latch.

tools for the job

pencil
combination square
cordless drill/driver
chisel

fitting the latch

1 Hold the latch on one face of the door at the required height. Allow the latch plate to overlap onto the edge of the door, so that the main latch casing sits flush against the door surface. Make a pencil mark along the top of the latch, one at the bottom, and two at the sides to show the height of the spindle position and the height of the keyhole.

2 Using a combination square, make horizontal guidelines to the marked-off points on the door face. Ensure that the combination square is held tight against the edge of the door so that the guidelines are accurate. Continue these lines onto the edge of the door and round to the other face, thus making a mirror image of the guidelines.

3 Measure the exact width of the door edge and lock the combination square to half this measurement. Use it to draw a central guideline vertically through the horizontal guidelines on the door edge.

4 Use the combination square again to measure the distance between the front of the latch plate and the centre of the spindle hole. Lock the square in position at the correct measurement. You may allow a fraction extra to this measurement in order to compensate for the depth of the latch plate as it will be recessed into the door edge.

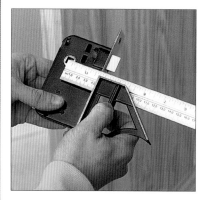

5 Transfer this measurement to the door edge, lining up the square with the pencil guideline, which denotes the spindle height on the door face. Make a vertical line through the horizontal one to provide a pin-point cross. Repeat this on the other side of the door. Repeat steps 4 and 5 to mark the exact position of the keyhole on the appropriate horizontal guidelines on the door. Double-check both measurements as mistakes are difficult to rectify later.

👍 tips of the trade

Accuracy is key when fitting latches, so it is essential that the chisels you are using are razor sharp. Therefore, before you start fitting the handles, make sure that you have serviced these tools as it will certainly help to ensure that the job is completed to a high standard. See also the General Tool Care section on page 19.

6 Use an auger or flat drill bit to bore into the edge of the door along the vertical pencil guideline. The size of the bit should correspond to the width of the latch casing, not the width of the latch plate. Measure the depth of the latch and transfer this length to the drill bit, marking it with a piece of insulation tape. This way, it is possible to drill accurately to the required latch depth. Work down the vertical guideline, making a series of overlapping drilled holes. Ensure that the drill bit enters the door edge at right angles to the door so that the depth of holes remains consistent.

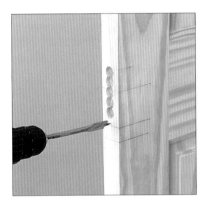

7 At the marked-off crosses for the spindle and keyhole, drill through the door using the correct size of auger or flat bit. It may be necessary to drill two overlapping holes to accommodate the keyhole. To avoid splitting the wood, drill from the marked-off points on both sides of the door, as drilling all the way through from one side can cause damage to the face of the door when the bit breaks through the surface.

8 Use a chisel to straighten the edges of the overlapping drilled holes along the door edge. Work methodically to produce clean and accurate cuts. Make safety cuts horizontally against the grain at the top and bottom of the hole. This will prevent the splitting of the wood.

9 Push the latch into the hole and carefully draw a precise pencil guideline around the latch plate on the edge of the door. There is little room for error at this stage and therefore take time to ensure that the latch is perfectly vertical, with the spindle and keyhole exactly aligned, before marking off.

10 Take out the latch and chisel around the guideline, removing a depth of wood equal to that of the depth of the latch plate. Take care not to split the wood, by again using safety cuts to slice across the grain at the top and bottom horizontal guideline, before making cuts along the vertical guideline, and therefore along the grain of the wood.

Carefully remove the loosened wood until the correct level has been achieved and the plate sits flush.

11 Reposition the latch, allowing the chiselled-out area to accommodate the latch plate. The plate should be vertical and sit flush with the door edge. Drill pilot holes for the screws.

12 Finally, screw the latch in place, securing it in position with screws at top and bottom of the plate. Ensure the screws are done up well, but do not overtighten and risk distorting the face of the latch plate.

241

fitting handles – 2 ⚒

With the latch in position, the next step is to fit the handles to the door. Most handles are made to fit on a standard spindle, which in turn is inserted through the door and latch. This allows you to choose handles according to your own personal tastes. In this case a lever lock handle has been used to demonstrate the general technique required for fitting purposes.

tools for the job

bradawl

cordless drill/driver

screwdriver

tape measure

pencil

combination square

chisel

fitting the handles to the door

1 Initially, position the spindle through the door and latch, to check that it fits precisely. If the position is slightly off, the spindle movement may be hindered and therefore it is essential to check that its positioning is free from obstruction of any kind.

2 Fit one handle onto the spindle and hold it in the correct position, vertical to the door surface. This can be checked with a torpedo level, but it is usually possible to

check its position by eye by judging the distance at the top and bottom of the handle plate relative to the door edge. Use a bradawl to make marks or indentations on the door surface through the handle plate screw holes.

3 Remove the handle and use a small drill bit to create pilot holes in the marks. Do not penetrate the surface much, as the holes are just a starting point for the screw insertion.

4 Reposition the handle and carefully screw it in place. It is best to insert the screws in a particular order to ensure that the handle stays level. Start at the top,

THE OTHER SIDE

Repeat steps 2–4 on the other side of the door to fix the other handle in place. If, when you first position this handle, the length of the spindle prevents the handle plate from sitting flush against the door surface, it will be necessary to remove the spindle and cut it down to size. Spindles are supplied as multi-purpose items to fit all depths of door, so it is often the case that spindle cutting will be required. This is a simple process, which can be achieved with the use of a standard hacksaw. Once trimmed down, reposition the spindle and fit the handle.

inserting a screw in one corner and then fix the second screw in the opposite diagonal corner at the bottom of the handle plate. Finish with the other top screw followed by the final bottom one. This makes it easier to ensure that the handle is precisely aligned throughout the process of screw insertion.

👍 tips of the trade

When screwing handles in place, it is always best to use a hand held screwdriver, rather than a power driver. You have greater control to ensure that the handle is positioned vertically and there is less chance that the screwdriver head can slip and scratch the surface of the brass. Such scratches are irreparable.

fitting the strike plate

Once the latch and handle are fitted, attention can be turned to the catch mechanism, or strike plate, which requires fitting to the door lining.

1 In a locked position, close the door onto the door lining, allowing the latch and lock to rest against the lining. Then make pencil marks on the lining edge to denote the top and bottom positions of the latch and lock. Make these guidelines as clearly as possible for accuracy is very important.

2 Open the door and continue the marked-off pencil lines on the lining edge, around and onto the face of the door lining.

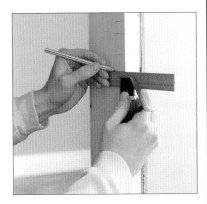

3 Holding the door in an open position, it is now necessary to measure the precise depth of the latch and the lock and along the door edge in order to gauge the correct position of the strike plate. Lock the

combination square at this depth measurement by tightening the ruler retaining screw.

4 Transfer the depth measurement, making a vertical guideline for the front of the latch and the lock respectively, between the appropriate horizontal lining guidelines.

5 Hold the strike plate in position. Mark around the strike plate to give its exact position requirement.

6 Chisel out inside the latch and lock guidelines and the external guideline for the strike plate. Position the strike plate, drill pilot holes and then screw it in place.

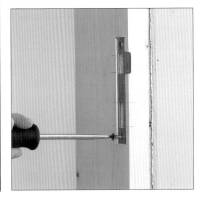

Once door furniture is fitted and the doorstop and architrave are fixed in place, the entire area may be decorated to reveal an attractive finished product.

finishing the frame ✂✂

A door should be finished off with a doorstop and architrave. The doorstop prevents the door from closing further than flush with the wall surface. Failure to fit one will mean the door can be closed too far and you will risk damaging the hinges. The architrave, however, fulfils a purely decorative role, adding a finish to the lining and an overall frame to the door.

external doors

Most external doors do not require a doorstop to be fitted as there is one already built into the frame. Similarly, the exterior of the frame does not need an architrave, but the interior can be surrounded with one if required.

fitting the doorstop

Doorstops vary in dimension, but are normally about 3.75cm x 1cm (1½in x ⅜in) in cross section. Sizes vary according to the door dimensions and between manufacturers. Normally a doorstop is supplied as part of the door lining kit.

1 Close the door so that you are on the inside side of the door lining. Carefully draw a pencil guideline on the lining at the position where the door meets the lining. Open the door, and cut lengths of doorstop to fit the head of the lining and down the two stiles. Start by positioning the doorstop at the head of the lining.

Check that it fits precisely before proceeding to fix it in position. Use wire nails for fixing.

2 Nail the head doorstop in place so that its front edge aligns precisely with the pencil guideline. Do not knock the nails all the way in at this stage – simply insert them far enough to be secure, but so that the nail head is still protruding. This allows removal and repositioning to be achieved easily, if it is necessary.

3 Cut and fit the length of doorstop on the strike plate stile. Then cut and fit the doorstop on the hinge side of the lining. Instead of

positioning this length along the pencil line, fix it slightly back from the line. This deviation will allow the hinge edge to shut easily and prevent it catching on the doorstop. Finish off by knocking the nails right in after opening and closing the door to check the action.

fitting the architrave

Once you have chosen the architrave style, fitting is relatively simple as long as cuts are accurate and a mitresaw or mitre block is used during this process. Remember that, for the best decorative effect, the architrave should be chosen to match with the other mouldings in the room such as the skirting board and dado or picture rails, if appropriate.

1 Use an offcut of the architrave to determine corner positions. Hold the piece in place above the door, approximately 0.5cm (³⁄₁₆in) to 1cm (⅜in) away from the lining edge. This distance is often decided by aesthetic preference and is a matter of personal

choice. However, once you have chosen it, you must ensure that it remains consistent around the entire door lining. Draw a pencil guideline along the top of the architrave, which extends out onto the wall surface to the side of the door, as this will help you to maintain consistency.

2 Hold the offcut vertically along the hinged side of the lining, keeping the same distance between the architrave edge and the door lining edge as per the distance that was employed at the top of the door. If you draw another pencil guideline along the outer edge of the architrave, it will then cross over the horizontal pencil guideline. Next, repeat steps 1 and 2 at the other corner of the lining. These pencil lines will now provide you with the precise guidelines for what will be the outside corners of your architrave.

3 Measure the length requirement for the top section of architrave by measuring between the two points where the pencil guidelines cross

above each corner of the door. Mark off this distance along the back edge of a piece of architrave. Then use a mitresaw to cut your architrave accurately to size.

4 Position the architrave above the door lining and nail it in position. Ideally, attach the length so that the nails protrude into the edge of the door lining and into the studwork around the lining. For block or brick walls, some masonry nails may be required.

5 Continue by measuring off the vertical architrave requirements. This can be done very precisely by holding a length of the architrave, which is slightly longer than the door height, wrong side out and butted against the edge of the top length of fixed architrave. Then make a mark with a sharp pencil where the vertical length meets the horizontal one, and use this as an accurate guideline when you use the mitresaw to cut the length to the required size.

6 You can now nail the vertical lengths in position. Add one further nail into each architrave corner joint, inserting the nail through one section of the architrave and into the adjacent piece. This helps to hold the mitred joints tightly together and reduces the risk of them splitting open at a later date.

7 Finally use a hammer and nail punch to ensure that nail heads are knocked in below the surface level of the architrave.

tips of the trade

• Although a mitresaw has been used to cut the architrave in the example shown here, an alternative method is to measure the distance required and use a panel saw and mitre block to achieve a clean 45 degree cut.

• When preparing a finished door frame for decoration, use a flexible filler to seal the gap along the outside edges of the architrave and the mitred joins, to allow for any slight movement in the door frame once it is in use.

front door fittings ✂✂

Aside from the basic handles, front doors often require further fittings, which are not necessary on internal doors. Although these fittings have a functional job to perform, they also add a decorative aspect to the front door and exterior of the house as a whole. Extra care should always be taken when working on them as mistakes can be very costly.

tools for the job

tape measure

pencil

combination square

cordless drill/driver

jigsaw

pliers

hammer

fitting a letterbox

The positioning of a letterbox is to a large extent determined by front door design. Fitting can take place when the door is hung in position, but it is often easier to carry it out with the door laid flat on trestle supports.

1 On the outer side of the door, mark out a rectangular guideline slightly larger than the plate of the letterbox on the middle of the central rail. Then mark crosses far enough in from each corner to accommodate the diameter of the drill bit. The drill hole should be large enough to accommodate a jigsaw blade.

2 Drill through the door at each cross with an auger or flat drill bit, ensuring that the hole does not extend outside the guideline. When drilling through, hold a block of wooden offcut tightly against the other side of the door where the drill point will emerge. This will prevent any wood being split or blown out on the other side.

3 Cut along the pencil guideline with a jigsaw, beginning each cut from one of the drilled holes. Remove the block of wood, then smooth any rough edges with fine grade sandpaper. Next, mark out the position of the retaining bolts.

4 Drill holes for the retaining bolts, holding a wooden block on the opposite side of the door to prevent splitting. Often letterbox design requires holes on the exterior of the door to be widened slightly at, and just below, surface level in order to accommodate the letterbox plate, so two sizes of drill bit may be required.

5 Attach the retaining bolts to the letterbox and thread them through the holes to the other side of the door.

6 Turn the door over and screw the retaining nuts onto the bolts. (Tighten with pliers if necessary.)

fitting a doorknocker

A doorknocker is fixed using a similar principle to a letterbox, again involving bolts that extend through the door and are secured by nuts on the inside face. Positioning is again affected by door design, but for panel doors, a central position where the top door rail crosses the vertical central stile is always a suitable place for a doorknocker.

1 Measure out the central position for the knocker and strike plate, making a clear pencil cross to act as a guideline for drilling.

2 Drill through the door, holding a wooden offcut on the other side to prevent damage to the wood. You may need to use a second, slightly larger drill bit to open up the entrance holes in order to accommodate the knocker and strike plate design.

3 Screw the supplied bolts into the retaining holes of both the knocker and strike plate, ensuring that the bolts are inserted straight, so that the risk of crossthreading is thereby reduced.

4 Insert both the knocker and strike plate through the appropriate holes, turn the door over and tighten the retaining bolts to secure the doorknocker in place. When positioning the knocker, a tap with the butt end of a hammer or a wooden mallet may be required, as the knocker is often designed with a small point behind its face which pierces into the door surface and adds to the security of the fixing. It is also best to cover the face of the knocker with a cloth when carrying out this process to prevent scratching or damaging the knocker surface finish.

The practical and aesthetically pleasing combination of external door furniture can add tremendous decorative appeal to the overall look of a front door.

installing cylinder locks ⁄⁄⁄

Cylinder rim locks are among the most common types of lock for front doors. From a security angle they are very effective, but are always best when combined with other door security features (see pages 250–1). Designs do vary but the basic principle of cylinder rim locks remains the same, in that a locking barrel extends through the door and combines with a latch to form a closing mechanism operated by key from the outside and with a lever from the inside.

tools for the job

pencil
combination square
cordless drill/driver
screwdrivers
hammer
mini hacksaw
chisel

1 On the inside of the door, draw a horizontal pencil guideline across the closing stile of the door. Use a combination square to continue this line around the edge and onto the front of the door. The exact height positioning for a cylinder rim lock is not standardized, but it should be on the upper half of the door – 130cm (4ft 3in) from the floor is generally an acceptable height to fit it.

2 Use the combination square to measure the distance between the lock edge (closest to the latch) and the hole that will accommodate the flat connecting bar. Lock the combination square in position at this exact point. Then transfer this measurement to the door, opening it slightly and resting the edge of the combination square against the door edge, whilst marking off the position on the horizontal pencil guideline.

3 Use an auger or flat bit to drill through the door at the marked point. The size of bit required will normally be suggested on the lock packaging and relates directly to the size of the cylinder for the lock. It is best to drill from both sides to make the holes because otherwise the re-emerging drill bit can make splits in the wood surface. Alternatively, whilst drilling, hold an offcut tight against the other side of the door, corresponding to where the drill bit will appear.

4 On the exterior of the door, insert the cylinder through its brass ring and the drilled hole, so that the flat connecting bar extends through to the other side of the door.

5 Fix the mounting plate to the cylinder and the inside of the door ensuring that it is level, and that the edge of the plate is aligned precisely with the door edge. It may be necessary to make pilot holes for the screw fixings, especially if you are using a hardwood door, which is what is shown here. When drilling the pilot holes, be sure that you are extremely accurate and also make certain that the drill bit goes into the door surface absolutely level.

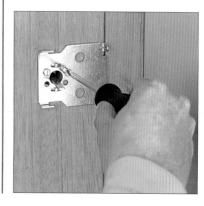

6 Depending on door depth, the flat connecting bar may be too long to allow for the easy positioning of the lock. It may therefore be necessary to trim the bar back so that the lock may be fitted. A mini hacksaw is the ideal tool for this purpose. Double-check your cutting measurements because you will not be able to rectify mistakes later.

7 Push the lock case onto the mounting plate, shifting it along until it catches firmly in position. This precise fitting procedure may vary slightly between different designs, and although the fit itself is very tight, there is normally a simple procedure for sliding the casing in place. Once in position, insert the two retaining screws to secure the lock casing firmly on the door.

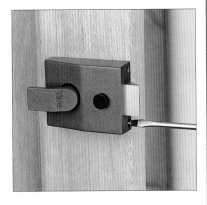

8 Next, close the door and draw a straight guideline above and below the lock casing on the door frame. A torpedo level can be used for this process, but space is very often confined, and therefore you may find

that it is actually easier to use the straight edge of the staple itself to aid you in this marking-up process.

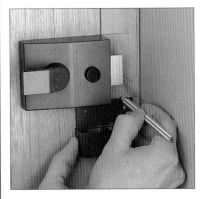

9 Open the door and hold the staple in place, following the guidelines you have just made. Continue the guideline round onto the internal facing of the door frame.

10 Measure the recessed part of the staple and transfer the measurement to the frame. This shows what wood must be removed to accommodate the staple. Use a chisel to cut the area, taking care not to damage the surrounding wood.

11 Finally, position the staple in the recess and screw it in place on the frame. Test the door to make sure the rim lock closes and opens correctly, making any minor adjustments as required.

RIM LOCK GUIDELINES

- **Standards** – Only ever fit a rim lock that is supplied in packaging and displays the relevant approval badges and assertions. Also check that the lock comes with a guarantee.

- **Dual use** – Although rim locks are a common front door feature, they are ideal for any other external door.

- **Decorative choice** – Security features such as this are never going to be attractive, but do consider that, like most fittings, locks can be bought in a number of different finishes.

- **Stile check** – Check the dimensions of the door stile to make sure the lock casing will fit onto it. Otherwise, a slimmer lock than that shown here will be required.

- **Dead lock** – The rim lock shown here has a dead lock option so that, once it has been locked with the key, it will not be possible to open the door. This is essential for doors with glass panes, so if a thief does break a pane and reach the lock, they will still be unable to open the door. For obvious safety reasons, key-operated dead locks must not be used when people are inside the home.

fitting extra security ↗

Security fittings for doors, and front doors especially, stretch further than just rim locks, and there are a number of other systems which may be used to add to the security offered by a rim locking mechanism. It is not necessary to use all the features shown here on a single door, but a combination of these items will make you feel safer in your own home.

tools for the job

pencil
tape measure
cordless drill/driver
chisel
bradawl
screwdrivers
torpedo level

mortise door bolts

Mortise door bolts are straightforward to fit and offer an excellent security mechanism for external doors. They are operated by a specially shaped key which extends the bolt between the door and frame when moved to the locking position. These door bolts may be fitted on a hanging door or on one of its hinges, as shown here.

1 Holding the barrel of the door bolt, draw a guideline around its faceplate on the door edge. Ensure that the rectangular guideline drawn is central to the edge of the door.

2 Using the correct size of auger or flat drill bit (size should be on the packaging), drill vertically down into the door edge. Make sure that the drill remains completely vertical, otherwise operation of the bolt will be hindered. Drill to a depth equal to that of the door bolt.

3 Chisel out inside the rectangular pencil guideline to a depth equal to that of the door bolt face plate. Make cuts with the chisel along the shorter dimensions of the rectangle (across the grain) before making cuts along the longer dimensions (with the grain). This will help prevent any splitting of the wood.

4 Hold the door bolt on the face of the door, aligning it with the drilled hole in the edge. Use a bradawl to mark the face of the door at the position on the bolt where the key will be inserted. Drill into the door at this point, allowing the drill to extend only as far as the door bolt hole in the edge of the door. Make sure you do not continue to drill through to the other side of the door.

5 Fit the door bolt in place in the edge of the door, securing it in place with the retaining screws. It may be necessary to drill pilot holes for the screws before inserting them.

6 Finally, fit the key plate on the face of the door so that its hole aligns directly with the one in the door. Another mortise door bolt may now be fitted at the bottom level of the door, before it is rehung on the door frame. Both bolts will need holes and cover plates positioned in the door frame. A similar technique to that for fitting a door latch strike plate is used here, where the position for the plate

is marked off and the appropriate amount of chiselling out is carried out to accommodate the door bolt.

door bolts

Simple door bolts offer a further option to the mortice door bolt. These are surface mounted and are even simpler to fit. Again, it is wise to have door bolts positioned at both the top level and bottom level of the door.

1 Hold the bolt in position on the door, using a torpedo level to make sure that it is perfectly horizontal. Use a bradawl to mark the positions for the screws on the face of the door.

2 Pilot drill holes and then screw the bolt in place. The same marking procedure can be used to position the catch plate for the bolt on the door frame. Take great care when using screws with solid brass fittings because a simple slip with the screwdriver may scratch the brass

surface and therefore detract from the finished look of the job once it has been completed.

peep holes

Door security does not necessarily have to involve a lock or mechanical barrier of some nature, as the use of peep holes demonstrates. These security items are simply used to check the identity of a caller even before opening the door.

1 Peep holes are normally supplied with both sections screwed together. Undo the two components and select a drill bit slightly larger than the size of the thread in the peep hole.

2 Drill a hole in the door centrally at eye level on the middle door stile. On the outside of the door insert the correct piece of the peep hole.

3 Turn the door over and insert the other section of the peep hole, screwing it in position into the other

section. The flat edge of a screwdriver may be required for tightening purposes. Although this peep hole has been installed with the door off its hinges, these security devices can also be installed with the door still hung in place.

door chains

These useful fixtures allow the door to be opened slightly, so that visitor identity can be checked before the door is opened fully. Door limiters are another version of this system.

1 The chain is best positioned at an appropriate height around the middle section of the door. Just below the rim lock is ideal. Use a bradawl to mark the position and then screw the main chain plate onto the door.

2 Attach the chain and retaining plate to the door frame, positioning it so that the chain can be conveniently slipped in place on the main chain plate.

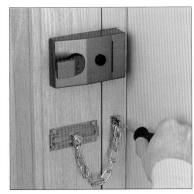

changing door appearance ⁄⁄

From time to time, it can be desirable to change the appearance of doors in your home without going to the effort and expense of full replacement. Methods for painting doors are outlined on pages 410–15, but it is possible to renovate doors, or change their appearance to something more appealing, in ways other than simply painting. These pages explain how to make and fit decorative panels to a flush door, adding simple, but attractive texture to the door surface.

renovating a flush door

Flush doors can be considered relatively featureless examples of door design. In some cases, this may be the minimalist look required. There is always the option, however, of adding panels to an existing flush door, which provides greater character at half the cost of full replacement with authentic panel doors. Expense can even be saved by adding panels to a relatively cheap new flush door.

panel considerations

Before starting you should first consider how many panels are going to be required on the door surface. Choices are normally either four panels of a similar size or six panels with the top two being around half the size of the lower four. Bear in mind that the greater the number of panels, the larger the amount of moulding and the greater the number of cuts that will be required. This is a particularly important consideration if you are panelling throughout your home and on both sides of doors, because the expense can escalate rapidly.

The choice of moulding also varies in style as well as price. The most ornate varieties can be expensive and often the cheaper, simpler designs are all that is required to achieve an effective panel door. As mouldings are normally painted, wood quality is not an essential consideration, so long as the mouldings are not split.

tools for the job

paint brush
combination square
pencil
tape measure
spirit level
mitresaw
scissors or craft knife

1 On a new door, it is always best to prime the surface before attaching the panels. The primer improves adhesion between the mouldings and the door when the double-sided tape is applied and the mouldings are positioned.

2 In addition to the door itself, it is also worth priming the moulding lengths before they are cut to fit. This saves time later, and also improves adhesion for the same reasons as explained in step 1.

3 Once the primer has dried, accurately measure the door size and begin by marking off what will be the outer corner points of the panels. A combination square is an ideal aid for this process and helps to keep measurements precise.

👍 tips of the trade

If the mouldings are to be picked out in a different colour from the rest of the door surface, it is best to apply undercoat and top coat to the mouldings before they are cut to size, and to paint the flush door surface with undercoat and top coat as well. This done, the mouldings can be attached so that the only paint requirement will be a 'touch up' of the coats already applied. Thus the very fiddly 'cutting in' requirement of the two differing colours on the door will be avoided, speeding up the time taken to complete the task by a considerable margin.

4 Use a spirit level to draw the pencil guidelines. Keeping these lines vertical or horizontal as required makes the panelling process much easier to achieve. Once all the panels are marked out on the door surface, measure each panel dimension separately and use a mitresaw to cut lengths of moulding to size. Accuracy at this stage will help to eliminate the need for any filling on mitre joins once the panels are in place.

PANELLING TIPS

- **Filling** – So long as measurements are accurate, there should only be limited filling requirements on the mouldings before decoration can take place. Use flexible filler or caulk to fill any slightly open mitre joints, and along any open joins between the moulding edges and the door face.

- **Nailing alternative** – Instead of using double-sided tape, it is possible to attach the mouldings using panel pins. However, the panel pin heads will require filling and sanding once they are hammered in place. Apply a small amount of wood glue to the back of the mouldings before they are positioned, to ensure that a good bond is achieved.

- **Ready-made panels** – Some manufacturers produce completed panels which can be attached directly to the door surface, eliminating the need for you to make mitred cuts. However, while these kits are very useful they can be expensive.

5 Apply double-sided tape to the back of the moulding. Ensure that the tape runs all the way, centrally, along its length and that there are no wrinkles or unevenness in the tape surface. Remove the backing from the tape once positioned, so that it may then be stuck to the door surface. The double-sided tape can be cut using scissors or a craft knife.

6 Attach the mouldings, with the outside edge of the moulding running along the pencil guidelines. The adhesive properties of the tape should allow for some adjustment of position when first placed on the door surface, though the glue will soon set, creating a tight bond between moulding and door surface. Continue to apply lengths until all panels are complete.

Combining colour can help to enhance the appearance of a panel door and draw further attention to its texture and design.

fitting door closers

Door closers are essential pieces of equipment used primarily in the domain of fire doors, whereby the automatic door closer mechanism acts to shut the door to maintain the desired fire barrier at all times. Door closers may also be used on standard doors where automatic closing is needed. These closers can either be visible or concealed from view.

tools for the job

bradawl
....
cordless drill/driver
....
chisels
....
tape measure
....
combination square
....
pliers
....

fitting a hydraulic door closer

These are the most common of the visible variety and are generally positioned at the top of the door and frame. The hydraulic mechanism is enclosed in a casing, which is attached to the top of the door and joined to the frame by a pivoting bar. As well as pulling the door shut, the mechanism also controls the speed at which the door closes. Designs can vary slightly, but most are based on principles similar to those demonstrated here.

1 Most such door closers will come supplied with a paper template to help position the casing. Attach the template to the door, securing it in place with some masking tape. Ensure the template is the right way round for the way the door is opening, and that its edges are perfectly aligned with those of the door. Use a bradawl to mark the fixing positions for the casing, making slight indents through the template and into the door surface. At the same time,

mark the positions for the retaining bracket for the door closer arm on the architrave.

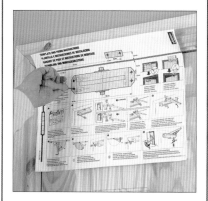

2 Pilot drill holes for the casing and screw it in position on the door surface. Take extra care to ensure that the door closer casing is the right way up and accurately positioned using the template hole guidelines.

3 Depending on the architrave design, it may be necessary to cut out a small section of wood from the architrave, so that the door closer arm bracket can be fixed flush in position. Draw an outline for the bracket and drill pilot holes, so that

once wood has been chiselled out it will still be possible to see the holes for screw insertion.

4 Attach the first section of the closer arm to the bracket and screw it in place on the architrave. Again, check that the bracket and arm are positioned the right way up, as subtle differences may hamper you from determining this.

5 Attach the other section of arm to the door closer casing and join it to the first arm with the nut and bolt supplied. Small adjustments may be necessary for exact positioning.

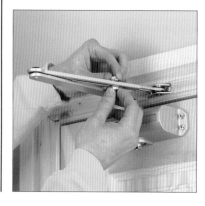

6 Open the door and allow it to close. It may be necessary to adjust the tension to suit your requirements. Most such door closers can be adjusted with a slot-head screwdriver, inserted at a special point on the side of the door closer.

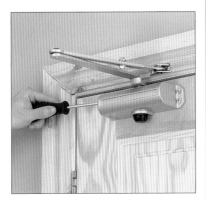

concealed door closers

With the function and workings hidden whilst the door is closed, this variety of door closer can be considered far more aesthetically pleasing than the type shown opposite. However, depending on door weight and its overall dimensions, more than one concealed door closer may be needed to fulfil the automatic closing function.

1 Open up the door and mark a cross in the middle of the door edge, central to the door's middle rail.

2 Drill at right angles and perfectly horizontally into the door at the point of the cross just marked. Use a drill bit equal to the size of the barrel

of the door closer. Drill bit size will normally be printed on the packaging. An auger or flat bit may be used for this purpose. Only drill in as far as the length of the door closer itself.

3 Insert the door closer in the hole and use a pencil to mark around the edge of the face plate. Ensure that the face plate is precisely vertical for the pencil guideline.

4 Chisel out a recess to accommodate the depth of the face plate. Working close to the door edge like this means that extra care is required not to split the wood.

5 Use the face plate of the door closer to draw another guideline on the door lining surface. Chisel out this area to the depth required for the door closer anchor plate.

6 Use pliers to pull the anchor plate away from the face plate, and insert the retaining bar across the chain to prevent it closing. Now insert the door closer in the door.

7 Finally, screw the anchor plate in place. Carefully remove the retaining bar from the chain and allow the door to close automatically. Tension may be adjusted if necessary.

insulating doors ✐

Most doors suffer from draught problems, especially given that the opening and closing mechanism will not function efficiently without gaps around the door edges. PVC and double glazed doors offer the best insulation, but with wooden doors it is often necessary to take further measures to improve insulation and reduce unwanted draughts. Such insulating techniques may be applied to both exterior and interior doors, although the materials used tend to differ.

exterior strips

An effective option used on many exterior doors is to attach draught excluder strips to the door frame. When the door is closed, a slight overlap of the strip from the door onto the frame effectively closes the gap that a draught may otherwise penetrate through. Designs vary, but most draught excluder strips are fitted using the technique shown below.

tools for the job

tape measure
craft knife
hammer
nail punch

1 Cut the strips to size so that you have one for each upright of the door frame and one length for the top of the frame. Mitred corners provide a good join between the strips. Position them ensuring that the more flexible edge of each section touches and follows the profile of the door surface.

2 Pin the strips in place, ensuring contact between them and the door surface when the door is in a closed position. Since the nails or pins used are so small, it is often easier to knock them into their final position using a punch. This also reduces the risk of damaging the strip with the hammer.

insulating tape

An alternative to the exterior strips is to use insulating tapes which are positioned on the internal part of the frame or on the doorstop. The advantage of these is that they are not visible when the door is in a

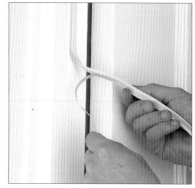

closed position and are also particularly easy to apply. Always read the manufacturer's guidelines to determine their recommended positioning, as tape design does vary and they may be used in slightly different positions on the frame or door surface.

Most insulating or excluder tapes are self-adhesive and are secured in place by peeling away the backing and pressing the strip into position. The adhesive used on these tapes is quick acting, so take care to position the tape correctly on first application as later adjustment is not always possible.

frame/wall junctions

Another area for draught penetration can be between the door frame and surrounding masonry. It is particularly important to close up such gaps, as these are also areas where damp or moisture can penetrate, leading to further problems.

tools for the job

sealant gun
masking tape

1 In order to make a neat finish, it is best to use masking tape. Apply separate strips of tape along the length of the junction on both the wall and frame. Even though the wall or masonry surface may be slightly rough or undulating, try to smooth

the tape into all depressions and recesses, whilst still maintaining a precise vertical edge to it.

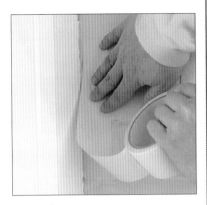

2 Load the sealant gun with a tube of silicone sealant. Cut the nozzle so that its diameter is slightly wider than the gap between the two lengths of masking tape. Depress the trigger and expel an even bead of sealant along the junction.

3 Smooth the sealant with a wetted finger, and proceed to remove the masking tape. The tape must be removed immediately after application, before the sealant dries.

interior options

A common measure to reduce draughts and improve insulation is to use draught excluder strips on internal doors.

tools for the job

tape measure

mini hacksaw

bradawl

screwdriver

1 Strips are supplied in lengths greater than standard door size so it is therefore necessary to cut them down to size before screwing in place. Measure the width of the base of the door and cut down the metal section of the excluder strip using a mini hacksaw.

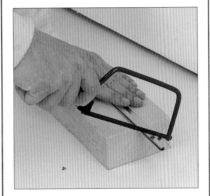

2 Insert the supplied brushes into the strip and position at the base of the door. Make pilot holes for the fixings using a bradawl. Make sure the strip is positioned so that

when the door is in a closed position the brushes rest on the floor, thereby cutting out any draught penetration under the door.

3 Screw the strip in place, again to ensure that the brushes make good contact with the floor surface. If need be, make adjustments before tightening the screws.

SOUND INSULATION

As well as insulating for draught reduction, it is possible to insulate with sound reduction in mind. All the measures shown here will certainly help with sound insulation but there are further methods that can be employed.

• Door quality – If sound insulation is a priority then door quality must be a consideration. As a general rule, doors of higher quality will tend to be more solid and therefore their sound insulating properties are enhanced. So door replacement is always an option.

• Increasing depth – As a less drastic measure, door depth can sometimes be increased to improve sound insulation. Simply fitting ply sheets to the surface of the door will help reduce sound transference between rooms.

• Sound insulation strips – Proprietary sound insulation strips can be purchased and fixed in a similar way to that shown for the draught excluder strips.

fitting windows

Fitting windows involves both internal and external considerations, so there are many areas to be considered when working on their installation. In many cases the projects may involve replacing more than one window and therefore planning your work and adhering to a timetable becomes a crucial factor. Remember that aesthetic considerations are just as important on the outside as they are on the inside, and there are the added factors of ensuring that the best security is employed, and that the window is able to deal with all manner of attack from the elements, through weatherproofing measures such as insulation and draft proofing. This chapter looks at all these concerns and explains the best techniques for installation of both full window units, and the various accessories which are used to complete the window function.

This window has been fitted with wooden beads to leave a neat finish between the framework and panes.

window furniture & security fittings

Most new wooden windows are supplied with window furniture, but it is often relatively cheap and simple in design, and there is always the option to change it for something more decorative. Security fittings will also need to be added to wooden windows to ensure they are easy to lock and safe from intruders. PVC and metal windows tend to be supplied with window furniture as part of the window design and therefore options should be chosen at the same time as the windows.

security fittings

Security fittings are required for both casement and sash windows, and in a growing market there are many options to suit particular needs and window designs. Some are combined with window opening and closing mechanisms, such as locking casement fasteners or locking sash window fasteners. Other fittings operate independently of the main fittings and represent a supplementary mechanism.

sliding sash window lock

sliding sash window bolt with plate casement

casement locking stay pin

sliding sash window bolt

casement window lock (automatic locking)

locking casement fastener (mortise)

locking casement fastener (wedge)

INSURANCE

It is worth bearing in mind that many insurance companies will specify the lock type to be used on windows and doors. You should therefore check your policy to see if there is any stipulation before going ahead and fitting security systems.

locking sash window fastener

casement window lock

safety advice

Make sure that all members of the household know where the window keys are kept. Ideally, there should be one in each room for in the event of an emergency quick access may be vital.

sash window stop

mortise window bolt

Casement fittings are based on fasteners and stays, primarily because these are the tried and tested mechanisms for both closing and opening windows and allowing them to be opened and locked at a certain distance. Trickle vents are also now installed in new windows to increase room ventilation. When choosing window furniture, ensure that the dimension of window rails is suitable for the furniture you choose as the size of the fixing plate for fasteners and stays does vary.

scroll fastener

black wrought iron fastener

telescopic sliding friction stay

Victorian fastener

trickle vent

screw-up stay for casements

black wrought iron stay and pins

brass casement stay and pins

Sash fittings have to operate in a completely different fashion to casement equivalents as the opening and closing mechanism for the window is very different. Since the distance a sash window can be opened is secured in position by the sash cord balance mechanism itself, the main function of sash window furniture is to fasten the window when shut, or to provide an area to grip onto for opening or closing. There is a wide selection of options available.

sash lift

sash eye

sash pulley with nylon wheel

sash lifting handle

ring sash lift

FANLIGHTS

Fanlights also require a catch mechanism similar to sashes and this has no involvement in the distance a window stays open. These catches normally fall into two categories:

sash stop

sash fastener – unsprung

sash fastener – fitch

sash fastener – quadrant arm

fanlight – catch plate

fanlight – catch box

fitting a window – 1

Fitting a window, or replacing an old one with a new, is a two-part process of initial removal followed by installation – removal often being the more arduous part of the project. Before removal always check that the new window is the right size: discovering that it does not fit after the old one has been taken out may mean you have to board up the opening temporarily.

window removal

Before starting work it is best to check that the weather forecast is favourable, since opening your home to the elements is an inescapable consequence of window replacement. In this example an old metal window is being taken out. Wooden windows tend to be much simpler to remove as they can be sawn or cut out much more easily than metal, which requires the use of more heavy duty cutting equipment. However, in both cases the aim must be to remove the entire existing window and frame, back to the masonry surround.

tools for the job

| protective equipment |
| grinder |
| hammer |
| old chisel or screwdriver |
| nail punch |
| hacksaw |
| wrecking bar |
| dusting brush |

1 Remove any opening casements from the window. On wooden windows, this can be achieved by unscrewing the hinges to release the casements. On metal windows, the hinges are normally externally positioned and cannot be undone in the same manner as for wooden ones – they must be physically cut

away from the main frame. The best tool for this is a grinder whose rotating blade can be used to cut though the metal hinge. Grinders can be hired quite cheaply from your local hire shop. Remember to follow all the manufacturer's instructions and guidelines for use.

2 Once all opening casements have been removed, apply masking tape over the glass in the remaining fixed casements. Proceed to remove the glass panes by initially knocking away any loose putty around the edges of the panes, using a hammer and old chisel or screwdriver. At the same time, you should be

looking for the screw or bolt heads on the horizontal rails that join the various sections of the metal window together. Look for fixings on the outer side of the window frame as well – these are for attachment to the wall surface. Generally, most of the glass has to be removed to expose these fixing points.

3 When fixings are found, use a hammer and nail punch to knock the screw or bolt out of the frame. A few firm knocks with the hammer should loosen it.

4 Once the head of the screw or bolt is exposed, it can be easier to use the claw of the hammer to lever it out of the frame. Alternatively, the claw end of a wrecking bar may be used to do this.

5 Almost invariably, the fixings around the edge of the window, which are attached to the wall, are not so easy to shift. This is mainly because they are longer and more heavy duty in order to secure the

window in place. You may therefore need to use a grinder to cut off the fixing heads. Once the head is off, a few knocks with a hammer and punch on the remaining fitting should knock it clear from the frame, releasing the window edge from its fixed position.

6 The fixed sections of the window may be further broken down by once more using the grinder to cut through the uprights of the vertical rails.

7 If vibration of the rail or window unit as a whole becomes too intense to make use of the grinder

effective, it may be easier to finish these cuts using a normal hacksaw.

8 The removal of the fixings in the horizontal part of the window frame, combined with the cuts in the vertical framework, now makes it possible to pull the relevant sections of the window frame apart. A wrecking bar is the ideal tool to help lever the sections apart.

9 Once the central areas have been broken down, it now becomes easier to lever the frame away from the masonry surround of the window. Again, a wrecking bar is ideal for this job. You may find the odd frame fixing which you missed during the initial removal process. Simply use the grinder to remove fixing heads as necessary and pull the frame from the wall surface.

10 Check around the edge of the window opening to ensure that no remnants of frame fixings are still attached. Remove them with a claw hammer should any be

found, at the same time taking care not to cause damage to the masonry surface. Any fixings that are likely to remove large portions of masonry when levered out should be removed using the grinder instead.

11 Once the entire window framework has been removed and the aperture is totally clear, brush and then dust around the entire frame to remove any debris and loose material. A standard decorator's dusting brush may be used to provide a totally clear surface for the installation of the new window.

safety advice

Taking out windows requires some caution as glass will almost certainly be broken. It is therefore essential to wear gloves and goggles for protection against glass and other flying debris. Also, hang a dust sheet close to the window inside the house to keep mess to a minimum, and always tidy away any broken glass as soon as possible, both inside and outdoors.

fitting a window – 2 ⁄⁄⁄⁄

The technique for fitting wooden or PVC windows is very similar – the most important part of installation being to ensure that the new window is positioned in exactly the same place as the old one. In houses that have cavity walls, it may also be necessary to renew the damp-proof course around the edge of the opening before inserting the new window.

fitting a new PVC window

Windows may arrive glazed or partially glazed. Check the instructions, as some will advise removing glass before installation and others may suggest only removing glass from fixed casements. You may also need to attach the windowsill to the frame before installation.

tools for the job

spirit level
cordless drill/driver
sealant gun
hammer
mini hacksaw

1 Windows will almost certainly be supplied covered with protective tape to prevent any scratches or damage in transit and prior to installation. This can now be removed before the window is fitted – the protective layers should simply peel away from the main PVC frame.

2 Position the window in the aperture and use a spirit level to ensure it is vertical and horizontal. For large windows two people may be required for this process, with one checking the spirit level while the other makes minor adjustments. Once you are satisfied the positioning is correct, use small wooden wedges to hold the window in place.

3 Secure the window in position with frame fixings that will penetrate at least 4cm (1½in) into the surrounding brick, blockwork or stone. Drill a pilot hole for the fixings directly through the window frame, using the correct size of drill bit.

4 Insert the frame fixing and, using a sealant gun, place a dab of silicone on the fixing hole – this will provide a seal once the fixing has been secured in place. Frame fixings will normally require one or two knocks with a hammer to position them in the hole. Stop using the hammer once the wall plug becomes flush with the surrounding frame.

5 Drive the screw into place, ensuring that the thread bites firmly into the wall plug and therefore the wall surface. Be careful not to overtighten the screw because this can cause the frame to bow and distort its shape. As you apply more frame fixings, keep checking with the spirit level that the window has not moved out of place, because it must be maintained in a vertical position.

6 Once all frame fixings have been inserted, attention can be directed towards glazing. This will generally require the use of packers in the rebates of each casement. These will be supplied with the window and

should be positioned as per the manufacturer's guidelines, before the glazed units are inserted.

7 With packers in place, the glazed units can be slotted into place. A little pressure is often required to position the units. Also, if the unit has integral glazing bars, as the example here shows, ensure that they are straight. Snap the internal glazing beads into position once you are happy with the positioning of the glazed unit.

8 Once the whole window is glazed, it is necessary to deal with the junction between the window

frame and masonry. To hide any rough masonry edges, apply a bead of silicone around the sides of the frame, and press a PVC cover strip along the bead to secure it firmly in place. Cut the cover strips to size using a mini hacksaw. Make good the recesses inside the house, with a bead of silicone around the frame.

9 Some windows may have drainage holes to let out any moisture from around the frame. Caps can be snapped in position on these holes to provide a more attractive finish to the window frame.

10 Finally, seal around the outer edge of the window frame and cover strips with a further bead of silicone sealant. The surface of the masonry is generally undulating, so it can be difficult to maintain an even and continuous line of sealant. The process can be aided by ensuring that the nozzle of the sealant tube is cut to the correct size, and if possible you can use masking tape to prevent excess sealant from spreading across the frame or masonry surface. Take plenty of time for this task as it certainly affects the finished look of the window.

PVC windows are a practical alternative to traditional wooden varieties. They are maintenance free and they have become a common option for many homeowners.

measuring & cutting glass ⟩⟩⟩

In most cases, it is advisable and often more convenient to have glass cut by a supplier, especially if a considerable number of panes are required. Some varieties of glass, such as toughened or laminated, should always be cut by a professional. However, situations may arise where it is necessary to make glass cuts of your own, so it is important to understand the correct principles and techniques for carrying out this procedure.

measuring glass

It is vital that any measurements you take are extremely accurate, since glass has no flexibility and cannot easily be trimmed to size. Nor is it possible to join glass if a mistake in measurement has been made. A few simple guidelines must therefore be followed when obtaining measurements for cutting needs.

Bear in mind that glass is always bedded into a window or door frame, whether this be into putty or silicone (PVC windows are clearly excluded from this category). Any measurement must therefore leave a 1–2mm ($\frac{1}{16}$in) tolerance around the edge of the glass for this purpose. In apertures that have never had glass fitted, it is a simple case of measuring dimensions and subtracting the tolerance allowance.

For old windows where a cracked pane may need replacing, measurement is made more difficult as putty may obscure the exact edge of the aperture rebate, and therefore some estimation is required in making an accurate measurement. It is also worth remembering that, in older windows especially, the frame or apertures may not be totally 'square', so be sure to measure all the separate dimensions in order to reach the correct size requirements.

Since accuracy is so important, take extra care when measuring glass requirements and double-check everything before any cut is made. A little extra vigilance at this stage may save a great deal of time later on in the project as a whole.

tools for the job

cutting board
felt tip or Chinagraph pen
combination square
standard glass cutter
circular glass cutter
tape measure
scissors

cutting a simple pane

Cutting down a large pane of standard clear glass to a smaller size is a very straightforward process, provided you use a good quality glass cutter. Make sure that you have a firm, totally flat surface to work on – a piece of MDF board is ideal.

1 Use a felt tip or Chinagraph marker to mark the dimensions of the cut on the glass. A simple mark on the edge of the glass is all that is required, and always double-check the measurement as mistakes cannot be rectified. A combination square is an accurate measuring tool.

2 Holding a straight edge across the pane – again a combination square is an ideal tool here – score the surface of the glass with a glass cutter. Only score the surface once, making a precise line from one edge of the pane to the other.

3 Wear goggles during the cutting process as a precaution against flying splinters of glass. Pick up the pane and position it on top of the combination square, so that the scored line runs precisely along the edge of the ruler of the square. Apply downward pressure to either side of the scored line, which will cause it to crack precisely along the line. The glass is now ready for fitting.

cutting circles

A circular cut can often be required in such instances as vent installation in a window pane. Although this may sound difficult, cutting a circle uses the same principles as for cutting a straight line, except that the type of glass cutter used is slightly different. To achieve a circle, the head of the cutter needs to be fixed at right angles to the shaft, and there must also be a rubber sucker on the other end of the glass cutter to secure and pivot the cutter when in use.

1 Measure the radius requirement of the circular hole and transfer it to the glass cutter. It will be possible to adjust the position of the rubber sucker pad accordingly before securing it in place at the position required on the glass.

2 Secure the pad in the centre of the pane and carefully rotate the cutter around this central position to provide a scored outline. Again, this should only be done once, applying even and constant pressure to the

glass cutter head. You may also need to apply downward pressure to secure the rubber sucker in position.

3 Fix the glass cutter head back into a position perpendicular to the shaft, and make further scores in the glass surface inside the bounds of the scored circular guideline.

4 The scored glass circle will rarely come free in a single piece, so weaken the glass further, enabling it to be removed in smaller pieces. To do so, use the butt end of the glass cutter and tap in the central area until sections of glass begin to break free.

dealing with awkward shapes

The design of a window or door will sometimes demand glass panes of an irregular shape. This can make measurements for glass installation slightly more difficult. For such awkward shapes, the best technique is to make paper templates which may then be used as a guide for cutting purposes.

1 Tape a piece of paper or card over the aperture and draw a guideline around the edge of the aperture to provide an image of the required shape.

2 Cut out the shape accurately, making allowances for bedding in if required. Position the template in the frame aperture to check that it fits. When correct, take the template to a glass supplier who will have the specialist equipment to make such a complex cut. Do not try to cut a shape like this yourself.

fitting glass

Fitting standard glass panes is a straightforward procedure which usually falls into one of two categories – installing either using putty or, alternatively, wooden beads. The former method is demonstrated in more detail on page 290, where a broken pane of glass is being replaced. The latter method is shown below and demonstrates the best technique for securing wooden beads.

demonstrated in more detail on page 290

fitting glass with beads

For new windows, manufacturers will often supply beads with the window, but in some cases it may be necessary to cut your own. The essential point to remember is that the beads must have a chamfered edge, so that when they are positioned water is taken away from the glass surface and prevented from collecting on the window rebates. Aside from this design necessity, the bead can be hardwood or softwood, which should generally be determined by the make-up of the window itself. Beads may also be used to secure double glazed units into wooden frames or apertures.

tools for the job

tape measure

sealant gun

cloth

mitresaw

hammer

card

nail punch

1 Even on a new window, check the dimensions of apertures to ensure that they are 'square'. On a window with multiple panes, it is often the case that not all will be of the same size. Often, those on the smaller opening casement are of a different size to the rest of the window, so be sure to check this situation before ordering or cutting glass. Once the

glass has been cut or supplied, check that the panes fit before proceeding any further.

2 With a sealant gun, run a bead of silicone around the complete rebate of the aperture. Make sure that the bead is continuous and there are no gaps. Silicone is supplied in a large range of colours – the clear variety is the most suitable for glazing purposes.

3 Take a pane of glass and position it in the aperture, by firstly bedding the bottom edge of the pane in the silicone sealant along the bottom rebate. From this starting

point, move your thumbs up the face of the pane, but close to its edges, gradually pressing it into place.

4 Carefully press the pane of glass in place ensuring that it fits correctly. Use a dry cloth to remove any excess silicone sealant.

safety advice

Take care to keep your hands away from the very edge of the glass as the edges are sharp and can cut you. Also, never apply pressure in the centre of the pane when positioning it. Instead, keep to the face of the pane, but near the edges.

5 Use a mitresaw with a fine blade to trim any beading as necessary. Apply another bead of silicone around the glass aperture rebate, and position the first wooden bead along the bottom edge. Push the bead into position, so that its face is flush against the glass surface and its base is sitting flush on the bottom wooden rebate.

6 Fit the top wooden bead followed by the side ones. The side beads may be a slightly tight fit, and you might need to tap them in place using the butt end of a hammer. However, take care not to force the beads as this could crack the glass (if they are simply too tight, saw off a sliver and refit them). Once the beads are fitted, again use a cloth to remove any excess sealant from the glass.

7 The beads should be secured in place using some glazing pins. Two on each bead is all that is required. Protect the glass surface from the edge of the hammer with a piece of card.

8 Finally, ensure that the glazing pins are flush with the wooden bead surface by using a nail punch for the final taps with the hammer.

pre-painting

In the example shown here, a natural wood finish means that there is no need to think about paint when installing the glass. Where a window requires painting, it is worth considering painting the beads before installation to reduce the time otherwise taken to cut-in paint next to the glass. It may also be advisable to paint the rebates before glass insertion. Depending on the thickness of glass used, it may be possible to see the bare wood at the bottom of the rebates, through the edge of the glass once it has been installed. Painting the rebates with the same colour as the window can help to avoid such an unsightly edge to the finished product. Also, it is worth bearing in mind that paint will not adhere to silicone so it may be worth pre-painting the beads before application. This means that any overspill of silicone will not affect the finished look of the final painted surface.

Wooden beads create a neat finish for wooden windows, making a clear and defined line between glass and frame.

installing window furniture

Clearly, for windows to function correctly they require some sort of window furniture to allow them to be opened and closed. Some new windows will come with window furniture fitted, and there is the option to use these or to change them to suit your personal tastes. A large selection of different types are shown on pages 260–1, but always undertake a few checks before making your final selection, as not all window furniture is suitable for every type of window.

fitting a casement fastener

Decide whether the fastener closes by means of a hook or mortise action. The former only requires surface mounting, whereas the latter needs to be cut into the window frame central upright. This is shown below.

tools for the job

bradawl
screwdriver
craft knife
chisel

1 Old furniture or, as in this case, the window furniture supplied with the new window, may simply be unscrewed and set aside before fitting new furniture. Hold the arm of the new fastener in the centre of the vertical casement rail. Use a pencil to mark through the screw holes onto the wood below. The height up the window will depend on window design. About halfway but below two-thirds is generally suitable.

2 Use a bradawl to make pilot holes at the pencil marks, then screw the fastener arm into position. Use a hand held screwdriver since a cordless driver has less control, and you risk allowing the driver head to slip off the head of the screw and scratch the brass fastener surface.

3 Bring the window to a closed position and hold the mortise plate of the fastener in place on the vertical casement frame. Position it so you can tell that the fastener arm will be able to close into the mortise, once the frame has been chiselled out. Draw around the plate with a sharp pencil, ensuring that the plate is in a precisely vertical position.

4 Cut around the pencil guideline with a craft knife, taking care not to allow the blade to slip. Cut to a depth equal to that of the fastener mortise plate. Use a chisel carefully to remove wood down to the depth of the mortise plate. This should be easily achieved by hand and not require the services of a hammer. Then hold the plate in place and draw a guideline inside the central area of the plate. Remove it once more and chisel the area out down to a depth that will allow the insertion of the fastener arm end.

5 Finally, place the mortise plate back in position, use a bradawl to make pilot holes once again, and screw it in securely.

hook fasteners

The main alternative to using mortise fasteners is to use hook fasteners. A similar technique is used to fit hook fasteners, except that the hook point of the fastener is surface mounted and does not need to be cut into the casement surface, unless the fastener design demands this to be the case. It is still important to position the hook point vertically on the central part of the casement frame and check that the fastener will close securely before screwing the hook point in place.

fitting stays and pins

As well as fasteners, most casements require stays to complete the opening and closing mechanism. Again, old or unwanted new window furniture should be removed, so that your chosen stays and pins may be fitted.

tools for the job

pencil
bradawl
screwdriver
cordless drill/driver

1 Close the window, securing it in place with the fitted fastener. Hold the stay in place along the bottom rail of the casement, marking the rail with a pencil through the screw holes in the stay securing plate.

2 Use a bradawl to make pilot holes and then screw the stay in place, again by hand rather than cordless driver to avoid the risk of scratching the stay surface.

Mark the positions of the stay pins with a pencil. It may be necessary to hold the stay in a closed position to find the exact location required for fixing the pins in the correct place.

3 Make pilot holes at the pencil marks using a bradawl or fine drill bit as shown here. Screw the pins in position by hand and check the completed opening and closing mechanism of the window in its entirety. It is still possible at this late stage to adjust the pin position slightly to ensure that the stay closes onto the pins securely.

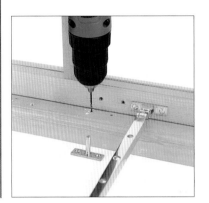

Although window furniture has a primarily functional role, it can also add a decorative edge to the finished look of a window.

adding security fittings ⁄⁄

Although security fittings are usually seen as additional to standard opening and closing mechanisms, window furniture for security purposes ought to be regarded as equally important and just as 'standard', whilst issues of security should be considered for all varieties of window, not simply wooden casement windows. Again, there is a wide selection of fittings and you should choose according to the design of your windows and the finish of the other window furniture.

windows & doors

fitting casement locks

Some casement fasteners are supplied with an integral locking system (see page 261), but whether or not your windows have these fitted, casement locks further enhance the overall security set-up. Normally, two casement locks should be fitted to each casement with one at the bottom and one at the top of the vertical rail.

tools for the job

bradawl

cordless drill/driver

screwdriver

1 Hold the two sections of the lock mechanism in place on the window casement and frame. Use a bradawl to mark the fixing points for the lock on the casement.

2 Use a cordless drill to drill pilot holes accurately in the casement. Ensure that the drill bit

used is smaller than the diameter of the screw shafts used for fitting the casement lock.

3 Screw the first part of the lock into position on the opening casement. Use a hand held screwdriver to provide better control than the cordless driver equivalent and reduce the risk of scratching the lock fitting.

4 Hold the second part of the casement lock in position on the vertical rail of the frame. Check its correct position by opening and closing the lock and, using a bradawl to mark its position, pilot hole these marks and screw the plate in place.

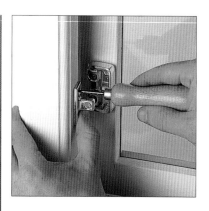

5 Finally, shut the window and use the supplied lock key to check that it closes correctly. Employ the same procedure to fit a further casement lock at the top level of the window.

fitting stay locks

There are many differing designs of stay lock available today, but one of the more common and most simple to fit is that which involves locking pins. In this situation, the original pins are being replaced by locking varieties, thus making the window more secure once it has been shut and locked.

tools for the job

bradawl
....
screwdriver
....

1 Release the stay from its closed position and unscrew the pins.

2 Hold the new locking pins in place and use a bradawl to mark new holes if necessary.

3 Screw the locking pins in place, ensuring that they are secured firmly in position on the frame.

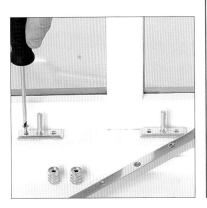

4 Close the stay and screw the locking barrels onto the threaded pins, securing them in place with the key supplied. These barrels will now rotate in position, unless a key is used to release them.

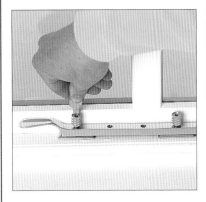

PVC windows

PVC windows are usually supplied with both the standard furniture and security mechanisms built into the window design itself. Most PVC windows have locking fasteners, which in many designs have a number of locking points around the edge of any opening casements. These points are released or locked by the handle opening mechanism. So although security is in general already taken care of with PVC windows, there are few, if any, alternatives for changing window furniture after initial installation.

sash windows & security

Most sash window fittings have security built into their design, as demonstrated by the variety of fittings and options shown on page 261. However, the illustration below helps to demonstrate how sash window fittings act together to form a security system aimed at preventing or discouraging forced entry.

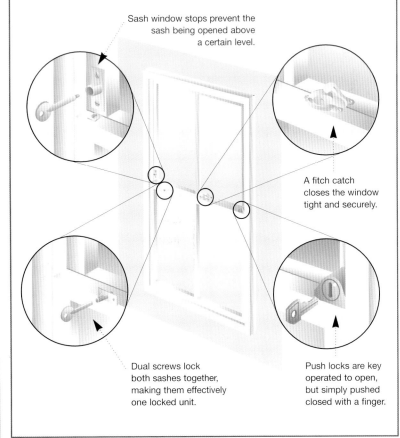

Sash window stops prevent the sash being opened above a certain level.

A fitch catch closes the window tight and securely.

Dual screws lock both sashes together, making them effectively one locked unit.

Push locks are key operated to open, but simply pushed closed with a finger.

insulating windows

The most effective form of window insulation is clearly to choose the PVC option and have new window units installed. In many cases, however, this can prove too expensive and other ideas need to be considered when looking at the best way of improving insulation in your home. Fitting a further window layer or insulatory barrier to an existing window offers a cheaper form of insulation than full double glazing, and is therefore often referred to as secondary double glazing.

fitting secondary double glazing – sliding doors

Sliding secondary double glazing tends to be fitted in window recesses, and its design still allows access to the main window so that it may be opened and closed as required. These units tend to be supplied in a kit form by manufacturers, which is then cut to size and fitted to your particular requirements.

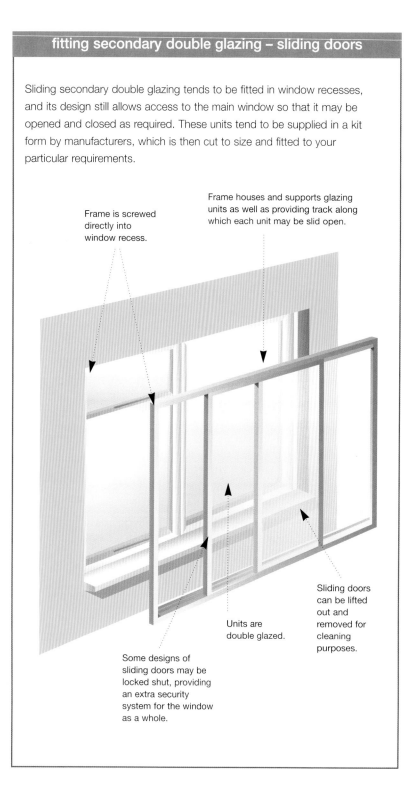

Frame is screwed directly into window recess.

Frame houses and supports glazing units as well as providing track along which each unit may be slid open.

Units are double glazed.

Sliding doors can be lifted out and removed for cleaning purposes.

Some designs of sliding doors may be locked shut, providing an extra security system for the window as a whole.

OTHER INSULATION OPTIONS

● **Polythene sheets** – One of the most economical ways of providing insulation is to use thin polythene sheeting, secured across the window or recess. This can be bought in kit form, and the sheet is initially secured around the window frame with tape. A hairdryer is then directed at the sheet which tautens the polythene and provides an insulatory barrier. The obvious drawback is that it is not possible to get to the window without breaking the sheet of polythene, but as a seasonal option or for windows that are rarely opened or simply do not open, this easy method is ideal.

● **Double glazed panes** – On existing wooden windows, insulation may be improved by replacing the panes of glass with double glazed units. Since these units are much thicker than normal panes, it is important first of all to check that the rebates of the windows are large enough to house the panes.

● **Draught excluders** – A further, very economical option for existing windows is to use one of the many freely available designs of draught excluder strips. Different manufacturers provide different products and designs. The two most common systems are either self-adhesive foam-based strips or more substantial plastic brush strips. The latter are mitred at the corners of the frame and fixed in place using panel pins. Different designs are suited to different types of windows.

A simpler system than the sliding doors can be found by using single PVC sheets fixed across the entire window surface. This provides an effective insulatory system, which is much simpler to fit than the sliding door mechanism shown opposite. Access is also possible in terms of opening windows if required. This is a cost effective and simple option that can either be applied on a seasonal basis or on windows which do not require frequent opening.

tools for the job

tape measure

mini hacksaw

craft knife

screwdriver

1 Accurately measure the dimensions of the entire window frame, as these will form the measurements for the plastic retaining track used to hold the PVC sheet in place. In this instance the sheet is being fitted directly onto the window frame inside the recess, but it may also be fitted on the wall surface outside, thus covering the whole recess. Prior to fitting the secondary double glazing, it is worthwhile cleaning the window on the inside and outside as access is more limited once the secondary glazing sheet is positioned.

2 Cut the track to size with a mini hacksaw or craft knife, mitring the ends to form neat joins in each corner of the window. Remove the backing of the adhesive tape on the back of the track.

3 Press the track firmly in position on the window frame, ensuring good contact between the tape and frame surface. There is normally a short period of time before the adhesive secures the track permanently in position, so minor movements or adjustments should be made quickly.

4 Once the track is in position all around the frame, lever it open. A screwdriver may be needed to help open up the track initially, but once it has begun to open it can normally be finished by hand. Measure the exact dimensions of width and height required for the PVC glazing sheet.

Transfer the measurements onto the sheet and use a mini hacksaw to cut it to size.

5 Insert the glazing sheet into the retaining track, sliding it carefully into position. Again, it is worth cleaning the sheet before positioning it, as access is limited to the inside face once it is fixed in place.

6 Finally, snap the retaining track closed onto the PVC surface, creating an effective form of insulation.

repairing doors & windows

Doors and windows are expensive yet essential elements in the make up of your home, and therefore need to be looked after to as great a degree as possible. Normal issues of wear and tear must be addressed to understand how problems occur and what are the best techniques for repair and restoration. Many of these problems are simple and fall into the category of nothing more than general servicing to ensure that operation of doors and windows is maintained. However, other repairs may be more extensive, requiring more detailed measures when it comes to restoration. The following chapter covers a wide range of topics in this area, and helps to demonstrate the best and most suitable techniques for dealing with the most common problems likely to be experienced.

These window panes feature a water lily stained glass design that complements the bathroom function of this room.

recognizing problems

An appropriate diagnosis is the first step to addressing any problems, and because doors and windows almost always include an opening and closing function and mechanism, many of their problems relate to the various ways in which this function is either hindered or prevented. The second major consideration is that although many problems are caused by general wear and tear, problems mostly occur in wooden doors and windows.

problem areas on doors

There are a number of areas on doors where problems may occur, with some being far more serious and more difficult to fix than others. This example shows many of the areas and points where problems may occur.

Door sticking at top can be caused by one of the door hinges loosening and thus allowing the door to drop one end whilst raising the other. The door will need to be removed and re-hung or excess planed from the top.

Door sticking at sides is, more often than not, caused by paint build-up over the years. Planing is therefore all that is required. Alternatively, it may be down to hinge movement and the door may need to be re-hung.

Door sticking at bottom is normally caused by hinges dropping or, on external doors, damp penetration at the base could cause the wood to swell and expand. The door will need to be removed and re-hung or excess planed from the bottom. Alternatively, an uneven floor surface may cause this problem, and changing normal butt hinges to rising butts should clear it up.

CAUTION

• **General sticking** – Sometimes sticking doors can point to more serious problems, as wall subsidence may knock a door frame out of line, creating a misshapen aperture for the door to close into. If in any doubt, therefore, seek professional advice on this matter, but remember that this sort of problem is relatively rare and sticking doors are more likely to result from the other explanations provided.

• **Warping doors** – This can occur with relatively cheap doors soon after installation. To avoid this happening, ensure that the doors are stored flat before installation and are left in the room they are to be put in for a number of days before being hung. This enables them to get used to the prevailing atmospheric conditions.

• **Sticking latch** – Gradual movement over time, or an old door which has slowly been planed and planed to fit the frame, may eventually reach a point where planing cannot continue because the latch plate is proud of the door edge. It is therefore necessary to recess the latch plate further into the door edge.

• **Hinge bound** – Where hinges have not been recessed into the door lining and/or door edge, a situation arises where the door is unable to close onto the doorstop. As a result pressure is put upon the hinges, which may eventually cause the door lining or door edge to split or damage. Resetting the hinge position is therefore necessary.

Due to the fact that casement windows work on a hinge mechanism, many of their problems are similar to those suffered by doors. The reasons for sticking casements are therefore often similar to those for doors. However, windows will always have an external aspect and the diagram below illustrates some other problems that may occur.

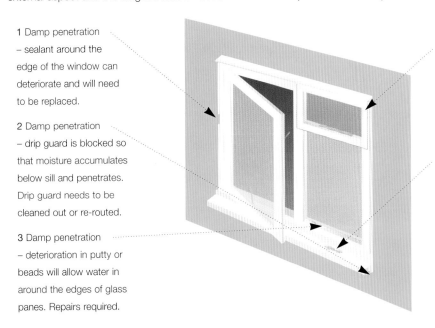

1 Damp penetration – sealant around the edge of the window can deteriorate and will need to be replaced.

2 Damp penetration – drip guard is blocked so that moisture accumulates below sill and penetrates. Drip guard needs to be cleaned out or re-routed.

3 Damp penetration – deterioration in putty or beads will allow water in around the edges of glass panes. Repairs required.

Sticking casements are caused by paint build-up or swelling during damp conditions or sometimes hinging problems. Normally a little planing will fix the problem, but in some cases re-hinging will be required.

Sometimes damp and/or insect attack can cause problems with wooden windows. If caught early enough small, localized areas can be treated, filled or partially replaced with new wood. Failure to carry out repairs quickly may lead to total window replacement being necessary.

Many of the problems found with sashes are the same as those illustrated for casement windows. In other words, rot and damp problems are just as likely to occur. However, there are some other problems that relate specifically to sash windows, as shown in the illustration below.

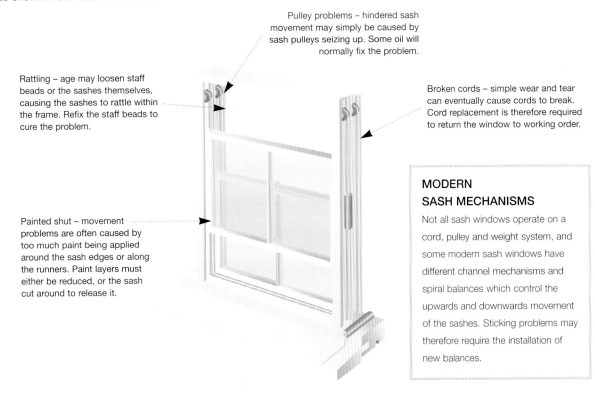

Pulley problems – hindered sash movement may simply be caused by sash pulleys seizing up. Some oil will normally fix the problem.

Rattling – age may loosen staff beads or the sashes themselves, causing the sashes to rattle within the frame. Refix the staff beads to cure the problem.

Broken cords – simple wear and tear can eventually cause cords to break. Cord replacement is therefore required to return the window to working order.

Painted shut – movement problems are often caused by too much paint being applied around the sash edges or along the runners. Paint layers must either be reduced, or the sash cut around to release it.

MODERN SASH MECHANISMS

Not all sash windows operate on a cord, pulley and weight system, and some modern sash windows have different channel mechanisms and spiral balances which control the upwards and downwards movement of the sashes. Sticking problems may therefore require the installation of new balances.

releasing sticking doors & windows ✓✓

Once diagnosed, sorting out window and door sticking problems becomes a comparatively straightforward task of simply choosing the right technique to deal with the particular problem at hand. As in all instances, it is best to start by trying the easy cures before moving on to the more complicated.

simple solutions

With sticking doors, especially along the sides, it is best to begin by trying the simpler solutions before taking more dramatic action, which may entail extensive wood removal from the door edge. Sometimes slight seasonal changes in response to atmospheric conditions can cause minimal expansion and contraction of door surfaces, and minimal easing is therefore all that is required.

tools for the job

candle

sandpaper or sanding block

wood plane

jigsaw

craft knife

1 Rub a candle down the leading edge of the door. Sometimes, this small transference of wax onto the

door edge can help to ease its operation, allowing the door to open and close more easily.

2 If this does not work, use some sandpaper or a sanding block down the edge. Start on the rough side and progress to the smooth side.

3 If still more easing is required, resort to using a wood plane and gradually shave off sections of wood along the door edge. Take care not to work all along the door edge as it may only be sticking in one localized area. It is normally possible to see

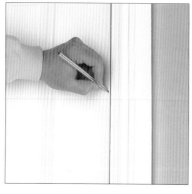

where the door is sticking by closing it and making a mark with a pencil to show where the obstructing areas are.

4 Set the plane so that only small amounts of wood are shaved off each time. Keep opening and closing the door to monitor the situation until ease of function is restored. The door edge may then be repainted.

tips of the trade

In some circumstances, paint build-up on a door edge must be reduced to help the opening and closing mechanism of the door. A heat gun can be used to remove excess paint initially, before employing a wood plane to smooth the surface. Paint may otherwise clog up the workings and blade of the plane, making it difficult to move along the door edge, so removal of the paint first is a good option. Remember when using heat guns to adhere to all safety rules and guidelines, and never to leave a heat gun unattended when switched on.

bottom of door sticking

When a door is sticking at the bottom it is best to use a scribing technique to measure how much wood needs to be removed in order to ease movement.

Put the door in a closed position. Cut a block of wood with a height representing the required clearance between the bottom of the door and the floor. Hold a pencil tight on top of the block, with its point resting on the block edge. Draw the block and pencil across the floor surface at the base of the door, leaving a pencil guideline along the bottom of the door. The door may now be removed from its hinges and trimmed to this guideline. For small cuts a wood plane may be used. For larger sections, a jigsaw is the ideal tool. Re-hang the door once the wood has been removed.

sash sticking

Sticking sashes is a common problem, and before attempting to take any mechanisms apart it is worth checking whether the window has simply been 'painted shut'.

If a window has been painted without allowing any movement of the sashes, it is likely that as the paint dries it will form a bond between the sashes and runners and therefore prevent the window from being opened. To cure this situation, simply use a craft knife to run around the edge of the sash, thus breaking the bond or seal and freeing up the window so that it may freely be moved up and down once more.

door furniture

On occasion, the door furniture itself may be responsible for preventing doors from opening and closing easily. This is usually due to the latch mechanism sitting proud of the door edge and catching the door frame or catch plate as it closes.

tools for the job

screwdriver

chisel

1 Remove the door handles and unscrew the latch plate. With some latches this may be a two-stage process, with a second cover plate actually covering the main latch.

2 It can be tricky to pull the latch out of the door, for if it has been fitted correctly it should be held tightly. Therefore position a screwdriver where the door handle spindle would

normally be, and pull on both the handle and the shaft of the screwdriver simultaneously, to pop the latch out from its recessed position.

3 Once out, use a sharp chisel to remove more wood from the recess, gradually scraping the recess surface back and taking care not to remove too much wood. If a lot of wood removal is required, you will need to reposition the hole for the handle and lock, as any adjustment in latch plate position will push the handle position away from the door edge and across the door surface.

4 Once you are happy with the amount of wood removed, replace the latch and check that the door closes before fixing it back in place. Remember that because the handle is not yet in position, once the door is shut it will not be possible to open it unless you have a flat-head screwdriver available to insert into the latch and act as a temporary handle, whilst you check the door opening and closing function.

fixing loose doors & windows ✂✂

As well as the common irritants relating to sticking doors or windows, there are also problems of equal inconvenience when doors or windows are loose and do not function properly. Whereas sticking problems tend to require removal of wood or recessing of fittings, 'loose' ones require the opposite remedy, with an addition of material needed to restore function.

adjusting a catch plate

As explained below, addition of wood strips is an extreme measure, and, for a door that is loose, a simpler solution is to adjust the position of the catch plate. Bringing the plate fractionally away from the door frame is usually all that is needed to allow the latch to hold in position once the door is shut.

ADDING WOOD

Where there is a huge difference between the width of a door and its frame, there is clearly a need to actually add wood to the edges of the door. This situation may only arise in extreme circumstances, or where a door that is obviously too narrow is moved to fit into a wider frame. In these cases, it literally becomes a procedure of cutting strips to the depth and width requirement, and screwing them to the door edges. It may be necessary to screw strips to both edges to maintain the balanced look of the door, especially if it is a panelled design. For smaller additions, joining on one side may be all that is required. If attempting this technique, remember that accuracy is vital in order to keep joins unnoticeable, and it is likely that the door will require a painted finish, because a natural wood coating may highlight the joined strips and make the repair too obvious.

tools for the job

screwdriver

scissors

craft knife

1 Unscrew the catch plate from its fixed position. It may require a little persuasion by levering it free with the end of a flat-head screwdriver.

2 On a piece of card, draw a pencil guideline around the edge of the catch plate itself.

3 Cut out the catch plate template precisely using scissors, but do not worry about cutting away the extended front section as this is an area which is not required when you fit the card in the recess itself.

4 Position the cardboard template in the catch plate recess, trimming as necessary to make any final adjustments for fitting precisely and tightly in place.

5 Screw the catch plate back in place, through the template and into the screw fixing holes below.

Use a craft knife to cut out the holes for housing the latch and lock. Try closing the door to see if the movement of the plate has affected the closed position. If the door is still loose, remove the catch plate and add a further piece of card to increase the 'packing'. Continue to add and test until the door closes properly.

rattling doors

Rattling doors provide another example of how a door may be loose fitting, but in this case the door itself may be a perfect fit in terms of its position in the frame, with the actual problem relating to the position of the doorstop. In other words, the doorstop has been positioned too far from the latch, so that even small gusts of wind or draughts cause the door latch to rattle rather than being held firmly in place by the latch position and doorstop combined. Conversely, the door may not close properly, because the doorstop is positioned too far forward or too close to the catch plate, and therefore the door cannot physically be shut in place. The remedy for this problem is fortunately very simple.

tools for the job

old chisel

pencil

hammer

Remove the doorstop by carefully levering it out of position using an old chisel to assist you.

Close the door and mark a line on the door lining to show where the ideal position for the edge of the doorstop will be, to allow the door to close tightly but still easily. Simply reopen the door and nail the doorstop back in place according to the new guidelines.

It may also be necessary to move the doorstop on the head and hinged side of the frame, so check for this once the first piece of doorstop has been repositioned.

loose casements

The opening casements in windows may also rattle or become loose, often as a result of them warping slightly or losing shape through age and weather attack. This situation may often be helped by adjusting the window closing mechanism and more specifically the position of the window

---

stays. The fixing plate of a window stay is usually positioned closer to the hinging edge of the casement than the opening edge. This allows the window to be opened further. However, where a window has warped, by moving the fixing plate closer to the opening edge greater leverage is gained when closing the window and therefore the stay helps to pull the casement back into shape.

tools for the job

screwdriver

bradawl or pencil

cordless drill/driver

Simply unscrew the stay fixing plate from its position near the hinged edge of the casement.

Reposition it, using a bradawl or pencil to mark the new fixing position. Pilot drill holes and screw the stay in place. There is normally no need to reposition the stay pins.

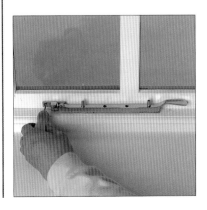

repairing hinges ✐✐✐

Many of the problems associated with doors and windows failing to open and close efficiently are caused by faulty hinging mechanisms, such as hinges not positioned correctly or not working in the appropriate manner. Outlined here are some common remedies for malfunctioning hinges on both doors, as shown, and casement windows.

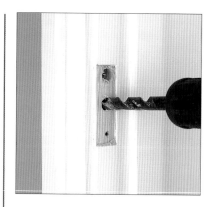

tools for the job

hammer
craft knife
screwdriver
cordless drill/driver
wooden mallet
chisel
pencil
scissors
saw
wood plane

loosening stubborn screws

When dealing with hinge problems, the first obstacle to overcome can in fact be removing the screws from their position. When hinges have not been painted removal tends to be relatively simple, but for painted ones the process can be much more difficult.

1 Begin by using the head of a flat-head screwdriver to scrape out paint from the slot in the screw head. A craft knife may also be used here.

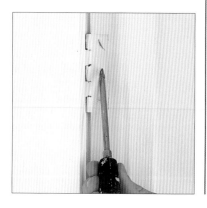

2 As further encouragement to moving the screws, give each one a few taps with a hammer on the screwdriver to dislodge it fractionally from its painted solid position. If the screw head is too corroded to make undoing possible, it may simply be necessary to drill out the screw and use a new fixing.

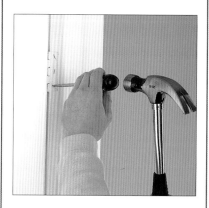

strengthening a hinge fixing

Through general wear and tear, hinges can become worn and their fixings can loosen, which results in a door moving out of position in its frame. Re-tightening screws may fix this situation, but normally the holes have become too enlarged for the screws to bite firmly. It is therefore necessary to fill the holes and redrill the fixings.

1 Remove the door from the frame. Make the existing screw holes much larger by using a large drill bit to bore into the door lining at each screw position. The size of the drill bit should be similar to that of the

diameter of the wooden dowel which will be inserted into the holes.

2 Insert lengths of wooden dowel into the bored holes, ensuring that the dowel is a tight fit. Apply some wood glue around the dowel before putting it in position.

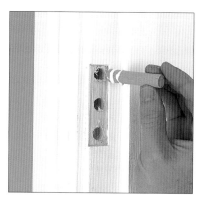

3 Knock the dowels in place using a wooden mallet, tapping carefully until the dowel extends a good distance into the hole. Avoid using a hammer for this process as it is likely to split the dowel. Use a cloth to wipe away any excess wood glue from around each dowel.

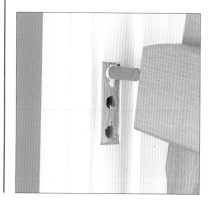

4 Leave the dowels to dry overnight so that they are glued firmly in position. Then, using a sharp chisel, cut off the dowel ends so that they are back flush with the surface of the door lining.

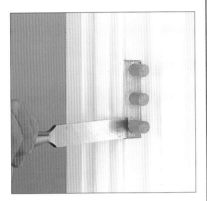

5 Holding a hinge back in position, use a pencil to mark the exact points for the screw fixings. This stage is especially important if you have changed or renewed the door hinges.

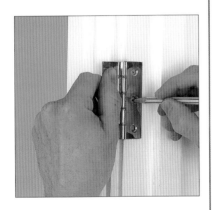

6 Using a fine bit, drill some pilot holes at each newly marked position. Finally, reposition the hinges and re-hang the door.

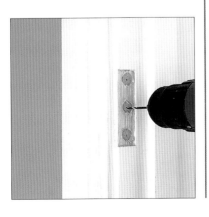

packing out a hinge

In a similar way to packing out a catch plate as shown on page 282, hinges may also be packed out to adjust the door position to close more efficiently. Instead of introducing a card template behind the catch plate, the hinges are removed and cardboard is positioned behind them.

1 Remove the door and hinges and cut some thick card to the size of the hinge recess. Be as accurate as possible with the card size to ensure that it fits snugly into the hinge recess. Try adding different thicknesses of card to aid this process. As an alternative to card, thin plyboard may also be used.

2 Position the card in the recess before screwing the hinges and door back in position. Test the door to see if closing has improved. If not, add more packing as required. You may find that the other hinge on the door will also require packing out.

patching a removed hinge

For many reasons a door may be removed from an entrance, or the side it hinges on the frame may be changed. Whatever the reason, the recesses of the old hinges in the door frame need to be repaired so that the frame may be redecorated. This is achieved by a simple patching technique that fills the recess and repairs the frame.

1 Having removed the hinge and cleaned up the hole with a chisel, cut a piece of softwood down to as close to the dimensions of the hinge recess as possible. Test it fits before applying some wood glue to it and positioning it in the frame.

2 Once the glue has dried, use a wood plane to smooth the surface of the patch and bring it flush with the surrounding door frame. Finally, some fine filling may be required before repainting the area to blend in with the rest of the frame.

renovating sash windows – 1

The opening mechanism of sash windows has traditionally been based on a cord, pulley and weight system, which balances the weight of the window as it is moved up and down for opening and closing purposes. When it comes to renovating and repairing these mechanisms, the process is fairly complex in the number of stages required but relatively simple to do if tasks are undertaken in the right order. The most common form of damage involves a broken sash cord.

removing the sash & replacing the cord

The balance of a sash window is such that the frame really only acts as a guide for moving the sashes. The sashes themselves are free running, using the pulley and cord mechanism as its only attachment to the frame as a whole. In other words, there is no solid or hinged attachment between a sash and the frame. However, releasing them from their operating position can be tricky.

tools for the job

old chisel or screwdriver
hammer

1 Lever away the staff bead from the main part of the frame using an old chisel or screwdriver. The bead is normally pinned in position with relatively small nails, so by moving the position of the chisel up and down the junction, gradually the fixings are loosened and the bead removed. It is

important to try not to damage the bead as it will be repositioned once the window repair is complete.

2 Remove the cover that hides the weights inside the frame of the window. These are sometimes metal plates that unscrew, but in this case the cover is made from a wooden panel. Again, use an old chisel or screwdriver to lever and ease the cover out of the frame.

3 Pull the top of the weight out from inside the frame and remove the broken section of sash cord. In some cases it may be necessary to reach right down inside the frame to locate the weight.

4 Remove the sash from the frame, remembering that when you pull the side of the sash (with the damaged cord) away from the frame, the other side of the sash will still be attached to the frame. It can thus be tricky to move the sash into a position that is clear from the frame and allows access for repairs. It is best to manoeuvre the undamaged cord so that the sash can be rested on a workbench in front of the window.

5 With the sash out of the way, this is a good opportunity to service the pulley and confirm that it is in good working order. Apply some oil to the pulley mechanism to ensure its moving parts are lubricated.

6 Take a piece of string and tie it onto a nail. Instead of using a straight nail, ensure that the one you use is slightly curved. This can be achieved with a few hammer blows.

7 Holding the untied end of the string with one hand, thread the end with the curved nail over the pulley. If the nail does not go through on the first attempt – as it is still too straight – simply increase the curve of the nail until it threads through easily.

NEW SASH SYSTEMS

Sash window design has been varied slightly in modern times with the introduction of different mechanisms to balance the sashes, but the opening principle remains the same, with the sashes still sliding along runners. Modern sash windows have vinyl or PVC linings for the runners and spiral balances in place of the traditional mechanism. However, cords and weights are still the most common sash opening mechanism.

8 Once the nail appears in the hole revealed by the removal of the weight cover, turn your attention to the other end of the string and tie a new section of sash cord to it.

9 Now thread the sash cord end, whilst tied to the string, over the pulley and into the window frame. It is important that the end of the cord is trimmed, because if it is in any way frayed it will be difficult to thread over the pulley mechanism.

10 Pull on the other end of the string (the end with the nail on it), thus pulling the cord down to

the weight cover hole. Once you can grab the end of the cord, pull it out from the hole and remove the string.

11 Thread the cord into the securing hole on the weight and tie it off tightly. Weight design will vary slightly, but generally the cord must be threaded through a hole in the top of the weight, pulled through a hole in the side of the weight, tied off and then pushed back into the side hole to wedge the knot in place.

12 In some cases, if the weight is designed to drop down into the window frame, it will be necessary to tie a knot at the other end of the cord to prevent the weight pulling it over the pulley and down into the window frame, which will oblige you to start the threading process again. Make a simple knot which can be untied easily when it is time to attach this end of the cord to the sash. Alternatively, tie off the cord onto a screwdriver, which may then be positioned next to the pulley and will prevent the cord pulling through.

renovating sash windows – 2 ↗↗↗

With the sash removed and the new cord threaded over the pulley and into the frame, attention can be turned to re-attaching the sash to the cord and getting it back into a running position. Once again it is best to follow a particular order of tasks, so that the window is, in effect, re-assembled in a good running order.

tools for the job

long-nose pliers
pencil
marker pen
scissors or craft knife
hammer
sealant gun

attaching the cord and replacing the sash

It may be worth checking the running mechanism of the other part of the sash window, to ensure that the internal parting bead allows the sash to run freely. If not, re-position it while the other sash is out of its place before tackling the broken sash.

1 Remove the remaining part of the broken sash cord. The method required will depend on the exact type of sash design. In this case, a pair of long-nose pliers is ideal to pull the old knotted section of cord out of its position in the side of the sash. If the cord is nailed or stapled, use pliers or a claw hammer to lever out any fixings.

2 Use a pencil to mark on the front of the sash (being repaired) the exact position of the cord retaining hole located on the side of the sash.

3 Reposition the sash in the frame, so that it is in its totally open position, with the top of the sash up close to the pulley

mechanism. Untie the new section of sash cord and hold it in the appropriate position, feeling the tension of the weight balance on the cord, and use a marker pen to mark on the cord next to the position of the cord retaining hole (marked in step 2).

4 Pull the sash out of its position in the frame once more and thread the cord through the top of the sash and out through the cord retaining hole, until you see the marked-off point on the cord. This task may be better suited to two people, so that one can take the weight of the sash window whilst the other threads the cord.

5 Tie a secure knot in the cord at the marked-off point and allow it to position itself inside the retaining hole. Check your measurements again before cutting off the excess cord with a pair of scissors or a craft knife, once the knot has been securely tied. Once again, two people may be required for this process with one holding the sash window whilst the other ties off and cuts the cord.

windows & doors

288

6 Reposition the repaired sash back in the frame. Ensure that the running mechanism is working correctly by opening and closing the sash a few times, checking that the movement is smooth and that the window does not jam or become hampered in the runners. It may sometimes be necessary slightly to re-adjust the sash cord length to reach optimum levels of movement.

7 Once you are happy with the smooth-running system, the weight cover can be replaced. Wooden ones often simply lever back in position and may require one or two taps with the butt end of a hammer. Take care not to damage the cover even though the fit may be tight, because making an exact replacement is a fiddly task.

8 The staff bead may now be replaced in its original position and part-nailed in. This is a suitable time to test the running of the sash in relation to all the front staff beads. If the sash has tended to rattle, for

example, it may be necessary to take out and move the beads slightly closer to the sash surface. Conversely, if the sash has generally been too tight in the runners, the beads may need to be moved away from the sash by a fractional amount. The beads can now be fully nailed in.

9 Finally, refill any nail holes in the staff bead with all-purpose filler and sand to a smooth finish once the filler has dried. Run a bead of flexible filler or caulk between the bead and the frame, and smooth with a wetted finger before it dries. The window frame may now be re-decorated.

Sash windows provide both an attractive and efficient type of window, as long as the running mechanism is kept in good order so it moves freely up and down.

replacing a broken pane ✂✂

Broken panes are probably the most common window problem that prevails in most households. Rectifying the situation comes down to a straightforward case of glass replacement, though the technique required for this task will be dependent on the way in which the glass pane is secured in the window. Glass is commonly held in position by wooden beads or putty, and it is replacing a pane in a puttied window that is demonstrated below.

tools for the job

hammer
hacking knife
pliers
paintbrush
putty knife
tape measure
protective gloves
goggles

broken pane in a puttied window

1 Tape up the outside of the broken pane with masking tape, keeping the tape only on the glass surface and not encroaching onto the putty or wooden frame of the window. Take care not to apply too much pressure on the glass surface and risk shattering the glass further at this preliminary stage.

2 On the inside of the broken pane, tape a folded plastic bag to the wooden rails of the window frame. Ensure a total seal around the edge of the tape, making certain that there are no gaps or holes. The bag will prevent glass splinters from being scattered inside the house when the old pane is removed.

3 From the outside of the window, use the butt end of a hammer to tap the glass pane, knocking it inwards and allowing it to break away from the rebates of the frame. Always wear protective goggles when carrying out this process to shield your eyes from any flying glass or debris.

4 Remove the largest sections of broken glass and place them in a bucket for safe disposal later. Some putty on the window rebates may also come away during this process, and should also be disposed of. Remove only the loose material by hand and leave the more secure pieces until later.

5 Use a hacking knife to scrape around the edge of the window rebates to remove any last pieces of glass and debris. If you do not have a hacking knife, a hammer and old chisel may be used to equally good effect. Remove old sprigs or pins in the rebates with a pair of pliers.

6 Remove the plastic bag and dust off the rebate to remove any debris. Seal the surface by priming all the bare wood in the rebate and on its edges. Allow this to dry before continuing. The paint seals the surface and provides a base for the putty.

7 Apply a small amount of putty around the rebate. Make sure that the putty has been well 'worked' in your hands, to mix it up and remove any lumps before application. The putty should have a similar texture to very pliable plasticine.

CHOOSING GLASS

Measuring size requirements is considered on pages 266–7, but it is also important to consider what frame the glass is being fitted into. Although the example here shows a window, a similar technique is used for doors, though the glass used in doors must be thicker, and sometimes toughened, compared to the thinner regulations pertaining to windows. So whether cutting your own glass or leaving it to a supplier, remember to choose the correct thickness for the particular replacement pane required.

safety advice

Replacing a pane will require access to both the inside and outside of the window. Therefore if the window is higher than ground floor level, be sure to use the appropriate access equipment for safe work on the exterior. Broken glass is extremely sharp and dangerous to handle, so wear protective gloves and goggles.

8 Press the glass into position in the frame, inserting the base first and applying pressure only near the edges of the pane. Allow the edges to become well bedded into the putty, squeezing excess out onto the interior rebate.

9 Hammer a few sprigs or pins into the rebate, next to but not touching the glass surface. This prevents any possibility of the pane falling out before the putty dries. Use a piece of card to protect the glass surface from the edge of the hammer during this process.

10 Apply another putty bead around the glass/frame junction. This bead should be of more generous proportions than the first, covering the entire rebate area.

11 Use a putty knife to 'finish' the putty surface. Rest the edge of the knife on the glass on one side and rebate edge on the other. Applying a little pressure on the blade, drag the knife across the putty surface. It may take more than one run of the knife to achieve a smooth finish. Finally, trim any excess putty from the interior rebate of the pane. Allow it to dry before re-decoration.

REPLACEMENT OPTIONS

For wooden beads, you need to remove the beads and broken glass before following installation guidelines as detailed on pages 268–9. Double glazed units in wooden frames require a similar process, but in PVC windows professional advice is advisable if a pane or unit replacement is required.

restoring lead lights ⟋⟋⟋

Some windows may be composed entirely of lead lights, whilst others have sections. The technique usually involves different glass colours being used in a pattern. Repairing broken panes is undoubtedly a fiddly job, which in some cases is best left to the professionals. However, as long as there is easy access to the damaged area, it is more than possible to make the repair yourself. If possible, remove the damaged casement section first so that it can be treated on a flat surface.

repairing hairline cracks and leaking panes

Small cracks in panes are often relatively inconspicuous to the naked eye, but will become worse unless attended to. The pane can be fully replaced, but this is generally not required as weatherproof properties can be restored by simply using some silicone sealant to seal any such problem areas.

tools for the job

dusting brush

sealant gun

cloth

1 Dust out any loose material from the glass/lead junction and apply a small but continuous bead of sealant around the junction.

2 Use a clean cloth to remove any excess sealant from the glass surface and smooth the sealant to a finish. Turn the entire

casement over, and repeat steps 1 and 2 before repositioning the casement in the window as a whole.

replacing a broken pane

tools for the job

craft knife

chisel

goggles

putty knife

cloth

1 The method for knocking out a broken pane shown on page

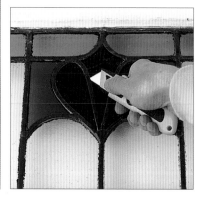

290 cannot be applied to lead lights, as this will almost certainly damage the lead, and access is required right into the lead rebate. First of all, cut the putty seal between the lead and the glass, using a craft knife.

2 The pliable nature of lead allows you to fold it back away from the glass surface to reveal the glass edge. A chisel is the ideal tool for this purpose, but take care only to fold the lead back and not to cause it to tear.

3 Turn the casement over and repeat steps 1 and 2, followed by a further cut around the edge of the glass with a craft knife.

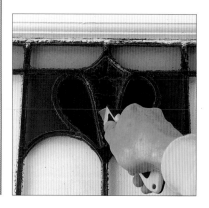

4 Turn the casement once more and tap out the broken pieces of glass. A little pressure with a cut-off piece of wood is a good tool to dislodge areas that do not come away easily. Wear protective goggles, just in case any splinters of glass are propelled from the broken pane.

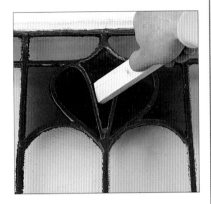

5 Apply a small bead of putty around the lead rebate. Ensure that it covers the entire rebate.

6 Carefully position the new pane in the light, pressing gently to form a good contact between the glass and the putty.

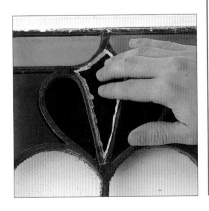

7 Use the chisel to fold the lead back in place (on both sides of the casement), using the flat face of the chisel over the lead strips, moulding it back to its original finish.

8 Use a putty knife to trim away the excess putty, providing a neat finished edge to the glass/lead junction. Finally clean the glass with a clean cloth.

Lead lights, whether in doors or windows, are an attractive option for a simple casement structure. Colour variations and designs add further to the look of this finish.

renovating metal ⚒

Restoring lead lights has been dealt with on pages 292–3, but there are many other window and door areas which display metal surfaces that at some time may require repair or renovation. Many metals used in designs for doors and windows are meant to be left simply with a metallic finish, such as the brass in door or window fittings.

repainting metal windows

Traditional metal windows have always required painting, but more modern versions which are normally incorporated with double glazed designs should not be painted and only require simple cleaning for restoration purposes. However, in order to obtain a satisfactory finish on metal windows that are designed for paint, it is important to follow a simple but necessary preparation procedure.

tools for the job

scraper
....
sanding block
....
wire brush
....
dusting brush
....
paintbrush

1 Remove as much flaky paint as you can from the window surface using a scraper. Applying pressure with the blade will remove much of the loose material on the rail surfaces.

The corner of the scraper blade may also be used along the joints of the window for further paint removal from these more inaccessible areas.

2 Use some rough grade sandpaper or a sanding block to smooth some more the surface of the window and further remove traces of old coats of paint.

3 For preparing metal windows, a wire brush is also useful in areas which are not flat, such as around the edge of the window casements which often demonstrate a curved profile and can render the use of a scraper ineffective.

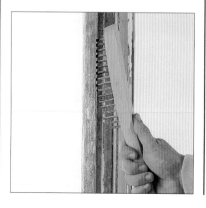

4 Prime the bare metal with a proprietary metal primer immediately after scraping and sanding has been finished. Otherwise, exposure of the metal surface to the open air, even for a short time, may encourage corrosion of the surface to begin again. Once primed, the window may be undercoated and top coated as desired.

putty replacement

Where putty has decomposed or come loose from the glass/rebate junction, remove the affected area and replace with a new section of fresh putty. Before re-application of the putty, ensure that the window rebates are free from dust and debris and that they are primed with a metal primer. This will improve the adhesion between the putty and the window rebates. Putty should be applied using a similar technique to that for wooden windows shown on pages 290–1.

using a heat gun

The flat surfaces of metal windows are ideal for stripping using a hot air gun, and therefore this is an option or addition to the methods described above. If you do choose to use a hot air gun, remember to follow the manufacturer's guidelines and obey all safety instructions.

metal window security

As part of a general metal window renovation, it is worth introducing security systems if they are not already in place. There are proprietary locking mechanisms available for metal windows which cover both the stays and pins, and the fasteners as shown in the diagram below.

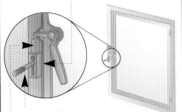

lock secured to metal frame using self-tapping screws

key used to move locking bar

bar locked in position below opening catch of fastener

Other proprietary systems may also be purchased to lock window stays in position. These are similar to the locking stays for wooden windows shown on page 273. Remember to keep keys in a safe place so that you have easy access in the event of an emergency. Ideally there should be a key in every room.

repainting window furniture

The window furniture on wooden windows is generally metal based. Brass fittings or those which have a 'brassed' finish should not be painted, but it can be possible to revive the look of other metal window furniture by painting it. Some fittings may have a type of paint finish on them already, and the way that a new coat of paint takes to a particular surface is variable. It can therefore be worth testing a piece of window furniture first before committing to painting it all. However, in most cases paint can be applied to these surfaces with good effect. The best method for application tends to be using aerosol paints.

tools for the job

screwdriver

wire wool

1 Always remove the window furniture from the window, and clean it down using some fine grade wire wool.

2 Place the stays and fasteners on a board, and holding the aerosol nozzle at 15–20cm (6–8in) away from the window furniture, spray it with several thin coats of paint.

3 A good way of painting the screw heads for the window furniture is to insert them in an old sponge, so that the heads point upwards, and spray them in the normal way. Once dry, all the window furniture may be refitted.

brass fittings

Many door fittings are brass or given a brass effect. For a thorough clean down it is always best to remove the particular article from the door or window, since proprietary polishes can damage the finish on other parts of the door or window surface. Always use a soft cloth when buffing up the brass to a finish.

wrought iron

Many door and window fittings are made from wrought iron and are often finished in a matt black coating. They can be revived by simple preparation and repainting. For particularly corroded pieces, immerse in an appropriate paint stripper overnight before thoroughly rinsing them down and repainting the following day.

repairing a windowsill 🪚

As well as being exposed to all the elements, sills come in for particular weather attack because of their function of collecting all water run-off from the window and diverting it away from the exterior walls of the house. Due to this more concentrated exposure to damp, decay is often more prevalent in sills. Unless damage is dealt with quickly, rot can spread to other parts of the window and therefore can require extensive repair or even total window replacement.

minor repairs

tools for the job

hacking knife
dusting brush and paintbrush
cordless drill/driver
protective gloves

1 Cut away loose material from the sill with a hacking knife. Give the area a clean with a dusting brush.

2 Apply a generous coating of wood hardener to the bare wood of the sill, ensuring that you

apply good coverage. Make sure to flood the area, and allow the wood to soak up the hardener.

3 Once the wood hardener has dried, mix up some wood filler and apply it to the hole concerned, making sure that it is pressed into every crevice. Wood filler is difficult to work with, and dries very quickly. It is therefore worth making more than one application, to build up layers to the level of the sill.

4 Directly adjacent to the filled area, in the sound part of the sill, drill some holes into the sill using a drill bit of equal diameter to some preservative pellets.

5 Insert the preservative pellets into the holes so that they are pushed deep into the sill. Wear protective gloves to do this as the pellets are normally very toxic so you must avoid all contact with your skin.

6 Mix up some more wood filler, and fill over the pellet holes. Once all the wood filler has dried, it may be sanded to a smooth finish and the sill repainted. Over time, the preservative pellets will break down and secrete a preservative solution into the sill. Therefore the combination of wood hardener and preservative pellets acting in tandem provide double protection against possible further wood decay.

major repairs

In some cases, sill damage becomes so extreme that the use of filler and preservatives is ineffective, and more drastic action is required.

tools for the job

old screwdriver
pencil
combination square
panel saw
cordless drill/driver
paintbrush
wood plane

1 Decide on the boundaries of the decaying area by inserting a screwdriver into the sill. If the sill is rotten, the screwdriver will penetrate the wood easily. If it is sound, the screwdriver will not break the sill surface.

2 Mark out the limits of the rotten area, extending your guideline slightly further onto the sound wood.

Draw the guideline so that the section you produce cuts into the sill at a 45° angle.

3 Beginning at the front of the sill, saw along the angled guideline back to the other guideline on the sill. Keep your cut as vertical as possible.

4 Saw along the back guideline to join with the other cut. The saw will usually be very close to the wall surface and this can make sawing quite difficult. Ensure that the cut is as straight as possible.

5 Use the cut-out section to mark off the replacement requirement on a new piece of prepared timber.

The timber should be of a dimension slightly larger than the cut-out section, so that once it has been fitted, it may be planed and sanded to the shape of the sill.

6 Saw down the new piece of wood to the marked-off size and pre-drill holes in the new front side of the sill. Also, use a countersink drill bit to open up the entrance point for the screws. Use wood preservative on the cut-out area on the old sill, and ensure that the new section of wood has been treated with preservative before it is fitted to the windowsill.

297

7 Screw the new section in place, ensuring that the screws bite deep into the existing sound section of the sill. Complete any final fitting requirements by planing the section to size. Use some wood filler to cover any joints and screw holes. More than one application of filler followed by sanding and wiping with white spirit will be required before repainting, to provide the very best finish.

refurbishing a doorway 🔨🔨🔨

Exterior doors clearly experience more punishment and wear and tear than interior doors, with much of this being due to normal weathering processes. It is therefore important to keep them in a good state of repair. Ensuring that surfaces are well decorated, and therefore preserved, is one of the best methods of preventing problems, but there are also other more structural ways in which doors may be protected.

attaching a weatherboard

Weatherboards are sloped sections of wood designed to increase run-off away from the base of an exterior door. If exterior doors do not have these fitted as part of their original design, they may be fitted later.

tools for the job

pencil
....
tape measure
....
spirit level
....
chisel
....
mallet
....
panel saw
....
cordless drill/driver
....
paintbrush

1 With the door in a closed position, hold a cut-off section of the weatherboard up against the door frame. Use a pencil to draw a guideline along the profile of the board and onto the hinging side of the frame. Repeat this procedure at the leading or opening edge of the

door. In each case, ensure that the base of the board is held slightly above the door threshold strip.

2 Draw a level guideline across the door, joining the top mark of each profile guideline. There may have to be some adjustment here, especially if the door is out of shape or was not hung properly. However, any adjustment must still ensure that the base of the weatherboard guideline is above the threshold strip.

3 Along each guideline on the door frame, chisel out the section of wood back to the main stiles of the frame. A small chisel is ideal for this particular job as the

size of the blade will allow you to follow the curved guideline as accurately as possible.

4 Saw the weatherboard to the length required and hold it in position, with the door still closed. Drill pilot holes through the board and into the door. Visually, it is best to place the holes in the concave part of the moulding. Five to six pilot holes should be drilled equidistantly along the weatherboard length.

5 Before fixing the weatherboard in place, paint the underside of it with a good quality primer. The priming must be done first, for once the board is fitted access to this part

of it will be impossible, and the underside is also a particularly vulnerable area for damp attack.

6 Once dry, reposition the board and fix it in place. Ensure that each pilot hole has been countersunk so that when screws are inserted, their heads will sit below the surface level of the moulding. The holes may then be filled and sanded before painting. Check the action of the door as you may need to shave a bit of wood off the leading edge of the weatherboard, so that it opens and closes smoothly into the frame.

frame problems

tools for the job

tape measure
pencil
panel saw
wrecking bar
paintbrush
cordless drill/driver
hammer

Many decay problems on exterior doors tend to occur more often in the frames than in the doors themselves. This is normally caused by damp penetration, which spreads up through the main body. It then becomes necessary to cut out the affected area and replace it with a new section of wood.

1 Determine how far the rot has progressed up the frame and make a diagonal cut slightly further along, into a sound section of wood.

2 It is likely that the section of frame to be discarded is held in position with frame fixings, and so a wrecking bar may be required to lever the section free.

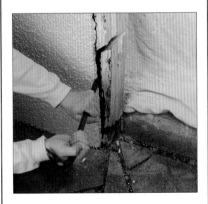

3 Use the old section as a template to draw a guideline on a new piece of wood of equal dimensions to that of the door frame. Ensure that the new wood has been well treated with preservative.

4 Saw the section to the correct size and position it in the frame. Pilot hole some fixing points, ensuring that at least one fixing will penetrate through the diagonal join made by the new section and old part of the frame.

5 Screw the new section in place – concrete anchor screws have been used in this case, but it is possible to use standard frame fixings with a wall plug.

6 Cut to size and refit the missing section of doorstop. Pin this in place with nails. Fill, sand and prime the entire section before repainting.

kitchens & bathrooms

Kitchens and bathrooms are working rooms in the home where specific tasks are performed, and as a result many of the features found in these rooms, whether they are sink units and worktops or baths and basins, are common to all kitchens or bathrooms. It is important to understand how these features interact so that they can be positioned to ensure that best use is made of available space. This section considers the vital components that make up the majority of kitchens and bathrooms and shows how design is tailored to meet those requirements.

the basic shape of a kitchen

Obviously, the size and dimensions of a room set constraints on the shape of a kitchen, but how space is utilized will also determine both its look and efficient operation. Kitchen design is based around three main areas: food storage and preparation, cooking, and washing. All three need to be positioned to enable the efficient and safe preparation of meals. The 'working triangle' of kitchen design reveals how these three areas best interact, showing the ideal positions for fridge and preparation areas in relation to the cooker and the sink. The illustrations on these pages demonstrate how this working triangle applies to three common kitchen shapes.

U-shaped kitchens

This type of kitchen shape provides probably the most satisfactory example of all for a working triangle. Distances between all three points are kept almost equal, which allows for optimum movement and access. The U-shaped design is most commonly found in large kitchens, although the same principles may also be applied to smaller kitchens where floor space is much more limited, and a similar working triangle shape can still be maintained.

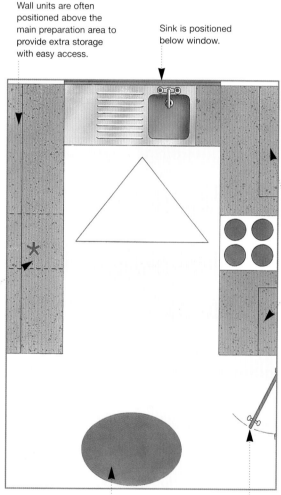

Wall units are often positioned above the main preparation area to provide extra storage with easy access.

Sink is positioned below window.

Wall units may be used in these areas as long as they do not extend over the cooker.

Fridge is centrally positioned beneath the main worktop area.

Eating area is away from the main working triangle, but within easy access of the food serving area next to the cooker.

Door can be opened without danger of knocking into anyone working in the kitchen.

GALLEY KITCHENS

A galley-style kitchen is another popular design, similar to the U-shaped kitchen but more suitable for a narrow room. Galleys have units on the opposing longer walls but not on the opposing shorter walls. The working triangle in this situation does still bear similarities to that of the U-shaped kitchen, indeed some U-shaped kitchens are often referred to as galley kitchens, especially when the 'U' is particularly elongated and floor space between the two opposing longer runs of units is limited. In a traditional galley kitchen, however, the sink would be moved onto one of the longer walls, while still ensuring that a good working triangle, with fairly even dimensions, is maintained.

As the name suggests, the units in an L-shaped kitchen cover the majority of two adjacent walls in the room. The working triangle can still be maintained, although distances between the three points are no longer equal. Depending upon room size, it should still be possible to include an eating area in the kitchen.

tips of the trade

Sink position – In most kitchens the sink tends to be positioned underneath a window. The main reason for this is to provide a view when menial tasks are being carried out at the sink. However, positioning a sink below a window also guarantees that it is on an outside wall, and this makes it much easier to link the waste pipes to an outside drain.

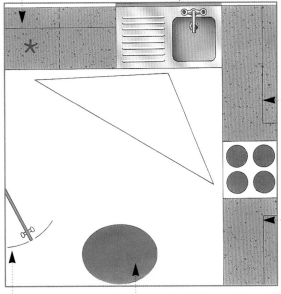

Storage space is above preparation area – although this may block off some light, it is a good compromise when extra storage space is needed.

Sink is positioned below window.

Extra wall units provide storage but must not extend over the cooker – the cooker is positioned centrally in the worktop and has plenty of space on either side for serving up meals.

Door can be opened without danger of knocking into anyone working in the kitchen.

Eating area makes the best use of available space and is still close to the food serving area of the worktop.

These are simple in design and are often used in long, narrow kitchens where the inclusion of double-facing units is impossible due to space limitations. In some cases, however, this choice of kitchen shape is used when budgetary concerns are paramount, and a simple limited stretch of units is all that is required. Despite the fact that the units and accessories are positioned along one wall, it can still be possible to maintain a working triangle, although the dimensions of the triangle will have to be considerably elongated to fit in with the kitchen design.

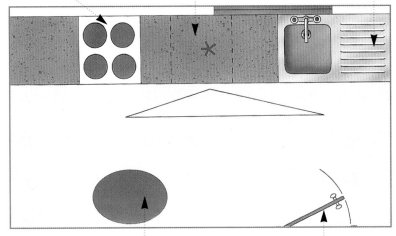

Cooker is positioned with room on either side for serving up meals.

Fridge is situated beneath central part of food preparation area.

Sink is positioned to share natural light with food preparation area, and fitting the sink butted up against the wall leaves a larger continuous food preparation area.

Eating area is positioned so as much access as possible is made available, while still being close to the serving area.

Door can be opened without danger of knocking into anyone working in the kitchen.

fitted kitchens

The term 'fitted kitchen' is used to describe a type of kitchen where the units are fixed in place to create the impression they are built into the room, and the majority of modern kitchens are of the 'fitted' variety. Naturally, the appearance and function of individual units will vary between manufacturers, but all units can be categorized according to whether they are handmade or standard, and whether they are fixed to the floor or attached to the wall above a worktop.

handmade units

Handmade items are traditionally more expensive than standard items, as the labour costs are greater and the materials used tend to be of higher quality – kitchen units are no exception to this rule. All the doors, drawers and carcasses of handmade units are constructed using traditional jointing methods, such as dovetail jointing, and tend to be made from solid soft- or hardwoods, which guarantees durability, rather than particle board and laminate. Fitting handmade kitchens is a highly specialized job and most people do not attempt to undertake it themselves.

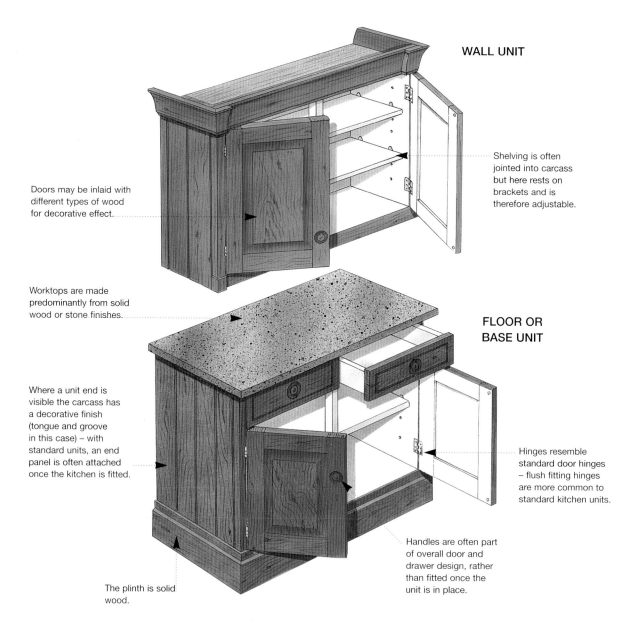

WALL UNIT

Doors may be inlaid with different types of wood for decorative effect.

Shelving is often jointed into carcass but here rests on brackets and is therefore adjustable.

Worktops are made predominantly from solid wood or stone finishes.

FLOOR OR BASE UNIT

Where a unit end is visible the carcass has a decorative finish (tongue and groove in this case) – with standard units, an end panel is often attached once the kitchen is fitted.

Hinges resemble standard door hinges – flush fitting hinges are more common to standard kitchen units.

The plinth is solid wood.

Handles are often part of overall door and drawer design, rather than fitted once the unit is in place.

Standard kitchen units are much cheaper than handmade varieties because they are mass-produced and usually made from particle board with a laminate finish, although quality and price do vary considerably. As well as aiming to achieve a pleasing appearance, modern designs are increasingly geared towards specific needs in the kitchen.

self-assembly

Commonly known as 'flat-pack', self-assembly units are supplied broken down into their constituent parts, and, as their name suggests, it is up to the individual to put them together. Self-assembly units occupy the lower end of the price scale, but there are some exceptionally good quality units available and by choosing carefully you can produce a very fine kitchen. Greater time will be needed for installation, but this can be set against the financial gains.

rigid

The main difference between rigid units and flat-packs is that rigid units are supplied factory assembled to reduce the time for installation. As a rule, however, only the carcass is supplied ready-made from the manufacturer and you will still need to fit the doors, drawer fronts and other accessories to the carcasses. This allows the manufacturer to supply general carcass units that can be adapted to suit the finished look of any style of kitchen.

combination

Combination units are supplied semi-assembled, so that part of the unit may be considered rigid, while the other part is in effect self-assembly. Corner units and carousels are often combination, as well as carcasses that are used to house accessories such as fridges or ovens. By being semi-assembled these carcasses can be adapted to fit different types of accessories and to house a greater variety of appliances, offering more choice to the customer.

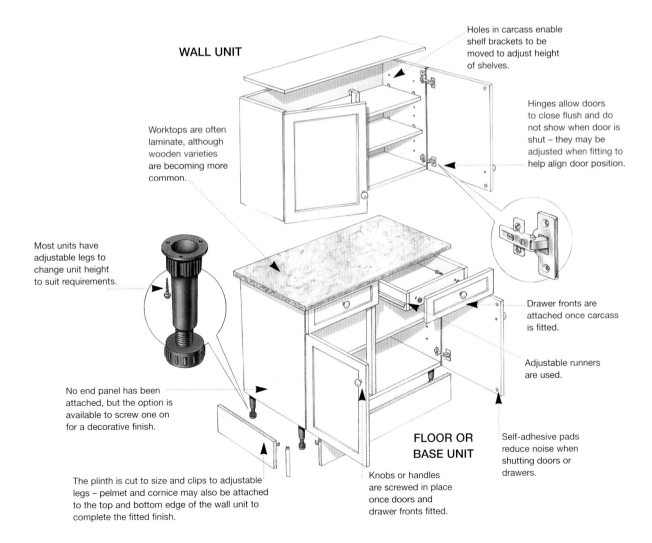

WALL UNIT

Holes in carcass enable shelf brackets to be moved to adjust height of shelves.

Hinges allow doors to close flush and do not show when door is shut – they may be adjusted when fitting to help align door position.

Worktops are often laminate, although wooden varieties are becoming more common.

Most units have adjustable legs to change unit height to suit requirements.

Drawer fronts are attached once carcass is fitted.

Adjustable runners are used.

No end panel has been attached, but the option is available to screw one on for a decorative finish.

FLOOR OR BASE UNIT

Self-adhesive pads reduce noise when shutting doors or drawers.

The plinth is cut to size and clips to adjustable legs – pelmet and cornice may also be attached to the top and bottom edge of the wall unit to complete the fitted finish.

Knobs or handles are screwed in place once doors and drawer fronts fitted.

unfitted kitchens

Unfitted kitchens offer a more traditional look since they refer back to an era when kitchen furniture and worktops were separate items not permanently fixed to walls or ceilings, with individual dressers and sideboards comprising the main utility items in the kitchen in addition to sink units. The unfitted look has enjoyed something of a revival with many manufacturers now offering semi-fitted ranges that imitate this type of traditional kitchen design.

free-standing units

The main visible difference between free-standing units and standard kitchen units is that the former tend to resemble more closely the look of everyday furniture found elsewhere in the house. Thus a storage unit may have a closer connection in terms of appearance to a wardrobe or cabinet than to modern base and wall units. However, the actual way in which free-standing units are now constructed and fitted is similar to that of standard kitchen units. For example, the doors and drawers in free-standing units will have been constructed using exactly the same method as their 'fitted' counterparts, even though the sizes may be slightly more unusual, and they will still need to be attached to the unit carcass once it is in place. The diagram below provides an example of a free-standing unit and also points out the various features it shares with a standard kitchen unit.

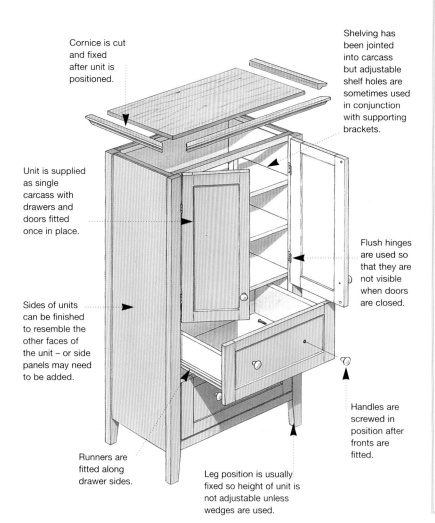

Cornice is cut and fixed after unit is positioned.

Shelving has been jointed into carcass but adjustable shelf holes are sometimes used in conjunction with supporting brackets.

Unit is supplied as single carcass with drawers and doors fitted once in place.

Flush hinges are used so that they are not visible when doors are closed.

Sides of units can be finished to resemble the other faces of the unit – or side panels may need to be added.

Runners are fitted along drawer sides.

Leg position is usually fixed so height of unit is not adjustable unless wedges are used.

Handles are screwed in position after fronts are fitted.

ACCESSORY UNITS

It is also possible to purchase free-standing accessory units, such as units for holding sinks, although it is likely that the unit will be supplied still requiring a substantial amount of assembly and the worktop will also require cutting to fit the sink. Thus although the unfitted look is now being catered for by manufacturers, it must be understood that there will still be a fair amount of fitting and assembling in order to achieve the finished unit look.

TRADITIONAL IDEAS

It is also possible to achieve an unfitted look by using more traditional pieces of furniture such as sideboards or dressers. New reproductions may be purchased or older items can be decorated to meet your preferences. This is an attractive option, especially when using a 'distressed' paint effect, as older items lend themselves well to creating this type of look. Also consider combining new units with old to create a more haphazard look, which can still provide a pleasing design.

Provided that access is not hindered, positioning an island unit in the central floor area of a kitchen is a sensible use of space. The simple kitchen table represents the most traditional and basic form of island unit, and this type has always been popular due to the variety of functions it can fulfil – acting equally well as a food preparation area, a dining area and more often than not an activity area for the whole family. The only difference with modern kitchens is that a greater choice of designs is now available, with additions being made to enhance utility and the aesthetic appeal. Island units usually do not need to be fixed in place owing to their weight, which means that they are also still moveable. The diagram below shows a typical island unit that incorporates a hanging rack to provide a further storage area in what would otherwise simply be redundant ceiling space.

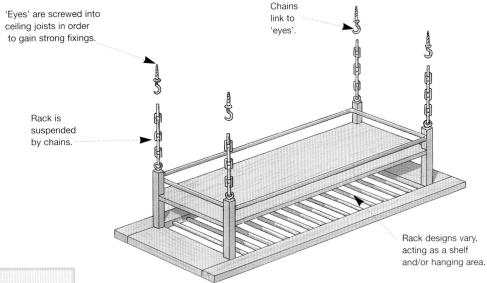

'Eyes' are screwed into ceiling joists in order to gain strong fixings.

Chains link to 'eyes'.

Rack is suspended by chains.

Rack designs vary, acting as a shelf and/or hanging area.

safety advice

When deciding on the position for hanging racks it is important to use a joist and cable detector. This will ensure that fixings are inserted into joists to provide adequate support, while avoiding any cables or pipes that run across the ceiling space.

ALTERNATIVE ISLANDS

Standard kitchen units can also be used to create islands in the centre of a room. These are fixed in place and have the characteristics of standard unit design. It is also possible to fit sinks or cooking areas into island units, but this will require water or gas and/or electrical supplies to be fed to these areas, which can be a tricky job. However, in the right size of kitchen the effect of such units can be well worth the work involved.

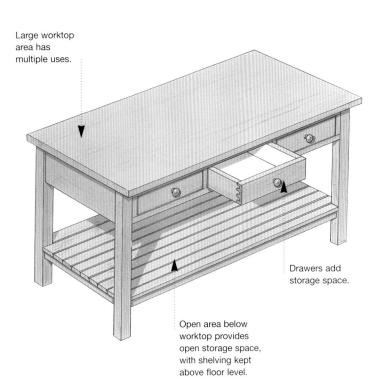

Large worktop area has multiple uses.

Drawers add storage space.

Open area below worktop provides open storage space, with shelving kept above floor level.

the basic shape of a bathroom

The basic shape of a bathroom is primarily affected by the size of the room and the number of items comprising a chosen suite. The number of bathrooms in a household, and thus the extent to which each bathroom is used and by how many people, will also have an influence. The bathroom is a very functional part of the home and it is important to position appliances so that they may function with optimum efficiency. The ideal area for ease of use of a particular item is referred to as 'standing room' or the 'working area', and these are demonstrated by the red boxes in the diagrams below. However, a bathroom is also a room for relaxing in, and it is important to incorporate a degree of comfort and aesthetics into the overall design.

spacious bathrooms

The larger the bathroom, the greater the choice available for design, but this still means that careful planning is essential. In fact, smaller bathrooms are often easier to design because options are limited. In general, where there is a large bathroom the available space tends to be filled with as many fittings as possible, which is satisfactory provided working areas are available for each particular fitting. Large bathrooms can be used by more than one person at the same time and it is therefore necessary for standing areas to be as separate as possible.

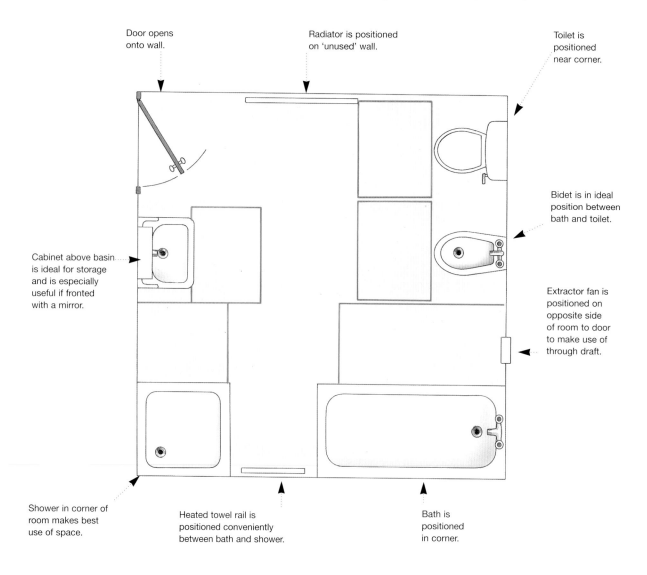

Door opens onto wall.

Radiator is positioned on 'unused' wall.

Toilet is positioned near corner.

Bidet is in ideal position between bath and toilet.

Cabinet above basin is ideal for storage and is especially useful if fronted with a mirror.

Extractor fan is positioned on opposite side of room to door to make use of through draft.

Shower in corner of room makes best use of space.

Heated towel rail is positioned conveniently between bath and shower.

Bath is positioned in corner.

In households with a single bathroom used by the entire family, there may need to be some compromises depending upon the available space. There are opportunities to choose fitting designs aimed at space saving, such as quadrant shower trays and a heated towel rail that also acts as the radiator in the room. Working areas may need to overlap in family bathrooms, but this can be limited to a certain extent, so that efficiency is maintained and the bathroom can still be used by more than one person at a time.

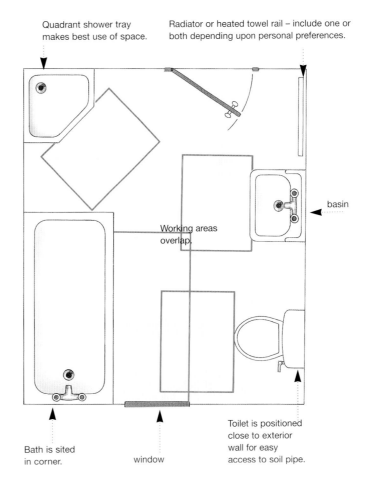

Quadrant shower tray makes best use of space.

Radiator or heated towel rail – include one or both depending upon personal preferences.

basin

Working areas overlap.

Bath is sited in corner.

window

Toilet is positioned close to exterior wall for easy access to soil pipe.

tips of the trade

Toilets should ideally be located on external walls, or close to external walls, so that the amount of plumbing required to get from the toilet to the exterior soil pipe is kept to a minimum.

En-suite bathrooms tend to be small in size, and as such many design choices will be dictated by the space available. Since this type of bathroom is not as 'busy' as others, the idea of working or standing areas tends to become redundant. Instead, a single central space becomes the working area for all items in the bathroom. Attention is more focused on providing easy access to the fittings in the bathroom by one person at any one time, hence the bath working area can become the basin working area depending upon which item is in use. Fitting a shower cubicle instead of a bath will allow for more space.

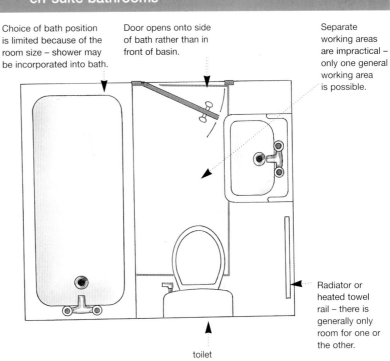

Choice of bath position is limited because of the room size – shower may be incorporated into bath.

Door opens onto side of bath rather than in front of basin.

Separate working areas are impractical – only one general working area is possible.

Radiator or heated towel rail – there is generally only room for one or the other.

toilet

the basic shape of a bathroom

309

fitted bathrooms

Clearly all bathrooms are 'fitted' in as much as the main items are permanently plumbed in and fixed in position. When the term fitted is applied to bathrooms, therefore, it usually indicates that those items are housed in specially designed units. The units usually have a collective finish and produce a continuous visual link that gives the bathroom a pleasing overall look. The term fitted is also used to indicate that pipework is boxed in and hidden from view.

bathroom units

You can build your own units if you wish or purchase custom-made versions. Manufacturers produce many different designs that can be fitted into most bathroom layouts. Although quality and price can vary dramatically,

there are a number of common features in the way that units are designed and constructed. The example below shows the way in which a basin unit – sometimes called a vanity unit – is constructed.

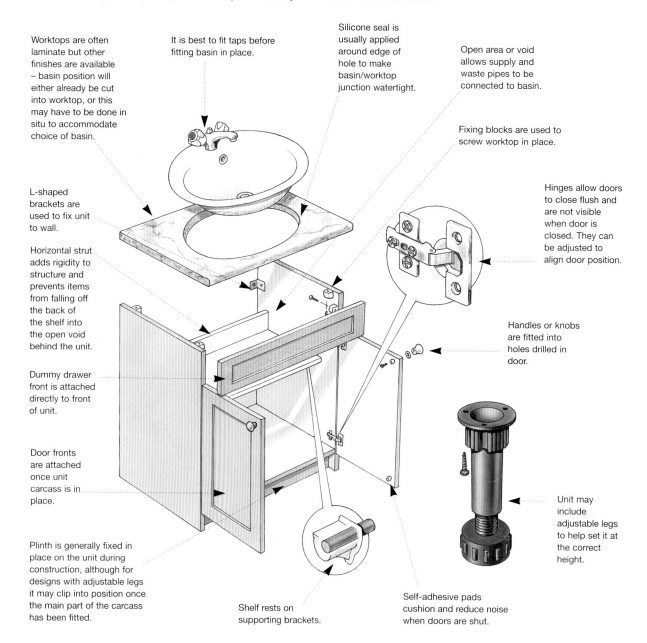

Worktops are often laminate but other finishes are available – basin position will either already be cut into worktop, or this may have to be done in situ to accommodate choice of basin.

It is best to fit taps before fitting basin in place.

Silicone seal is usually applied around edge of hole to make basin/worktop junction watertight.

Open area or void allows supply and waste pipes to be connected to basin.

Fixing blocks are used to screw worktop in place.

L-shaped brackets are used to fix unit to wall.

Hinges allow doors to close flush and are not visible when door is closed. They can be adjusted to align door position.

Horizontal strut adds rigidity to structure and prevents items from falling off the back of the shelf into the open void behind the unit.

Handles or knobs are fitted into holes drilled in door.

Dummy drawer front is attached directly to front of unit.

Door fronts are attached once unit carcass is in place.

Unit may include adjustable legs to help set it at the correct height.

Plinth is generally fixed in place on the unit during construction, although for designs with adjustable legs it may clip into position once the main part of the carcass has been fitted.

Shelf rests on supporting brackets.

Self-adhesive pads cushion and reduce noise when doors are shut.

It is possible to achieve a fitted look in one of two ways. One method is to house all the bathroom fixtures, such as the basin and toilet, within carcass units and to connect these units with extra storage and display units so that units run from wall to wall. Panelling can be applied around the bathtub to match the unit finish. The bath is the largest fixture in the bathroom, so panelling is an effective way of incorporating it into the decoration of the rest of the room rather than allowing it to dominate. The aim of this type of bathroom design is to hide all the pipework and connections within the runs of units, while still maintaining maximum practicality and a modern, attractive appearance.

RIGHT *Unit design may be linked with other decoration in the room to enhance the fitted look. The blue colour of some of the door and drawer panels of the units in this bathroom is repeated in the colour of the walls.*

The other method for achieving a fully fitted look is to box in all unsightly elements. As well as disguising or hiding areas of pipework from view, the boxing can also be designed to provide extra shelving that is useful for both storage and display purposes. As long as the frameworks are well constructed, boxing can be just as pleasing to the eye as manufactured units. You can also apply a decorative finish to boxing frameworks, such as tiling, in order to produce a well-integrated and built-in effect. Full instructions on boxing in are given on pages 354–5.

LEFT *Decorating the boxed in areas with the same tiles used for the floor enhances the fitted look and gives the impression of a made-to-measure overall bathroom design.*

fitted bathrooms

311

plumbing & electricity

Installing a new kitchen or bathroom, with all the relevant fixtures and fittings, requires a certain amount of skill with plumbing and electricity. There will probably be some areas where you need to seek professional advice, but as far as the basic tasks are concerned, most jobs are relatively straightforward as long as the correct order of work is followed and appropriate techniques used. This chapter shows the best techniques for installing a selection of fittings. Be sure to plan jobs thoroughly so that you have all the right connections for a particular installation before you start.

313

Bathroom fixtures, such as the toilet and bath shown here, need to be assembled, then positioned and plumbed in.

preparing plumbing & electrics ⟋⟋⟋⟋

When new fittings are to be positioned in a different place from the old ones, you will need to reroute supplies. It is therefore important to have some understanding of the different types of pipe available and the various ways in which they can be joined. Before embarking on any pipework, always turn off the water supply and drain the pipes. In terms of electrical supplies, major overhauls are not usually required, although some cables may need rerouting.

cutting copper pipes

tools for the job

pipe cutter

wire wool

1 Clamp the pipe cutter around the pipe and rotate it in the direction designated by the arrow until it cuts all the way through. You can use a hacksaw to cut the pipe if you wish, but a pipe cutter gives a cleaner cut.

2 Clean the pipe using wire wool before making any connection.

connecting copper pipes

There are several ways of making a connection or joint between copper pipes. The simplest is to insert a compression joint. However, it may be unsightly if it is in a position that can be easily viewed. The other methods involve using solder and a gas torch. They are slightly more difficult but produce a neater finish.

compression joints

Compression joints are easy to fit because the process does not require the use of a gas torch.

tools for the job

adjustable spanners

1 Separate the compression fitting and slip it in place on the two ends of the cut pipe. To begin with, position it hand tight with the olives (small rings) situated on the pipe inside the fitting.

tips of the trade

Pipe connectors are made in many different shapes, for example elbow joints and T-connectors, so that it is possible to reroute most pipes.

2 Use adjustable spanners to tighten the joint, allowing the threaded section to tighten onto the olives to create a watertight seal.

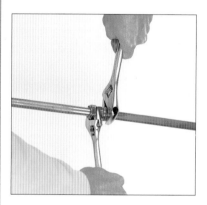

solder ring joints

Solder ring joints are the easiest type of joint to make because the solder itself is already inside the connector.

tools for the job

gas torch

heat-resistant mat

1 Apply flux to the ends of the pipes and inside the connector. The flux helps to clean the copper and achieve a watertight joint.

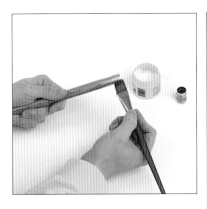

2 Slot both ends of the pipe into the connector. Holding the pipe over a heat-resistant mat, use a gas torch to heat the joint gently, allowing the solder ring inside it to melt and form a watertight seal.

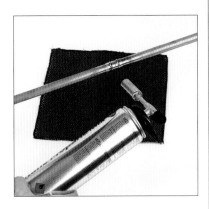

safety advice

When using a gas torch, always read the manufacturer's guidelines to ensure safe use. Gas torches should never be left burning unattended and a heat-resistant mat should be positioned next to the joint to avoid burning or singeing adjacent surfaces.

end feed joints

The other type of solder joint is referred to as an end feed joint. It does not contain a ring of solder inside and, therefore, the solder must be applied during the heating procedure with the gas torch. Flux is still used to clean pipe ends, but solder wire must be applied around the joint to create a watertight seal.

connecting plastic pipes

Plastic pipes are usually very easy to connect since many have push-fit joints or are threaded with rubber washers. However, in some cases solvent weld joints have to be formed using a special type of cement to fix the pipes together.

tools for the job

hacksaw or hand saw
cloth

1 Cut the pipes to the required size with a hacksaw or hand saw and clean the ends thoroughly.

2 Apply solvent weld cement around the end of the pipe. Push the end of the pipe into the required connector. Remove excess cement with a cloth and allow the joint to dry before continuing with the next section.

electrical rerouting

In hollow walls or ceiling voids, cables can be fed into place, but with solid walls the procedure is more laborious. Leave the actual electrical work, such as wiring, to professionals.

tools for the job

club hammer
bolster chisel
hammer
protective equipment

1 Draw pencil guidelines where the cable will run. Use a club hammer and bolster chisel to cut through the wall, removing material to a depth of around 2.5cm (1in).

2 Position the cable well below surface level. Cover it with an impact-resistant plastic channel held in place with galvanized nails, then apply a surface finish such as plaster.

plastic plumbing ⚡⚡⚡

Although copper pipe is still used as the main type of water supply pipe in the home, plastic pipe is becoming much more commonplace because the way they are jointed makes them incredibly easy to work with. Pipe and fitting designs can vary slightly between manufacturers, so it is best to use the same type of plastic plumbing throughout your home. However, all manufacturers produce adaptors to join their plastic pipes with the more conventional copper pipe systems.

tools for the job

pipe cutter or mini hacksaw
adjustable spanners
screwdriver
cordless drill/driver

cutting & joining plastic

Before you can build up any sort of plastic supply pipe system, you need to understand how to form a simple joint or connection between two lengths of pipe.

1 Plastic supply pipe can be cut with any fine-toothed saw – a mini hacksaw is ideal. Alternatively, you can buy proprietary cutters. Whatever you use, try to make the cut as square as possible. Remove rough edges with fine abrasive paper.

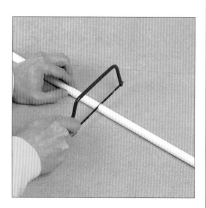

2 Push both ends of the pipe into the ends of the connector. Push each pipe in as far as it will go, making sure they have both been grabbed by the rings inside the joint.

3 Pull the pipes away from the joint to create a watertight seal.

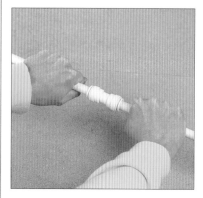

4 If you need to undo the joint for any reason, simply push the end collar on the joint to loosen it and pull the pipe free from the fitting.

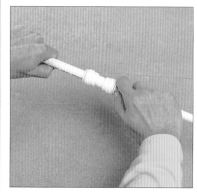

joining copper & plastic

Joining a section of copper and plastic pipe together can be achieved very simply using a specially designed adaptor. It is fitted in a similar way to a compression joint.

1 Fit one section of a copper compression joint onto the end of the copper pipe and remove the securing nut from the other end of the joint.

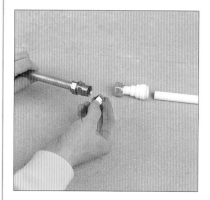

2 Fit the plastic adaptor onto the copper compression joint and use adjustable spanners to tighten the joint and make it watertight.

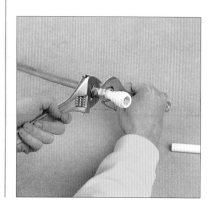

3 Insert and secure the plastic pipe as shown in steps 2 and 3 of 'cutting & joining plastic' on the opposite page.

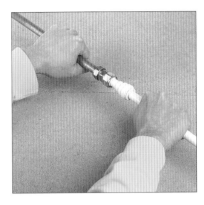

fitting a shut-off valve

Shut-off valves are available for both copper and plastic pipes. Designs vary – the one shown here is operated by a slot-head screwdriver.

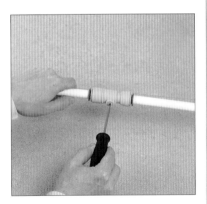

inserting a stop end

It is sometimes necessary to close off the end of a pipe. For example, when changing bathroom fittings there may be a time delay between removing the old fitting and installing the new one. Therefore the water may have to be turned back on in the meantime to provide a supply for other areas in the house. Whatever the reason, the method used is to push a stop end into the opening of the pipe and then pull it back to secure it in place.

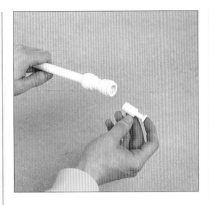

using reducers

When a larger bore of pipe needs to be joined to a smaller bore, use reducers to connect them. Reducers are manufactured in all sizes to cope with a variety of needs.

1 Insert the end of the reducer into a connector for the larger pipe bore. Pull it back to lock it in position.

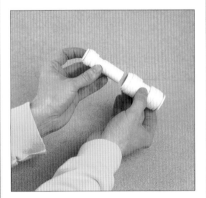

2 Insert the small bore pipe into the reducer and pull it back to lock it in position. Insert the larger bore pipe into the large bore.

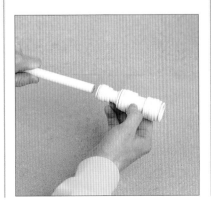

supporting pipes

All supply pipes have to be supported at intervals along the course of their route. However, because plastic pipe is more flexible than copper pipe, more clips are needed to provide adequate support to the pipe once the water supply is in use.

1 Position pipe clips along the route of the pipe at intervals of no more than 30cm (1ft).

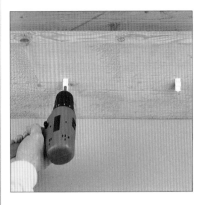

2 Make sure that the pipe is clipped firmly in place before the water is turned on so that there is no danger of the pipes sagging and thereby placing joints under unnecessary stress.

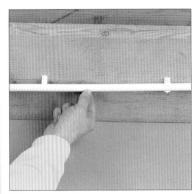

tips of the trade

To ensure that clips are aligned, use a spirit level to draw a pencil line along the joists to act as a fixing guideline.

installing a basin & pedestal ⚒⚒⚒

Most of the hard work involved in installing a basin and pedestal is concerned with making sure that the water supply pipes and waste pipe are appropriately located for easy connection. If you are merely replacing a basin, you will usually be able to reuse the existing supplies and waste when it comes to reconnection. However, if the new basin is situated in a different area to the original basin position, it will be necessary to adjust the lengths of the supply and waste pipes, as discussed earlier in this chapter (see pages 314–15).

monobloc taps & pop-up wastes

Whatever the type of taps or waste being fitted, the basic technique for installing a basin and pedestal remains the same. It is best to attach the taps and waste to the basin before fixing the basin to the wall, as it is much easier to gain access. In this case, a monobloc tap and pop-up waste are being fitted.

tools for the job

slip-joint pliers
screwdriver
spirit level

1 Position the sealing washer at the base of the tap, so that a watertight seal will be formed when the tap is positioned on the basin. If the taps you are using are not supplied with a washer, apply silicone sealant around the base of the tap before fitting it in place.

2 Fit the copper supply pipes by screwing them into the base of the tap. A rubber washer is generally supplied to form a tight seal between the threaded part of the supply pipe and the tap. You will also need to insert the threaded bolt, which is used to hold the tap in position.

3 Thread the supply pipes and threaded bolt through the hole in the basin. Position a rubber gasket on the underside of the basin hole, followed by a retainer ring, threading both over the threaded bolt. Secure them with a lock nut, which can be done by hand but may need tightening with pliers. Do not over-tighten.

tips of the trade

Basins can easily be chipped or cracked, especially when working on a concrete floor, so you should always protect the basin by laying a dust sheet on the floor.

4 Attention may now be turned to the waste. A pop-up waste system is constructed from a number of components. Thread the top section of the waste outlet through the outlet in the basin ensuring that the correct gasket has been fitted over the outlet tail. If a gasket is not supplied with the outlet, the waste may be seated on silicone sealant. If using sealant, be sure to wipe away any excess before it dries.

5 Screw the bottom section of the waste in place on the underside of the outlet. Once again, ensure the correct gasket has been positioned between the waste section and the underside of the basin outlet. Do not over-tighten, just make sure the waste is securely fitted and watertight.

position the pedestal exactly. However, positioning the pedestal before the basin will ensure a good contact between the two, making the overall placement as secure as possible.

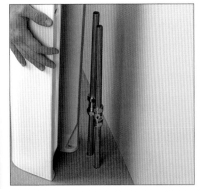

you may need to use wall plugs. Over-tightened screws may crack the basin, so use a hand-held screwdriver for greater control.

11 Secure the pedestal through the holes inside the base. Do not over-tighten and make sure the screws are long enough to hold firm in the floor, but not so long that they damage underfloor services.

6 Insert the pop-up waste rod and screw the waste lever into the base of the waste outlet. Fix the waste lever with a threaded nut, which is secured hand tight.

9 Carefully lift and position the basin on top of the pedestal, adjusting pedestal position to ensure the basin sits correctly. Use a spirit level to check the basin is level, with its back face flush against the wall.

12 Position the waste bung adjusting the level so it will provide a watertight seal. Connect up the outlet and water supply pipes, before turning on the water supply.

7 Join the lever and pop-up waste rod with the supplied clamp by threading the rod and lever into two retaining holes in the clamp. Fix the rod and lever firmly in place with two well-tightened screws.

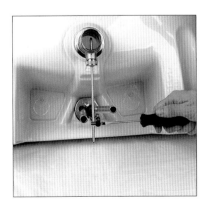

10 Fix the basin in place with retaining screws inserted through the back of the basin and into the wall surface. If it is a solid wall,

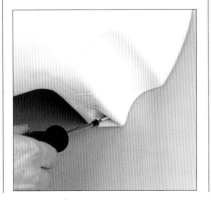

8 Position the basin pedestal in front of and covering any supply pipes. Until the basin is in place and levelled up you will not be able to

ALTERNATIVE TAP DESIGNS

Some taps have tails that connect to the water supply with braided steel supply tubes. These tails are secured in place with backnuts on the basin, before the supply tube is attached. You will still require a gasket and/or washer barrier between the metal surfaces of the tap and the basin.

installing a wall-mounted basin ⟋⟋⟋⟋

There is little difference between a wall-mounted basin and a basin and pedestal in terms of connections and function. The different installation processes centre around the way in which the basin is fixed to the wall, and the manner in which supply and drainage pipes are either hidden or made more decorative. This need to hide supplies can make installing a wall-mounted basin awkward because access to connections is more limited.

solid walls

You need to provide an appropriate route for the required pipes to reach the basin. In a solid wall, this involves chasing out a channel.

tools for the job

> tape measure
> pencil
> spirit level
> club hammer
> bolster chisel
> protective equipment

1 Mark the basin position on the wall and draw pencil guidelines down the wall to demarcate a channel to accommodate pipes. Allow space for connecting with existing supplies.

2 Use a club hammer and bolster chisel to remove this channel. Wear gloves and goggles to protect from flying debris. Once the channel is deep enough, supply pipes may be routed to the correct position.

hollow walls

Pipework can be routed through the cavity in hollow walls. However, access holes often need to be so large to accomplish this that cutting out a section of plasterboard may be the easiest option. In addition, you may need to fix an extra nogging in the studwork to provide adequate support for the basin.

tools for the job

> tape measure
> cordless drill/driver
> pipe cutter
> adjustable spanners
> panel saw
> hammer
> plastering or dry lining equipment

1 Check height measurements to be sure of the exact position of the basin and where brackets will need to be fixed to support it. Fix one or more extra noggings in place at the correct height for the brackets.

2 You may have to drill holes through studwork to provide for pipe rerouting.

3 Position the pipes and add appropriate connections as required (see pages 314–17).

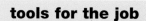

4 Insert an insulation blanket between the studs. Nail a plasterboard sheet over the area, then dry line or plaster as required. Make access holes for the pipe tails to protrude into the room.

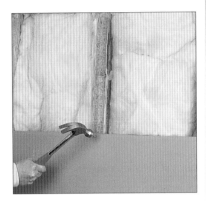

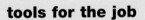

installing the basin

tools for the job

spirit level

tape measure

pencil

cordless drill/driver
and/or screwdriver

hacksaw

adjustable spanners

1 Draw a level pencil guideline where the brackets require fitting to correspond with the supporting points on the back of the basin. Screw the brackets directly into the wooden stud in hollow walls, or use wall plugs and screws in solid walls.

2 Attach the taps and waste pipe to the basin before hooking it in place over the supporting brackets. Screw the basin in place through the pre-drilled holes on its underside. Sometimes a plastic washer is supplied to produce a barrier between the screw and basin. Do not over-tighten the screw.

3 Hold the waste assembly in place and measure the length of pipe required to connect between the basin and trap. Cut the pipe to the appropriate length and make the necessary connections. You can now connect the taps to the hot and cold water supplies and the basin is ready for use.

Wall-mounted basins provide a compact and elegant finish. The chrome waste system matches the taps so that it does not detract from the decorative effect.

installing a bath ⤸⤸⤸

Before installing a bath, make sure that the necessary provision has been made for supply pipe and drainage pipe connections. In many cases, the existing pipework will be sufficient, but if the new bath is to be located in a different place from the old one, pipe adjustment will be required. Installation tends to be a two-part process. First, the feet and supportive framework is put in place, then the taps and drainage system are connected.

tools for the job

screwdriver and/or
cordless drill/driver
adjustable spanners
spirit level
pencil
tape measure

attaching the feet

Most baths have feet and supporting legs so that the underside of the bath is raised from the floor. The legs can be adjusted to take into account any unevenness across the floor surface. Most manufacturers supply baths without the feet attached.

1 Lay the bath upside down on a dust sheet to protect its surface. Most new baths are coated with a protective plastic film but this is really only meant for protecting against dirt and will not prevent scratches or scrapes. Position the bath legs in the sockets situated around the rim of the bath. These are generally secured in

tips of the trade

Older bath designs may not have adjustable feet and the feet that they do have may already be attached to the main bath body. In such instances, you may need to insert wooden wedges below the feet to ensure that the bath is perfectly level. A level bath is important for the safety of users as well as a good finish.

the socket by a grub screw, which passes through the outside of the socket and into the leg.

2 Position the feet in the holes at the base of the legs using a nut on either side of the leg framework to hold them in place. Adjust the position of each foot to approximately the same height – these can be adjusted more accurately when the bath is in place. Most leg frames can also be screwed into the base of the bath through pre-drilled holes in the centre of the leg framework. Take care to use screws of the correct length so that they penetrate the chipboard base but not the bath itself.

3 Most bath designs have a central leg to provide extra support. This is much smaller in size and is screwed, with a foot attached, in the middle of the bath base. Again, take care to use the correct length of screw.

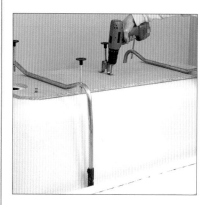

fitting & levelling

Once the legs and feet are attached, turn the bath right side up. Two people are needed for this because even very light baths are awkward to handle on your own. The next step is to fit the taps and waste pipes before finally levelling the bath once it is in position.

1 First attach the waste and overflow system to the bath. Pop-up waste designs for baths differ slightly from basins in that the waste is operated by a circular handle above the overflow outlet. A cable runs from the handle to the waste so that the plug hole can be opened and closed as required. Fit the supplied gaskets to both the waste outlet and overflow.

2 Holding one part of the waste outlet in one hand, screw the second part into the underside section through the outlet in the bath. Make sure that the appropriate gasket is positioned on this side of the outlet. If one is not supplied, apply a bead of silicone sealant instead.

3 Hold the back section of the overflow outlet in place in the same way, screwing the visible section of the assembly into position on the inside of the bath. Again, a gasket is generally supplied to create a watertight seal on this side of the assembly. Otherwise apply sealant.

4 Attach the overflow pipe between the overflow outlet and the underside of the waste assembly. Screw fitting collars with rubber washers are generally used for this.

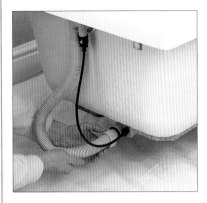

5 Lower the taps through the pre-cut holes in the bath and secure them in place with a backnut. Most taps are seated on a gasket (as here) but, if one is not supplied, silicone sealant can be used instead.

6 Ease the bath towards its final position using a spirit level to help adjust leg heights to ensure that the bath is completely level.

7 The bath must be held securely in position. You can do this by cutting a channel in the wall and allowing the extreme edge of the bath to be supported in this channel. Alternatively, as shown here fix some supportive brackets into the wall and some corresponding brackets on the bath rim, then fit the rim over the brackets. Always double-check that the two halves of the brackets will align before screwing them in place.

8 Finally, connect the taps to the water supply and connect the drainage system (see pages 314–15), then screw the bath feet to the floor.

tips of the trade

It is important that baths are stable in order to avoid accidents. You can add extra support by inserting blocks of wood between the floor and underside of the bath. Weight can also be spread more efficiently if the feet are positioned on top of planks of wood. In many cases the extra height this produces is advantageous.

fitting a toilet & cistern ⁄⁄⁄

A cursory glance at a toilet and cistern tends to suggest more complicated plumbing than is actually the case. Supply and drainage systems are in fact fairly simple and, as long as the toilet is not being moved too far from the original position, a changeover is a relatively straightforward process. Problems only tend to occur if soil pipes need lengthening or repositioning to accommodate a completely new toilet location.

close-coupled toilets

Most modern toilets follow a close-coupled design, whereby the cistern sits directly on top of the pan. This type of design is the easiest to fit and provides fewer complications than low-level or high-level toilets. The instructions provided here show the general principles involved in the fitting of a close-coupled design.

tools for the job

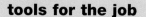

screwdriver

slip-joint pliers

1 First, assemble the internal cistern mechanism. Position the siphon unit inside the cistern by allowing the bottom threaded section to pass through the hole in the base of the cistern.

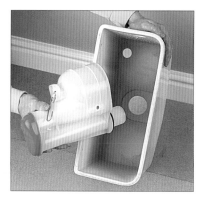

2 Fit the supplied rubber gasket over the threaded section, then position the connecting plate.

3 Secure the cistern connecting plate in position with a large threaded collar, then insert bolts in the holes on either side of the plate.

4 Insert the flushing mechanism or water control assembly into

the cistern, again allowing the threaded end of the water supply pipe to pass through the hole at the bottom of the cistern.

5 Secure it in place using the supplied washer/gasket and threaded collar. It is usually only necessary to tighten by hand the collars for the supply pipe and the siphon. Take care not to cross-thread either collar during the tightening process.

6 Fit the flushing handle to the cistern, holding it in place with a threaded collar. Make sure that the handle is linked to the flushing mechanism.

7 Ease the toilet pan into position, allowing the outlet pipe to marry with the soil pipe.

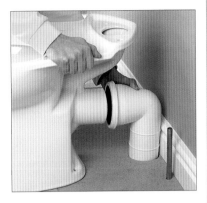

8 Lift the cistern onto the pan so that the connecting bolts thread through the retaining holes on the pan. Position a rubber gasket at the flush entrance so that the threaded section of the siphon unit is inserted through the gasket.

OTHER TYPES OF TOILET

• **Low-level toilets** – These have cisterns mounted on the wall above the pan, with a connecting pipe from the bottom of the cistern to the pan. The cistern must be attached to the wall with substantial fixings because, unlike a close-coupled toilet, the pan does not support any of its weight.

• **High-level toilets** – The cistern is fitted high up the wall so the flush pipe needs to be much longer. Again, wall fixings must be sturdy enough to support the cistern weight.

9 Fit the nuts supplied by the manufacturer to the cistern connecting bolts using both rubber and metal washers to hold the cistern securely in place. This will provide a barrier between the metal and ceramic surfaces.

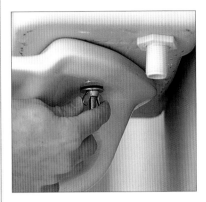

10 Connect the supply pipe for the cold water supply to the cistern using slip-joint pliers.

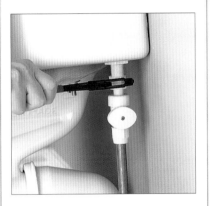

11 If the cistern has pre-drilled holes in its back, next to the wall, insert screws to secure the cistern in place. Again, use both metal and rubber washers.

You should also insert retaining screws through the holes at the base of the pan in order to hold it securely in position.

12 Finally, fit the toilet seat by securing it in place through the pre-drilled holes at the back of the pan. Turn the water supply back on – the toilet is now ready for use.

REPOSITIONING A TOILET AGAINST AN INTERIOR WALL

Complications will occur if a toilet is to be moved from an exterior wall to an interior one. The reason that toilets are usually located on or close to an exterior wall is because there is easy access to the soil pipe, which tends to run down exterior walls and into the sewer system. Having the toilet on an interior wall necessitates extending the large drainage pipe from the toilet out to the soil pipe. Clearly, the dimensions of the drainage pipe make routing difficult because it is unlikely to fit and have the required run if it is positioned below floor level. The alternative method of running the pipe around interior walls is unsightly and is also unlikely to provide the necessary run. As a result, keeping the new toilet position close to the existing one or at least situated on an external wall will always make fitting procedures much easier.

installing a bidet

If you have the luxury of a spacious bathroom, a bidet is a very useful fitting. There are two types: over-rim and rim supply. The former is illustrated here and has water coming from taps above the bidet rim. A rim supply bidet fills from below the rim and as such warms the seat as water is pumped into the bowl. This system has a risk of back siphonage, which means a dedicated hot and cold water supply is essential, making it a more complicated undertaking.

over-rim supply bidets

In many ways an over-rim supply bidet is installed in a similar way to a bathroom basin. First, make sure that both hot and cold water supplies have been routed for bidet connection (see pages 314–17). The waste pipe can be joined directly to the soil pipe or connected to the basin or bath waste pipe. A simple T-connector can be cut into either one of these waste outlets for this purpose. However, consider waste heights carefully because there can be a danger of water from a basin running back into the pan of the bidet if the waste is much higher than the bidet. Also, waste from the bidet could run back into the bath if it is much higher than the bath waste. You need to adjust the run of waste pipes to account for such potential problems.

tools for the job

slip-joint pliers

adjustable spanners

screwdriver

tape measure

pipe cutter

1 Thread the top section of the pop-up waste outlet through the outlet in the bidet, making sure that the correct gasket has been fitted over the tail. If a gasket is not supplied with the outlet, it can be seated on a layer of silicone sealant

to produce the necessary watertight seal. If using sealant, be sure to wipe away the excess before it has a chance to dry.

2 Screw the bottom section of the waste onto the top section underneath the bidet. Again, make sure that the correct gasket is positioned between the waste section and the ceramic surface of the bidet.

3 Turn your attention to the monobloc tap for the bidet. Position a sealing washer at the base of the tap – again, if the taps you are using are not supplied with sealing washers, they can be seated on silicone sealant.

4 Fit the copper hot and cold water supply pipes to the base of the tap fitting, screwing them firmly in place, but taking care not to over-tighten them. Fit the threaded bolt that will be used to secure the tap in position.

5 Thread the copper pipes of the tap assembly through the hole in the bidet. Secure the tap assembly in place using the supplied washers or backnuts. Fit a locking nut onto the threaded bolt, tightening by hand. You may have to give the nut one or two turns with an adjustable spanner to ensure the taps are securely in place. Take care not to over-tighten.

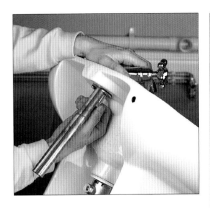

6 Screw the pop-up waste lever into the base of the waste outlet. Tightening by hand is usually sufficient, although you may need to use adjustable spanners.

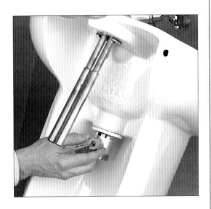

7 Insert the pop-up waste rod into the waste lever and join it to the lever with the supplied clamp. Fix them in place, using a screwdriver to tighten the connection. Adjust the fixing if necessary so that the waste bung sits correctly in the outlet. The pop-up waste bung itself is also adjustable to ensure a watertight fit in the outlet, so make any necessary adjustments now.

8 Make sure that all the necessary supply pipes and waste pipes are in place, ready for the bidet to be positioned and connected. In this case, a swept T-connector has been used to make the appropriate connection in an existing waste pipe. Shut-off valves have also been fitted to the supply pipes so that water can be turned off in an emergency. See pages 314–17.

9 Position the bidet, connecting the supply pipes and waste outlet and trap. Secure the bidet in place by inserting screws at the base of the bidet through the pre-drilled holes. Take care not to over-tighten these fixings and use washers if supplied by the manufacturer. The water supply may now be turned on and the bidet used.

Providing an extra dimension of hygiene and comfort, bidets can also be a highly ornate element of a bathroom design.

installing a shower ⁄⁄⁄⁄

Showers are convenient and efficient bathroom fittings that consume a fraction of the water used by baths. Shower types vary, as do the mechanisms by which they are controlled – our main concern here is the installation procedure. A shower that is sunk into a wall tends to create a more aesthetically pleasing finish, but surface mounting the shower is generally easier to implement. In this example, a shower unit is being fitted into a stud wall.

recessed shower units

tools for the job

tape measure
cordless drill/driver
slip-joint pliers
adjustable spanners
plasterboarding & tiling equipment

1 You will need to install an extra nogging inside the wall to act as a mounting position for the shower. If it is a new wall, do this during the construction process. If it is an existing wall, strip the plasterboard and fix a nogging at the required height and at a depth that will allow the shower unit to sit behind the wall surface, with the controls protruding beyond it. Route hot and cold water supply pipes to the correct position in the wall.

2 Secure the shower unit in place on the supporting nogging so that the connections for the water supply marry with the unit. Cut the

pipe length with a pipe cutter if necessary. Use an adjustable spanner to tighten the connections between the supply pipes and shower unit.

3 In many cases you will need to connect an additional length of pipe from the unit to the shower head. Follow the guidelines provided by the manufacturer.

4 You should now complete the wall. Marine plywood makes a good background for a tiled shower enclosure, but plasterboard can be used as long as it is sealed and/or plastered. Screw the decorative part of the shower head supply pipe onto the recessed part of the pipe.

5 Fit the appropriate collars and/or washers over the unit and supply pipe. These generally push into place.

6 Fit the shower head retaining bracket on the wall and connect the hose to the supply pipe.

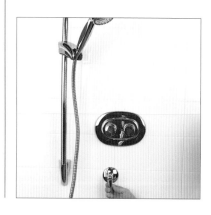

installing a bath screen

If a shower is being installed above a bath, you must fit a bath screen to protect the room from water spray.

1 Use a spirit level to fix the channelling for the frame vertically above the edge of the bath. If fixing into tiles, use the correct type of drill bit to make pilot holes so that you do not damage the tiled surface.

2 Fix the hinging mechanism to the channelling. Designs vary but in many cases the hinge is a two-part assembly. The first part is used to create a secure wall fixing, to which a second section is added.

3 Fit the corresponding hinge sections onto the screen. These are normally of a decorative design. Take care to place any gaskets or protective barriers between the metallic part of the hinge and, in this case, the glass surface.

4 Here, a retaining bolt is pushed through the hinge barrel. It holds the door in place while allowing the hinging mechanism to push the door backwards and forwards from the bath edge. Fit rubber sealant strips to the under edge of the screen.

Simple bath screens provide a physical barrier that prevents water overspray. Different shapes and designs can be chosen to match your bathroom layout.

fitting kitchens & bathrooms

To a greater or lesser extent, most modern kitchens and bathrooms are based on a fitted design that makes the best use of the available space, while still being functional and attractive. This chapter demonstrates the techniques used for constructing and combining units to produce a fitted kitchen and bathroom. There are always slight differences in unit design between manufacturers, which means techniques will need to be refined. However, this chapter helps to demonstrate that most of the general principles involved in fitting kitchens and bathrooms remain constant, irrespective of manufacturing variations. For those instances where unit design does require a change in technique the different options available are also explained.

This stylish kitchen was constructed by building up carcasses, fitting worktop, attaching fronts and finishing.

assembling flat-pack units ⌐

'Flat-pack' is the name given to a unit or carcass that requires assembly before being fitted, so called because of the way they are delivered. Methods for construction will always vary slightly between manufacturers and for different types of unit, but general principles of assembly do remain constant. This chapter demonstrates how to construct a large base unit and covers almost all the techniques you are likely to come across.

There can be a surprising number of components in a flat-pack. It is best to lay out all the unit sections and panels first, then check the fixing pack to ensure you have the correct number of sections and the appropriate choice and quantity of fixings.

tools for the job

slot-head screwdriver
cross head screwdriver
cordless drill/driver
hammer

tips of the trade

It can be worth undertaking one or two dry runs putting the unit together without fixings. This helps to work out how each section relates to the other once the whole unit is complete. Always check each new section has been positioned the right way up.

1 Many flat-packs are assembled following a system of cam studs and screws in pre-drilled holes. This offers an efficient connection as the

holes are drilled with great accuracy in a factory. Position studs according to the guidelines and screw them by hand into the pre-drilled holes. Some studs may need a few turns of the screwdriver to fit securely.

2 Fix drawer runners on the side panels of the unit, following the marked-off positions. Only attach a runner on each side panel if the unit includes two drawers. Choose correct screws for the runners – if they are too long you risk going all the way through and damaging the outer surface.

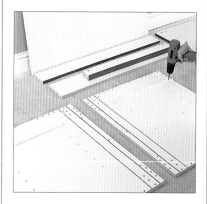

3 Position plastic threaded dowels in pre-drilled holes on the base section and the ends of connecting

sections. These dowels simply push into place and will make joints much stronger when the unit is assembled. Some manufacturers use wooden dowels, which will require gluing (see drawers in step 10).

4 Insert cam screws in the appropriate holes indicated (these will eventually correspond with the holes that have had the cam studs already inserted into them). Again, you should be able just to press these screws into position by hand. Make sure the open side of the cam screw faces the edge of the section, so that it will be possible to join the section to the side panel with the corresponding cam stud. Ensure that the head of the cam screw fits flush with the surrounding panel surface.

5 Use the central strengthening upright as the starting point for full assembly. Connect the base of the upright to the base section, and screw the top strengthening rail in place on top of the upright. Continue to check that each section is being positioned the right way up.

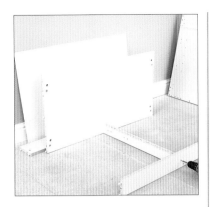

6 The side sections of the unit can now be put in place using the position of the dowels, and cam studs and screws, as a guide. Tighten the cam screws to produce a rigid structure. To encourage the cam fixings and dowels to align, you may need to make one or two gentle blows with the butt end of a hammer on the outside of the side sections.

7 The back panel may now be added. This normally slides into position in purpose-made channels in the side panels. You will find that back panels are more often than not thinner than the other section, since they provide no structural strength to the unit as a whole. Secure them in place by nailing panel pins along the bottom edge of the back panel into the edge of the base section. Ensure that the pins are inserted perpendicular to the base panel edge rather than at an angle – If you make an angled insertion, this can cause the pins to break through the surface of the base panel, which results in a weak fixing and unsightly blemish.

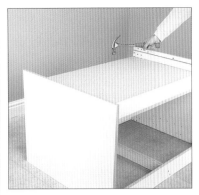

8 Clip the shelf supports in place. These should push in by hand but you may need to apply one or two knocks with the butt end of a hammer. Now insert the central shelf, allowing it to come to rest on the supports. The shelf will either be held in position by the force of gravity or it will have a clip design, resting both below and on top of the shelf to hold it in position.

9 Screw the central drawer runner(s) in position. Two central runners will be needed for a unit with two drawers (one either side of the central vertical upright), otherwise only one will be required.

10 Drawers are usually assembled with dowels, often made of wood and therefore require gluing before the drawer unit is fitted together. If no glue is supplied, normal PVA will suffice. Wipe away any excess with a cloth before it dries.

11 Allow the dowelled joints to dry before fixing runners to the drawer. Screw them in position, perpendicular to the drawer edge.

12 Finally position the drawer(s), and the unit is ready for the first stage of the kitchen-fitting process.

getting level

When installing a new fitted kitchen, it is vital to ensure work begins from a level starting point. From this point the whole kitchen is developed and any inaccuracy at this stage will be magnified as work continues. The importance of taking time to get a level starting point cannot be emphasized enough.

measuring & marking

The aim is to mark a horizontal level guideline at a height corresponding to the top of the base units, which should always be fitted first. If the units are rigid with no feet to allow height adjustment, the guideline will be equal to unit height. Where units have adjustable feet, a good height is 87–9cm (34–5in). To make the guideline you will need to measure up the highest point in the floor level. Not all floors are perfectly 'true' and you will need to make adjustments at this stage to counteract the situation.

tools for the job

spirit level
tape measure
pencil

1 In most kitchens at least one unit will be fitted in or around a corner (see pages 338–9). This makes an ideal starting point and you should try to fix the level guideline from one of the corners. If you have a choice

of corners, take your level line from the highest. If there are no corner units, simply find the highest point along the floor. Lie a long length of batten on the floor, up against the skirting board, then position a spirit level on top to gauge which way the floor is 'running'.

2 Mark off at the desired unit height, measuring from the floor up the wall surface.

3 No further measurements need be taken up the wall surface, but simply use the spirit level to draw a horizontal guideline on the wall. This will represent the height at which the kitchen units will be fitted.

4 Make an accurate plan of the position of units by marking off along the guideline where one unit ends and the next will begin. Refer to your kitchen plan in order to gain accurate measurements.

using a batten

Attaching a batten along the level guideline will facilitate the process of fitting units, but is not always specified by manufacturers. However, the batten approach creates an excellent fixing point for units and provides extra support for the worktop once fitted. If the units are not particularly deep, and as such will be set away from the wall, you will definitely need to attach batten to support the worktop. With deeper units personal choice comes into play. Techniques for fixing units to a wall with or without batten are discussed more fully on pages 336–7.

tools for the job

panel saw
cordless drill/drver
power drill
hammer

using concrete anchors

For solid walls, concrete anchors are the ideal choice as they offer by far the quickest method and create exceptionally strong fixings.

1 Cut a piece of batten to length, then drill through it directly into the wall surface below. Drill bit size should correspond to that of the concrete anchor screws being used.

2 To create a solid fixture, simply screw the concrete anchors directly through the batten and into the solid wall below. Continue to make fixings about 30–45cm (12–18in) apart along the length of the batten.

using wall plugs

Wall plugs can be used for making fixings in both solid and hollow walls. A different type of plug is required for each type of wall surface and you will need to check the packet. In this example a solid wall is again shown.

1 Drill into the wall through the batten. In some cases an electric power drill may be a more suitable choice than a cordless drill/ driver, especially if the wall is made from particularly strong material.

2 Press a wall plug into the hole and then insert a screw into the plug. Use a hammer to gently tap the screw and plug further into the wall, until the screw will go no further without a considerable increase in the force applied with the hammer. You will need to tighten up the screw after hammering it in to make absolutely sure the fixture is solid. Employ a cordless drill/driver for this. Continue to add further wall plug fixtures along the batten as required.

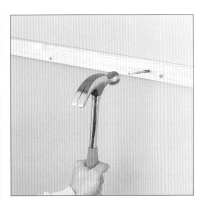

fitting legs

Whether you have purchased a flat-pack or solid carcass kitchen, the manufacturer will almost certainly have left you with the job of attaching legs to each unit.

tools for the job

cordless drill/driver

1 Screw up the legs so that they are in the half-way position along the adjusting thread.

2 Position the legs in the pre-drilled holes on the underside of the unit.

3 Fix them in place with the screws supplied. The units are now ready to be fitted.

positioning base units

Having gained a level guideline, attention may now be turned to the job of positioning and fixing the actual units. A spirit level is again the most important tool here, for although the back edge of the units can be aligned against the batten guideline, the front edge must also be resting at the same level. Thus positioning the units before fixing becomes a methodical process of adjusting leg height to ensure the unit is level across all dimensions.

unit fixings

As a final preparation before the units are positioned, any fixing brackets supplied will need to be attached to the units. There are usually just two types of fixing bracket – those for the worktop and those for the wall.

tools for the job

hammer

cordless drill/driver or screwdriver

worktop fixing brackets

These are small plastic blocks that are knocked into pre-drilled holes in the side of the unit. To form the fixing mechanism between the unit and worktop, a screw is inserted through the bracket into the worktop.

wall fixing brackets

These are L-shaped brackets that are fixed to the back corner of the side panels on a unit. Their L-shape means that once the unit is in position

against the wall, a further screw is inserted through the bracket to hold the unit in place.

NON-ADJUSTABLE UNITS

For units without adjustable legs, small wedges should be used to adjust height as necessary. You can cut your own wedges from 5 x 2.5cm (2 x 1in) batten.

---

positioning & levelling

The kitchen design featured is of a single run of units along one wall. It is best to begin in the corner of the room if possible, and although kitchen units are not too heavy, you might want to employ a helper to lift the larger units into position.

tools for the job

spirit level

cordless drill/driver

clamp

1 Lift the first unit into place in the corner, addressing the back edge to the batten guideline.

2 Adjust leg height by unscrewing or screwing up the legs as required. This will raise or lower the unit as a whole, thereby bringing it to the correct height for levelling with the batten guideline.

3 Hold a spirit level across the top of the unit to make final adjustments on height. The top of the unit should sit flush with the top edge of the batten. Check the position of the unit by holding the level across all directions on top of the unit, adjusting leg height as required.

4 Move the next unit into position adjusting leg height as required and repeating the levelling procedure. Be sure to hold the level across both units to check they are positioned at the same height.

5 Continue to add further units until the entire run is complete, checking they are all level with each other. Clamp adjacent units together for fixing purposes. If the design of your unit does not include pre-drilled holes for joining, then make your own by drilling through the unit at a point that will be hidden by the hinge plate once it is fitted.

6 Screw all the units together to form a tight fixing. Provided they are all level, this will turn what were single units into a rigid, seamless row.

7 Fix the units to the batten by firmly inserting screws through the wall fixing brackets and into the batten on the wall.

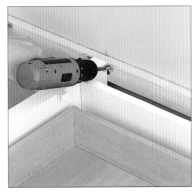

wall fixing alternatives

The method demonstrated above is not the only way of fixing units to a wall and some manufacturers may specify their own particular guidelines. Much of this will be due to the depth of the units. The technique shown will work for most unit types. It is vital, however, to check that the depth of worktop you have will not be too shallow if the units are brought forward from the wall surface using only the batten technique. For kitchen units that are either relatively shallow or particularly deep, you may need to consider applying the following alternative techniques.

shallow units

For shallow units, follow the steps described on pages 334–5 for attaching batten guidelines to the wall. In order to account for standard worktop depth, however, the units will have to be set slightly further away from the wall. Use the technique described on the left to gain the correct height of the units. Then attach additional, shorter lengths of batten to provide a solid fixing between the unit and the wall.

deep units

For deep units it is very likely that the depth of the worktop will be only slightly larger than the actual depth of the unit. As a result, it is essential that the units themselves are positioned as closely as possible to the wall. In this scenario, simply refrain from using a wooden batten to act as a guideline, and instead attach the units directly to the wall, still using wall fixing brackets but carefully following a pencil guideline.

beginning with corner units

On pages 336–7, beginning in the corner of a room was demonstrated using a straight run of base units. However, it is often the case that kitchen layout will require the units to extend around an internal corner. In this situation it is still best to begin in the corner of the room, but clearly the unit used will be a corner base unit rather than a standard base unit. The technique for fitting will therefore need to be modified slightly to account for this variation in design.

Corner units can be supplied ready-made, but they are more often supplied part-assembled and require further assembly and levelling, as shown here. Some corner units are designed to have a simple shelf storage system. Another storage option, however, is a carousel system that facilitates access once the unit is fitted. Although a carousel system can be more complicated to fit, the space saving possibilities make it very worthwhile.

tools for the job

cordless drill/driver

hammer

cross head screwdriver

spirit level

1 Add an extra leg to the assembled part of the base unit carcass. This leg is generally positioned directly below the pivotal point for the carousel unit, and will provide extra support for both the unit and carousel when loaded. Adjust leg height to a similar level to that of the other four legs on the unit.

2 Before the unit carcasses are transported they will often be fitted with an internal temporary support to maintain their shape and reduce the risk of damage. Once the extra leg has been fitted and the unit is turned up the correct way, this temporary support may be removed. Following the guidelines provided by the manufacturer, use a hammer to knock in shelf connectors along the edge of the carcass. These will correspond to the attachment of the self-assembly part of the unit.

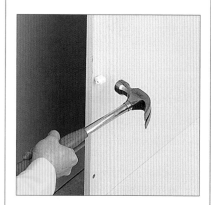

3 Fix the carousel brake ring into the pre-drilled section at the base of the carcass. Ensure the ring is the correct way around.

4 Thread the top shelf of the carousel onto the supporting pole. Position a supporting dowel or pin through the pole to stop the shelf from slipping down the pole. Then take the second (lower) carousel shelf, and thread it into position. If required, fit a supporting dowel to prevent slipping, as for the first shelf. Attach the lock roller to the underside of the lower shelf, making sure that the arm of the roller is in the correct position as indicated by the manufacturer's guidelines.

tips of the trade

A particularly useful tool to use when you are attempting to align and position kitchen units is a 2m (6ft 6in) spirit level. The length makes it much easier to check the level of a number of units at the same time once they are in position. This is especially useful in L-shaped kitchens where you may wish to allow the level to span from one wall of units across to the other. Although these extended spirit levels are quite expensive, if you are a home improvement enthusiast this tool will prove invaluable for both kitchen installation and future projects.

5 The secured carousel shelves may now be positioned inside the corner unit carcass. Thread the pole up through the top of the carcass before allowing the base of the pole to rest inside the carousel brake ring. Once in position, knock the securing bung in place through the top of the unit. This will hold the pole and carousel securely in place, whilst still allowing it to rotate fully for ease of access.

6 With the carousel securely fitted inside the pre-assembled unit, attention may now be turned to assembling the flat-packed section of the corner unit. Before making a start, however, it is important to take a little time to lay out the pieces in front of you on the floor. This will allow you to identify the different sections as required and make sure each section is around the right way. Once you are familiar with the layout, use a hammer to knock in connectors along the edges of the sections that correspond to the connectors inserted in step 2.

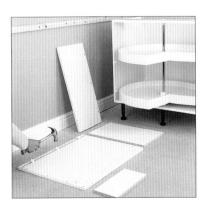

7 Where indicated in the manufacturer's instructions, use corner connecting blocks to join the back section of the unit to what will become the side section of the corner unit as a whole. You will probably find it easier to use a hand-held screwdriver rather than a cordless driver in this situation, since it allows you to maintain greater control while holding the relevant sections in position.

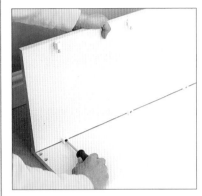

8 Added strength is often given to the join in the floor sections of these units by creating a dowelled join between the floor and side sections. Glue and insert dowels, ensuring that when the floor section is positioned it joins neatly with the side panel. Use a damp cloth to wipe away any excess wood glue before it dries.

9 To complete the self-assembly section of the corner unit, add two further legs to supply support for the unit as a whole once it is assembled. Screw these in place in the usual way.

10 Stand the self-assembled corner section up on its legs and marry up the connectors positioned in steps 2 and 7. Corresponding connectors should simply screw into each other. Again, a hand-held screwdriver is often the best tool for this purpose.

11 Position the finished unit in the corner of the room, adjusting the legs to gain the correct level. Use the spirit level across all angles on top of the unit to ensure precise positioning, as all the other units will take their lead from the position of the corner unit.

fitting wall units ⤢

As with base units, wall units must also be fitted precisely level to achieve the best possible appearance and in order to function properly, allowing the doors to be opened and closed smoothly. Wall units are reliant on wall fixings to secure them in position, so it is vital that these fixings are correctly installed. Most units are hung on wall brackets and for further strength tend to come already fitted with a fixing rail, where screws can be inserted directly through the back of the unit and into the wall surface. This combination of wall brackets and fixing rail provides the best method for securely positioning wall units.

tools for the job

cordless drill/driver

tape measure

pencil

spirit level

screwdriver

clamp

1 Before taking measurements for wall bracket position, drill some pilot holes in the fixing rail on the back of each of the wall units – two or three holes per unit should be adequate.

2 Measure up from the top of the base units to what will be the bottom edge of the wall units. This distance can vary according to personal preference, but you should bear in mind certain safety issues. Where a wall unit is directly above a hob, the distance must be at least 60cm (2ft). Where units are either side of a hob, a minimum distance of 46cm (1ft 6¼in) is required.

Therefore a good base height for wall units is somewhere between 45–50cm (1ft 6in–1ft 8in). Remember to adjust your measurements to account for the depth of the worktop. The height is measured from the top edge of the worktop, so you will need to add worktop depth on top of unit height.

WALL UNIT HEIGHT

To determine the position of wall units you will need to decide what height best suits your needs. A key factor is the stature of the person or persons who most frequently make use of the kitchen facilities – they should not need to overstretch when reaching into cupboards or bang their head when preparing food. Issues of safety should, however, be accounted for. As discussed in step 2, units above and either side of a hob must accord to a minimum height. This minimum often then dictates the height of the other units, as it is better to have an even run of units rather than incorporating a 'step' for the hob.

3 Use the mark made to indicate the height of the units to draw a level pencil guideline. Use a spirit level as a straight edge so that you do not need to make further marks along the wall – simply ensure the bubble remains level. This guideline identifies the base position of all the wall units.

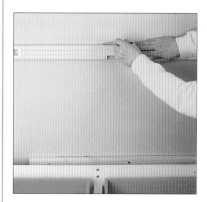

4 Measure up from the base guideline a distance equal to the height of the wall units and draw a further level line to denote what will be their top edge once in place. Paying close attention to the kitchen plan, draw vertical lines to separate the positions of the different wall units.

Follow the manufacturer's guidelines to gain the correct distance between the vertical and horizontal guidelines and the edges of each bracket. Mark this position with a pencil.

5 Hold the brackets in place and fix them to the wall with suitable fixings. Remember to choose the correct type of wall plug depending on whether it is a solid or hollow wall. Continue to fit wall brackets for each unit. Most units will require two brackets, one for each corner.

safety advice

When drilling and fixing into walls, take care not to coincide fixings with supply pipes or cables. Use a pipe and cable detector to help avoid such instances.

6 Simply hook the wall unit over the brackets to hold it in position on the wall. For larger units it may be worthwhile employing a helper to lift the unit into place.

7 Once all the units are in place, some minor adjustment may be required for final levelling purposes. In the top internal corner of the units, there is normally an adjustment block that has two functions: one screw can be tightened or loosened to adjust the height of the unit, the other is used to tighten the unit against the wall bracket once you are satisfied that it is totally level. In order to gain access to these screws, it may be necessary to remove a shelf from inside the unit.

8 Wall units should always be mechanically joined together to ensure they create a rigid storage structure. To make a fixing, clamp together adjacent units and drill directly through the side panel of one unit into the next. Position the hole close to the front edge, in line with the hinge fixings.

9 Use two-part steel connection screws to join the units together, inserting two fixings along each unit edge. Tighten with a screwdriver.

10 As an extra precaution to ensure the unit structure is solid, fix directly through the back of the unit by inserting screws through the holes drilled in step 1.

tips of the trade

The methods recommended in order to achieve a strong fixing with screws inserted in the fixing rail will vary according to the type of screw and wall surface.

• If the wall has to be plugged, you will need to pre-drill holes in the wall surface, so that the screw may be inserted once the wall unit is in place. To make this plugged fixing, after step 7 mark through the drilled hole in the fixing rail, remove the wall unit and then drill and plug the wall before repositioning the unit.

• On solid walls, use concrete anchor screws so that plugging is not necessary.

• Where the drilled hole in the fixing rail coincides with wooden studs in a hollow wall, there is no need for plugging as a standard screw will fix directly into the stud.

fitting doors & drawer fronts

Doors, drawer fronts and handles add the finishing touch to a kitchen unit. Although the fixing procedure for all these items is very straightforward, because they contribute so much to the finished look of a kitchen it is important to take the time to ensure correct technique is employed.

cupboard doors

Most manufacturers pre-cut holes on the inside of doors to indicate the exact hinge position, and pre-drill holes on the unit for the hinge plate. Nevertheless, precision is still vital when inserting screws to ensure the door functions smoothly.

1 Position hinges on the inside of the door and screw them in place securely.

tips of the trade

Always select the correct size of screw for each item. If the screws are too long they will penetrate through to the front of the drawer or door front.

2 Fix hinge plates in the pre-drilled holes in the carcass. A cordless drill/driver is the ideal tool to use so that the screws bite firmly, but set it on a low speed to maintain good control with the driver.

3 Position the door so the hinges slip over the hinge plates, then tighten the retaining screws.

4 If the door height needs to be adjusted to level up the edges,

this can be done by loosening off the hinge plate screws allowing the door to be moved up or down.

5 Tightening or undoing the hinge screw allows further adjustment of door position to gain a level when the door is closed. One screw may require tightening while the other screw needs loosening.

fitting handles

Manufacturers generally make a small indentation on the inside of doors as a guide for fixing handles.

1 Using the correct-sized drill bit – it should match the shank of the handle screw – drill through the

door from the inside out to the front. Hold a block of wood against the door front at the point where the drill bit will break through. This will prevent the surface of the door splintering. You may need to drill more than one hole depending upon your chosen handle design.

2 Insert the handle retaining screw(s) through the hole(s) just drilled.

3 Secure the handle in place by tightening the screw(s).

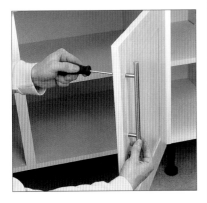

corner unit doors

The door fronts of corner units tend to require slightly different fitting techniques, due to the variety of designs that facilitate access to the awkward storage space. Technique will also vary according to whether the doors are 'full height', in that they make up the total height of the unit, or whether dummy drawer fronts need to be attached prior to fitting.

full height option

With corner units, a post is attached to the inside edge of one of the doors for a seamless appearance when the doors are closed. Secure the post in place by attaching fixing plates to the back of the door that overlap onto the corner post. Follow the same procedures described above for fixing doors and handles to the corner unit.

170°-opening option

Alternative hinges are available for corner units that are slightly more complex in design in that they can be opened to 170°, making access to inside the unit much easier.

dummy drawer option

In this situation, further fixing plates are used to overlap between the door and drawer front. Thus when the unit is in a closed position it appears to function like separate cupboards and drawers, where in fact the corner unit is only a cupboard.

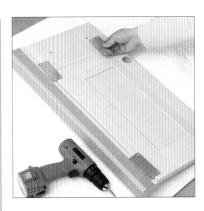

fitting drawer fronts

Check the manufacturer's guidelines as to whether handles need to be attached before the drawer fronts are screwed in, or afterwards.

1 Marry up the pre-drilled holes and double check the drawer front is the right way around.

2 Screw through the pre-drilled holes inside the drawer into the drawer front to secure it in place. Hold the front in position to ensure a good tight fixing.

fitting wooden worktop ⁄⁄⁄

Most varieties of worktop are fitted using similar techniques, although techniques can vary in particular cases. For example, wooden worktop is not always supplied with a moulded edge, so if you want a moulded edge, choose carefully or you will have to create it yourself on your worktop. You may also need to take into account variations in cutting techniques and plan so that the best use is made of the factory edges on the worktop material.

deciding on cut positions

Factory cut edges on a worktop will be much more accurate than those cut at home, so the best use should be made of them. The diagram opposite shows the ideal arrangement of cut edges for a typical worktop formation. The ends you cut yourself should form junctions with the walls, so that their edges will be covered by final finishing on the walls. In this design, only one cut end is exposed as a visible edge, and with further finishing the cut will in effect be hidden. It is best to join the sides to factory cut ends in order to achieve a precise fit.

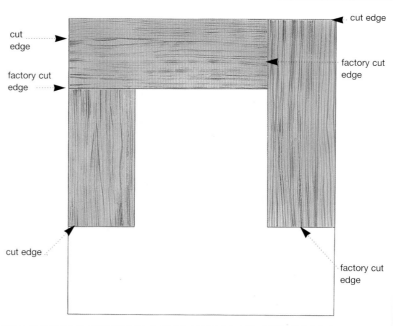

cut edge

cut edge

factory cut edge

factory cut edge

cut edge

factory cut edge

tools for the job

panel saw or jigsaw
tape measure & pencil
clamp
router

fitting a straight run

A straight worktop run is the easiest to fit, but the same techniques can be used for more complex designs.

1 Cut the worktop to length and position it approximately on top of the units. Measure the overhang at the front. If the units have been fitted correctly, this distance should

be slightly more than the required overhang. Normal overhangs are between 0.5 and 2cm (⅛ and ¾in), measuring from the door or drawer front. Undulations in the shape of the wall may cause the initial overhang to vary slightly along the length of the worktop. Rather than simply trimming a specific length off the back of the

worktop, therefore, you may need to cut away a more graduated portion. To do this, first position the worktop so that its front edge overhangs by the same amount along the entire run of units, while ensuring that the back edge is touching the wall in at least one place.

tips of the trade

Cutting to length – Wooden worktop can be cut with a jigsaw or panel saw. Make sure the correct blade has been fitted if you are using a jigsaw as anything too coarse will splinter the edges of the cut. If using a panel saw, keep the angle of the blade shallow in relation to the worktop surface to produce the cleanest possible cut.

2 The next step is to make a scribing block to help work out how much of the back edge requires cutting away. The size of the scribing block will be equal to the distance between the front edge of the work surface and the carcass, less whatever distance you wish for the finished overhang of the worktop. Cut a small block of wood to this exact size. Hold a pencil next to the block and draw a guideline by sliding the block along the back wall. You may wish to clamp the work surface in position to ensure it does not move during this procedure.

3 Cut along the guideline using a jigsaw or panel saw. Accuracy is important, but any small splinters caused by the jigsaw can be sanded away and will, in any case, be hidden when the worktop is fitted against the wall surface.

4 Reposition the worktop so that the cut back edge is tight against the wall, with the front edge forming an even overhang along the

front of the unit. Clamp the worktop in position, screwing through the brackets if supplied. Also fix up into the underside of the worktop through the front fixing rail of the units.

dealing with corners

Corners should not present too many problems, provided that the ideal positioning for cut edges has been taken into account – follow the layout indicated by the diagram opposite. Separate lengths should be cut to size and scribed as required, before joining together.

1 At the corner join, apply a generous amount of wood glue or PVA along the joint.

2 Move the sections into position, creating a strong bond. Wipe away excess glue with a cloth before it dries. Some manufacturers supply fixing plates that can be attached on the underside of the joint to help hold it firmly in position.

finishing the edge

A router is the ideal tool to add a decorative edge to the worktop. Choose the cutter according to the type of finished edge you require.

1 Follow the manufacturer's guidelines for the router and lock the cutter in position.

2 Run the router along the edge of the worktop to create a moulded edge. Work in smooth, continuous motions – by dwelling in particular areas you can singe the wood.

fitting other worktop ⌐⌐⌐⌐

Aside from the many wooden varieties, there are a number of other types of worktop available in a range of materials, including laminates and synthetic or natural stone. Fitting natural and synthetic stone worktops should really be left to the professionals, but laminate worktop can be fitted using a similar technique to wooden worktop, with only slight changes in terms of planning and procedure.

deciding on cut positions

The arrangement of cut edges for laminate worktops is similar to that indicated for wooden worktops on page 344. It equally follows that cut ends should, if possible, be positioned against wall junctions so that their edge will be covered by whatever finish is applied to the wall. However, since laminate worktops cannot be sanded and their edges are not finished by routing, it is even more important to position factory cut edges at the exposed ends. Joining strips can be used to neaten the effect of inaccurate cuts in corners.

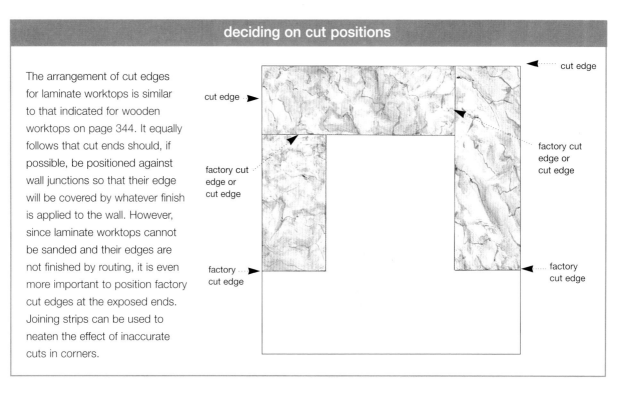

cut edge

cut edge

factory cut edge or cut edge

factory cut edge or cut edge

factory cut edge

factory cut edge

tools for the job

tape measure & pencil
straight edge (batten)
panel saw or jigsaw
hacksaw
cordless drill/driver

cutting worktop

Laminate worktops may be cut with either a panel saw or jigsaw. If using a jigsaw it is vital to choose a blade designed for cutting through laminates, otherwise the surface of the worktop can splinter. Cutting the worktop with the underside uppermost further reduces the risk of splintering.

1 Mark off the required length and draw a precise guideline across the width of the worktop using a length of batten as a straight edge.

2 Move the batten to one side of the guideline, a distance equal to that between the edge of the jigsaw and its blade. Screw the batten in

place, securely but temporarily, at this point on the underside of the worktop. Cut through the worktop holding the jigsaw against the batten. This method produces a perfectly straight cut. Ensure the worktop is well supported when cutting, as any shift in position will risk splitting the laminate surface.

dealing with corners

It is extremely difficult to make an accurate cut across the laminate worktop so that it can be glued and fixed in the same way as for wooden worktop. Even the slightest blemish in a cut or unevenness in positioning will magnify any problems with the join. To overcome this problem, joining strips are commonly used to create a strong join between sections.

1 Cut the joining strip to the exact width required for the laminate worktop – strips are usually made from aluminium, which can be cut using a hacksaw.

2 Apply some silicone sealant along the cut edge of the worktop, and then screw the joining strip in place along the edge.

3 Add a further quantity of silicone sealant along the facing edge of the adjoining worktop section, which should already be fitted in place on the unit. Then slide the section with the joining strip into position flush against the edge covered with sealant.

4 Screw through the fixing rails in the carcass into the underside of the worktop. Pay special attention at the corner. Wipe away any excess silicone then allow it to dry and create a watertight bond.

👍

tips of the trade

Fitting straight lengths – To fit straight lengths of laminate worktop follow the same technique described for wooden worktop on pages 344–5. Check the correct jigsaw blade is installed for cutting laminate finish.

finishing edges

The manufacturer will have provided laminate strips to finish the worktop ends. These are applied using a warm iron, which melts and activates an adhesive on the back of the laminate strip sticking it securely in place.

tools for the job

iron
scissors
craft knife

Heat the iron to the temperature specified by the manufacturer. Cut the laminate strip to size with scissors and hold it against the worktop edge. Gently run the iron across the surface of the strip until it bonds. Once the adhesive has dried and the strip is securely positioned, trim the edge of the strip to ensure a neat and precise finish – a craft knife is ideal for this purpose.

WORKTOP OPTIONS

• **Natural stone** – To fit a natural stone worktop, such as granite, create a template of the area required first and give this to the factory for them to cut it to the correct size and polish. The worktop is fitted in large sections, and this is best carried out by professional fitters. An epoxy-based resin is normally used for dealing with joints. Since the stone has no elasticity, it is vital that the units are exactly level – any undulations will cause the stone to crack under its own weight.

• **Synthetic stone** – This type of worktop also needs to be templated for fitting, which is best undertaken by professionals. A level surface is similarly crucial for fitting.

fitting cornice, pelmet & end panels ✂✂

Cornice, pelmet and end panels provide finishing touches to units and are used as decorative embellishments to improve the overall appearance of the kitchen. These items have no structural role to play and are primarily concerned with hiding fixings and 'rounding off' the edges and sides of units, to create a pleasing finished appearance.

tools for the job

tape measure & pencil
mitresaw
cordless drill/driver
sealant gun
clamp

fitting cornice

Cornice is the decorative edging fitted around the top edge of wall units to provide a moulded and framed finish to the run, enhancing the 'built-in' look. Fixings are hidden from view when inserted through the cornice top down into the unit tops. Fitting cornice is a process of careful measuring and fixing, and accuracy is especially important for fitting cornice round a corner.

1 Observe how the design of the cornice will relate to the fitting process, then measure the required length and cut the two pieces to size. Mark on the end of each piece the

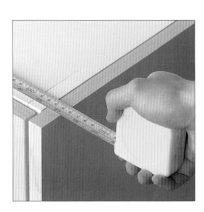

45°-angle cut required to form the mitre joint. You will usually need to align the cornice with the 90°-angle made by the corner of the wall unit carcass. However, if the unit includes an end panel and/or door extending out slightly from the carcass, you will need to take this into account.

2 Make the angled cut on the cornice using a mitresaw for accuracy. Ensure the saw is well supported to prevent tearing the cornice surface as the cut is made.

3 Screw the first section of cornice in position allowing the screws to bite firmly into the wall unit. Be sure

to use screws of the appropriate length so that they do not penetrate through to inside the unit.

4 Apply some wood glue or PVA to the end of the fixed section before attaching the next piece.

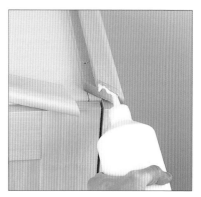

5 Position the next cornice piece, forming the mitre joint by hand initially, allowing the glue to produce a tight bond. Continue by screwing the cornice in place employing the same technique described in step 3.

6 In some cases a tiny gap may appear in the mitre joint. Fill the gap with silicone sealant of a similar

colour to the cornice. Wipe away excess with a cloth before it dries.

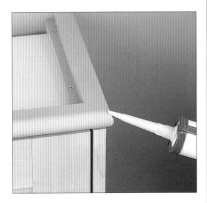

fitting pelmet

Many manufacturers produce one shape of moulding that can act for both cornice and pelmet, such is their similarity. The main difference is that pelmet is attached to the bottom rather than top edge of the unit. As you would expect, the technique for fitting is very similar. Measure and cut the pelmet as for cornice; however you will need to clamp the pelmet in place to allow it to be fixed to the underside of the units.

fitting end panels

End panels are an optional fitting applied to the ends of both wall and base units. They are generally chosen to match the door and drawer fronts.

1 Cut the panel to height, then position it at the end of the unit, overlapping the front edge. Pull the drawer out to allow access for a tape measure and measure the distance required for the panel to overhang the front of the unit. Cut away any extra from the back edge. Most walls are not totally 'square', so it is best to scribe the back edge of the panel to create a neat fit. While measuring the overhang at the front, therefore, allow the panel to touch the wall in at least one place. Then measure and

cut a scribing block, which will produce the required overhang.

2 Draw a guideline along the back edge of the panel using the scribing block to maintain distance.

3 Cut away the unwanted section of panel with a jigsaw using a blade suitable for laminates. Position and clamp the panel at the end of the unit, then insert screws from inside the unit into the back of the panel. Screwing from the inside ensures no damage is visible.

tips of the trade

As an alternative method, apply bonding adhesive or silicone sealant to the end panel before screwing it in place. Thus you will only need one or two screw fixings while the adhesive or sealant dries.

End panels, cornice and pelmet help to lift the appearance of what are essentially functional units in a kitchen design.

fitting plinth ⤢

As cornice and pelmet provide a finished edge to wall units, so plinth provides the finished edge to the bottom of base units. For units with legs, plinth is fitted by means of clips attached to the back of the piece of plinth and then clipped in place on the legs.

tools for the job

tape measure & pencil

mitresaw

panel saw or jigsaw

combination square

cordless drill/driver

iron

scissors

craft knife

1 Plinth is generally supplied in standard lengths of a set height. In most cases, the height will not need to be cut down as units tend to be manufactured so that the plinth fits comfortably underneath. A slight gap in-between the top of the plinth and the underside of the unit should not cause a problem, since this area is not in general view. Before cutting plinth to the correct length, check to see whether you will also need to reduce the height at the same time. Remember this gap may not be consistent under all units, especially if the floor has a slope. You should therefore check the height measurement in several positions.

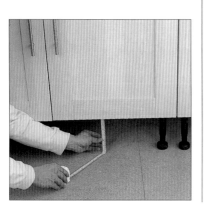

2 Cut the plinth to the correct length and, if necessary, reduce in height. You can use a panel saw or jigsaw to cut the plinth across its width, but a mitresaw, set to a 90°-angle, will provide a cleaner and more accurate cut, ensuring the best possible joins with other sections. Use a panel saw or jigsaw to adjust the plinth height.

3 Lay out the cut length of plinth in front of the base units allowing its bottom edge to rest against the unit legs (the front of the plinth should be facing down). Use a combination square and pencil to draw a series of lines on the back of the plinth to correspond with the centre of each base leg.

4 Fix clip brackets in the centre of each guideline. Make sure the screws being used are not too long. Otherwise they will penetrate through to the front face of the plinth and cause unsightly damage.

5 Position the clips in each of the brackets so they are still aligned with the base unit legs.

6 If a sealant strip is supplied, turn the plinth upside down and attach the strip to the bottom edge. The purpose of a sealant strip is to create a neat, watertight seal that facilitates cleaning.

7 Having applied the sealant strip – if applicable, otherwise after the clips have been positioned – turn the plinth back up the right way and clip it in position on the base unit legs.

8 Once again check the plinth height. If flooring is yet to be laid, bear in mind it is best for the flooring material to extend under the units, with the plinth fitting neatly on top. Use a piece of card or board similar in height to your choice of flooring to check for adequate tolerance. If you find there is not enough, unclip the plinth and cut down the height further.

internal corners

Internal corners present a slight problem when dealing with plinths, as it is unlikely that a leg will fall precisely on the point where the plinth requires joining. You will therefore need to use another type of bracket, which joins the two plinths together to form a rigid enough connection so that both ends are held securely in place.

1 Cut the two lengths of plinth so that one length extends slightly further under the units than would be the case for an exact corner join. Lay this longer length on the floor so that the front is facing upwards. Secure a fixing bracket on the front face in a central position slightly back from the point where the two sections of plinth will ultimately join.

2 Fix the connecting clip for the corner bracket at the end of the shorter length of plinth on the back face. When the two lengths are positioned, the clip on the back edge of the shorter length will join with the fixing bracket on the longer length, clipping together to form a tight internal joint in the corner.

dealing with cut ends

In some cases the cut end of a length of plinth may be visible, for example, on external corners where there is often no option but to have an exposed end. If this situation arises, employ a similar technique for dealing

with the cut ends of a worktop and cover over the end with a thin strip of laminate (see also page 347).

1 Measure and cut the laminate strips to size with scissors.

2 Position the strip on the end of the plinth, then smooth over the strip with a warm iron – the heat from the iron causes the adhesive to bond with the cut end. As it is a contact adhesive there is no need for clamping. Once it is secure, trim the strip with a craft knife for a neat finish.

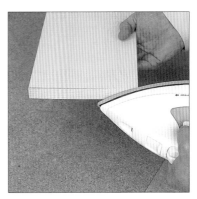

PLINTH OPTIONS

Although fitted kitchens normally include specially manufactured plinth, it is possible to make your own using either MDF or prepared softwood planks. The same procedure is used for fixing the plinth in place, but the main benefit with this method is that more options for finishing are available. For example, planking can be stained to provide a natural look.

fitting breakfast bars

Breakfast bars are becoming an increasingly popular addition to kitchen design. They can be built separate and free-standing or integrated into a run of fitted units, thus transforming a worktop into a multi-purpose area that can be used for both food preparation and eating. What fundamentally changes a worktop into a breakfast bar is the ability to sit comfortably at the worktop so that meals may be taken.

separate bars

Separate breakfast bars are ideal for individuals or couples and are a good way of using worktop offcuts.

tools for the job

tape measure & pencil
panel saw or jigsaw
cordless drill/driver
spirit level
hacksaw

1 Cut 5 x 2.5cm (2 x 1in) batten to a length equal to what will be the back edge of the breakfast bar. Chamfer the ends of the batten so that they will not be visible when the worktop is in position. Screw the batten to the wall at a suitable height. This need not be standard worktop height – the ability to sit comfortably should be the deciding factor.

2 Attach L-shaped fixing brackets along the batten at roughly 20cm (8in) intervals. Make sure that the top section of the brackets extends horizontally and flush with the top edge of the batten.

3 Cut a section of worktop to size. Adding a curved edge to the corners will help soften its appearance. To form the curved edge, make a guideline – you can use the base of a paint can for a template – then cut along the guideline with a jigsaw.

4 Hold the worktop in position, sitting on the batten, and rest a spirit level on the surface. Make any adjustments needed to get the worktop level, then measure the distance from the underside of the worktop to the floor.

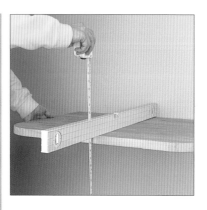

5 Using a hacksaw, cut a length of stainless steel tubing to this measurement. With suitable brackets, attach the pole to the underside of the worktop and floor. Fix the worktop securely in place through the L-shaped fixing brackets along the back edge. The edge may now be routed for final finishing (see page 345).

integrated bars

An integrated breakfast bar is basically a continuation of the kitchen worktop, but it can be much deeper or wider than standard size. As such, much of the fitting procedure is similar to that demonstrated on pages 344–7.

tools for the job

tape measure & pencil

hand saw or jigsaw

cordless drill/driver

spirit level

hammer

1 It is always best to fit a breakfast bar before the rest of the kitchen worktop, because of its greater size, even though it may not be fixed as the first section. Breakfast bars are often supplied in a specific size, although wooden ones may be cut down and the edge finished yourself. Measure the worktop to work out the different overhangs. As with a normal worktop, the non-seating edge should have an overhang of between 0.5cm (⅛in) and 2cm (¾in). The opposite overhang should be deep enough for people to be seated comfortably.

2 On the seating side of the bar, it will be necessary to provide some sort of finish to the back of the

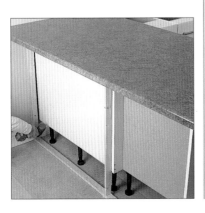

kitchen units. Tongue and groove panelling offers an attractive and hardwearing option. You will need to build a framework to attach the panelling – 5 x 2.5cm (2 x 1in) or 5 x 5cm (2 x 2in) batten is ideal for this purpose. Gain a secure fixing by the wall and continue to build up the framework.

3 Horizontal struts will need to be included in the batten framework to provide additional strength and extra fixing points for the tongue and groove panelling.

4 Once the framework is complete simply build up the panels by fixing through the tongues of each board into the batten struts below. Join each new length over the previous panel to hide the fixing points.

👍 tips of the trade

Breakfast bars with a considerable overhang may need to be fitted with extra support. This can be provided by screwing a length of batten at the wall junction underneath the overhang.

353

Here a run of floor units has been fitted with a worktop that overhangs on one side so that it may be used for both dining and food preparation.

boxing in

One of the attractive features of a fitted kitchen or bathroom is that most of the exposed cables and pipes are hidden by the units themselves. Sometimes, however, a small amount of boxing in may be required to cover unsightly features still exposed after the units have been fitted. There are two main types of boxing – that which covers over permanently and that which incorporates a built-in access hatch of some variety.

without access

Boxing in without access is by far the easiest to build of the two types, as it is simply a case of making the most unobtrusive boxing design possible. The most versatile materials for building any type of boxing are MDF in conjunction with 5 x 2.5cm (2 x 1in) batten.

tools for the job

tape measure & pencil

panel saw or jigsaw

cordless drill/driver

hammer

1 Pipes are one of the most common obstacles to be dealt with by boxing and are often found in the corners of rooms. First of all, fix cut lengths of batten to the wall surface on either side of the pipes.

2 Measure the dimensions required to make a box with two pieces of mdf. Remember that one piece will have to overlap the other in order to create a right-angled join.

3 Cut the MDF to size using a jigsaw or panel saw. If using a panel saw, remember to keep the angle of the blade shallow in relation to the surface of the MDF – this will improve both the ease of cutting and the accuracy of the cut.

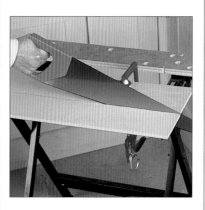

safety advice

MDF creates more dust when sawn than other fibreboards, so whether cutting with a jigsaw or panel saw, always wear a dust mask.

4 Nail the MDF sheets in place with panel pins. Start off the pins by knocking them along the edge of the MDF before it is in position. This makes the final nailing much easier and reduces the chance of damaging the wall with the hammer.

5 Nail the second piece in place, then add further pins along the edge of the overlapping sheet to form a strong corner joint. The boxing can now be painted or tiled as required.

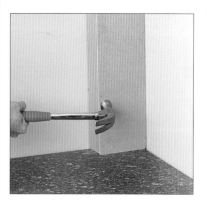

tips of the trade

Cracks along the junction made by the boxing can be filled with flexible caulk before decorating. Flexible filler reduces the risk of cracking, especially important when boxing over hot water pipes where temperature changes cause the boxing to expand and contract slightly.

with access

Access is generally required when a stopcock or stop valve is present in a section of pipework. Whatever the situation, access panels can be hinged, fitted with magnetic catches or can even be built as free-standing units that are positioned without any permanent fixing. Free-standing units are a common type of boxing for below boilers in kitchens, where access is required – a small free-standing boxing unit is placed over the pipework to shield it from view.

tools for the job

tape measure & pencil

panel saw

cordless drill/driver

jigsaw

screwdriver

hacksaw

hammer

hinged access

1 Having cut an MDF panel to fit your boxing framework, mark off the size of door required in the face of the MDF. A tile makes an excellent template and is an ideal size for a hatch that needs to be large enough for hand access.

2 Using a flathead drill bit, drill through the MDF at each corner of what will be the access panel

opening. Be careful not to allow the edge of the drill bit to extend over the pencil guidelines.

3 The drilled holes will act as an access point so for a jigsaw to cut out the panel.

4 Cut a door to fit in the hole in the panel from another piece of MDF. Then use a hacksaw to cut a length of piano hinge and screw it into the hinging edge of the panel door.

5 Fit a small handle to the door before finally screwing it in place on the hinging edge of the panel.

The entire panel may now be attached to the boxing framework following the same method described opposite.

free-standing access

1 Cut pieces of MDF to size and fix them together along one edge to create a right-angled unit.

2 On the inside of the unit, glue additional blocks to the right-angled junction, thereby enhancing the structural strength. The unit can now be tiled over or painted and positioned on a worktop, covering pipework that needs periodic access.

fitting shelving

Shelves are usually fitted to provide storage in addition to wall units. Where budgets are limited, however, shelves can be used as a straight alternative to wall units, and in small rooms where space is at a premium and wall units would create a rather cramped atmosphere, simple shelving is a suitable option. Whatever your reasons may be for choosing to install shelving, it is vital to employ adequate fixing techniques to ensure the shelves are level and secure enough to support the weight of whatever you place on them.

making use of worktop

A good way of making use of the inevitable leftover pieces of worktop is to make extra shelving. Moreover, the width and depth of worktop material allows for hidden fixings.

tools for the job

tape measure & pencil

jigsaw or panel saw

cordless drill/driver

router (optional)

hacksaw

disposable resin applicator

1 Mark the outline of the shelf on the worktop. Then cut around this guideline – a jigsaw is ideal for this purpose but you can also use a panel saw. Using a flathead bit, drill holes at a point outside the guideline to accommodate the jigsaw blade. A router may be used to shape a decorative moulded edge around the front of the shelf if desired (see page 345 for further instructions).

2 Firmly clamp the cut-out shelf to a workbench and use a drill with a flat bit to make two holes in the back edge of the shelf, relatively close to either end. The holes need to be just wider than the circumference of a threaded bolt, which will be used as the wall fixing mechanism.

3 Cut the two bolts to length using a hacksaw. The bolts should penetrate inside the shelf to a depth of at least half the shelf width, and should penetrate into the wall to an equal distance. Measure and mark off the position of the holes on the wall, checking they are aligned, and drill the holes required.

4 Insert resin into the holes in the wall with the disposable applicator. Push the threaded bolts into the holes and allow the resin to dry out. Once the bolts are secured, use the applicator to insert resin into the bolt holes in the shelf itself.

5 Lift the shelf into position fitting the holes in the back edge over the threaded bolts in the wall.

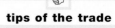

tips of the trade

Resin drying times will vary. Follow the guidelines to ensure you get the timing right when making the fixing.

hidden fixing brackets

The more traditional approach to fitting shelves involves a visible bracket, but it is still possible to hide the fixings. Once again, discarded worktop may be used to create the shelving.

1 Again, measure and mark the outline of the shelf on the worktop. Use this guideline to cut the worktop to size, ideally using a jigsaw but otherwise a panel saw will be adequate. Drill holes outside the guideline for initially inserting the jigsaw blade. Having cut the shelf you may turn your attention to attaching the hidden brackets. Hold the housing section of one of the brackets against the wall and employ a mini level to ensure that it is precisely vertical. Then mark the fixing position with a bradawl.

2 Drill the correct size of hole in the wall and fit wall plugs. They may push in by hand, or require some additional encouragement with one or two taps of the butt end of a hammer.

3 Now reposition the housing section and screw it securely in place. Check it once more with a mini level to ensure that it has not shifted out of position.

4 Position the second housing section on the wall next to the section already fixed in place. It will need to be positioned at the correct distance to accommodate the shelf. Place a spirit level across the top of both sections to ensure that they are precisely level and aligned. Once again mark with a bradawl through the second section to indicate where you need to screw.

5 Screw the section in place, then slide the support brackets into both the housing sections.

6 Finally, position the shelf and secure it in place by using a hammer to knock one or two panel pins through the top of the shelf and into the brackets below.

ALTERNATIVE SHELVING SYSTEMS

In both the examples shown, leftover wooden worktop has been used to create extra shelving, thereby helping to create an overall integrated look to the kitchen. However, most DIY outlets will stock a wide selection of shelving systems, and you may prefer to choose a material or design that provides a contrast with the other kitchen surfaces. Whatever system you ultimately choose, the secret of successful shelving remains the same – make sure the shelves sit level and that the brackets and fixings will be able to bear the weight requirements.

installing fitted bathroom units ⟋⟋

Fitted bathroom units are becoming increasingly common. They are sometimes supplied ready-assembled but, in many cases, they are flat-packed and require assembly before being installed. Some units are designed to form part of a run of units, while others, such as a vanity unit, are used singly as separate features. Whatever the case, the principles for assembly are similar. Many flat-packs are put together using cam studs and plastic connecting blocks, as shown here.

tools for the job

hammer

screwdriver

cordless drill/driver

1 Organization is the key to assembling units – so lay out all the relevant sections to make sure you have the required number of components and the correct fixings to put them together. Follow the manufacturer's guidelines for assembly – in most cases, the first step is to hammer plastic connectors into pre-drilled holes along the edges of the panels. In this case, the connectors are being inserted in the two side panels of the unit.

2 Insert wooden dowels into the appropriate holes on the edges of the shelving sections. Insert cam screws into the pre-drilled holes, pushing them in position by hand and making sure the open end of the screw thread is pointing towards the edge of the shelf or unit section. Insert the cam studs that will attach

to the screws in the corresponding part of the unit. Some may need a turn of the screwdriver to fit them securely in place. Since the pre-drilled holes have been accurately made in a factory, cam studs and screws offer an efficient connection mechanism that ensures precision and eliminates the chance of errors.

3 Assemble the unit by marrying the corresponding sections at the appropriate fixing points. The cam studs connect with the cam screws by inserting the stud into the screw, then turning the screw to lock the fixing in place. Continue to add sections of the unit until the basic carcass is complete.

4 Now work on the unit doors. Most manufacturers use recessed hinges that are hidden from external view when the door is closed. Their exact positions are generally pre-marked and cut into the back of the doors, so fitting is a simple process of positioning the hinge and screwing it in place.

5 Hinge plates may also be attached to the carcass of the unit, again using the pre-drilled holes made in the manufacturing process. Most hinge plates are reversible but in some cases there is a right and wrong way up, so always check before attaching them to make sure that the door hinges will fit.

6 Fit the doors in place by hooking the hinges onto the hinge plates and tightening the central retaining screw to hold them in position. These types of hinges are always adjustable, so once the unit is in place it is still possible to move the door position slightly to make sure they are level and open and close correctly, although it usually takes a little trial and error to get them right.

7 Now fit the basin section of the unit. In this case, the moulded basin section is screwed in place using the plastic connecting blocks on the edge of the carcass. Screws are inserted through the blocks into a chipboard section that is an integral part of the basin unit. There will inevitably be variations between manufacturers regarding how the basin is fitted, so it is important to follow their guidelines.

8 With this unit a drawer front is used to finish the front section, which that is held in place with connecting blocks.

9 You will need to make some sort of provision at the back edge of the carcass for fixing the unit to the wall. L-shaped brackets are ideal for this purpose and are usually supplied by the manufacturer as part of the flat-pack. Screw them into position along the back edge of the unit.

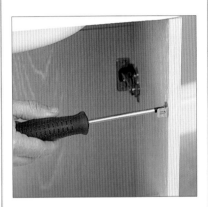

10 Attach door handles by drilling through the door at the marked points. Be sure to use an appropriate size drill bit or the handles will be loose. To prevent splitting or damaging the doors, hold a block of wood at the position where the drill bit will emerge from the door.

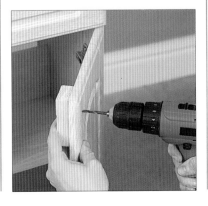

11 Screw the handles in place using one hand to hold the handle while the other hand operates the screwdriver.

LEVELLING A RUN OF UNITS

In many cases it will be necessary to connect a number of units in a row. In such circumstances, assemble the units separately and position them along the wall, using a spirit level to check that they are correctly aligned horizontally and/or vertically, according to the planned layout of the room. A 2m (2yd) spirit level is particularly useful for this job because it can span several units, making this procedure much easier.

FINISHING TOUCHES

Once the unit is assembled, it can be positioned against the wall. If necessary – for example, for a vanity unit, as shown here – make sure that the relevant water supply and drainage outlets are ready for connection. You will also need to install the fittings for the basin (this is covered in greater detail on pages 318–21). It is often best to fit taps to a unit before it is installed in its final position so that you can gain easy access to the underside of the basin. When you have completed all of the above, final fitting is a case of doing up connections and securing the unit in position against the wall.

fitting a bath panel ⚟

Traditional or roll-top baths did not usually have a bath panel, so the underside of the bath was always visible once installation was complete. However, most modern bathrooms employ some type of bath panel to box in the underside of the bathtub and so hide the framework and plumbing. This panelling can take the form of a permanent structure but it is always best to create a bath panel that can be easily removed for inspection purposes.

tools for the job

spirit level

pencil

tape measure

cordless drill/driver

panel saw or jigsaw

screwdriver

making a frame

In order to fit a panel, there must be a framework onto which it can be attached. For acrylic panels, this framework is normally integral. However, for more heavyweight alternatives such as wooden bath panels, wooden batten makes the ideal support.

1 Hold a spirit level vertically against the edge of the bath, allowing one end to touch the floor. Position a length of 5cm x 2.5cm (2in x 1in) batten on the floor parallel with the bath rim. Position a small block of wood (the same depth as the bath panel) between the bottom

of the spirit level and the batten. Move the spirit level and block along the edge of the bath and batten until the batten is in the precise position required for the base framework. Draw a pencil guideline along the edge of the batten.

2 Use the same method described in step 1 to work out the position for the base batten at the end of the bath. Again, mark the edge of the batten with a pencil guideline. Measure the distance between the walls and the intersection of the pencil guidelines and cut the battens accordingly.

3 Fix the longer batten in place. Cut a piece of 5cm x 5cm (2in x 2in) batten long enough to reach from the top of the base batten to the underside rim of the bath. Fix it at right angles to the shorter base batten. Fix the shorter base batten to the floor so that the thicker section of batten runs up under the rim of the bath at the corner for extra support. Alternatively, join two pieces of 5cm x 2.5cm (2in x 1in) batten together and use it for the same purpose.

4 Fix a batten to the wall at both the tap end of the bath and the opposite wall corner. These will be used as fixing points and support for the corresponding panel ends.

fitting the panel

With the framework in place, you can turn your attention to fitting the panel. Bath panels are generally supplied in standard sizes that must be cut down to meet your specific requirements.

1 Panels often need to be scribed so that they fit flush against both the walls and the skirting boards. Holding a small block of wood, cut

to the thickness of the base of the skirting, rest a pencil so that its point draws a guideline for cutting on the panel surface.

2 Cut along the pencil guideline with a panel saw or jigsaw. Choose a fine cutting blade so that the edges of the panel do not splinter.

3 Fix the main panel in place by screwing it into the batten framework. Do the same with the smaller end panel. Drill pilot holes through the end panel and into the edge of the main panel. Take care not to damage the surface of the panels.

4 Insert mirror screws into the pre-drilled holes to secure the panel.

5 Snap the covering cap on the screws to produce a neat finish.

ALTERNATIVES TO WOODEN PANELLING

There are many different methods of panelling a bath in addition to the simple moulded wooden panel featured here. For example, a sheet of MDF (medium-density fibreboard) can be tiled and used as a bath panel. You will need to use a special tile drill bit to make pilot holes through the tiles, so that the screw fixings can be inserted through them to hold the panel in place on the framework. Another option is to attach sections of tongue and groove directly to a framework around the bath, although you will need to build inspection hatches into the design. Alternatively, the tongue and groove can be fixed to a sheet of MDF and used as a removable panel in the same way as the wooden one shown in the illustrated example. Yet another option for fixing the panel in place is to use magnetic catches instead of screw fixings.

Bath panels provide an attractive finishing feature and can be specifically chosen to complement the overall decorative scheme in the room.

fitting kitchen & bathroom accessories

Once all the main kitchen and bathroom fittings are in place, you can turn your attention to the accessories that complement them. Kitchen sinks and cookers, mirrors, cabinets and towel rails are all items that serve both a functional and decorative purpose. They must therefore be fixed in place correctly if they are to fulfil both these roles. This chapter also covers the fitting of fans and ventilation systems so that the kitchen and bathroom are comfortable as well as attractive and functional.

The main accessories in this bathroom are a pair of mirrors, which give the illusion of space, and a stylish towel rail.

fitting sink units

The first stage of the procedure for fitting a sink unit is to measure and cut a hole for the sink in the worktop. Attention is then turned to the different elements of the sink itself, with the taps needing to be attached and waste system installed. Finally, connect the unit to water and waste pipes.

safety advice

If you have a metal sink, and/or any metal pipes, they must be earth bonded for safety reasons. Contact a qualified electrician to carry this out.

tools for the job

tape measure & pencil
cordless drill/driver
jigsaw
paintbrush
screwdriver
adjustable spanners

1 Often a paper template will be provided as a guide for cutting. If not, turn the sink upside down on the worktop, then measure to ensure it is fitted equidistant from the front and back edges of the worktop. Make sure the sink is correctly positioned in relation to the base unit below.

2 Draw a pencil guideline around the edge of the sink, making sure it does not slip as you do so.

3 Take a further measurement of the overlap where the sink edge will rest on the worktop once fitted. Mark this guideline inside the first.

4 Use a slot-head drill bit to drill holes through the worktop in

the corners of this second pencil guideline – these holes will allow access for a jigsaw blade. Be careful not to allow the drill bit to break the bounds of this guideline.

5 Cut around the inside guideline to remove the internal area of worktop. When you approach the finishing cut, ensure the worktop is well supported so that you do not risk damaging or splitting it.

6 If the sink is being fitted in a wooden worktop, as shown here, apply a coat of oil around the cut edge to seal it from the possibility of water penetration once the sink is in use. Attention may now be turned to the sink unit itself.

7 Insert your chosen taps into the sink unit. Make sure that the backnut and required washers are fitted to the underside of the tap and that supply pipes are attached. Although tap designs do vary and you should take account of the manufacturer's specific guidelines.

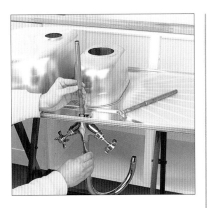

8 Now attach the waste system to the sink, again following the manufacturer's guidelines.

9 Fix retaining clips around the raised strip on the underside lip of the sink unit.

👍

tips of the trade

You will find It is much easier to carry out the procedures for inserting taps and attaching the waste system and retaining clips (steps 7–9) before the sink is fitted in place, as access to the unit is clearly much easier then.

10 Turn the sink the correct way up and lower it into the cut hole in the work surface. It should be a tight but comfortable fit.

11 Screw up the retaining clips on the underside of the sink – these should bind with the worktop to form a watertight seal. The sink and taps may now be connected to the waste and water supply, respectively. If the sink is similarly positioned to the old one then this is quite a simple procedure as the pipes will be in close proximity. For instructions on how to connect and, if necessary, re-route these services, see pages 314–15. If in any doubt seek professional advice.

REVERSIBLE UNITS

Some units include a reversible feature, whereby a tap hole is cut on both sides so that the sink can be positioned with the drainer on either side. If you have such a unit then you will need to fit a bung in the front of the sink before final connection.

This fitted sink unit features false drawer fronts to maintain the illusion of a continuous bank of storage units. Dummy drawer fronts are fixed with special brackets.

fitting an integral hob & oven

If you are looking to create a compact and neat overall appearance to your kitchen, then fitting an integral hob and oven will help considerably to realize this aim. The integrated effect is achieved by the fact that the oven and hob are housed, or appear to be housed, within the general make-up of a run of units. Some manufacturers produce specific units to hold these appliances or, in the case of ovens especially, brackets are used to suspend the appliance between two units. Whatever design you choose, the correct electrical and/or gas supply will need to be connected. Professional help will almost certainly be required for this purpose.

hobs

Cutting the worktop to accommodate a hob requires a very similar technique to that used for fitting sink units. The same basic method for measuring guidelines and cutting out the worktop can be applied to hobs. Refer to pages 364–5, adapting as required.

tools for the job

tape measure & pencil
cordless drill/driver
jigsaw
screwdriver

1 It is usually the case that the manufacturers will stipulate a minimum distance between the back wall and the edge of the hob. This minimum is required for obvious safety reasons and practicalities – adequate space must be left in order to connect up electrics and/or gas pipes, and for cooking the hob needs to be positioned far enough away from the wall so that pans can sit comfortably on the back rings.

2 Once the hole has been cut, lower the hob in place and use clips to secure it in the worktop. The hob may then be connected up to the gas or electric supply as required – a job for a professional. Even if the hob is gas powered, as shown in this example, it is likely that an electrical connection will also be required to supply the ignition system.

ovens

Although ovens are often housed in purpose-made units, they may also be suspended using a system of runners, as demonstrated here. With this system, the worktop and all the carcasses of a run of units must first be fitted, leaving the appropriate size of gap between units into which the oven can be fitted. The runner system is a simple and effective way to create an integrated appearance.

tools for the job

cordless drill/driver
tape measure & pencil
screwdriver
spirit level

1 The first step is to fix the two vertical runners (or rails) along the front edge of the units on either side of the gap left in the run for inserting the oven. To ensure accuracy, you may find it useful to form pilot holes with a cordless drill before inserting the screws.

2 Fix both of the vertical rails in place, screwing through the ready-made holes provided along the length of each rail.

3 Mark off the positions for the bottom horizontal runners – this will normally be slightly back from the front edge of the units. Make sure the runners are positioned precisely level and at the height recommended by the manufacturer, according to the type of oven being fitted.

4 Again, drill pilot holes for the fixings and secure the horizontal runners in place.

5 Check that there is enough depth between the front of the worktop and back wall so that the oven will fit comfortably.

6 Attach further runners to the oven itself, along the bottom edge of both side sections – these runners will be supplied along with the oven. Follow the manufacturer's guidelines to ensure that they are fitted using the correct technique and at precisely the right level.

7 Lift and slide the oven in place, allowing the oven runners to rest on the runners attached to the unit.

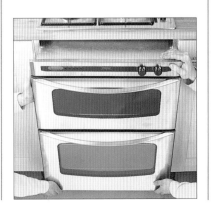

8 The front edge of the oven should overlap onto the vertical runners fixed to the sides of the units. Drill a pilot hole through the marked positions on the oven edge and into the rails. Use a drill bit suitable for cutting through the metal surface of the runners.

9 Finally, insert screws in the pilot holes through the overlap and into the vertical runners, thereby securing the oven in place.

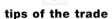

tips of the trade

Supply connection – To allow for access, electrical and gas supplies will need to be connected before the oven is finally installed. Fitting a kitchen is an exact process, however, and prior to connection it is necessary to ensure that the correct tolerance has been built in behind the oven to accommodate gas and electrical supplies. Therefore, it is best to fit the oven first to check for tolerance, then remove the oven temporarily to allow access for connection.

fitting an extractor fan & hood

Installing appliances designed to ensure adequate ventilation is now a crucial aspect of fitting a modern kitchen, largely due to the increased effectiveness of general household insulation. Natural drafts prevalent in houses before such innovations as double glazing were generally sufficient to dispel the build-up of fumes. Today, however, a mechanical means of ventilation is usually required for adequate air circulation. Early designs in this area were uninspiring, but attractive ventilation systems that greatly contribute to kitchen appearance are now available.

Kitchen ventilation systems are generally available either in an integral design, whereby the appliance is built into a run of units, or based on a hood-and-chimney design as shown in this example. Each of the two basic designs can be used with either a ducting or filter extraction system. A ducting system involves the installation of a physical channel from the hood to the outside of the house. A hole large enough to fit a ventilation shaft through an exterior wall will need to be drilled, and as a consequence this system requires a fair amount of work. The alternative is to use a 'recirculator' system that circulates the air through charcoal filters. These filters are easily fitted in the extractor hood, and no ducting is required. Most hood designs are built to accommodate both options and final adjustments can be made during the fitting procedure.

tools for the job

tape measure & pencil

spirit level

cordless drill/driver

screwdriver

1 The manufacturer will stipulate a precise distance requirement between the worktop and bottom edge of the hood. Measure up and mark off this distance on the wall surface. Make the mark central to the position of the hob. You may require a spirit level for this purpose.

2 Attach the supplied template to the wall with masking tape, and mark through at the fixing points.

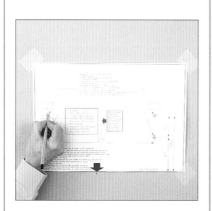

safety advice

It is vital to ensure your kitchen has sufficient ventilation, especially if it includes gas appliances. If you are in any doubt about the adequacy of a particular system, you must seek professional advice.

3 Drill holes into the wall surface at the marked-off points and insert the correct size of wall plug, according to whether the wall is hollow or solid.

4 Screw hood-retaining brackets into the wall ensuring they are precisely vertical and secure.

5 Lift the hood into place and clip it over the wall retaining brackets.

You may need another person to help with the lifting. Check it is positioned centrally in relation to the hob below.

6 Further retaining screws will normally need to be fitted inside the hood to tighten the fixings between the hood and wall bracket. Connect up the electrical supply for the hood at this stage. Professional help will be required for this purpose. If you have chosen a ducted ventilation system, the ducting should also be fitted and connected to the outside vent at this point.

7 Fit the chimney by slotting it into the top of the hood. You will normally also need to attach a bracket to the ceiling. Draw a level vertical guideline from the centre of the hood top to the ceiling, then fix the bracket.

8 Slide the hood into place, and extend the sections to join with the ceiling bracket. Hoods tend to be supplied in two sections so that one slips over the other, making height adjustment a simple procedure.

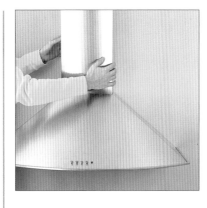

9 Fix through the holes provided at the top of the chimney into the ceiling bracket to secure it in place.

10 With the chimney in place, the only thing remaining is to fit the charcoal filters to the underside of the hood.

A large hood-and-chimney extractor fan system is an impressive feature, and if a light fixture is included this will make cooking on the hob much easier.

fitting a dishwasher & washing machine

Either a washing machine or a dishwasher, or often both, are commonly found in most modern kitchens. Both appliances need to be connected to a water supply and drainage facility and as such are normally situated close to the kitchen sink. Connecting up each appliance involves a similar procedure, with the bulk of the work involved in getting the supply and drainage pipes to the appropriate joints.

plumbing in appliances

Washing machines usually require both a hot and cold water supplies, whereas the majority of dishwashers require only a cold water supply. The most ideal set-up is to have the supply pipe(s) branching off the pipes that supply water to the kitchen sink. These supply pipe(s) are generally situated between the shut-off valves and the taps by means of a 'T'-connector, which directs the supply pipes horizontally away from the main vertical pipes for the sink. A threaded tap connection is needed on the end of these horizontal supply pipes so that the machine supply can be connected easily and the tap turned on to provide water. In order to connect the discharge hose and water supply pipe(s) to the appropriate joint below the sink, access must be made in the back of the kitchen sink unit.

tools for the job

cordless drill/driver

slip-joint pliers

screwdriver

1 Use a hole saw or large flathead drill bit to make holes of the correct diameter for the pipes in the back panel of the unit. In this case a dishwasher is being fitted, which requires two holes to be drilled, one for the cold water supply pipe and the other for the discharge hose.

2 Thread the discharge hose and supply pipe through the holes. For this process the dishwasher needs to be positioned close to the wall, which often makes access tight, though the pipe and hose normally allow enough length.

3 A rubber filter will generally need to be fitted inside the connecting joint for the cold water supply. This filter helps to keep damaging impurities away from the washing mechanism. Once in place, the filter can quite simply be screwed onto the threaded end of the cold water supply pipe.

4 Connect up the discharge hose to a waste adaptor on the sink trap. Ensure the hose leaves the dishwasher vertically, joining the sink trap at a height between 30cm (12in) and 80cm (32in). Never cut down the hose from the supplied length.

fitting integral dishwashers

Integral dishwashers enable separate doors to be attached, so that the dishwasher unit does not detract from the finished look of a fitted kitchen. The plumbing remains the same, but some care will be needed to adjust the washer level and fix the door.

tools for the job

cordless drill/driver
....
pencil
....
slip-joint pliers

1 To protect the work surface above the dishwasher from steam and water attack, it is best to fit a condensation strip along the underside. A plastic self-adhesive strip has been used here, but some manufacturers supply a metal strip that requires screwing in place.

2 If necessary, screw the feet of the dishwasher into the threaded holes on its base. Try to set the feet at approximately the same height. The machine will need to be leant back for this process. Then position the dishwasher in front of its alcove and adjust the feet to gain a perfect level at the correct height. Levelling is vital to ensure the optimum working position and ensure that the door fits correctly and blends with other units.

3 Connect up the water supply and fit the discharge hose using the method already described, then ease the dishwasher into position. You may now turn your attention to fitting the door. Fitted kitchen designs will either provide full doors or, as is shown here, combine the drawer and cupboard front look. In this last case, the false drawer and cupboard fronts need to be connected to each other with metal plate connectors. Simply screw these in place along the joint between the drawer and cupboard fronts, ensuring that edges are kept flush and the joint is tight.

4 Use the template supplied by the manufacturer to mark off the correct positions for the securing brackets on the back of the door.

5 Screw the securing brackets in place following the marked-off screw insertion points indicated by the template. Then fit both the drawer and cupboard handles employing the same techniques as demonstrated on pages 342–3.

6 Press the 'door' into position on the front of the dishwasher, marrying up the fixing brackets with the fixing holes on the dishwasher.

7 If appropriate to the door design, fix from the inside through the dishwasher door and into the back of the unit front.

INTEGRAL DOORS

Integral doors may also be fitted to fridges and freezers. Washing machines usually have a separate hinged door, which is attached in a similar way to base units.

fitting cabinets ⌐

Most bathrooms have at least one cabinet that is used for storing toiletries and/or medicines. Many fulfil an additional function by having a mirror on the door of the cabinet, hence the ideal location for installing such a cabinet is above a basin. If a bathroom cabinet is to be used for storing medicines, make sure it is positioned out of the reach of children or has a locking mechanism so that you can control access.

cabinet design

Along with all bathroom accessories, there is a wide choice of cabinet designs. As well as size differences, they are available in numerous finishes. Many cabinets have open storage areas which are ideal for storing items that are in everyday use, so that you do not have to keep opening and closing the cabinet.

single door mirror cabinet
with shelf

corner cabinet

single door
mirror cabinet

double door mirror cabinet
with shelf

double door cabinet with
colourwash effect

ornamental
antique cabinet

PAINTING CABINETS

Many cabinets are supplied varnished or stained, but there is nothing to stop you from painting the cabinet to match other decorations in the room. Simply sand back the wooden surface thoroughly, then prime it and apply your chosen paint finish.

fixing in position

Even lightweight cabinets will put a considerable strain on the wall fixings once they are filled with toiletries and the like, so all cabinets must be fixed securely to ensure there is no danger of their falling off the wall. Most cabinets are supplied with fixings and instructions, and the example shown here demonstrates a typical technique for securing a cabinet in place. When positioning a cabinet, it is always best to have a helper so that one person can hold the cabinet roughly in place while the other checks it for height suitability. This is especially important if the door(s) of the cabinet include a mirror, because it will need to be positioned at a height that is ideal for all members of the household.

tools for the job

tape measure

pencil

spirit level

cordless drill/driver

screwdriver

1 This cabinet has pre-drilled holes in the back, so it is necessary to measure the distance between the holes as accurately as possible. There are two holes near the top of the cabinet and two near the bottom. You need to measure the distance between the holes from side to side and from top to bottom.

2 Transfer these measurements onto the wall using a spirit level to draw horizontal lines representing the distances between the holes. Mark the required hole positions on the lines, then drill and insert wall plugs at these points.

3 Hold the cabinet in position and screw through the inside into the wall plug fixings. In this case, fixing blocks have been supplied to add greater strength to the fixings. A hand-held screwdriver has been used here because it can be difficult to gain access to the corners of the cabinet using a cordless drill. Shelving may or may not be fixed in place in the cabinet at the time of manufacture. If it is not, tap the supporting brackets for the shelves into the sides of the cabinet at the appropriate positions, then slide the shelves into place.

4 Attach handles if required, screwing them through the pre-drilled holes on the doors.

If the holes for handles have not been pre-drilled at the manufacturing stage, use a cordless drill and an appropriate size drill bit to make pilot holes. Hold a block of wood on the other side of the door so that the drill bit goes into the block when it emerges and does not cause the door surface to splinter.

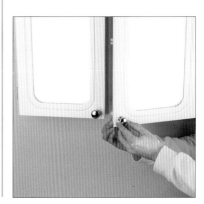

Cabinets fulfil an important bathroom function by providing essential storage and also act as interesting features on open wall surfaces.

fitting mirrors ⁄⁄

Mirrors are an integral part of bathroom layout and there is a wide range to choose from, both in terms of design and the methods by which they are fixed to wall surfaces. The main problem when installing mirrors is that it is not possible to fix through them unless pre-drilled holes have been made at the time of manufacture. Specially designed brackets or adhesive must be used instead to hold the mirror in place on the wall.

heated mirrors

tools for the job

pencil
tape measure
spirit level
cordless drill/driver

1 In this example the mirror is positioned above a splashback using flush fixings screwed into the wall. Begin by marking the fixing points for the two lower clips by drawing a level line on the wall using a spirit level. Here, the line is drawn above the splashback because the recesses into which the clips will insert are set back slightly from the edge of the mirror on its reverse side.

2 Fix the two bottom clips in place on the drawn guideline, making sure that their distance apart corresponds with the distance between the insertion points on the back of the mirror.

3 Measure upwards from the two bottom clips to mark the position for the top two. Again, make sure that their distance apart corresponds with that of the insertion points on the back of the mirror. It is a good idea to draw a vertical line upwards from the lower clips to mark the position of the top ones, in which case you should use a spirit level to ensure accuracy.

4 Screw the top two clips in place. These have a slightly different design from the lower ones, in that they have an elongated oval-shaped hole for the screw fixing rather than a round hole. This is so

that they can slide up and down on the screw fixing. Insert the screw through the bottom of the oval.

safety advice

Do not attempt to carry out electrical wiring and connection yourself. This must always be done by an electrician.

5 Once the wiring is complete, position the mirror on the wall surface. Fit the bottom edge of the mirror into the lower clips, then lay the mirror flat against the wall and slide the top clips down into the insertion points on the back of it.

using adhesive

Another way of fixing a mirror to a wall surface is to use mirror adhesive or a strong bonding adhesive. These are available in tubes and are expelled with the aid of a sealant gun. You will need to support the weight of the mirror while the adhesive dries.

tools for the job

tape measure & pencil
panel saw
mini level
cordless drill/driver
sealant gun or dispenser

1 Cut a length of batten equal to the width of the mirror. Fix it to the wall at the position where the base of the mirror will be. Use a mini level to check that the batten is level.

2 Apply adhesive generously to the back of the mirror.

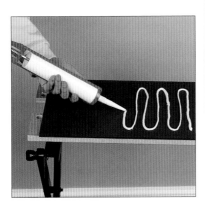

3 Position the mirror with its bottom edge on top of the batten. Once the adhesive has dried, remove the batten, fill the screw holes with filler and decorate the wall.

mirror tiles

tools for the job

pencil
tape measure
spirit level

1 Use a spirit level to draw a pencil guideline on the wall at the point where the bottom edge of the first row of tiles will sit. Draw a vertical guideline to help you position the first column of tiles precisely. Attach self-adhesive pads to the backs of the tiles. One on each corner is usually sufficient, but you should read the manufacturer's guidelines because some heavier or larger tiles may need more pads to support them.

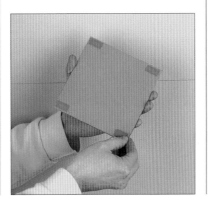

2 Use the pencil guideline you have drawn to position the tiles on the wall, gradually building up your chosen design. In most cases you can butt the tile edges up against each other, although some manufacturers may recommend leaving a small gap.

MIRROR SCREWS

Mirror screws are the best option for fixing mirrors with pre-drilled holes in their surface. The screws are specially designed so that decorative caps can be fixed over the screw head once the mirror is in place. Like many fixings, different manufacturers produce different designs, so you are likely to find variations in the types of mirror screw available. Some designs include a rubber grommet that should be positioned in the mirror hole before the screw is inserted. This helps to minimize the risk of the mirror cracking when the screw comes into contact with the edge of the hole (although you still need to be careful when inserting the screw to make sure that you do not over-tighten it). In the same way that screw designs vary, so do the actual caps that fit over the screw heads. Designs range from rounded domes to more flattened, squarer shapes. Some caps actually screw in place onto the mirror screw, while others are snapped or clipped in position like a popper fastening.

fitting accessories ⤢

All the small accessories in a bathroom, such as soap dishes, toothbrush holders and non-heated towel rails, supply additional storage areas that make the best use of space. They also provide the finishing touches to the overall look of the bathroom, which will make your decorative scheme look complete and the room welcoming. Many of these accessories are available as sets so that you can achieve a coordinated finish.

safety advice

Always check for pipes and wiring using a cable or joist detector prior to drilling into walls.

The fitting mechanisms on accessories vary but it is usually the case that specially designed brackets are attached to the wall surface first, then the actual fitting is attached to the bracket and held in place with a discreetly positioned grub screw. This two-part fitting process can be difficult because you need to make sure that brackets align correctly with fittings. Alternatively, the actual fixing bracket is integral to the fitting and, once in place, a cover or cap is fitted over the bracket to provide an attractive finish.

Installing accessories on tiled surfaces requires a specific technique to make the appropriate pilot holes for wall plug and screw fixings.

fixing into tiles

Fixing accessories to plaster walls, whether solid or hollow, can be achieved using the correct wall plugs and screws, and the same is true for tiled surfaces. However, you need to use a specially designed drill bit that is strong enough to penetrate a tile accurately. Accuracy is the key point here because a hole drilled in the wrong place cannot simply be filled and repainted in the way that you would with plaster walls. Also, even though tiles have a very strong surface, they can shatter or crack

if the wrong technique is used. A standard masonry drill bit may well go through some tiles, but it is often the case that while piercing the tiled surface, the coarseness of the bit can break away glazed sections of tile around the hole.

tools for the job

felt-tip pen

tape measure

cordless drill/driver

screwdriver

1 Take your time when deciding on the precise position for the fitting – in this case a towel ring – because mistakes are not easy to rectify on a tiled surface. The bracket for the accessory should be fixed in as central a position on the tile as possible. The closer you move towards the edge of a tile, the more likely that drill vibrations will cause it to crack. Hold the fitting in place with one hand and use a felt-tip pen to mark through the screw holes onto the tile surface below.

2 Remove the fitting from the tile surface and cover the marked points with masking tape. It should still be possible to see the marks through the tape, but if they are not obvious renew them on top of the tape. The reason that masking tape is applied over the drilling points is that the shiny surface of the tile can cause the drill bit to slip, which makes accurate drilling impossible and can lead to scratching. The masking tape adds some grip and keeps the point of the bit in place.

3 Insert the tile drill bit into the drill, making sure it is securely held in place. A tile drill bit looks like a miniature javelin or spear.

4 Holding the drill bit against the marked point on the tile, start up on the drill a low speed. This will create a tiny indentation in the tile surface that will allow the bit to gain a good grip before the speed is increased. Once this initial break is made, use the drill in the normal way to penetrate through the tile surface and into the wall below. Holding a vacuum cleaner nozzle below the hole while you drill will improve the aesthetic finish of the tiled surface, because it prevents the dust produced when drilling through tiles from falling down and resting in grout joints or sealant beads at the base of the wall. Even if this dust is wiped off, there is often unsightly staining of the grout or sealant. By using the vacuum to remove dust as you drill, there is no need to clean up afterwards and the grout or sealant cannot become stained.

5 Once the holes are drilled, remove the masking tape from the tile surface. Insert wall plugs into the holes. These are usually supplied with the fitting – if not, choose some suitable ones from your supply or buy some if you do not have any already. The plugs will generally slip into the holes, easily tightening as the head of the plug becomes flush with the wall surface. In some cases, you may need to use the butt end of a hammer to knock the plug into position. Be sure to use only the butt end of the hammer, because using the other end will risk breaking the tile.

6 Reposition the fitting and screw it in place. It is always best to use a hand-held screwdriver for this because it offers greater control regarding the amount of pressure exerted. If a cordless screwdriver is used, there can be a danger of over-tightening, which could crack the tiled surface so that the tile will need to be replaced.

7 Finally, screw the covering cap in place to obscure the fixing mechanism. This may attach with a grub screw or simply be a threaded fitting that is screwed into place by hand.

tips of the trade

• **Levelling up** – Sometimes, on final viewing, the accessory you have just installed may not appear to be precisely level. Most manufacturers take this into account and design their accessories so that small adjustments can be made after installation. Where two screws are used to secure a fitting, one of the holes is often of a slightly elongated shape, which allows the screw to be loosened and the fitting rotated to a different position. This is usually enough to rectify it.

• **Waterproofing** – By drilling a hole in a tiled surface, you are in effect piercing the watertight barrier created by the tiles and grout. It can, therefore, be worth applying a small amount of silicone sealant to the end of screws before they are inserted so that this watertight barrier is maintained.

INSTALLING TWO OR MORE BRACKETS INTO TILES

In the example shown here, only one bracket is required to hold the fitting in place. However, for larger fittings such as horizontal towel rails, more than one bracket will be needed. When two brackets are required, it is vital that they are positioned perfectly level so that when the rail, or other accessory, is fitted in the brackets you achieve the best possible finish. In such instances, always use a spirit level to draw a horizontal pencil guideline along the tiles, and measure along this line to mark the exact positions where holes need to be drilled for the fixings. You can then use the drilling technique shown in steps 3 and 4. Once the holes have been made, rub out the pencil line with an eraser and then finish fixing the brackets in place. The way that accessories are inserted into the brackets varies between manufacturers, so always pay close attention to their specific instructions to ensure that all fixings are secure.

377

installing ventilation ⌐⌐⌐

Ventilation is important in bathrooms because of their damp, moist atmosphere. This type of environment suffers from condensation, which can damage decoration and finishes unless adequate ventilation systems are installed. The advent of double-glazing has increased the problem and made ventilation systems essential since the somewhat draughty nature of older windows and doors did at least allow some flow of air.

mechanical ventilation

Mechanical ventilation is usually in the form of extractor fans. These fittings remove the damp air from the room and help to produce a less humid atmosphere. They can be positioned in either walls or ceilings. The latter is particularly common in shower cubicles. Most are operated by an electrical supply that switches the fan on automatically when the light is turned on in the room. This mode of operation varies according to the manufacturer, and many designs incorporate automatic cut-off switches after a set period of time. It is worth bearing in mind that building regulations in new properties specify that an extractor fan must be fitted in a bathroom.

WALL-MOUNTED FAN

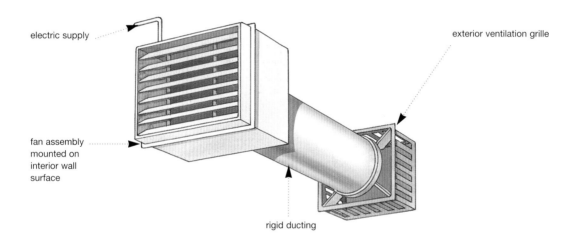

electric supply

exterior ventilation grille

fan assembly mounted on interior wall surface

rigid ducting

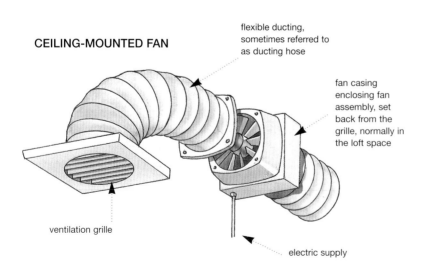

CEILING-MOUNTED FAN

flexible ducting, sometimes referred to as ducting hose

fan casing enclosing fan assembly, set back from the grille, normally in the loft space

ventilation grille

electric supply

WINDOW-MOUNTED FANS

Fans that can be fixed into a circular hole in a windowpane are readily available. You will need to cut the hole using the correct type of glass cutter, although it may be easier to get your local glass merchant to perform this task. You should never attempt cutting holes in double-glazed windows. The actual fan assembly is fitted on the inside of the pane, with an inner casing covering the moving parts. An exterior grille is used to finish the outer part of the assembly.

For wall-mounted fans, a hole must be cut through the wall to the exterior of the house. In order to cut a hole through masonry with any degree of accuracy, you will need to hire a core drill bit and drill. It is not worth buying this type of equipment because it is extremely expensive and will only be needed for very occasional use – it is much more cost effective to hire from a local supplier. For ceiling-mounted fans, the equipment required is not as heavy duty since there is no masonry work involved. The simple technique for making an access hole in a plaster ceiling is demonstrated here.

tools for the job

pencil & tape measure

pipe, cable & joist detector

padsaw

screwdriver

1 Work out the position of the fan, using a cable, pipe and joist detector to check that there are no

supply pipes or cables in this area. These will obstruct the fan and could be dangerous if cut. There should also be no ceiling joists because they would make it impossible to install the fan. You may, therefore, have to make a small compromise when deciding on a position. Hold the grille in place on the ceiling and use a pencil to draw around the circumference of the circular section of the grille. This provides a cutting guideline.

2 When you have determined the the position of the fan, use a padsaw or dry wall saw to cut out the circular section of ceiling.

3 Secure the first part of the grille assembly in the hole with retaining screws. Clip the grille in place, then fit the ducting hose and extractor above the grille assembly.

379

static vents

Static vents are an alternative type of bathroom ventilation that do not involve any mechanical parts. They simply allow air to flow in the room, using natural draughts to create the circulation. Some examples of static vent systems, and covers that are used to neaten the finished look, are shown here.

Louvre vents act as the interior covers for ventilation holes or ducts in exterior walls. Different designs and finishes are available. Plastic and aluminium examples are shown here. Plastic vents can be painted to blend with wall finishes. As with the air brick, the grille is permanently open.

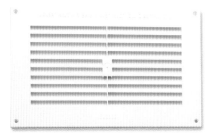

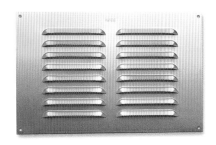

Hit-and-miss vents are interior covers for holes or ducts that have an opening and closing mechanism.

Air bricks are positioned in the wall structure and are permanently open.

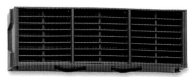

repairs to kitchens & bathrooms

No matter how fine the quality of fixtures, fittings and finishes in the kitchen and bathroom, you will almost certainly need to make repairs at some stage. In most cases the incidence of repairs is determined by frequency of use, but that said, it is not uncommon to find tap washers need changing, door handles fixing or worktops resealing in even relatively underused kitchens and bathrooms. This chapter demonstrates how to make all these repairs and remember it is important to make repairs as soon as the need arises, since regular maintenance helps to extend the life of the room and will save you money in the long term.

All kitchens need repairs over time – with
this kitchen, for example, you may need
to replace a broken tile on the worktop.

reviving worktop ⚒

Worktops are invariably the most used of all kitchen surfaces and as a consequence will probably require frequent repairs to maintain their condition. Outlined below are a number of common problems experienced with different types of worktop and guidance on the best techniques for returning them to good order.

Use masking tape to hold the section securely in position while the glue dries.

scratches

artist's brush
dry cloth

To deal with surface scratches, simply dust and clean the area then paint along the groove with a fine artist's brush using an oil-based paint such as eggshell. Try and match the worktop colour as closely as possible. For a patterned worktop it is best to choose one of the darkest colours in its design. Wipe away any excess.

repairing the front edge

Where damage to a laminate worktop is so extreme that minor repairs would have little effect, you may need to consider replacing the front edge with

---

wooden worktop

Wooden worktop should receive occasional reoiling, but you may also need to make localized repairs caused by spillages that have been allowed to soak in and stain, or through surface scarring caused by knives or other cutting implements.

tools for the job

electric sander (optional)
cloth

1 Sand the affected area until the stain has been removed. An electric sander is ideal for this purpose but take care not to dig the edge into the worktop, which will cause undulations in the wood surface.

2 Apply a small amount of oil to a dry cloth and gently rub it into the sanded area. You may need to make two or three applications to blend the area back in with the existing worktop.

laminate worktop

Damage to a laminate finish cannot be simply sanded away – it is more a case of effective camouflaging.

repairing edges

tools for the job

small fitch
masking tape

1 If the edge has chipped, glue the broken piece of laminate back in position, if possible, using neat PVA.

an alternative finish. In this example, a wood moulding has been used to create a new decorative edging on the front of the worktop.

tools for the job

clamps
combination square
jigsaw
hammer (optional)

1 Clamp a section of batten along the front edge of the worktop. It needs to be positioned so that a jigsaw can rest against the side, then use the batten for a guide as it is moved along the worktop, producing a straight cut along the edge.

2 Remove the damaged worktop edge with a jigsaw. Keep the blade tight against the batten to make sure of a dead straight cut.

3 Cut and glue a length of moulding along the newly cut edge of the worktop. Fix the moulding

with either wood glue or PVA. Nail one or two panel pins through the moulding to hold it in place while the glue dries, if necessary. Stain and varnish the batten to seal the surface and provide a decorative finish.

tiling over

If damage to the worktop is excessive, then a further option is to tile over the entire worktop surface to provide a completely new look.

tools for the job

tiling equipment

Attach moulding along the front edge of the worktop, and stain and varnish it to your preference. Then apply tiles directly on top of the worktop (see pages 420–1 for further instructions). Remember that sink or hob height may have to be adjusted so that the tiles can be lipped under the edges of such appliances.

resiliconing

The overall appearance of a worktop can often be let down simply by staining or damage over time to the silicone seal. By periodically replacing the seal, you will not only revive the look of the worktop, but also renew the waterproof seal between the worktop/wall junction.

tools for the job

paintbrush
window scraper
craft knife
sealant dispenser or gun

1 Paint a proprietary sealant removal solution onto the silicone allowing it to soak in as much as possible.

2 Use a window scraper to ease the old seal away. Then clean the area thoroughly before reapplying a new silicone bead.

fixing doors & drawers

Hinges and handles on drawers and doors are the areas that most commonly suffer damage on kitchen units. As moving parts, it is inevitable that hinges will eventually wear out and the daily tugging on handles will similarly loosen the fixing or even pull off the handle altogether. In some cases, once these sort of breakages begin to occur it can signal the time for a new kitchen. Generally, however, only the most frequently used doors or drawers in a kitchen will experience any major problems. Fixing such one-off problems can therefore return the kitchen to optimum working level and does not have to signal the need for a complete kitchen refit.

tools for the job

cordless drill/driver
pencil
combination square
hinge cutting bit
mini level

A sagging or off-level door will often indicate that there is a problem with hinges. The movement of the hinge is likely to have caused the fixing holes of the hinge plate to widen, so that the plate comes away from the side of the carcass. The best way to fix this problem is to relocate the hinge plate to a slightly higher position on the door, which will require refixing both the plate and hinge mechanism itself.

1 Unscrew the door from the unit and remove both the loose hinge plate from the carcass and the hinge mechanism from the door.

2 Use a combination square to measure up from the original hinge position to a new location further up the door. Mark the central point for the new recess required to house the hinge.

3 The next stage is to cut the new hinge recess in the door. This can be done using a cordless drill by attaching a hinge cutting bit. Make sure that the point of the hinge cutter is precisely inserted at the marked-off point for the centre of the new recess. Gradually cut into the door taking care to drill to the exact depth requirement for the hinge.

4 Thoroughly dust out the hole and then screw the hinge into the new recess, ensuring that it is correctly aligned with the door edge. Before rehanging the door, fill the old recess with matching wood filler.

5 Use the same measurement to mark off on the inside of the carcass the change in position of the hinge plate. Then reattach the hinge plate by screwing it securely in place. Rehang the door and screw together the hinge and plate. Finally, fill the old holes on the door and unit and, if necessary, paint over them for a finish almost as good as new.

quick fix

As an alternative to cutting a new hinge, it may sometimes be possible to refix a hinge plate with the aid of some resin.

1 Remove the loosened hinge plate and then carefully expel some resin into the old fixing holes.

2 Reposition the hinge plate and screw it back in place, holding it in position until the resin 'goes off'. Excess resin will probably squeeze out around the edge of the hinge plate when it is screwed in place. Remove this with a cloth before it has the chance to dry. Rehang the door once the resin has fully hardened.

drawer problems

Whereas hinge problems are common for unit doors, the main problems encountered with drawers tend to relate either to the loosening of screw fixings for the handles or the drawer fronts themselves. In either case, adhesive can be used to reinforce fixings and return the drawers to good working order.

tools for the job

cordless drill/driver
clamps (optional)
screwdriver

fixing fronts

1 Drawer fronts often become loose, as the effectiveness of the screw fixings lessens with constant use. To remedy this problem, simply unscrew the drawer front and apply a generous amount of wood glue or PVA to the back face.

2 Screw the front back onto the drawer carcass. It is important for the back face of the drawer front and the front face of the carcass to be pressed together very tightly, in order to ensure proper adhesion.

You may therefore need to attach some clamps to hold the front firmly in position. Although the screw fixings for the drawer front will remain slightly loose, the combined effect of the glue and screws will hold the drawer front back in the desired position.

fixing handles

1 Again, the daily opening and closing of drawers will take its toll on the screw fixings for handles, which may become loose or fall off completely. For obvious aesthetic reasons it will not be possible to reposition the handle and make new fixings altogether. To repair a loosened handle, therefore, you will need to unscrew it and apply a small amount of resin to the thread of the fixing bolt.

2 Screw the handle back in position using washers to help spread the force put on the handle when the drawer is opened. This technique can also be applied to door handles and handles with only one fixing point.

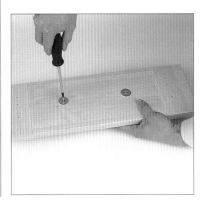

changing doors & handles

The style of a kitchen is often created by the types of doors, drawer fronts and handles that have been used in its design. The carcasses themselves have little to do with the look of a kitchen, so in order to change style, as long as the carcasses are in a good state of repair, it only becomes necessary to make changes to the more obvious areas, such as cupboard fronts and/or handles. Changing handles is clearly a very economic way of altering a kitchen look, whereas door and drawer front replacement is certainly more dramatic, but will greatly increase the cost.

design options

There are always many options to choose from when making such unit changes, and personal preference will be the determining factor in the choice you make. Below are just a few examples of cupboard fronts and handles, showing slightly different designs and finishes. Remember when making choices, especially with doors, ensure that the new ones will fit the existing units in your kitchen. Subtle differences in size may not be immediately obvious when choosing between manufacturers and you should always double-check that dimensions will be suitable.

DOORS

wooden panel door

laminated wood effect panel door

painted finish panel door

solid wood flush door

KNOBS

brass

wood

ceramic

porcelain

HANDLES

brass

wood

antique brass drawer pull

brass drawer pull

brushed steel

tools for the job

cordless drill/driver

screwdriver

combination square

pencil

wood block

changing doors

Replacing doors is a simple process where the old ones may be unscrewed at the hinge and the new ones fitted. In some cases, it may be suitable to reuse the old hinges, but if there is a difference in manufacturer's designs, you may need to fit new ones. Likewise, the hinge plates themselves may need changing on the carcass unit.

changing handles

Nearly all kitchen handles are interchangeable in that manufacturer's differences tend not to create too many problems. If you are changing a knob to a handle, however, you will need to drill an extra hole and if you are changing a handle to a knob, you will need to fill the leftover hole and repaint the unit to conceal it.

simple changeovers

1 Firmly hold onto the knob, or handle, while you undo the retaining screw(s).

2 Position the new knob, or handle, and screw it in place. Start this process by hand before using a screwdriver for final tightening.

changing from knob to handle

1 Use a combination square to measure down from the existing hole to a position that mirrors the distance between the threaded fixing points on your chosen new handle.

2 Mark this position accurately – if it is out of place, the thread of the screw may not engage correctly with the thread of the handle.

3 Drill through the marked off point. Be sure to position a block of wood on the other side of the door so that when the drill bit emerges it cannot split or 'blow out' the hole and damage the door side.

4 Line up the new handle over the drilled holes and tighten the fixings securely with a screwdriver.

DRAWER FRONTS

When you are replacing a drawer knob or handle, you may encounter a separate set of problems. Replacing one knob with another is a simple changeover, but it is more difficult to change a knob to a handle, as two new holes will require drilling, thus leaving a central hole in the drawer front. This creates another scenario whereby the drawer front must be painted in order to cover the old fixing holes. Even with a simple changeover of one handle for another you must check that the distance between the fixing holes is the same.

unit makeovers ↗↗

As an alternative to replacing doors, handles or drawer fronts, it is possible to work on or add other finishes to existing units and fronts in order to change their appearance. As for all unit makeovers, it is important that the existing units are in a sound condition so that your efforts will be long lasting, and that adequate preparation is put into these tasks so that the finish itself is durable. Ideas and materials for unit makeovers are constantly being updated by manufacturers and below are just some examples of the options available.

adding panels

tools for the job

pencil
tape measure
combination square
cordless drill/driver

To increase interest on a flat or flush cupboard front, panels may be used to produce a more textured or three-dimensional finish. Mouldings may be bought and cut to length or, as shown here, proprietary kits may be purchased where the panels are already made up and simply require fitting. Although this latter technique adds a little expense, it does save a lot of time and ensures that the mitred corners of the panels are precise.

1 Use a pencil and combination square to measure the ideal position for fixing the panels to the doors. It is easier to remove doors and lay them out flat for this purpose.

2 Most panels are fixed in position with double-sided tape. Peel the tape off the back of the mouldings.

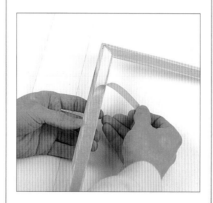

3 Position the mouldings so they are aligned with the pencil guidelines. The adhesive is very strong, but you can make any necessary minor adjustments in positioning before it finally sticks.

4 It is likely that the new moulding position may make it necessary to move handles. Simply remove the existing ones and fill in the screw holes. Then measure for an appropriate position to drill through the door and fix a new handle.

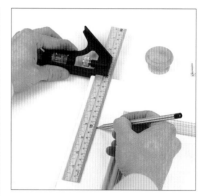

tips of the trade

• In order to get the best possible adhesion between the moulding and door, make sure that the door surface has been both thoroughly cleaned and well dried before you apply the panel.

• If you are using mouldings that are not fixed with self-adhesive tape, panel pins can be used to secure the mouldings in place. It can also be worth using a little PVA adhesive on the back of the mouldings to add further strength to the fixing. The heads of the panel pins will need to be punched in and filled before you go on to decorate.

• Normally, the newly panelled door will require painting. Be sure to use esp to prepare the door surface if it is of a laminated or melamine finish. A varnished wooden door should be sanded back and primed before painting. If your preference dictates that panel colour is to be different to the background door colour, it is worth painting the panels and the doors separately before positioning the panels. In this way the dividing line between each will be as sharp as possible, and no time-consuming and fiddly cutting in will be required.

MOULDED UNITS

Instead of adding panels to flush doors, another method for producing a panelled effect is to use a router. By fitting the correct type of cutter, the router can be used to channel out a moulded pattern in the front of doors. This technique is for the more advanced woodworker.

covering doors

An alternative to adding mouldings to a flush door is simply to cover the whole face with a decorative wallpaper. There are companies that specifically manufacture for this purpose. Such paper is self-adhesive and the technique for fitting is similar to that of general wallpapering.

tools for the job

tape measure & pencil
scissors
craft knife
sanding block
cordless drill/driver

1 Remove the handles and sand down the door surfaces to provide a key for the adhesive.

2 Use a damp sponge to wipe away any dust from the door surface and allow the surface to dry.

3 Use scissors to cut the paper to a size slightly longer than that of the door. (The width of the paper roll should be slightly greater than the door.) Peel back a small amount of the self-adhesive backing paper and position the roll at the top of the door.

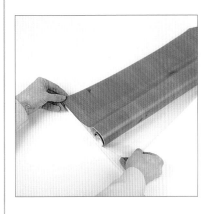

4 Gradually unroll the paper, pulling the backing away, and allowing the paper to stick to the door. Use the factory cut edge of one side of the length to follow the door edge.

5 Smooth the surface of the paper to remove any air bubbles, and use a craft knife to trim off any excess.

6 Use fine grade sandpaper to sand the edges of the door gently to ensure that the paper edges will not lift away from the surface.

7 Screw the handles in place. If you are changing handle design, fill the original holes before applying the paper, then drill new holes.

DRAWER UNITS

In both these examples, a door has been used for illustrative purposes. The same techniques may also be applied to drawer fronts in order to blend in the whole finish.

repairing a bath ⚒

Baths can be given a new look by simply changing the panels or choosing a new design of tap to update the style. In addition, the actual bath surface can be repaired to hide scratches or defects as long as the correct materials and techniques are used. Proprietary re-enamelling kits are easy to apply and can make an old bathtub look like new. Replacing the sealant around the edges of the bath is also very effective in brightening up general bath appearance.

re-enamelling a bath

Although enamel baths are very hardwearing, they eventually tarnish, with their surface becoming stained or losing its enamel finish in places. A professional re-enamelling is an expensive business but there are now proprietary kits available that have some success returning old enamel baths to their original condition. They are easy to use but careful application is necessary to achieve a reasonable finish. Often these kits can be used on more than just enamel surfaces – sometimes ceramic, iron or plastic baths can be recoated using the same procedure, however the kits cannot be used on acrylic baths. Read the manufacturer's guidelines carefully to make sure that the kit is suitable for your particular bath surface. In this example, an old enamel bath is being renovated using one such proprietary kit.

tools for the job

sponge
cloth
proprietary re-enamelling kit
cordless drill/driver

1 First, clean any dirt or grime off the bath surface using a mild detergent and allow it to dry thoroughly. Cover the taps and waste outlets with masking tape or remove these items temporarily while re-enamelling takes place.

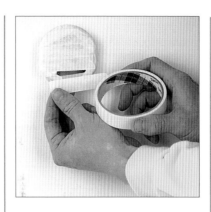

2 Clean the bath using the cleaner and sponge supplied with the kit. Rinse and allow to dry.

3 Sand the bath surface using fine-grade abrasive paper. Rinse with warm water and allow to dry.

safety advice

Make sure that the bathroom is adequately ventilated when using re-enamelling kits because the fumes can be quite overpowering.

4 Most kit systems involve mixing a hardener with the coating prior to application. Follow the manufacturer's guidelines.

5 Use a brush to paint all the detailed areas around outlets and taps, and generally those places where a roller would be unable to gain access. Take care to apply the coating as evenly as possible.

6 Pour some of the coating mixture into a roller tray or the tray supplied with the kit, and distribute the coating evenly over the roller surface.

7 Apply the coating to the bath as evenly as possible, reloading the roller at appropriate intervals. Try to cover any unsightly brushmarks.

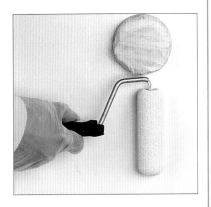

8 Once the coating is dry, apply another coat. Again, try to cover previous brushmarks and roller marks in order to produce an even finish. When the surface is dry, remove the masking tape.

tips of the trade

• **Sealant removal** – Where the bath is in contact with wall surfaces, be sure to remove any sealant so that the new coating extends right up to the edge.

• **Drying time** – Coatings may need to dry for 48 hours before the bath can be used, so make sure you read the manufacturer's guidelines for any specific instructions.

• **Future cleaning** – After the bath has been coated, only use liquid, non-abrasive cleaners on its surface, applied with a sponge or cloth.

• **Further protection** – As a further protective measure, apply a coat of car wax to the bath once or twice a year to help maintain its finish and keep it as clean and bright as possible.

• **Change sleeves** – Use a different roller sleeve for each coating because it is not possible to clean the roller between coats. If you attempt to use the same roller sleeve for the second coat it will produce a very rough and unsatisfactory finish.

USING SILICONE SEALANT

First, apply masking tape along each side of the joint to be sealed, then expel the sealant along the joint. Smooth it with a wet finger. Remove the tape while the sealant is still wet, smoothing the edges of the sealant if necessary with a wet finger.

replacing seals

The sealant around the edge of a bath will need to be repaired at some point during the lifetime of the bath. Removing the old seal and replacing it with a new one is a simple process.

tools for the job

small paintbrush

window scraper

sealant gun or dispenser

1 Use a small paintbrush to apply a proprietary sealant removal solution along the sealant bead. Allow this to soak into the sealant according to the manufacturer's guidelines.

2 Use a window scraper to ease the sealant away from the wall and bath surface, taking care not to scratch the surface of the bath.

3 Use a cloth to clean away any remaining sealant. Dampening the cloth with methylated spirits will help to prepare the surface for reapplication of sealant to give a watertight finish.

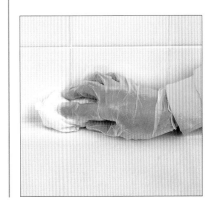

making tile repairs ⤢

It is almost inevitable that the tiles in a bathroom will become damaged and that their appearance will deteriorate over time. Rather than completely retiling, you may prefer to carry out some sort of repair or renovation to restore a good finish to the existing tiled surface. The degree of damage may vary in seriousness, from broken or cracked tiles to simple grout discoloration. Whatever the damage done, carrying out a repair is a relatively straightforward process.

Condensation, general moisture levels, and wear and tear over time, are all factors that contribute to the gradual deterioration of grout joints between tiles. Often the main reason people choose to change tiles in their bathroom is because the old grout has become discoloured and detracts from the overall appearance of the tiled surface. However, it is not always necessary to retile and often tiles can look good as new by either reviving or replacing the grout.

regrouting

tools for the job

grout raker
vacuum cleaner
grout spreader
sponge

1 Employ a specially designed grout raker to remove old grout from joints. The serrated, roughened edge digs out the grout as you apply pressure to the surface. Take care not to scratch the edge of the tiles.

2 Once you have raked out all the joints from around the tiles, it is important to remove any dust or debris from both the tile surface and within the joints. Wipe the surface down and use a vacuum cleaner to remove debris from the tile joints.

3 With the old grout completely removed from the joints, regrout the tiles using the usual techniques (see page 421). However, for a slightly different look you might like to consider using a coloured grout as a change to the standard white varieties. Grout colouring is usually supplied in a powdered form, which is mixed with white grout until the desired colour intensity is achieved.

grout reviver

Reviving grout is in many ways a simpler and quicker way of restoring grout to a clean finish when compared to regrouting. Total regrouting does tend to last longer and is the more hardwearing option, but because the task of grout revival is quick, it can be performed on a more regular basis. Grout reviver tends to be supplied in proprietary kit form.

tools for the job

grout reviving kit
sponge

Make sure the tile surface has been thoroughly cleaned and is completely dry. Apply the reviver along all the grout joints in the same way that you would apply paint. Wipe away any excess reviver using a damp sponge. There is normally a critical timing between application and wiping away excess, so you should always refer to the manufacturer's guidelines in order to attain the best finish.

replacing a tile

Tiles can be broken by accident, or they can simply crack over time due to weaknesses in their manufacture. Whatever the reason, the process for replacing a broken tile is the same. It can be difficult to find an exact match for the tile being replaced and even small colour variations are noticeable in the finished product, so choose carefully. This is a good reason for always holding onto a few tiles when you finish any new tiling project.

tools for the job

cordless drill/driver
scraper
club hammer
cold chisel
protective gloves
goggles
adhesive spreader
grout spreader
sponge

safety advice

When drilling into tiles and removing them, always wear goggles to protect your eyes from any flying debris.

1 Drill a number of holes into the broken tile surface to weaken its structure. Use a tile drill bit if possible, but since accuracy is not paramount a masonry bit should break through

the tile just as well. Make sure the drill does not slip onto surrounding tiles and risk damaging them.

2 The next step is to loosen the grout around the edge of the broken tile with a grout raker.

3 Remove the damaged tile with a club hammer and cold chisel. Again, take care to position the point of the chisel so that it cannot slip and damage the surrounding tiles.

4 Use a scraper to remove any remaining tile adhesive from the wall surface.

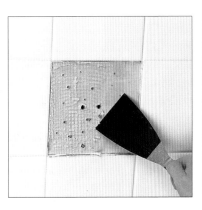

5 Apply adhesive to the space left by the old tile and position the new one. Use spacers to maintain a consistent gap around the edge of the tile for the grouting joints. The spacers will have to be applied at right angles to the tile surface.

6 Hold a batten across the tile surface to check that the new tile sits flush with the surrounding tiles. If necessary, adjust adhesive levels until the tile sits flush.

7 Once the adhesive has dried, remove the spacers and grout the tile joints in the usual way.

fixing dripping taps ///

Dripping taps are a common problem but repairs are usually simple to carry out. Leaving a tap that is dripping is not only a waste of water but can also lead to stained fittings, so it is best to deal with the problem immediately. Although manufacturers regularly update tap designs, the way in which leaks and drips are repaired remains relatively unchanged. Rubber washers are the most common type of seal used in tap design – the more modern alternative is ceramic cartridges.

Rubber washers are situated at the base of the headgear deep inside the tap design. In order to gain access to the washer, you must disassemble the tap. There will always be slight variations in the dismantling procedure depending on the tap design. This usually relates to whether the tap handle is held in place with a retaining screw or simply push fit. Retaining screws may also be covered with caps, so gaining access to them may not be instantly obvious. The example below shows a common tap design and demonstrates the main principles of gaining access to washers and the way in which they are replaced.

Before beginning work, you will need to turn off water at the mains or by closing the shut-off valve below the relevant tap. Make sure that you allow any water left in the pipes to run off before dismantling. If you forget to do this, it will spill out when you remove the tap headgear from the tap body.

replacing washers

tools for the job

screwdriver

adjustable spanners

long-nose & slip-joint pliers

craft knife

1 Remove the tap handle. In this case, it simply pulls away from the main body of the tap.

2 Unscrew the retaining screw at the top of the plastic cover that is fitted over the tap headgear.

3 This cover acts purely as a mounting for the tap handle, so simply pull it off the headgear.

4 Use an adjustable spanner to undo the headgear from its position in the main tap body. You may need to clamp another spanner or some slip-joint pliers onto the tap body to hold it in place while you apply the necessary pressure to undo the headgear. If this extra support is required, either tape the jaws of the pliers or wrap a cloth around the tap body to prevent scratches.

5 With the headgear removed, you can gain access to the washer. In this case, it is secured in position with a nut. This can be removed with a pair of long-nose pliers or a small adjustable spanner, as shown here.

6 Remove the old washer. You will probably find it easiest to do this by using a slot-head screwdriver to flick it off. Replace it with a new washer before reassembling the tap.

tips of the trade

• **Avoiding losing parts** – Make sure the sink plug is in place when changing a washer, because the various small screws and parts of the tap can easily be dropped in the sink and disappear down the plughole.

• **Easing washers** – In many cases, the washer will not be held in place with a nut but simply pushed onto the end of the headgear. The old washer can be cut away using a craft knife if it is difficult to remove. Soaking the new washer in hot water can make it more pliable and easier to press into place.

OTHER TYPES OF LEAK

Replacing washers will deal with leaks from the spout of the tap. However, leaks that occur further up the tap body are more likely to be caused by the failure of a different type of seal. This seal is referred to as an O-ring and can be found in a number of places in the tap, on both the tap headgear and within some spout designs. If leaks become apparent around the shrouds that cover the tap headgear or at the base of the spout on a monobloc tap, the O-ring seal usually needs to be replaced.

replacing ceramic disc cartridges

This modern type of water-control system is very efficient and it is unusual to have to replace a disc cartridge because of leakage. In fact, it is so rare that there are no small parts such as washers that can be changed. Instead, the whole cartridge must be exchanged for a new one. There are many different designs of cartridge so it is important to know the correct type for your particular bathroom before purchase.

Before beginning work, make sure that the water is turned off at the mains or that the shut-off valve below the relevant tap has been closed. Run off any water left in the pipes before you start work.

tools for the job

screwdriver

adjustable spanners

1 Remove the tap handle. In this case, a cap is unscrewed off the top of the handle to gain access to the retaining screw below. The tap shroud can then be unscrewed. This will often come away by hand but adjustable spanners or pliers can be used if greater pressure is required. Protect the surface of the shroud to prevent it from being scratched, if using spanners or pliers.

2 Unscrew the cartridge from the main tap body using an adjustable spanner. You may need to grip the tap body in order to provide the necessary leverage.

3 Pull the old cartridge out of the tap body and replace it with a new one. The tap may now be reassembled.

OTHER TAP MECHANISMS

The repairs shown here relate to two different types of tap design. However, there are other mechanisms used to control water flow. Some modern taps are controlled with a ball-type mechanism in which one handle is used to control the flow of both the hot and cold taps. Washers and O-rings are still used in their design, however, so methods of repair are similar. There are sometimes small differences between designs from different manufacturers, who often produce specific repair kits for each type of tap.

dealing with shower problems

Showers can suffer damage to both their functioning and finish. In terms of finish, most repairs are caused by the constant action of water hitting wall surfaces, combined with the humid atmosphere. Whether the shower is enclosed in a separate cubicle or positioned in a bath, steam can have a marked effect on surrounding painted surfaces. As far as function is concerned, there are a few simple maintenance procedures that will ensure the best performance from your shower.

installing a PVC ceiling

The ceiling directly above the shower is the area that suffers most from water damage. Moisture accumulates there and can lead to a breakdown of the decorated surface (normally paint). To prevent this, a sheet of PVC (polyvinyl chloride) can be fitted to form a totally waterproof area.

tools for the job

pencil

tape measure

panel saw

sealant gun or dispenser

1 Measure the dimensions of the ceiling area above your shower. For an enclosed shower, this will be the entire ceiling inside the cubicle – otherwise, you will have to judge what size area you need to cover.

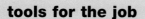

2 Mark the dimensions on the sheet of PVC and cut it to size using a panel saw.

3 Apply a generous quantity of silicone sealant across the back of the PVC sheet.

4 Hold the sheet securely in place and the sealant should adhere quickly.

5 Once the sealant has dried, apply a further bead of silicone around the edge of the sheet to create a neat seal. You may wish to use masking tape to help you achieve a neat sealant line (see box on page 391). Once this has dried, the shower may be used, after leaving this last application of sealant to dry for 24 hours.

FIXING PVC WITH SCREWS

If the PVC sheet does not adhere easily to the ceiling, you may need to hold it in place with some sort of mechanical fixing. Drill pilot holes through the sheet and into the ceiling, then insert screws to hold it in position. Ideally, snap some PVC caps onto the screw heads to disguise them and make the sheet more pleasing to the eye. To ensure a good seal around the screws, apply a small quantity of sealant to the screw head before inserting it. In this way, as the screw is driven into place, the sealant wraps around the thread of the screw and creates a watertight seal.

painting the ceiling

Problems with peeling paint, build-up of mould and staining are often the result of the type of paint used and the fact that the area is not often wiped. Wear protective gloves when carrying out this process.

1 Sand the area, then wipe with a fungicidal solution to kill mould. Allow it to dry, then rinse with water.

2 Oil-based eggshell paint is more durable and resistant to moisture and condensation than standard emulsion paint and so is the preferred paint for use in a bathroom. Apply two or three generous coats and allow to dry thoroughly.

maintenance

Many of the problems associated with shower fittings are related to the shower head itself or the hose. These elements of the shower are in frequent use, so regular maintenance should be undertaken.

head cleaning

Shower jet holes can often become blocked with limescale, and this is particularly true if you live in a hard-water area. If this happens, you should disassemble the head and descale the holes. Always wear protective gloves when handling descaling fluid.

1 The way in which shower heads are dismantled varies between manufacturers, but in most cases there is an obvious screw fitting that is simply undone in order to gain access to the inside of the shower head.

2 Clean the jet holes with a descaling fluid. Use an old toothbrush to apply the fluid to all of the intricate mouldings of the

shower head. Be sure to read the manufacturer's guidelines carefully for the solution you are using, and check that it is suitable for plastic- or metal-based shower heads.

tips of the trade

Some blockages in shower holes can be removed using a pin (although take care not prick yourself while doing so). However, you should avoid this method if your shower head contains plastic diaphragms because these can be damaged by the pin.

hose replacement

Another common problem with showers is when the hose begins to leak around the connection with the head itself. In some cases the problem can easily be fixed with a washer, but in general a new hose is required. Be sure to get the correct size of replacement hose, then simply unscrew the old one and screw the new one in place.

dealing with blockages & leaks ↗↗↗

Many problems in bathrooms and kitchens are hidden away from view but their effects can be devastating if not acted upon quickly. Blockages of any nature should be dealt with as soon as they are noticed, because any delay could lead to repairs that incur a much greater cost. Likewise, any leaking pipes should be repaired immediately because once water does begin to drip from a joint or hole, it will not stop unless an adequate repair is made.

sink & basin solutions

There are two methods of dealing with these blockages, both of which are outlined here.

using chemical cleaners

There are various chemical cleaners available. Most are caustic (generally containing sodium hydroxide) and, as such, protective gloves should always be worn. They are best used when the first signs of a blockage become apparent. Read the manufacturer's guidelines carefully, but in general one or two spoonfuls of the cleaner need to be poured into the plug hole in the basin. Run a small amount of water to ensure that none of the granules are allowed to rest on any exposed part of the sink bowl. Leave the cleaner to work for 20–30 minutes, before flushing the system with more water. One further application may be required to clear the blockage. Make sure there is adequate ventilation when carrying out this procedure because the fumes can be quite overpowering.

safety advice

For homes with a septic tank as part of their drainage system, chemical-based caustic cleaner cannot be used. Instead, a bacteria-based treatment must be employed. As usual, always follow the manufacturer's instructions.

using plungers

When chemical cleaners are ineffective, the next option to try is a plunger. First, you must create an airlock in the drainage system. This can be achieved by inserting a rag or cloth in the overflow outlet. When you have done this, position the suction pad of the plunger over the basin outlet. Move the plunger handle rhythmically up and down, which should put enough pressure on the blockage to loosen it. In this example, a modern design of plunger has been used. It works on a similar principle to traditional designs except that water is sucked into the plunger cylinder and forced at high pressure into the blockage below, thereby dislodging it.

unblocking toilets

Toilets can be unblocked using a plunger in the same way that you would unblock a sink, as long as the head of the plunger is large enough to cover the outlet in the toilet pan. Alternatively, use an auger as demonstrated below.

1 Pull out the spring section of the auger to a suitable length for extending around the U-bend of the toilet.

2 Push the spring section into the U-bend of the toilet and turn the handle on the back.

removing traps

If attempts to clear blockages with chemical cleaners and plungers are not successful, it may be necessary to turn your attention to the drainage pipes and trap below. In that case you may have to undo the trap and clean it out by hand in order to remove a blockage.

1 Most traps simply unscrew by hand. For particularly stiff or solid joints, however, it may be necessary to use some slip-joint pliers to provide a good grip and extra leverage for undoing purposes. Before you start unscrewing, always position a bowl below the trap to catch any excess water inside.

2 Flush out the trap with water and use your fingers to remove any large pieces of material that could be contributing to the blockage. This can be a bit of a messy business, so you may wish to wear some gloves to protect your hands.

3 Before you replace the trap, you could take the opportunity to replace any washers in order to renew the seals.

using an auger

Augers are extremely effective tools for dealing with all manner of blockages, and where a sink is blocked, or rather a sink drainage system is blocked, an auger might be the best piece of equipment for rectifying the situation. The long spring and handle mechanism give you good access to the blockage and provide the force you will need to break it up and release it.

1 Remove the trap on the sink to leave access to the drainage pipe. Pull out the sprung section of the auger to a length that can be inserted into the drainage pipe. When removing the trap from the sink, remember to have a bowl close at hand to catch the excess water that will be released.

2 Insert the sprung section into the pipe and turn the handle of the auger so that it screws into the pipe void and eventually comes into contact with the blockage. Keep turning the auger handle to allow the sprung section to burrow into the blockage, gradually breaking it down, making it much easier to wash away down the pipe.

tips of the trade

Where a trap is 'weeping', or leaking water around the threaded section, if you are unable to find a suitably-sized replacement washer, it is possible to employ silicone sealant in order to stop the leak. Simply remove the section, dry it thoroughly, and apply sealant around the thread before screwing it back into position. Allow the sealant to dry before using the sink again.

MACHINE MAINTENANCE

Washing machines and dishwashers require little general maintenance, other than occasionally checking to ensure that the supply and drainage pipes are in good working order and that there are no visible leaks or drips. However, it is worth referring to the manufacturer's guidelines for the particular appliance as, for example, in some situations filters may need cleaning or replacing to enable the machine to function at optimum levels.

decorative finishes

However well constructional tasks have been carried out, the decorative aspect of any renovation work is the deciding factor in determining how good the finished product will look. Therefore, attention to detail at this stage of a project will turn an ordinary finish into an outstanding one.

This section provides options and instruction on many decorative processes while supplying the crucial information on how to achieve good finishes through preparation and planning. Take time to choose decorative schemes, and use this section as a guide for selecting the most appropriate materials and techniques.

choosing finishes

Decoration is very much an issue of personal preference. In general, most people tend to have particular opinions on certain finishes – for example, many people have wallpaper in every room whereas others cannot bear the thought of wallpaper anywhere. Some use strong colours in every room scheme, whereas others shy away to more neutral shades. There is no right or wrong and it can be worth trying out a range of options.

design aspects

When considering any decorative option, design or period features may influence the type of decoration you use. Both period homes and ultra modern apartments are similar in this respect, because both have some limitations on the types of materials that can be used, if the home is to retain its style or design. Therefore some research or thought gathering on authenticity should take part in your final decision-making process.

Knocking two rooms into one or widening entrances between rooms is a way of creating a more open plan layout. While providing a lighter, more spacious atmosphere, consideration needs to be made of the feasibility of removing whole or partial walls, especially if they are loadbearing. However, this sort of renovation can dramatically change the look of your home and totally transform a cramped, rather gloomy atmosphere into a design of far greater appeal.

RIGHT *Period design features, such as fireplaces, help to create extra interest in the decorative scheme.*

wallpaper

The modern DIY revolution has also increased the range of options open to people who wish to use wallpaper. Manufacturers now produce papers in a greater range of designs, colours and textures than ever before. Wallpaper has an instant effect, which often makes it an attractive option for many people, but it is important to paint any surrounding woodwork or surfaces in colours that will complement the paper. It's also important to ensure that furnishings in the room will make a suitable contrast or complement to the paper design. Different wallpapers may have markedly different effects on the atmosphere of a room, so choose your pattern carefully.

LEFT *Stripes are a particularly effective wallpaper design and can help to create the impression of height within the room by making the ceiling appear higher.*

ABOVE *Tile designs can be used effectively on both walls and floors to create a well-integrated scheme.*

RIGHT *Large, open plan room designs provide a broad canvas for atmospheric colour schemes.*

BELOW *Strong colours are a particularly effective way of picking out the different types of surfaces and features in a room.*

tiles

Tiles form part of the decorative scheme in most bathrooms or kitchens, even if their primary use is for practical purposes. Design choices may be influenced by a desire to tie in colours with other wall decoration, or you may opt for neutral colours that will complement any number of alterations to the surrounding decor.

paint

Paint is the most versatile of all decorative products, and is used in most rooms on at least some surfaces. Colour availability stretches through every imaginable shade, which means that all tastes are catered for – to the point that there can sometimes be so much choice that it is difficult to decide between closely matched colours. This vastness of range presents plenty of options for co-ordinating colours and producing complementary or contrasting schemes to suit personal choice.

painting details

Contrasting colours can enliven surfaces, particularly when they are used to pick out certain details or features in a room. The right combinations can create greater texture and add interest to various architectural features. However, the greater the range of colours used, the greater the amount of time that should be spent planning the scheme to ensure that the correct blend is chosen.

choosing materials

Having made decisions on the type of finish you require, it is necessary to choose the best materials for that particular finish. The best materials are those that have the most suitable properties and the right decorative attributes – some finishes are suited to some surfaces more than others, and these factors should be considered before materials are purchased and used.

tiles

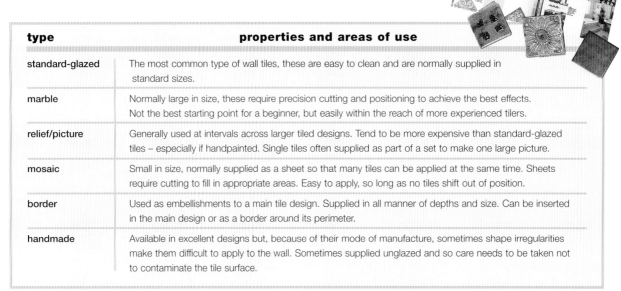

Tiles are the most hardwearing of decorative materials, making them suitable for most areas in the home.

Able to withstand knocks and regular cleaning, they are most commonly used in kitchen and bathroom areas.

type	properties and areas of use
standard-glazed	The most common type of wall tiles, these are easy to clean and are normally supplied in standard sizes.
marble	Normally large in size, these require precision cutting and positioning to achieve the best effects. Not the best starting point for a beginner, but easily within the reach of more experienced tilers.
relief/picture	Generally used at intervals across larger tiled designs. Tend to be more expensive than standard-glazed tiles – especially if handpainted. Single tiles often supplied as part of a set to make one large picture.
mosaic	Small in size, normally supplied as a sheet so that many tiles can be applied at the same time. Sheets require cutting to fill in appropriate areas. Easy to apply, so long as no tiles shift out of position.
border	Used as embellishments to a main tile design. Supplied in all manner of depths and size. Can be inserted in the main design or as a border around its perimeter.
handmade	Available in excellent designs but, because of their mode of manufacture, sometimes shape irregularities make them difficult to apply to the wall. Sometimes supplied unglazed and so care needs to be taken not to contaminate the tile surface.

wallpaper

Different wallpapers have surprisingly varied properties, which means that they can be used in a range of areas

around the home. When choosing a design, do make sure that the actual paper make-up is also suitable.

type	properties and areas of use
lining	Dead flat and available in various thicknesses. Either used as an underlayer for patterned wallpaper or can simply be painted over. Smooths wall surfaces, and provides a softer texture than cold plaster walls.
textured	Relief is built into the paper structure in order to provide pattern and/or texture. Excellent for covering over rough wall surfaces. Some varieties can be painted while others have a vinyl finish already applied.
standard-patterned	Machine-patterned, and made in vast quantities and ranges of designs. Ideal for most wall surfaces. Often requires lining first. Available as ready-pasted or paste-the-back varieties.
vinyl	Hardwearing paper designed to be easily cleaned or wiped down. The vinyl layer makes it suitable for bathrooms and kitchens.
natural	Composed of natural fibres such as silk or hessian. Difficult to hang and best left to the professionals. Provides an outstanding finish, but not particularly hardwearing.

This table contains some of the most common finishing paints for walls and ceilings, and explains their relevant properties. In addition to these common varieties, it is possible to choose specialist, proprietary finishes.

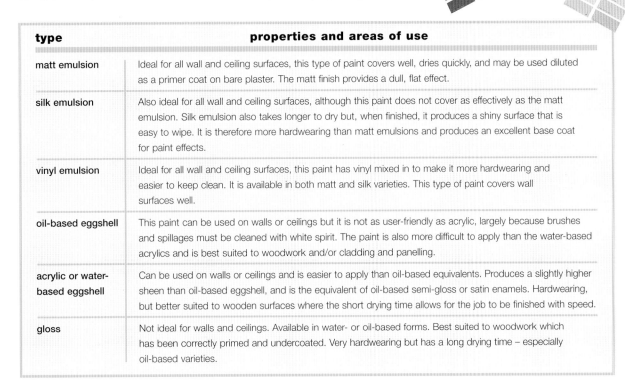

type	properties and areas of use
matt emulsion	Ideal for all wall and ceiling surfaces, this type of paint covers well, dries quickly, and may be used diluted as a primer coat on bare plaster. The matt finish provides a dull, flat effect.
silk emulsion	Also ideal for all wall and ceiling surfaces, although this paint does not cover as effectively as the matt emulsion. Silk emulsion also takes longer to dry but, when finished, it produces a shiny surface that is easy to wipe. It is therefore more hardwearing than matt emulsions and produces an excellent base coat for paint effects.
vinyl emulsion	Ideal for all wall and ceiling surfaces, this paint has vinyl mixed in to make it more hardwearing and easier to keep clean. It is available in both matt and silk varieties. This type of paint covers wall surfaces well.
oil-based eggshell	This paint can be used on walls or ceilings but it is not as user-friendly as acrylic, largely because brushes and spillages must be cleaned with white spirit. The paint is also more difficult to apply than the water-based acrylics and is best suited to woodwork and/or cladding and panelling.
acrylic or water-based eggshell	Can be used on walls or ceilings and is easier to apply than oil-based equivalents. Produces a slightly higher sheen than oil-based eggshell, and is the equivalent of oil-based semi-gloss or satin enamels. Hardwearing, but better suited to wooden surfaces where the short drying time allows for the job to be finished with speed.
gloss	Not ideal for walls and ceilings. Available in water- or oil-based forms. Best suited to woodwork which has been correctly primed and undercoated. Very hardwearing but has a long drying time – especially oil-based varieties.

choosing materials

405

Paint effects are produced by the use of a coloured glaze which allows for the creation of broken-colour finishes on a wall surface. So the materials used are more concerned with achieving pattern and effect, rather than actually containing finishing properties in their own right.

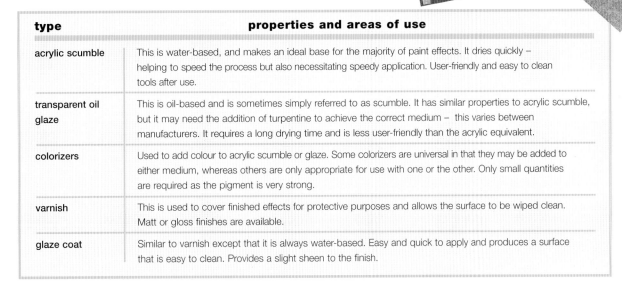

type	properties and areas of use
acrylic scumble	This is water-based, and makes an ideal base for the majority of paint effects. It dries quickly – helping to speed the process but also necessitating speedy application. User-friendly and easy to clean tools after use.
transparent oil glaze	This is oil-based and is sometimes simply referred to as scumble. It has similar properties to acrylic scumble, but it may need the addition of turpentine to achieve the correct medium – this varies between manufacturers. It requires a long drying time and is less user-friendly than the acrylic equivalent.
colorizers	Used to add colour to acrylic scumble or glaze. Some colorizers are universal in that they may be added to either medium, whereas others are only appropriate for use with one or the other. Only small quantities are required as the pigment is very strong.
varnish	This is used to cover finished effects for protective purposes and allows the surface to be wiped clean. Matt or gloss finishes are available.
glaze coat	Similar to varnish except that it is always water-based. Easy and quick to apply and produces a surface that is easy to clean. Provides a slight sheen to the finish.

ceiling & wall preparation ↗

The quality of a decorative finish depends on thorough surface preparation. This stage of the renovation procedure is one of the most important in terms of ensuring that the constructional work you have carried out will be shown off to its best possible potential. It is important not to rush surface preparation and to ensure that any defects are corrected at this stage so that defects will not appear in the final surface.

filling

Filling cracks, joints or holes in wall and ceiling surfaces can be considered a relatively simple, methodical task, achieving the best results by following an uncomplicated order of work. There are three main types of filler: all-purpose filler, flexible filler and expanding filler. Each type is designed for a particular kind of task, and all proprietary products currently on the market are based on one of these varieties.

all-purpose filler

Manufacturers describe this type of filler as all-purpose, and although it can physically be used for most things, it is still best suited to particular types of hole. It can be bought ready mixed or as a powder to which water is added and a smooth creamy filling paste created. It is most effective in small divots and dents on open wall or ceiling surfaces.

1 Remove any dust in the hole and dampen it slightly to improve the filler's adhesion. Use a filling knife to

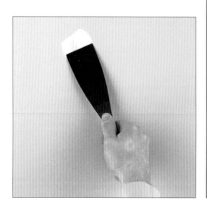

press the filler into place, applying pressure with the knife's flexible blade. Leave the filler slightly proud of the hole – it shrinks slightly as it dries – but remove excess from around the outside.

2 Once dry, sand to a smooth finish, flush with the surrounding wall. For deep holes, a second application of filler may be necessary because excessive shrinkage can pull the first application down below the hole surface. A second, thinner coat therefore builds up the level and allows for a sanded flush finish to be produced.

flexible filler

Although some all-purpose fillers claim to have flexible qualities, they tend not to achieve the standards set by tubed, flexible filler or caulk. This type of filler is used along corner or ceiling junction cracks where slight movement is always prevalent. Although all purpose filler can be used in these areas, it tends to crack after time whereas flexible filler or caulk tolerates more stress through movement. However, take care to smooth the filler before it dries, as it is not possible to sand it.

safety advice

Always wear a dust mask when using an electric sander, and preferably use a sander which has a built-in dust extraction bag.

1 Use a sealant gun to apply sealant along the corner cracks, allowing the filler to bead over and cover the crack beneath.

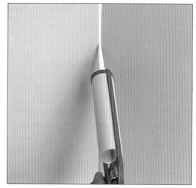

2 Before the filler dries, use a wetted finger or a sponge to smooth the filler into the junction. Keep a cup of water handy to wet or clean your finger as you work on shaping the filler.

3 For storage purposes, insert a nail or screw into the nozzle of the filler tube to prevent it hardening in the nozzle and making it difficult to use when next required.

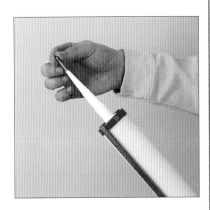

expanding filler

In large gaps or holes, especially around awkwardly shaped inlets such as pipes, the use of flexible or all-purpose filler is neither suitable nor economic. Expanding fillers are ideal as they get into all the small crevices, adhere well, and make a neat finish. However, it is best to use them with all-purpose filler because expanding filler or foam has a rough texture. So, once the major filling process is complete, finish off the surface with a final skim of all-purpose filler.

Expanding fillers are aerosol-based, and are guided into a hole using an extended nozzle. As their name suggests, once out of the aerosol the chemical make-up of the filler expands and takes up the entire area that requires filling. This leads to the filler protruding from the hole. Once dry, this can be trimmed back with a craft knife to a neat finish. When using expanding filler, follow the manufacturer's safety guidelines.

caulking blade

A caulking blade or caulker (not to be confused with caulk in terms of flexible filler) is ideal for speeding up the all-purpose filling process. On walls with a number of small holes, draw the wide, filler-loaded blade of the

caulker across the surface. This enables you to fill several holes simultaneously, rather than having to attend to each one separately with a small filling knife.

tips of the trade

Although it is important not to jeopardize the quality of the finish by rushing the job, there are a number of practical, time-saving measures that can be taken. Various tools have been designed to speed up DIY tasks, and electric sanders, in particular, are useful pieces of equipment. Sanding is never the most inspirational or invigorating of tasks and so using an electric sander helps to speed up the process. Suitable for wide open wall surfaces, it covers the area far more quickly than can be achieved with a hand sanding block and paper.

---

cleaning and sealing surfaces

Once the necessary filling and sanding of surfaces has been completed, it is important to clean surfaces with warm water and mild detergent to remove dust and impurities. Finally, rinse the surfaces with water and allow it to dry. Depending on its condition and the decorative layers to be applied, it may also be necessary to seal the surfaces before painting or decorating, In the chart shown on the right, the PVA solution referred to comprises a standard mix of 5 parts water to 1 part PVA. Mix the solution thoroughly before application.

type	surface treatment
surfaces which have been stripped of paper	Must be sealed with a PVA solution
dry lined	Proprietary sealer must be applied to the surface before further decoration
new plaster	Seal with PVA solution before papering, or apply a dilute acrylic coat before further painting
old painted	Ensure the surface is completely clean. PVA solution is required if paper is to be applied
old papered	Inadvisable to paint over an old papered surface unless you are sure the paper is firmly stuck down
wood panelling	Prime and paint as required, or apply a natural wood finish

painting techniques ✂✂

The quality of a painted finish is dependent on both the type of paint used and the method of application. Therefore, having purchased quality materials, it is important to develop a good painting technique, to ensure you achieve the best possible finishes. There are a number of different tools which may be used for applying paint, and many are suited to particular areas and tasks, but a certain amount of personal preference can also influence your choice.

tools for the job

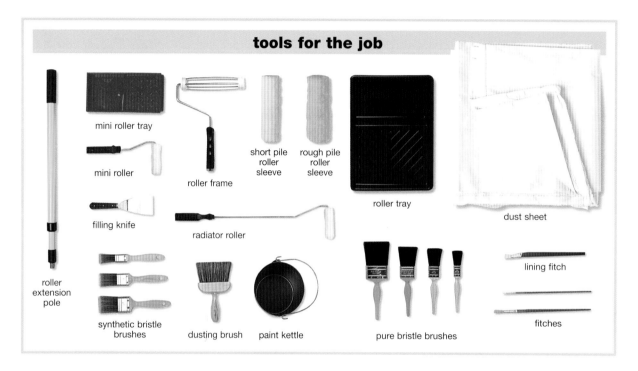

mini roller tray

mini roller

roller frame

short pile roller sleeve

rough pile roller sleeve

roller tray

dust sheet

filling knife

radiator roller

roller extension pole

synthetic bristle brushes

dusting brush

paint kettle

pure bristle brushes

lining fitch

fitches

ceilings

Painting ceilings always tends to produce the initial problem of gaining the best access. Although using a stepladder and brush is an option, there are far more efficient and easier ways of going about this task.

1 Attach an extension pole to the roller so that the ceiling can be painted with your feet on the floor. An extension pole is also useful for walls, as it helps gain access to the top area of a wall and reduces the need to bend over for lower wall areas. Using an extension pole also produces a more even pressure during paint application, and therefore improves the quality and evenness of the finish.

2 Having used a roller, it is still clearly necessary to finish or 'cut in' around the edges of the ceiling. A brush is the best tool for this purpose. If the walls in the room are to be painted, allow the ceiling colour to extend slightly down on to the wall surface – when the wall is painted, you may then paint over the excess ceiling colour and cut in precisely into

the wall/ceiling junction. This technique ensures you do not waste time cutting in the ceiling colour.

tips of the trade

New equipment is always being devised and while some people prefer traditional tools, it can be worth experimenting.

improving technique

There are a number of factors that can affect the final appearance of a painted surface. Practising your painting technique will always help to ensure a good ceiling or wall finish, as will considering the following points.

number of coats

Probably one of the key factors in producing a good finish, it is always best to have a flexible attitude when deciding on coat requirement. As a rule, no surface should receive fewer than two coats of paint and new plaster surfaces should get three. The quality of paint you are using will also determine requirement – hence the false economy of buying cheap paint. Refreshing a previously painted room with the same colour as before will only require one coat. So flexibility is the key but, as a general rule, the greater the number of coats, the better the finish.

wet edges

The chemical make-up of modern paints often includes such substances as vinyl (making them easily washable), which can be a problem when painting. The slight sheen that the vinyl produces can cause highlighting of areas where paint layers are greater than in other areas. This occurs when the central areas of a wall are painted, left to dry and then the edges cut in later. So as coats are applied, the slight overlap between the edge of the central wall areas and the cut-in edges acquire a build-up of paint layers, which can cause a noticeable colour difference. To prevent this, paint one wall at a time so that both the edges and central area of the wall are painted and therefore dry at the same time. This is especially important for dark colours which can be more noticeable than lighter shades.

roller trails

The texture of rollers leaves a slight imprint in the paint and surface finish. Make sure you avoid paint build-up at the ends of rollers, as this can lead to thicker paint lines or trails on the ceiling or wall surface.

priming

Prime areas which have been filled with an all-purpose filler using your chosen wall colour. Otherwise, the

varying absorption properties of the filler and the wall can cause shading differences when further coats of paint are added.

For troublesome stains on an older painted surface area, it is best to use a proprietary stain block to coat the area before continuing with finishing paint.

Where flexible filler or caulk has been used, it is always best to prime it with an oil-based undercoat, as water-based acrylic applied directly to the caulk can sometimes crack as it dries.

spraying

In some circumstances, a spray gun is a useful tool for painting large open areas. However, always mask off areas that do not require painting, and wear goggles and a respiratory mask. Apply a number of thin coats rather than a few thicker ones, as this will help to prevent runs in the finish.

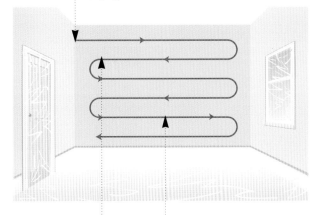

Start the gun slightly to the side of the section to be painted and then progress on to the area.

Begin at the top of the wall and work down to the bottom.

Allow each level of paint to overlap slightly as you progress.

painting doors ✎✎

Quite simply, there is a right and a wrong way to paint any item, and doors are no exception – you must refine your technique so that the best possible quality of finish is achieved. Once preparation and priming has been completed, application of undercoats and finishing coats follows the same system or order of work. Doors vary in design, but one of the more common varieties is the panel door, and the best way of achieving a good finish is demonstrated below.

tools for the job

38mm (1½in) paintbrush
25mm (1in) paintbrush

painting a panel door

Panel doors vary in design from two large panels making up their surface, to as many as eight panels. However, the best system for painting them stays the same and here a six-panelled door has been used. Choice of brush size is very important, and a 375mm (1½in) brush is ideal in most cases.

1 Begin by painting the panels themselves, starting at the top. As well as painting the central flat area of the panel, also complete the moulded area and try not to allow paint to encroach onto the rails or stiles.

2 Continue to work down the door, completing all the panels, using the bristles of the brush in line with the direction of the wood grain. Even if you are painting a pressed

panel door which does not have any 'grain' as such, still direct the brush in the direction of what would be the perceived grain.

3 Once the panels are complete, move on to paint the central vertical stiles down the middle of the door. Try not to allow the paint to extend on to the horizontal rails, and if any excess encroaches on the painted panels, ensure that you brush the paint out to prevent a paint build-up.

4 Move on to coat the horizontal rails to complete the central portion of the door. Take care when creating the join between these rails and the painted vertical stiles to

ensure a precise defining line. This will maintain the principle of painting in line with the grain and therefore provides the neatest possible finish.

5 Finish the face of the door by painting the two outer vertical stiles on the hinge and opening edge of the door. Again, make precise divisions at the point where the vertical stiles cross the edges of the horizontal rails whilst still brushing the paint out in the usual manner.

6 Paint the leading edge of the door using a 250mm (1in) brush to avoid overspray. Take care to paint precisely down the edge of the door only and not on the door face.

7. Now that the door itself is complete, turn your attention to the door architrave. The hinge edge of the door in this instance need not be painted as it should be the same colour as the other face of the door. Begin on the architrave by painting the edge.

8. With the architrave edges complete, paint the face of the mouldings, returning to the 375mm (1½in) brush for quicker coverage.

9. Paint the inner door stop and remaining side of the frame, and check for any areas that you have missed. Finally, turn attention back to

the face of the door to make sure there are no drips on the paint surface. 'Brush in' such areas as required.

flush doors

Flush doors do not have the complicated surface of panel doors.

Hence they may be treated more as an overall open surface, which is best painted by mentally dividing the door area into eight equal-sized sections, beginning with two at the top and three further rows of two areas as you go down the door surface. It is important to maintain a 'wet edge' in the paint as you move from each area to the next, so that there is no visible join between each of the eight areas. The architrave and door frame may be painted as for panel doors.

glazed doors

When painting a glazed door it should be treated more like a casement window than a solid door surface.

A well painted door forms an integral part of any room decoration. Attention to detail and precise dividing lines help to enhance its look and provide a good quality finish.

painting windows

Just as with doors, it is necessary to follow a particular order of work to achieve the best possible finish for windows. But accuracy is even more important as it is vital to prevent paint being transferred or oversprayed onto the glass surface. Therefore, as we have seen is the case with doors, windows must be 'broken down' into different sections and painted systematically, according to the order listed below.

tools for the job

25mm (1in) paintbrush

casement windows

Casement windows provide a good example of how all window painting should be approached. Casements themselves vary in design, with different types and sizes of opening section, but a similar principle regarding the order of work applies. Remember to look back continually to painted areas and brush out any drips or runs that you find before the paint dries. Make sure that you pay particular attention to the numerous joints and corners, which provide areas where paint could build up.

1 Initially, attention should be aimed towards the smallest opening casement. Begin by painting the rebates using a 25mm (1in) brush. Take care to bead the paint directly along the rebate/glass junction, creating a precise edge.

tips of the trade

- **Preparing the sill** – Before painting a windowsill, wipe over it with a cloth dampened in white spirit and allow it to dry before applying paint. This removes dust particles and improves the overall finish.

- **Window guards** – If you find producing a precise edge between rebate and glass particularly difficult, it may be worth using a window guard. These specially designed pieces of metal or plastic can be held along the junction of glass and wood, positioned to shield the glass surface so that paint is applied only to the wood. However, after painting each rebate, the edge of the window guard or shield should be cleaned with a cloth to remove excess paint, and prevent it being transferred to the glass surface when it is next positioned.

- **Drying time** – Always allow sufficient drying time for paint. Closing the window too early will almost certainly lead to it sticking shut.

2 Move on to complete the rest of the small opening casement, first painting the horizontal rails, and then the vertical ones. Remember always to keep the brush bristles in line with the direction of the wood

grain, depending on which section of the casement is being painted. This creates a neat finish between vertical and horizontal rails.

3 Now move on to the larger opening casement, beginning once again with the window rebates. Start painting the top panes and work down the window rebates to the bottom level of the pane.

4 You can now finish painting the opening casement by completing the central horizontal and vertical rails. The very last parts that are left to be painted are the outer vertical rails on the hinged side and the leading edge of the casement.

decorative finishes

412

5 Then paint the fixed casements, starting on the rebates first before finishing with the open faces of the rails.

6 Next, paint around the internal rebates of the main window frame, between the outer edge of the frame and the casements themselves. When working next to the opening casements, be sure to paint a precise dividing line so that there is no untidy overspill on the window edges.

7 Finally, complete the main face of the window by painting the outer frame. Similar accuracy is required here for painting the rebates

next to the glass. Always produce a precise dividing line between the window frame and the wall surface.

8 With the window complete, the sill may be painted to provide the overall finished product.

It is worth noting that painting the exterior of a window is very similar to the interior, except the rebates may be putty or wood. The technique used will remain very much the same.

sash windows

Painting sash windows follows similar principles as for casements, starting next to the glass and working out towards the frame being the best method. The main problem with sashes is when painting the runners, as this tends to be the area where sticking may occur and hinder the mechanism of the window. It is therefore worth inspecting the runners closely before beginning to paint – if they do not require re-coating, then it is not worth painting them purely for the sake of it. Bear in mind that the runners are obscured most of the time, and it is better to have them functioning easily than stuck fast because of layers of paint build-up. From an aesthetic point of view as well, efforts should be concentrated on window parts that are most visible.

A well painted window provides clean, crisp lines which show good attention to detail, enhancing the overall look of the room decoration.

paint effects ⚲

The popularity of paint effects has never been greater and manufacturers are responding to this demand by producing various tools, equipment and materials. One of the most important materials is the scumble – quality paint effects tend to be as dependent on this as they are on the technique or correct equipment. Some techniques are slightly more difficult than others, so it is worth bearing in mind the level of skill required, when choosing which effect to have.

tools for the job

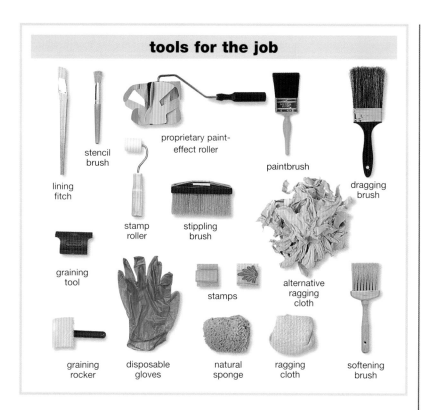

lining fitch

stencil brush

proprietary paint-effect roller

paintbrush

dragging brush

stamp roller

stippling brush

graining tool

graining rocker

disposable gloves

stamps

natural sponge

alternative ragging cloth

ragging cloth

softening brush

colour, which then cannot be mixed 'back', and so leads to unnecessary wastage of materials.

dilution considerations

Remember that the strength of colorizer pigment in a small area will be diluted when added to a large quantity of glaze. Therefore, bear in mind that although the pigment of colorizers is very strong, once applied to the wall there will be some dilution of the effect.

quantities

Directions will vary between manufacturers in terms of how much pigment is required and how much coverage the glaze will provide on the wall surface. However, although glaze does go a lot further than traditional paints, remember that if you run out it will be nearly impossible to re-mix a glaze exactly the same. Therefore, always mix up more than the required amount, to ensure that this situation cannot arise. Any leftover mixture can always be stored in an airtight container for future projects.

mixing colours

The majority of paint effects are created using transparent glaze. This is the medium that provides the textured or three-dimensional effect that makes paint effects appealing. Traditionalists would argue that the glaze should be oil-based, but by far the most user-friendly are acrylic- or water-based equivalents. These can simply be bought off the shelf so that mixing colour becomes a basic process of adding pigment or colorizers to the glaze in order to achieve the shade you require.

However, some caution and instruction is required for this process, in order to avoid wastage and be sure

that the colour you mix will actually be the colour you require on the final wall surface.

adding colorizer

Before adding colour to the scumble, mix colorizers to produce the shade you require. It is unlikely that your perfect colour requirement will be that of a particular tube of colorizer so mixing is nearly always necessary. Then add some of your mixed colour to a small quantity of scumble on a mixing palette, so that you can test it on a discreet area or spare board. Skipping this process, and adding colorizer directly to large quantities of scumble can lead to a scumble being mixed to the wrong

techniques

Most paint effects are categorized by whether they involve 'on' or 'off' techniques. The former involves using a tool to apply the effect directly to the wall, whereas the latter involves applying glaze to the wall with a normal paintbrush before using a tool to apply an effect in the glaze. The same tool may be used in both techniques, but with a completely different finished effect. For example, the finish produced by sponging 'on' is markedly different to that of sponging 'off'. However, not all tools can be used for both methods and some are more clearly suited to one technique or the other.

sponging 'on'

Dip a dampened natural sponge into wet glaze and remove any excess before lightly applying the sponge to the wall surface. Change your wrist angle and sponge direction as you progress across the wall in order to achieve a totally random effect. Wash out the sponge periodically.

ragging 'off'

Apply glaze to the wall with a paint brush and use a crumpled, dampened rag to make impressions of the rag in the glazed surface. Change your hand angle and the position of the rag to maintain a random effect. Only work

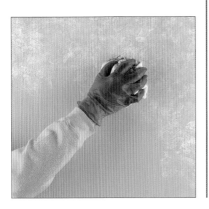

in areas of 1m² (1yd²) at a time, otherwise the glaze will dry before you get a chance to make the impressions. Use a new rag (or wash the old one) when it becomes clogged with glaze.

stippling

Really only an 'off' technique, apply glaze to the wall before using a stippling brush to make fine, textured imprints in the glaze surface. Keep the bristles of the brush at right angles to the wall surface at all times. Again, only work in areas of 1m² (1yd²) at a time, and remove excess glaze from the bristles at regular intervals.

colourwashing

Probably the most simple of 'off' paint effects, colourwashing involves brushing on the glaze and using the texture of the brush to produce the finished effect. Brush strokes can be used randomly or in a uniform manner depending on taste. Also, more than one coat may be applied to build up the overall depth of finish.

STAMPING

Stamps (like stencils) provide a method of applying a definite image to a wall surface. The design can be anything decorative and may be combined with other types of paint effects – used over the top of them – or applied direct to plain, painted walls.

● Apply paint to the back face of the stamp using a specially designed foam roller. Test the stamp on scrap paper before applying it to the wall, in order to check that you have the correct amount of paint for the depth of finish you require.

● Apply the stamp to the wall, ensuring that it is at right angles and does not slip on the wall surface and therefore smudge the image. Remove the stamp at right angles from the wall surface, and then move on to the next position. Paint can be reapplied between each stamp application or, alternatively, every two to three applications, which helps to produce a softer, more random effect.

wallpapering techniques ⁊⁊

Wallpapering requires a methodical approach, with close attention to detail. It is important to take time when choosing your paper, ensuring that it suits aesthetic requirements and that you will feel confident applying it. Some papers are easier to use than others and subtle patterns can make accurate lining up particularly difficult, but careful practice should make the process easier.

tools for the job

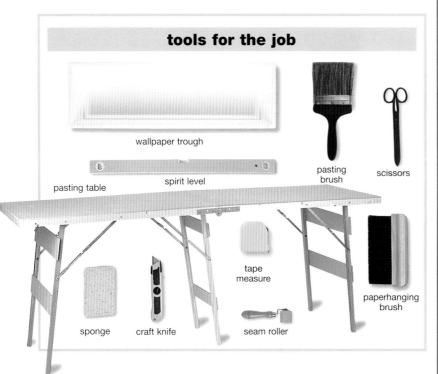

wallpaper trough

spirit level

pasting brush

scissors

pasting table

tape measure

paperhanging brush

sponge

craft knife

seam roller

Try to decide on a starting point that allows the first length of paper to be a full one – that is to say, the only trimming required will be at the top and bottom edges. The exact starting position will depend on the particular room shape. With most papers it is best to start near a corner, because if a join is required it is least noticeable when positioned on a corner junction. With large patterns, the design should be centred on any prominent walls such as a chimney breast, so that a balanced effect will be created.

1 Use a spirit level to draw a vertical line from ceiling to floor – this will provide a guideline for positioning the first length.

2 Apply paste to the back of the first length of paper (if required) and position it so that the edge runs down the vertical guideline. Use a paperhanging brush to remove air bubbles, brushing the paper out from the centre towards the edges.

3 Use a craft knife to trim lengths at both ceiling and floor level. For the best results, trim slightly on to the ceiling and skirting board respectively, so that when the paper is brushed into place, the best looking finish is produced.

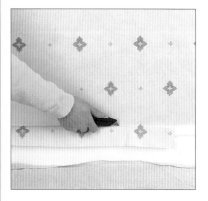

4 Always butt join the lengths and make the pattern meet at eye level. It normally follows that the pattern will match along the entire length, but occasionally 'pattern drop' does occur. In these instances, it is better to have the best match where the paper is most seen, in other words at eye level.

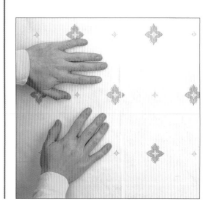

ceilings

Ceilings are sometimes lined to improve their finish, or they may be wallpapered as a further decorative option. In both cases, it is important to begin in the correct place and to paper across the longest dimension, thus minimizing the number of joins. Obstacles, such as light fittings, must also be taken into account. You will need at least two pairs of hands and should pay extra attention to safety:

- Construct a safe access platform with planks over stable trestles spaced every 1.5m.
- Turn off electricity at the consumer unit when working around electrical fittings.

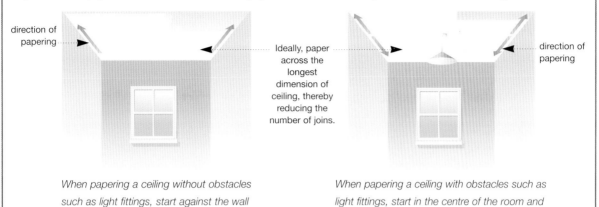

direction of papering

Ideally, paper across the longest dimension of ceiling, thereby reducing the number of joins.

direction of papering

When papering a ceiling without obstacles such as light fittings, start against the wall and work across the surface area.

When papering a ceiling with obstacles such as light fittings, start in the centre of the room and work away from the pendant in both directions.

invisible joins

In some circumstances, butt joining lengths may be impossible. On an external corner, for example, the length of paper becomes slightly creased because it cannot round the corner and still remain vertical.

1 Allow the length to overlap on to the previous one, matching the pattern on the overlap.

2 Using a craft knife and straight-edge – a spirit level is ideal – cut through the centre of the overlap from ceiling to floor.

3 Peel back the edges of the full lengths and remove the two strips of excess paper. Then brush the edges back into place to reveal a perfect join between the two lengths.

PREPARING TO PAPER

Before applying paper to the walls, it is necessary to run through a few standard checks and procedures.

- **Paper type** – Determine whether the paper is ready-pasted or whether the back requires paste application. Although the technique for hanging both is similar, the tool and material requirements vary slightly.

- **Batches** – Always check that the rolls display the same batch numbers. This is because there may be a slight shading difference between manufactured batches.

- **Cutting** – When cutting paper, always allow for the size of the pattern repeat and a small excess for trimming purposes at each end.

- **Lining** – Walls should generally be lined with lining paper before wallpaper is applied. Check the manufacturer's guidelines on the particular wallpaper you are using for their recommendations.

417

applying decorative wall panelling ⚒⚒⚒

Proprietary decorative wall panels offer a lightweight alternative to wooden cladding such as tongue and groove. The application procedure is more similar to that of wallpaper than constructional wood panelling, although the panels are supplied in specific sizes and are generally designed to cover only the dado level in a room.

planning

The pre-determined size and patterning of this type of panelling means that you will need to plan its positioning quite carefully. The aim should be to keep joins in discreet areas, so try to join full panels in corners that are seen every day, and join half panels in corners that are less obvious.

tools for the job

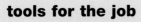

spirit level
pencil
tape measure
pasting brush and table
sponge
paperhanging brush
craft knife
hammer

1 Decide on the best starting position and draw a vertical guideline on the wall with a spirit level.

2 The back of the panels must be soaked with water and left for approximately 20 minutes before paste can be applied. A systematic approach therefore needs to be developed so that while one panel is soaking, another is being applied. It can be a good idea to pencil the timings on the back of the panels, so that you can guage accurately when each one is ready for pasting.

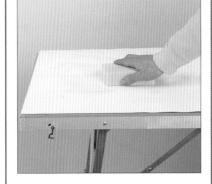

3 Use a proprietary paste on the back of the panels, taking care to ensure that the entire surface has an even coverage of the paste. Work

the brush from the centre out to the edges of the panel, and try to avoid getting any paste on the table. Any overspill should be removed with a damp sponge.

4 Apply the first panel to the wall using the pencil guidelines for positioning. Use a paperhanging brush to remove air bubbles as you run the brush across the entire panel surface. The bottom edge of the panel should sit flush along the top of the skirting.

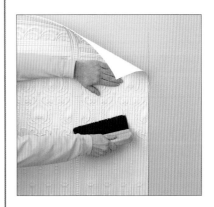

5 Join subsequent panels using the same technique, butting the edges tightly together. However, take care not to allow any overlaps because these will show up clearly in the finished effect – a slight gap is actually preferable to overlap.

👍 tips of the trade

Once in position, panels must be primed with an oil-based undercoat before further coats and decorative effects can be applied.

fielded panelling

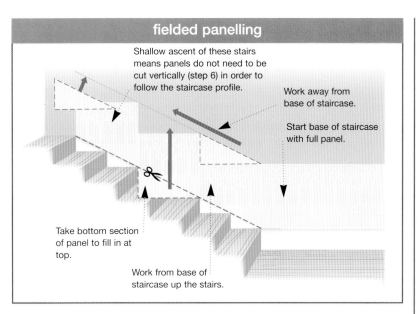

Shallow ascent of these stairs means panels do not need to be cut vertically (step 6) in order to follow the staircase profile.

Work away from base of staircase.

Start base of staircase with full panel.

Take bottom section of panel to fill in at top.

Work from base of staircase up the stairs.

6 At the stairwell, cut panels vertically in half and continue to apply them up the staircase. Use the paperhanging brush to mould the bottom section of the panel into the staircase profile. Trim any excess along the junction with a craft knife.

7 Take the trimmed excess from the bottom section of the panel and butt join it at the top of the same

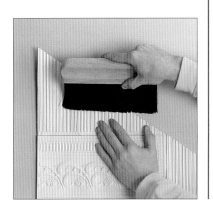

panel. The angle of ascent of the 'panelling' edge should relate directly to the angle of ascent of the staircase. (The diagram above illustrates how these panels should be cut and fitted.)

8 To finish the top edge of the panelling, apply a dado rail (see pages 428–9). The rail should slightly overlap the panelling, so that a neat, precise finish is produced.

9 Finally, caulk all the joints in the panelling to produce a smooth finish and prevent edges lifting at a later date. Remove excess caulk with a damp sponge.

Decorative wall panelling makes an attractive finish in any room, and looks particularly effective when used on stairwells with a matching dado rail.

tiling techniques ✗✗✗

In addition to being decorative, tiles clearly offer a practical wall covering option. Easy to clean and hardwearing, their use tends to be concentrated in areas such as the kitchen and bathroom. When applying tiles to the wall, emphasis must be put on keeping the level or vertical line to ensure a balanced effect, in much the same way as wallpapering. Actual application requires a methodical technique combining meticulous planning as well as accurate measuring and cutting.

PREPARING TO TILE

Before tiling, it is important to be fully prepared, organizing your order of work, to minimize mistakes and confusion.

- **Checking tiles** – Always open boxes of tiles before purchasing to ensure that there are no breakages.

- **Shuffling** – When using single-coloured tiles for the entire or major part of a design, mix up or shuffle the tiles between boxes so that any slight colour variations will be evenly spread across the tiled surface and therefore invisible to the naked eye.

- **Tile gauge** – To help decide on starting points, make a tile gauge from a piece of wooden batten. Lay a line of tiles out dry on a flat surface (allowing for spacers) and hold a piece of batten along their length. Use a pencil to mark off the joints between the tiles on the batten. Now hold the batten against the wall and use it as a gauge to determine the most suitable position for the tile layout. It also lets you plan cuts at the most suitable places and achieve a balanced effect.

- **Spacers** – Spacers are normally supplied in sheets which need to be broken up before use. It is therefore best to break up a number of sheets before you begin to tile, so that time isn't wasted when actually applying tiles to the wall surface.

- **Keeping clean** – Tiling can be a messy business: always keep a bucket of clean water to hand so that surfaces and tools can be kept clean at all times.

tools for the job

tile saw

tile cutting machine

grout spreader

sponge

grout raker

tile nippers

grout shaper

adhesive spreader

There are a few simple guidelines which may be applied to the majority of tiling projects.

1 The top of skirting board is rarely precisely level, nor is it the best point to apply the first row of tiles. Therefore, nail a piece of batten in position above the skirting board using a spirit level as a guide. This acts as a support for the tiles, preventing them from slipping down the wall surface. Once the main body of tiles is complete and dry, the batten is removed and cut tiles can be used to fill the area above the skirting board.

2 Spacers must be used to maintain the distance between tiles. On the open wall surface, these

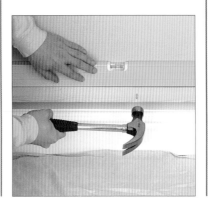

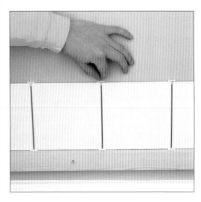

tiling sequence

Although each room differs, there is a basic order of tiling that will help to achieve the best finish.

1 Apply full tiles.
2 Fill in around obstacles.
3 Complete corners.
4 When main design is dry, fill in cut tiles at bottom of wall.
5 Apply border tiles if required.

1 Lay full tiles.

2 Fill in around obstacles.

5 Apply border tiles if required.

4 Use cut tiles at the bottom of the wall.

3 Complete corners.

definite scratch through the glazed surface of the tile.

2 Design varies between tile cutters, but the general principle of breaking the tile along the scored line involves applying weight to either side of the line, causing it to crack precisely along the cut.

will remain in place and can be grouted over. At the bottom level, they can be positioned flat on the batten, and remain in position until the tile adhesive has dried. They may then be removed along with the batten.

3 When grouting, always use a grout spreader (never your fingers), moving it in all directions across the tiles to press the grout firmly into every joint. Remove the excess from the tiles as you progress.

4 Wipe down the tiled surface with a damp sponge before using a grout shaper to tool the joints and provide a neat finish. Run the shaper

along the joint to smooth the grout between each of the tiles.

cutting tiles

Cuts can be divided into two simple categories – those that are straight and those which have a curve.

straight cuts

1 Although hand held tile cutters can be used for this purpose, a tile cutting machine is the ideal tool for accuracy and ease of use. Measure off the size of the required cut and score along this line to produce a

curved cuts

Cutting curves involves the use of a specially designed tile saw. Clearly mark the curved guideline on the tile and clamp it in a workbench before cutting through the tile using the saw.

tiling a splashback ⚞⚞⚞

If bathroom or kitchen walls are not fully tiled, a splashback may be necessary behind a basin, hob or kitchen sink. The key to achieving a good result is to make sure that the splashback is centrally positioned in relation to the basin. You can then centre the first tile on this central point and tile outwards from there, or use the centre point as a joint between the first two tiles, again working outwards.

tools for the job

tape measure & pencil
mini level
notched spreader
electric tile-cutting machine
grout spreader (optional)
protective gloves
sponge
sealant gun or dispenser

1 Measure the back edge of the basin and mark the centre point.

2 Draw a pencil guideline upwards from this point. Use a mini level to make sure that the line is vertical.

3 Mark the middle of the first tile along its top edge. This mark is only required for positioning purposes so it can be wiped off later. Apply some adhesive to the back of the tile using a small notched spreader.

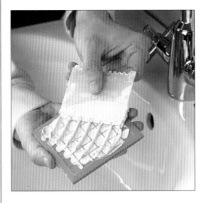

4 Position the tile by making sure that the pencil mark corresponds exactly with the vertical pencil guideline on the wall.

5 Continue to apply tiles to the wall, using spacers in joints to maintain a consistent gap between tiles. The back edge of many basins is curved. This makes tiling slightly more difficult because you will need to place card beneath the edge of

the first row of tiles to maintain the correct level for the tiles. The amount of card used at a particular point depends on how much is required to keep the row level. Likewise, when border tiles are added, card will need to be used under the first ones on either side of the design in order to maintain the correct height.

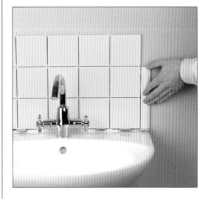

6 It is usually necessary to cut border tiles at the corner of the splashback. A good effect is achieved by making mitred joints. For relief border tiles, as shown here, it is best to use an electrically operated tile-cutting machine. Again, wear protective goggles and follow the manufacturer's instructions.

7 Once the first mitred tile has been positioned, measure the next tile by holding it in place and marking the points at which the tile needs to be cut.

8 Position the tile, judging a joint between the mitre that is equal to the gaps between the tiles in the main part of the design.

9 Once the design is complete, allow to dry, then grout. It can be easier to use your fingers rather than a spreader to push the grout into place on tiles with a raised surface, but always wear protective gloves.

10 When you have finished grouting, apply a silicone sealant strip along the back edge of the basin. Use the technique described on page 391.

tips of the trade

• **Full tiles** – Ideally, you should only use full tiles in a splashback design because there is no way of hiding from view cut tiles that can mar the overall look of the basin. It does not usually matter if tiles overhang the edge of the basin slightly and, in many cases, a row of border tiles can provide an attractive frame.

• **Spacers** – When using spacers in conjunction with relief border tiles, it is not possible to insert them into joints flat against the wall. Instead, insert them at right angles to the wall surface and remove them once the adhesive has dried.

A tiled splashback provides a practical and decorative feature that highlights and complements a basin design.

adding to existing tiles ✂✂

An easy way to change the look of your bathroom or kitchen is to alter the existing tile layout. In many instances, even if tiles still look new and bright, a slight update in appearance can work wonders. The examples shown here should only be carried out on sound existing tile surfaces. If tiles are coming away from the wall or are poorly fitted, then you should remove the old ones and begin from scratch (see also pages 392–3 for how to remove tiles).

tile transfers

A bank of clean white tiles may look good in some bathrooms, but using tile transfers to add pattern to a bland tile surface can be an attractive option if you wish to brighten up the room. The exact method of application can vary slightly between manufacturers but the principles of soaking and positioning transfers remains similar.

tools for the job

sponge

bucket

cloth

1 The first job is to make sure that the tile surface is completely clean by wiping away all traces of dirt or grime with a sponge.

2 Soak the transfer in a bucket of clean warm water making sure that the entire sheet is immersed. Read the manufacturer's guidelines for the required soaking time.

3 Remove the transfer from the bucket and shake off excess water. Position the transfer on the tile.

4 When happy with the position, slide off the backing paper to leave the transfer image on the tile.

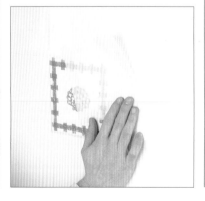

tips of the trade

Do not position transfers in areas that are prone to abrasion. Although they are fairly robust once dry, they cannot withstand regular rigorous cleaning. It is a good idea to buy a few extra transfers so that you can replace any that may get damaged, although this problem will not arise if you choose to apply a selection of designs.

5 Dab the image with a dry cloth to remove excess water and smooth away air bubbles.

painting tiles

A simple way of changing tile appearance is to paint them a new colour or a combination of colours. Tile primers are now available that make this process possible and allow a durable finish to be achieved.

tools for the job

sponge

paintbrush

1 Sand the tiled surface to provide a key for the paint. Clean any dust or grime with a mild detergent and rinse with clean warm water. Allow the surface to dry completely.

2 Paint tile primer over the entire tiled surface. When dry, you can apply your chosen emulsion, eggshell or gloss paint.

👍

tips of the trade

If you use emulsion paint, varnish over the top to increase its durability.

adding picture tiles

Another way to liven up an existing area of tiles is to remove some of them and replace them with picture or patterned tiles. The technique for removing tiles is shown in more detail on pages 392–3, where broken tiles are removed before new ones are put in their places.

---

tools for the job

grout raker
cordless drill/driver
protective gloves & goggles
club hammer
cold chisel
notched spreader
grout spreader

1 Use a grout raker to scrape away as much grout as possible from around the edges of the tiles that are to be removed. Drill a number of holes through the surface of the tiles to weaken their structure, then use a club hammer and cold chisel to knock out the broken sections of tile. Remember to wear protective gloves and goggles.

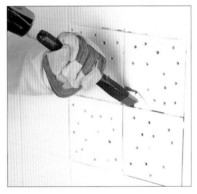

2 Apply adhesive to the wall and press the new tile into position. Use spacers to maintain the gap around its edge while the adhesive dries. When completely dry, remove the spacers and grout the joints.

A quick, inexpensive way of changing the appearance of a tiled surface is to use plastic tile sheets. These are easy to apply and can be used over existing tile surfaces.

tools for the job

notched spreader
scissors
grout spreader

1 Use a notched spreader to apply adhesive to the back of the sheets making coverage as even as possible.

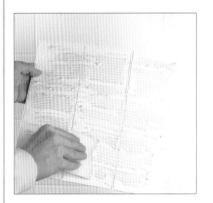

2 Press the sheets into position. The number of tiles on each sheet means that a large area can be covered very quickly. The sheets can be cut with scissors to fill in gaps around the edge of a design. Once the adhesive has dried, apply grout.

adding to existing tiles

425

fitting tongue & groove panelling

The use of tongue and groove panelling is an extremely effective way of transforming a wall surface and making a room feel warm and inviting. The panelling can be applied across entire walls or just up to dado level, as in the example demonstrated here. Applying panelling is a two-part process – first you need to build a framework onto which the boards will be applied, then you must cut the boards to fit the space and fix them in place.

tools for the job

pencil

tape measure

spirit level

panel saw

cordless drill/driver

hammer

nail punch

mitresaw

building the framework

Tongue and groove panelling should be attached to a batten framework. Although 5 x 2.5cm (2 x 1in) battens are often ideal, it can be advantageous to use slightly larger battens such as 5 x 5cm (2 x 2in) so that a shelf can be formed across the top of the panelling for extra storage. Another advantage is that they produce deep panelling, which means that pipes attached to the wall can often run beneath the framework.

1 A good height for dado panelling is approximately 1m (1yd) above floor level. For these dimensions, three horizontal battens should be fixed to the wall surface, one at floor level, one at the required height for the top of the panelling and one about halfway between the two. Draw guidelines for these battens using a spirit level to make sure that they are horizontal.

2 Fix the battens to the wall surface using the guidelines for positioning. In this case, concrete anchors are inserted directly through the battens into the masonry wall below. For hollow walls, use the correct wall plugs and screw fixings to hold the battens in place.

3 To deal with any pipes, cut batten lengths so that a gap is left to allow the pipe to run down through the framework.

attaching the panelling

The structure of tongue and groove panelling allows it to be fitted in place so that the actual fixing points are hidden from view. In simple terms, small nails or panel pins (depending on the thickness of the panelling) are inserted at 45° angles through the tongue of a board to hold it in place. The groove of the next board covers this tongue and, therefore, the fixing. When applying boards it is best to start at an internal corner and have a number of boards cut to size before you begin so that progress is swift. However, be aware of the fact that small undulations or slopes in the floor may mean that you need different heights of board if the top of the panelling is to be neat and level.

tips of the trade

Remember to make access hatches in the panelling for any stopcocks or shut-off valves, so that the water supply can be turned off easily in an emergency.

1 Position the first board using a spirit level to check that it is completely vertical.

2 Fix the first board to the battens through the top, middle and bottom of its face. Only hidden fixings should be necessary with all subsequent boards.

3 Knock nails through the tongue of the board and use a nail punch to make sure that the head disappears below wood surface level.

tips of the trade

• **Selective panelling** – On walls that have a number of kitchen or bathroom fittings, building a framework and panelling can be a complicated procedure. It is often worth panelling only those walls that are relatively free from obstacles.

• **Decoration** – Tongue and groove panelling can be finished with paint or coated with a natural wood stain or varnish to complement the existing decoration in the room.

4 Keep adding boards, slipping the groove of the new length over the tongue of the previous one, and inserting nails along the tongue of the new board.

5 You will need to add a decorative moulding at external corners to cover the joint. This can either be glued or nailed in position.

6 To finish the top of the panelling, cut some 7.5 x 2.5cm (3 x 1in) batten, mitring the joints neatly at the corners. This produces a much more attractive and professional finish than butting the straight edges.

7 Fix the 7.5 x 2.5cm (3 x 1in) batten in place by inserting screws or nails through the batten into the 5 x 5cm (2 x 2in) batten below to secure it in position.

8 Add a decorative moulding around the underside of the 7.5 x 2.5cm (3 x 1in) batten for a more attractive result.

ALTERNATIVE EDGING

Instead of using moulding, you can achieve a simpler finish by routing the edge of the top batten.

fitting decorative rails ↗↗

Decorative rails present a further way of adding character to walls. The rail shape tends to be determined by its function – a picture rail usually has an upturned top edge to provide a stable base for the hook, while dado rails are traditionally used to prevent chairs from damaging the wall surface and so have a rounded surface. Generally, dado rails are fitted about 1m from floor level and picture rails are positioned between 20cm (8in) and 50cm (20in) from the ceiling.

decorative finishes

fitting a dado rail

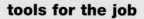

Dado rails tend to be the most popular choice of fitting, as many modern houses do not have the height to accommodate picture rails. Dado rails can be applied in rooms with low or high ceilings, and still produce an excellent effect.

tools for the job

tape measure
pencil
spirit level
mitresaw
hammer or cordless drill/driver
nail punch
sealant gun
sponge

1 Draw a horizontal guideline around the wall perimeter using a pencil and spirit level. Measure the wall dimensions and calculate the required lengths for each wall. Be sure to get the end of the tape measure right into the corner junctions.

2 Clamp the rail into the mitre saw (to ensure a precise cut) and cut the required lengths.

3 Apply bonding adhesive to the back of the rail. Allow the adhesive to run down the central portion, so that when it comes into contact with the wall it will spread from the centre towards the edges.

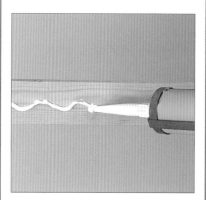

4 Press the rail in position allowing the pencil guideline to run along the bottom edge of the rail. Continue to press in position along the rail length, so that total contact between the rail and wall is achieved. Use a sponge to remove any excess adhesive that squeezes out.

5 Nail or screw fixings along the length of the rail to hold it firmly in position, and punch in the nail heads below the rail surface level. Continue to join lengths around the rest of the room.

👍 tips of the trade

When a rail is to remain unpainted and have a natural appearance, avoid using permanent nail fixings which will be easily visible. Instead, just apply a strong contact adhesive that will hold the rail permanently in position while it dries. Some extra support may be given during the drying process by taping over the rail – the tape will help to bear the weight of the rail.

6 Apply a bead of caulk along the top edge of the dado rail, smoothing it into the joint with a wetted finger. This will help to cover any small cracks and produce a better surface finish for decorating.

7 Also apply caulk to corner joints, especially where mitre joints are not totally tight. Nail heads may then be filled with an all-purpose filler and carefully sanded to a smooth finish before decoration.

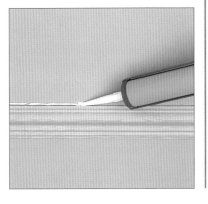

Decorative rails provide an attractive feature which divides wallspace while adding character to a room design and decoration.

tips of the trade

Strongly coloured wall surfaces or rails tend to eliminate the need for caulking along the edges of the rail/wall junction. This is because the strong colour should overshadow any slight cracks along the joint.

DECORATION

• **Wallpapering** – If the rail is to divide two types of wallpaper, or there is to be a particularly strong contrast between the rail colour and the wall, it can be best to paint or stain the rail before it is fixed in position.

Apply wallpaper to the surface before fitting the rail. Even if the rail is to divide two different papers, it is possible to use only rough joins, as the rail will cover this area.

• **Staining** – For a natural wood finish such as a stain, apply two coats to the rail before cutting and fitting it, so that there is no need to encounter a particularly fiddly staining process along the edge of the rail. This early staining means that you should not have to cut in too closely to the paper when applying a final top coat. This theory doesn't just apply to natural wood finishes, but can also be applied to painting.

• **Painting** – If you plan to paint the rail in a strong colour, mask off both sides of the wall surface.

Remember that applying rails after wall decoration does make reparation of any scrapes or wall damage more difficult, so take extra care when offering up and applying the rail.

fitting decorative rails

429

creating a textured ceiling finish ⚒

Various types of finish may be added to flat ceiling surfaces to produce a textured or patterned effect. These coatings can be used on dry lined or plastered ceilings, or even over rougher, undulating surfaces, helping to create a more attractive finish. However, textured coatings should never be applied over the top of wallpaper or lining paper, and they must only be applied to ceilings that have been sealed and are therefore stable enough for this type of coating.

tools for the job

There are various specific tools available for creating a textured finish. Not all of these pieces will be required – the tools you use depend upon the the type of texture or pattern you are planning to create (see below).

block brush

standard comb

combination comb

mixing tool

stippler

rough trowel

pattern roller

caulking blade

such imperfections will affect the ability of the textured finish to adhere to the ceiling properly.

2 Mix the textured coating in a bucket. Follow the manufacturer's instructions regarding the amount of water required to add to the powder. Although the coating can be mixed by hand, it is much easier to use a mixing tool attached to a drill.

stippling a ceiling

Once the coating has been applied to the ceiling, a specific tool is required to create the finish. Combs or trowels may be used, but in this case a stippler has been employed to produce a stippled ceiling effect.

👍 tips of the trade

If possible work from a sturdy platform, moving gradually across the ceiling surface. Stepladders may be used, but this will involve a lot of effort getting up and down.

1 On plasterboarded ceilings, make sure that all the joints between the separate boards are taped with self-adhesive jointing tape. Check that the tape is firmly stuck down and that there are no ripples or creases, as

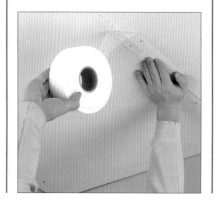

TRADITIONAL TAPING

Instead of using self-adhesive tape, it is possible to use a more traditional method of taping, with standard jointing tape. Standard jointing tape needs to be soaked in water before use. It is then applied to the joints between the plasterboard sheets in a similar way to the tape above.

3 Use a caulking blade to apply a band of textured coating over the plasterboard joints and any nail heads in the ceiling surface. Allow this area to dry thoroughly before coating the rest of the surface.

4 Use a block brush to apply the main coating to the ceiling surface. Apply a thick, even coat to ensure total coverage and a consistent depth. Work in areas of approximately 1m² (1yd²) at a time, in order to prevent the mixture from drying.

👍

tips of the trade

It is a good idea to have two people working on the surface at any one time – as one person applies the coating, the other can use the stippler. This helps to ensure the coating always has a wet edge and that the job is finished in one go, without any dried, patchy areas. It may also pay to practise the technique on a scrap piece of plasterboard, before commencing work on the ceiling. This is especially important when using combs, as the technique can take time to master.

5 Take the stippler and press it into the surface coating at right angles to the ceiling. Lift away, again at right angles to the surface, and move to the adjacent coated area. Overlap the stippled impressions slightly to produce an even, random effect. Change the angle of the face of the stippler on the surface for an even greater random effect. Repeat steps 4 and 5 across the ceiling surface until the whole area is complete.

6 Finish off around the ceiling edge by dampening a 2.5cm (1in) brush and drawing it through the wet coating. This provides a neat border to the coating.

👍

tips of the trade

Once dry, textured coatings can be left uncoated, but you can add a matt or silk finish if you prefer.

These coatings provide an effective finish on a ceiling, giving depth and texture to what is normally a flat, rather two-dimensional area in a room.

fitting curtains & blinds ✂✂

Your choice of window dressing will depend on the decorative style you want for your room, as well as the amount of space you have available for the window dressing. You will also need to consider the amount of light and privacy required.

The type of room in which the window dressing will hang also requires some thought. Voluminous, billowing curtains can be very attractive in a living room or bedroom but would not be a practical option in a kitchen or bathroom. They are particularly unsuitable over a worktop, unless the hanging system and length of curtains is considered very carefully. In those situations blinds that fit into the window recess and can be adjusted to provide light and privacy as required are more practical.

tools for the job

tape measure & pencil
straight edge &/or spirit level
cordless drill/driver
screwdriver

curtains

When choosing fabric for curtains also consider practicality. For kitchens, bathrooms and other rooms subject to variable humidity, hard wearing and washable fabrics are essential. Curtains may be hung on either a track or a pole.

curtain tracks

Tracks tend to be regarded as the less attractive type of curtain rail and as such are normally kept discretely hidden by ensuring that the head of the curtain covers the track as much as possible. Tracks represent a good

choice where space is limited, however, since they hold the curtain tight against the wall or window.

1 Draw a level guideline above the window to indicate the position of the track. Using a spirit level for a straight edge is the easiest way to ensure a level line. Curtain tracks require frequent fixing points in order to support the curtain weight. Mark off equidistant points along the line and drill and plug these positions.

2 Screw in the brackets along this line making sure the brackets are the right way up and that they bite firmly into the plugged holes.

3 Once all the brackets have been fixed in place, clip the curtain track onto the front of them. You will need to position the track so that it overhangs either side of the window by an equal amount. Now simply fit track gliders and hang the curtain.

curtain poles

A curtain pole offers a more ornate hanging system than tracks. You will usually find that the ends of the pole are embellished with finials, and in many cases the curtain head is deliberately made to hang below the pole so that its decorative qualities are always in view. A major drawback is that a pole will cause the curtain to encroach further into the room, but provided space is not a problem in your room, then poles can be an ideal choice for hanging curtains.

Fit a bracket at each corner of the window to hold the pole in place. For large windows you may need to fit a central bracket as well to support the

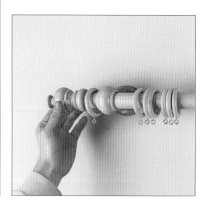

weight of the curtain. The curtain is usually hung with rings, with a finial attached to both ends of the pole in order to prevent the curtain from falling off.

blinds

Types of blinds include simple roller blinds and roman blinds that can be raised or lowered to control light, as well as venetian (or slatted) blinds and vertical blinds, both of which are ideal where privacy is an issue.

Blinds are normally made from some form of easy-to-clean material. They are generally supplied in a kit form that involves fixing brackets to the window frame.

1 Measure the width of the window before buying your blind to make sure of the correct requirement. It is very important to take measurements all the way down the window, not just at the top, as distortions in the shape of the recess may result in the window being narrower at the bottom. If there is significant distortion then the blind must be bought with the narrowest measurement in mind so that it will fit comfortably within the window recess.

2 Fit the fixing brackets in the top corners of the window, screwing into the wooden frame. Make sure that each bracket is positioned the correct way up and at the right corner for each end of the blind.

3 Position the roller blind and then insert each end into the correct bracket. You will notice one bracket is of a different shape to the other, as the fittings on each end of the roller are made to fit with only one of the brackets. Finally, attach a cord pull to the blind so that it may be put into operation.

tips of the trade

Blind kits are sometimes supplied with the blind material separate from the roller. Join the blind to the roller with staples, double-sided tape or double-sided velcro, which is useful for taking the blind down again for cleaning.

A blind was the ideal choice of window dressing for this kitchen, as it rests tight against the window frame and does not intrude into the working area of the sink.

making changes outdoors

While your scope for executing masonry projects indoors is fairly limited, no such restrictions apply in the garden. Here, you can build walls to your heart's content – along boundaries, around a patio, as barriers to retain soil in terraces on a sloping site, or simply to hide a garden eyesore. You can add features such as a garden arch, and link different levels with flights of steps. You can build in brick or stone, creating formal or informal structures to suit the style of your garden. The two key points you need to remember are that every garden structure needs good foundations, and because you are building outside, everything you construct must be thoroughly weatherproof.

planning outdoor
masonry projects ↗↗

Whatever you plan to build in your garden, you need to do some planning and preparatory work first, even if you are just building a straight stretch of wall. This involves deciding what you want to achieve, where to site the various components of your scheme, what materials to use and how to organize the job into practical and achievable stages. You can then estimate and order materials with confidence, and tackle the job in an orderly fashion. You can also prepare the foundations that are essential for any garden structure.

making drawings

If you have a clear idea of what you want to create, buy some graph paper and pencils and start measuring things so that you can make a detailed scale drawing to work to. Begin with a plan so that you know where walls, steps and other features will be built. Add elevations to help you estimate materials accurately. Work to a sensible scale – 1:20 is suitable for most gardens – and use metric measurements for accuracy. Make sure you know the sizes of the various materials you will be using, so that you can use your drawings for estimating quantities.

preparing the site

When you have decided what to build and where to site it, you must do some basic site preparation. Mark out the area of the work with string lines tied to pegs. Remove all plants, grass, weeds and other vegetable matter, and dig away the topsoil, moving it to another part of the garden for redistribution. Cut back the roots of any large trees or shrubs well clear of the working area. As you dig, keep your eyes open for any buried services. Professionally laid cables and pipework should be buried at least 450mm (18in) down, but amateur supplies to garden buildings may have been laid at a far shallower depth.

laying foundations on a sloping site

The foundations should be laid as linked and overlapping steps. Each step should be a whole number of bricks in length, and the step height should be equal to a maximum of three courses of brickwork or one of blockwork (225mm/9in). The upper step should overlap the lower one by the length of two bricks or one block (about 450mm/18in). Peg a board across the trench at the step position to form the edge of the upper step and lay each concrete step in the same way that you would lay a concrete slab on a flat site (see opposite).

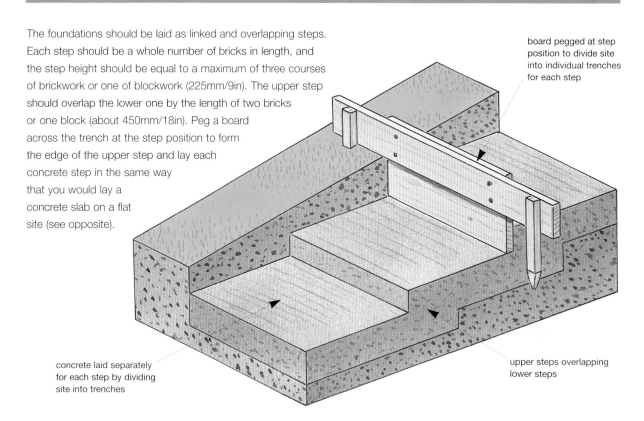

board pegged at step position to divide site into individual trenches for each step

concrete laid separately for each step by dividing site into trenches

upper steps overlapping lower steps

For most garden walls, a concrete strip foundation is all that is required, but its size and positioning are important. It should be a minimum of 150mm (6in) thick, and up to 200mm (8in) thick on clay soils because of the tendency for clay to shrink and swell.

The strip should be placed in a trench 350 to 400mm (14 to 16in) deep, with its top one course of blockwork or three courses of brickwork below ground level. This allows soil to be placed right up to the foot of the wall, and helps protect the foundation from frost or accidental damage by digging close by. The width of the foundation strip should be twice the thickness of the wall you are building, up to a height of about 750mm (30in). For higher walls, increase the strip width to three times the wall thickness.

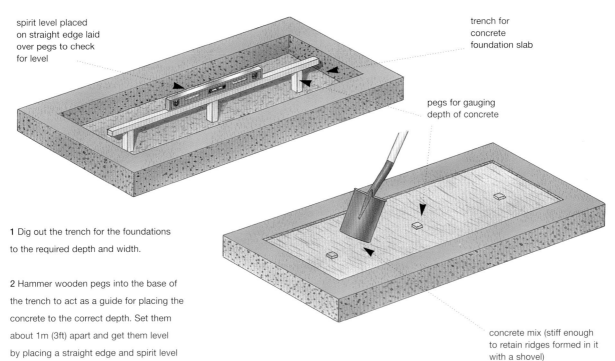

spirit level placed on straight edge laid over pegs to check for level

trench for concrete foundation slab

pegs for gauging depth of concrete

concrete mix (stiff enough to retain ridges formed in it with a shovel)

437

1 Dig out the trench for the foundations to the required depth and width.

2 Hammer wooden pegs into the base of the trench to act as a guide for placing the concrete to the correct depth. Set them about 1m (3ft) apart and get them level by placing a straight edge and spirit level on adjacent pegs.

3 Estimate how much concrete you need for the foundation. For example, the strip for a wall 4m (13ft) long and 1.5m (5ft) high, built in 230mm (9in) thick brickwork on sound subsoil, should be 4.5m (15ft) long, 700mm (27in) wide and 150mm (6in) thick. Its volume is 4.5 x 0.7 x 0.15 cubic metres (15 x 2.25 x 0.5 cubic feet) – that is, 0.47cu m (16.87cu ft). To make this quantity, you will need about two-and-a-half 50kg (110lb) bags of cement and just under 900kg (2000lb) of all-in aggregate.

4 Mix the concrete (see pages 470–1 for more details). For in-ground foundations you should use a mix of 1 part cement, 2.5 parts sharp (concreting) sand and 3.5 parts of 20mm (¾in) aggregate (gravel). If you are buying all-in aggregate (mixed sand and gravel), mix 1 part cement to 5 parts aggregate. Use a bucket to measure the quantities accurately by volume, mix them thoroughly by hand or in a cement mixer, and add water until the mixture is stiff enough to retain ridges formed in it with a shovel.

5 Barrow the concrete to the trench, tip it in and compact it around the pegs. Use a piece of fence post or similar wood held lengthways in the trench to tamp it down, and add more concrete as necessary to get the surface level with the tops of the pegs. Do not worry about any slight irregularities in the surface. You can compensate for these when bedding the first course of masonry on the foundation.

6 Cover the concrete with polythene sheeting if rain or frost threatens, and allow it to harden for at least three days before starting to build on it.

FOUNDATIONS FOR STEPS

If you are building a flight of steps against a retaining wall, calculate its overall size. Then lay a concrete slab 100mm (4in) larger all around than the size of the flight and 100mm (4in) thick (150mm/6in thick on clay soils). See pages 470–3 for more details about laying concrete slabs. If you are building steps in a bank, only the bottom step needs a foundation strip. It should be 300mm (12in) wide, 150mm (6in) thick and 200mm (8in) longer than the width of the steps.

garden walls

Garden walls can mark property boundaries, act as dividers between different levels of the garden on sloping sites, or form self-contained planters and other garden features. Their method of construction varies according to whether their purpose is structural or merely decorative, and whether you are building in brick or blocks. If you are building a garden wall from scratch, its foundations below ground level are as important as its structure above.

foundations

Even the lowest garden wall needs proper in-ground support. In most cases this means excavating topsoil and subsoil, and laying a concrete strip foundation using a mix of 1 part cement to 5 parts combined aggregate (mixed sharp concreting sand and 20mm/³⁄₄in gravel). The strip should be twice as wide as the wall for masonry up to 750mm (29½in) high, and three times the width for higher walls. It should be at least 150mm (6in) thick on all soil types except clay, in which case it should be 200mm (8in) thick because clay is prone to subsidence. Its top surface should be about 230mm (9in) below ground level, so that three courses of bricks or one of blocks can be placed below ground level and planting or turf can be laid next to the wall.

brick walls

The simplest brick garden walls are built as a single layer of brickwork, one brick (102mm/4in) thick. The bricks are laid in stretcher bond, with each brick overlapping those in the course below by half its length. The maximum safe height for this type of construction is 450mm (17³⁄₄in) – six courses of bricks – unless it is supported by piers one brick square at the ends and at 3m (10ft) intervals in between, when a further three courses can be added. A taller wall needs brickwork twice as thick – the length of a brick (215mm/8½in) instead of the width of one. You can build a wall like this to a height of 1.35m (4ft) without piers, and to 1.8m (6ft) with end and intermediate piers one-and-a-half bricks (about 330mm/13in) square. Building a thicker wall means having to adopt a different way of arranging the bricks (see box).

TYPES OF BOND

Three different bonding arrangements are commonly used for garden walls.

• **English bond** – The first course has two rows of parallel stretchers, the second course is formed by headers (bricks laid end-on to the face of the wall). Alternate stretcher and header courses build up the wall. In header courses, a brick split lengthways (queen closer) is used at corners.

• **Flemish bond** – Each course has two parallel stretchers followed by one header. The headers are centred over the pair of stretchers in the course below. Queen closers are used at the ends and corners in alternate courses.

• **English garden wall bond** – The first three, four or five courses are laid as parallel stretchers, followed by a single course of headers. This type of bond is similar to English bond, but it is not as strong because there are not so many courses of headers.

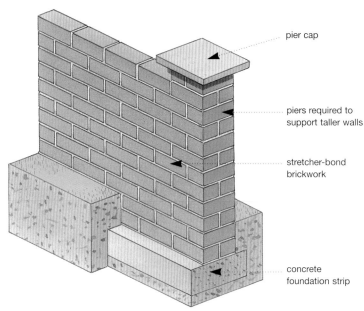

pier cap

piers required to support taller walls

stretcher-bond brickwork

concrete foundation strip

Two types of manufactured blocks are commonly used for garden walls. The first is reconstituted stone. These blocks have one face and one end moulded to resemble natural stone, while the other faces are smooth so the blocks can be laid just like bricks in level courses. Some ranges include blocks of different lengths and heights, creating the appearance of random stonework when laid. The same height restrictions apply as for brickwork, with the provision of piers being necessary for high walls.

The second type is the pierced screen wall block. This is a square block pierced with a variety of simple designs. They are commonly 300mm (11¾in) square and 90mm (3½in) thick, and are designed to be laid in stack bond – in columns and rows with no overlap between the blocks, which obviously cannot be cut to size. The resulting wall is comparatively

weak unless piers are built at 3m (10ft) intervals and metal mesh reinforcement is used in the horizontal mortar joints. Piers can be of brick or solid block, or can be constructed using special matching end, corner and intermediate pier blocks that are

200mm (8in) high and have hollow centres so that they can be erected around reinforcing rods set in the foundation concrete. The maximum wall height is 600mm/23½in (two blocks) without reinforcement, and 1.8m (6ft) with it.

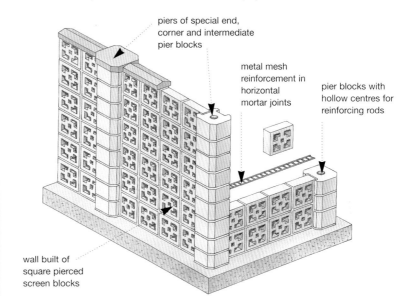

piers of special end, corner and intermediate pier blocks

metal mesh reinforcement in horizontal mortar joints

pier blocks with hollow centres for reinforcing rods

wall built of square pierced screen blocks

Walls used to terrace a sloping garden have to be strong enough to hold back the weight of earth. A low brick wall up to 600mm (23½in) high can be built in 215mm (8½in) thick brickwork, without reinforcement, in one of the bonds described opposite. For a wall up to 1.2m (4ft) high, the wall is built as two layers in stretcher bond, with reinforcing rods set in the foundations and sandwiched between the two walls. For extra strength, the walls are bonded together with cavity wall ties, and the cavity is filled with fine concrete. Walls higher than 1.2m (4ft) must be built by professionals to ensure that they are strong enough to withstand collapse. For this reason, it is better to terrace a sloping site with several low walls forming a series of shallow tiers, rather than to have a single high retaining wall.

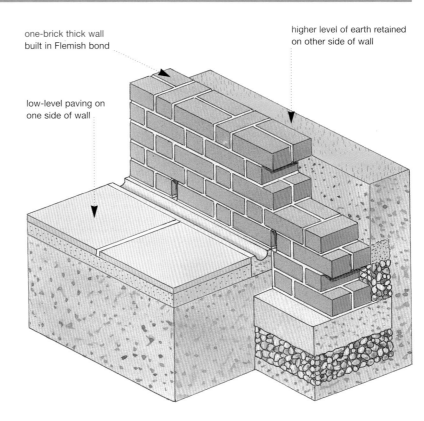

one-brick thick wall built in Flemish bond

higher level of earth retained on other side of wall

low-level paving on one side of wall

building a brick wall – 1 ⚒

For your first attempt at bricklaying, it is best not to be over-ambitious. Plan to build a straight section of wall no more than about fifteen bricks long and about eight bricks high, with the bricks laid end to end in stretcher bond. This will enable you to practise laying bricks level and in line, handling mortar, getting even joints and building to a true vertical. When you have mastered that, you can progress to forming corners and piers and building thicker walls.

tools for the job

string & pegs
hammer
bricklaying trowel
spirit level
brick bolster
club hammer
gauge rod (see box page 441)
bricklayer's pins
pointing trowel

1 The first step is to lay a foundation strip (see page 437). When you have done this, drive a peg into the ground just beyond each end of the strip and tie a length of string between the two to act as a guide for aligning the faces of the bricks in the first course of the wall. Position the string so that the bricks will sit centrally on the foundation.

2 Mix some mortar and trowel a strip about 150mm (6in) wide onto the foundation or patio. Level it roughly with the tip of a bricklaying trowel. Place just enough mortar to enable you to lay three or four bricks.

3 Working from one side of the foundation, set the first brick in place (some bricks have a recess, called a frog, which some people prefer to bed into the mortar, while others position it uppermost). Tamp the brick down into the mortar with the handle of the bricklaying trowel until it looks level. You can check this and adjust the level if necessary once you have laid several bricks.

4 Butter a generous amount of mortar onto the end of the next brick, pressing the mortar on firmly with the trowel held at 45° to the edges of the brick. If the mortar keeps falling off, try dipping the end of the brick in a bucket of water first.

5 Lay the second brick in line with the first, butting it up to the first brick so that the mortar on its end is compressed to a thickness of about 10mm (½in) between the two bricks. You may need to hold the first brick in place as you do this so that it cannot move. Tamp the second brick down level with its neighbour and check that the two bricks are in line. Continue in this way until you reach the end of the first course. Lay a spirit level along the top and against the faces of the bricks, and tap any that are high or projecting back into line. Then turn the spirit level through 90° and check that each brick is level across its width.

6 To ensure that the vertical joints are staggered in subsequent courses, you need to start the second course of the wall with a brick cut in half. To cut a brick, score a line across the flat side and place the brick on a soft surface (a bed of sand or the lawn will do). Align the edge of a brick bolster with the scored line and strike it firmly with a club hammer. The brick should cut cleanly with a single stroke.

7 Spread some mortar onto the first course of bricks and set the half brick in place to start the second course. Lay as many whole bricks as needed to complete the course, finishing it off with the other half brick that you cut in step 6. Trim off excess mortar from the joints as you work, then check line and level with a spirit level as before.

8 Add bricks at one end of the wall to start the third, fourth and subsequent courses, building upwards until the wall is eight bricks high. You will have to lay four bricks

in course three, three-and-a-half in course four and so on, up to one-and-a-half bricks in course eight. After laying each course, use a gauge rod to check that the horizontal (bed) joints are the same thickness (see step 10). The bricks now form even steps half a brick long running down from the end of the wall. This process is called racking back, and the object of the exercise is to build the wall by working from the ends towards the middle. Repeat the process at the other end of the wall.

9 Before proceeding any further, use a spirit level to check that the ends of the wall are truly vertical and that the face of the wall is flat. To check that the vertical joints are a standard width, rest the spirit level on the sloping brickwork. It should just touch the corner of every brick.

10 Hold the gauge rod against each end of the wall to check that the joint thicknesses are even all the way up. If not, knock down the faulty section and rebuild.

MAKING A GAUGE ROD

To check that mortar joints are the same thickness, make a tool called a gauge rod from a length of softwood. Mark lines on it to indicate the bricks or blocks and the mortar joints between them. In this project, for example, you should mark alternate brick widths (65mm/2½in thick) and joints (10mm/½in thick).

11 Push a bricklayer's pin into the mortar between the third and fourth courses at each end of the wall and tie a string line between them. Use this as a guide for laying the rest of the bricks in course three. Move it up a course at a time and complete another course of bricks, finishing with the eighth and final course laid with the frog down. You do not need a string line to lay this course. Once again, use a spirit level to check line and level, and make sure that all the vertical joints in the wall line up from course to course. You have just built your first wall.

building a brick wall – 2

Once you have mastered the basics of handling bricks and mortar and building up courses, you can move on to turning corners and adding piers – essential supports if you are to build walls longer or higher than the one on the previous page. As with building a straight wall, the object of the exercise is to maintain the bond – the overlap of half a brick's length from course to course – to ensure that corners and piers do not form weak points in the wall structure.

tools for the job

string & pegs

hammer

bricklaying trowel

spirit level

builder's square (see box below)

brick bolster

club hammer

rubber mallet

gauge rod (see box page 441)

bricklayer's pins

pointing trowel

MAKING A BUILDER'S SQUARE

Cut three lengths of 50 x 25mm (2 x 1in) softwood – 400, 500 and 600mm (16, 20 and 24in) long. Glue and screw the two shorter pieces together at a right angle with a corner halving joint (formed by crossing the two lengths of wood and removing half the thickness of the wood from each piece to form a flush joint). Make a mark on the outside edge of the shorter length 300mm (12in) from the corner and on the longer one 400mm (16in) from the corner. Check that the distance between the marks is exactly 500mm (20in). Lay the 600mm (24in) length across the angle with its outer edge in line with the pencil marks. Glue and screw it to the other pieces, then cut off the overlaps at each end flush with the shorter pieces.

A simpler alternative is to cut a large triangle from the corner of a machine-cut sheet of plywood.

turning corners

If you build walls in stretcher bond, turning corners is straightforward. You simply place each corner brick at right angles to the one beneath it. This ties the two sections of the wall together and maintains the bond pattern in each course. The only cut bricks needed are in alternate courses at the open ends of the two sections, as for a straight wall.

1 Lay two foundation strips at right angles to each other (see page 437), then lay the first course of bricks forming one section of the wall (see page 440). Place the first brick of the second section at right angles to the corner brick of the first section, after buttering some mortar onto its end, and tamp it down level.

2 Place several more bricks in the first course of the second section of wall, and use a spirit level to check that they are truly horizontal and in line. Hold a builder's square in the internal angle between the two sections to check that they are at

right angles to each other, and adjust them if they are not. Complete the rest of the first course.

3 Start the second course by bedding two bricks in place at the corner, laid the opposite way around to the two in the first course. Tamp them down and get them level in both directions – along their length and across their width.

4 Build up the brickwork on both sides of the corner until the wall reaches its final height and you have just a single brick in the topmost course. This is the same process of racking back that you used in building a straight section of wall.

5 Hold a gauge rod against the corner to check that the joints are even, rebuilding the affected section if they are not (ideally you should check after each course). Build up the brickwork in the same way at each open end of the wall, and check the coursing there as well.

6 Place a spirit level or gauge rod on the sloping steps of brickwork to check that the racking back is even and the joints between the bricks are uniform – the level or rod should just touch the corner of each brick. Build up each section of wall as shown in step 11 page 441.

building piers

Piers are also bonded into the wall structure for strength. In stretcher bond brickwork they can be one brick square and projecting from one face of the wall or, for maximum strength, one-and-a-half bricks square and centred on the wall. For walls built in stretcher-bond brickwork more than 450mm (18in) high, you need a one-brick pier at the end of the wall and at 3m (10ft) intervals along it. Position the larger piers in exposed locations. The maximum safe height for a stretcher bond wall with piers is 675mm (26in) – nine courses. Higher walls should be built 215mm (8½in) – one brick length – thick. This can be used up to 1.35m (4ft) without piers and up to 1.8m (6ft) with two-brick (440mm/17¼in square) piers.

projecting piers

To build piers one brick square at the end of a stretcher bond wall, place a brick alongside the last whole brick laid at the end of the first course. Place the first brick of the second course at right angles to them, then lay bricks in the second course as usual. Complete the pier with a half brick in this and every alternate course.

To build intermediate piers one brick square, place two bricks side by side at right angles to the wall face in the first course. To avoid the vertical joints aligning in the second course, centre a half brick over the two whole bricks in the first course, then lay a three-quarter brick at either side of the half brick. Complete the second course of the pier with a whole brick. Repeat this arrangement for alternate courses.

centred piers

You can build centred one-and-a-half brick piers in one of two ways. The first uses whole bricks for all courses of the pier, and the wall is tied to the piers with strips of expanded metal mesh bedded in the mortar every two or three courses. The second, stronger method bonds each course of the wall into the pier. This requires the use of half and three-quarter bricks in the pier structure to maintain the bond pattern.

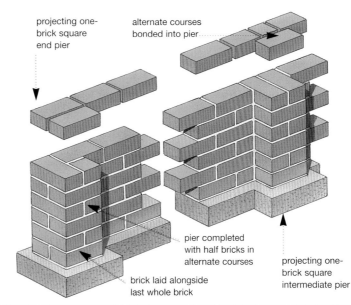

projecting one-brick square end pier

alternate courses bonded into pier

pier completed with half bricks in alternate courses

projecting one-brick square intermediate pier

brick laid alongside last whole brick

building a stone block wall ⚒

Reconstituted stone walling blocks allow you to build natural-looking stone walls just as easily as if you were laying bricks. The blocks have faces and ends shaped to look like rough-hewn stone, but the top and bottom of the blocks are flat so that they can be laid in level mortar courses. Most ranges of blocks offer a choice of different lengths and heights, enabling you to build walls with the appearance of random stonework.

Visit suppliers such as garden centres and builders' merchants to select the blocks you want to use for the stone wall. There you will find the range of blocks available on display, giving you the opportunity to look at colour, texture and size options before deciding. The next stage is to plan the wall layout and estimate how many blocks are required. Accurate estimating is especially important if the wall is to comprise a mixture of block sizes. Design the wall on paper first and then count up how many blocks of each size will be needed to create the arrangement. Blocks tend to be sold in complete packs, but most suppliers will split packs if necessary. The smallest quantity they will supply is generally enough to build about 1sq m (10sq ft) of wall. In most cases suppliers will deliver direct.

tools for the job

bucket & mixing equipment
hawk
rubber mallet
bricklaying trowel
spirit level
gauge rod (see box page 441)
bricklayer's pins
builder's square (see box page 442)
pointing trowel

1 Lay the foundation strip (see page 437), then lay out the blocks dry. This enables you to check that the drawing translates correctly into three-dimensional reality, and provides an opportunity for correcting

any errors before actual construction begins. You can then pick up the blocks, course by course as you build up the wall.

2 Prepare a standard mortar mix, made from 1 part cement to 5 parts soft (building) sand. Then set up string guidelines as for building in brickwork, and trowel enough mortar onto the foundation slab to lay the first three or four blocks. Bed the first block in place on the mortar and tamp it down until it looks level. Butter mortar onto the end of the next block and lay it in the same way. Repeat for the next two blocks, then check with a spirit level that they are truly horizontal and aligned.

tips of the trade

Whatever the mix, there is a correct method for preparing mortar. Measure the proportions by volume, using separate buckets for cement and sand. Always mix the ingredients dry before adding water and make sure the mortar is not too sloppy or it will run and stain the faces of the stones.

3 Complete the first course by spreading more mortar on the foundation and laying further blocks. Start laying the second course, placing any double or triple-height blocks according to your sketch plan and checking that all the blocks overlap those in the first course to maintain the correct bonding pattern.

4 Place smaller blocks alongside the larger ones. There will inevitably be some alignment of the vertical joints where two or three smaller blocks butt up against a larger one. Use a gauge rod to check that the mortar joints between the stacked blocks are uniform in thickness. Add further mortar to the joints if required.

the faces of the blocks with a stiff brush when they have dried. Finish the wall by adding a layer of coping stones. These protect the top courses of the wall from rain and frost damage, and help to throw water clear of the faces of the blocks below. Set the coping stones in a generous mortar bed, tamping them down level with each other, then fill the joints with a further quantity of mortar.

5 Continue building up the wall course by course, mixing large and small blocks according to your sketch plan. Make frequent checks with a spirit level as you build to ensure that the courses are truly horizontal and that the face and ends of the wall are both rising straight and not leaning or sloping too much. Complete the main part of the wall by adding the final course. The maximum recommended height for reconstituted stone block walls built with piers every 3m (10ft) is 625mm (2ft) in 100mm (4in) thick blockwork and 1.8m (6ft) in 210mm (8¼in) blockwork. It is advisable not to build any higher or the wall will become structurally unsound.

6 Now turn your attention to the pointing. Use a fairly dry mix for the pointing mortar in order to avoid staining the faces of the blocks. Take a sausage of mortar off the hawk with a pointing trowel and bed it well into the joint. Neaten the surface with the point of the trowel and leave to harden. Remove any droppings from

BLOCKWORK WITHOUT MORTAR

Some manufacturers offer reconstituted stone blocks that are designed to be laid without mortar in low walls up to 625mm (2ft) high. The blocks have grooves on their undersides and ridges on their top surfaces, which interlock as the wall is built up. Other blocks are moulded to imitate drystone walling, with each manufactured block having the appearance of several interlocking stones. These can be laid with special thin-bed walling adhesive instead of mortar to give the appearance of a wall hand-built using individual stones. Matching coping stones are also available, moulded as stones set on edge so that you can finish the wall in the traditional way.

Coping stones add the finishing touch to a stone block wall and protect the blockwork from frost and damp. Simply tamp them down on a thick bed of mortar.

building a retaining wall

If you have a sloping garden or you want to create raised planters, you will need to build walls that hold soil behind them, so-called earth-retaining walls. These obviously have to be stronger than a free-standing wall because they act as a kind of dam, holding back not only the soil but also the considerable amount of moisture that it can contain after wet weather. This means building in 215mm (8½in) thick masonry, making provision for trapped groundwater to drain away.

When you are planning the design and siting of earth-retaining walls to terrace a sloping site, it is preferable to construct several shallow terraces rather than one or two tall ones (if you do build tall ones, they will need reinforcing; see box opposite). Smaller walls will be under less stress, and building steps to link the levels (see pages 452–3) will be much simpler. If you are creating several terraces, build the retaining wall that is furthest from the house first, so that you do not have to move materials from one terrace to the next. Earth-retaining planters are unlikely to be higher than about 900mm (3ft), and their box-like structure gives them more than enough strength to contain the soil that will be held within them, so reinforcement is unnecessary.

Get professional advice before building earth-retaining walls higher than about 1.2m (4ft).

bonds for earth-retaining walls

It is possible to build a retaining wall with two parallel skins of stretcher-bond brickwork – known as double-thickness running bond – but the wall will not be very strong, even if the two leaves are tied together with cavity wall ties in the mortar beds. A stronger structure results if some of the bricks are laid end-on as headers, when they act as ties to hold the wall together. Two bonding arrangements commonly used for walls 215mm (8½in) – one brick length – thick are English and Flemish bonds.

In English bond the wall is built with different alternate courses, the first of stretchers laid side by side in running bond, the second of headers. At corners, a course of stretchers becomes a course of headers in the return wall, and vice versa. At ends and corners, a brick cut in half lengthways (a queen closer) is fitted before the last header to maintain the bonding arrangement. A variation called English garden wall bond has from three to five courses laid as stretchers, followed by a single course of headers. It is sometimes used instead of pure English bond to reduce the amount of pointing required in the header courses, but is marginally less strong.

In Flemish bond, each course consists of a pair of stretchers followed by a single header, so that on the face of the wall each header is centred on the stretcher below. Again, queen closers maintain the bond at ends and corners. The resulting wall is a little stronger than English bond because every course contains headers as through ties. A variation known as Flemish garden wall bond has a header after around three pairs of stretchers in each course, again to reduce the amount of pointing required.

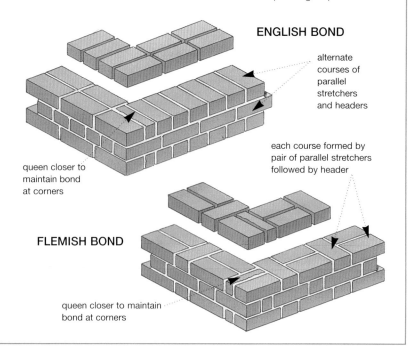

ENGLISH BOND

alternate courses of parallel stretchers and headers

queen closer to maintain bond at corners

each course formed by pair of parallel stretchers followed by header

FLEMISH BOND

queen closer to maintain bond at corners

building an earth-retaining wall

Any earth-retaining wall needs solid, secure foundations. Excavate a trench to a depth of about 450mm (18in) and pack down a 150mm (6in) layer of hardcore using a fence post as a ram. Then drive in timber pegs to act as a depth guide for the foundation strip, and place a 150mm (6in) thick layer of concrete (1 part cement to 5 parts all-in aggregate) over the hardcore. Tamp it down with a beam held lengthways in the trench, level it and cover it with polythene. If you have clay soil, dig deeper so that you can put in a 300mm (12in) thick concrete strip. Allow the concrete to harden for at least three days.

tools for the job

spade
wheelbarrow
string & pegs
hammer
bricklaying trowel
spirit level
rubber mallet
brick bolster
club hammer
gauge rod (see box page 441)
bricklayer's pins
builder's square (see box page 442)
pointing trowel

1 You need to use special-quality frost-proof bricks for retaining walls. Reconstituted stone wall blocks are naturally frost-resistant. Lay the first course of brickwork, adjusting the thickness of the mortar bed to correct any unevenness in the foundation. Begin with a course of stretchers laid in running bond if you are building in English bond, as shown here, or pairs of stretchers followed by a single header if you are building in Flemish bond.

2 If the wall turns a corner, lay the first course of the return section of wall next. Place a queen closer behind the last stretcher at the face of the wall to maintain the bonding arrangement in the return wall. In English bond, the course continues along the return wall as a course of headers. In Flemish bond, place a pair of stretchers next to the queen closer, then a header and another pair of stretchers alternately along the rest of the course.

3 To allow water trapped behind the wall to drain away, either leave every other vertical joint open

in the bottom two courses of the wall to act as weepholes, or build short lengths of copper or plastic overflow pipe into the mortar bed above the first, second or third course of bricks – the first course is usually best.

4 Continue building the wall up to its required height in your chosen bond. Line the back of the wall face with heavy-duty polythene sheeting or give it two coats of liquid damp-proofing solution. This will prevent the masonry from becoming saturated, causing white efflorescence to appear on the exposed face of the wall – a problem that spoils the appearance of many retaining walls. Backfill behind the wall with gravel to a depth of at least 300mm (12in) to assist with drainage behind the foot of the wall. Allow the mortar to harden for a week before back-filling with soil.

REINFORCING WALLS

Walls higher than about 900mm (3ft) should be built around vertical steel reinforcing rods set into the foundation concrete. Build the wall in double-thickness running bond with the rods between the two leaves of the wall. Tie the two leaves together with cavity wall ties placed 450mm (18in) apart in every alternate bed joint, and in every course at wall ends and corners. Fill the space between the leaves with fine concrete.

building a screen block wall

Pierced screen walling blocks allow you to build walls that act as a screen rather than a solid barrier. You can use them on their own or incorporate them as decorative panels in brick or block walls. Unique among building blocks, they are laid in vertical columns – an arrangement known as stack bonding – which means that a screen block wall is inherently weak unless it is reinforced during construction to compensate for the lack of bonding between the individual blocks.

Screen walling blocks are made to a standard size of 290mm (11½in) square, giving a modular unit 300mm (12in) square with a 10mm (½in) thick mortar joint. This means that any wall you build with them must be a multiple of 300mm (12in) in length and width. The maximum height for a wall built solely using screen walling blocks is 1.8m (6ft) – six courses. The blocks are usually 90mm (3½in) thick, and are white or off-white in colour.

Block manufacturers also make matching hollow pier blocks. These are 200mm (8in) high, so that three pier blocks coordinate with two walling blocks. They are made in four types – to form end piers, intermediate piers, corners and T-junctions – and, depending upon the type, they have one or more recessed faces into which the walling blocks fit. Any wall built with pier blocks must therefore have an even number of courses. Matching pier caps and 600mm (2ft) long wall coping stones complete the range.

tools for the job

bricklaying trowel
club hammer
rubber mallet
spirit level
pointing trowel

To build a free-standing wall, lay a foundation strip (see page 437), then spread a bed of mortar on it long enough to bed three blocks. Set the first pier block in place at one end

and tamp it down with the handle of a club hammer. Use a spirit level to check that it is standing squarely.

Butter some mortar onto one face of the first block and rest it on the mortar bed so that you can lower the mortared edge into the groove in the pier block. Tap it along gently until it engages, then tamp it down gently into the mortar bed. The blocks are fairly fragile, so try to tamp them close to the corners so that the force of the blow is transmitted down through solid material.

Butter the edge of the next block and bed it against the first, again tapping it horizontally until

the vertical joint is 10mm (½in) thick. Tamp it down level with its neighbour and trim off any excess mortar to prevent it from staining the block surfaces. Continue placing blocks in this way to complete the first course of the wall, finishing off with an end pier block. If the wall is longer than 3m (10ft) – ten blocks – incorporate intermediate piers at a maximum of 3m (10ft) intervals.

Spread some mortar on top of the first pier block at one end of the wall. Place the second pier block on it, tamp it down to a joint thickness of 10mm (½in) and check with a spirit level that it is level in both directions and that the pier is vertical.

5 Repeat the process to place the third pier block. To reinforce the pier, fill its hollow central section with mortar, bedding it down inside the pier with a softwood offcut.

6 Place the second course of blocks on top of the first. Make sure that the first block engages fully in the groove in the pier blocks, and that subsequent blocks are perfectly aligned with the ones below. The top of the second course should be level with the top of the pier.

7 If you intend to build a wall higher than two courses, the pier blocks must be built around a steel reinforcing rod set in the foundations. Tie the wall blocks to the pier with a strip of expanded metal mesh bedded into the mortar in alternate courses and hooked over the reinforcing rod.

Add pier and pierced screen wall blocks as necessary to complete the wall. If the finished wall will be more than four courses high, add two more courses now and allow the

mortar to harden overnight before adding the next two.

Finish the wall by placing pier caps and coping stones on top of the wall. These could be matching or contrasting in colour, depending on taste. Check that the coping stones are level and that they overlap the wall blocks by an equal amount on each side of the wall. Mortar the joints between the coping stones.

tips of the trade

• **Matching mortar** – Since screen wall blocks are white or cream in colour, ordinary mortar will look much darker and will spoil the appearance of the wall. To get around the problem, order white Portland cement and the palest sand available from your walling supplier, and use these to make a matching mortar. If these materials are not available, the only alternative is to paint the wall with masonry paint or exterior-quality emulsion paint when the wall is complete.

• **Infill panels** – If you intend to use screen walling blocks as infill panels in solid masonry walls, remember that one block coordinates with four courses of brickwork. The blocks are a little narrower than a brick – centre the blocks on the brickwork if the wall will be viewed from both sides, but fit them flush with the face of the brickwork if only this face of the wall is visible.

Use a rubber mallet to tap the pier caps and coping stones into the mortar on top of the wall, and check with a spirit level to make sure that they are perfectly level.

building a brick arch ⟋⟋⟋

A brick arch is a striking way of framing a gateway or an opening in a high boundary wall (although building the latter is best left to the professionals). The structure is self-supporting once built, but you need the help of some timber formwork to support the arch bricks while the mortar sets. A two-ring arch is the best choice for a free-standing archway. A one-ring arch is weak and looks rather insubstantial, while a three-ring arch is too overpowering and looks better in a wall.

An arch works by transferring its weight downwards into the wall or piers that support it. If the arch is free-standing, the piers must be at least 215mm (8½in) – one brick – square, and it is generally best to err on the side of safety and build the piers measuring 330 x 215mm (13 x 8½in) with three bricks in each pier course. Each pier should have its own concrete foundation pad, 450mm (18in) square and 150mm (6in) thick.

tools for the job

bricklaying trowel
....
spirit level
....
tape measure & pencil
....
jigsaw
....
hammer
....
arch former (see step 2)
....
pointing trowel
....
raking tool or small cold chisel

1 Build the two piers, checking after each course that they are rising at the same level. Continue until you reach the springing point – the level at which the arch will begin. For

an archway 900mm (3ft) wide, piers of twenty-two courses of brickwork will give adequate headroom.

2 Measure the width of the opening at the springing point and cut two semicircles of plywood to that diameter with a jigsaw. Nail them to wood offcuts to make an arch former measuring about 200mm (8in) from front to back. Set the former on props so that it sits level with the tops of the piers.

3 Place some mortar on top of each pier, next to the former, and set a brick in place on each one. Butt it up against the former and tamp it down in the mortar.

BUILDING A SEGMENTAL ARCH

You can use a variation on the brick arch technique to build a flatter arch, known as a segmental arch because its curve is a smaller segment of the circle's circumference than a semicircle. Use a pencil, some string and a drawing pin as improvised compasses to draw the curve you want on a sheet of board. Cut it out, check its appearance across the opening and use it to mark and cut a matching piece for the other side of the former. Remember that the flatter the arch, the more upright the bricks will be at either side of the opening. You will probably have to build the tops of the piers up level with the end bricks to improve their appearance.

4 Add bricks to each side of the former one by one, making sure that each one is butted against the former and that the wedge-shaped mortar joints between the bricks are the same width – around 10mm (½in) thick on the inside of the curve, and about 20mm (¾in) on the outside.

5 If you have spaced your bricks carefully, there should be room for a single brick – the keystone – at the top of the arch. Butter mortar on both sides of it and slot it into place.

6 When the keystone is in place, hold a spirit level against the face of the arch to check that all the bricks are perfectly aligned.

7 Spread mortar on top of the first ring of bricks and build up the second ring in the same way, with wedge-shaped mortar joints. The second ring will have a slightly larger radius than the inner one, so the brick joints will not align after the first brick.

You will need more bricks for the second ring – twenty-three (compared with nineteen for the inner ring) for an arch 900mm (3ft) wide. When you have added the second keystone, neaten all the visible mortar joints.

8 Leave the former in place for 48 hours to give the mortar time to set hard (if rain or frost threatens,

cover the top of the arch with polythene sheeting). Then remove the props carefully and let the former drop out without disturbing the brickwork. Point the joints on the underside of the arch to complete the job. Rake out the dried mortar to a depth of 4–5mm (1/8in) and replace it with fresh mortar using a pointing trowel.

When the arch is built, rake out the dried mortar from the joints and fill them with fresh mortar, either flush with the face of the bricks or recessed slightly, for a perfect finish.

building steps in a bank ⚒⚒

In a steeply sloping garden, the safest way of getting up and down sloping lawns is via a flight of steps, and the simplest way of building them is to use the bank to provide the step's foundations. As long as the subsoil is firm and has not been disturbed recently, careful cutting of the step shapes will provide a perfectly stable base for the flight. All you need is a single concrete foundation slab to anchor the lowest tread of the flight.

Garden steps should have treads at least 300mm (1ft) from front to back and 600mm (2ft) wide. Increase this to at least 1.2m (4ft) to create enough room for people to pass each other on the steps. The height of the risers will be governed by the bricks or blocks you use – two courses of brick or standard walling block topped by a paving slab will produce a step height of just under 200mm (8in). The treads should overhang the risers by about 25mm (1in). If the flight will be more than ten treads long, incorporate a wide landing halfway up the flight.

safety advice

Treads and risers should be the same size throughout the flight and the treads laid with a slight slope from back to front so that rainwater drains off them and cannot freeze there.

tips of the trade

To count the number of treads you will need, use a horizontal string line and a long garden cane stuck in the ground at the foot of the bank to measure the bank height. Divide this by the height of each tread to calculate how many steps you will need. Divide the length of the string line by the number of steps to check that the tread depth will be at least 300mm (12in).

preparing the site

1 Use pegs and string lines to mark out the sides of the flight and the positions of the tread nosings on the bank. Remember that treads need to be at least 300mm (12in) from front to back. Using paving slabs 450mm (18in) square gives a tread about 350mm (14in) deep, allowing for the depth of the riser that will be built off its rear edge.

2 Remove the transverse string lines and use a spade to cut out step shapes in the bank. The pegs will act as a guide to where the front of each tread should be. Work from the top of the slope downwards so that you do not break down the edges of the treads you have cut by standing on them.

3 Dig a trench at the foot of the flight and cast a 100mm (4in) thick concrete strip foundation about 300mm (12in) longer than the width of the flight and about 300mm (12in) wide (see page 437). Allow the foundation slab to set for three days before starting to build the flight of steps.

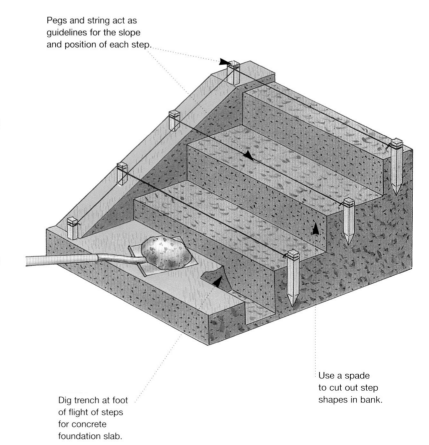

Pegs and string act as guidelines for the slope and position of each step.

Dig trench at foot of flight of steps for concrete foundation slab.

Use a spade to cut out step shapes in bank.

building the steps

1 Spread a bed of mortar across the centre of the concrete foundation strip and bed the first course of bricks or blocks in it. Four bricks laid in stretcher bond make a flight of steps that is 900mm (36in) wide, ideal for paving with two 450mm (18in) square slabs per tread. Then cut a brick or block in half to start the second course of the riser. Bed it in place at one end of the riser and then complete the second course.

2 Infill behind the brick or blockwork of the first riser with crushed aggregate, which compacts better than hardcore because it contains a mixture of large and small pieces. Tamp it down well with a fence post or a similar sturdy, thick piece of timber, taking care not to disturb the bricks or blocks that you have just laid.

3 Spread a bed of mortar on top of the first riser and over the infill below where the edges of the paving slabs that are to form the treads will be. Bed the first slab in place, checking that it is level from side to side and has a slight slope towards its front edge to allow rainwater to drain off. Set the second slab of the tread alongside it, tamp it down level with its neighbour and trim off excess mortar from beneath the fronts of the treads.

4 Build the brick or blockwork of the second riser up at the rear of the first treads. Spread a mortar bed and set the bricks or blocks in it as before. Infill behind the riser and bed the next two treads in place, using the same method as before. Continue building risers and placing treads until you have completed the flight of steps. Finally, neaten the pointing and brush dry mortar into the gaps between the treads.

5 If the cut edges of the treads show signs of crumbling, build dwarf brick walls at each side of the treads to contain the soil.

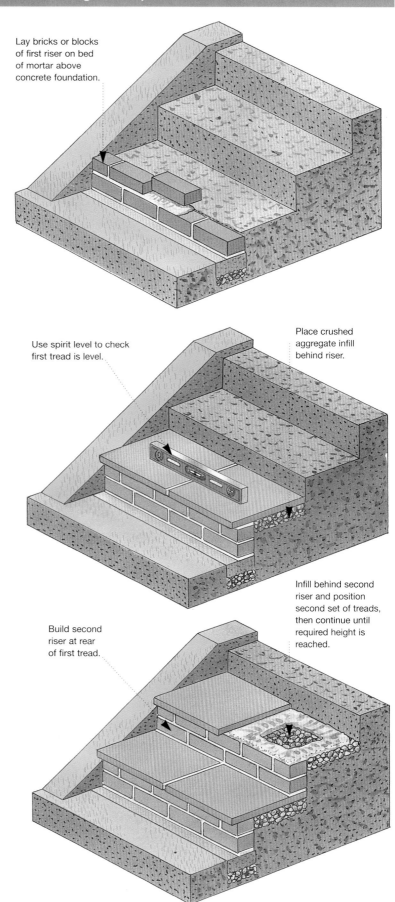

Lay bricks or blocks of first riser on bed of mortar above concrete foundation.

Use spirit level to check first tread is level.

Place crushed aggregate infill behind riser.

Infill behind second riser and position second set of treads, then continue until required height is reached.

Build second riser at rear of first tread.

building steps in a bank

453

building free-standing steps ✂✂

If you are creating different levels in your garden through the use of retaining walls, you will need to build some steps to give you easy access from one level to the next. The easiest way to do this is to build a flight of free-standing steps between the two levels. This is more complex than building steps in a bank, since you have to create the entire structure yourself instead of letting the bank do the work of supporting the steps.

Plan the shape and dimensions of the new steps around the paving and walling you intend to use. It makes sense to match the bricks or blocks to those used for the existing retaining walls, and to choose paving that matches what you have elsewhere in the garden. Most paving ranges offer slabs in several different sizes, so you can choose whichever best suits the dimensions of your steps.

A free-standing flight of steps needs foundations to support the perimeter brickwork and the internal brickwork that supports the edges of the treads. Clear the site for the steps of vegetation and topsoil, and excavate to a depth of about 200mm (8in). Ram in a layer of hardcore about 100mm (4in) deep, and use sand to fill in the voids. Then place and level a 100mm (4in) thick concrete foundation slab about 100mm (4in) larger in each dimension than the flight of steps. Refer to pages 470–3 for more information on laying concrete slabs.

The flight of steps in the example illustrated here is built against a brick retaining wall four bricks high. It is four bricks wide, has risers two bricks high and treads formed of two 450mm (18in) square paving slabs. The top tread sits on the wall and the earth retained behind the wall.

tools for the job

pegs & string

garden spade

wheelbarrow

bricklaying trowel

spirit level

builder's square

(see box page 442)

brick bolster

club hammer

timber straight edge

1 Spread a bed of mortar along the line of the perimeter brickwork and lay the first course. Tamp them down with the handle of a trowel. Use a spirit level to check that they are level, and a builder's square to check the corners. Finish each course with a half brick.

2 Start the second course with a whole brick. On flights more than 450mm (18in) high, you need to tie the steps to the wall to prevent cracks from developing between the steps and the wall as time goes by. You can either chop out a half brick

in the wall and bond a whole brick from the steps into the recess, or use metal wall extension profiles (see pages 50–1).

3 Complete the second course of bricks. Once again, use a spirit level to check that the course is perfectly level, with all the bricks correctly aligned, and that the face of the brickwork is vertical.

4 Build transverse walls inside the brick box to support the second riser brickwork and the meeting edges of the slabs that will form the first tread. These can be of honeycomb construction (that is, the vertical joints do not need pointing).

5 Add two more courses of brickwork to form the second riser and the sides of the flight, and build up the rear internal support wall to the same height to support the meeting edges of the slabs that form the second tread. Use a spirit level to check that the wall is level.

6 Spread some mortar on top of the brickwork that forms the first step. Position the two slabs that will form the tread of the steps. Tamp them down level with each other, and with a slight fall towards the front of the step. Once again, use a spirit level to check the position.

7 Point the joints between the slabs and along their rear edges, and trim off excess pointing between them and the brickwork below. Place the slabs that form the second tread in the same way. If this tread is at the top of the flight, as in this example, rest the rear edges of the slabs on the wall behind.

POSITIONING HIGHER FLIGHTS OF STEPS

The picture sequence illustrated on these pages shows steps ascending at right angles to the face of the wall. If the retaining wall is more than six courses of brickwork in height, however, extra steps will be needed and the flight will have to extend farther away from the wall as a result of this. If this is not acceptable, either because you do not have sufficient space for them or simply for aesthetic reasons, turn the flight of steps through 90° so that the flight rises parallel to the wall face. Such a flight will then project onto the lower level by just the width of the treads.

Use the point of a bricklaying trowel to scrape away excess mortar from all the joints. The quality of the pointing can make a big difference to the finished look of the steps.

creating & repairing outdoor surfaces

Most householders want to do more than just admire the garden from the house. They want to walk around it without getting their feet wet, sit outside without chairs and tables sinking into soft grass, and perhaps create decorative features with gravel or cobbles. They may even want areas of concrete to provide foundation slabs for garden buildings, or just to provide an inexpensive parking bay for the car. The most popular materials for creating patios, paths and other outdoor surfaces are paving slabs and interlocking paving blocks. Both come in a wide range of styles, shapes and colours and are very easy for the amateur landscape gardener to lay. All you have to decide is which to choose and where to lay them.

For areas with light traffic, such as patios or paths, slabs may be laid on sand rather than a mortar base.

patios, paths & drives

Apart from walls, garden landscaping also requires hard surface areas for traffic and to take garden furniture. Patios, paths and drives can be surfaced in a variety of materials, including individual slabs or blocks laid on a sand or mortar bed, and areas of concrete, cobbles or gravel. The key requirements of any hard surfaces outside the house are that they should provide a stable, firm surface that drains freely in wet weather and is laid on a solid base so that it does not subside and become uneven as time goes by.

slab paving on sand

Paving slabs come in a range of shapes and sizes, and sets are available that build up into circular features with up to three concentric rings around a central stone. Slab texture may be smooth, moulded to simulate split slate or York stone, or finished with a fine gritstone or coarser aggregate surface. Colours range from buff and grey through various shades of terracotta to red. For areas that will get only light traffic, such as patios and garden paths, the slabs can be laid on a raked and compacted sand bed about 50mm (2in) in depth. This provides continuous support for the undersides of the slabs, accommodates any unevenness in the subsoil beneath and makes it easy to get neighbouring slabs level. The sand bed can be laid directly over well-compacted subsoil, but if it is unstable or has been dug recently, a 75mm (3in) thick layer of well-rammed hardcore (broken builder's rubble) or crushed rock will be required below the sand to provide a firm base that will not subside. The joints between the slabs are filled with brushed-in sand or soil.

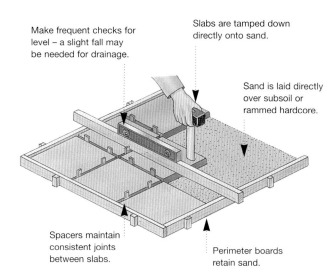

Make frequent checks for level – a slight fall may be needed for drainage.

Slabs are tamped down directly onto sand.

Sand is laid directly over subsoil or rammed hardcore.

Spacers maintain consistent joints between slabs.

Perimeter boards retain sand.

slab paving on mortar

For areas such as drives and parking bays that have to take vehicles, slabs must be laid on a mortar bed otherwise the weight of the vehicle will make individual slabs subside and crack. The mortar bed needs a firm and stable sub-base – either a 100mm (4in) thickness of well-rammed hardcore or crushed rock, or an existing concrete drive. The slabs are laid on lines of mortar placed beneath their edges and across the centre, leaving space for the mortar to be compressed and squeezed out sideways into an almost continuous bed when the slab is placed and levelled. Joints between slabs are filled with a very dry, stiff mortar mix to avoid staining the slabs when they are placed.

Crazy paving is a form of slab paving laid using the same method as for normal paving, but with broken paving slabs as the raw material, which are laid on a continuous bed of mortar rather than mortar being applied under each one.

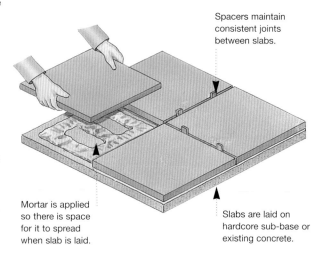

Spacers maintain consistent joints between slabs.

Mortar is applied so there is space for it to spread when slab is laid.

Slabs are laid on hardcore sub-base or existing concrete.

concrete

Concrete is a mixture of cement, sharp sand and fine aggregate' – stones up to 20mm (¾in) across – which makes an ideal surface for patios, paths and drives where the emphasis is on economy and hardwearing properties, rather than a grand appearance. When formed into strips and slabs, the concrete is contained in a timber mould called formwork. This ensures that the cast slab will have clean vertical edges, and also acts as a levelling guide when pouring in the final layer of concrete. The correct mix for exposed slabs is 1 part cement to 3.5 parts combined sand and aggregate.

Once the trench has been dug and formwork established, a firm sub-base of compacted hardcore or crushed rock is laid, followed by a thin layer of sand or ballast to fill in gaps in the hardcore, with the concrete laid on top. The combined depth of the two sub-base layers should be approximately 75mm (3in) for a path or patio, and 100mm (4in) for a drive, rising to 150mm (6in) on clay soils. Similarly, the concrete layer should be 75mm (3in) thick for paths and patios, 100mm (4in) thick for drives and 150mm (6in) on clay.

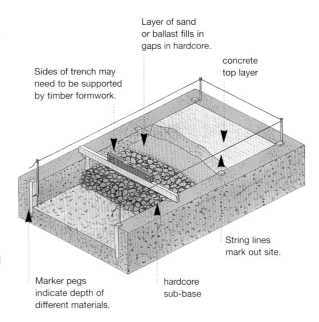

Layer of sand or ballast fills in gaps in hardcore.

concrete top layer

Sides of trench may need to be supported by timber formwork.

String lines mark out site.

Marker pegs indicate depth of different materials.

hardcore sub-base

gravel & cobbles

Gravel is river stone typically sieved to a diameter of 20mm (¾in). It is loosely laid over a firm sub-base of well-rammed subsoil or crushed rock (hardcore is too coarse), ideally with a weed-proof membrane laid under the sub-base. A depth of 50mm (2in) is required for a garden path and 100mm (4in) for a driveway. The area will need some form of edge restraint, such as kerbstones or pegged timber boards, to prevent the gravel from transferring to adjacent lawns or flowerbeds. Cobbles are larger rounded pebbles up to 75mm (3in) in diameter. They can be laid loose but are more commonly set to around half their depth in a continuous mortar bed. They make an attractive surface but one that is relatively uncomfortable to walk on, so they are usually laid only as small feature areas within other paving or as a trim.

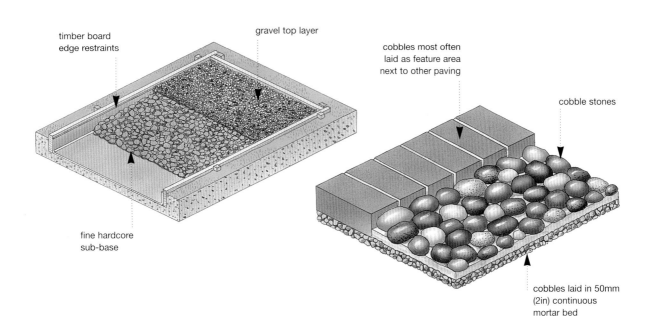

timber board edge restraints

gravel top layer

fine hardcore sub-base

cobbles most often laid as feature area next to other paving

cobble stones

cobbles laid in 50mm (2in) continuous mortar bed

laying slabs on sand ↗

The simplest way of creating hard surfaces in your garden, such as patios and paths, is to lay paving slabs on a sand bed. Sand is easy for bedding and levelling and will provide a firm support for slabs as long as they are subjected only to pedestrian traffic. As the individual slabs are quite large, you can cover a sizeable area surprisingly quickly once the site is cleared and sand bed prepared. However, large slabs are heavy and anyone with back trouble should avoid laying them.

SLAB SIZES & FINISHES

Most paving slabs are square or rectangular, but sets are also available that build up to form circles. Square slabs range from 225 or 300mm (9 or 12in) up to 600mm (24in) in size, while rectangles start at 450 x 225mm (18 x 9in) and go up to 900 x 600mm (36 x 24in). This last is often used for laying pavements, but is perhaps too large for a small garden and certainly too heavy for one person to lift and lay. Finishes available include smooth, textured and riven – which is an imitation of split natural stone. Colours range from off-white and buff to red, granite and slate. Cheaper slabs are simply formed from cast concrete. These are relatively brittle and very difficult to cut accurately. More expensive slabs are hydraulically pressed, which makes them stronger and more easy to cut.

👍 tips of the trade

You need to plan the number of slabs you will need. To avoid unnecessary and time-consuming cutting, plan an area that is a whole number of slabs in length and width. Take rough measurements of the site, select the slabs you want to use and note the sizes in which they are manufactured. It is then a simple job to plan the layout in squares, rectangles or a mixture of the two, using graph paper to produce a scale drawing of the arrangement. Not only will this help when it comes to laying, it will also enable you to order precisely the right number of slabs in each size and so avoid unnecessary wastage.

tools for the job

tape measure
pegs & string
spade
hammer
wheelbarrow
shovel & rake
levelling board (home-made)
spirit level
mallet
brick bolster & club hammer
stiff-bristled broom

1 Mark out and clear the site, then excavate to a depth of 100mm (4in). Compact the subsoil if it has not been disturbed recently. If it has, dig a further 75mm (3in), then spread and compact a 75mm (3in) layer of gravel or crushed rock over the site. Tamp it down firmly with a length of fence post. Unless the paving will finish flush with an existing grassed area, edge the area with 100mm (4in) wide perimeter boards to retain the sand bed. Use sawn preservative-treated 25mm thick timber, nailed to timber pegs hammered into the subsoil.

2 Bring the sand to the site in a wheelbarrow and rake it out to a thickness of 50mm (2in). Use a piece of perimeter board as a levelling board to smooth over and level off the sand. Rest a spirit level on top of the board as you work to check that the sand bed has a slight fall away from the house for drainage purposes. Kneel on a board offcut as you work so that you do not disturb the sand.

tips of the trade

To estimate how much sand to order, measure the length and width of the paved area in metres and multiply the two together to get the area in square metres. Then divide this by 20 to get the volume in cubic metres for a layer 50mm (2in) thick. Add 10 per cent to the total volume to allow for uneven subsoil and filling joints.

3 Place the first slab at one corner of the area and tamp it down into the sand bed using either a mallet or the handle end of a club hammer. Check that the slab is level in one direction and has the correct slope in the other.

4 Lay the next slab, either butting it up to the first one if you want close joints, or use wooden spacers if you prefer wider joints. Tamp it down and check that it is level with its neighbour, with the same fall away from the house. If the slab sits too low, lift it and add a little more sand underneath, then reposition.

5 Continue laying slabs along the first row, removing the spacers as soon as each slab is surrounded by further slabs on either side. Follow your plan unless you are laying only square slabs in a chequerboard pattern of rows and columns.

6 Once each row is complete, lay the levelling board along the row to check the slabs are lying level. Then check the fall down each row, and make any adjustments.

7 If your design is such that you need to cut a slab, mark the cutting line in pencil or chalk and use a brick bolster and club hammer to make a shallow cut across the slab. Then place the slab on the sand and strike the slab harder so that it snaps along the cut line. If you have a lot of cutting to do, it is a good idea to hire an angle grinder, which will make the cuts quickly and cleanly. When you have laid all the slabs, remove

the last spacers and shovel some sand onto the surface. Use a soft-bristled broom to brush the sand into all the joints between the slabs, then brush off the excess.

tips of the trade

If you are laying paving in an area that has a manhole, do not simply pave over it. The sand will enter the drains, and you will have an awkward job of lifting slabs to gain access. Get a builder to raise and reposition the frame so that the cover will be level with the new paving (or tackle the job yourself by adding a course of bricks around the top of the chamber).

There is no need to fill the joints with mortar when laying slabs on sand – it is enough simply to brush a further quantity of sand into the joints.

laying block pavers ✗✗

Block pavers are the most popular choice for outdoor surfaces. Their advantages are that they are small and easier to handle than slabs, they are designed to be laid on a sand bed, and there is no pointing to be done as they are butted closely together. In addition, unlike other dry-laid paving materials, they will withstand the weight of a car. The only drawbacks are that it takes longer to cover an area with blocks than slabs, and the paved area must have edging to retain the sand bed.

Block pavers are generally rectangular and 50–60mm (2–2½in) thick. The most common size is 200 x 100mm (8 x 4in), but many other sizes are available. They also come in a wide colour range. The surface is slightly textured, with the block edges bevelled to emphasize their outline when laid. Either the blocks themselves or matching kerb blocks may be used as perimeter edging – these will need to be set in mortar.

Block pavers can be laid in various designs, from simple basket-weave to intricate herring-bone patterns. Most designs are laid square to the edge restraints, but you can also lay the blocks at an angle – generally 45° – running across the site. Note that the sand used for the bedding layer should be sharp (concreting) sand, not soft (building) sand, which does not compact as well and may also stain the blocks.

tools for the job

garden spade

tape measure

pegs & string

wheelbarrow & shovel

rake & tamping beam

levelling board

hired plate compactor (drives only)

spirit level

bricklaying trowel

rubber mallet

brick bolster

club hammer

hired block splitter (optional)

broom

1 Clear the site of vegetation and mark the area to be excavated. Dig out the area to a depth of about 100mm (4in) for patios and paths, and compact any disturbed subsoil – a thick fence post is used here. For a drive, excavate an additional 100mm (4in), then add a 100mm (4in) layer of hardcore or crushed rock. Compact this layer using a hired plate compactor (see box).

2 Position the edge restraints around the area to be paved. Set block or kerbstone edging in a mortar bed or, alternatively, nail preservative-treated timber edging to stout pegs. Allow mortar to harden for 24 hours before laying the blocks.

3 Fill a wheelbarrow with sand and tip the sand into the area to be paved. When all the sand is in place, rake it to a uniform depth of about 50mm (2in). Use a levelling board to smooth and level the sand across the area, working from a board so that you do not compact the sand bed by treading on it. Form stacks of blocks at intervals around the perimeter of the site.

LAYING BLOCK DRIVEWAYS

If you are laying block pavers as a driveway, you need to settle them into place to prevent them from subsiding under the weight of vehicles. To do this, hire a power tool called a plate compactor. This vibrates as you run it over the laid blocks, settling them into the sand bed and also compacting this so that it cannot itself subside. You should make one pass of the machine after placing the blocks, and another after brushing sand into the joints. This tool is also ideal for compacting any hardcore and crushed rock that is being used as a sub-base for any paving project.

4 Place the first blocks against one edge restraint, following whatever laying pattern you have chosen. If you are laying a patio or path, tamp them down into the sand bed using a rubber mallet. If you are creating a drive, simply set them in place. Make sure the blocks are butted closely together.

5 After laying about 1sq m (10 sq ft) or so of blocks, lay a spirit level on the levelling board and place it across the blocks in various directions to check that they are level and sitting flush with one another. Tamp down any that are proud of their neighbours.

6 Carry on laying blocks across the area, checking regularly that you are maintaining the pattern correctly. Depending on the pattern chosen and the shape of the site, you are likely to have to cut some blocks to finish the surface. Lay as many whole blocks as you can first of all, then insert the cut blocks, tamping each one into place.

7 You can cut block pavers with a brick bolster and club hammer, as shown here, but you will save time and effort (and spoil fewer blocks) if you hire a hydraulic block splitter for the day. Mark the cutting line in chalk, position the block in the cutter and pull down on the handle to split the block.

With all the cut blocks in position, lay a spirit level across them to check the levels once more and tamp down any that are proud of their neighbours. When you are satisfied, spread some fine, dry sand liberally over the surface and brush it this way and that until all the joints are filled. Sweep off the excess sand.

Make sure that you move the brush across the whole paved area, bending the bristles into all the joints to ensure that they are filled with sand for a perfect finish.

laying slabs on mortar ⚒

If you want to use paving slabs for a drive or other area that will get more than just pedestrian traffic, you need to bed them on mortar over a concrete sub-base to ensure that the slabs have a continuous solid support and will not crack under the load. You can also lay slabs on mortar rather than sand for patios and paths. In this instance, a concrete base is not required but the subsoil beneath the slabs must be firm and well compacted.

Laying concrete from scratch in order to place slabs on top to create a driveway is an expensive way of creating this type of outdoor feature, but if the concrete is there already the job becomes a more economical proposition. As long as an existing concrete base is sound – in other words, not riddled with cracks and subsiding in places – and is at least 100mm (4in) thick, it will make the perfect foundation for a paved drive.

As with laying slabs on sand (see pages 460–1), the secret of success lies in careful planning. Take time choosing the slabs you want – you will have to live with the results for some time – and work out the layout to avoid having to cut slabs unless it cannot be avoided. On an existing concrete base you may have to mix slab sizes to ensure that you have whole slabs along all open edges of the base. Increasing or decreasing the spacing between the slabs may also help you avoid having to cut slabs.

tools for the job

tape measure

shovel

bricklaying trowel

rubber mallet

spirit level

timber straight edge

watering can

pointing trowel

stiff broom

brick bolster

safety goggles

work gloves

patios & paths

After planning (and if necessary sketching out a scale drawing) the slab layout, clear and mark out the site. If laying onto subsoil, make sure it is well compacted. Mix a fairly sloppy mortar mix in the proportions 1 part cement to 6 parts soft (building) sand. Compact the subsoil thoroughly and place five pats of mortar in the place where the first slab will be positioned, one under each corner and one in the centre. Lay the slab in place on the mortar and tamp it down with the handle of a club hammer or a rubber mallet so that it is perfectly level. Then repeat the process to lay other slabs across the area, checking the level from time to time with a spirit level resting on a timber straight edge. When you have laid all the slabs, brush a mixture of cement and sand into the joints and sprinkle water onto the paving with a watering can to dampen the mortar and make it set hard between the slabs. Once dry, the mortar locks the slab in place and ensures that it does not move.

driveways

1 If you are laying a driveway on a concrete base, brush the surface of the concrete with a stiff broom to remove any loose material, and treat it with a fungicidal wash to kill any weeds, lichen and algal growth. This should prevent any weeds or other plant growth from emerging through the joints in the paving for some time, though you will have to take measures to control this problem in the future. Spread a generous square of fairly sloppy mortar where the first slab will be positioned, and add two lines of mortar at right angles across the centre of the square – this is called box-and-cross bedding in the trade.

2 Place the first slab on the mortar and tamp it down well with a club hammer. This will compress the bedding into a continuous layer of mortar and bond the slab securely to the concrete. Use a spirit level to check that the slab is level (assuming that the concrete base beneath it is level, of course).

3 Place more box-and-cross mortar for the next slab, position it and put two 10mm (½in) wood spacers between it and the first slab. This ensures that the pointing gap remains constant across the whole paved area. Then tamp the slab down and check that it is level and aligned with the first slab.

4 Lay the rest of the slabs in the same way with spacers between them, working your way across the area row by row. You can remove the spacers as soon as each slab is surrounded on all sides by other slabs.

5 Allow the mortar to harden overnight. Mix a fairly dry mortar mix so that it does not stain the slabs, and work it into the joints with a pointing trowel. Use an offcut of wood to pack the mortar down well. Allow mortar droppings to dry on the slabs, then brush them off.

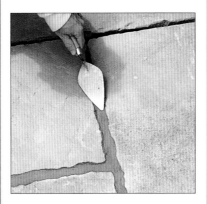

cutting slabs

1 If you have to cut just a few slabs, do it by hand. Wearing safety goggles and gloves, mark the cutting line and cut a shallow groove along it with a brick bolster and club hammer. Alternatively, score the line with repeated passes of the corner of the brick bolster.

2 Place the scored slab on a bed of sand and position the brick bolster in the centre of the line. Strike it firmly with the club hammer and the slab should split along the scored line. If you have to cut a lot of slabs, consider hiring an angle grinder for the day.

ENSURING EFFICIENT SURFACE DRAINAGE

With mortar-pointed slabs, rainwater will not drain away between the slabs in the way that it does when slabs are bedded on and pointed with sand. You should therefore build the slabs on a slope in order to prevent puddles from collecting and standing on the surface after it has rained. The slope should be of a continuous uniform gradient across the paved area.
If the paved area is next to the house, lay the slabs so that the slope falls away from the house. Aim for a slope of about 1 in 40 – that is, a 25mm (1in) drop for every 1m (3ft) of patio or drive width.

tips of the trade

• **Seal the concrete** – If the existing concrete slab is dusty, treat it with a solution of PVA (polyvinyl acetate) building adhesive, diluted as recommended by the manufacturer for use as a sealer. Not only will this bond the concrete surface together, but it will also help the mortar to bond well to the concrete, ensuring that the slabs do not work loose as time goes by.

• **Plant the gaps** – If you want your paving to have an informal look, lay the slabs with wider than usual joints and fill them with soil rather than mortar to encourage grass, moss and low-growing plants. Using slabs in a mixture of different sizes also looks less formal than same-size slabs laid in carefully regimented rows.

laying crazy paving 〃〃

Crazy paving is a paved surface created by bedding irregularly shaped pieces of stone in mortar and then pointing the gaps between the pieces. The stone is usually broken paving slabs, although natural stone can also be laid as crazy paving in the same way. It may have got its name from the crazing that affects the glaze on old pottery, as the appearance of well-laid crazy paving is similar. The stones have to be well fitted and the pointing carefully detailed to avoid a piecemeal finish.

The main attraction of crazy paving, apart from its rustic and informal look, is that the paving is cheap – broken slabs are widely available in large quantities from demolition contractors and also some local authorities. As a rough guide, one tonne of broken slabs will cover an area of 9–10sq m (100sq ft), but this depends on the thickness of the slabs. Ask your supplier for advice when ordering. You may be offered a choice of stones in one predominant colour and texture, or as a random mixture. Generally speaking, crazy paving looks better if all the pieces are more or less the same shade.

When the delivery arrives, sort the stones into groups. Pieces with two square adjacent edges will form corners, while those with one straight edge will serve as perimeter stones. Separate what is left into large irregular pieces for the centre of the paved area, and small infill pieces. Stack the groups around the paving site so that you have got them to hand while you work.

The best base for crazy paving is an old concrete slab in need of a facelift. The alternative is a layer of crushed rock or hardcore, laid over well-rammed subsoil. Brush old concrete to remove loose bits from the surface, treat it with a fungicide if it is covered in lichen and green algae, and seal its surface with diluted PVA (polyvinyl acetate) building adhesive if it is very dusty. Clear a virgin site of vegetation, skim off the topsoil and bed down a 75mm (3in) layer of crushed rock, ready for the mortar bed that will take the paving.

tools for the job

shovel
wheelbarrow
hired cement mixer
bricklaying trowel
rubber mallet
spirit level
timber straight edge
club hammer
brick bolster
pointing trowel
spot board for mortar
stiff broom

1 Mix your first batch of mortar using a hired cement mixer – you will need so much mortar for bedding and pointing that hand mixing is not really an option for this job. Use a mix of 1 part cement to 5 parts sharp (concreting) sand, and make it relatively sloppy. Start work at one corner of the site, shovelling enough mortar onto the area you are paving to cover about 1sq m (10 sq ft) at a time. Trowel it out to a thickness of about 50mm (2in).

2 Select a corner stone and tamp it down into the mortar bed using a mallet or the handle of a club hammer. Use a spirit level to get it level, and make sure it is aligned with the edges of the slab if you are laying on concrete. Otherwise, use string lines to help you keep the edge stones accurately in line.

3 Choose a large perimeter stone that fits well against the corner stone – aim for a pointing gap of no more than 25mm (1in) in width, or your crazy paving will look very gappy. Set it in place and tamp it down, using a mallet or the handle of the club hammer, then check that it is level and in line with the corner stone.

4 Continue laying perimeter and corner stones all the way around the site until the edge is complete. As you bed the stones, mortar will squeeze up between them. Leave it, as it will reduce the amount of pointing needed later, but make sure it does not sit proud of the surface of the stones.

5 Shovel in more mortar, spread it out and start bedding large irregular stones in the centre of the area, working from one end to the other. Use a brick bolster and club hammer to trim stones to improve their fit. Check that each stone is level as you tamp it down by placing a timber straight edge across the paving with its ends on the perimeter stones. Kneel on a board as you work across the site to avoid disturbing the pieces you have already laid.

6 Use smaller pieces of stone to fill in the remaining gaps, again trimming them to size first if necessary. Use any remaining mixed mortar to fill the gaps between the

stones to within about 5mm (¼in) of the surface of the paving. Allow the mortar to harden overnight before starting on the pointing – the most time-consuming part of the job.

7 Make up a pointing mortar of 1 part cement to 5 parts soft (building) sand. It should be somewhat drier than the bedding mortar to avoid undue staining of the stone surfaces. Trowel it into the joints from a spot board, then draw the side of the trowel blade along the edge of each stone to recess the mortar about 3mm (⅛in) below it and leave two sloping bevels meeting at a central ridge.

8 Allow any loose mortar that you have dropped to dry on the stones – lifting this when it is wet will leave stains. Once the pointing mortar has set hard, brush the paving surface to remove the debris.

Crazy paving has a rustic, informal look that is perfectly enhanced by a busy planting scheme, with flowers and shrubs allowed to overlap onto the paving.

laying gravel & cobbles ↗

A gravel path or drive makes an attractive contrast to flat paving materials, especially if the aggregate is chosen with care. Strictly speaking, gravel is made up of small water-rounded pebbles and is available in a range of natural earth shades. Crushed stone aggregates have rough-edged stones and are available in colours ranging from white and grey through reds and greens to black. These can be laid as a single colour or can be mixed if preferred.

tools for the job

tape measure

spade

handsaw

club hammer

claw hammer

bricklaying trowel

shovel & wheelbarrow

garden roller or tamping beam

rake

timber straight edge

using cobbles

Cobbles are large rounded river stones. They make an uncomfortable surface to walk on but can look very attractive when used in the garden to provide a visual counterpoint to flat surfaces – perhaps as a border to a path. They can be loose-laid, but are better bedded in mortar.

1 To create a cobble feature, complete the surface that it will complement – a brick or block border, for example. Then spread a bed of

fairly sloppy mortar about 50mm (2in) deep and start placing individual cobbles in it to about half their depth.

2 Use a timber offcut and a club hammer to tamp them down into the mortar bed until they are reasonably level. This will ensure that they do not work loose as time goes by. When the mortar has dried, brush away any excess and apply a coat of clear silicone masonry sealant to the stones to give them a permanent wet look and enhance their colours.

using gravel

Gravel surfaces are satisfyingly crunchy to walk on or to drive over, and are an excellent burglar deterrent – you cannot cross gravel quietly, even on tiptoe. However, they do have several practical drawbacks. For a start, they need some form of edge restraint, such as pegged boards or concrete kerbstones, to stop the gravel from migrating onto lawns or into flowerbeds. You also have to rake them regularly to keep them looking neat and tidy, and they

will need treating with weedkiller from time to time. Another drawback is that they can attract local cats and dogs, which regard gravel as an ideal outdoor litter tray. Last of all, pushing a laden wheelbarrow across gravel is like wading through quicksand.

If you decide to create a gravel feature in your garden, first choose which type of aggregate to use. Then measure the area you intend to cover and the depth to which you want to fill it so that you can calculate the volume you require. A depth of 50mm (2in) is adequate for a path, but 75mm (3in) is better for a drive.

You will need a bulk delivery for all but the smallest projects. A cubic metre (35cu ft) of gravel or aggregate will cover about 20sq m (215sq ft) to a depth of 50mm (2in), and 13sq m (140sq ft) to a depth of 75mm (3in). If your supplier delivers by weight, one tonne will cover about 7.5sq m (80sq ft). Bulk loads are delivered loose or in large canvas slings – these are preferable to a big heap because the gravel is contained better while you move it to its final destination. For small projects, you can buy gravel and other decorative aggregates in 25, 40 and 50kg (45, 90 and 110lb) bags.

1 Measure out the site and clear vegetation and topsoil. Compact the subsoil thoroughly. Put the edge restraints in place, either nailing preservative-treated timber to stout pegs or bedding kerbstones in a fine concrete mix. If you are using boards, secure them with pegs every 1m (3ft) or so to prevent them from bowing.

2 Lay a proprietary weedproof membrane over the site to discourage deep-rooted weeds from growing through the gravel. Overlap strips of membrane by at least 100mm (4in), and trim the edges.

3 You can lay the gravel directly over the membrane, but if the subsoil is soft it is best to put down a layer of crushed rock or fine hardcore first. Shovel it onto the membrane to a depth of at least 50mm (2in).

4 Compact the crushed rock with a heavy garden roller if you have one. Otherwise, use a heavy timber

tamping beam such as a length of fence post to pack down the layer of rock. To test whether you have tamped it down sufficiently, walk on the surface – if you do not leave footprints, then the rock has been tamped down enough.

5 Use a wheelbarrow to transport the gravel to the site and tip it out in heaps. When you have done so, spread out the gravel shovelful by

shovelful up to the level of the edge restraints. Take care not to disturb the compacted base layer. Rake the gravel out level, then place a timber straight edge on the edge restraints and draw it across the site to identify any high or low spots. Rake off the former and fill the latter with more gravel. Once the gravel is level, roll or tamp it to bed it down well and leave the finished surface about 25mm (1in) below the tops of the edge restraints.

It is important to rake the gravel level in order to achieve an attractive finish, and it is a good idea to do this regularly to keep your gravel feature looking as good as new.

laying concrete – 1 ↗

Concrete can be used to create a driveway, a patio or a path but suffers by comparison with paving slabs and blocks as far as appearance goes. It can also form bases for lightweight garden buildings such as summerhouses, sheds and workshops, and is the material used to create foundations for all sorts of garden structures such as walls, arches and steps. Its main advantage over other materials used for creating outdoor surfaces is that it is very economical.

ingredients

Concrete is a mixture of coarse and fine aggregates – stones up to around 20mm (¾in) in diameter with smaller stones and coarse sand – that is bound together into a solid matrix by cement. You can buy the ingredients separately from builders' suppliers and mix them yourself, buy dry ready-mixed bags of cement and aggregate (ideal for small jobs) or order ready-mixed concrete (best for large areas).

Ready-mixed concrete may be delivered by a large truck mixer with its familiar slowly turning drum, or by a smaller vehicle that carries dry cement, aggregates plus a cement mixer and can mix the amount you need on the spot. Truck mixers can deliver up to about 6cu m (200cu ft) of concrete from their chutes directly to the site. Smaller vehicles mix by the barrowload, which you then have to move from truck to site.

The ingredients of a concrete mix depend on the use to which the material will be put. The three standard formulae are given in the table below, along with the quantities you need to make 1cu m (35cu ft) of concrete. All-in aggregate is a mixture of sharp sand and 20mm (¾in) aggregate. Always mix ingredients by volume, using separate buckets or similar containers of the same size for cement and aggregate. Mix batches based on 1 bucket of cement plus the relevant numbers of buckets of sand and aggregate.

USE	MIX	PROPORTION	AMOUNT PER CU M (35.3CU FT)
General-purpose cement (most uses except foundations and exposed paving)	cement	1	6.4 bags (320kg/700lb)
	sharp sand	2	680kg/1500lb (0.45cu m/15.8cu ft)
	20mm (¾in) aggregate	3	1175kg/2600lb (0.67cu m/23.6cu ft)
	OR all-in aggregate	4	1855kg/4100lb (0.98cu m/34.6cu ft)
Foundations (strips, slabs and bases for paving)	cement	1	5.6 bags (280kg/615lb)
	sharp sand	2.5	720kg/1600lb (0.5cu m/17.6cu ft)
	20mm (¾in) aggregate	3.5	1165kg/2560lb (0.67cu m/23.6cu ft)
	OR all-in aggregate	5	1885kg/4150lb (1cu m/35.3cu ft)
Paving (exposed slabs, especially drives)	cement	1	8 bags (400kg/880lb)
	sharp sand	1.5	600kg/1320lb (0.42cu m/14.8cu ft)
	20mm (¾in) aggregate	2.5	1200kg/2640lb (0.7cu m/24.7cu ft)
	OR all-in aggregate	3.5	1800kg/3960lb (0.95cu m/33.5cu ft)

mixing your own concrete

For hand mixing you will need a hard, flat surface. A sheet of exterior-grade plywood is ideal for protecting drives or patios, which should not be used unprotected because the concrete will stain them, however promptly you hose them down. Plastic trays 1m (3ft) across may be bought for mixing small quantities.

tools for the job

shovel

clean bucket

wheelbarrow

hired cement mixer

by hand

1 Measure out the sand and aggregate into a compact heap. Form a crater in the centre with a shovel and add the cement. Mix the ingredients dry until the pile is uniform in colour and texture. If you are using dry ready-mixed concrete, tip out the sack and mix thoroughly.

2 Form a crater in the centre of the heap and add water. The aggregate will contain a certain amount of water already, so the amount you need to add will be trial and error to begin with. After two or three batches, you will be better able to gauge how much to add.

3 Turn dry material from the edge of the heap into the central crater. Keep on mixing and adding a little more water in turn until the mix reaches the right consistency – it should retain ridges formed in it with

the shovel. If it is too sloppy, add dry ingredients, correctly proportioned as before, to stiffen it up again.

with a mixer

If you are using a cement mixer, set it up on its stand and check that it is secure. Put some aggregate and water in the drum and start it turning. Add most of the cement and sand, then water and solid material alternately, to ensure thorough mixing. Run the mixer for two minutes once all the ingredients are in, then tip out some of the contents into a wheelbarrow. The mix should fall cleanly off the mixer blades.

preparing formwork

Concrete foundations for walls can generally be poured straight into a prepared trench, since they will be hidden once the wall is built. However, surfaces such as paths, patios and bases for buildings need to have straight vertical edges, and the way to provide these is to lay concrete within what is known as formwork or shuttering – lengths of timber supported by stout pegs to form a mould for the concrete. The top edges of the formwork provide a levelling guide for the concrete, while its inner faces give the finished slab a neat moulded edge.

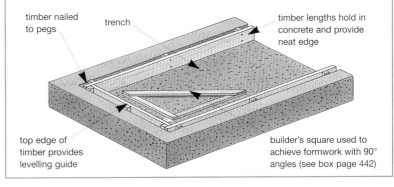

timber nailed to pegs

trench

timber lengths hold in concrete and provide neat edge

top edge of timber provides levelling guide

builder's square used to achieve formwork with 90° angles (see box page 442)

laying concrete – 2 ✂

With the concrete mixed and the formwork in place, you are ready to start laying your concrete feature. Make sure that you have excavated the site to the correct depth and that you have placed and compacted a layer of crushed rock or hardcore if this is required – see pages 458–9 for details. Check that the formwork is square and level, or has a slight fall if drainage of rainwater is needed away from the house.

Large areas of concrete cannot be laid as continuous slabs or they will crack due to expansion and contraction. You must therefore divide the work into bays, each separated from its neighbour by an expansion joint of hardboard or similar material, if the concrete is being laid as a continuous operation. Where the area being concreted has a curved edge, make sure that expansion joints meet the curves at right angles. If you are using the alternate bay technique (see opposite page), an expansion joint is not necessary – simply remove the formwork between filled and unfilled bays before concreting the unfilled bays. The recommended maximum size of each bay is around 4 x 4m (13 x 13ft). On paths less than 2m (6ft 6in) wide, incorporate an expansion joint every 2m (6ft 6in).

see pages 458–9
(see opposite page)

👍

tips of the trade

It is best not to lay concrete if frost is forecast because permanent damage will be caused if the water in fresh concrete freezes. If an unexpected frost sneaks up on you, lay polythene sheeting over the concrete and cover it with a layer of earth or sand. Leave this in place until a thaw sets in. Never lay concrete on frozen ground.

compacting the concrete

The most important part of concreting is compaction. For a concrete slab, the ideal compacting tool is a length of 100 x 50mm (4 x 2in) sawn timber used on edge, long enough to span the formwork. If you wish, add angled timber handles to each end of the tamper so that you and a helper can operate it in tandem.

Shovel concrete into the formwork, then rake it out level. Make sure that corners and edges are well filled. Add more concrete until the level is about 12mm (½in) above the top edges of the formwork.

Set the tamper in place across the formwork at one end of the slab and start tamping the concrete down. Use the beam with an up-and-down motion until the concrete is level with the top edge of the formwork, moving it along by half the beam's width after each tamping stroke. Do not simply scrape the tamper along the formwork. Continue tamping in this way until you reach the far end of the concrete slab, then repeat the process using a side-to-side sawing action to remove excess concrete. If the surface of the concrete still contains small voids, spread a thin layer of extra concrete and use the tamping beam again.

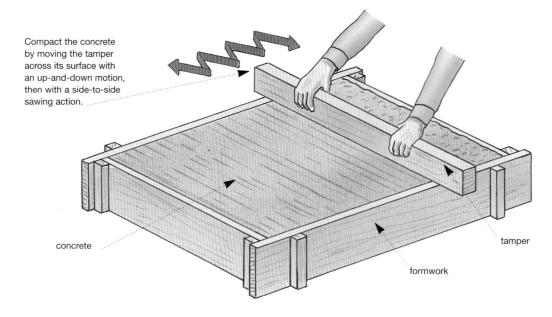

Compact the concrete by moving the tamper across its surface with an up-and-down motion, then with a side-to-side sawing action.

concrete

tamper

formwork

Cut strips of hardboard to match the thickness of the concrete and set them on edge with dabs of concrete against their sides. The top of the strip should be level and just below the top edges of the formwork. Then lay concrete up to the strip, working from both sides at the same time so that placing and compaction do not push the strip out of position. Incorporate similar joints where concrete slabs meet buildings. If there is an inspection chamber within the area being concreted, first place formwork around the chamber so that you can place a box of concrete around it. When it has set, remove the formwork and fit expansion strips all around it before concreting the rest of the slab. For concreting irregular-shaped areas, set formwork boards across the area to divide it into bays. These boards should always be at right angles to the perimeter boards.

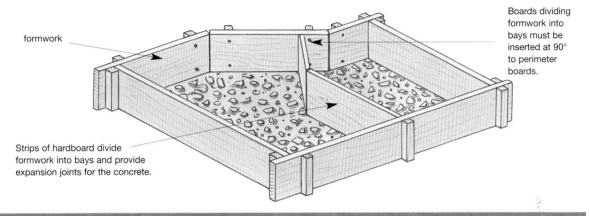

formwork

Strips of hardboard divide formwork into bays and provide expansion joints for the concrete.

Boards dividing formwork into bays must be inserted at 90° to perimeter boards.

alternate bay technique

If a slab adjoins a wall, you will not be able to use the tamper at right angles to the wall. Instead, you will have to lay alternate bays along the wall. Set up formwork as usual, with timber stop-ends dividing the bays. Place an expansion joint next to the wall and fill alternate bays, tamping the concrete parallel to the wall. Remove the stop-ends after 48 hours and concrete the remaining bays, using the hardened concrete edges of the first set of bays to guide the tamping beam. There is no need to fit expansion joints between the bays.

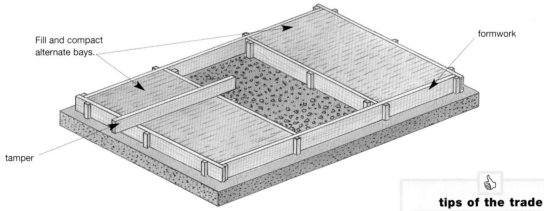

Fill and compact alternate bays.

formwork

tamper

FINISHES FOR CONCRETE

You can leave concrete with the rippled finish created by tamping but this is not very attractive. You can create a finer rippled finish if you do the final tamping by working the beam backwards and forwards with a sawing motion at right angles to the formwork. Brushing the tamped surface with a soft broom will flatten the ridges and leave a fairly smooth finish. A wood plasterer's trowel will give a fine sandpaper texture, while a steel float will create a fine, flat finish.

tips of the trade

Fresh concrete will weaken and crack if it dries too quickly, and this is a particular risk with thin slabs of large surface area. As soon as the concrete slab is laid and finished, cover it with polythene sheeting weighted down all around with bricks or baulks of timber to stop wind from blowing under it. Leave the sheeting in place for about three days.

patching concrete ↗

Concrete is the most widespread – and economical – material for laying drives, paths, patios and other surfaces around the house and garden. Although it produces a highly durable surface, it can crack if overloaded by heavy vehicles, or if the ground subsides or swells beneath it. These cracks let in water that then freezes, widening the crack and opening up further cracks that can eventually lead to the complete break-up of the surface.

If you have a concrete surface that is looking a little the worse for wear, inspect it more closely to get an idea of the true extent of the damage. Cracks, potholes and broken edges are all relatively straightforward to repair using the techniques outlined in the step-by-step sequence below, but if the surface has cracked and partly subsided, you will probably be better off breaking up the sunken section and laying new concrete in its place (see the box on the opposite page for advice on how to deal with subsidence).

tools for the job

safety goggles

work gloves

brick bolster

cold chisel

club hammer

pickaxe

spade

bucket & mixer

pointing trowel

tamping beam (for larger repairs)

plastering trowel

stiff broom

rake

1 Break away all loose material from the site of the damage, using a cold chisel, a brick bolster or even a pickaxe if necessary. Always wear protective safety goggles and thick work gloves to do this kind of work. Pick the debris out of the hole or crack piece by piece. Do not disturb any hardcore that was

beneath the concrete. If there is none and the slab was laid directly on the earth, excavate to a depth of about 100mm (4in).

2 If you had to dig out the subsoil in step 1, pack some hardcore (pieces of broken brick, flints from the garden or similar solid material) into the hole and tamp it down firmly with the handle of the club hammer.

3 Mix some concrete using 1 part cement to 3.5 parts all-in aggregate (combined sharp sand and gravel). For small patching jobs, buy a dry ready-mixed bag of concrete and just add water. Shovel it into the hole, or place it alongside a crack.

4 Tamp the concrete down into the hole using a piece of timber that is long enough to span it on edge. By moving this from side to side as you work your way across the patch, you will automatically rule off excess concrete. Fill cracks using a pointing trowel, pressing the concrete well down into the crack and finishing it flush with the surrounding surface.

5 Tamping with a timber straight edge will leave the repair with a ribbed surface finish. Flatten this with a plastering trowel if you want a smooth finish, or use a stiff-bristled broom to create a more definite textured effect. Cover the repair with

polythene sheeting weighted down with bricks. Allow it to harden for 24 hours before walking on it, and for 48 hours before driving a car over it.

DEALING WITH SUBSIDENCE

If an area of concrete has cracked and subsided slightly, you cannot simply lay more concrete on top of it to bring it back level with the rest of the slab because a thin screed will always be prone to break up and delaminate. Break up the area that has subsided using a pickaxe or a hired concrete breaker, then excavate to a depth of at least 150mm (6in) and pack in a 150mm (6in) thick layer of hardcore or crushed aggregate. The latter is better than hardcore because it compacts more fully and provides a denser and more stable base for the new concrete. Peg some timber formwork around the area you are replacing, and add more aggregate to fill the edges and corners of the mould, tamping it down well. Mix some concrete using 1 part cement to 3½ parts combined aggregate, shovel it into the mould and rake it out. Over-fill the mould slightly, then rest a tamping beam across the formwork and tamp the concrete down level with it. This will also remove any high spots. Fill any hollows that appear, and tamp again. Then finish the concrete surface to match the rest of the slab, cover it with polythene sheeting and allow it to harden for 48 hours.

6 If an edge of the concrete has broken away, remove all loose material and cut the concrete back to a sound vertical edge. Cut a piece of wood or board deep enough to match the thickness of the concrete

and long enough to span the patch, and hold it in position against the edge of the concrete with a couple of bricks or with timber pegs driven into the ground.

Pack concrete into the mould, tamping it down well with a timber straight edge to ensure that the mould is completely filled and well compacted. Finish the surface of the patch to match the surrounding concrete, cover it with polythene sheeting and allow it to harden for 24 hours. Before removing the timber the next day, run the blade of a pointing trowel between the timber and the edge of the concrete.

Use a timber straight edge to tamp the patch of concrete down well in order to achieve a flush, even surface that is safe to walk on and attractive to look at.

levelling uneven paving ↗

Paving slabs and interlocking paving blocks are very popular for giving hard surfaces around the garden a decorative finish. Although level when first laid, both slabs and blocks can become uneven due to ground movement, subsidence of the base on which they were laid or overloading by heavy traffic. Once this occurs, every raised edge is a trip hazard and the whole area soon begins to look unsightly, with weeds starting to grow through cracked joints.

Uneven paving is often the result of inadequate preparation and incorrect techniques when the slabs or blocks were first laid, especially if they were placed dry on a sand bed with joints also filled with sand. Water running off the surface of paving slabs can slowly erode the sand beneath, allowing the paving to settle. Settlement is also a common problem with block paving that was laid by hand, rather than being bedded into its sand base with a plate vibrator. The solution to this problem is to lift and re-lay the affected slabs or blocks.

tools for the job

safety goggles & work gloves

pointing trowel

brick bolster & scrap wood
(for lifting slabs)

shovel

club hammer

bucket & mixer

bricklaying trowel

spirit level

long timber straight edge

chalk

rake & stiff broom

cold chisel

dealing with uneven paving slabs

1 If a paving slab has subsided, rake out any sand or mortar pointing between the affected slab and its neighbours. Alternatively, use the tip of a pointing trowel to do this.

2 Drive a brick bolster into one of the gaps, lay a piece of scrap wood on the edge of the adjacent slab to protect it, and use the wood as a fulcrum to lever the slab up. Slide the wood underneath the raised edge so that you can get a grip on the slab and lift it out. Wear a pair of thick work gloves to give your fingers some protection while lifting out the heavy slab.

3 If the slab was laid on sand, add a little fresh sand to the bed and replace the slab. Stand it on edge at one side of the hole in which it fits, lower it to the horizontal and slide it slightly so that it drops into place without disturbing the sand

bed. Tamp it down with the handle of a club hammer until it sits level with the neighbouring slabs. If it still sits a little low, repeat the process to add more sand.

If the slab was laid on mortar dabs, chip the old mortar off the back of the slab with a brick bolster and club hammer. Take care not to crack the slab – it does not matter if a little mortar stays stuck to it. Then mix a small batch of bricklaying mortar (a bag of dry ready-mixed mortar is ideal for this sort of job) and use a bricklaying trowel to place five dabs on the bed of the hole – one near each corner and one in the middle. Drop the slab back into place and tamp it down with a hammer to the required level.

4 Lay a spirit level across the relaid slab and its neighbours to check that they are correctly aligned, then fill the joints around the relaid slab with sand or dryish mortar to match the rest of the area. If you are using mortar, lay strips of cardboard alongside the joint to prevent mortar from staining the slabs while you fill the joint.

Shovel some fresh sand onto the affected area and rake it out evenly, then start replacing the blocks one by one. Tamp each block down firmly into the sand bed so that it is flush with the neighbouring blocks. Use the straight edge to check that you have eliminated the subsidence after replacing every four or five blocks.

If the individual pieces of stone have begun to crack and break up, lift them and replace them with new pieces of stone, trimmed to fit.

1 Wearing safety goggles and a pair of thick protective work gloves, cut out all the failed pointing with a cold chisel and club hammer. Take care not to disturb the individual stones of the paving when you do this unless you are planning to replace damaged pieces. Brush away the debris.

dealing with uneven paving blocks

1 Identify the extent of the subsidence by laying a long timber straight edge across the paving in different directions. Mark any blocks that have sunk below the straight edge with chalk.

4 Finish replacing the blocks, check they are level once again and complete the job by brushing fine, dry sand into the joints. This will help to lock the blocks together and prevent subsidence from recurring.

2 Place new pieces of stone on a mortar bed and tamp them down level with their neighbours. Point the joints with a dryish bricklaying mortar, taking care not to get any on the faces of the stones. Fill the joint almost flush with the surface, then draw the tip of a pointing trowel along each edge of the joint in turn, letting it follow the contours of the stones. The aim is to highlight the edges of the stones and give the pointing a raised V-shaped profile.

2 Wearing protective gloves, prize up several blocks at the edge of the area of sunken blocks. Work your way block by block towards the area that has subsided, and lift these blocks too.

repointing crazy paving

Crazy paving is usually bedded in mortar, so it is not generally prone to subsidence. However, the pointing between the individual stones can crack and break out, leaving unsightly paving that can also be a trip hazard. The solution is to repoint the joints with fresh mortar.

glossary

Access hatch – section cut out of floor, wall or ceiling and made into a hinged door or removable panel.

Acrylic (or water-based) – describes the make up of paint or glaze used for open areas such as walls or ceilings.

Aggregate – broken stone, pebbles, gravel or similar material that forms the largest part of compounds such as concrete and mortar (finest aggregates are better known as sand); aggregate is also referred to as ballast.

Air brick – brick containing a number of holes and used for ventilation into a room or under a floor.

Angle bead – a moulding made from galvanized steel and expanded metal mesh that is used as reinforcement for plaster on external wall corners.

Architrave – decorative strips of moulding fitted around a door frame to create a finish over the joint between frame and wall.

Baluster – part of a balustrade, the correct term for stair spindles between string and handrail.

Base unit – a kitchen or bathroom unit that is sited at floor level.

Bath panel – decorative panel attached to the side of a bath; is normally removable for access to the area under the bath.

Batten – thin pieces of wood used for boxing in and for sundry other construction requirements.

Blinding – sand spread over hardcore layer in concrete floor to prevent the damp-proof membrane being pierced.

Block – a masonry unit, usually larger than a brick, used to build house and garden walls.

Block paver – brick-sized paving unit, made in a variety of colours and designs, that is laid on sand in an interlocking pattern.

Blocking in – 'filling in a space' (e.g. to disguise the construction details under a staircase) by adding flat panels of hardboard or plasterboard.

Bond – the way in which bricks are arranged in a wall; different bonds are used for different types of walls.

Boxing in – technique of employing a framework to cover up unsightly items, such as pipes; usually constructed as a frame of wooden battens and covered with building board.

Breakfast bar – length of worktop used for both food preparation and serving meals; incorporates a seating facility created by an overhang on one or more sides.

Brick – a masonry unit made from burnt clay and other materials that is used for building house and garden walls and other structures; a standard brick measures 215 x 102 x 65mm (8½ x 4 x 2½in).

Bulkhead – partial wall that often hangs over a stairwell or to one side of the staircase, and which is not directly supported by a floor.

Butt - alternative name for hinge.

Carcass – the basic structure of a bathroom or kitchen unit where no embellishments such as doors or drawer fronts have been added.

Carousel – circular shelving system used in corner units; rotates in order to aid access.

Casement - name given to a section of window or used to refer to an entire window made of a number of casements; normally, casement windows contain both opening and fixed sections.

Caulk - acrylic or water-based flexible filler supplied in tube and dispensed from a sealant gun; must be smoothed to finish before it dries.

Cavity wall – house wall consisting of two layers, or 'skins', of masonry held together with metal or plastic wall ties, and with a gap (the cavity) – commonly 50mm (2in) wide – between them; common in construction of external walls of modern homes.

Ceiling centre – ornamental plaster or foamed plastic moulding fixed in the centre of a ceiling for decoration.

Ceiling unit – kitchen unit that is fixed to the ceiling.

Cement – binder in powder form that bonds sand or aggregate together to form mortar for bricklaying or concrete.

Chipboard – manufactured board made of compressed wooden fibres and supplied in sheets which are normally joined with a tongue and groove mechanism.

Cistern – water storage tank for entire household supply or smaller tank such as that used to supply a toilet.

Cladding – name given to a material which covers the main structural element below it.

Cleat – small, short length of timber that supports another larger piece.

Closed tread – type of stairs that includes a riser in each step; the opposite to open tread.

Cobble – rounded pebble, up to 75mm (3in) in diameter, laid loose or in a mortar bed.

Colorizer – concentrated colour that is supplied in small tubes or containers, designed to add colour to paint or scumble for paint effect purposes. Some can be added to either acrylic and solvent-based paints or glazes.

Concrete – building material made from cement, sand, aggregate and water that sets to a hard, stone-like mass and is used for floors and subfloors, wall foundations and as cast slabs for laying patios, driveways and the bases for outbuildings.

Concrete anchor – screw designed to fix into masonry without the need for a wall plug.

Condensation – moisture that forms when the air is completely saturated and unable to absorb any more; most likely to collect on surfaces that are colder than the surroundings, such as cold windows.

Coping – a brick, stone or concrete strip, usually overhanging, set on top of a wall to protect it from exposure to the weather.

Cornice – decorative moulding fixed around top or bottom edge of wall units, or along wall/ceiling junction; generally more ornate, and greater in depth than coving.

Coving – a plain moulding, generally concave in cross-section, fitted in the angle between a wall and ceiling for decorative purposes; a cornice is a more ornate type of coving.

Crazy paving – a paved surface created by bedding irregular-shaped pieces of stone or paving slab in mortar and then pointing the gaps between the pieces.

Cutting in – term used to describe painting in the corners, or at the different junctions on a wall surface, or between walls and wooden mouldings.

Dado – lower area of a wall.

Dado rail – wooden rail or moulding denoting the top of the dado and therefore dividing up the wall surface into a lower and upper area; sometimes referred to as a chair rail.

Damp-proof course (DPC) – a continuous layer of impervious material (formerly slate, now usually plastic) built into a house wall just above ground level to stop ground water soaking into the wall and causing rising damp; concrete ground floors include a damp-proof membrane (DPM).

Damp-proof fluid – means of repairing a failed DPC or substitute if none exists, whereby proprietary liquid is injected at numerous points into an exterior wall at the level of a damp-proof course in order to form an impermeable layer.

Damp-proof membrane (DPM) – common abbreviation for damp-proof membrane; a sheet material laid between subfloor and flooring to prevent moisture from rising up through concrete and screeds.

Datum mark – mark on a wall, or other immovable part, of a known height and from which all other measurements are taken.

Dead lock – locking system that requires a key to open; some require a key to be put in the locked position, while others may be locked without a key but still require one for opening.

Distressing – paint effect designed to give surfaces an aged look.

Door lining – the wooden lining (the internal part of a door frame).

Door stop – strip of wood which runs around the internal part of a door frame or lining and acts as a barrier for the door edge to close on to.

Dry lining – a wall lining formed from tapered-edge sheets of plasterboard fixed to a framework of timber battens; the joints are taped and filled but the board does not require plastering.

Dry rot – type of fungal attack to timber and other building materials; starts as minute silky threads covering the timber surface, then changes to what looks like cotton wool balls and finally dark red sponge-like bodies.

Dummy drawer front – drawer front that is not attached to a drawer but is fixed to a unit carcass to imitate drawer position in order to maintain the decorative finish of a run of units.

Efflorescence – powdery white salts left on a wall surface as it dries out after construction or plastering. (They should be brushed, not washed, off.)

Eggshell – hardwearing paint that has a dull matt finish; available in acrylic or solvent-based forms.

Emulsion – acrylic or water-based paint used for open areas such as walls and ceilings.

Enamel – hardwearing decorative coating for bathroom fittings, traditionally used on old iron baths.

End panel – a decorative panel attached to the exposed sides of both wall and base units at the end of a run of units; often matches finish of door fronts.

English bond – an arrangement of bricks in a wall with alternate courses laid as headers and stretchers; the wall is one brick (215mm/8½in) thick.

En-suite – term normally applied to bathroom directly adjacent to, and serving, one particular room.

Escutcheon – small plate used as decorative finish to a keyhole; may have a cover for insulation/privacy.

Esp – common abbreviation for 'easy surface preparation'; a primer applied to laminate, melamine and tiled surfaces.

Expanded metal mesh – perforated metal sheet or strip used to support plaster when patching holes in partition walls and ceilings.

External corner – a corner that extends out into the room.

Extractor fan and hood – kitchen ventilation system that is housed in a decorative unit designed to imitate a chimney; positioned directly over the hob at a set distance in order to remove steam and cooking fumes.

Factory cut edge – a cut edge that has been produced as a result of the manufacturing process and is therefore cut with precision; the exposed edges should be factory cut edges rather than those cut by hand.

Fan – mechanical ventilation system, either ceiling- or wall-mounted.

Filler – plaster powder used to fill small holes and indentations and to cover nail and screw heads before decorating.

Fitted – term used to describe a kitchen or bathroom that comprises similar units fixed in a permanent position, usually integrated together in 'runs'.

Flat-pack – also known as 'self-assembly', a unit supplied in sections that needs to be assembled before fitting in place; name refers to the mode of packaging for delivery.

Flemish bond – an arrangement of bricks in a wall where each course consists of a header followed by a pair of stretchers; the wall is one brick (215mm/8½in) thick.

Floor grille – metal cover fitted over a hole in the floor to allow air into the room and the area under the floor; can be fixed or with a shutter design.

Floor unit – a bathroom or kitchen unit that is installed at floor level.

Flush – where two or more surfaces create a seamless join.

Flush door – type of door, available in both hollow or solid forms.

Flush lighting – lighting systems that are recessed into a surface, such as sunken spotlights on a ceiling.

Flux – cleaning material used on joints prior to soldering.

Formwork – timber boards fixed to pegs in the ground to form a mould for a cast concrete ground slab; formwork is removed when the concrete has set.

Foundation – a strip of concrete cast in a trench to support a wall or other masonry feature; it is sometimes referred to as a footing.

Galley kitchen – a long narrow kitchen with units on opposing walls, similar to a 'u'-shaped kitchen.

Gauge rod – a bricklaying aid made by marking brick and joint heights on a timber batten and used to check that courses in a wall are being built evenly.

Glaze – medium to which colorizers are added to create paint effects; acrylic or solvent-based alternatives can be referred to as scumble.

Gloss – highly decorative, hardwearing and shiny paint finish.

Glue block – triangular wooden block fitted at the back of the stairs between tread and riser.

Glue wedge – timber wedge fitted to stairs so that the tread is held tightly into the string.

Gravel – washed river stone that is typically sieved to a maximum stone diameter of 20mm (¾in); used in concrete.

Gripper – wooden strips with nails sticking up to hold in position the traditional type of carpet.

Grout – waterproof compound that fills the gap between tile joints.

Handrail – rail fixed either to wall or open side of staircase that may be gripped to provide support as you climb and descend the stairs.

Hard tile – ceramic wall or floor tile as opposed to softer varieties such as cork or vinyl.

Hardboard – thin building board often used on floors to provide smooth subfloor below further floor covering.

Hardcore – layer of concrete floor made up of broken brick, concrete and other masonry rubble; laid to build up the level and provide a stable base before the concrete is poured on.

Hawk – a metal or plywood square with a handle underneath that is used to carry small amounts of mortar or plaster to the work area.

Head plate – horizontal wooden stud that creates a ceiling fixing for stud wall framework.

Header – a brick laid in a wall with only its ends visible; timber around a fire surround to support cut joists.

Headgear – term denoting the internal mechanism of a tap.

Hearth – area in front of and at the base of a fireplace.

Herringbone struts – wooden or metal diagonal braces that are attached between joists to prevent movement in floors.

Housing – shallow groove into which another section of timber is fixed.

Internal corner – a corner that points away from the centre of the room.

Island unit – single unit or run of units positioned in the centre of the room, separate from the units around the perimeter of the room.

Jointing compound – similar to plaster or filler and used to join gaps between plasterboard when dry lining.

Jointing tape – tape used to join plasterboard sheets prior to dry lining or plastering; self-adhesive varieties are available.

Joist – a wooden or steel beam supporting a floor and, in upstairs rooms, the ceiling below.

Joist detector – electronic metal detector that finds the line of nails fixing timbers in place, and hence the joist positions; some may also have a different mode to trace the position of electric cables or pipes.

Joist hanger – metal bracket used to support the ends of floor joists at wall junctions, with varieties specifically designed for attaching to masonry or timber, or some can be built-in.

Joist socket – hole in wall or heavy beam to support joists when joist hangers are not used.

Junction box – box in which electrical cables are joined together.

Keystone – the central brick or stone at the top of an arch.

Laminate – term used to describe the process whereby a thin layer (plastic or wood veneer) is bonded to another surface, such as fibreboard, to create one solid piece.

Landing – the area halfway up a staircase that links different flights to change direction; also commonly used to refer to the area of the upper hallway immediately at the top of the staircase.

Latch – retractable lever which allows doors to open and close into a frame.

Latex – rubber-based material used as a levelling and adhesive compound.

Lath and plaster – a lining for ceilings and stud partition walls in older houses, consisting of plaster applied to closely spaced wooden strips (the laths) that are nailed to the ceiling joists or wall studs.

Leading edge – vertical edge of door or window furthest from the hinges.

Lever handle – handle designed in the shape of a horizontal bar; it is pushed down to operate the latch in a door.

Lever latch – latch mechanism of a door operated by a lever handle.

Light – another word for casement when referring to a window section and normally used to describe small parts of a window, either fixed or opening (e.g. 'the small light in a casement window' would be a small opening section); also a term used in conjunction with lead light windows.

Lighting rails – lighting system where a number of lights are positioned along a rail; light position is generally adjustable along the length of the rail.

Lining – the application of lining paper to wall surfaces.

Lintel – a steel, wood or concrete beam spanning the opening of a door or window.

Locking lever latch – latch mechanism with separate locking system built into overall latch casing.

Low-level lighting – lighting system where lighting position is well below ceiling level.

L-shaped – term used to describe the layout of a kitchen that resembles the shape of an 'L'; the units extend from one wall around to the adjacent one.

Masonry nail – hardened steel nail that can be driven into masonry with a hammer.

Mastic – non-setting filler used to seal joints between building components, such as between a window frame and the surrounding masonry; also known as caulk.

MDF – common abbreviation for medium-density fibreboard, a manufactured building board made from compressed wood fibres.

Mitre – angled joint, normally involving two lengths of material joining at a right angle, hence each piece must be cut at a 45° angle.

Monobloc – tap comprising one spout where hot and cold water is mixed to provide the required temperature.

Mortar – mixture of cement, sand and sometimes other additives used for bricklaying and rendering.

Moulding – length of plaster or wood that is used as a detail in order to create a decorative finish on either a wall or ceiling surface; also used on doors for interest.

Nap – slope of the carpet pile.

Naplocks – metal strips with a similar function to gripper rods but used at door openings.

Needle – a short horizontal timber or steel beam inserted through a wall and supported by adjustable steel props in order to carry the weight of the wall while part of the wall is being removed.

Newel post – main post at the top and bottom of stairs to support the handrail.

Niche – moulded plaster feature, built into or inserted into wall surface to provide decorative display area.

Nogging – short horizontal timber fixed between wall studs or ceiling joists to stiffen the structure.

Nosing – the rounded-over edge of a timber tread.

Open plan – home design where rooms are either very spacious, or where smaller rooms have been knocked through to form one large room.

Open tread – type of stairs constructed without riser; opposite of closed tread.

Outlet pipe – waste pipe leading from a particuler fitting trap into the drainage system.

Padstone – a masonry unit used to support the end of a beam or lintel in a wall.

Parquet – flooring composed of wooden blocks arranged in a geometric pattern; another name for a woodblock floor.

Party wall – shared wall that divides two properties.

Paving slab – a masonry unit, usually square or rectangular and 35mm–50mm (1½–2in) thick, laid on sand or mortar to form a patio, path or drive.

Pebble-dash – a finish formed by pressing small stones into rendering while it is still wet.

Pedestal basin – a basin that is partially supported by a pedestal.

Pelmet – decorative moulding fixed around the bottom edge and top edge of wall units to provide a neat finish; also at top of window dressing.

Penetrating damp – moisture entering a building through some defect in its structure and waterproofing.

Peninsula unit – kitchen unit that extends out from a run of units fitted against a wall into the centre of the room but is still integrated into the run; storage areas and worktop may thus be accessed from both sides.

Picture rail – wooden moulding positioned on upper part of wall and traditionally used to hang pictures; now mainly used as purely decorative feature to break up a wall surface.

Pier – a buttress projecting from one or both sides of a wall to increase the wall's stability, sometimes at the freestanding ends of the wall and at regular intervals along its length.

Pile – short tufts of material that actually form the carpet layer; can be plain or patterned.

Pilot hole – a small hole allowing a nail or screw to start into the wood.

Pinch rod – two sticks taped together and held in a gap to transfer dimensions from one side to the other.

Planning permission – legal permission that must be sought from the local authority to carry out some types of building work.

Plaster – a powder mixed with water to form a plastic material that is applied to wall and ceiling surfaces and hardens to form a smooth surface suitable for decorating.

Plasterboard – a sheet material formed by sandwiching a plaster core between sheets of strong paper; used for lining ceilings and stud partition walls.

Plasticizer – a mortar additive that will make mortar easier to use and work with.

Plinth – board attached between the underside of base units and the floor in order to create a decorative finish;

often clipped onto the feet of units using special brackets.

Plumb – perpendicular, upright.

Plywood – building board formed by bonding together thin veneers of wood with the grain of alternate veneers usually at right angles to one another.

Pointing – mortar filling the joints between brickwork; formed into different edge profiles using a variety of pointing tools.

Polishing – technique of finishing a plastered surface with a plastering trowel or float.

Pop-up waste – where the plug for a waste outlet is connected to the waste system and is positioned in, or removed from, the waste outlet through the operation of a connecting rod or cable.

Primer – type of paint used to seal surfaces before adding further coats.

Prop – adjustable telescopic steel tube used to support needles or the floor above when removing all or part of a wall.

Proprietary – referring to a material, tool or technique that is produced specifically by one manufacturer or group of manufacturers.

Ptfe – polytetrafluoroethylene tape used for mending leaking joints.

PVA – short for polyvinyl acetate, an all purpose adhesive used to bind and/or stabilise surfaces; used in concentrated and dilute forms.

PVC – short for polyvinyl chloride, this is a plastic used for pipes, windows and so on, although modern PVC windows are more accurately referred to as uPVC, with the 'u'

standing for unplasticised (this more modern material does not de-nature in a way that some PVC windows do).

Quarry tiles – hard tiles that have been fired in a kiln; used as a floor covering material.

Queen closer – a brick cut in half along its length and used to maintain the bond pattern in English and Flemish bond.

Render – mortar-based coat used as undercoat for plaster on solid block walls internally; externally may be used to form the finished surface, which may be left untreated or painted.

Resin – extra-strong adhesive.

Riser – the upright part of a step that joins two treads together.

Rising damp – moisture entering the building from the ground due to the failure of the damp-proof course in a wall or the damp-proof membrane in a concrete floor.

Rock wool – generic term for an insulating material made from mineral fibres.

Rose – ceiling fixing for electrical light fitting; also plaster accessories used as ornate ceiling decoration.

RSJ – rolled steel joists that are in essence heavy duty lintels; used mainly over an opening when a loadbearing wall is removed and two rooms are converted into one.

Sand – fine aggregate mixed with cement to form mortar; coarse (sharp) sand is used for concreting, while finer (soft) sand is preferred for bricklaying and rendering.

Sand plugging – technique of soundproofing where sand is

introduced into a floor space in order to insulate and reduce noise travelling between floors.

Sash – type of window or one section of a sash window.

Screen wall block – a square building block pierced with cut-outs and used to form decorative screen walls in gardens where complete privacy is not required.

Scribing block – small piece of wood cut to a size that helps to mark off the trimming requirement on a section of worktop or panelling, so that it may be cut to a precise size.

Scrim – traditional type of jointing tape used to cover joints between plasterboard sheets.

Sealant – any tubed silicone or mastic used for sealing along joints such as those between walls and window frames.

Self-levelling compound – compound applied to concrete floors in order to provide a level surface for further floor covering.

Self-smoothing compound – a powder mixed with water and other additives to form a liquid coating: it is poured onto uneven concrete floors and left to find its own level before hardening to a smooth surface.

Silicone sealant – waterproof sealant used along junctions.

Skew – nailing or screwing at an angle through wood or masonry in order to provide a fixing.

Skim – apply top coat of plaster to wall surface.

Skirting board – decorative and protective wooden moulding that is fitted at the junction between floor and wall.

Soft tile – decorative tiles that are made from pliable materials such as cork or vinyl.

Soil pipe – large diameter waste pipe into which waste from toilet is expelled; normally positioned on exterior wall of the house.

Sole plate – the wooden stud creating the base or floor fixing for partition wall.

Solvent cement – adhesive used when joining some designs of plastic waste pipe.

Solvent-based or oil-based – terms used when referring to the make up of paint or glaze.

Soundbreaker bar – metal strip attached to walls or joists, onto which plasterboard is fixed instead of fixing it directly to the wall.

Spacer – divider used between ceramic tiles to keep a consistent distance between them.

Spandrel panelling – special panels to fill in the triangular space immediately under a staircase.

Spindle – a metal bar, normally square in section, which extends from one side of the door to another through the latch casing, with each end inserted into door handles; an essential part of mechanism which transfers handle movement to the latch, thus opening and closing the door; also a baluster.

Splashback – area on wall surface subject to splashes from basins, sinks or hobs and covered with an easily wipeable material, such as tiles, stainless steel or glass.

Split level room – a room with a step in either the floor or the ceiling level.

Springing point – the point at which the curve of an arch begins.

Stain – oil- or water-based chemical for changing the colour of wood.

Static vent – ventilation grill with no mechanical parts.

Steam stripper – machine used to aid wallpaper stripping by expelling steam onto the wall surface, causing the paper to bubble so that it can be removed more easily.

Stretcher – a brick laid in a wall with its side faces visible; in stretcher bond brickwork, bricks are laid end to end, with each brick centred over the joint between the bricks in the course below.

Strike plate – metal plate situated on door lining to accommodate the latch, and lock if appropriate, when the door is in a closed position.

String – part of the staircase structure that supports the ends of the treads and risers (if fitted).

Stud – wooden uprights used in the construction of a wall framework.

Stud wall – wall consisting of wooden studs and covered in plasterboard; used for partition walls in houses and finished with plaster or dry lined.

Subfloor – the base floor material beneath a floor covering, usually floorboards, chipboard or concrete.

Subsidence – foundation problems in a house, which cause serious cracks and movement in its structure.

Suspended floor – a floor that is suspended between walls.

Tamp down – action of applying pressure to compact materials in order to consolidate them together.

Tongue and groove – interlocking mechanism used to join some types of planking, or building or panelling board.

Trap – area directly below drainage outlet where waste is typically directed through a u-shaped section of pipe.

Tread – the horizontal part of a step that you walk on as you go up and down a staircase.

Trowel – any one of several tools used for bricklaying and plastering; a bricklayer uses a large bricklaying trowel and a smaller pointing trowel, while a plasterer uses a rectangular steel trowel and a gauging trowel as well as both internal and external corner trowels.

Undercoat – the first coat of plaster or paint, also known as the base coat; a top coat of finish plaster or paint is added to it.

Unfitted – term used to describe kitchen or bathroom layout where units are not permanently fixed.

U-shaped – description of kitchen layout where the units are arranged to mimic a u-shape.

Vinyl – manufactured substance used to produce decorative, easy-to-clean floor coverings; also, protective covering on some wallpapers or additive used in paint, to improve their hardwearing and wipeable properties.

Vinyl emulsion – water-based paint ideal for a bathroom environment as it contains vinyl and is therefore easier to wipe down and keep clean.

Wall extension profile – system of wall-mounted track and interlocking metal ties that is used to bond new masonry at right angles to an existing wall.

Wall plug – plastic or metal sheath inserted into pre-drilled hole in wall to house screw.

Wall profile – metal plate used to support and tie-in block or brick wall when a new wall is being joined to an existing one.

Wall tie – metal or plastic tie used to join internal and external layer of a cavity wall together.

Wall unit – cabinet mounted on wall surface.

Wall-mounted basin – basin mounted directly onto a wall with bracket fixings, rather than being fixed with screws and resting on a pedestal.

Washer – a rubber ring that prevents water leaking from joints within taps.

Weatherboard – length of wooden moulding fixed at base of external doors to divert water away from the base of the door.

Weedproof membrane – sheet material laid over subsoil beneath gravel or decking to prevent weed growth while allowing rainwater to drain through it.

Wet rot – wood damage from the moisture content being too high; not as serious as dry rot but still leads to the destruction of timber.

Wick – action whereby moisture is absorbed into the ends of timber by capillary attraction.

Window dressing – a decorative finish used for windows, such as curtains and blinds.

Wood glue – adhesive for joining together wooden sections.

Woodblock – constituent section of a parquet floor.

Woodboring insects – bugs that live on the cellulose found in timber; an infestation of such insects can seriously damage the wood to the point where it will become structurally unsound.

Worktop – work surface positioned on top of fitted kitchen or bathroom units.

index

the authors

Julian Cassell and **Peter Parham** have run their own building and decorating business for several years, having successfully renovated a variety of large and small scale properties around the UK. These award-winning authors have written a number of books covering all aspects of DIY, and their innovative approach has made them popular television and radio guests. They wrote the sections on walls and ceilings, doors and windows, kitchens and bathrooms (pp. 8–15, 20–67, 72–89, 104–7, 116–17, 122–5, 176–9, 220–431)

Mark Corke began his career with the BBC, working in both TV and radio. During this time he maintained a strong interest in woodworking and DIY and successfully renovated several houses. Since 1989 he has worked as a freelance journalist specializing in practical subjects, has written several books and makes regular appearances on national TV and radio. He wrote the sections on floors and stairs (pp. 16–19, 134–75, 182–219)

Mike Lawrence is a long-standing and highly respected writer in the field. He is the author of numerous DIY project books and manuals and is currently the technical consultant on the highly successful BBC1 television programme 'Changing Rooms'. He wrote the sections on masonry and plastering (pp. 68–71, 90–103, 108–15, 118–21, 126–33, 434–77)

acknowledgements

The authors would like to thank the following individuals for supplying props, advice and general help: Michael and Sue Read, Mike O'Connor, John and Margaret Dearden, Adrian Moore, Steve Harris, Nick Pennison, Gary Woodland, Craig Rushmere, Kevin Hurley, June Parham, Adele Parham, David House at Hewden Hire in Bruton, Bill Dove, Andrew Toogood at Bradfords in Yeovil, Colin and Ros Lawrence, John White and Richard Hooper at B.J. White in Yeovil, Marina Sala, Jakki Dearden, Emmanuelle Baudouin, David Bevan at Aristocast, Trevor Culpin at Screwfix, David Hayward, Mark Eminson at Bradfords, Martin and Mandy Tilly, Michael and Judith Levett, Simon and Sandra Levett, Johnny Koolang.

The publisher would like to thank the following: Magnet Ltd, Screwfix, A&H Brass Ltd, Armitage Shanks, Axminster Power Tools, Richard Burbidge, Ideal-Standard, Armstrong DLW, Fired Earth, Junckers and MFI.

First published in 2003 by Murdoch Books®

Reprinted in 2004

Text, diagrams and commissioned photography copyright ©2003 Murdoch Books

ISBN 1 90399 245 1

Commissioning Editor: Iain MacGregor

Editors: Alastair Laing, Angela Newton, Natasha Treloar, Michelle Pickering

Compilation Editor: Christine Eslick

Design Concept: Laura Cullen

Designers: Shahid Mahmood, Tim Brown

Compilation Designers: Sarah Rock, Annette Fitzgerald

Managing Editor: Anna Osborn

Design Manager: Helen Taylor

Photo Librarian: Bobbie Leah

Illustrations: Mike Badrocke, John Woodcock

Photography: All photography by Tim Ridley and copyright Murdoch Books® except: Armitage Shanks: 150 left, 177 bottom right, 311 top and bottom, 312, 361 bottom right; Armstrong DLW: 134, 164; Axminster Power Tools: 17 top right; Dominic Blackmore: 4 (copyright Murdoch Books®); Richard Burbidge: 146, 182, 187 bottom right; Graham Cole: 34, 35; Corbis: 10, 11 bottom left, 12, 13; Elizabeth Whiting Associates: 67 bottom right, 81 bottom right, 144, 147, 247 bottom right, 289 bottom right, 413 bottom right, 431 bottom right; Fired Earth: 150 right, 151 bottom right; Simon Gilham (copyright Murdoch Books®): 16 right, 17 left and bottom right, 18–19, 148, 152–63, 166–75, 180–1, 184–7 (except bottom right), 188–97, 204–19; Ideal-Standard: 151 top right and left, 327 bottom right, 329 bottom right, 362; Junckers: 198; Magnet Limited: 258, 269 bottom right; Ray Main: 90; MFI (Hygena): 300, 330, 353 bottom right, 433 bottom right; MFI (Schreiber): 380; Murdoch Books Books®: 123 bottom right, 220, 276, 293 bottom right, 402, 403, 429 bottom right; Howard Rice: 6, 434; Juliette Wade: 456, 467 bottom right; Rentokil: 16 left, 202–3

Chief Executive: Juliet Rogers

Publisher: Kay Scarlett

PRINTED IN CHINA by Sing Cheong Printing Co. Ltd

Murdoch Books UK Limited

Erico House

6th Floor North

93–99 Upper Richmond Road

Putney, London SW15 2TG

Phone: + 44 (0) 20 8785 5995, Fax: + 44 (0) 20 8785 5985

Murdoch Books UK is a subsidiary of

Murdoch Magazines Pty Ltd

Murdoch Books® Australia

Pier 8/9, 23 Hickson Road

Millers Point NSW 2000

Phone: + 61 (0) 2 4352 7000, Fax: + 61 (0) 2 4352 7026

Murdoch Books® is a trademark of

Murdoch Magazines Pty Ltd